SOCIAL
CREATURES

2008
Lantern Books
128 Second Place
Garden Suite
Brooklyn, NY 11231

Printed in the United States of America

Library of Congress Cataloging-in-Publication Data

Social creatures : a human and animal studies reader / Clifton P. Flynn, editor.
    p. cm.
 ISBN-13: 978-1-59056-123-2 (alk. paper)
 ISBN-10: 1-59056-123-6 (alk. paper)
 1. Human-animal relationships. I. Flynn, Clifton P.
 QL85.S62 2008
 304.2'7—dc22
                                2007050601

green press INITIATIVE

Lantern Books has elected to print this title on Joy White a 30% post-consumer recycled paper, processed chlorine-free. As a result, all printings of *Social Creatures* to date we have saved the following resources:

28 Trees (40' tall and 6-8" diameter)
13,246 Gallons of Wastewater
9 million BTU's of Total Energy
807 Pounds of Solid Waste
2,766 Pounds of Greenhouse Gases

As part of Lantern Books' commitment to the environment we have joined the Green Press Initiative, a nonprofit organization supporting publishers in using fiber that is not sourced from ancient or endangered forests. We hope that you, the reader, will support Lantern and the Green Press Initiative in our endeavor to preserve the ancient forests and the natural systems on which all life depends. One way is to buy books that cost a little more but make a positive commitment to the environment not only in their words, but in the paper that they were published on. For more information, visit www.greenpressinitiative.org

Environmental impact estimates were made using the Environmental Defense Paper Calculator. For more information visit: www.papercalculator.org.

"This logo identifies paper that meets the standards of the Forest Stewardship Council® FSC®is widely regarded as the best practice in forest management, ensuring the highest protections for forests and indigenous peoples."

SOCIAL CREATURES

A HUMAN AND ANIMAL STUDIES READER

CLIFTON P. FLYNN, EDITOR

Lantern Books • New York
A Division of Booklight Inc.

To Jill—
The love of my life

Acknowledgments

This volume would not have been possible without the contributions of several other individuals. I thank Martin Rowe at Lantern Books for his faith in me and this project and for his enthusiastic support throughout; Ken Shapiro, for his encouragement and sound advice; Anthony Podberscek for his generosity; the University of South Carolina Upstate, for providing me with a sabbatical leave to work on this book, as well as financial support; my human children, Harrison and Clay, and my nonhuman ones—Maya, Teddy, Bob, Sarah, and Annabelle—for their inspiration and example; and finally, my wife, Jill, for her support, patience, guidance, and love.

Contents

Social Creatures

An Introduction

Clifton P. Flynn

Social Creatures—indeed we are. Human beings are distinctly and necessarily social. From birth to death, our experiences, our emotions, the very essence of who we are— all depend on our interactions and relationships with others. But which others? Until fairly recently, scholars' examination of the social lives of human beings was limited only to interaction with other humans; our relationships with other animals had been almost completely ignored. This was true despite the fact that:

- animal references and representations flood our culture: in literature (Brer Rabbit, Old Yeller), in the movies (*Bambi, Free Willy, Jaws*) and television and cartoons (Lassie, Mickey Mouse, Barney); in advertising (Tony the Tiger, Charlie the Tuna, the Geico Gecko), in art, in religious ritual and symbolism ("Lamb of God," kosher foods, animal sacrifice) and in our language ("sly as a fox," "stubborn as a mule," "there's more than one way to skin a cat," "kill two birds with one stone")
- more homes have companion animals than children, and in the vast majority, the animals are regarded as "family"
- millions of humans work in occupations that involve animals, both living and dead, including some people who love animals and have to kill them (e.g., shelter workers)—and some who kill animals without appearing to let it bother them at all (e.g., slaughterhouse workers)
- animals have been used to make statements about and distinguish between people of different social statuses, whether it be class (pure-bred dogs and fur coats for the wealthy), race (derogatory use of animalized language and images toward members of oppressed minorities—blacks as monkeys or Jews as rats), or gender (sexist language that degrades women—"chick"—and rewards men—"stud")

These are just a few of the myriad ways in which our lives involve and intersect with the lives (and sometimes the deaths) of other animals.

Although most of the academic world was ignoring our social relations with other creatures, a few others began to seriously consider this forgotten arena. Over the last two decades, in both the social sciences and the humanities, a growing number of scholars have investigated our interactions with animals and what we can learn about ourselves from observing how we think about and treat other animals. This book presents some of the best work that has been published in Human–Animal Studies (HAS). *Social Creatures* is an attempt to provide a vehicle for those who want to seriously study human–animal relationships. It contains an array of articles, using varied theoretical and methodological approaches, representing multiple disciplines—sociology, anthropology, history, philosophy, psychology, criminology, social work, feminist studies, and literary studies. The readings have been chosen because of their quality and significance to HAS.

The "A-Words"

Our failure to study our relationships with other animals has occurred for many reasons. Many scholars argue that our beliefs about human superiority and animal inferiority—speciesism—have caused us to dismiss or ignore the role of animals in our lives. Historically, humans have justified beliefs about our superiority over other animals in a variety of ways. Sometimes we have used religious arguments suggesting that animals don't have souls, and therefore aren't worthy of moral consideration; or that God gave humans dominion over the animals, to use in any way we saw fit. Other thinkers decided that animals lacked the ability to reason, and thus couldn't participate in the moral community, or lacked the ability to feel, so they couldn't really suffer. Still others attributed animals' inferior status to their lack of language. Without language, so the argument went, animals couldn't think, couldn't use symbols to create shared meanings with others, didn't have a "self," and therefore were not capable of participating in meaningful interactions with human beings.

So, in psychological terms, much of it can be boiled down to two rather unattractive human qualities: arrogance and ignorance. These qualities are the natural result from the unequal relationships that humans have with other animals. Our arrogance concerning other animals contributed to our ignorance about them. If we perceived them in a particular way, then that was how we tended to see them, irrespective of reality. Our power over other animals and our attitudes toward them, made it possible for us to see them as trivial, unimportant, or tangential at best and to ignore them, leaving them out of the picture altogether, at worst. And these notions of superiority prevented us from learning about the lives of animals as individuals, and about the role they play in our own lives. These qualities are related to three important and interrelated notions that have thwarted human attempts to study other animals and that must be acknowledged and dealt with in any serious attempt to study human–animal interaction. These notions are: anthropocentrism, anthropomorphism, and anecdotes. Criminologist Piers Beirne (1995, 23) refers to anthropocentrism and anthropomorphism as the "twin bastions of speciesism." And for cognitive ethologist Mark Bekoff (2006, 88), anthropomorphism and anecdotes are the "a words."

Anthropocentrism

Anthropocentrism means "human-centered." And that has been the approach to the study of the social lives of human beings. Research that has included animals typically has studied them as objects or as a group, rather than recognizing their individuality. Or, it has included animals only in the periphery, not as the main focus of the study. Seldom, until recently, has our interaction with other animals been the centerpiece of our investigation. This book tries to bring animals to the center of our study of social behavior.

Anthropomorphism

Anthropomorphism refers to attributing human qualities to animals. In the scientific community, using language that suggests animals have intentions, desires, and emotions has been severely criticized as lacking objectivity. One of the worst sins a biologist could commit was to assume that animals shared some of the same mental, social, and emotional capacities that humans do. Scientists would go out of their way to overlook evidence of mindedness, selfhood, personality, and agency. The irony, of course, is that the more we have studied other animals, even in this detached way, the more we have learned about their complex cognitive and emotional capabilities. We have learned that many animals do have preferences and intentions, can solve problems, do display emotions and read our own, are self-aware and do have an active mental life, and can create shared meanings with humans. (All caretakers of companion animals knew this already!) And the discovery of these qualities has serious moral implications for how we treat our fellow social creatures, including issues related, but not limited to, animal experimentation. If animals have a biography, if they are a some "body" and not a some "thing," what are our ethical obligations to them?

Of course, we have to be careful not to go too far. Other animals are not "little people in fur." They are who they are, with their own unique needs, desires, and interests. Attributing human qualities too freely or inappropriately to other animals could lead to misunderstanding them and worse, mistreating them. So anthropomorphism, if used wisely, doesn't have to be one of science's most serious transgressions. If we can employ it critically to reach reasonable conclusions, without misrepresenting the animal's nature or needs, then it could help us not only understand other animals and our relationships with them better, it might influence how we think about and treat them as well.

Anecdotes

The third "a word"—anecdotes—like anthropomorphism, is employed negatively by critics in order to dismiss claims of animal consciousness or mindedness as unscientific, subjective stories, rather than "real," "objective" data. But as Marc Bekoff (2006) rightly points out, the plural of anecdote is data. As Bekoff says, "Anecdotes, like anthropomorphism, can be used for the betterment of science if we carefully assess how we are using them" (2006, 89). Case studies are needed to provide a solid data base for theory building and for stimulating future research.

What Human–Animal Studies Is—and What It Is Not

Let's start with what it is not. First, HAS is not biology or animal behavior. There the focus is on the animals in a technical and specific way—their habitat, their feeding habits, their reproduction patterns, etc.—and particularly, on their characteristics as a species, not as individuals. Neither is the emphasis on other animals' social relationship with human animals. Similarly, those who study animal science or welfare center on how the use of animals for human purposes can be improved. Other disciplines or studies that approach animals on the periphery, as commodities, as passive objects, as tools, as property—without examining and questioning those statuses, without respecting their lives, and without attempting to understand ourselves via investigations of our relationships with other animals—cannot legitimately be considered Human–Animal Studies.

So what is Human–Animal Studies? The focus of HAS is the study of human–animal interaction. Ultimately, HAS asks: What can we learn about ourselves from our relationships with other animals? What does the way we think about and treat other animals teach us about who we are?

Yet not only does HAS merely include other animals in the scholarly realm; it conceptualizes them in a qualitatively different way. As Shapiro (2003, 332) has written, HAS investigates all aspects of our relations with other animals, "respecting animals other than human by treating them as beings with their own experience and interests—not exclusively as cultural artifacts, symbols, models, or commodities in a largely human-centered world. Doing so . . . secure[s] the place of animals other than human in the 'moral landscape'. . . ." And as HAS widens the scope of academia to include other animals, it is anticipated that we will learn more about them as well, and that our knowledge could come to benefit not only ourselves but the other social creatures who are such a vital part of our lives.

Part I: An Emerging Field

Our behavior, our lives, and our destiny are directed in part by the shadow of the beast.

Clifton Bryant

1 An Introduction to Human–Animal Studies

Kenneth J. Shapiro

The opening selection comes from the editor's introduction to the first issue of Society and Animals, *one of the premier journals in Human–Animal Studies. In his 1993 article, Kenneth Shapiro identifies the purpose and significance of both the new journal and the emerging new subfield. Shapiro sees the study of human–animal interactions as teaching us much about ourselves. Research in this area, he argues, will contribute to changing attitudes about other animals and our relationships to them. Finally, Shapiro emphasizes the power of language to shape how we think about, and treat, other animals.*

When we pause to reflect on it, the continued broad scope, pervasiveness, and varied form of animals in our lives is surprising. The dominant image of the modern world is a human-centered and technologically dense landscape. The baying of horses in the streets has long been drowned out by the whirring of motors. Yet our world is still replete with animals in the street, home, nursing home, consulting room, at the "feeder," in the city alley and city park, in the lab, on the farm, in the stream, in the wild. . . . In addition to these living relations, our lives are saturated with former animals— the animal-based products and byproducts with which we feed, medicate, and clothe our bodies. And our thought and language remains suffused with fictional animals— the symbolic animals that provide images and metaphors for our rituals, pastimes, names, fables, character analyses. . . .

As social scientists we are interested in how all these animal presences inform our psychology, sociology, and anthropology. The main purpose of *Society and Animals* is to foster within the social sciences [and humanities] a substantive subfield, animal studies, which will further the understanding of the human side of human–nonhuman animal interactions.

Renewed interest in human–nonhuman animal relations is also prompted by the

Originally published in 1993 as "Editor's Introduction to *Society and Animals*," *Society and Animals*, vol. 1, no. 1, pp. 1–4. Reprinted with permission from Brill Academic Publishers.

current debate over the ethics of our use of animals. In addition to better understanding ourselves, through animal studies we wish to understand our varied relations to them, and to assess the costs—economic, ethical and, most broadly, cultural—of these relations. For those impacts are complex and often of mixed consequences for both parties, human and nonhuman.

On the face of it, this emerging field itself might contribute to the anthropocentrism that many discussants contend is the root cause of animal exploitation. For animal studies is the investigation of nonhuman animals as they influence and are present to us human animals. However, as social scientists we believe that we can provide a relatively independent set of information so that people can make more informed judgments about practices and policies involving nonhuman animals.

Most social scientists now agree that their work is itself a powerful influence on the society that we study. Whether we like or intend it, the topics we investigate, the questions we ask, and the results we generate all affect the institutions that develop policy and promulgate values. Like it or not, we are important players in the current debate over our use of animals.

The emergence of an academic field of study has paralleled each of three recent progressive social movements (Civil Rights, Women's and Environmental Movements). This strongly suggests the inevitability of an animal studies subfield that will parallel the Animal Rights Movement.

In addition to providing substantive information, these cross-discipline fields also foster changes in sensibility and point of view, and the adoption of a critical interpretive stance. We can no longer read Jansen's introduction to the history of art and fail to see that there are virtually no women artists represented there, or a history of the rise of a civilization without becoming aware of the fall of a habitat, or an experiment on maternal deprivation in primates without registering the consequences to the animals involved.

Already we are seeing the emergence of programs in animal studies at universities and of academic journals such as *Society and Animals*, *Anthrozoös*, and *Centaur*—all of which provide both substantive information and critical perspective.

. . . Finally, this first experience as editor of *SandA* sharply raised the issue of our use of language regarding animals. Consider the journal's title: The term "society" refers to human society, but why should we expect you to take it that way, as many nonhuman animals are social and have a society—by most definitions of that term? Conversely, the term "animal" refers to nonhuman animals, but, again, why should you take it that way, as humans are animals as well? Should we call the journal the cumbersome *Human Society and Nonhuman Animals*? This has its own problems:

why should we make the primary categorical cleavage, human and nonhuman, and why should we name all nonhuman animals by the negation of all but ourselves?

Of course, the more general problem is that historically we have come to use "animal" to refer to all animals except humans. Etymology notwithstanding, (*anima* for enlivened with a soul; *humus* for soil or dirt), the appropriate generic term for all animate life has been demoted to a sub-category of that life. "Human" is given equal standing with that formerly generic term so that we have humans and animals for humans and other animals. Ironically, dating from the Enlightenment this humanistic discourse replaced the then regnant discourse of religion that had its own self-valorizing categories (Christian/heathen). Today, we have other categorical cleavers that perpetuate other us/them and in-group/outsider divisions—white/Black, man/woman. The latter displays the further linguistic sleight of hand of making a subcategory, male, into a superordinate category under which the categorically equivalent term, female, is then subordinated.

Other features of the linguistic degradation of animals other than humans extend to the level of species. We have "human being" but not "deer-" or "dog being." In fact, we further reduce the species-specific being of animals other than humans to a generic process with terms like "organism" and "preparation." We also deny species their being through reference to animals based on their function or site from our human point of view—we have pet animals, lab animals, and farm animals. "Companion" is a bit of an improvement for it at least names an apparently reciprocal arrangement. "Animals in the lab" would be an improvement over lab animal, but would *Lab Animal* (a trade magazine of laboratory technicians) accept that new title?

On the level of individual being, we say "he" or "she" for a human individual, but, in most contexts, "it" for an individual other than a human. We, thereby, depersonalize and deindividualize animals other than humans. More subtly, we erase individuality by reifying animal species other than *homo sapiens*. We speak of "the deer" as a supraindividual, forgetting that the actual referent is an aggregate of individual deer.

Of course, we social scientists have contributed to this linguistic degradation through taking our concern with scientific objectivity to mean that the objects of our study must be denied their subjectivity and individuality (Noske 1989). We insist that our relation to them be subject to object not subject to subject.

One of the ways a field of study can raise consciousness is through changes in language habit. I hope that through the publication of *SandA* we can arrive at a language and a concomitant sensibility and practice that will increase our respect for individual animals other than humans.

Questions for Discussion

1. Based on this reading, how would you define Human–Animal Studies?
2. How does Human–Animal Studies parallel the rise of other academic subfields such as Women's Studies or African-American Studies?
3. Why does Shapiro think that our use of language regarding other animals is so important?

2 The Zoological Connection

Animal-Related Human Behavior

Clifton D. Bryant

Nearly three decades ago, sociologist Clifton Bryant criticized his discipline for ignoring the overwhelming presence and significant influence of other animals in our lives. In this piece, Bryant challenges his colleagues to pursue research in this area, and lays out a number of examples of possible topics of investigation. He reminds us of how our culture and language are flooded with animal images and symbols. Some of the more fruitful areas for research, he suggests, include the animal as social problem, the animal as sentient creature, animals and occupations, animals as surrogate humans, and animal-related crime. Interestingly, despite Bryant's argument, it was over a decade later before his fellow sociologists began to seriously study human–animal relationships.

Sociologists, among the practitioners in most of the behavioral sciences and many of the humanities, have been singularly derelict in their failure to address zoological component in human interaction and attendant social systems. We have tended not to recognize, to overlook, to ignore, or to neglect (some critics might say deservedly so) the influence of animals on, or their import for, our social behavior, as well as our relationships with other humans and the directions that our social enterprise often takes.

Humanists have long explored the presence, function, and symbolism of animals in art, literature, and theater at various periods of history (as illustrations, see Antal and Harthan 1971; Clark 1975; Hastings 1936; McSpadden 1972; Toynbee 1973; Zuelke 1965). Social historians in both trade and scholarly treatises have addressed the relationship of man and various beasts in myriad social contexts, and including a wide variety of species, such as the wolf (Lopez 1978), the horse (Dent 1974; Hooper 1976), the elephant (Scullard 1974; Wilson and Ayerst 1976), the whale (Robertson

1954), the crocodile (Graham 1973), and the dog (Leach 1961; Sloan 1971), to mention only a few. Other writers (Carson 1972; Dembeck 1965) have spoken to the human–zoological interface among animals in general.

Animals are often a constituent indirect factor in human illness and, in this connection, social epidemiologists have documented the epizootic relationship between man and beasts. . . . Similarly, behavioral scientists other than sociologists, have examined the interface of animals and human social behavior. Economists have spoken to the question of the financial consequences of many modes of animal-oriented activities from sheep raising to horse racing, to the consumption of fried chicken. Likewise, there is an extensive anthropological literature ranging from Levi-Strauss's (1962) statement on totemism to Wissler's (1914) classic paper on the influence of the horse in the development of plains Indian culture in the United States, and from Williams's (1974) comments on animal references and themes in the communication among members of a black Pentecostal church to Jordan's (1975) insightful analysis of the relationships of the dog and human in the rural South. Psychiatrists have also probed the relationship of animals and humans (Heiman 1956), as have veterinarians (Leigh 1966).

Sociologists, on the other hand, have often been myopic in their observations of human behavior, cultural patterns, and social relationship, and unfortunately have not taken into account the permeating social influences of animals in our larger cultural fabric, and our more idiosyncratic individual modes of interaction and relationships, in their analyses of social life. With very few exceptions, the sociological literature is silent on this topic. This discussion seeks to move sociological attention in a more zoological direction. To this end, I hope the following comments, illustrations, and suggested investigative directions will be sensitizing to the researcher.[1]

Animals and Language Saturation

An extensive behavioral science literature indicates that the language of a given society may well reflect the cultural preoccupations of the society, as evidenced by the inclusion of an inordinate number of words, expressions, and nuances pertaining to these concerns and preoccupations in the language repertoire (as an illustration, see Lindesmith and Strauss 1956). Eskimos, for example, preoccupied with survival in their cold environment, have elaborate sets of words that refer to minute distinctions among different kinds of snow and snowfall (Hiller 1933). The Arabs are said to have approximately six thousand words that refer in some fashion to camels (Klineberg 1954), and the Solomon islanders, presumably as with other societies in the South Pacific, have numerous terms that refer to the coconut (Lewis 1936). . . .

Less recognized, however, is the fact that the language of our own society is heavily saturated with zoological references, which suggest a greater influence of, and involvement and preoccupation with, animals than we are prone to recognize or admit. Words, phrases, metaphors, similes, analogies, etc., redolent of animals are abundant in our language to a degree that invites sociological explanation. In appearance, we have "buck teeth," a "pony tail," are "pigeon-toed," have "crow's feet under our eyes," or look "ratty." A blind date may be a real "dog." In physical ability, condition, or characteristic, individuals may be "fat as a hog," " an old goat," "hungry as a bear," strong as an ox," "smell like a goat," as "busy as a beaver," "eat like a horse," "like a bird," "blind as a bat," or "sick as a dog." In temperament, we may be "gentle as a lamb," or "mean as a snake," "pig-headed," "bull-headed," stubborn as a mule," lion-hearted," "quiet as mouse," or a real "son-of-a-bitch." In terms of demeanor, behavioral proclivity, and/or attitudinal persuasion, one may be a "night owl," "book-worm," "silly-goose," "sex-kitten," "cool cat," "stud," "scaredy cat," "foxy lady," "catty," "sly as a fox," "slippery as an eel," or "quick like a bunny." We may be "hot to trot," make an "ass of ourselves," "horse around," "cat around," "cry wolf," "be a scapegoat," "get our feathers ruffled," "get the lions' share," "be a monkey's uncle," a "lame duck" politician, "bark up the wrong tree," throw "snake eyes" in dice, be "henpecked," or "let the cat out of the bag." We live in a "dog eat dog" world, get our information "straight from the horse's mouth," have a "whale of a time" at a party, take a "Mickey Mouse" course in school, "butt out" in combat, "live high on the hog" in affluent times and, if we are really confronted with a problem, we may well be able to "weasel out of it."

Time and space limitations obviously preclude an exhaustive recitation of animal-related language components in our society's culture. It suffices to say that our language does have an extraordinarily high saturation level in this regard. This strong zoological flavor in our language would suggest a considerable animal influence in our cultural fabric.

Other Zoological Dimensions in Culture

Preoccupation with animals does not stop with zoological analogies and metaphors. We are inordinately prone to label much of our material culture with animal labels, titles, designations, and other appellations, again to a degree that begs explanation. Our children play with teddy bears, eat animal crackers (more recently our pets eat people crackers), and save their allowances in piggy banks. We adults wear Hush Puppy or Bass-Weejun shoes, alligator shirts, turtleneck sweaters, and sharkskin suits; we smoke Lark or Camel cigarettes (or use Bull Durham tobacco if we roll our own) or White Owl cigars, which we light with a Cricket lighter. For those of other nicotine persuasions, a plug of Red Fox or Bull of the Woods chewing tobacco may hit the spot. We refresh ourselves with Gatorade, and for something stronger may imbibe cold duck wine, White-Horse scotch or Wild turkey bourbon, with perhaps a bit of longhorn cheese for a hors d'oeuvre. One of our favorite foods is a hot dog. We drive Rabbits, Impalas, Foxes, Mustangs, Firebirds, Jeeps (jeeps, as older persons will recall, were originally small animals in Popeye cartoons), and put "tigers in our tank," according to a well-known gasoline commercial. We shine our shoes with Kiwi polish and our automobiles with turtle-wax, and wash ourselves with Dove soap and our pots and pans with 20-Mule Team Borax. You can always tell a good ol' boy—he'll be wearing a Caterpillar Tractor cap.

At another level our literature and art forms are also heavily linked with animals. Basic to children's literature are stories such as Goldilocks and the Three Bears, the Little Red Hen, The Three Little Pigs, and Little Red Riding Hood and the Big Bad Wolf, not to mention the Uncle Remus stories and Brer Rabbit.

One of the most enduring novels in the English language is *Black Beauty*, a story purportedly told by a horse in the first person; *Bambi* was a book-of-the month selection in 1928, and a recent best selling novel made into a very popular movie was *Watership Down*, a story whose main characters are rabbits. . . . Like our books, many of our movies have had zoological themes, plots, or references. Examples here would be *Day of the Dolphin*, *The Birds*, *Born Free*, *King Kong*, *Jaws*. . . .

Theater also reveals the zoological connection. One of the most beloved plays of our time is *Harvey*, where a seminal character is an invisible seven-foot rabbit. . . . Among other plays that either involve animals or use similes or metaphors in the title are *Cat on a Hot Tin Roof*, *Night of the Iguana,* and *The Voice of the Turtle*, to mention a few.

Similarly, many of our most popular television programs have involved animals in some fashion. Here could be listed *Lassie*, *Mr. Ed*, *Gentle Ben*, *The Muppets*. Some of our most famous actors and performers have been animals. Consider Rin Tin Tin, Trigger . . . and of course Cheeta (Tarzan's chimpanzee), not to mention Arnold (the pig in *Green Acres*). Among the most famous Americans in history (and in all the world) are imaginary animals—Mickey Mouse, Bugs Bunny, and Donald Duck. . . .

A substantial number of our songs over the years have had zoological titles or references. Here could be included . . . "How Much Is that Doggie in the Window?", "Bye Bye Blackbird," "Turkey in the Straw," and "Hound Dog." Perhaps the most popular musical group in history was The Beatles. For those persons of classical taste there are *Swan Lake* and *Madame Butterfly*.

Our leisure activities are very much dominated by animal oriented behavior. Among our favorite recreational pursuits are . . . hunting and fishing, bird-watching, horseback riding . . . visiting zoos, attending circuses and rodeos,[2] . . . and leering at Playboy bunnies. Even some of most celebrated athletic teams have animal names in totemic fashion. Consider the Chicago Bears, the Atlanta Falcons, the Detroit Lions, and the Miami Dolphins.

Animals are seminally constituent to many of our holidays and special occasions. We have Santa's reindeer at Christmas, the Easter Bunny, the thanksgiving turkey, the black cat at Halloween, and Ground Hog Day.

The Zoological Influence on Behavior

Encyclopedic volumes might be written listing zoological elements and traits in our culture. But the animal influence in our social life goes beyond mere semantic novelty. There is virtually no area of social life that is untouched by animals. The particular configuration that our social behavior assumes results in many instances from a zoological consideration. The crowing rooster wakes us up in the morning and the last thing we do at night is walk the dog, or let the cat out. Animals and insects sometimes interfere with our picnics, and in institutionalized fashion we eat fish on Friday. Taking home a doggie bag has become constituent to the ritual of restaurant behavior, and a mink coat may break up a marriage or save one, depending on whether it is given to the mistress or the wife. In some rural parts of the country, most work stops and schools let out on the opening day of deer season, and the table fare of many families depends on whether the husband is a hunter.

A recent scientific study showed that people who have a dog (or other kind of pet) are more likely to survive a heart attack (Friedmann and Katcher 1978). Some individuals bankrupt themselves betting on the ponies, and other may legitimate their high social status by riding to the hounds. The apartment one rents may depend on whether pets are allowed. Our social relationships are often shaped by animals. It may be easier for boy to meet girl (or vice versa) if they are both walking their dogs. Two individuals may sustain a friendship over time by being hunting companions, and a young childless couple may find that their mutual concern for a pet dog or cat gives them a shared interest that strengthens and nourishes their marriage. . . .

An individual whose tom cat yowls all night may well discern that his neighbors are less than cordial in their interaction with him. . . . Individuals who collect snakes seem to have fewer friends who visit them than do most people, and persons who have a moose head hanging over their fireplace mantle are probably less likely to be asked to join exclusive upper-class clubs. . . . One can lose the respect of friends . . . by mistreating a pet, gain public admiration by riding a bucking bronco or a Brahman bull, become newsworthy by catching an inordinately large fish,[3] enhance one's political chances in an election by appearing on television with a dog, and become a social outcast (at least temporarily) by having an encounter with a skunk.

The Sociological Study of Human–Animal Relations

In spite of the evident prominence of zoological influences in our culture and the subsequent import for our social lives, the sociological literature is largely silent on animal-related human behavior. This is an unfortunate oversight that handicaps our acquisition of a comprehensive understanding of our social enterprise. Sociological research on animal-related human behavior might well yield additional valuable insights concerning: the interaction process; social motivation; the influence of value systems on perception, socialization, and personality development; human violence and its sublimation; and the social dynamics of anthropomorphism. In this connection, several investigative directions in studying animal-related behavior would seem to hold particularly sociological promise and the remainder of our comments will address such directions.

The Animal as Social Problem

Historically and cross-culturally animals have sometimes been social problems, or key elements in social problems. Man-eating tigers disrupt village life in rural India. Locusts destroy crops everywhere and precipitate famines. Contaminated oyster beds in Chesapeake Bay may put large numbers of watermen out of work. The infants of the poor in slum areas are sometimes attacked by rats. Discovery of an endangered species in a strategic location may halt a technological project that might have brought employment to thousands and progress to millions, and an insect like the boll weevil impoverished an entire region for decades. Human behavior and values are often inextricably interwoven with animal behavior in convoluted configurations that may assume dysfunctional dimensions for the social enterprise. . . .

In our own country, we are confronted with both extant and potentially serious animal-related social problems.[4] Our dog and cat population, for example, is approximately one-half that of the human population and growing at a much faster rate (2,000 to 3,500 puppies and kittens are born each hour as compared to 415 human beings) (see Djerassi, Israel, and Jochle 1973). . . .

Our dogs are biting hundreds of thousands of persons each year—38,000 in New York [city] alone. This is an increase of 43% over the past eight years in New York.

Each year persons, and especially children, are attacked by dogs, and savagely mauled, maimed, and even killed. . . .

There are other animals and other problems, but the social import of much animal-related human behavior would seem to be a sociologically fertile realm of study and research for students of societal dysfunctions and disorganization.

The Animal as Sentient Creature

Certain operative value systems in our society mandate conceptualizing the animal as a sentient creature, possessed of sensibilities and sensitivities, and endowed with certain inalienable basic rights to be free from pain and suffering imposed through human tyranny and exploitation. Such value systems have recently crystallized into a concerted social movement bearing the name "animal liberation" (Singer 1977). This movement is gathering considerable impetus and its recent momentum is increasingly bringing it into conflict with various value systems, of technological, economic, or social mode, with which it is unalterably incompatible. The collision of such value systems is not without significant social and economic implication. It may be recalled that concern for whales in our society, and activism in this regard, resulted in legislation that caused the demise of an entire industry, the American whaling industry. Similar concern for dolphins is having its impact on the tuna fishing industry because of resultant legislation that severely handicaps tuna fishing techniques. In Europe, "animal liberation" already has achieved considerable success and animal husbandry there is burdened by an incredible array of regulatory legislation motivated by animal welfare concerns. In Denmark, for example, laying hens must now by law be maintained in a yard rather than in a wire cage. . . .

There are other incipient dilemmas in the "animal liberation" controversy. Major recreational and occupational activities such as trapping, hunting, horse and dog racing, greyhound coursing, rodeo, and cock-fighting, to name some, are all threatened by the controversy and possible legal reforms that may be generated by animal welfare concerns and the attendant efforts of its adherents. Our technology makes heavy use of animals for laboratory testing but longstanding opposition to the practice, such as the antivivisectionist movement, is intensifying. . . . In 1973, a story became public that indicated that the U.S. Air Force intended to use 200 beagle dogs to test poisonous gases. As a result, "the Defense Department received more letters of protest that it had received about the bombing of North Vietnam" (Regan and Singer 1976). Some countries have moved to severely restrict and regulate the use of animals for laboratory purposes. . . . The animal welfare dialogue is well rooted in history. René Descartes, the seventeenth century French mathematician and scientist, conceptualized animals as a kind of beast-machine, as it were. Inasmuch as animals could not speak, it was assumed therefore that they could not think, and accordingly, could not feel. . . . In opposition to the Cartesian view of animals as machine, a formidable social opposition arose and continues to gain momentum until this day. The neo-Cartesian perspective survives, however. Interestingly, Pope Pius XII, for example, in speaking on the subject of lower animals killed in a slaughterhouse or a laboratory, indicated that, "their cries should not arouse unreasonable compassion any more than do red-hot metals undergoing the blows of the hammer, seeds spoiling underground, branches crackling when they are pruned, grain that is surrendered to the harvester; wheat being ground by the milling machine" (quoted in Carson 1972).

. . . Although sociologists have traditionally found social controversy of engaging scientific interest, they have apparently viewed animal-related controversy, social movements, or collective behavior as possessing little sociological relevance. The emerging social dilemmas and conflicts in this regard would surely seem to offer sociological vistas of tantalizing dimensions. From the standpoint of national need and the cultural equilibrium, sociologists would almost seem to have an implicit mandate to become involved in this morass of convoluted social-value conflicts. There is an inconsistency and lack of logic in much of our societal animal values that invites analysis. After all, as one author put it, "Beat a cat and go to prison. Chase and kill a fox and become conceivably Master of the Hunt" (Carson 1972).

Man, Beast, and Work

Sociological students of work and occupation have found little to interest them in the human–animal interface attendant to work, even though the systemic linkages are not inconsiderable. The history of the social enterprise is, in large measure, a history of man and animal working together. In various societies we encounter horses, cattle, camels, water buffalo, llama, reindeer, elephants, or dogs, to name only a few species, as ubiquitous work animals. The resultant dyadic arrangement between man and beast is a most singular interactive relationship and could undoubtedly provide enlightening and significant insights concerning personal identity, dyadic behavior, and the interface of anthropomorphic processes and social linkages, if probed sufficiently. The cowboy and his horse, the farmer and his mule, the organ grinder and his monkey, the miner and his jackass, the mahout and his elephant, and the shepherd and his dog, to mention some of the vagaries of man–animal work teams to be encountered, are classic examples of task-oriented assemblages involving a human and one or more beasts. Inasmuch as the company of, and interaction with, an animal especially in some work-linked aggregations and attendant behavioral configurations, appears to satisfy at least partially, certain human interactive and communicative needs, it might well be that a better understanding of the sociopsychological parameters of loneliness and alienation, and the ameliorative mechanisms that most effectively address such states, can be obtained through systematic study of such aggregations.

At a less abstract level, another man–animal work linkage with sociological import is the occupational specialty that is animal oriented or animal related. It should be recalled that a substantial proportion of our extant vocations, in fact, directly involve animals. The vocations range from professional specialties such as veterinary medicine to unskilled workers in poultry-processing plants, and include occupations with widely varying concerns such as fisheries' biologists who undertake to maximize zoological aquatic resources, game wardens who seek to optimize the extant populations of wild game and fish through the enforcement of hunting and fishing laws, exterminators who attempt to minimize the number of unwanted and undesirable animal and insect populations, and taxidermists who strive to create the illusion of life in dead animals and fish through various preservative techniques. It is only in recent years that sociologists have undertaken to study occupations because of the animal connection.[5]

. . . The zoological component of some types of work has other sociologically important implications. Animals may contribute to, or detract from, the relative occupational prestige of particular vocations, depending on the public context. The animal dimension may even be a significant factor in the degree of work satisfaction or disaffection that people experience on the job. . . .

It should not be overlooked that animals can and have successfully displaced humans in some work situations. Perhaps the most sociologically fascinating example of animals being employed in human work systems is the intriguing efforts of Verhave (1966) to train pigeons to work on a pharmaceutical company assembly line performing quality-control inspection work.[6] This researcher was able to train the birds "to discriminate 'defective' gelatin capsules from nondefective capsules." The results of the experiment were extremely encouraging and the way might well have been paved for a new industrial revolution where man was freed from monotonous and disaffective work by the employment of birds and beasts. Sociological considerations, unfortunately, brought the project and prospect to naught. As one writer describes the outcome:

> However, the pharmaceutical company sponsoring the research decided to abandon the project for a variety of reasons unrelated to the efficiency of the technique. The major deterrent to continuation was, as one

might expect, the concern about public reaction. What consumer would be confident in the reliability of a drug, part of whose quality control was supervised by a pigeon? (Lubow 1977, 34)

. . . . In our subsequent research studies of work and the social context, it might be profitable to examine more fully the interpretive meaning and behavioral import of animal-related work for practitioner and public.

The Animal as Surrogate Human

Animals serve numerous functions in human society, but perhaps sociologically the most interesting function is filling statuses in social groups. Many animals, in effect, are required to play the role of surrogate humans in many social contexts. . . . Almost every conceivable kind of creature from snake to cat, and from horse to chimpanzee has been made to play the role of companion to human. It is the dog, however, that has been the principal in this regard, in our society. . . .

We often take the view that a child needs a companion to grow up and interact with, and to provide an object of emotional attachment. The dog that the child receives becomes in effect, a surrogate brother or sister and usually plays the role well. Each may become protective of the other and both are intensely loyal. They may play together, sleep together, and even "talk" to each other. It has been noted that "communication may be established more easily with a pet than with a parent or relative" (Siegel 1962). Children sometimes have imaginary pets before they have real pets. It has been suggested that a dog or other kind of pet is an essential component in the socialization of a child. The care of the pet develops responsibility, and the child can better "explore the environment" (Levinson 1972a). . . . Although it is popularly believed that a dog or pet has some impact on a child's socialization, sociologists have not seen fit to explore such a possibility. . . .

For the young childless couple, or in the years prior to having children, the pet dog often becomes a surrogate infant, and it is the dog who is the recipient of the love, affection, and attention that the infant would have received. . . .

For the older couple, the dog may play the role of surrogate child to replace the grown child that has moved away. For many elderly persons, and especially widows or widowers, the dog or other pet may become their major social contact and the majority of their interaction may be with the pet. . . .

The seeing-eye dog becomes a surrogate caretaker for the blind, and dogs have recently been used as surrogate therapists for the mentally disturbed (Rynearson 1978), or at least "co-therapist" (Levinson 1972b). The attachment of dogs and people is so great that the death of the owner may cause the dog to grieve itself to death, or the death of the dog may be as traumatic to the family as the loss of a child. The widespread presence of pet cemeteries is vivid testimony to the degree of anthropomorphism involved in most human–dog relationships. It is not unusual to encounter tombstones, caskets, and even graveside services in the repertoire of human response to the death of a dog (or other pet).[7]

We simply tend to use animals, and especially dogs, as replacement actors for people in our understaffed social groups. As Rynearson (1978) has phrased it, "It is natural for the child who has left home or the spouse who has died to be warmly surrogated by a pet." There is an increasing psychological and psychiatric literature on the emotional attachment of humans and pets, and the social role of animals in human groups.[8] Unfortunately, sociological interest in such topics has been minimal. Given some of the incipient trends in childless marriages, singlehood, widowhood, and the increase in the number of couples where children no longer live in the home, there would seem to be good reason to predict the increased reliance on pets as surrogate humans. In the face of such prospects and the increasing significance of human–pet relationships for the maintenance of emotional equilibrium and the amelioration of loneliness and alienation, within a context of more burdensome societal crises and pressures, would not a concerted sociological research effort focusing on individuals and their pets likely yield handsome insights concerning this neglected dimension of human relationships and social interaction?[9]

Zoological Crime

It is the area of crime, delinquency and deviancy that sociologists may perhaps encounter the most fertile phenomenological fields to plow. Animal-related social norms in enormous variety are constituent to all societies, but seemingly especially our own. Violations of such norms may well be among the most ubiquitous of any social deviancy. With only a few recent exceptions (see for example Bryant and Palmer 1976), the area of animal crime has been almost completely ignored by researchers. Animals can be the perpetrators of crime, the instigators of crime, and the victims of crime. They may also be the object of crime, the motivation for crime, the instrument of or for crime, and even the mechanism for the punishment of crime.[10]

. . . Animal-related crime may well be among the oldest form of sanctioned social norm–violation. Prehistoric man, like primitive folk peoples today, presumably had a well-developed conceptualization of fishing and hunting rights, prerogatives, privileges, and obligations. Encroachment on another's hunting or fishing rights, failing to observe appropriate amenities or obligations attendant to hunting or fishing—such as the appropriate distribution of killed game, or the theft of another's kill—would all constitute serious breaches of normative mandate and would disturb community equilibrium, precipitating serious sanctions in many instances. Among agricultural or pastoral peoples, the theft of livestock or invasion of grazing space constitutes extremely serious deviant acts.

In contemporary society the involvement of animals in the social enterprise has become increasingly convoluted and complex, and the proliferating number, and elaboration of, proscriptive and prescriptive norms relevant to animals and animal-related human behavior, has reached an incredible stage. Where in an earlier era one might be hanged as a horse thief, it is now possible to be prosecuted and punished for a bewildering array of animal-related offenses ranging from parrot smuggling to annoying a whale. These can be arranged in at least five categories.

Animals as Personal Property

As mentioned above, horse theft was an endemic criminal activity on the American frontier, as was cattle rustling. Miscreants were dealt with swiftly and harshly. Animal theft is still a major mode of criminal activity. Cattle rustling is still wide-spread, as is the theft of other livestock. Florida ranchers alone, for example lose $3,000,000 worth of beef cattle each year (Bryant and Palmer 1976). Expensive race-horses are tempting targets for thieves and extortionists. "Dognappers" steal dogs for ransom and other thieves steal dogs for resale to pet shops or scientific laboratories. . . . The theft, appropriation of, or assault on, a man's beast, be it elephant or fish, is a crime against property and is a relatively frequent and widespread criminal offense.

Animals as personal property may also be assaulted or killed. The owner of a pet poodle in Florida claimed that a dog groomer cut her pet while clipping the dog's hair causing the dog to "become traumatic" and frightening it out of its playful personality. She sued for $15,000 damages and the jury awarded $9,000. . . .

Animals as Public Property

Fish and wildlife, in this country, are considered to be the corporate property of the public, and accordingly hunting, fishing, and trapping are regulated and controlled by both State and Federal legislation. Jurisdiction usually depends on whether the game in question is migratory or nonmigratory. The vagaries of game-law violations are among the more prevalent of all criminal offenses, and game wardens who enforce such laws wage a relentless war on "camouflage-collar criminals" (Palmer 1975; Snizek *et al.* 1975). Crimes against publicly owned creatures are recently assuming new and unusual configurations, however. This past year in Texas, three men were fined $6,000 in federal court for conspiring to kill at least 70 federally protected golden eagles from a helicopter. The men had violated the Airborne Hunting Act, in addition to killing protected birds. The men apparently were killing the eagles because they thought the birds were a menace to baby sheep and goats (United Press International 1978a). Several years ago, three corporations and four individuals were tried in federal court for illegal international trafficking in American alligator hides worth $700,000. At the time, American alligators were on the endangered species list (*New York Times* 1977). Federal law protects various undersea growths in national parks and elsewhere, but scuba divers are now stealing coral from the ocean floor because of the new jewelry fad, and facing prosecution as a result (United Press International 1978b). Today it is illegal to annoy or attack any marine mammal. . . . The broadening purview of animal-related laws will surely dramatically increase the number of persons who violate these laws and are legally punished for their offenses.

The Animal as Hazard or Nuisance

Within some contexts, the animal is viewed as a hazard or a public nuisance and appropriate laws are enacted in an attempt to ameliorate the nuisance and prevent the hazard, and persons subsequently violate these laws. Perhaps the best know example of such offenses is the serpent handling of various Appalachian fundamentalist religious sects. Persons maintaining some patently dangerous animals as pets are often legally punished. One man in New York State, for example, was fined for keeping a mountain lion (Associated Press 1997f). . . . In Dallas, Texas, a woman was fined for keeping 50 monkeys as pets. It was charged that "the monkeys create an offensive odor, excessive noise and cause severe devaluation of the property." (Associated Press 1977a). . . .

Anti-Cruelty to Animal Laws

As noted earlier, there is a long history of organized groups and informal efforts to ameliorate the plight of the animal and to regulate the treatment of animals in order to protect them from human cruelty. Anti-cruelty statutes have both proliferated and expanded in their scope and coverage of animal-related human behavior. Contemporarily there are anti-cruelty laws covering animals in agriculture, being processed into meat, in entertainment, and in laboratory experimentation, to name but a few areas. Dog-fights and cockfighting are illegal in some contexts, in many states, but avidly pursued underground as clandestine sport by fans who are in violation of the law (Bryant 1971). . . . Laws prohibiting a human from having sexual relations with an animal exist in most states and some carry very severe penalties. These laws generally view bestiality as cruelty to animals.

Crimes against Ecology

The concern with ecology in recent years has precipitated an elaborate extension of animal-related laws and regulations. A significant proportion of such laws have addressed animals or fish that are threatened with extinction—"endangered species," as it were—and generally prohibited the hunting or killing of such animals if indigenous to this country, and the importation or ownership of the animals or any products derived from them, if the creatures are native to other countries. Examples of such laws are the prohibitions against importing certain types of furs, hides, and skins, as well as whale products and some kinds of ivory. The importation of certain rare kinds of birds and animals is also illegal but there is widespread smuggling of these creatures in spite of severe penalties. Interestingly, even noted scientists and zookeepers are violating such laws. The director of Yale University's Peabody Museum, an internationally known ornithologist and research pioneer in the study of egg-white protein, was fined $3,000 for illegally importing bird eggs from Britain (*New York Times* News Service 1974). In recent years some of the most prestigious zoos in the nation have been investigated for possible violation of federal laws concerning the importation of rare animals (Associated Press 1977e). . . .

Crime is a behavioral phenomenon relative to time and technology, and to social values and interpretive context. It would appear that such laws and patterns of social control attendant to animals and animal-related human behavior are proliferating at a significant rate, and will continue to do so in the future. In the face of social constraints to the contrary, violations of such normative systems will also likely persist, if not accelerate, producing much more widespread modal patterns of "zoological crime." There would seem to be little rationalization for sociologists to continue to disregard animal crime. Such criminal configurations may have far more significant social consequences than might be generally believed. . . .Animal crime is ubiquitous. It is encountered in city and farm, factory and laboratory, and its offenders come from all walks of life and social classes. Animal crime involves powerful public sentiments from all concerned parties. Animal crime with all of its implications may be as potentially divisive and as disruptive to the social enterprise as any other form of deviancy.

Summary

Our social enterprise is not composed of humans alone. Creatures of all variety are inextricably involved in many of our behavioral activities and play important interactive roles in society. The animal influence in our lives is enormous and our culture is richly infused with zoological components. The profusion of animal-oriented or related human behavior in which we routinely engage is important in its consequences and significant in its import. It would seem to well justify the research attention of sociologists. As students of society and social behavior, we can no more appropriately ignore the zoological dimension, than an analysis of drama can ignore seminal actors in a play. To truly understand human social behavior in all its vagaries, and to be completely sensitive to the full array of its nuisances and subtleties, we must enhance our appreciation of its zoological dimension. Accordingly, we might all be well advised to add animals to the lexicon of our discipline. We may come to perceive whole new vistas of behavioral linkages by taking into account the "zoological connection." Our behavior, our lives, and our destiny are directed in part by the shadow of the beast. Let us, therefore, turn our sociological attention to this neglected area of social causation.

Questions for Discussion

1. Bryant chastises sociologists for having ignored our relationships with other animals. What might we learn about ourselves from studying our interactions with nonhuman animals?

2. Why do you think sociology and many of the other social sciences have been so slow to study human–animal relations?

3. Bryant suggests that for some people, animals may serve as surrogate humans. Do you think animals replace human companionship or can they also help facilitate human social relationships?

3 The Animal Question in Anthropology

Barbara Noske

How have anthropologists traditionally studied other animals? That is the question that Barbara Noske asks and answers in this essay. For Noske, anthropology has been decidedly anthropocentric (human-centered) in its approach—overlooking, objectifying, and ignoring the role of other animals in human societies. Interestingly, those scientists who caution us not to reduce social and behavioral differences between groups of humans to biological explanations (based, for example, on race or sex) have continued to rely almost exclusively on biology to conceptualize other animals and to explain their behavior. But once animals are brought to the center of the scientific investigation, and studied more like social subjects than biological objects, then perhaps we can learn to see them (and ourselves) more accurately.

Anthropologists commonly define their discipline, anthropology, as the study of *anthropos* (humankind) and think it perfectly natural to pay little or no attention to the nonhuman realm of animalkind. Of course, animals do figure in anthropological studies but they do so mainly as raw material for human acts and human thought. Anthropology has a long tradition of studying the ways in which human groups and cultures deal with and conceive of their natural environment, including other species. Such studies usually confine themselves to humans in their capacities as agents and subjects who act upon and think about animals.

Consequently, animals tend to be portrayed as passive objects that are dealt with and thought and felt about. Far from being considered agents or subjects in their own right, the animals themselves are virtually overlooked by anthropologists. They and their relations with humans tend to be considered unworthy of anthropological interest. Most anthropologists would think it perfectly natural to pay little or no attention to the way things look, smell, feel, taste, or sound to the animals involved.

Originally published in 1993 in *Society and Animals*, vol. 1, no. 2, pp. 185–190. Reprinted with permission from Brill Academic Publishers.

Consequently, questions pertaining to animal welfare in the West or in the Third World rarely figure in anthropological thought.

Anthropologists treat animals as integral parts of human economic constellations and human-centred ecosystems: They are economic resources, commodities and means of production for human use.

Animal-based human economies have been studied extensively by anthropologists, who have regarded as their main question whether or not various human practices with animals are economically or ecologically rational (seen from the human point of view). Only in those cases where semi-wild animals still retain some control over their own whereabouts do anthropologists sometimes look at the advantages of existing human–animal arrangements for the animals.

The discipline of anthropology is blatantly anthropocentric. At best, humans and animals are taken to interact within one communal ecosystem and most anthropologists' attention is directed toward understanding humans rather than animals. Questions focus on humans and humans alone. Do animal population dynamics, diet, and mobility have no influence on human culture?

Apart from animals that function as subsistence factors, anthropologists have duly called attention to animals that are made to serve non-subsistence human purposes, for instance as objects of prestige or sacrifice or as totems. Animals in this capacity have been vested with religious significance and with symbolic and metaphorical power. In addition, anthropologists have focused on the roles that animals play in human ceremonial and religious life.

Anthropological interest in animal totems or animal symbols is no guarantee against an anthropocentric approach. More often than not such interest serves as an excuse to stop at human constructs instead of paying attention to the animals themselves. When challenged on this issue most anthropologists argue that for questions about animals *per se* one had better turn to sciences such as biology or ethology. To point out to them that in addition to a *human–animal relationship* there also exists something like an *animal–human* relationship, and that totally ignoring the latter will lead to a one-sided subject–object approach is a waste of time. As present the anthropocentrism in anthropology goes virtually unchallenged.

Understanding Anthropology's Anthropocentrism

The reason for this is the commonly held view that animals in themselves have nothing to offer a science that is concerned with the social and the cultural. Anthropologists and sociologists as well as scholars in the humanities generally assume that sociality and culture do not exist outside the human realm. These phenomena are taken to be exclusively human, a view which lands anthropologists and their colleagues in the circular argument that animals, not being human, cannot possibly be social or cultural beings.

Social scientists characterize humans in terms of the material and social arrangements these humans make and by which they are also shaped: as beings who socially constitute and are constituted.

Humans are taken to make their own history and while their natural history was once believed to be made for them, modern humanity increasingly tries to shape that history as well. By contrast, animals are believed to have only a natural history, which is made for them and which has caused them to evolve in the first place.

Unlike human beings, animals tend to be regarded as organisms primarily governed by their individually based genetic constitutions. But this conviction turns out to be an *a priori* one, given the circumstance that almost no student of human society and culture asks the same questions about animals as are asked about humans. One does not look for the social and the cultural where surely it cannot be found, outside the human sphere! However, if one preconceives humans to be the sole beings capable of creating society, culture, and language, one excludes animal forms of society, culture, and language by definition. On the whole, animals figure in anthropology not only as objects for human subjects to act upon but also as antitheses of all that according to the social sciences makes humans human. The social sciences present themselves preeminently as the sciences of discontinuity between humans and animals.

There are few social scientists willing to ask what animal–human continuity might mean in terms of their own field. Thus sociologists do not bother about a sociology of animals. Neither do most social scientists question the common hierarchical subject–object approach to the human–animal relationship; least of all do they pose questions as to the ways in which animal subjects might relate to human subjects. Social scientists tend to treat our continuity with animals as a purely material residue from a pre historical past. At the most our "animalness" (our body) is taken to have formed the material base upon which our real "humanness" (mind, sociality, culture, language) could arise. Our humanness is built on an animal basis of sorts, with a vital addition.

Biological Essentialism: For Animals Only

At the same time social scientists tend to be on their guard against any form of biological essentialism. They hasten to point out the dangers of explaining social differences between people in terms of biological essences such as race or sex (and rightly so).

Ironically, many scientists who hold this view still gravitate toward those essentialist positions they claim to detest—as soon as another biological category comes into view, our species barrier. Suddenly clear-cut notions as to what *is* human and what *is* animal crop up among anthropologists and other social scientists. Their outspoken criticisms of those who think in terms of other biological essences lose credibility in the face of their own assumptions about human and animal essences. Implicitly, anthropologists do have conceptions pertaining to a universal human essence: It seems first and foremost to be embodied in our "non-animalness" and in the animal's "nonhumanness." But if humanness is identical with non-animalness, then what constitutes animalness and what are animals?

As we have noted before, hardly any social scientist shows interest in animals for their own sake, let alone cares to ask sociological and anthropological questions about them. Given the exclusion of animals from their respective fields, what grounds do these social scientists have for making such confident statements about animals, especially about what animals are not? What conceptions do these scientists have of animals and where did they get them?

In an earlier work (Noske 1989), I described the extent to which the social scientific image of animals and animalness has been shaped by sciences that are often denounced as reductionist and objectifying. Such reductionism is only denounced, however, when directed at human beings. The natural sciences, particularly the biobehavioral sciences, are responsible for creating the current animal image. The biobehavioral scientific characterization of animals is presented in terms of observable traits and mechanisms thought to be encoded in the animal's genetic make-up. Unlike genetic transmission, human cultural transmission does not pass over the heads of the individuals concerned. It involves the active if not always conscious participation of the transmitters (the teachers) as well as that of the recipients (the learners). It is not as if the former are active and the latter passive.

Biology and ethology have somehow become *the* sciences of animalkind. It is from these sciences that social scientists (the sciences of humankind) uncritically and largely unwittingly derive their own image of animals and animalness. Animals have become associated with biological and genetic explanations.

This has led to an "anti-animal reaction" among scholars in the humanities. They bluntly state that evolutionary theory is all right for the interpretation of animals and animal actions but not for humans. Hardly any critic of biological determinism will stop to think whether animals indeed can be understood in narrowly genetic and biological terms.

Many people in or allied with the social sciences err in accepting biology's image of animals as *the* animal essence. They fail to appreciate that that image of animals is a de-animalized biological construct. The anthropocentric social sciences view their own subject matter, humans, as animal in basis plus a vital addition. This view turns animals automatically into reduced humans. The argument goes as follows: If biologists and ethologists are reductionists this is because animals, as reduced beings, prompt them to think so.

However, it may well be that animals continue to be objectified because biologists prefer to remain reductionist and because social scientists for their part prefer to remain anthropocentric.

Reexamining Human–Animal Continuity

Does the current image of animals really convey all there is to animals? Having rejected the caricatures reductionists have made of humans, why take their animal caricatures at face value?

To acknowledge human–animal continuity is not necessarily to indulge in biological reductionism (Noske 1989). Another obstacle to the recognition of human–animal continuity is the fear among biologists of being accused of anthropomorphism, the attribution of exclusively human characteristics to animals. For their part, social scientists have been jealously guarding what they see as the human domain and so tend to applaud the biologists' fear of anthropomorphism. What is currently denounced as anthropomorphism are those characterizations which social scientists are keen to reserve for humans. In their critique of biological determinism social scientists point an accusing finger at anyone who credits animals with personhood. But again, how can one know how animals differ from or are similar to humans if one declines to ask the same questions about the two?

There are some courageous animal scientists who do say that animals are more human-like and less objectlike than their own science will have us believe. However, they will often say such things off the record or rather apologetically. This is understandable since they are committing a sacrilege both from the perspective of the animal sciences and from that of the human sciences. Those scientists who have actually studied animals as participant observers, the common anthropological approach to human societies, reveal a tension in their writings between the accepted biological codes and their own experiences with animal personhood. Jane Goodall who is working with chimpanzees, Dian Fossey who lived and died among mountain gorillas, the Douglas-Hamilton couple and Cynthia Moss who are living and working among elephants, all write about touching experiences with animal personhood. Their science cannot handle these forms of animal reality and tends to belittle or ignore them. The animal sciences are simply not equipped to deal with those characteristics in animals which according to the social sciences make humans human.

Faced with the shortcomings of their own tradition a number of dissatisfied animal scientists, such as Donna Haraway and Donald Griffin, have called for a tentative anthropological approach to animals. What attracts them in anthropology and particularly in its method of participant observation is its intersubjective, nonreductionist way of acquiring knowledge, a method contrasting strongly with the subject–object approach applied by animal scientists in their laboratories. Anthropologists treat the Other with respect and are wary of ethnocentrism. Even though the Other cannot be fully known nor understood, anthropologists have been trained to tread upon this unknowable ground with respect rather than with disdain.

But all this pertains only to the *human* Other. It is curious that scientists who have learned to beware of the dangers of ethnocentrism so easily lapse into another kind of centrism—anthropocentrism. We are sadly stuck with two seemingly unrelated images: one of humankind and one of animalkind conveyed by two totally separate brands of science, the one typifying humans as social subjects, the other typifying animals as biological objects. The newly emerging discipline of human–animal relations will find this a formidable obstacle to overcome.

Questions for Discussion

1. How has anthropology traditionally studied other animals?
2. Give several examples of what Noske refers to as "anthropology's anthropocentrism."
3. What does Noske mean by biological reductionism?

Part II: Studying Human–Animal Relationships

Few exchanges are as intense and emotionally involving as those we have with companion animals. Despite the frequency and importance of relationships between humans and animals, analyses of interspecies interaction are noticeably rare in the social scientific literature.

Clinton Sanders

4 Understanding Dogs through Kinesthetic Empathy, Social Construction, and History

Kenneth J. Shapiro

The previous selection called for researching human–animal interaction in a way that attempts to capture the perspectives of the animals themselves. In this reading, psychologist Ken Shapiro outlines one way to do just that. Shapiro, drawing on phenomenological psychology, proposes a three-pronged strategy for taking the role of the animal other. Primarily, the researcher tries to assess the experience of other animals by sensing or empathizing with the bodily movements or intentions of the animal, which Shapiro refers to as "kinesthetic empathy." Yet this understanding of the animal's bodily experience must be informed both by "social constructions"—the cultural meanings of the animal—and the "history" or biography of the specific animal as understood by the human investigator.

Introduction

In her recent book *Buffalo Gals* (1987), Ursula Le Guin presented a collection of stories about our relation to nonhuman animals. Her work demonstrates the advances that we have made in the sophistication of our accounts of such matters since Kipling's charming but homocentric *Just So Stories* ([1912] 1950). Le Guin succeeds in walking a line between a sloppy identification that humanizes and homogenizes animals and an alienated and often cruel relation to animals. While respecting the differences between human and nonhuman animals, the "space between us," she also acknowledges our commonality: in terms of our thesis, the bodily experiencing that we have in common and that is the basis of our access to each other. She does this by inviting us to "come into animal presence," a term she takes from the title of a Denise Levertov poem.

Originally published in 1989 in *Anthrozoös*, vol. 3, no. 3, pp. 184–195. Reprinted with permission, International Society for Anthrozoology (ISAZ).

That poem reads, in part, "What joy when the insouciant armadillo glances at us and doesn't quicken his trotting across the track into the palm bush. What is this joy?" This joy comes from being in the presence of a creature who "has some intention to pursue in the palm forest." This joy lies in dwelling in that presence, in inhabiting that intention, the armored but guileless world of the armadillo. I will attempt to show that it is instructive to so inhabit nonhuman animals, while recognizing that our dwelling there, as in all other presences, whether human-animal, human-human, or human-divine, is necessarily imperfect.

In the less mythopoetic but nonetheless influential literature and practice of my own field of psychology, we have not typically been interested in the experience of nonhuman animals. In fact, at least apparently, psychology got along for over a generation without interest even in human experience. Recently, there have been a number of calls to initiate (Nagel 1974; Griffin 1981; Burghardt 1985) or, really, reinitiate (Grene 1965) such a focus. But why should we be interested in an animal's presence or experiencing? In his paper on animal awareness, Burghardt states: *Let us retain an open-minded delight in animal abilities, a respect for what they may be experiencing, and a balance between skepticism and incredulity. And we must not forget, nor ignore, the use, or misuse, to which our findings will be put in the growing debate on the treatment of our fellow creatures* (his emphasis, 918). Here are three reasons—delight or joy, respect, and concern for their welfare.

Of course, it is not only what we understand of animals, whether of their abilities or experiencing, that affects them; it is how we arrive at that understanding—our method. For any method constrains us to certain living arrangements for the objects of our study and requires them to undergo certain procedures. As importantly, that treatment of animals influences attitudes and practices toward animals in noninvestigatory settings. This paper describes a method that is respectful of animals both in that it does not require constraining them in cages and in that its goal is to describe the structures of their experience as they are lived by them.

I present the method primarily through its application to the study of an individual dog. Following that application, I will provide a fuller discussion of the method. I believe that this reversal of the more usual order of presentation is justified here because a phenomenologically based method, particularly one applied to nonhuman animals is undoubtedly unfamiliar to most readers.

Phenomenology in Psychology

By way of a brief introduction, the development of phenomenology as a method in psychology began with Giorgi (1970) as an attempt to explicate the structures of mundane human experience. In this human science approach to psychology, the researcher usually elicits a combination of written and oral protocols from subjects on a particular phenomenon of interest. Each protocol is then analyzed to extract the constituent features pertinent to the phenomenon. Through reflection on his or her evolving sense of the phenomenon, the researcher develops a typical description that identifies structural—that is, constituent—features of the phenomenon.

Obviously, there are considerable problems with any direct application of this method to the study of nonhuman animals. However, I have attempted to retain some emphases consistent with the spirit of the approach: the focus on the meaning of the experience to the subject, the participation of the investigator in that experience, and the attempt to locate essential features of the experience. The primary shift is from verbal discourse to bodily experience—the meanings implicit in a subject's gestures, postures, and attitudes. To use another phenomenological term, bodily experience refers to the way in which the animal is "intending" the world at any moment.

Since there are problems both in locating and in explicating the intended world whether of a human or a nonhuman animal, the present method, following Ricoeur, is necessarily mixed. In his study of psychoanalysis (1970), the philosopher Paul Ricoeur argued that Freud's theory proceeds on two levels of discourse at once: that of the natural sciences, in which phenomena are thinglike, causally determined, and, hence, to be explained; and that of an interpretative science in which the object of study is an autonomous subject, more textlike than thinglike, and, hence, to be understood rather than explained. Ricoeur argued further that such a mixed discourse, and a correspondingly mixed method, is necessary in the study of human beings because we are both objects and subjects.

Following the lead of this dual or ambiguous ontology but extending it to nonhuman beings, the method I present is mixed. It centers on an interpretative investigative posture, which I term kinesthetic empathy. However, that empathic move into the world of the animal, the animal as subject in the original sense of that term, is supplemented by consideration of the social and historical contexts that shape the animal (and the investigator's experience of the animal).

The method has three moves. The primary posture is one of kinesthetic empathy through which the investigator attempts directly to sense or empathize with the motor intention or attitude or project of the animal. This emphasis on the investigator's bodily sensibility is an extension of an earlier effort of my own, which described a method based on bodily reflective modes (Shapiro 1985). The empathic move is informed in two ways that constitute the mixed methodology. First, the investigator reads relevant texts in both popular and scientific literature to assay pertinent social constructions of the animal under investigation. The reading must assess the social construction in terms of both the investigator's preconceptions and its likely impact on the actual experience of the animal. Second, the investigator must become a historian of the individual animal or animals under study. In effect, he or she develops a biographical account. This also informs the attempts at kinesthetic empathy.

Description and Reflection

Background

Sabaka (the name comes from the Russian for dog) is a five-year-old male dog of mixed breed. He has been in our household since he was about four weeks old, when we got him at a local animal shelter. He had been abandoned at a town dump. Three months or so after he joined us, we obtained a second dog, a female collie mix, probably four years old, also from a shelter. We had decided on two dogs so that they would be company for each other. Undoubtedly influenced by the local Maine practice of keeping dogs outside even in winter, to serve as watchdogs, we planned to raise the dogs primarily in an outdoor yard with a run joining a shed in the barn. Elkie, the collie, adopted Sabaka, and the two were inseparable for about a year, when Elkie died from an illness contracted before we acquired her. That event changed our relation to Sabaka significantly, as I will describe. A second major event in Sabaka's life, in his third year, was our absence from the house for a six-month period, during which Sabaka was left with a housesitter.

Sabaka at Play

When Sabaka was about two years old, before he took on the activities of guarding the house and keeping up on the latest movements of the local wildlife—the red squirrel in the yard and the woodchucks across the way—playing was the order of the day. We had furnished him with a bucket, located in our playroom, in which were kept all manner of items—discarded knotted socks, a partial upper of an L.L.Bean shoe, a rubber watermelon, dead tennis balls, and a plastic bone. Sabaka could initiate play with one of us by pulling out, say, an old sock and approaching coyly. Alternatively, we, or one of the two neighbors' dogs who often visited, could in like manner get a sock and approach him. Typically, play commenced in earnest when I, for example, went down on all fours and attempted to catch Sabaka and get the sock from him. By custom, the playing field was largely limited to a couch that he could fit under but I could not (at least, not without injuring myself) and sundry other combination obstacle/hideaway/out-of-bounds pieces of furniture, all in the playroom.

Occasionally, the play could break out into a hallway that made a circuit around the stairwell and then back to the playroom.

At first glance, this activity hardly seems worth mentioning—a simple game of keep-away and chase. However, on reflection, the invitation ritual, the play itself, the implicit rules and regulations governing the legitimate play area, permitted and prohibited moves, and the object of the game, as well as the conditions ending it, were all quite intricate and yet easily maintained by both players. Even more subtle were the postures, feints, and deceits, the half-executed moves during what might look, to the uninitiated, like timeouts from the game.

In reflecting, I can evoke some of the actual moves and postural intimations of moves and give an account of them. I also can evoke and then reflect on the way that I recognize those moves, his and mine, in the moment of the play. From this reflection, it is clear that I typically do not understand and respond to his moves through a simple inferential posture. Rather, in the midst of the game, my understanding of his moves and of the plays he makes—of the paths traversed, of the paths prohibited or unlikely, of his inclinations, temptations, irritations, intimidations, and intimations with respect to possible moves—in short, my understanding of his bodily experience is more direct and immediate. As the language I have employed suggests, it is comparable to the way a tennis player anticipates an opponent's next shot and prepares for his or her own return. However, here I stay with the opponent's shot, with Sabaka's move, rather than going from it to the move it invites from me. I can know Sabaka's actions and incipient intentions and stay with them, at least at some moments, by empathizing with them, by taking up his bodily posture and attitude.

Through this investigatory posture, I can have an immediate sense of the move he is about to make. But *move* is too weak a term: the thrust of the present discourse is to show that I have more than merely a sense of his physical movement; I can know what is significant to him and what and how he is experiencing in a certain moment. Through this involvement and reflection on it, I realize that his experience is of a phenomenal field. He is embedded in a lived rather than an objective space. It is a space shaped and oriented by his own position, interests, and projects, rather than the homogeneous space of, for example, Euclidean geometry. Sabaka's space during our play is shaped by the objects that are more or less accessible or prohibited to one or both of us and also by another mobile body that he knows puts constraints on and also proffers invitations to his own moves—that is, with respect to which he is a center of potential action. He remains embedded in this field, unable to reflect on it. His knowledge is a "knowing how" not a "knowing about" (Ryle 1949). In the terms being developed here, his is a bodily sense of the field. His experience consists of invitations from the objects configurationally present to him, in relation to him as a lived, mobile body.

His action is addressed to a certain milieu that has vital significance to him (Merleau-Ponty 1963, 151). As a lived body, he has the power paths and barriers, and is able to enact his inclinations with respect to it. For example, he has a sense of my incipient intention to pursue him one way around the stuffed chair and, correlatively, of the way that he can move to avoid me. He knows bodily and immediately my possible moves. They are meaningful with respect to a complex field of barriers and accesses, themselves meaningful with respect to his own particular capacities, his own possible moves. In effect, he lives in a region of bodily experience that is and remains prelinguistic—always only implicitly meaningful.

His experience is not thoughtful in the sense that he knows or can register as a fact, for example, that I cannot follow him under the couch. He does not depict or represent or give an account to self or other. Neither can he refer to nor indicate an object merely for the sake of drawing attention to it (Terrace 1985). His is not ectothinking, that is, he cannot utilize schema that are available independent of circumstance (Lyons 1987). It is closer to endomesothought, a mixed mode of practical and impressionistic but nonetheless thoughtful understanding. He is embedded in an always implicitly significant world; his is a concernful absorption, as Cave (1982, 253) puts it, applying Heidegger's notion of caring to animals. He is interested, he cares about and intends a world, but one in which he is always absorbed. His concerns are directed and enacted but without thoughtful mediation. Meaning for him resides in the shape and kinetics of the objects of his world in relation to his concerns.

In Buytendijk's (1936) rereading of Pavlov, he suggested that a dog's looking for something is intelligible neither as Pavlov's reflex machine nor as a clear and positable imaginative life. Rather, a dog has a "vital phantasy" (174), which Buytendijk likens to our familiar experience of looking for something without deliberately intending to look and without positing what we are looking for, guided only by a vague bodily sense of having forgotten something. Similarly, the dog's experience is a form of sensorimotor judgment.

Consistent with the emphasis here on movement and possible movement as Sabaka's primary form of understanding, the intelligence of Clever Hans, the famous counting horse, did not lie in his capacity to count (although animals have been shown to have some capacity to "summate"—defined as judgment to choose among different quantities [Rumbaugh, Savage-Rumbaugh, and Hegel 1987]). Rather, it was in his extraordinary sensitivity to the subtle movements of Von Osten's head and posture (Katz 1937). More recently, Vicki Hearne (1986) corroborated this capacity for bodily rapport between horse and trainer-rider. Finally, the chimpanzee Moja, when given repeated opportunities to draw a given set of objects, consistently drew the typical movement of one particular object, a basketball, rather than a representation of the object's shape. The basketball was drawn as vertical zigzag lines (Beach, Fouts, and Fouts 1984).

The important role of perceived movement in a dog's constitution of his world would seem to have some ethical implications for research in which a dog is restrained in a body harness, for example, as in the learned helplessness paradigm (Seligman 1975).

Sabaka's Sense of Space and Place

When he is outside, Sabaka spends much of his time lying in a certain spot at the head of the drive that allows him an optimal view both down the driveway to the street and through the windows of the kitchen. It also allows him to be in the sun. From this spot, he can comfortably doze while vigilantly smelling, listening, and watching, ready to bark, bay, and half-charge at passers-by. He also can watch family comings and goings. Other places within the house offer some of these features—under the couch in the playroom, on the second-floor landing, at the threshold between the dining room and the kitchen.

Currently, Sabaka sleeps overnight on the landing. My original plan for him to sleep outside had been derailed by Elkie's premature death, after which he slowly moved to sleeping arrangements closer to us, in a shed attached to the main house. However, during our six-month stay abroad, we instructed the housesitter to let him spend the night inside, since she was away during the day, during which time he was outside. It was very cold at night, and we felt guilty about leaving him. Also, in retrospect, it is clear that a conflicting construction of "pet"—namely, that of dog as an integral member of the family—was vying here with the Maine woodsman construction of outdoor watchdog. Apparently, it took our absence to give that construction formative power. In any case, Sabaka now sleeps on the landing twelve feet from my bedroom.

When he is in the house, during the day and early evening, Sabaka stays under the couch, sometimes to be away from us, for example, when he has done something he should not have, and sometimes to be near, for example when I am on the couch. When we eat in the dining room, he remains on the threshold of that room, although, over the years, that threshold has edged almost imperceptibly closer and closer to my soup, as the sleeping arrangement has edged closer to my bed. At almost any time of day or night he may, if given the chance, sleep on a second favored couch in my study. It would seem that I cannot (or perhaps do not really wish to) train him other-wise. While he generally takes a somewhat distant position of surveillance with respect to us, he will quickly occupy a bedspread or cushion left on the floor and, when curled up next to one of us, will immediately commandeer the apparent choice center of another family member's resting spot, even as he or she is setting it up or rolling over for a second to change the channel.

Let me now offer some reflections on these actions. Apparently, Sabaka lives space in various ways. Some of these have been described in ethological literature on dogs and their evolutionary ancestors, wolves. With respect to the instinctive behav-ioral patterns of the latter, both Scott and Fuller (1965) and Fox (1978b) assert that dogs and wolves retain much in common. Most of the activities I have just described fit between a dog's territorial space, that space which is defended, marked and tracked, and the "personal space" (Katz 1937, 95) at the border of which, and within which, a dog performs numerous complex greeting, courting, dominance determina-tion, and care-soliciting behaviors. Between the roughly territorial and personal spaces is what I will call the space of place.

Within the literature on *Canidae*, instinctive patterns are described under the rubric of lair behavior—shelter and care seeking, building and maintenance behav-iors (Scott and Fuller 1965, 64–65). Informed by these descriptions and their typical-ly functional—that is, evolutionary—explanatory accounts, I return to the animal under study and attempt to empathize kinesthetically with his lived sense of these activities. What is Sabaka's bodily experience of the space of place?

I want to appreciate directly Sabaka's bodily experience, his posture, attitude, incipient and actual moves and be carried along toward them as features of his own intended world. As I watch him in this way, I sense that he spends much time seek-ing and checking on previously established places. As he approaches a prospective place, his bodily posture already begins to assume the contour that the prospective place would offer as well as appreciating the lookout potential. He begins to circle it and to curl and lower his body. There is more to this behavior than the vestigial instinctive grass-flattening or snake-checking behavior of his wolf ancestors. His bodily attitude communicates his sense of how this space could contain him; he is, as it were, trying it on for size. He is seeking a space that he already knows bodily: an optimal resting place that offers the sense of protection and the lookout advantage of a partial enclosure while simultaneously providing comfort—the warmth of the sun or the softness of the carpet. As a vantage point, it is a lookout, or, rather, a smelling station or listening post, both for detecting outside threat and for keeping track of us. At the same time, it is a place that gives him a sense of being with or close to us; in it, he is in the family lair. Once in that space of place, he lives it in a certain bodily way. He curls his body in the recess for physical warmth and for closeness to the pack or family of which he is a member; he sighs and purrs with contentment and security much as he does when petted; he lies oriented to keep watch both for strangers and for the possibility of gaining even more access to the family hearth. But, again, he already assumes this posture as a kind of set, as the project of finding such places. The bodily posture of place seeking and place sought are correlative, and, by kinesthetically empathizing with his body, I can direct myself from it to the intended place, the way of being and point of view that it, in turn, intends.

More generally, I sense that Sabaka's bodily experience intends objects in the world as possible sites for his inhabitation: He is looking for potentially secure places. He tries them out by virtually dwelling in them in anticipation of the actual. Once established, they are his habitations, places he has and holds—etymologically, from *habere*, to have and hold (Jager 1983, 156).

Adding to our description of Sabaka in the first vignette, the structure of his bodily experience consists of possible habitations as well as possible moves. In addition to the bodily attitude that intends objects as occasions for his action, he assumes a bodily attitude that intends complex configured objects as to be lived in and lived from, as optimal vantage points and advantages. One way that Sabaka lives space is "as to be appropriated," "as to be incorporated," so that it serves as and becomes his point of view. The historical account of the journey of his primary sleeping place moving closer and closer to the family lair shows that this appropriation of place can be an ongoing project. Sabaka slowly, over a long period of time, whittled away at the boundaries of permissible sites to establish his preferred space of place.

While the emphasis on spatiality here admittedly may reflect the peculiar construction of pets in the Western world and/or the investigatory posture being promoted, I would speculate that spatiality may ground the being of Sabaka in the way that it is often claimed that temporality grounds human beings (Heidegger 1962). This is not to say that there are not temporal structures operative in his experience, but I would suggest that place primarily grounds being for him. He belongs in the place and relates to others from and through that place. He can just lie there for hours because he is not primarily waiting, he is not primarily anticipating, he is not thinking in our sense; he is already arrived, he is at home.

Correlatively, his is a spatial identity. In contrast to a reflective self that is constituted and developed as a unity through and over time, his is a self constituted through association with a space. Sabaka's habitat is his self. The space he has and holds is his appropriated self. He is radically, ontologically place dependent. His being is not a being in question; it is not continually thrown forward and resynthesized in and through temporal ekstases.

This peculiar ontological dependence on space is a vulnerability that has ethical implications for the practice of housing animals in cages whether in laboratories, shelters, or kennels.

Sabaka Being OK

When Sabaka has been given a special treat (e.g., a bone) or has brought one in from outside, and Zeke, the neighbor's dog, visits, Sabaka will growl at him even if the bone is nowhere in sight and has been left unattended for hours. He will then maintain a position between Zeke and the bone, by aggressively snarling if necessary. However, more commonly, Zeke's arrival signals the beginning of play as an old sock long gathering dust suddenly becomes, once again, the object of an extended tug-of-war.

While I eat breakfast, Sabaka lies, not on the threshold of the dining room, but out in the hall leading to my study. After breakfast, as I pass through the hallway, he gets up and heads toward the study, turning frequently to establish whether I am following him. I usually do so, opening the far door of the study to let him up the stairs to a favored sunroom.

On a walk recently, Sabaka went off sniffing, nose to ground, tail wagging high in the air. I continued my walk and, although I called for him from time to time, did not see him again until I returned to the house. This was an unusual occurrence, and Sabaka looked at me a bit sheepishly. I was mean enough to confirm his concern by speaking to him sharply and withholding his usual postwalk cookie. I went about my business, only returning a half hour later to the playroom where he was lying. I did not greet him, and he looked at me continuously but without moving. I relented finally, saying, "OK, Sabaka; it's OK." He immediately approached, solicited me to kneel, stood up on his hind legs, and licked my chin. Then, he went about his business, trying to find a warm spot in the sun.

Sabaka will seek affection or solicit care as a complex function of a number of conditions, such as the amount of time we have been apart or, as in the incident just related, his sense of my feelings toward him. He also stays closer and begins to be a bit oversolicitous of affection when the rest of the family is away. Also, when he thinks I am hurt or when I act in a way not familiar to him, he will approach and sniff at me, preferably at my face, and will stay closer to me than usual, watching me more. In a sense, these three examples suggest a functionalist or behaviorist way of thinking about relationships. It is as if Sabaka's action in relationship to others is adequately intelligible in terms of contingencies of reinforcements or some "what's in it for me" payoff matrix. Zeke's visit is merely a threat to Sabaka's prize bone or, at best, an occasion for play; my anticipated entry into the hallway is an opportunity for access to a comfortable place.

These modes of understanding can be applied as well to the third set of examples. Here, while food and physical comfort are less directly at stake, the interactions between Sabaka and me could be reduced to learned security operations or even further reduced to an early bonding maintained largely through instinctive patterns of behavior. Certainly, the face licking itself has a clear instinctive component—as a pup licks the face of its mother upon her return to the den. While taking these explanations, as well as other less scientific but also pervasive social constructions, into account, the present method results in a different sort of discourse and purports to raise and attempts to answer other questions. For example, in what sense may Sabaka be said to seek and maintain relationships, whether with a conspecific or with a human? Is the term *relationship* applicable and appropriate in its full meaning? If so, what is Sabaka's experience of a relationship? What is Sabaka's experience of me? How am I present to him?

When I have reprimanded Sabaka, or I am upset, or when the rest of the family is away, Sabaka is clearly riveted on me. I directly sense his searching for my bodily attitude to him. He is, as it were, studying my kinesthetics—my posture, bearing, incipient movements, and the like. I realize, then, that this is a habitual way in which he knows me. He also rivets on me when it is near his dinnertime or when I am getting ready to take him for a walk. However, what he is checking on here is different and is perhaps more indicative of what might be termed a relationship concern. He is checking to see if it is all right between us or with us. When I say "it's OK, Sabaka," sometimes he will simply walk away without approaching to lick my face. But the way he walks away differs from the way he approached or was riveted on me. His posture is no longer sheepish, or intimidated, or tight, or tentative. He walks away secure.

Secure in what? Perhaps, for him, I am simply another secure place, if a more mobile one. It would follow, then, that relationship for him is reducible to place, so that his experience of checking on me has the same structure as checking to see if the landing is available. Or is this posture not reducible to that related to place but indicative of a different, perhaps more originary, structure? As it is for many of us, is being sure that the primary relationship is "OK" so important that, without that certainty, Sabaka cannot play, or go for a walk, or even seek security of place in anything like the same way?

After sensing that it is "OK, Sabaka," does he walk away with a different sense of me, of Sabaka, of us, or of some generalized atmosphere? Is he in relationship; is he carrying "us" with him, if not as an image, then as a different bodily sense of it being OK with us? Perhaps, then, the converse is the case: Place is reducible to, or is a substitute for, or predicated on our relationship being OK.

Of course, as was established earlier, Sabaka does not predicate or register or refer or depict or represent. He is, rather, always concernfully absorbed. The question that we are raising here is whether that concernful absorption can contain a sense of a relationship. My empathetic sense of Sabaka suggests that it might—that Sabaka carries with him a sense of how it is between us and that this is an important feature of his world.

Method

Empathy Defined

The primary investigatory posture in this mixed methodology I refer to as "kinesthetic empathy." The term *empathy* is overfreighted and loosely used in both popular and social scientific contexts. I will begin with a working example to illustrate concretely the referent that I intend here.

I have, of necessity, spent much time in hospitals this past year—not as a patient but as a "visitor." After watching a simple procedure—the doctor giving the patient an injection, for example—I find that my body had arched, pelvis forward, as had the patient's body, the other's body—let us say, your body. I had not been aware directly that you had moved, let alone that I had. Now, as I reflect on that bodily attitude, I sense that it embodies a refusal of the illness on your part. With the posture that I unwittingly imitated, you are closing yourself off, not just from the pain of the treatment but from the treatment itself, because it implies that you have the disease.

A kinesthetic empathy, consisting of the meaningful actual or virtual imitation or enactment of bodily moves, is possible. It is possible because we both have living, mobile, intending bodies. Further, the particularity, richness, and confidence of the meaning of my empathic sense of your experience in any moment is a function of my knowledge of both a general social construction of disease metaphors and hospital situations in a given culture and a knowledge of your history. The body can be already informed, relatively, through such implicit prior understandings.

Empathy is the direct apprehension of the intent, project, attitude, and experience of the other. It is not limited to "sensory feeling," as I wince when the door catches your or the dog's foot. Instead, it includes a more general sense of your situation, such as your refusal to accept your illness, or Sabaka's sense of place, of security, and of comfort. More generally, I can also directly apprehend your or a dog's project, purpose, or anticipated intent.

Empathy is a general access to the intended world of the other. However, that access is not accomplished by inference. It is not a function of the form—that action in that context implies this intention. Nor is it gained through analogy—if I made that kind of move in relation to that kind of object, I would be having this kind of intention, and so you probably are, too. More subtly, I do not use empathy to refer to self-identification, to an act by which I put myself in your shoes. Finally, empathy does not refer to a bodily complementarity, as when your body invites mine to adopt a certain fit with yours—to support you while you lean or to be encompassed by your position. Of course, all of these postures are possible and potentially informative. However, here I take empathy to refer to a moment in which I, if only focally, forget myself and directly sense what you are experiencing. We all have at least fleeting moments of this.

However, in reflection, we discover that the structure of the empathic moment is more complex than a momentarily leave-taking of the self. The forgetting of the self is relative because implicit in the empathic moment are several features that point back to that momentarily passed-over self: a variable sense of confidence as to whether the empathically given meaning is accurate; a sense of control that allows me to stop experiencing what you are experiencing, to have some distance from it. More generally, then, there is the sense in empathy that this is the experience *of the other*—as direct and poignant as the given sense of refusal is, it is not *my* refusal, it is not *my* experience.

Empathy as Process

As imperfect as empathy is, how is it possible at all? Here I can only suggest an outline to an answer through a set of concepts adopted from several phenomenological thinkers. All experiencing is sensuous in that it involves bodily sensibility (Sokolowski 1985, 23). Thought as well as perception, ideas as well as sights, states of mind as well as tickles, can be "registered." In contrast to a reported fact, a registered thought or a registered percept is "grasped" or "appropriated" or allowed to "sink in" (34–36). I can think that the house is abandoned and merely report it to myself or to you, or I can actually let that thought sink in, actually have some intuitive presentation of an abandoned house, a beached whale, or even a complex concept. This potential or implicit sensibility, bodily presence, or possibility of "taking up" is a helpful first step in thinking about how empathy is possible. All experience is at least potentially embodiable, because the lived body is our access to objects

(Merleau-Ponty 1962). To perceive is to live the object, to inhabit it through the potential mobility of the lived body (67–68).

We attend *from* that lived body to the object of our experience (Polanyi 1967). Intentionality, defined as that feature of experience because it always intends or takes an object, has this from/to structure. To perceive an object is to dwell in it as a primary focus, while my own body is present only as a secondary or subsidiary awareness (10). In these terms, empathy is a second-order application of the notion of intentionality. Empathic experience involves appropriating a second body that then becomes my auxiliary focus. Through my lived body, I accompany yours as it intends an object.

To solidify this possibility, consider the following progression. We can readily extend our effective arm so that it becomes coterminous with our tennis racket. The tennis racket is integrated into our forgotten body for the effective return of service. However, I can extend the sensational as well as the manipulative power of my body. For example, I can directly know the obstacles in my path by extending my body into my blind person's cane, which is then part of my auxiliary focus or "forgotten body." Finally, I can transform my body, so that I incorporate not only the width and length but also the complex mobile capacities of my automobile, which I then realize in the directly and immediately given sense that that truck heading toward me cannot be avoided. If I can appreciate how I, as it were, can become a Buick, it is not a much greater leap to conceive of experiencing, at least momentarily, another's experience.

Still, how can we understand the possibility of inhabiting another person's body? Following the critique found in much phenomenological literature, it is helpful to rethink the common Cartesian ontology that locates us holed up in our bodies as some mental stuff and, instead, to recognize that we are out there in the world *through* our bodies. Our bodies do not encase us; rather, we are our bodies. Given that identity, we are radically in touch with things and also with other living bodies in the world. It is also helpful to recognize that we human animals have the same basic bodily possibilities—to move toward and away from, to effect, manipulate, gesture, posture, and the like. This is consistent with the familiar observation that an infant can immediately take up the postures and moods of others. In a sense, much of our later development is learning not to do so, not to be imitative and empathic so that we can attain the distance and externality presumed necessary to make inferences and think logically.

With these briefly noted considerations, we can begin to understand the possibility of empathizing with or inhabiting the body of a being of another species. For, like us, nonhuman animals are intentional beings who move in purposeful ways, who run into barriers, reach for things and find other things unreachable; who also posture, gesture, effect, and manipulate. In fact, the notion that difference and inaccessibility across species lines constitutes a more radical cleavage than that across culture, history, or even developmental period is often an unexamined and speciesist prejudice.

Unlike us, however, nonhuman animals live more exclusively in a prelinguistic region where meaning is and remains implicit, embodied, and more consistently enacted directly. Whereas signification for us more typically involves a complex dialectic between signifiers and the signified, we also live in and have access to a prelinguistic bodily region and, in fact, arguably must do so to experience meaning (Gendlin 1962). Not only are nonhuman animals sufficiently similar to us in that we have a lived body in common with them, the comportment through which an animal's intention (in the ordinary sense of "purpose") is embodied is less deceitful, more visible, and, therefore, more directly inhabitable by us. In fact, an animal's incipient postures are so reliable that they have evolved a secondary signaling function (Daanje 1972). If empathy can be conceptualized largely at the level of the lived body, as I am arguing here, then nonhuman animals are likely a more propitious object of study for a methodology featuring empathy than are humans.

A final argument for the possibility of empathizing with animals is from common experience. Most of us do relate to nonhuman animals, particularly so-called companion animals, as though we do, at least at times, immediately apprehend their concerns, projects, and experience—at least, until we are trained not to do so.

Influences on Empathy

I have argued that empathy refers to a directly given sense of another being's experience. However, I do not imply with this claim that the immediately given apprehension of another's world is free of influences from the investigator's own history, biases, intended project, and the like. In the same way that, as a postmodernist, I reject the possibility of an unbiased objectivist stance, particularly in the social sciences, I do not conceive of empathy as a transparent access, a pure mirroring of what we seek to understand. On the contrary, empathy must be understood in the context of an interpretative act. The understanding that I bring to the object of study necessarily affects and is affected by that object such that I am involved in a progressive circle of further understanding—what is called the hermeneutic circle. While the empathic act aims to deliver just what the object of study is experiencing, that act is necessarily informed by my "preunderstanding" of the object. My lived body is continually informed by the world and subsequently takes up that world, including the other's world, differently. That is why it is critical to the present method that the investigator reflectively evaluate the product of his or her kinesthetic empathy. I have distinguished two regions of such reflection: social construction and history.

Social construction. I use "social construction" broadly to refer to that inclusive set of attitudes and beliefs that jointly constitute a particular social group's perception of reality (Berger and Luckmann 1967). As investigator, then, I must clarify the social construction of the object of study, since the animal and I are embedded in that construction. Clearly, I know Sabaka through complex and sedimented layerings of, among other categories, "animal," "pet," and "dog."

For example, one important although subtle contemporary attitude toward animals is that a nonhuman animal is, as it were, a species not an individual. Influenced by this construction when we refer to a particular dog, we often mean the reified, deindividuated, generic collectivity, "the dog," rather than the individual. Another example of a contemporary attitude is that of the pet as a "minimal animal"—as sanitized, neutered, neotenized, fixated at adolescence (Shepard 1978). Finally, an interesting, relatively recent social construction of "dog" is as an extension of human eyes or hands, as therapeutic companion, as stress reducer.

In addition to the social constructions of the popular culture, as investigator, I am also embedded in an additional reality—the meanings of animal, pet, and dog in the scientific literature. This literature is itself pluralistic and constructs the object of study differently not only in substance, through findings, but also through radically different methods that imply different forms of access and relationship to animals. Ethology, comparative psychology, the behaviorist program, physiological psychology, and an emerging cognitive psychology of animals define different ways of knowing, treating, and relating to animals. For example, for the behaviorist Seligman (before he became cognitivist), the dog is intelligible in terms of contingencies of reinforcement. When that contingency system is broken down, the dog is reduced to a radically ineffectual, huddled mass.

The investigator must take both the popular and the scientific social constructions into account. They cannot simply be subtracted or bracketed because many are formative of the dog's experience as well as of the investigator's approach to the study of that experience. We actually have bred dogs to realize certain social constructions. More subtly, in the context of the present study, Sabaka's experience of other dogs and of humans may have been affected by the construct of the rugged outdoor dog prevalent in Maine, for this influenced my early socialization of him.

When I kinesthetically empathize with Sabaka, these social constructions, both on the side of the investigator and on the side of the dog, come into play. As investigator, I must attempt to clarify and make judgments about their presence. However, in the present method, the investigative goal is the description of a dog's experience, not of the social constructions as such. While empathy is not independent of social construction, we refuse to limit a dog or our study of him or her to a projection, a human construction, a reading of ourselves.

Generally, social constructions bias our perception toward an emphasis on "typifications," toward features purportedly common to the *class* of individual objects under study (Wagner 1970). Influenced by their operation, we are less apt to be open to the individuality of the object of study. This necessitates as a corrective the second region of reflection in the present method—individual history.

History. While empathy is a direct apprehension, unmediated in the moment, what I apprehend when I empathize is necessarily informed by history. This is the case even when my emphasis is on kinesthetic empathy and even when the object of my empathy is a nonhuman animal. In addition to reflection on social constructions, then, the investigator must reflect on his or her understanding of the history of the individual under study, for that history is already informing the empathic move. When I know Sabaka's early history of abandonment, for example, I approach his experience of moments of possible separation informed by that history.

Our position here is that it is not possible somehow to leave the historical dimension behind while empathizing. However uninformed I may be of a particular animal's history, part of what I carry when I empathize, part of my preunderstanding, is a historical understanding. A sense of the animal's past is necessarily present to me. In fact, to the degree that I am ignorant of the individual's history, I probably fill in my understanding of it with a more general, purportedly ahistorical account. The investigator, then, must reflect on his or her empathic apprehension in the light of his or her knowledge of the history.

History also informs the experience of the animal. This may seem self-evident, but often we fail to give specific major events the standing of "true historical particulars" (Gould 1987), particularly when dealing with nonhuman animals. Instead of, a concrete individual history, we limit the historical to the developmental—for example, to an account of more species-general developmental milestones. Goodall's work (1986) is an exception and shows clearly that a given individual's personality and behavior are often largely intelligible in terms of historical events involving his or her immediate family group, the larger social group, and even that group's interaction with other social groups. In like manner, certain major events had significant impact on Sabaka—his abandonment at the dump, our adoption of him and of Elkie as his companion, the death of Elkie, and our trip abroad without him.

One implication of the recognition of the importance of an individual's history is that it undercuts an emphasis on the status of any study's findings as universal. If we take seriously the importance of individual history, we cannot claim to be analyzing the essential dogginess of the dog. "Individuality does more than matter; it is of the essence" (Gould 1987, 23). Any particular dog is an individual in that his or her life is historically embedded. Adding to Regan's (1983) critical phrase, more than the "subject of a life," an individual animal is the subject of a particular life.

Returning to the role of history on the side of the investigator, recent developments in narratology are pertinent (Polkinghorne 1988). In addition to providing a contributing context necessary in understanding a dog, history or historical narrative also provides a form of understanding. When I eventually describe Sabaka, that description is itself shaped by the constraints of a "life history narrative" (Runyan 1984). As an interpretative act, empathy is informed by the individual animal's history as it affects his or her experience, by my evolving understanding of that history, and by the forms of narrative understanding.

Conclusion

Invitations to move and bodily sensibility are the basis of meaning in Sabaka's experience. For him, meaning does not occur in or consist of a semantic field of, say, differences, similarities, and associations. Rather, meaning occurs in and is the contexts of possible moves, of possible ways of living and maintaining space, and, as the last reflection suggests, of forms of relationship with others. For Sabaka, meaning consists of and is known through bodily experience. To understand the complex, intimate, and wonderful choreographies of that world, it is helpful for an investigator, informed in reflection by social constructions and historical considerations, to assume a posture of bodily sensitivity to it—to empathize kinesthetically with Sabaka.

Questions for Discussion

1. Explain what Shapiro means by "kinesthetic empathy."
2. How do social constructions and history help the investigator to interpret the bodily intentions of an animal?
3. Apply Shapiro's model to understanding the viewpoint of your companion animal and the relationship between the two of you.

5 Future Directions in Human–Animal Bond Research

Alan M. Beck and Aaron H. Katcher

Research has revealed a host of physiological, psychological, and social benefits from our interactions with companion animals. Alan Beck and Aaron Katcher summarize many of these positive outcomes, yet remind us that there is much more to learn about the human–animal bond. Future research must examine which factors, groups, and circumstances influence whether and to what degree our lives benefit from interactions with other animals. One important area of investigation concerns animal-assisted therapy (AAT). Much promise has been shown with certain populations (e.g., the elderly), but there are problematic aspects of AAT as well. Beck and Katcher conclude by calling for an interdisciplinary approach that employs better methodological designs and that acknowledges and promotes the significance of the other animals on human health.

> *A small pet animal is often an excellent companion for the sick.*
> —Florence Nightingale (1820–1910)
> (*Notes on Nursing* 1860)

More than 15 years ago, the National Institutes of Health (NIH) convened the NIH Technology Assessment Workshop on the Health Benefits of Pets (National Institute of Health [NIH] 1988). At that time, the major evidence for such health benefits was a report that pet owners experienced increased one-year survival after discharge from a coronary care unit (Friedmann, Katcher, Lynch, and Thomas 1980). This was widely noted in popular literature and served as the first study published in a medical journal that documented animal ownership as a factor that contributes to the prevention of disease. A decade later, Anderson, Reid, and Jennings (1992) reported that pet owners had slightly lower systolic blood pressures, plasma cholesterol, and triglyc-

Alan M. Beck and Aaron H. Katcher, *American Behavioral Scientist* (vol. 47, no. 1) pp. 79–93, Copyright © 2003 by Sage Publications. Reprinted with permission from Sage Publications, Inc.

eride values than non–pet owners and an independent ancillary study to the Coronary Arrhythmia Suppression Trial (CAST), a National Institute of Health (NIH) clinical trial, found that dog ownership, lower anxiety, and human social support are all associated with an increased likelihood of one-year survival after a myocardial infarction (Friedmann and Thomas 1995). It appears that pet ownership reduces the incidence of cardiovascular disease because it influences psychosocial risk factors (Patronek and Glickman 1993).

The final presentation of the NIH Technology Assessment Workshop proposed that

> all future studies of human health should consider the presence or absence of a pet in the home and, perhaps, the nature of this relationship with the pet, as a significant variable. No future study of human health should be considered comprehensive if the animals with which they share their lives are not included. (Beck and Glickman 1987)

Theoretical Perspective

Two complementary ways of interpreting the health data are the biophilia hypothesis and social support theory. The Biophilia Hypothesis was suggested by E. O. Wilson (Kellert and Wilson 1993; E. O. Wilson 1984, 1993) and posited that throughout most of human evolutionary development, fitness was increased by an ability to hunt animals and locate sources of vegetable food. Thus, the brain was hardwired with a predisposition to pay attention to animals and the stimulus properties of the surrounding environment. In seeking to deploy this theoretical framework to understand the putative health benefits of animals and the effects of AAT, three limitations should be noted. The theory does not imply that we have an inborn tendency to maximize the welfare of animals because our survival for almost all of the past three million years was dependent on sneaking up on animals and killing them (Katcher and Wilkins 1993). Second, the theory cannot be tested in its general form, it can only be tried in specific cases that will prove or disprove the specific instance. Third, it is almost impossible to separate out cultural influences from biologic ones without extensive testing in diverse social groups.

Social support theory, another theoretical perspective, is buttressed by a large volume of research describing the positive health effects of human social companionship (Lynch 1977, 2000). This kind of support ranges from the positive benefits of marriage, having a confidant, being in a community of faith, perceiving ones neighbors to be friendly, or even receiving a telephone call from a helpful nurse. Animals are demonstrably a source of social support, as indicated by the number of Americans who say that the pet is "a member of the family," talk to their pet as they would a person, or consider their pet a confidant (Cain 1983; Katcher 1981), although what people mean by the trope "a member of the family" has not yet been clearly defined (Cohen 1998, 2002). Companion animals also increase the frequency of human social support (Eddy, Hart, and Boltz 1988; Messent 1983). Indeed, it is difficult to separate out biophilia, the cultural response to animals of different kinds (Lawrence 1993) and the effects of social support on both animals and humans. These theoretical approaches can be used alternatively or in combination to enlarge the focus of research and obviate to narrow a focus on companion animals as the sole source of health benefits from contact with the nonhuman environment. With this ecological approach we can pursue research to determine how we can enrich the human environment by inclusion of a variety of experiences and suggest that gardens, houseplants, the availability of a view of trees and park land, and the way in which natural spaces are used in walks could all play a role in human well-being. The role of both the animal and the "green" component of the environment cannot be tested apart from multivariate epidemiological studies that would inquire about both an environmental and animal impact. Yet, the epidemiological studies of the health effects of animal contact have narrowly focused on companion animals. By way of illustration, pet ownership is strongly associated with single-family ownership and the chance for confounding the effects of pets and gardens is very real.

Failure to take a theoretical perspective based on biophilia has led to some important omissions or oversights in the literature. Are avocations such as hunting or fishing or bird watching done in a family or social context as protective of health as keeping a pet? Does raising a farm animal for a 4-H competition improve the social facility of children the way it that has been reported for pet keeping (Guttman, Predovic, and Zemanek 1983; Melson 2001)? In therapy, the prevalent use of dogs has obscured the research literature suggesting that animals to which the patient is not bonded improve health status. Finches in a communal cage (Beck, Seraydarian, Hunter 1986) and fish in tanks (Katcher, Segal, and Beck 1984) as well as trees in a park (Ulrich 1984, 1993) all have demonstrable effects on health and well-being.

Animals and Children

Future research also should focus on healthy populations because there are indications that animal contact is beneficial; at the very least, there are theoretical reasons to believe so (Beck and Katcher 1996). Such is the case with young children (Davis 1985; Levinson 1964, 1969; Melson 2001; Melson, Schwarz, and Beck 1997). European investigators have demonstrated that animal contact may favorably influence the development of communication skills in young children (Filiatre, Millot, and Montagner 1983; Guttman *et al*. 1983). Animals are so much a part of children's lives and their literature that it is reasonable to assume that animals have some affect on their development. As an example, the *Diagnosis and Statistical Manual of Mental Disorders* (DSM IV), the official manual of mental disorder classification, notes that stuttering is often absent during oral reading, singing, or talking to inanimate objects or pets (American Psychological Association [APA] 1980). Melson (2001) suggests that caring for pets is a way children learn to nurture, especially important for male children in our society who have few, if any, games that mold caring and nurturing. Animals play important roles in motivating children and shaping how they view the world (Beck, Melson, da Costa, and Liu 2001; Katcher and Wilkins 2000; Rud and Beck 1999, 2000). However, the biophilia hypothesis suggests that keeping pets is only one way that children can be engaged with animals and nature. As noted above we need studies of a wide variety of contacts with animals and nature. At this stage in our knowledge, we do not know if the value of animals for children is resident in the animals' ability to focus attention as predicted by the biophilia hypothesis, participation in the adult roles of caring for another, the human social support from family or community that it generates, animal social support from the bond between children and pets, or a combination of all of those factors (Beck and Meyers 1987).

The Physiological and Psychological Studies

The short-term physiological responses to looking at animals, or pictures of animals, undergoing stressful tasks, with and without the animal present, and interacting with animals have been recently reviewed by Friedmann (2000). She did not include in that review the similar effects of looking at natural scenery or pictures of such scenery and modulation of stress by such sights (Frumkin 2001). Research is needed to assess the physiological effects of animal interaction beyond measures of blood pressure and overt behavior. This is already possible with reliable, minimally invasive techniques of measuring immune function, patterns of brain activity, and endocrine function.

There is some evidence in the literature that pets should be prescribed for certain vulnerable populations (Rowan and Beck 1994). Before it is possible to make so strong a recommendation, certain real discrepancies in the literature need to be addressed.

There is a suggestion in the literature that dogs are more valuable for the protection of health than cats (Friedmann and Thomas 1995; Serpell 1991; Siegal 1990). However, the literature is not uniform in this observation (Anderson *et al*. 1992;

Friedmann *et al.* 1980). Part of the problem is the tendency of women enlisted in these studies, who are more likely to be the owners of only cats, to have poorer health and less social support (Friedmann 2000). It would be desirable to have this question resolved by a larger trial in which it is possible to match health and human social support status of cat and dog owners.

One group of investigators has produced evidence that pets, including cats and dogs, are so effective in reducing the response to stressors and lowering ambient blood pressure in mild hypertensives that a case can be made for treating hypertension with pet ownership (Allen, Blaskovich, Tomaka, and Kelsey 1991; Allen, Shykoff, and Izzo 2001). However, their data is not supported by other investigators who have observed only a modest decrease in ambient blood pressure with pet ownership and a smaller and less consistent protection from the effects of stressors (Baun, Bergstrom, Langston, and Thomas 1984; Friedmann, Katcher, Thomas, Lynch, and Messent 1983; Friedmann, Locker, and Lockwood 1993; Katcher 1981; Katcher, Friedmann, Beck, and Lynch 1983; Straatman, Hanson, Endenburg, and Mol 1997; Watson, and Weinstein 1993; C. C. Wilson 1987; 1991). Before we can confidently prescribe pets for hypertension, we need the conflict resolved by investigators using comparable methodologies, including studying people in their homes (Friedmann, Katcher, and Meislich 1983; Katcher, Friedmann, Goodman, and Goodman 1983; Voith 1985).

If we think pets are beneficial for some people, we have to accept the evidence that they are associated with decreased health and morale in others. The reports of Ory and Goldberg (1983); Lago, Knight, and Connell (1983); Miller and Lago (1990); and Stallones, Marx, Garrity, and Johnson (1990) have all reported no effect of pets or evidence of decreased morale and health in some populations. It would be important to more precisely define those populations. Simon (1984) has suggested that a close attachment to pets can attenuate bonds to people. People with an impaired capacity for intimacy with other human beings would be at risk for lack of human social support. Recent information bearing on this issue has been found in the observation that in some populations a high attachment to pets is associated with high scores on a dissociation index (Brown and Katcher 1997; 2001). Dissociation as a defense mechanism and the dissociative disorders are often associated with an impaired capacity for intimacy with people. Thus, this population might be vulnerable because of a lack of human companionship despite the presence of animal companionship.

The Cultural Significance of Animals and Nature

The symbolic role of animals in society may be as important as the physiological impact on people. For example, many police forces carry teddy bears in their cruisers as part of their trauma kits. Advertising is full of animal images, as are our everyday lives and speech, and yet very little attention has been given to trying to understand how these symbols are important to us as individuals and to society as a whole. In the real world, even rabbits and turtles can encourage approaches by other people and stimulate conversations between children and unfamiliar adults (confederates) in a community park setting. This is an example of animals as "social lubricants" (Hunt, Hart, and Gomulkiewicz 1992). Each year, people visit area zoos more than they go to professional sporting events (E. O. Wilson 1993). Animals are important to people; we must study how to better use that interest at times of physical and psychological need.

Animal-Assisted Therapy (AAT)

The public health implications of animal ownership may be particularly important to older adults, whose family and friends may live at some distance or have even died. In the United States, about 95% of the elderly live in the community and 30% of those live alone (Harris, Rinehart, and Gerstman 1993). The evidence is that animals play a positive role for elderly persons living alone (Siegel 1990; 1993). Animal owners appear to experience improvement of life satisfaction and levels of personal safety after retirement compared to nonowners (Norris, Shinew, Chick, and Beck 1999).

Although older adults appear to derive at least some benefit from animal contact, they frequently are not pet owners (American Pet Products Manufacturers Association [APPMA] 2003). This may be a function of their economic situation and housing constraints. Future studies with older adults should clearly document the value of animal contact and, where possible, record the costs or cost savings involved. Such information will help older adults keep their animals and may even help subsidize the care. It would be important to study the social and psychological characteristics of those senior citizens most likely to benefit from an association with a companion animal.

Although most older adults live in the community, others reside in independent living facilities and nursing homes. These institutional settings have been used for a variety of AAT programs that use varying assessment instruments and interventions, including resident mascots and visiting animals (Banziger and Roush 1983; Brickel 1979, 1984; Corson, Corson, and Gwynne 1975; Fick 1993; Francis, Turner, and Johnson 1985; Harris *et al.* 1993; Hendy 1984; Kongable, Buckwalter, and Stolley 1989; Perelle and Granville 1993; Robb 1983). Presently, Alzheimer's disease is an area of great interest because it now affects one in ten people age 65 and nearly half of all people age 85 and older (Hingley and Ruggeri 1998). There is evidence that the presence of a dog can increase social behaviors when the animal is available temporarily or permanently. Behaviors including smiles, laughs, looks, leans, and touches were more normal for many people and those who did not appear to benefit from the animal were always the same individuals (Batson, McCabe, Baun, and Wilson 1997; Kongable *et al.* 1989). Often, animals other than dogs are more appropriate in such settings and more programs are using fish tanks to improve morale and even improve eating habits (Edwards and Beck 2002; Hundley 1991; Riddick 1985). There is evidence that older people with Alzheimer's disease would benefit from contact with animals in whatever their living environment (Verderber 1991). Future research should be directed toward identifying how to alleviate the more common problems facing patients in their home environment, including lack of stimulation, social isolation, agitation, and staff morale.

AAT Can Be Problematic

There are risks associated with any animal contact; although there is little indication that animal programs are particularly dangerous, there are few reports of adverse effects (Schantz 1990; Walter-Toews 1993). AAT has a good safety record, but the potential for problems increases as programs involve more people and more animals (Beck 2000). To justify any risk associated with animal contact, we must demonstrate a value to the patients. The most common criticism of animal-facilitated therapy programs is that they are not goal oriented and even when goals are identified, evaluation is often unclear (Beck 2000; Beck and Katcher 1984; Draper, Gerber, and Layng 1990; Hundley 1991). To justify any risk and secure acceptance within the health care industry, programs have to be assessed with appropriate methodology, including studies of moderate or long duration and especially multi-centered studies using comparable protocols. Choosing the best animal for a particular subject in a given therapeutic setting requires more information than is currently available. It is also important to understand the attributes of a pet that are most likely to positively impact the health and well-being of people of different cultural backgrounds and histories. Without this knowledge, we may make generalizations that lead to false expectations and failure in AAT.

If clear demonstration of efficacy remains a problem, specificity is a variable of treatment for which there is little evidence in the AAT literature. We do not know under what circumstances and for what patients it is to be the treatment of choice and how it compares to other alternative therapies. It will be difficult to obtain this data as long as AAT remains a volunteer activity by therapists dedicated to one particular species of companion animal (Katcher 2000).

It is important to identify the people or situations where contact with animals is potentially problematic or inappropriate for either the people or the animals. Resident animals, often institutional mascots, pose some of the ethical problems that face all owned animals, that is, they must be well maintained with appropriate food, water, shelter, social interaction, and veterinary care. For animal welfare and basic scientific reasons, it is time to conduct studies on the possible health effects that people have on animals, that is, look at the animal side of the human–animal bond. For social animals such as dogs and many birds, interaction with people may produce many of the same health benefits that animals afford humans or it may increase stress. Objective assessment of physiologic stress and a better understanding of captive behavior may provide new insights into the human–animal bond and the management of captive animals. There is a growing literature on how to define and measure stress in animals (Moberg 1985), but more work in this area is needed. Assessing the most ethical and safest way to include visiting and residential animals in any setting should be an area on continuing study (Beck 2000). Last, future studies should include a focus on the health benefits and risks for the animals involved in human–animal interaction. Such an expansion of the study scope would not only be humane but might provide a better model for understanding the impact of animals on humans. There is some support for the idea that human–animal interactions benefit the animals as well as the people (Lynch, Fregin, Mackie, and Monroe 1974; Lynch and McCarthy 1969; Odendaal and Lehmann 2000; Sato, Tarumizu, and Hatae 1993). If social companionship is an evolutionary development, then it is only logical that both sides of the social interaction will benefit.

Because of the intimacy of the relationship between pets and people, the sudden death of a pet also can have deleterious consequences. More research is needed to identify people likely to have an excessive grief response, how to best deal with bereavement, and how this population may help us to better understand human loss as well. In addition, there is a great need for longitudinal studies on bereavement after pet loss to determine its immediate and long-term consequences. Research is especially needed in how prolongation of a chronically ill animal's life affects mourning. The development of newer treatments in oncology that prolong life but do not necessarily cure and the growing popularity of hospice care within veterinary medicine has generated a need for research in this area. We do not know if it is in the best interests of all pet owners to prolong an ailing animal's life. Moreover, we do not know which owners would benefit and which would suffer. If AAT encourages or creates new human animal bonds, we can no longer ignore the consequences should the bond be broken due to death or illness of the pet. The loss of a mascot animal, for whatever reason, impacts on the welfare of the human residents and more study is needed on how to best address the problem.

There are published and well-recognized links between animal abuse and abusive behavior toward other humans (Arluke, Levin, Luke, and Ascione 1999; Ascione and Arkow 1999; Lockwood and Ascione 1998), but there are also indications of the opposite effect. For example, children exposed to humane education programs displayed enhanced empathy for humans compared with children not exposed to such programs (Ascione 1992). Although there is growing literature on the relationship between animal abuse and human violence, there is little directed research on understanding the underlining social and psychological mechanisms and even less on how to use animals to reduce antisocial behavior.

There is also a need for more study on some of the difficulties that can occur in human–animal contact. We need a better appreciation of the diseases and injuries that are or might be associated with animal interactions as well as more data on the problems of human psychological dependence on companion animals. Potential problems include excessive grief responses on the death of a companion animal and the accumulation of large numbers of "companion" animals to the point where they constitute a threat to animal and human welfare; people who accumulate excessive numbers of animals believing they are serving those animals is a serious and understudied aspect of the human–animal bond (Patronek 1999; Worth and Beck 1981).

Conclusion

After reviewing available data, we conclude that animals do play a significant role in the lives of many people. However, the resources available to those doing basic human–animal bond research are not sufficient to answer the questions raised here today. Future knowledge into the specific health benefits of pets must come from the many studies of human health that will be conducted by other scientists over the next few years. Think of how much more we would know about the effects of animals on human health if questions regarding pet ownership had been included in the well-known longitudinal Framingham Heart Study, the Health and Nutrition Examination Survey (NHANES), or the Systolic Hypertension in the Elderly Program pilot project (Siegel *et al.* 1987).

In addition, the U.S. Census also should begin to include questions on the number and types of animals in people's homes and how people use gardens and green spaces. If this were done, we could begin to address a wide variety of public health issues, including potential zoonoses with long incubation periods and subtle positive effects of animals on chronic and stress-related diseases. Just as tobacco and coffee consumption are considered important because they alter the risk of many diseases given their widespread use, we must be alert to the health promoting potential of pet ownership as well as the characteristics of those groups for which it might not be beneficial. Encouragement of the inclusion and consideration of pet exposure as a possible risk factor in NIH-funded studies of human health would be cost-effective and is an idea whose time has come.

To accomplish this, we must first generate an increasing awareness of the potential importance of human–animal, human–nature interaction and involve scientists from a wide variety of fields for interdisciplinary collaborative research. All future studies of human health should consider the presence or absence of a pet in the home, the nature of this relationship with the pet, and how the occupants interact with other aspects of the living environment as a significant variable. No future study of human health should be considered as comprehensive if the animals with which they share their lives are not included.

In sum, there is solid evidence that animal contact has significant health benefits and that it positively influences transient physiological states, morale, and feelings of self-worth; however, there are many inconsistencies in the literature. We do not know the magnitude of the health benefit, the populations that are beneficially or adversely affected, or even how pet ownership compares to other ways of enjoying the living environment, such as gardening, walking in green and tree-shaded spaces, bird watching, hunting, fishing, or raising animals for production. The AAT literature is badly in need of carefully controlled experiments in which the control group shares some of the appeal or attractiveness of animal contact. If AAT is to progress beyond its current state and earn reimbursement from the companies managing medical care, there needs to be multicentered therapeutic trials and comparisons with other kinds of alternative therapies, including horticulture, nature study, dance, music, and psychodrama, to name but a few. At present, most of AAT is conducted by volunteers who are devoted to particular animals, which almost precludes developing precise criteria for specificity of any kind of AAT. Research is needed to identify the scope of the influence of animal contact and how to better focus the effect for people at large and at risk. This will require an interdisciplinary approach by veterinarians, biologists, psychologists, and medically trained personnel.

Questions for Discussion

1. What two hypotheses are used to explain the health benefits of the human–animal bond? Briefly explain each.
2. What are some of the physiological and psychological consequences of interaction with other animals?
3. What are some of the benefits and criticisms of animal-assisted therapy (AAT)?

6 Understanding Dogs

Caretakers' Attributions of Mindedness in Canine–Human Relationships

Clinton R. Sanders

In one of the first studies to use ethnographic methods to examine human–animal relationships, Clinton Sanders looks at how dog owners construct the identities of their companion animals. Previous research on severely disabled individuals has shown how their family members draw on their intimate knowledge and unique history to socially construct the identities of the disabled, thereby allowing the disabled to continue to participate in social interaction. Sanders contends that a similar process occurs with humans and their animal companions. By constructing a human-like identity for their dogs, people are not merely projecting personalities on their animals, but rather see them as real partners in authentic social relationships.

> *Words are the source of misunderstanding.*
>
> —Antoine de Saint Exupéry
> (*The Little Prince*)

Few associations are as intense and emotionally involving as those we have with companion animals. Despite the frequency and importance of relationships between humans and animals, analyses of interspecies interaction are noticeably rare in the social scientific literature (for exceptions, see Arluke 1988; Bryant 1991; Crist and Lynch 1990; Helmer 1991; Hickrod and Schmitt 1982; Mechling 1989; Nash 1989; Sanders 1990; Robins, Sanders, and Cahill 1991; Wieder 1980).

To a major degree, this lack of attention to animal–human exchanges is due to the conventional sociological belief that "authentic" interaction is premised on the abilities of social actors to employ conventional linguistic symbols. Language

Clinton R. Sanders, *Journal of Contemporary Ethnography* (vol. 22, no. 2), pp. 205–226, Copyright © 1993 by Sage Publications. Reprinted with permission from Sage Publications, Inc.

enables interactants to construct and share a mutually defined reality and provides the vehicle for the internal conversation that constitutes mind.

Because they are presumed to lack the ability to understand and use shared linguistic symbols, animals are, in the conventional sociological view, excluded from all but the most simple social exchanges. Mead ([1934] 1964) presented nonhuman animals as ongoingly involved in communicative acts involving the use of natural signs. He conceived of animal exchanges as immediately situated and involved in direct references to physically present objects or intentions. The only connection between the sign/gestures presented by animals and the subsequent behaviors of their cointeractants was due, according to Mead, to instinct or conditioning.

In establishing this phonocentric view, Mead effectively excluded the routine encounters of people with their nonhuman companions from all but the most cursory of examinations. Because animals are not full-fledged social actors from the Meadian point of view, their encounters with humans are one-way exchanges, lacking the intersubjectivity at the heart of true social interaction. People interact with animals as objects. From the conventional perspective, dog owners'[1] babbling endearments to their canine companions are simply taking the role of the animals and projecting humanlike attributes onto them (see Pollner and McDonald-Wickler 1985). Interpreting the behavior of dogs as authentic social responsiveness is the same form of anthropomorphic projection in which people engage when they "interact" with a computer (Turkle 1984), automobile, or other inanimate object (Cohen 1989).

In contrast, caretakers of companion animals and others who live in everyday situations entailing frequent and intimate interaction with nonhuman animals and who have practical interests in making ongoing sense of their behavior consistently see animals as subjective actors and define interactions with them as being "authentic" and reciprocal social exchanges (see Crist and Lynch 1990; Griffin 1984; Hearne 1987; Shapiro 1990; Ristau 1990). People grant this (at least, limited) mindedness to animals even when the situation in which they encounter the animal-other is formally constrained by a reductionist ideology demanding that they be seen and dealt with as scientific objects. Arluke's (1988; 1990) studies of animal care technicians in medical research facilities and Wieder's (1980) work with chimpanzee researchers, for example, amply illustrate the persuasiveness of everyday encounters in prompting people to regard nonhuman animals as minded coactors.

This discussion focuses on dog owners' definitions of the companion animals with whom they have ongoing relationships. Based on routine, intimate interactions with their dogs, caretakers come to regard their animals as unique individuals who are minded, empathetic, reciprocating, and well aware of basic rules and roles that govern the relationship. Caretakers come to see their dogs as consciously behaving so as to achieve defined goals in the course of routine social exchanges with people and other canines. The dogs are regarded, in short, as possessing at least a rudimentary ability to "take the role of the other." This interpretation of the dogs' actions and reactions as "expressions of competence" (Goode 1992)—as thoughtfully constructed and reciprocating—requires owners, in turn, to take the role of the animal other in order to establish the "natural rituals" (Collins 1989) that constitute their ongoing relationship.

Following a brief presentation of the various sources of data on which this discussion is grounded, I expand on the key elements outlined above. Drawing parallels to the sociological work on interactions between able-bodied people and ostensibly less competent human others (e.g., Bogdan and Taylor 1989; Goode 1992; Gubrium 1986), I first describe how owners construct perspectives on their dogs as minded actors and what they see to be the nature of their subjective experience. Next, I present the owners' definitions of their animals as possessors of unique, historically grounded personalities. I then focus on the central emotional component of the canine–human relationship. Owners typically view their canine companions as having an emotional life and as being ongoingly aware of and appropriately responsive to the emotional experience of their human companions. The substantive discussion closes with a description of how caretakers incorporate their dogs into the social networks and key routines that encompass and comprise their intimate lives. The article's conclusion points to areas of further research and focuses on how investigations of animal–human relationships can expand sociological perspectives on such central issues as mind, identity construction, and interpersonal intimacy.

The Research

The data on which this discussion is based are drawn from three sources. First, I call on material included in an "autoethnography" constructed as I systematically observed and recorded personal experiences with my own dogs (three Newfoundland females) over a four-year period. As the term implies, autoethnography is a combination of autobiography and ethnography. As such, it rejects the traditional ethnologic convention of positioning the researcher as an objective outsider describing and interpreting observed events. Instead, autoethnography emphasizes the value of information drawn from the systematic examination of personal experiences, emotions, and interpretations (see Denzin 1989; Ellis 1991; Hayano 1979; Shapiro 1990).[2]

The second body of data was amassed during nine months of participant observation in a large veterinary clinic located in the Northeast. The field data of central importance to this article consist of detailed observations of owners and their dogs as they waited for a veterinarian to come into the examination room, the conversations that owners had with me during this time, and the exchanges that occurred between clients and veterinarians in the course of the service encounter. Unless asked directly who I was, I did not identify myself as a sociologist to the clients. In general, clients assumed that I was a veterinary student or a technician employed by the clinic. As a participant in the setting, I routinely made myself generally useful, holding animals for various procedures, fetching equipment and supplies, helping clean examination rooms, offering non-medical advice, and in a variety of other ways assisting with the business of the clinic.

Finally, information is drawn from relevant portions of a series of in-depth, semi-structured interviews conducted with 24 dog owners initially contacted when they presented themselves at the veterinary hospital or who agreed to be interviewed following their involvement in an eight-week-long puppy-training class sponsored by the clinic. These interviews averaged between 60 and 90 minutes in length and were tape-recorded with the interviewee's permission. All interviews were conducted in the interviewee's homes, and in all cases the owner's dog was present during the encounter, thereby allowing me to observe exchanges between the informant and his or her animal in their most familiar interactional setting.

I do not maintain that this description of owners' orientations toward and interactions with their dogs encompasses all such exchanges. It is certainly the case that owners construct a variety of identities for their dogs—from object through make-believe person to surrogate child—and consequently treat them in a variety of ways. I do contend, however, that the interactants and canine–human exchanges presented here are fairly typical of the people, dogs, and relationships one finds in the average American household.

The informants were drawn from and observations were made in a veterinary practice that provided services for a largely middle-class clientele. A recent national survey commissioned by the Veterinary Medical Association (1988) reveals that approximately 38% of American households include an average of 1.5 dogs and that close to 78% of dog owners visit a veterinarian an average of about 2.5 times a year. People with canine companions encountered in a veterinary clinic, therefore, can reasonably be seen as fairly typical dog owners. Certainly, one would expect to encounter rather different orientations and relationships (probably more on the functional/object end of the continuum; see e.g., Jordon 1975) were research done with lower-class owners and/or those who never seek veterinary services.[3]

Assigning the Dog a Humanlike Identity

The designation of another as "human" is an eminently social activity. The exclusion of certain people from this category has been a fairly common socio-historical phenomenon. "Primitives," African Americans, and members of various other human groups routinely have been, and continue to be, denied the status of human (see Spiegel 1988), and studies of interactions in total institutions (e.g., Bogdan *et al.* 1974; Goffman 1961; Goode 1992; Vail 1966) are filled with descriptions of the "dehumanization" of inmates by staff members, principally on the grounds that the inmates do not possess the requisite level of mind.

In their study of the interactions of non disabled people with severely disabled family members, Bogdan and Taylor (1989) discussed the ways in which the social meaning of humanness is created and the criteria used by "normals" to assign a human identity to severely disabled intimates.[4] This definitional activity entails attending to four basic factors. First, the nondisabled attribute thinking to disabled others. The latter are seen as minded-able to reason, understand, and remember. The caretakers regard the disabled individuals as partners in the intersubjective play of social interaction, interpret their gestures, sounds, postures, and expressions as indicators of intelligence, and are adept at taking the role of the disabled others.

Second, the nondisabled see the others as individuals. They regard the disabled persons as having distinct personalities, identifiable likes and dislikes, authentic feelings, and unique personal histories.

Third, the disabled persons are seen as reciprocating, as giving as much to the relationship as they receive from it. For nondisabled associates, the others are true companions who help to expand their lives by providing companionship, acting as objects of caring, and opening up situations in which they can encounter new people (see Messent 1983; Robins, Sanders, and Cahill 1991).

Finally, Bogdan and Taylor (1989) described how disabled persons are humanized by being incorporated into a social place. Through defining the disabled persons as integral members of the family and involving them in ongoing domestic rituals and routines, the nondisabled actively situate the others into the intimate relational network.

The owners I interviewed and encountered in the veterinary hospital engaged in a process of identity construction very similar to that described by Bogdan and Taylor. They routinely used their day-to-day experience with their dogs to define their animals as minded social actors and as having, at least, a "person-like" status.[5] Caretakers typically saw their dogs as reciprocating partners in an honest, nondemanding, and rewarding social relationship.

The skeptical reader of what follows may well discount caretakers' identity construction of their dogs as "mere" anthropomorphic projections. Even if this were the case, we should not disregard people's definitions of the other as the central element in understanding how human–animal relationships—or relationships between "normals" and alingual others more generally—are organized (see Pollner and McDonald-Wickler 1985).

Evaluating the subjective experience of others is always a tricky procedure (Schutz 1970; Goffman 1959). Most basically, the chaining of interactions is a practical endeavor; estimations of coactors' perspectives are assumed, altered, or discarded with regard to what works. Intimate familiarity with others—animal or human—is an effective teacher.

As I write these words, for example, one of my dogs comes to my study and stares at me. She then walks back down the hall to the door opening onto the porch and rings the bell she uses to signal her desire to go outside. Because I am not immediately responsive, she returns to my study, pokes me with her nose, and returns to the door. Grumbling about the intrusion, I get up, open the door, and she goes out to lie down in her usual spot.

I maintain, and the dog owners presented below would maintain, that the most reasonable interpretation of this mundane sequence of events is to see it as an authentic social exchange. My dog has encountered a problem, realized on the basis of remembered past events that my actions hold the potential for solving her problem, purposefully behaved in a manner that effectively communicated her "request," and, in so doing, shaped my behavior to her defined ends.

Seeing this simple encounter as involving communication of a definition of the situation, mutual taking the role of the other, and projection of a short-term future event does not, however, require that we literally see dogs as people. Defining companion animals as "people in disguise" (Clark 1984, 24) is as degrading to them as is the view that they are mere behaviorist automatons. My informants, in describing their dogs' humanlike qualities and actions, did not regard them as literally human. Nor did they facilely place them in a "keyed frame" as "pretend" people (Hickrod and Schmitt 1982). The point they were making, and the focus of this discussion, is that their animal companions were far more than objects; they were minded, creative, empathetic, and responsive. The animal–human relationships they shared were authentically social.

The Dog as Minded Actor

The owners with whom I spoke had little doubt of their dogs' cognitive abilities, and all could recount examples of what they defined as minded behavior. Dogs' thought processes were generally seen as fairly basic ("He's not exactly a Rhodes Scholar"), and, to a certain extent, thoughtful intelligence was seen as varying from animal individual to individual and from breed to breed. Because they were dogs and not humans, the companion animals were typically described as engaging in thought processes that were "wordless" (Terrace 1987). Thought was characterized as being nonlinear, composed of mental images, and driven largely by emotion (see Gallistel 1992). When asked if she thought that her malamute cross could think, an interviewee replied,

> Yes I do. I don't think [dogs'] heads are empty. I think their thinking process is different from ours. I think they think on emotions. If the environment is happy and stable, they are going to act more stable — pay more attention to what you are doing. They are going to be more alert. If everything is chaotic, they would not be thinking externally but be more concerned with themselves internally — protecting themselves and not paying attention to my cues. I would call that thinking, but it is not what you would call linear thinking. . . . They are making decisions based on emotional cues.

No matter what the mode of mental representation defined by caretakers, most agreed that the issues thought about were rather basic. The dog's mind was focused predominantly on immediate events and matters of central concern to his or her ongoing physical and emotional experience:

> I think that [my dogs] are here just to get approval. [They are here for] feeding or to get petted or get their ears rubbed. I think they think enough not to get yelled at, not to get into trouble. That's the way dogs are. I don't think they can reason like people.

On the other hand, some owners did see their animals as going beyond these basic physiological and emotional concerns. One typical type of example offered by informants focused on their dogs' play activities and the adjustments they made while being trained. The dog's purposive modification of behavior was seen as indicating a basic ability to reason. For example, one owner described the actions of his hunting dog in the course of learning to retrieve objects from the water:

> This is the smartest dog I have ever had. We are having him trained professionally, and we were with the trainer with my dog and some of the

other dogs he was trainding. He said, "Look here. I'll show you how smart your dog is." He threw the retrieving dummy out into the middle of this long pond there. My dog jumped in and swam to the thing, grabbed it in his mouth, and took a right turn. He swam to the land and walked back to us with the dummy in his mouth—all proud. He was the only one smart enough to walk back. The other dogs all swam out, retrieved the thing, and swam all the way back.

While watching my own dogs play, I was struck by the adjustments they made—behavioral alterations that, were they made by hairless bipeds, clearly would be seen as demonstrating thought. Soon after the introduction of a new puppy into my household, I made the following entry in my autoethnographic notes following a walk in the woods:

> Today Isis [my three-year-old Newfoundland] appeared to come to a realization about how she had been attempting to play "chase" and this prompted her to alter the play process somewhat—essentially altering the assumption of roles. On each of the walks so far, Isis has attempted to initiate chase by acting as the chaser. She runs off at a rapid pace, turns back, runs toward Raven [the puppy], bowls her over, runs past, etc. This doesn't work because of the size and strength difference. Raven just cowers, runs to one of us for protection, cries out. So, this time when Raven made a run at her at one point in the walk, Isis ran off a little ways until Raven followed. Isis then ran further and soon Raven was in hot pursuit. Isis led her on a merry chase over fallen trees, through thickets, into gullies. It was particularly interesting to watch because Isis was adjusting the game on the basis of her knowledge of Raven's, as yet, limited abilities. She would run just fast enough so that Raven wouldn't get more than a few feet behind and would occasionally slow down enough that Raven could grab hold of some hair on her side or legs. Isis would also toy with the other player by jumping over larger falls or into gullies with deep, vertical sides—obstacles she knew were beyond Raven's limited abilities.

Owners frequently offered stories in which their dogs acted in ways that were thoughtfully intended to shape the owners' definitions of the situation and to manipulate their subsequent behavior to desirable ends. A number of informants told of dog behavior such as the following:

> We have a beanpot that we keep filled with dog cookies. Every time the

dogs go out and "do their business" they get a cookie. They have interpreted this as "all we have to do is cross the threshold and come back
and we get a cookie." So it will be raining and they won't want to go
out and they will just put one foot outside the door and then go over to
where the cookies are kept: "Well, technically we went out."

Though rarely successful, this sort of behavior indicated for the owners an
attempt by the dog to deceptively manipulate their definition of the situation (dog
went out) so as to shape their behavior (give cookie). Caretakers also provided
descriptions of situations in which they observed their dogs engaging in deceptive
actions while playing with other dogs. For example, a veterinarian offered the following story when we were discussing the issue of whether or not dogs think:

I believe that dogs think. My dogs play a game called "bone." One of
them will get the rawhide bone and take it over to the other one and try
to get him to try and get it. Or one will try to get the bone if the other
one has it. One day I was watching and the youngest one was trying to
get the bone without much luck. So he goes over to the window and
begins to bark like someone is coming up the driveway. The other dog
drops the bone and runs over to the window and the puppy goes and
gets the bone. There wasn't anyone in the driveway—it was just a trick.
Maybe it was just coincidence but. . . .[6]

The Dog As an Individual

Although many caretakers did see certain personality characteristics as breed related,
they regularly spoke of their own dogs as unique individuals. Few informants had any
trouble responding at some length to my routine request that they describe what their
dog "was like." Owners currently living with multiple dogs or those who had had
serial experience with dogs often made comparisons in presenting their animals'
unique personal attributes. For example, an interviewee with two Springer spaniels
responded to my question about his dogs' personalities as follows:

It's interesting. A good way to look at this is to compare her with my
other dog. I look at my older Springer and she is always begging for
attention. Sometimes I misinterpret that as wanting something to eat.
I'll just be studying and she is happy just to sit there and have her head
in my lap while I scratch her behind the ears. On the other hand, Ricky
really likes attention and she seeks it. But if you're not willing to give
it to her, she'll go find something else to entertain herself. She's bold,

she's aggressive. At the same time she is affectionate—willing to take what you will give her.

Owners also were adept at describing their dogs' unique personal tastes. Informants typically took considerable pleasure in talking about individual likes and dislikes in food, activities, playthings, and people. For example, when asked by the veterinarian whether her dog liked to chew rocks (he had noticed that the dog's teeth were quite worn), a woman described her female Doberman's special passion:

> She just loves big rocks—the bigger the better. When she finds a new one she is so happy she howls. She'll lie and chew them all day. She puts them in her water bucket, and sometimes it takes two hands to get them out.

Owners also attributed individuality to their dogs by embedding them in a readily recountable narrative history. Interviewees took great pleasure in telling stories about their dogs' exploits and how they were acquired. In somewhat more abstract terms than those used by my informants, Shapiro (1990) presented the individuality of his own dog, stressing its embeddedness in their shared historical experience:

> History informs the experience of a particular animal whether or not it can tell that history. Events in the life of an animal shape and even constitute him or her . . . . [My dog] is an individual in that he is not constituted through and I do not live toward him as a species-specific behavioral repertoire or developmental sequence. More positively, he is an individual in that he is both subject to and subject of "true historical particulars". . . . I can not replace him, nor, ethically, can I "sacrifice" him for he is a unique individual being. (189)

The Dog as Emotional and Reciprocating

As mentioned above, owners typically understood their dogs as having subjective experiences in which some form of reasoning was linked with emotion. The most common theme that emerged from the encounters in the clinic and interviews with owners was that dogs are eminently emotional beings. Dogs were, for example, described as experiencing loneliness, joy, sadness, embarrassment, and anger. Interviewees often focused on this last emotional experience—anger—because it was linked to incidents in which dogs responded in ways which owners saw as indicating vindictiveness. For example, one owner described her Shar Pei puppy's displeasure at being abandoned and his playfully vengeful response to her absence:

> It's funny. Usually after I have been at work all Friday I don't go out
> unless I am sure that somebody is going to watch him. But one time I
> left him alone and when I got home HE WAS ANGRY. He just let me
> know. [How did he let you know?] He'd follow me around and he
> would look up at me and he would just bark. It was like he was yelling
> at me. And I would say, "What is it with you?" and when I would stop
> talking he would look at me and bark—like "You left me. How could
> you do that?" You could read it in his face. When he was younger and
> I would go to work and leave him during the day, he would find some
> way to let me know that he wasn't pleased—like he would shred all his
> newspapers. Every day was something new. He would move his crate,
> or he would flip his water dish, or something like that.

In the course of my research, I routinely asked owners whether they thought that
their dogs had a "conscience." Although there was some considerable difference of
opinion among informants about how effective their animals' consciences were in
constraining unwanted behavior, all saw their dogs as possessing a basic sense of the
rules imposed by the human members of the household. In turn, they all could offer
descriptions of incidents where their animals violated the rules and subsequently
responded in ways that indicated the subjective experience of guilt. Typical guilt
responses entailed clearly readable body language—bowed head, tucked tail, ears
down, sidelong glances. For example:

> Some major problems existed with Diz when he was younger and learn-
> ing the house rules—what's proper and what's not proper. [Do you
> think Diz has a conscience?] He knows what he should and shouldn't
> do. If he gets into something. . . . He came up the stairs with a big old
> flower in his mouth, this silk flower, and his ears go forward. That's his
> look, "Am I doing something I'm not supposed to be doing?" He'll get
> something in his mouth and he'll put his head down and his ears go
> down and his little tail is kind of wagging. It is a body language that
> says to me, "Am I supposed to be doing this?"

Because caretakers saw their dogs as experiencing a subjective world in which
emotion played a central role, they frequently understood their relationships with the
animals as revolving around emotional issues. The chief pleasure they derived from
the animal–human relationship was the joy of relating to another being who consistently demonstrated love—a feeling for the other that was honestly felt and displayed
and not contingent on the personal attributes or even the actions of the human other.

One indication of the intensely positive quality of their relationship with their animals were the owners' perceptions that their dogs were attuned to their own emotions and responded in ways that were appropriate and indicated empathy. A man and his teenage daughter, for example, spoke of their dog's ability to read their emotions and his attempts to comfort them when they felt sad:

DAUGHTER: He's just fun. He keeps us lighthearted. And he certain-
             ly senses our moods. If you're sad and crying he will
             come snuggle next to you.

FATHER: He just seems to sense it somehow, you can be in a dif-
             ferent room and be down. Recently when Mary was in
             her room he just seemed to know where to go. . . . He
             sensed that somewhere in this house—his doghouse—
             there was something that was not quite right. He sought
             Mary out and was just there. One day I was sitting on
             the front porch kind of blue about some things and he
             just snuggled in there—totally noninvasive, just "If you
             want to pet me, pet me. I'm here if you need me."

Owners saw their intimate relationship with their dogs as premised on intersubjectivity and shared emotion. However, caretakers defined the animal–human relationship as unique because it was free from the criticism and contingent feelings that typified relationships with human intimates. This prompted owners to feel intense emotional ties to their dogs. The centrality of emotional connectedness is obvious in this story offered by a client in the veterinary clinic as she responded to my request for her to tell me about how she acquired her dog:

A lady down the street had a litter. I went in and immediately he came
right over to me. It was love at first sight—he chose me. I remember it
was really snowing that night and we couldn't get to the grocery store.
My mother made him chicken soup. To this day he goes wild when he
smells chicken soup. Every time I make it he gets half. Sometimes this
annoys my roommate—"Hey, I wanted some of that." But he is more
important. He's not a dog to me. He's my best friend. He loves me and
I love him. When I come home from work he's happy to see me and I
am happy to see him. I try to spend quality time with him every day. .
. . He gives me love. He can't live without me and I can't live without
him. It's so hard to see him getting old. I just don't know what I would
do without him.

Affording the Dog a Social Place

Because their dogs were regarded by owners as displaying these essentially human-like attributes, they actively included their animals in the routine exchanges and the special ritual practices of the household. The dogs typically were considered as being authentic family members.[7] Shared family routines commonly centered around feeding and food preparation, playing with or exercising the dog, and some more idiosyncratic routines that evolved in the course of the shared relationship. One interviewee, for example, referred to her own childhood experiences while describing the daily breakfast routine she shared with her newly acquired puppies:

> I love these dogs. They are people dogs. We do have a set course of activities during the course of the day. We seem to meld very nicely with one another. Anywhere from 5:30 on, the dogs will start to bark which means to me that it is time to get up—the activities of the day have begun. I come downstairs and they are on the back porch waiting to come in for breakfast. I bring them in the house and I talk to them. We talk about what we are going to do today and what do you want for breakfast? Of course, they have no choice—they get the same thing every meal. But it is very important for me to talk to them, and I'm sure they know what I am saying because they will go into the pantry and get a biscuit. So I go in and get the bag of Purina®, and I show it to them and say, "This is what we're having for breakfast." They'll sit down and look, and I will go the refrigerator and get the . . . yogurt out, and I will put a spoonful in each dish, and I will always be sure that I leave a little on the spoon so the kids can lick it. I do that because it reminds me of when I was a kid, and whenever my mother made frosting she would leave a little on the spoon. That was always the highlight of frosting a cake—licking the spoon. Then I take the dishes out and they eat. I go get my coffee and read the paper and talk to them. They will walk around and poop. They will play for a while. The day has begun.

Informants regularly spoke of key ritual activities they shared with their animals. Most, for example, celebrated their dogs' birthdays. Cakes were baked, presents were bought, parties were organized, favorite foods were prepared, and other special steps were taken by owners to ritually commemorate their animals' births. The other typical ritual in which the dogs were included was that surrounding Christmas or other religious holidays. A young woman, for example, described her puppy's first Christmas:

He just loved Christmas. Somehow he figured out which were his presents under the tree and he happily opened them all himself. He had his
own ornaments on the tree—I got some that were unbreakable and put
them on the bottom branches. He would take one carefully in his mouth
and come running into the other room with it all proud to show it off. He
loved the tree. He thought we had brought it in from the outside just for
him.

At the same time that owners presented their dogs as thinking, emotional, creative, role-taking individuals they realized that conventional social definitions tended to situate dogs outside the bounds of humanness. Companion canines are customarily regarded as objects, toys, or creatures whose ostensibly human characteristics
are "actually" the result of anthropomorphic projection on the part of over-involved
owners. However, intimate experience and the practical recognition that treating their
animals as minded and competent coactors *worked* as an effective context in which
to understand and accomplish ongoing collective action convinced owners that rigid-
ly placing dogs outside the social category of "person" was unwarranted. The recognition that their views of their dogs violated conventional boundaries between
humans and "others" and could potentially be seen as stigmatizing was apparent in
the discomfort often expressed by my interviewees when I asked them if they regarded their dogs as "people." For example:

In a sense they are [people]. They have feelings. There is a mutual caring for one another and although they may hurt one another it is done
in a playful manner. Yeah, they are people, but I hesitate to say that to
too many individuals because they would think I am nuts. Because I
don't think many people think of animals as being people. The majority of people think of animals as pets and they are to be kept at a distance. It is very important to me to have these "kids" portrayed as part
of my family. Because they are part of my family. I do treat them as
people. I care about them and I would never deliberately hurt them. It
is very important for me to convey to them that I do care very much for
them. I'm sure they understand that.

Conclusion

This discussion has focused on the categories of evidence used by dog owners to
include their animals inside the ostensibly rigid but actually rather flexible boundaries
that divide minded humans from mindless others. The picture that emerges is of the
person experiencing his or her companion dog as an authentic, reciprocating, and

empathetic social actor. Canine companions are effectively involved with their care-takers in routine social exchanges premised on the mutual ability of the interactants to take the role of the other, effectively define the physical and social situation, and adjust their behavior in line with these essential determinations. In much the same way as the able-bodied construct identities of intimate human others who have severely limited abilities, caretakers use the evidence at hand to define their dogs as possessing minds, emotional lives, unique personalities, and readily identifiable tastes. These humanlike characteristics qualify dogs to be incorporated into the rituals and routines that sym-bolize and constitute owners' daily lives and intimate social networks.

This discussion of people and their dogs has touched on only one small segment of human interactions with nonhuman animals. Sociological attention could be directed at a wide variety of related issues and situations—for example, people's interactions with species other than canines; occupational and recreational settings incorporating animals; class, ethnic, and racial variations in human–animal interac-tions; and intensely interdependent relationships, such as those between people and guide dogs or other assistance animals.

Within the larger context of how animal "humanness" is constructed as a practi-cal accomplishment, this discussion has presented mind as similarly constituted. Much like those who intimately and regularly interact with Alzheimer's patients (Gubrium 1986), the owners on whom I focused regarded their dogs as possessing minds revealed in the knowledge drawn from intimate experience. The import of this view is that it moves away from the Meadian orientation toward mind as an individ-ual internal conversation/object. Instead, mind is reconceived as more fully social, enduring in its social classification by those who are most connected to and knowl-edgeable of the alingual other. Like Gubrium's (1986) Alzheimer's patient caregivers, dog owners actively engage in "doing mind": They act as agents who identify and give voice to the subjective experience of their animals. Dog caretakers also make claims for the minds of their animals because they, like the intimates of the severely retarded and those with Alzheimer's disease, can "listen with their hearts." Owners foster and value the emotional connections that bind them to their dogs. To a major degree, the intimate relationship and interaction that the owner shares with his or her animal is, as Gubrium put it, an "emotive discourse" (47).

The generative context within which this emotionally focused construction of animal mind takes place involves the accretion of mutual experience of what Collins (1989) referred to as "natural rituals." Caretakers and their dogs ongoingly share activities, moods, and routines. Coordination of these natural rituals requires human and animal participants to assume the perspective of the other and, certainly in the eyes of the owners and ostensibly on the part of the dogs, results in a mutual recognition of being "together."

Most broadly then, this discussion has been about how identities are constructed. Sociogenic identities (Goode 1992) are created and projected in immediate interactional contexts. Perspectives on the other and evaluations of his/her/its capabilities are affected centrally by preexisting expectations and ideologies. Those who routinely interact with alingual companions draw from their ongoing experience information about the other, effectively disconfirming folk beliefs, occupational ideologies, or academic doctrines that present the inability to talk as rendering one mindless and incompetent. Investigations of people's relationships with companion animals, like those focused on affiliations with speechless humans, emphasize the undue emphasis traditionally placed on language as the foundation of intimate interaction, mind and thoughtful behavior, and the generation of social identities.

This, then, is part of the promise of the investigation of people's relationships with companion animals—expansion of sociological perspectives on mind and modes of mental representation ("iconographic mind"), illumination of procedures whereby minded identities are socially generated and the interactional contexts which constrain these procedures, extension of analyses of "the other," and the opportunity to further develop our views of intimate relationships and the emotional elements which are central to these essential social bonds. Seen in this light, systematic attention to animal–human relationships offers symbolic interactionists a challenging and rewarding prospect.

Questions for Discussion

1. What does Sanders mean when he argues that human identity is socially constructed?
2. What are the four basic features caretakers employ in constructing the identities of their canine companions?
3. Do you believe that the identities of dogs are merely projections of their caretakers, or do they have a unique inner experience that enables them to have meaningful social relationships with humans?

Part III: Historical and Comparative Perspectives

We have now entered a new transitional period in our relation to the natural world, when we exercise power to an extent undreamed of at the beginning of the nineteenth century; most animals, not just those we have chosen to domesticate, depend upon us for their very existence.

Harriet Ritvo

7 Speciesism, Anthropocentrism, and Non-Western Cultures

Barbara Noske

Are non-Western cultures less speciesist and anthropocentric than their Western counterparts? Even though there is a tendency to see these non-Western societies' views and treatment of other animals in a more favorable light compared to our own, it doesn't mean that we shouldn't ask about speciesism and anthropocentrism in these cultures as well. In this selection, Barbara Noske does just that. She critically examines human–animal relations in hunter/gatherer, hunting, and herding societies, presenting examples of interactions that are both respectful and harmful to animals. And while she concludes that, in general, animals in non-Western cultures are less likely to be objectified, and humans less superior, anthropocentric beliefs and practices nevertheless can be found.

Introduction

Current debates on the human–animal relationship and animal ethics in the West highlight a number of things, among them the questions of *speciesism* and *anthropocentrism*.

Speciesism generally refers to differences in treatment of individual beings on the grounds of their belonging to different biological categories: species in this case. It amounts to judging animals, not as unique and sentient individuals, but solely by their species. They become specimens of a particular species that may be favored or abhorred by us, humans. (Noske 1993, 1994). The most common use of the term speciesism, however, centers on membership or, indeed, *nonmembership* of one particular species, the human one, with as consequence the discrimination and often harsher treatment of anything nonhuman. By its critics, speciesism has been defined as analogous to racism and sexism (Ryder 1989).

Originally published in 1997 in *Anthrozoös*, vol. 10, no. 4, pp. 183–190. Reprinted with permission, International Society for Anthrozoology (ISAZ).

Anthropocentrism, in addition, refers to the related idea that humanity is and should be the measure of all things. Others and "otherness" tend to be overlooked and fail to be taken into account (Noske 1990, 1997) Though not identical, the two— speciesism and anthropocentrism—tend to go hand in hand, the former pertaining a bit more to practice, the latter to attitude.

In debates about humanity's relationship with nature and with animals, non-Western cultures are often portrayed as some sort of reflecting mirror in order to provide contrasts with Western ways of dealing with, thinking and feeling about animals.

Since I am presently not in a position to collect first-hand data by means of participant observation, I shall examine a number of hunter/gatherer and pastoral societies as recorded in the anthropological literature. As it is, very few anthropologists, with Nanda Niemeijer (1994) a notable exception, have conducted their fieldwork from a position where both humans and animals are considered equally as subjects with individuality, integrity and agency.

While anthropologists typically have collected massive amounts of information on exotic human–animal relations in various cultural contexts (Evans-Pritchard 1940; Lévi-Strauss 1965; Rappaport 1967; Harris 1974) they hardly ever address questions pertaining to animal welfare and the animal as subject. Neither do they show much interest in the existence of speciesism or anthropocentrism in non-Western culture. Where animals figure in anthropological studies, they tend to be looked upon merely as passive raw material for human acts and human thought.

Anthropologists tend to accept speciesism and anthropocentrism as "given" in society and generally refrain from asking questions about them. In fact most social anthropologists argue that in order to answer questions about animals and their welfare it would be better to turn to sciences such as evolutionary biology or ethology. Few social anthropologists now study physical anthropology as part of their curriculum, a circumstance that has much to do with the inheritance of Nazism, which used arguments of physical continuity between animals and humans in order to justify racism and genocide (Noske 1997). Where physical anthropology is being taken into account, it tends to examine animals and animal–human relations from a biological, rather than a socio-ethical point of view.

Animals are frequently thought to be unworthy of anthropological interest. Elsewhere I have outlined the reason for this blind spot within social anthropology and its lack of sensitivity to the animal's fate in the world's cultures. It lies in the inherent speciesism and anthropocentrism prevalent in the discipline itself: human–animal interactions tend to be seen as subject–object relationships and it is only the human-subject side that anthropologists care to consider (Noske 1990).

Anthropologists prefer to treat animals as an integral part of the human economic constellations and human-centered ecosystems: that is, as economic resources, commodities and as means of production for human use. Animal-based human economies have been studied extensively by anthropologists who tended to ask whether or not various human practices vis-à-vis animals are economically or ecologically rational (seen from the human point of view). Only in a small number of cases, notably in those where semi-wild animals still retain some control over their own whereabouts, do anthropologists sometimes condescend to look at the advantages of existing human–animal arrangements for the animals in question (Leeds 1965; Ingold 1974).

One way in which the human–animal relationship has been explored, has been through the genre of cultural materialism. Harris (1974) has demonstrated underlying economic reasons for the worship and love of certain animal species in some cultures. For instance, he explains the Hindu veneration for the cow in India and the love of pigs in New Guinea in economic terms: both worship of cows and love of pigs eventually work to the economic advantage of the human social actors. This type of work focuses on reasons why human societies do not kill or eat their animals *more* or why they lavish so much care, affection and energy on them (Harris 1974, 1985).

Apart from animals that function as subsistence factors, there are practices in which animals are made to serve other non-subsistence human purposes: as objects of prestige, sacrifice or totems. Animals in this capacity have been vested with religious significance and with symbolic and metaphorical power (Lévi-Strauss 1965). Typically many scholars in the social sciences, especially cultural materialists such as Harris, would label the non-subsistence roles and functions attributed to animals as "irrational behavior" on the part of humans. To many of these scholars rationality clearly signifies economic usefulness only, and other underlying motives for human practices and ideologies regarding animals are consequently viewed as "irrational." As James Serpell so rightly points out—and not being an anthropologist himself he probably is in a good position to do so—it is amazing how little attention anthropologists have paid to the universal habit of pet keeping (Serpell 1986, 1988).

Rather than accepting non-economic and non-symbolic motives as real and legitimate reasons for humans to keep pets, anthropologists seem to have gone out of their way to detect the "hidden" reasons for Western and non-Western pet keeping. The idea that "lovability" and emotions like affection and tenderness could be legitimate bases for this intersubjective human–animal relationship still seems out of place and even shameful to many anthropologists.

There is a tendency in Western society not only among anthropologists but also among environmentalists—I happen to be both—to romanticize and idealize older, indigenous cultures. No doubt, we have much to learn from them. But this should not prevent us from asking critical questions as part of the ongoing debate on animal ethics, questions such as: "What about animal welfare in these cultures?" "And what about speciesism and anthropocentrism, do they exist in these cultures as well?" "And if so, in what form?"

Animal Dependent Cultures: The Aborigines and the Inuit

Admittedly, anthropologists have written extensively on the role that animals play in human ceremonial and religious life. In hunter/gatherer societies people tend to have an organic world view which leads them to place themselves *within* rather than *above* the natural world. Nature is in no way the Other or the Lesser. Indeed, in these societies categories like nature and culture tend to be nonexistent. For the Australian Aborigines nature can be said to have a direct spiritual, moral, and social significance: the moral system saturates the landscape and the ecological system pervades the religion (Stanner 1972). The Aboriginal concept of the *Dreamtime* or *Dreaming* refers to a kind of epoch in which mythical—often animal—ancestors lived but which is not thought of as a time that is past in the ordinary sense of the word. According to Stanner, one cannot fix the Dreamtime in time: it was, and is, everywhen; an intertwinement of humankind, society, nature, past, present, and future within a unitary system not easily grasped by minds too much under the influence of humanism, rationalism, and science. The Dreamtime, embodied in sacred and secret local sites, tells the people how they and other beings derived from the same stock, that was neither one nor the other. Continuity, balance, and "abidingness" (abiding by what is or what was previously) are the measure of all things rather than human distinctness and supremacy (Stanner).

Many other native peoples bear testimony in their stories as to how the world was made, how the animals came to be the way they are and how humans and animals are all part of the same ongoing life force. In these stories men and women transform themselves easily into animals and animals act like human beings. Thus, according to Inuit beliefs, humans and animals alike originated from the copulation of a woman and an animal (Rasing 1988).

In various Australian Aboriginal belief systems animals are thought of as kin. Certain humans and animals are taken to be part of the same totemic group. A mythical Dreamtime ancestor, for example a kangaroo, has made "dream tracks" upon the earth thereby creating the features of the landscape. When it died it left inexhaustible numbers of "spirit children" behind who live on eternally at specific localities that are therefore sacred. It is by leaving these places and entering the body of some woman that they temporarily transform themselves into Aboriginal children. Thus an Aboriginal individual is literally made up of substance that actually is part of the sacred kangaroo site and will after death once more suffuse with the site (personal communication from anthropologist Mark de Graaf, cf. also Hiatt 1978; Mountford 1981; Bennett 1991). The same process is said to take place when an animal individual is born.

For an instructed and initiated Aboriginal person, Australia is covered with a mosaic of cultural compositions in each of which a portion of earth (a place), a portion of life (a species) and a portion of society (a human group) are joined together. A clan and territory are connected with certain species whose prototypical powers were locally active in the Dreaming in creation (Maddock 1982). A kangaroo totemic group includes not only kangaroos and human men and women but also other species and perhaps the rain and the sun. It is much more than a classificatory device; implicated is a moral and ritual relationship. The human members of the group refrain from killing, plucking or eating their totem, and if extreme hunger constrains them to do so they commonly express their regret and perform some ritual act. Other persons with different animal totems may, and do of course, kill kangaroos (Elkin 1967). Moreover, people actually care for the animal species to whose totem they belong. The ecologist, A. E. Newsome, has found that in the mythology of the Aranda people of Central Australia the major totemic sites for the red kangaroo coincide with the most favorable habitats for this species. He also found that, according to the Dreamtime myths, the ancestral kangaroos made their so-called dream tracks overland by natural means and through the air or underground by supernatural means. In Newsome's opinion it is no coincidence that the best kangaroo habitat was traversed naturally (and thereby created) and the worst habitat, namely desert, was crossed supernaturally by these ancestral Dreamtime kangaroos. When the Aboriginal people approach the kangaroo totemic sites, they do so in silence and reverence. Hunting is forbidden near these sacred sites and weapons have been laid down some way off. Thus red kangaroos are protected near their best habitat. (Newsome 1980)

Hunting Animals

Many anthropologists have looked upon hunting as a mere technical device for making a living. Hunting, however, implies chasing, frightening, wounding, and killing other living beings. Dutch anthropologist, Willem Rasing, is exceptional in that he does not hesitate to state explicitly that hunting means killing (Rasing 1988). Hunting peoples have to inspire fear, wound, and inflict pain and death upon animals in order to survive but this does not stop them from strongly acknowledging their interrelatedness with the animal. There exists abundant evidence that people committed to hunting, torturing, and killing animals often do so with a certain reluctance and feeling of guilt. Throughout the procedures of hunting an attitude of ambivalence prevails, and the rationalizations and rituals so often surrounding the practice of hunting are all part of an overall effort to reconcile two conflicting tendencies.

Thus, according to Rasing, the Inuit generally claim that the animals they are hunting agree to be killed as they are made for human use. Greenland's native author, Finn Lynge (1992), points out that according to ancient myths, respectful hunters will never go hungry: the animals will seek them out, as if asking to be taken (in real life, however, animals often do resist their own killing). Inuit hunters believe that disrespectful attitudes toward the animals will bring misfortune, mediated by the spirit powers of the animals concerned (Lynge 1992). According to the Inuit, the animals depend on being hunted in order for their species to thrive; that is, that animals need to be killed. Thus the people take good care so as not to cause their prey animals unnecessary suffering, although many observers report that they do not extend this caring attitude to their sled-dogs who often are treated quite roughly (cf. personal communication anthropologist A. J. F. Köbben).

Incidentally, a number of Australian Aboriginal tribes equally adhere to the notion that nature, including animals, is not self-managing but that it needs people to perform rituals. Lack of human ritual participation is thought to lead to a deterioration of the natural status quo. Here too animals are said to depend upon human-performed acts (i.e. increase rites) for survival (Bennett 1983; Morton 1991). Laurens van der Post has written about the various ways by which Bushman people used to try and solve the ambivalences mentioned above, for example, by thanking the eland with a dance for letting itself be captured (van der Post 1966). The Bushman people show an intimacy with all nature which has been named "participation mystique," a sense not only of intimate knowing but also of *being* known by trees, clouds, and animals (van der Post 1966; Wannenburgh 1979).

There are also opposite accounts of human–animal relations among the Bushmen. Anthropologist Elizabeth Marshall Thomas describes the callous way in which a tortoise is being roasted by Gai, a Gikwe Bushman. She claims that Bushmen often ignore the suffering of animals and regard it with great detachment (Thomas 1989).

Herding Animals

Nomadic hunters are not the only people famous for their close relationship with animals. The 1940 classic by Evans-Pritchard, *The Nuer,* tells us about these African pastoralists who are—or at least were—profoundly influenced in their outlook by their dependence upon and their love of cattle. This love comes close to the affection people show toward pets. To the Nuer, cattle do not just have instrumental value as sources of meat, blood and milk but are also vital links in social relationships. However, while the Nuer spend their lives ensuring their animal's welfare, here too one may detect a certain ambivalence in their attitudes and practices. For instance, they skillfully manipulate cow psychology and cow sociology.

Cattle are not primarily raised for slaughter: the oxen are frequently made to play a sacrificial role in ceremonies. Although there are some special occasions when people gorge themselves on meat, it is thought generally that people ought not to kill an ox solely for food as the ox may even curse them. Eating an ox's flesh should only be done in severe famine. Nevertheless, any animal that dies a natural death is eaten. The Nuer are fond of meat, and declare that on the death of a cow "The eyes and the heart are sad, but the teeth and the stomach are glad. A man's stomach prays to God, independently of his mind, for such gifts." A man sometimes decorates the long horns of his ox with tassels, and the neck with bells. The horns are cut in a particular shape, during which operation the beast suffers a lot of pain. The Nuer sometimes compare this ordeal to the initiation of youths into manhood, thereby incorporating the oxen as conscious and active agents into a human socio-moral domain (Evans-Pritchard 1940).

Another African pastoral people, the Fulani, are reported to be well aware of the ambivalence in their day-to-day dealings with cattle herds. The milking and bleeding of animals evoke ambivalent ideas and usages, springing from the fact that milk and blood sustain the life of the animal or its offspring, as well as affording the pastoralists their subsistence (Stenning 1963). In some pastoral cultures people traditionally believe that sanctions exist on failure to perform certain duties, sanctions not wielded by gods but by the cattle themselves. They are thought to react not only to omissions of conduct concerning themselves but also against certain types of unsatisfactory personal relationships in the human community. They also actively visit sanctions upon those who do not fulfill their obligations. Cows are said to purposely withhold their milk because of their abhorrence of incest. Cattle are believed to place value upon and to entertain general notions about human conduct. People would talk in terms of "Cattle do not allow me . . ." etc. (Stenning 1963).

Another group of people intimately associated with animals are the Tuareg of Northern Africa. The Kel Ewey Tuareg make their living by means of camel and goat herding. They believe that their animal's social world is structured like their own. That is, that animals relate to each other in the same way that humans do, that they have friends like people do, that they enjoy being with their friends, and that each animal has a distinct personality. According to these Kel Ewey Tuareg the animal's willingness to be trained is therefore restricted. Humans as well as animals have their own will and consequently human exploitation of animals is therefore checked. The Tuareg typically do not control their camels' reproduction. The animals are only semi-domesticated; males and females mate far away in the desert and have to be chased and caught over and over again. Both camels and goats can and do at times refuse to cooperate with their masters. Female goats may occasionally refuse to give milk or so it is believed, especially when people have been known to sell that milk—which is considered immoral by traditional Tuareg (Spittler 1983).

Animal Suffering in Respectful Cultures

Does a strong dependence upon or a life shared with animals foster a respectful attitude toward them? And if so, does human respect or even veneration for animals always work to the animal's own advantage and well-being? The aura of sanctity that surrounds cows in Hindu areas of India is by no means universal, not even within India. Tribal India does not refrain from killing and eating cattle. To East Indian hunters/gatherers and peasants practicing shifting cultivation, bovines represent sources of meat, mediums of exchange, and objects for sacrifice.

The "mithan" in tribal India serves as a beast of sacrifice and is thought to be capable of all sorts of supernatural acts and is often worshipped. However, this does not safeguard it from human cruelty, partly because the people do not perceive their treatment of the mithan as cruelty. For various hill tribes in India the mithan used to be important as sacrificial animal, for instance, in marriage and death ceremonies, at times of illness and misfortune, in rites to maintain fertility and well-being, to mark important events, to seal friendship pacts, and in Feasts of Merit. These Feasts are held primarily to enhance a person's status.

There are three methods by which the mithan is sacrificed: strangulation; chopping, stabbing, cutting, or spearing; and beating on the head. Strangulation tends to be preferred where the breath is taken to be the seat of soul and life. Some people believe, however, that the soul and life reside in the blood, which has to flow accordingly, for example by means of stabbing or slowly killing the animal with knives or even by simply cutting the flesh off at random. The third method involves striking the animal continually with an axe until death results. In addition, a bamboo device is forced into the throat of the animal before death occurs. These slaughtering and sacrificial methods are connected with religious belief as well as the fear of retribution by the spirit of the animal. Sometimes forgiveness is sought or the blame passed on to someone else (Simoons and Simoons 1968).

Various peoples of the Indonesian archipelago are equally known for their intimacy with and veneration for a bovine: the water buffalo. Here too the people's good-
will and respect for the buffalo is not always conducive to buffalo welfare. Ritual
slaughtering, even though accompanied by a feeling of respect for the buffalo about
to be slaughtered, nevertheless is a cruel business—the blood must flow. To cut the
throat is a necessity; the buffalo should die slowly so that all the blood can leave the
body. The animal is stabbed with spears in non-lethal places so as to make the process
last. In order to prevent the buffalo from tearing itself loose in fear, its tendons are
sometimes cut before slaughtering takes place (Kreemer 1956). In Toradja society a
buffalo due to be sacrificed on the occasion of a human funeral used to be addressed
as follows: "Oh buffalo, your destined hour of death is not yet there, but we have
decided to end your life. Do not be angry, for from ancient times onwards you were
destined to carry our sorrow. Especially now that your master has passed on, as you
know. Your flesh is being prepared for your master, but may your soul remain with
your living companions" (Kreemer 1956, translation from the Dutch by BN).
Similarly, on Sumba hundreds of buffaloes used to die on the occasion of a human
funeral without any of these animals being eaten.

People may apologize for the slaughter so as not to anger the victim who then
may incite the other buffaloes to stampede and scatter and leave their masters. It is
believed a slaughtered buffalo must not bellow in agony otherwise many people will
die as a result. So at the moment that the spear enters its body a piece of cloth is tied
around its muzzle. This cannot but remind one of present-day laboratory practices
where researchers cut their animals' vocal cords so as not to hear the cries and moans
(Evernden 1993).

The underlying reason for the bloodiness of such sacrifices may be the need to
placate the spirits of the dead. However, blood is also taken to embody the life force.
In other words, the blood is viewed as the seat of life, an idea that would account for
the magical significance of blood and bloodletting. The victim's blood adds to this
vital force and the animal's dying should last as long as possible, resulting in a slow
death under torture. This is dictated not so much out of a sadistic lust for torment but
because of the socio-religious aura surrounding the act of sacrifice.

The animal victim is being flattered and apologies are offered so as to get the victim to undergo its fate willingly and not revenge itself. Before striking the buffalo down
the people would express sadness at its death and mourn as if it concerned a family
member. The Toradjas think of buffaloes as living in the same moral realm as themselves, as pursuing the same aims and interests, as yearning after the same things as
humans. Much like the cattle of African pastoral peoples, buffaloes are thought capable

of punishing humans with sickness and bad harvests. At times the buffalo is said to be clairvoyant and to reveal things in human dreams. An overall and close connection is perceived to exist between the human and the buffalo realm (Kreemer 1956).

General Discussion

To what extent can non-Western peoples be said to be less anthropocentric and less speciesist in their attitudes toward animals than people in the West?

In a society where humankind is not seen as the measure of all things, a particular construction of the world—a *human* construction—may nevertheless still count as the sole truth. And although an organic view of the world would in principle and potentially be more animal-sympathetic, this kind of worldview is not necessarily a safeguard against anthropocentrism. The notion, for example, that animals need people's actions, be it rituals or hunting, in order to survive and reproduce—however true in today's Western world—is basically an anthropocentric notion. Moreover, where a human moral and social system is projected onto the rest of nature, albeit in all sincerity, one runs the risk of losing sight of the animal as the Other. In that case, animals are in danger of being deprived of their own domain and their own way of experiencing the world. Failure to acknowledge the animal's own construction of the world (Watzlawick 1977) as well as humanity's limitation in fathoming such constructs, may result in yet another form of human-centeredness.

The animal Other does not and cannot live in the same socio-moral domain as humans do. Animals live in their own societies and in their own ecosystems, of which humans may or may not be a part. Presumably animals could not care less what sort of perceptions their human killers carry around in their heads when performing the act of killing or sacrificing. The only real thing to a wounded or dying animal are its own sensations and perceptions, the reality of pain and fear. To spear or knife an animal, while at the same time humbly asking its forgiveness or uttering an incantation, may be a sign of equality and respect on the part of the hunter, but may be infinitely more horrifying to the animal than a quick bullet would be.

Nobody can completely overcome his or her anthropocentrism since we hardly can "leap over" our own humanity. Animals are not things out there in the world, simply given to our senses. All representations of animals are human constructs but some leave more room for the animal Other to constitute its own world than do others.

As for speciesism, in many native cultures it is not so much the individual animal of flesh and blood that counts but rather the animal as a symbol of its species and as a representative for qualities that people attribute to that species. Consequently, individual animals tend to be pinned down by their species' traits regardless of their distinct personality and subjectivity: a situation that in modern terms could be listed as a form of discrimination on biological (species) grounds.

While certain popular preconceptions prevail about indigenous people having a comprehensive and harmonious relationship with all that is natural, in native cosmologies there actually exists a high degree of differentiation in treatment and ideology regarding various animal species. Some species are almost semi-gods (the Rainbow Serpent in Aboriginal mythology), others represent evil such as the hyena in Bushman cosmology. Some animals, notably totem animals, may be treated well, other not so well.

Questions for Discussion

1. Does respect for animals or dependence upon animals necessarily result in favorable outcomes for the animals?
2. Discuss Noske's contention that often it is the species and not the individual animal that is valued.
3. How does totemism lead to speciesism?

8 The Anthropology of Conscience

Michael Tobias

How does culture influence our attitudes toward other animals? And how is the treatment of other animals related to our treatment of our fellow human beings? In this essay, Michael Tobias examines three societies in India—the Jains, the Bishnoi, and the Todas—each of whom practices vegetarianism as part of a larger normative system of nonviolence. Tobias argues that these communities have something valuable to teach the rest of us about morality, suggesting that an ethical and peaceful life may require the respectful coexistence with other animals.

In this brief essay I invite consideration of an anthropological framework of moral analysis that takes as its blueprint observations on several human cultures and their concern, or lack thereof, for nonhuman life forms. I will focus on three communities in India whose strict vegetarianism is predicated upon their insistence on *ahimsa*, the Sanskrit term for nonviolence (Tobias 1992).

Vegetarian religions and tribes are extremely rare in the world today. But in India, there are approximately eight million adamantly vegetarian Jains, nearly one million (Hindu) Bishnoi of the northwestern deserts of Rajasthan, and approximately 1,200 Todas of the high Nilgiri mountains of Tamil Nadua state, in South India. I shall restrict my comments here to their specific perceptions of other species, and the astonishingly cohesive, community-wide compassion they bestow upon other species. This insistence upon *ahimsa*, or not harming other living beings, provides a methodological approach to gauging and appreciating another people's holistic attitude toward the environment and, by implication, the important variable of human conscience, however fraught with ethical relativity such moral high ground may be.

By understanding the integrity and sustained traditions of biophilia as practiced by these three separate communities in an otherwise ecologically war-torn nation, I

Originally published in 1996 in *Society and Animals*, vol. 4, no. 1, pp. 65–73. Reprinted with permission from Brill Academic Publishers.

believe we can divine important guiding metaphors for belief and action that are urgently appropriate for human beings everywhere (Montague 1978). Moreover, it is all the more remarkable that these three groups have maintained their active empathy toward nature when all around them meat eating, and the destruction of the environment, prevail. In fact, the government of India concluded a major anthropological survey in 1993 that showed (to the country's surprise) that 88% of the nation's people were non-vegetarian (Sing 1993).

The Jains

Jainism is one of the oldest religions in the world. By the time of its most recent sage, Mahavira (599–527 B.C.E.), Jain traditions had already been firmly documented for centuries, and Jain oral folklore comprises a theology extending thousands of years before Mahavira's time. Mahatma Gandhi was schooled by a Jain monk, and was to promulgate the first Jain principle of *ahimsa* as the core of his own philosophy in life. Gandhi consistently argued that "*ahimsa* limps: but it is the only way" (Tobias 1987).

The Jains will not partake of those industries, business practices, or professions that exploit animals in any way. Clearly, they cannot eliminate entirely the violence inherent to human nature, but they have taken extraordinary care in analyzing the nature of human harm and prescribing methods by which we can minimize our adverse behavior. These "fences" take the form of vows, hundreds of vows, that pertain to every aspect of daily life (Tobias 1995a). Every living organism, say the Jains, is endowed with a unique, precious soul, or *jiva*, a life force that must be respected, even revered. All souls are interconnected (*parasparopagraho jivanam*), thus invoking an ecological sense of stewardship under the prevailing Jain doctrine of universal reciprocity. Jainism is intent upon that sense of shepherding nature. Said Mahavira, " . . . a wise man should not act sinfully toward earth, nor cause others to act so, nor allow others to act so . . ." (Jacobi 1880).

Consistent with this Jain activist stance are its key behavioral norms: *ahimsa*, nonviolence; *aparigraha*, nonacquisition; *asteya*, patent respect for others' rights, property, territory, and integrity; and *satya*, truth (Tobias 1995b).

The Jains have no gods. Rather, they revere 24 early sages, of whom Mahavira is the most recent. Mahavira renounced his material possessions, including his clothing, at the age of thirty. For twelve years he wandered throughout India in search of truth. At the age of 42 he was enlightened, and spent the rest of his life (thirty more years) wandering from village to village promoting nonviolence. His first sermon was known as *Samavasarana* (Tobias 1994a), meaning in Prakrit, "a congregation of people and all other animals." We can read this same mythopoetic ecology in the much later communion between St. Francis and the birds, though it is unlikely that the Medieval Italians in Assisi had ever heard of Jainism. In fact, the West apparently was not to learn of the religion until the late eighteenth century, with one possible exception. Alexander the Great's first biographer noted that when the general and his army reached the Indian village of Taxila, during their conquest of Asia, Alexander encountered several naked men sitting quietly in meditation who would not speak with the young general until he, too, sat down in the dust, shed his armor, and quieted his heart. It is alleged that this incident convinced Alexander to give up his conquests and return home to Greece. Given their prominence in the Indian subcontinent at that time, those naked yogis were probably Jains. To this day, some 60 Jain monks (*Digambara*, meaning "sky clad") continue to wander naked throughout the country spreading the message of peace. Their nudity is a sacred institution that reflects their belief in nonpossession. In one of my first encounters with a Digambara *muni* (monk), he told me that he had been wandering nude most of his life and that this total freedom, this complete lack of material possessions made for the most exquisite happiness. Other Jain disciples throughout the country would provide him his one, vegetarian, meal each day (Tobias 1993).

Most Jains are vegetarian. It is the basis of their way of life: Over seven million consumers who will not wear leather, who will not keep pets, engage in agriculture, or participate in the exploitation of animals or, to some extent, even plants (Tobias 1991). Through a variety of ecologically sensitive professions, Jains have become wealthy—as teachers, lawyers, doctors who will not prescribe drugs derived from animals, scientists, environmental engineers, jewelers, accountants, publishers, judges, politicians, and religious leaders. As a community, they give back much of what they have earned. It has been estimated that the Jains, who account for less than one percent of India's nearly one billion people, in fact contribute as much as 50 percent of all social welfare in a country notoriously lacking in government support for basic health and human services.

Jains believe that all organisms are endowed with between one and five senses— human beings having five, a mango fruit one. Jains are only allowed to eat one-sensed beings, and in strict moderation, with frequent fasting. The Jains consume the banana, but spare the banana tree. This sensate principle is basic to Jain spiritual ecology. Mahavira expounded on the appropriate human attitude toward and treatment of other organisms. At a time when Greek biology (primarily in the hands of Aristotle) recognized about six hundred other species, Mahavira had already catalogued approximately 800,000 organisms. Such scientific acumen is astonishing. In fact, Jain literature comprises several million pages of scripture and analysis, comparable to

Talmudic scholarship. It is interesting to note that original Biblical precepts ordained vegetarianism among Jews, a practice that has recently been revived by many Jewish groups in the United States. Kosher came about as a compromise measure to insure at least some additional humanitarian treatment of animals, and to provision for the sacredness of the animal's blood, its life force (Tobias, Morrison, and Gray 1995).

Jainian ethics hinge on the belief that the liberation of the soul from ill deeds and negative thoughts requires active participation in creating the world daily and a recognition that the power of that creation is in every living being. Their community conceives of human nature as an island of conscience in a sea of tumultuous evolution. This challenge is accomplished through very specific techniques, an ecology of soul, if you will. Daily spiritual practice requires careful attention to all actions and thoughts, forgiveness, tolerance, critical self-examination, restraint, frequent fasting, 48 minutes of daily meditation (*samayika*), following a holy path that may lead to total renunciation. At the basis of these injunctions is the belief in the sacredness of all life. Today in India seven million adherents of an ancient, yet thriving, religion exercise a strict ecological consciousness in their consumption of goods, diet, professions, and charity in the midst of one of the most fiercely capitalistic countries in the world.

The Bishnoi

In 1988, about a hundred ecologists marched across the drought-ridden Tar desert to examine the strange immunity to such crisis enjoyed by one of the desert communities, the Bishnoi. These Hindus have, for centuries, worshipped the fifteenth-century environmental hero, Jangeshwar Baghwan, or Jamboje, born in the Rajasthani village of Pipasar. But, unlike other Hindus, the Bishnoi have no idols. They believe Jamboje to have been a descendant of the Hindu god Vishnu. The edicts of Jamboje, translated into a book known as the *Jamsagar* or "show people the light," prescribed strict vegetarianism and an ethos of desert husbandry that is remarkable for its calculating sustainability. Although dozens of tribes and communities around the world practice ecological sustainability, very few combine it with vegetarianism.

The Bishnoi are not vegan, but are known for showing great affection to their animals, particularly to their cows. Bishnoi eat curd, buttermilk, cooked vegetables, kddi made from graham flour, spices, sugar, breads, and a considerable amount of lentils. They live in small villages numbering no more than one hundred, typically nuclear families. They are strictly rural, and maintain a belief in the venerability of old age. Voting is a matter of pride to the Bishnoi, who saw the first Bishnoi woman elected to a political assembly outside their community in 1987.

In the eighteenth century, outside lumber interests came into Bishnoi territory with their eyes on the local thick-trunked khejare tree (*Prosopis cineraria*), which the Bishnoi continue to depend upon for its high protein fodder and use as thatch. They have always been emphatic in their conservation of this plant. When outside industrial interests threatened to denude the khejare forests, many Bishnoi hugged the trees in an effort to prevent such deforestation. Hundreds of them were massacred doing so. Recently, the Government of India honored those martyrs as the country's first ecological heroes, the precursors of the recent Chipko ("tree-hugging") movement across the Indian Himalayas (Tobias 1986).

If a Bishnoi is discovered to have eaten meat, or harmed an animal, he or she is socially boycotted. In such small villages, it is almost impossible to elude scrutiny and, hence, the religious edicts are not easily transgressed. Here again is an in-built mechanism for perpetuating an ecological ethic. One might be tempted to predict that when and if the Bishnoi are urbanized, as part of India's—and the world's—mad dash toward megacities, Bishnoi traditions will vanish. But the Jains have proven this not to be the case. Unlike the Bishnoi, Jains have virtually no rural tradition, but are strictly dependent upon an urban community of like-minded Jains. In fact, Jains would never condone the keeping of cattle, nor of any other animals. They believe that husbandry is a form of interference, of exploitation. It is rare to find a Jain household that has a pet.

As a result of their faith, Bishnoi villages swarm with wild animals. And while much of India periodically suffers from drought, the Bishnoi's ability to monitor water, harvesting dewdrops from plants, maintaining cisterns, and preventing overgrazing by their sheep, cows, and goats, predictably results in plentiful water for their villages. They do not suffer; their cattle have plenty of alfalfa, two varieties of millet grow throughout the hot summers, and through the winter radishes, carrots, garlic, onions, sorghum, wheat, and sesame oil are produced, at great profit.

I will never forget driving through Rajasthan and seeing one funeral pyre of buffalos after another, tens of thousands of animals that had perished, and hundreds of thousands of people forced into ecological exile. But in Bishnoi territory, there was no vision of hell, but rather one of modest paradise. The Bishnoi's emotional bonding with their animals, their love of life, has sustained them in a pragmatic as well as a spiritual sense.

The Toda

Among the five tribal groups of the Nilgiri massif, the 1,200 Toda (known as *Ahl* by the Toda themselves) are the most ancient and unusual. Over a thousand years ago, the entire tribe apparently converted to vegetarianism, a fact documented by the first appearance of their cattle worship. Since that time, that veneration has yielded a bewildering variety of practices oriented toward the preservation of life and the love of animals. The Toda consume cow's milk and sell it to other tribes in nearby markets. This commerce is their sole sustenance. Toda cattle worship is a complex religion with its own priests, cattle temples, and elaborate rituals that define the entire Toda civilization. None of the neighboring tribes is vegetarian.

One of the first serious ethnographers to make contact with the Toda was British anthropologist W. E. Marshall, who published the major study of these people in 1873 when the reported Toda population was 693. Permit me to quote extensively from his book, for reasons that will be apparent:

> The Todas have no sports or games, except the innocent tip-cat, corresponding in its play very much with our boys' game of rounders. No violent exercise. No means of settling disputes by scientific personal conflict, as in wrestling, fencing, or boxing. Nothing in fact pointing to natural turbulence of character and surplus energy. They wear no weapons of offence or defence. They do not even hunt, either, for the sake of providing themselves with food, or for the pleasure of the chase. They do not attempt to till the ground. The products of the buffalo form the main staple of Toda diet. . . . To what other cause but grievous national improvidence can we attribute their having acquiesced in promptings to part with an amount of meat sustenance, that would, if utilized, nearly double their food supply? And to permit skins and horns of vast herds—whose sale would have brought a very welcome addition to their revenue—to be removed . . . ? . . . If they will not trade, and to work are ashamed, yet why none of the ordinary short cuts to wealth and honor, by means well known in all ages, and to most nations? No exciting and glorious war, with plunder! The feathers of the chief, the titles of the hero! No women to be attached, or prisoners to be enslaved or tortured! No food but a milk diet and grain, whilst the woods are full of game, and flocks and herds to be had for the taking! What is the meaning of all this? Have we come on the tracks of an aboriginal reign of conscience? And was man originally created virtuous as well as very simple? It appears to my mind, that in this absence of vigorous qualities: in the disregard of gain and of thrift: as well as in their ultra domesticity, we have the attributes of a primeval race. (Marshall 1873/1989)

Marshall goes on to reveal his contempt for these primitive people whose natures he describes as "torpid and inefficient," unlike "more spirited" races who are "clever, and persevering through ages of strife with fellow-man."

Such sentiments were common in the nineteenth century, and are even more so today, though perhaps less disingenuously conveyed, in an era of the GATT, NAFTA, and an aspired-to fifty trillion dollar global economy. With the advent of the British in the southern Hill Stations, the Toda women were sexually sought after by foreigners, who succeeded in transmitting a variety of diseases. By 1927, according to anthropologist Anthony Walker, "49% of the Toda population was suffering from venereal diseases, and this was seen as the principal cause of the community's low fertility" (Walker 1986).

In the company of a local anthropologist, Tarun Chhabra, I filmed extensively among the Toda in the winter of 1995, particularly in the small villages of Toror and Inkity. The villages hold less than 30 inhabitants living in no more than five units.

Most family units have about a dozen buffalos, four of which are active milking buffalos producing something like fifteen liters of milk per day. The cattle range freely. They are the economy, the religion, the talk of the town. Buffalos are the primary source of exchange and gift giving, food, and interspecies companionship, along with dogs. Occasional elephants, the rare tiger, numerous monkeys, and a host of other species inhabit Toda lands. The dairies are communally owned, though villages belong to individual families (Chhabra 1995).

Whenever disputes do arise, the elders meet for a *noyim* at a hill called Asxwilyfem. There they honorably and rationally work out resolutions that—true to Marshall's complaint—involve no screaming, fighting, or killing. In fact, so mild-mannered are disputes that one is hard pressed to ascertain who has been wronged. Norms of justice among the Toda are similar to those practiced throughout rural India. But because the vegetarian approach to life is so ingrained among the Toda, as among the Bishnoi and Jain, the intensity of conflict appears greatly reduced, and the common language for conflict-resolution unanimously assured. Property and other economic issues all are adjudicated by an unquestioned ethical communion (Rivers 1906/1986). Those arenas that are perpetually charged with stark opposition elsewhere in the world never surface among the Toda.

This common language of ethical justice, couched in the unambiguously expressed context of conscience, is perhaps the key contribution of the Toda to the larger human community. At a time when cattle and other animal species are being slaughtered and tortured in the billions, it is extremely important to note that there is a human tribe that has persevered gently for over a thousand years (Tobias 1994b).

Neither felling the forests nor fouling the soil, harming no animal, the Toda worship their habitat, insuring for themselves an afterlife (Chhabra 1993).

Conclusion: The Relativity of Concern

Some may dismiss these statistically diminutive human cultures as mere anthropological oddities, irrelevant to national policy. Yet India's neighbor to the northeast, Bhutan, has in fact codified similar ecological ethics as those practiced by the Jains, Bishnoi, and Toda, incorporating the spirit and intent of such ethics into its Constitution. The Bhutanese have kept 63% of their forests in a virgin condition (versus 9% in the U.S. and far less in India). And while Bhutanese Buddhists (who constitute nearly all of the 1.3 million population) are not by definition vegetarian, they are largely so. They have resisted development and moved into the twentieth century with astounding precautions, to avoid the serious mistakes occurring, for example, in neighboring Nepal, where wildlife, forest cover, watersheds, and human cultures have been devastated (Tobias 1985).

Close observation of these three historically rooted animal protectionist groups allows social scientists to better gauge the integrity and effectiveness of groups elsewhere in the world who are increasingly attempting to engender sustainability. The Jains, Bishnoi, and Toda have formulated precise criteria of ethical behavior toward animals and in so doing should, perhaps, best be viewed in the context of the cultural variable of conscience. Their example of active compassion provides a provocative challenge to the rest of the world. As beacons of behavior, they suggest critical indicators of possible change, for a twenty-first century whose primary task a growing number of people believe must be the adoption of an ecological and humane conscience. That means, first and foremost, making lasting peace with other life forms (Tobias 1994c).

Questions for Discussion

1. What is *ahimsa* and how does it influence the Jain view and treatment of other animals?
2. What are the common principles of the Jains, Boshnoi, and Todas?
3. Are these three cultures merely interesting aberrations or do they have something valuable to teach the rest of the world about ethical living?

9 The Emergence of Modern Pet-keeping

Harriet Ritvo

Many of us forget that widespread pet-keeping is a relatively recent historical phe-nomenon in both English and American homes. In this account, historian Harriet Ritvo chronicles the development of attitudes toward animals and their domestica-tion. Although certain classes of elite individuals had owned pets for centuries— members of the church and the aristocracy—the emergence of pets in the households of ordinary people occurred only within the last two centuries. Ritvo analyzes the social and historical forces that led to middle-class pet-keeping, including scientific and technological advances that resulted in the belief that nature, formerly thought to be largely out of human control, was now seen as capable of human domination.

Nowadays few people feel the need to conceal their affection for their pets. On the contrary, many contemporary English and American households unashamedly include dogs and cats, and the owners of particularly elegant or surprising pets are inclined to flaunt them as symbols of discriminating taste or conspicuous consump-tion. The economic importance and social respectability of pet-keeping is further attested by the flourishing institutions—from animal hospitals to breed clubs to the pet food industry—that service pets and their owners. A great deal of our society's time, energy, and money is now devoted to satisfying pets' and pet owners' needs, physical and otherwise (Kellert 1983; Serpell 1986).

When thinking about the history of household animals, we are often tempted simply to project into the past the conditions that we daily observe in the present. Pets figure so prominently in contemporary American and European life that it is difficult to imagine earlier versions of our societies in which they did not enjoy similar appre-ciation. Yet if we look back as little as two centuries, the position occupied by domes-tic dogs and cats begins to seem unfamiliar. One measure of this difference is the paucity of evidence about the relationships between humans and their animal com-

Originally published in 1987 in *Anthrozoös*, vol. 1, no. 3, pp. 158–165. Reprinted with permis-sion, International Society for Anthrozoology (ISAZ).

panions. Because household animals were not considered objects of serious inquiry or widespread appeal, few authors and publishers were inclined to spend time and ink on them. These intellectual and economic disincentives were reinforced by more direct social coercion. Individuals who expressed untoward interest in or affection for pet animals might provoke disapproval, contempt, or suspicion.

An example of the kind of source in which information about eighteenth-century pets is apt to be embedded is the *History of the Ancient and Honorable Tuesday Club*, an extremely long satirical account of a club for upper-class men, which met regularly in Annapolis, Maryland, during the 1740s and 1750s. The author, a Scottish emigrant named Alexander Hamilton, apparently wrote for a restricted audience, since his narrative is only now being prepared for publication. Although the *History* has certain literary pretensions—for example, it is written in a high mock-heroic mode—it is primarily of interest today as a storehouse of social history. As he wryly chronicled the annals of the Tuesday Club, Hamilton touched on a variety of everyday topics, including attitudes toward pets and pet-keeping. For example, one of the leading figures in the Tuesday Club was fond of cats, and the satirist made this predilection the emblem of his target's luxurious and depraved character. The following is an excerpt from what is intended as a biting portrait:

> This celebrated Gentleman, Judging his own Species, unworthy to make constant companions and Intimates of, Chose a Society of Cats for his friends, fellows and play mates, both at bed and board, and so far did his extraordinary charity and benevolence extend to those Cats, that he would deign to converse with them in the most familiar manner, giving some of them a Christian like education . . . it is said, that he once buried a favorite Cat, with great form and ceremony, like a Christian. . . . Some may think it very Strange, that . . . a Gentleman born and bred in a Christian land, should pay so much deference and respect, to these brute creatures. . . . In fine, had he been a persian Dervis, who understood thorro-ly the Language of brutes, there might be some plausible reason for his amusing himself in this manner; but as he is an old Englishman, and a protestant, and a Christian of the Church of England, as by Law established, there is no other way . . . for accounting for this odd humor, but by ascribing it to mere whim and fancy. . . . (Hamilton 1990)

This selection, which is extracted from a much longer diatribe in the same vein, suggests that pet-keeping was not only unusual in the American colonies on the eve of Revolution, but was also an easy target for criticism and ridicule. Other contemporary sources corroborate the low esteem in which pet ownership was held. In England at about the same period Humphrey Morice, a gentleman of some distinction who had served as a Privy Councillor, wished to provide for the maintenance of his aged dogs after he died. Because he feared public opinion, however, he was reluctant to include this bequest in the main body of his will, hiding it instead in a secret codicil, which he cast in the form of a letter to a friend (Harwood 1928). More generally, the metaphorical or symbolic or connotative penumbra surrounding the dog, which was then as now the archetypal pet species, although not the only one, indicated the low regard in which both animals and their owners might be held. In the eighteenth century the main characteristics attributed to the dog were not the loyalty and affection that predominate in current iconography. Instead, as many of William Hogarth's satiric paintings and engravings demonstrated, the dog was more likely to represent bestiality, vulgarity, and subversion. Thomas Bewick, the author and illustrator of popular works of natural history, wrote that, although the dog was loyal to his master, "to his own species he is ill-behaved, selfish, cruel, and unjust." Earlier still, during the sixteenth and seventeenth centuries, the contrast with modern understandings of the dog's moral nature was still more striking. Shakespeare, for example, seldom referred to dogs except to express his distaste for them and for the people with whom he associated them (Bewick 1975; Empson 1951; Paulson 1979).

It is necessary to emphasize that English and American pets have only recently gained widespread acceptance because it is so easy to assume the reverse. Americans routinely think of their own culture, and especially the part of it that derives from Great Britain, as one that embodies a unique, intrinsic, and immemorial fondness for animals. English self-stereotypes echo this point of view. Thus when a publican in the western part of England was recently prosecuted under the anticruelty laws for advertising hedgehog-flavored potato chips, the media on both sides of the Atlantic reported it as typical, lovable English dottiness. And there is more solid, less anecdotal evidence for this understanding of Anglo-American attitudes. For example, the institutionalized animal protection movement originated in Great Britain with the foundation of the (not yet Royal) Society for the Prevention of Cruelty to Animals in 1824; the Cruelty to Animals Act of 1876 pioneered state regulation of animal experimentation (French 1975; Turner 1980). But this heightened sensitivity to animal suffering did not develop in a vacuum; the activists who crusaded on behalf of their fellow creatures were inspired not by benevolent abstractions but by repeated observation of violent physical abuse. However early nineteenth-century Britons may have stacked up in relation to the citizens of other nations, most of them were more notable for their indifference to animal pain, or even their enjoyment of it when it came in the guise of such sports as dog fighting, badger baiting, or rat killing, than for their abhorrence of cruelty to their fellow creatures (Ritvo 1987).

Thus the tradition of extravagant British concern for animals, like many other apparently ancient usages, turns out to have been a Victorian creation (Hobsbawm and Ranger 1983). Although at the end of the nineteenth century a humanitarian crusader named W. J. Stillman could celebrate the strength, "especially in Anglo-Saxon countries," of "this sentiment of tenderness for . . . the sentient lower creatures," English self characterizations of only slightly earlier offered quite a different impression. In the 1830s, for example, the naturalist Edward Jesse wrote that "of all the nations of Europe, our own countrymen are, perhaps, the least inclined to treat the brute creation with tenderness," and in 1868 Queen Victoria, who was herself both an enthusiastic partisan of animals and a devoted pet owner, complained that "the English are inclined to be more cruel to animals than some other civilized nations are." Even after the Victorian period, some human victims of oppression, especially women, but also members of the lower classes, found an easy metaphor for their sufferings in those routinely inflicted on laboratory animals (Jesse 1835; Stillman 1899; Hibbert 1984; Lansbury 1985).

In the unpropitious emotional or moral climate of pre-Victorian Britain (although most of the following refers specifically to Britain, it also applies to the history of pet-keeping in America, where, at least through the nineteenth century, developments tended after a slight time lag to parallel those across the ocean), it is perhaps not surprising that few people kept pets. That is, although domesticated animals, including dogs and cats, had been part of many households from Saxon and Celtic times, almost all of these creatures were kept because they performed some useful function, not simply because they were affectionate or ornamental. A sixteenth-century listing of English dog breeds divided the animals by function: for example, "Fynder," "Stealer," "Turnspit," and "Dancer" (Caius, undated). Even dogs that kept relatively elevated human company, such as those that appeared with their masters in the formal portraits of the seventeenth and eighteenth centuries—portraits are often adduced as evidence of the antiquity of pet-keeping—were not pets, but rather hunting dogs like setters and spaniels or, more rarely, coursing dogs like greyhounds.

Nevertheless, pet-keeping did have a long history among certain kinds of people. A medieval example, admittedly fictional but representative of a trend among her small group of peers, was the privileged prioress of Chaucer's fourteenth-century *Canterbury Tales*, who traveled with "smale houndes" that she fed prodigally "with rosted flessh, or milk." In Chaucer's view, and in that of the ecclesiastical authorities of his day, who tried to suppress pet ownership among monks and nuns from affluent backgrounds, such behavior was inappropriate. Despite this official censure, however, pet-keeping among the very privileged did not disappear, and, a century and a half later, the secular ladies attending the court of Henry VIII were allowed to bring their dogs (Thomas 1983). Beginning in the seventeenth century the owners of estates occasionally erected monuments in memory of deceased animals, although it is usually difficult to tell from the surviving inscriptions whether the commemorated animal was a genuine pet or merely a loyal servant (Lambton 1985). And during the latter part of the seventeenth century, King Charles II was renowned—or perhaps notorious—for doting on lapdogs, and his fondness has been preserved in the name of one of the major varieties of toy spaniels. When his pets were stolen, as seems to have happened with some frequency, he was inconsolable; once he went so far as to advertise in a newspaper for a favorite's return. (He may have been one of the first to avail himself of this method of repairing his loss, since newspapers were a recent innovation at that time.) Charles' brother and successor, James II, also enjoyed pet dogs, as did his successors, William and Mary. During their joint reign the pug, which was, like William, a native of the Netherlands, became established as the preferred lapdog of the English aristocracy (Ritchie 1981).

What these early pet owners had in common was privileged status in terms of both money and rank. This meant, on the crudest material level, that they could afford to maintain animals that did not earn their keep. It also gave them sufficient independence to ignore any criticism or derision that might be directed their way. And on a deeper level, they may have enjoyed a metaphorical security—a feeling of supremacy over nature—that was as unusual as was their exalted social position. For animals, even heavily domesticated pet animals, have always symbolized the natural world, and incorporating one into the intimate family circle would have presupposed an attitude of trust and confidence that few ordinary English citizens of the sixteenth, seventeenth, and even much of the eighteenth centuries were able to muster. Pet owners probably saw the nonhuman world as a less threatening and more comfortable place than did most of their contemporaries, who understood their relationship with the forces of nature primarily as a struggle for survival. That is why pet-keeping did not become a widely exercised prerogative until this struggle had been sufficiently mediated or attenuated by scientific, technological, and economic developments. Only at that point could ordinary people interpret the adoption of a representative of the elements (however tame and accommodating) as reassuring evidence of human power, rather than as a troublesome reminder of human vulnerability (Passmore 1975; Shell 1986; Thomas 1983).

Thus it is not surprising that widespread pet ownership among members of the middle classes can be dated from the late eighteenth and early nineteenth centuries.

This period saw a series of radical changes in the general relationship of human beings (at least European human beings) to the natural world. Whereas at the beginning of the eighteenth century natural forces had been perceived as largely out of human control, by the end of the century science and engineering had begun to make much of nature more manageable. Advances in natural history, and especially in taxonomy, signaled an increase in human intellectual mastery. On a more pragmatic level, progress in such fields as animal husbandry, veterinary science, and weapons technology made those who had to deal with animals less vulnerable to natural caprice. These technical developments were paralleled in the political sphere by the increase of English influence in those areas of the world—Asia, Africa, and North America—where nature was perceived to be wildest. Once it had become the subject of domination rather than a constantly menacing antagonist, nature could be viewed with affection and even, as the scales tipped more to the human side, with nostalgia. This shift had consequences throughout Western culture. For example, the art and literature of this period show an increasing aesthetic appreciation for wildness, which had previously been castigated as ugly, as well as new sympathy for peripheral experiences and points of view, including those of animals, as well as of the poor and of the human inhabitants of exotic territories.

In the less elevated sphere of the home, more and more people—especially members of the middle classes, which had especially benefited from the advances of the eighteenth century—indulged in sentimental attachment to pets as it became clear that they represented a nature that was no longer threatening. There are many indices of the increase in companion animals, especially dogs, from about the beginning of the nineteenth century. None of these indices is individually conclusive, but together they seem persuasive in their chronological location of the transition. For instance, the returns from the dog tax, originally imposed as a revenue measure during the Napoleonic wars, grew steadily. Publishers discovered a new market for books about dogs where none had previously existed; in addition, periodicals devoted generally to country sports began to feature dogs more prominently. Finally, well into the Victorian period, the official institutions of dog fancying appeared. The first formal dog show was held in Newcastle in 1859; the Kennel Club was founded in 1873, to be followed by a host of clubs devoted to individual breeds; and the first canine *Stud Book* appeared in 1874. Parallel organizations for cats appeared within a few decades (Ritvo 1987).

Although it was pervasive, the shift in attitudes that encouraged the expansion of pet ownership among ordinary people was not conscious. That is, when people, either in the nineteenth century or, for that matter, at more recent periods, decided to acquire pets, they did not do so with the conscious intention of reenacting a scenario of human conquest and control of nature. Instead, the voluminous Victorian literature of pet-keeping was saturated with the sentimentality characteristic of the period; at least on the surface it was a literature of love rather than one of domination. But this love presupposed, and even celebrated, a satisfactory resolution of the struggle between nature and civilization. Indeed, not only did the conquest of external nature make it possible for many people to own pets, but the safe, captive, and loyal pet reciprocally symbolized the appropriate relation between humans and nature under the new dispensation. One of the underlying attractions of pet ownership may have been the opportunity it offered people to express those unacknowledged or even subconscious understandings. An examination of a few of the standard concerns of enthusiastic nineteenth-century pet owners reveals that beside the rhetoric of affection and admiration in which they routinely described their relationships with their animals ran another rhetoric, one expressed in action as well as in language, that was explicitly concerned with power and control.

For example, many pet-keepers were producers as well as consumers of animals. The whole enterprise of maintaining and improving breeds embodied a metaphorical assertion of domination; the breeder assumed an almost godlike role in planning new variations. And on a more literal level, any attempt at breeding, at least unless pet owners were content to abandon their aspirations and let their animals be guided entirely by their own inclinations, immediately provoked a contest between human will and natural proclivities. On the most literal level, enforcing a predetermined choice of mate required close physical control of one's animal. Thus the fact that it was impossible to disengage dogs that managed to evade attempted restrictions was particularly troublesome, because it could produce a prolonged and public display of resistance to human authority. "Where they are permitted to run about and appear in such a state before the habitations of the respectable. . .it is a most disgusting shameful spectacle," objected one early nineteenth-century chronicler, who was motivated by disciplinary as well as prudish concerns; he continued, "there is, perhaps, no nuisance that stands more in need of compulsive correction" (Taplin 1803). To prevent such unedifying performances, bitches had to be locked up when they were in heat. Like masters whose moral standards for their families and servants were too lax, owners who neglected this responsibility failed in their duties to the community. (This was not the only way in which the exercise of authority over the natural world became metaphorically confounded with dominion within the human sphere.) The "quantities of bastards [canine bastards were meant here, but the ambiguity was not completely accidental], and the dwindled breed of Pointers and Setters" could be laid to the account of pet owners who exercised insufficient surveillance (Thornhill 1804, 35).

And physical isolation was not enough; if possible, bitches' sentiments and imaginations had to be controlled as well. An eminent Victorian dog fancier recalled a Dandie Dinmont terrier whose wayward emotions made her useless for breeding; she "became enamoured with a deerhound, and positively would not submit to be served by a dog of her own breed." Even bitches who were more compliant might defeat their owners' purposes, if they were allowed so much as to look at attractive dogs of different breeds. Delabere Blaine, who was sometimes known as "the father of canine pathology," had a pug bitch whose constant companion was a white spaniel. He claimed that all her litters were sired by pugs, and all consisted of undeniably pug puppies—but that in tribute to her infatuation one puppy in each batch was white, a color that was not desirable in pugs (Dalziel 1879).

If ensuring that pets consorted only with their chosen mates represented a victory over nature on its own terms—that is, overpowering it by brute force—the kind of manipulation involved in deciding which animals to pair exemplified a triumph of human intelligence. Thus aficionados of many modern dog breeds point with pride to their dogs' ancient origins, but in fact almost all of these origins were fabricated by nineteenth-century dog fanciers in search of distinctions that could be ratified by an elaborate hierarchy of pedigrees and dog show awards. Even the few breeds for which there is significant pre-nineteenth-century evidence, such as the toy spaniel, were transformed so radically by Victorian breeders as to practically obliterate their genetic connection with their alleged forebears. Most so-called traditional breeds simply did not exist as breeds in the modern sense of race or strain at all. For example, the word "bulldog" is old, but until the nineteenth century it referred to dogs that performed a particular function—that is, attacking tethered bulls—rather than to dogs that shared a particular ancestry or set of physical characteristics (Lytton 1911; Ritvo 1986). Thus Victorian dog fanciers were working with a relatively clean slate when they set out to develop breed standards. And the standards they developed suggest that what they valued was arbitrariness—the ability to produce animals with surprising or unnatural characteristics. Often the rarest traits, meaning those that were furthest from a strain's inherent inclinations and so offered the strongest evidence of the breeder's influence, provoked the greatest admiration; conversely, typical animals—that is those that displayed traits that would probably have been manifest without human interference—were frequently dismissed as merely mediocre.

Fortuitously, as the most plastic of domesticated animals, dogs were particularly vulnerable to this kind of manipulation; indeed, it was occasionally suggested that their genetic malleability was the gratifying physical analogue of their temperamental eagerness to serve their human masters. Thus, the inclination to celebrate animals that exemplified the human ability to reconstruct had an influence on the character of breed after breed. For example, until bull-baiting was outlawed in 1835, bulldogs were simply dogs of any appearance and ancestry with sufficient courage, strength, and ferocity to hold their own against outraged bulls. It is not surprising that bulldogs of this sort became uncommon once their primary function was abolished; but it may be somewhat surprising that animals of the same name reappeared as popular pets toward the end of the century.

However, the terms in which the resurgent bulldogs were described strongly suggested that their connection with their bloodthirsty namesakes was rather tenuous. They were said to be more pampered than other breeds, more "delicate" as puppies, and so indolent that it was necessary to coax them to eat. In disposition, they were alleged to be "peaceable" and "intelligent," also qualities for which their predecessors were seldom celebrated (Anon. 1894; Davies 1905; Lane 1900; Pybus-Sellon 1885). In physical character, the revived bulldogs also reflected the arbitrary manipulations of breeders rather than any adaptation to function. So apparently random were the standards prescribed for the breed that outsiders had great difficulty in making sense of them. Thus, although much printed advice about bulldog breeding was available, a correspondent who said he had "only quite recently entered the Bulldog Fancy" implored the editors of the *Sportsman's Journal and Fancier's Guide* to publish a brief description of "the points, general make and shape . . . of the bulldog" (Anon. 1879).

A sample of what this gentleman was up against was the Dudley nose question, which convulsed the Bulldog Club for over a decade. Dudley, or flesh-colored, noses occurred in some strains of fawn-colored bulldogs, usually in conjunction with light eyes and a yellowish face. In 1884, the Club voted to exclude all dogs with Dudley noses from competition, narrowly defeating a counterproposal that Dudley noses be considered mandatory in fawn bulldogs (Farman 1898). This issue was fought on aesthetic grounds, but breeders could be similarly whimsical in their selection of traits that had more serious pragmatic implications. Thus in the 1890s the conformation referred to as being "well out at the shoulder" became standard among well-bred bulldogs. Any dog lacking this feature was doomed to mediocrity in the eyes of show judges, but those lucky enough to display it were likely to end up as seriously crippled as Dockleaf, a renowned champion of this period, who could not walk two miles without collapsing (Anon. 1891a; Lee 1893).

Almost every dog breed provided occasion for this kind of arbitrary display of human ability to manipulate. The collie, which Queen Victoria's partiality made the most popular late-nineteenth-century dog breed, was also reconstructed to serve the figurative needs of fanciers. Collies were originally valued for the qualities they had developed as hard-working Scottish sheepdogs—intelligence, loyalty, and a warm shaggy coat. But once they were ensconced in the *Stud Book* and in comfortable homes, breeders began to introduce modifications and "improvements." As pedigreed collies became more numerous, breeding fashions became more volatile; breeders redesigned their animals and restocked their kennels in accordance with the latest show results. For example, the 1890s saw a craze for exaggerated heads with long, pointy noses, despite the objections of some conservative critics. In 1891, a *Kennel Gazette* reviewer complained that show judges had given all the prizes to "dogs of this greyhound type whose faces bore an inane, expressionless look." Others alleged that such dogs could hardly display the intelligence characteristic of their breed because there was "no room in their heads for brains" (Anon. 1891b).

Thus breeding offered dog owners the chance to stamp canine raw material with designs of their own choosing; it was a continually repeated symbol of the human ascendancy over nature. (Cat fanciers tried this too, but feline raw material proved much less pliable. This may explain, at least in part, the relatively limited popularity of pet cats during the nineteenth century.) And the theme of control surfaced more explicitly in connection with other pet-related issues. The relatively close coexistence of a large animal population and a large human population inevitably produced conflicts and problems that could only be resolved by regulation. But such regulation often seemed to address issues much more complex and far-reaching than was required merely to eliminate (usually canine) nuisances. Disciplining animals could be confounded with disciplining people, and the regulation in question might easily become the occasion for an unacknowledged redefinition of the boundaries of civilized or responsible society. Unreliable or inadequately disciplined groups of human beings could be grouped with animals rather than with their more respectable conspecifics; thus they frequently replaced nature as the object of manipulation.

Throughout the nineteenth century, for example, even as pets were made increasingly welcome at respectable domestic hearths, the pets of the poor were castigated as symbols of their owners' depravity—an unwarranted indulgence that led them to neglect important social duties. A typical complaint criticized colliers who "have more dogs than they know what to do with" and "starve their children and feed their dogs on legs of mutton." In addition, pet dogs were alleged to intensify the squalor of impoverished accommodations. An eminent veterinarian painted a distressing picture that conflated physical and moral contamination: "currish brutes . . . living with their owners in the most miserable and badly ventilated dwellings . . . and contributing to make these dwellings still more insalubrious by absorbing their share of the oxygen . . . and poisoning the atmosphere by their filthiness" (Anon. 1897; Fleming

1872). Thus reformist critics presented their efforts to deprive the poor of their pets as straightforward humanitarian efforts on behalf of suffering people and animals. But the juxtaposition of such efforts with explicit attempts to regulate the behavior of lower class humans suggests an additional dimension. For example, the regulations governing the Peabody Model Dwellings, part of a paternalistic late Victorian scheme to assist the worthy poor, combined prohibitions against keeping dogs with similar strictures forbidding hanging out laundry, papering the walls, and children playing in the corridors. By defining pets as an inappropriate luxury, which the poor had neither the financial means to support nor the moral means to control, more respectable members of society may have implied that pet-keeping was presumptuous for members of the lower classes (Jones 1984). The underlying symbolism of domination may have defined pet ownership as the prerogative only of those whose social position justified some analogous exercise of power over their fellow human beings.

These examples and speculations may help explain why large numbers of ordinary people did not begin to keep pets until something under two hundred years ago. With only slight extrapolation, they may also suggest why England, beginning in the last century, and the United States in the current century have been distinguished for the number of pets cherished by their citizens as well as for the generosity with which many of these companion animals are treated. Along the same lines, it is not surprising that the protection of wild animals first emerged as an issue in late Victorian Britain and attracts its most energetic and sustained contemporary support in North America and Europe (Doughty 1975; Fitter and Scott 1978). The concept of pet is not inevitably limited by species; pets do not even have to share our domiciles. Pets can also be understood as animals to which we maintain a certain relationship of domination mixed with responsibility and generosity (Tuan 1984). So defined, pets may prove to be nearly ubiquitous. We have now entered a new transitional period in our relation to the natural world, when we exercise power to an extent undreamed of at the beginning of the nineteenth century; most animals, not just those we have chosen to domesticate, depend upon us for their very existence.

Questions for Discussion

1. Historically, what role has social class played in pet-keeping?
2. Why did widespread pet-keeping among the middle class only appear in the last two hundred years?
3. How is human preoccupation with the domination of nature reflected in practices related to pets during this period?

Part IV: Animals and Culture

This is the sense in which the human–animal divide is a social construction: it is neither natural nor inevitable; it is the product of the power humans exerted and wished to maintain over other creatures. In other words, domination produced difference.

Leslie Irvine

10 Animal Rights as Religious Vision

Andrew Linzey

Throughout history, Christianity and other major world religions have generally been unsympathetic to the notion of animal rights. In fact, religious arguments have typically been used to oppose moral consideration for other animals, to justify their inferiority, and thus to legitimate their use by humans. In this chapter from his book Animal Gospel, *theologian Andrew Linzey suggests an alternative view; namely, that there are features of religion that are consistent with animal rights. What is needed, according to Linzey, is for "religious people to reexamine and rediscover the riches from within their own respective traditions which enable a morally positive view of animals."*

During the last twenty-five years, we have witnessed the growth of a new socially reforming movement called the animal rights movement.[1] Like others, this movement has been distinctly ideas-led. During the last twenty years there has been, as Andrew Rowan has pointed out, more philosophical discussion of the moral status of animals than there was during the previous two thousand years (Clarke and Linzey 1990). A revolution in ideas has been the major precursor to a fundamental shift of ethical sensibility.

I am reminded of a conversation between William Temple and his father, Frederick Temple, when William was a precocious schoolboy. At dinner one evening, William asked his father, "Why do not philosophers rule the world, Father? Would it not be a good thing if they did?" "They do," came the emphatic reply, "five hundred years after they are dead" (Iremonger 1948, 18–19). Almost without knowing it, we have inherited in Western culture certain ideas about animals that we seldom question and rarely scrutinize rationally. These ideas are almost entirely negative: Animals have no souls. They are not rational like humans, they are "put here" for our use. Each of these ideas has a long, predominantly Christian, history. Although many indi-

Originally published in 1998 in *Animal Gospel* (Chap. 6), University of Illinois Press. Reprinted with permission from the author.

vidual philosophers and thinkers have questioned these ideas, until quite recently they have gone unchallenged—at least politically and socially.

We are witnessing for the first time in Western history effective intellectual challenges to traditional views of animals based on these negative ideas. Although the media frequently present the animal rights movement as sentimental, antihuman, or anti-intellectual, the truth is almost entirely the reverse. The animal rights movement had its origin (in modern times) in the growth of the humanitarian movement in the nineteenth century which was, of course, concerned with improving living conditions for various oppressed subjects, children as well as animals—and has been spurred on during the last half-century at least by sustained philosophical and moral argument. Indeed, as early as 1977, the anti-animal rights philosopher Raymond Frey complained about the prevailing philosophical "orthodoxy" in favor of animal rights and vegetarianism (Frey 1977).

At the heart of the animal rights movement are, I suggest, two basic insights. The first we have already enumerated: It is that animals are not just commodities, resources, machines, things, means-to-human-ends, or beings here-for-our-use but rather sentient beings (capable of pain and suffering) with intrinsic value. The second insight is that there must be moral limits to what we may do to animals. This latter insight is most commonly expressed by saying that animals have "interests" or "rights." By positing animal rights, we insist that there are limits to what may be done to them morally. That doesn't mean, of course, that all animal rights are absolute (any more than it means that human rights are absolute), but it does mean that in normal situations at least there are certain limits that we should observe in our treatment of them. Clearly animal rights language is the language of strong moral obligation; it denotes checks and markers en route to a less exploitative way of living with nonhuman animals. Although our obligations to humans and animals are not identical, they are in essence the same *sort* of obligation.

These two insights—the apprehension of the intrinsic value of other sentient beings. and a keen sense of human moral limits in relation to them—have not been universally welcomed among religious people. Indeed, among Christians in particular there seems to be the most concerted opposition. To give just one example, in the journal *Trumpet Call*, published by the Peniel Pentecostal Church, the lead article argued that, "Meat eating and the acceptance that beasts are meant to serve humankind is not only justifiable in every moral consideration, but it is also biblical. The doctrinaire and unnatural decision to become vegetarian, or to put the rights of animals above those of man, is sinful and cannot be reconciled to a Christian life" (*Trumpet Call* 1995). The assumption is that animal rights is essentially a secular philosophy compromising religious, specifically Christian, perspectives. And generally there seems no getting away from it; animal rights philosophy does pose some apparently sharp challenges to elements within not only Christian but also other religious worldviews as well.

Let me select just two. The first is *humanocentricity*. By this I mean humanocentricity (of a bad sort) in which duties are seen as things that apply primarily, if not exclusively, to human subjects. With the possible exception of the Jain tradition, and mindful that it is hazardous to generalize about the world's religious traditions, it nevertheless seems generally true that even within such traditions in which concern for animals is engaged it is principally done on the basis that such concern is secondary and peripheral to that central concern appropriate for human subjects. At the very least, although there are some shafts of light—principally though not exclusively from Eastern traditions—animal rights philosophy appears to have no obvious religious tradition to which it can appeal and in which it feels unambiguously at home.

The second is *hierarchy*. By this I mean the tendency within all religious traditions to grade forms of life in such a way that human life and well-being are always seen as intrinsically more significant and more important than those of any other species. According to the Aristotelian hierarchy virtually taken over by St. Thomas Aquinas, within the Christian tradition there is something like an intellectual pyramid in creation, with humans placed at the top and the other animals in descending intellectual order. However difficult it may be to gauge the relative moral merits of other species, it must be clear that such hierarchical ordering by itself invariably leads to the disparagement of other (nonhuman) beings. We judge other beings by ourselves: our needs, definitions, aspirations, and complexes. Notwithstanding the need to make definitions and discriminations of various kinds, religious traditions have nearly always assumed and justified the moral priority of the human species.

Given these challenges, only two of which I have enumerated, it is perhaps not surprising that many religious people feel that animal rights represents a departure from at least some historically evolved religious perspectives. Or, ironically, some believe the very reverse, that animal rights is inseparable from a reprobate religious tendency—so-called animal worship. And, it must be said, there have been some Christian critics of animal rights who have not shrunk from arguing just that (Stott 1978).

And yet it seems to me to be entirely superficial to maintain an absolute juxtaposition between animal rights insights and world religious traditions. Although on the whole such traditions have been heavily humanocentric and hierarchical in their thinking and practice (as invariably have been the societies in which they emerged and developed), it is also true that many of these same traditions contain what I can only call elements of an inclusive moral vision—inclusive, that is, of specifically nonhuman beings. Let me try to articulate three basic notions that seem especially relevant here.

In the first place, within theistic traditions—and here I think primarily of Judaism, Christianity, and Islam—there is the familiar idea that animals are with us *common creatures* of the same God. All beings, according to a theistic perspective, originate with a Creator who is loving, just, and holy. In theory this means that animals are not completely separate from us; there is a common ontological basis for all life. This view alone can provide a strong theoretical framework for the commonly articulated sense of kinship and affinity which many humans feel instinctively with the natural world and animals in particular. In the Qur'an, there is an explicit acknowledgment that animals form communities like us and that they, too, praise their Creator. "There is not an animal on earth, nor a bird that flies on its wings, but they are communities like you . . ." (6:38). In the Hebrew Bible, the covenant is made specifically not only with human beings but with Noah, his descendants, and all living creatures (Gen. 9:8). One of the sayings of the Prophet explicitly accepts that this covenant has implications for the way in which one species should treat another. He says, "When a snake appears in a dwelling place say to it: 'We ask you by the covenant of Noah and by the covenant of Solomon, son of David, not to harm us' " (Robinson 1991, 49). In the Christian tradition, the notion of St. Francis of Assisi that animals are our "brothers and sisters" in creation predates Darwin and the discoveries of evolution.

If a theistic perspective is engaged, it follows that human needs or estimations of the value of other creatures cannot be the main or sole criterion by which we can base our understanding of their moral worth. That animals are creatures of God must imply that they (nonhuman animals) have a moral worth in themselves. Although this is an elementary and hardly controversial implication of creation doctrine, its moral ramifications are rarely considered.

In the second place, in Indian traditions, principally Hinduism, Buddhism, and Jainism, there is the central idea of *ahimsa*—translated by Gandhi as "nonviolence" or "non-injury"[2] Although this idea is variously understood, its extension to nonhuman life forms has never been in doubt. This has given rise, as we all know, to traditions of vegetarianism and abstinence from animal protein. It is striking from a Western Christian perspective how traditions that often derive little from a belief in the Creator should so clearly have grasped what most Western theists have overlooked: the self-evident worth of all life itself. In Buddhism the principle of no killing, or harmlessness, constitutes the first precept. In the Hindu tradition, it has been claimed that "almost all the Hindu scriptures place strong emphasis on the notion that God's grace can be received by not killing his creatures or harming his creation. . . " (Dwivedi 1990). Indian religions have frequently laid before us the goal of living nonviolently with our nonhuman neighbors, and in that sense have invariably included animals directly within the moral circle, in a way in which Western religious traditions have not.

And yet the principle of respect for all life has not been entirely lost even in theistic traditions, which are usually ambivalent about respect for animal life *per se*. One foundational text in this regard is Genesis 1:29, which requires vegetarianism. Although not formally requiring a meatless diet, Judaism has often viewed vegetarianism as the "ideal" diet commanded by God before humanity's descent into sin symbolized by the Fall and the flood. Although nonviolence toward animals has rarely been perceived as a Christian duty as such, the principle of *ahimsa* does find an echo in Albert Schweitzer's doctrine of reverence for life. The German word *Ehrfurcht*, correctly translated as "reverence" rather than simply "respect," preserves the religious, even mystical, aspect of Schweitzer's thought.

In the third place, almost all religious traditions have placed various emphases on the notion of *empathy* or *compassion* for those who suffer. "Kindness to any living creature will be rewarded" according to Muhammad (see Robinson 1991, 48). The Jewish tradition forbids cruelty to animals, a view summarized in the Hebrew phrase *tsa'ar ba'alei chayim*, the biblically based injunction not to cause "pain to any living creature" (Schwartz 1992). In accordance with this principle, Jews have consistently refused to participate in bloodsports, especially sport hunting. "Let a man feel hatred for no contingent being, let him be friendly, compassionate" declares the Lord Krishna in the *Bhagavad Gita* (Zaehner 1969). In Mahayana Buddhism, the Bodhisattva resolves to save all living things from the cycle of misery and death. This resolution is surely one of the most noble found within any religious tradition:

> I have made a vow to save all living beings. . . . The whole world of living beings I must rescue, from the terrors of birth, of old age, of sickness, of death and rebirth. . . . I must ferry them across the stream of Samsara. I myself must grapple with the whole mass of sufferings of all beings. To the limit of my endurance I will experience all the states of woe, found in any world system, all the abodes of suffering. And I must not cheat all beings out of my store of merit. I am resolved to abide in each single state of woe for numberless aeons; and so I will help all beings to freedom. . . . (Burtt 1955, 133–134)

I know of no religious tradition that teaches indifference to suffering as a matter of principle. Indeed, the meritorious acts within almost all religious traditions consist in their relief of unnecessary suffering. Even within Christianity—in some ways the most humanocentric of all religions—dogmatic orthodoxy has had to coexist with the tradition of saints East and West who have befriended animals, showed compassion for them, and even engaged in heroic acts of protecting them from cruelty.

Now, it is important that these general remarks should not be misunderstood. I am not claiming that, rightly understood, all religious traditions are unambiguously favorable to animals, still less to a modern doctrine of animal rights. I am not claiming that all religions are on the side even of moderate animal welfare. But I am claiming that there are within almost all religious traditions notions concerning the status of animals—and of the nature of our moral obligation—that can aid a more imaginative appreciation of their individual worth and lend support to the notion of moral limits.

While I am the first to admit that a great deal of Christian history and theology has been neglectful and callous toward animals, it remains true that even here there are rich resources within Christianity for a deeper respect for animals as creatures of God. But as I have pursued my own work, I have become increasingly aware of other scholars and thinkers within other traditions working simultaneously for similar goals. Within Islam, the late Al-Hafiz B. A. Masri, former Imam of the Woking Mosque, spent his life working publicly for the welfare of animals. Masri was deeply convinced that Muslim doctrine required a compassionate view of animals. His book *Islamic Concern for Animals*, published in English and Arabic, has become a standard text (Masri, 1987). Within Judaism, Richard Schwartz and Roberta Kalechofsky have been pioneers. Schwartz's book *Judaism and Vegetarianism* makes the case for vegetarianism derived from biblical teaching and the traditional mandate not to cause pain to animals (Schwartz, 1988). Kalechofsky has edited a seminal collection titled *Judaism and Animal Rights*, which includes her own essay on how experiments on animals anticipated and paralleled experiments on human subjects (Kalechofsky, 1991a; 1991b). Within Buddhism, Philip Kapleau, director of the Zen Center in New York, has been a leading advocate of Buddhist vegetarianism. His book *To Cherish All Life: A Buddhist Case for Becoming Vegetarian* takes issue with the Theravada tradition which sanctions meat eating, and argues that the Buddha was not only a vegetarian but admonished his followers to be so as well (Kapleau 1982).

Although it is wrong to suggest that religions are always the allies of animals, it is worth appreciating the religious, even mystical, insights in which the modern animal rights movement is grounded. The first of these is the mystical appreciation that what is given in the lives of other beings has intrinsic value—to be precise, a nonnegotiable, noninstrumentalist, nonutilitarian value. Such an insight, I suggest, finds its most natural home within a worldview in which humans are not the measure of all things or indeed the master of them. Similarly, the notion that there are moral limits to what we may do to animals presupposes a moral order in which human needs and wants are not by themselves the sole criterion of what is morally good. In other words, both animal rights insights belong morally to a *more than humanistic* view of the world. It is the worship of humanity, the deification of the human species itself, that prevents a proper understanding of animals, and indeed of ourselves. It is worth bearing in mind that if Western religion has been detrimental to animal rights, even more so has been the recent history of Western technology, which more than any other philosophy has regarded animals as machines and commodities.

It therefore seems to me to be possible to claim animal rights insights as at least a development of some notions that are implicit, if not explicit, in a religious way of looking at the world. Moral insight after all does not come from nowhere; all insight logically is rooted in a way of looking at the world. Some Christians seem astonishingly blinkered in their appreciation of their own tradition in this regard. After all, animal rightists have not invented the vision of the wolf lying down with the lamb in Isaiah 11:6, or the universal command to be vegetarian in Genesis 1:29, or indeed the vision of the earth in a state of childbirth awaiting its deliverance from suffering in Romans 8: in these, and in other ways, animal rightists can claim to be rediscovering and reactualizing visionary elements already present within the Western religious tradition.

What is urgently required is for religious people to reexamine and rediscover the riches from within their own respective traditions that enable a morally positive view of animals. The truth is that, until now, few within any of these traditions have seen the necessity or urgency of doing so. But if the animal rights movement is not to degenerate into just another fashionable secular movement divorced from the great traditions of religious thought, it is imperative that these great traditions engage with such insights in a thoughtful and reflective way. Arguably, within the Christian tradition at least, animal rights insights are correctives to a tradition that has failed to reflect sufficiently creatively on some of its own most cherished ideas. It is of course easy to deride the animal rights movement as "secular," but it has always seemed to me a great mistake to suppose that only religious people understand fully—or indeed fully reflect on—the basic insights of their own traditions.

My conclusion is that the basic insights of animal rights are consistent with many religious ideas and intuitions, and need to be brought into a much closer relationship with them. A spirituality that cannot or does not engage with contemporary moral movements is likely to discover itself increasingly irrelevant to people's deeply felt concerns. At the same time, moralism is not enough either. We need a spirituality that is open to new moral insights but which also saves us from the dangers of intolerance and self-righteousness. Moralism is not enough because for its very coherence and survival it depends upon a religious vision of how the world should be. The American naturalist Henry Beston in his book *The Outermost House*, published in 1928, posed the challenge in this way: "We need another and wiser and perhaps a more mystical concept of animals. . . . They are not our brethren, they are not underlings; they are other nations, caught with ourselves in the net of life and time, fellow prisoners of the splendor and travail of the earth" (Beston 1928, 25).[3]

Questions for Discussion

1. According to Linzey, what two features of Christianity and other world religions make it difficult to embrace the philosophy of animal rights?
2. What religious traditions does Linzey argue support the moral and ethical consideration of other animals?
3. Do you agree with Linzey that "the basic insights of animal rights are consistent with many religious ideas and institutions, and need to be brought into a much closer relationship with them?"

11 The Power of Play

Leslie Irvine

How our culture defines and distinguishes between humans and other animals depends on a long process of social definition. Over the last century, social and cultural forces have produced a new sensibility regarding our attitudes toward other animals. As an example, "pets" have become "companion animals" and "owners" have become "guardians." Sociologist Leslie Irvine argues that when adults play with their companion animals, this interaction is more than simple, carefree fun. These ordinary activities, referred to by Irvine as micropractices, challenge the ideology of animal inferiority and resist and reshape the human–animal divide.

A Short History of the Human–Animal Divide

The ontological divide between humans and nonhuman animals may be the oldest social construction. Early humans apparently made no effort to distinguish themselves from or set themselves above nature (Ingold 1994). With the transition from hunting and gathering to farming, however, people "adopt[ed] a radically different attitude to the natural world" (Serpell 1986, 217). Human communities began to define the natural world and the nonhuman animals within it "as fundamentally different and ontologically separate" from their own (Wolch 1998, 121). The process of civilization required an attitude of domination, justified through beliefs that animals were not only "other," but also inferior to humans (Thomas 1983; Tuan 1984; Franklin 1999). This is the sense in which the human–animal divide is a social construction: it is neither natural nor inevitable; it is the product of the power humans exerted and wished to maintain over other creatures. In other words, domination produced difference. Moreover, it produced not only difference but inequality, for in the case of nonhuman animals, "different" meant "inferior."

The primary justification for animals' inferiority was their supposed inability to reason.[1] In *Politics*, Aristotle ranked living creatures according to their rational abil-

---

Originally published in 2001 in *Anthrozoös*, vol. 14, no. 3, pp. 151–160. Reprinted with permission, International Society for Anthrozoology (ISAZ).

ities. His "ladder of life" placed humans at the top and inanimate things at the bottom. Following Plato, he differentiated humans into higher and lower groups, with those possessing lesser intellects (than Greeks) destined for slavery. Animals allegedly had even less intellectual ability than slaves, and, since nature does nothing in vain, they were "naturally" designed to serve the more perfect humans. This dualism of humans/nature percolated into Christian doctrine during the fourth century C.E., largely through the writings of St. Augustine. During the Middle Ages, Thomas Aquinas, who was trained in Aristotelian thought, solidified rationalist, antianimal dogma. Aquinas maintained that the only part of the soul that survived after death was the part that reasoned. Lacking this, the souls of animals died along with their bodies. Aquinas thereby relieved Christians of having to treat animals with kindness, since they would not meet the creatures they had exploited in the afterlife. He advised humans against outright cruelty, but not because of its inherent evil. Rather, its harm lay in its potential to lead to the more serious offense of cruelty to other humans.[2]

Aquinas stood at the forefront of what historian Keith Thomas (1983) calls a "breathtakingly anthropocentric spirit" that would peak in the seventeenth century. The dominant attitude toward animals at the time is perhaps best conveyed by Descartes, who considered them automatons: so thoroughly "other" that they lacked consciousness of their own pain. Even amidst pervasive anthropocentrism, however, there were detractors, for few discourses—even hegemonic ones—ever dominate totally. Cracks in the doctrine of human supremacy increased throughout the eighteenth and nineteenth centuries. Over time, attitudes toward animals would become less anthropocentric and more sentimental, resulting in, among other trends, increased pet-keeping. Scholars offer varying accounts of this transformation. In brief, Thomas examines the period from 1500 to 1800, attributing the change in attitudes largely (but not entirely) to urbanization. As vast numbers of people began to live at a distance from animals, the potential existed to romanticize them. Harriet Ritvo (1988, 20) argues that Victorian advances in animal husbandry, veterinary medicine, and weapons technology made "those who had to deal with animals less vulnerable to natural caprice." Once nature ceased to be a constant menace, human beings could view it with more affection. Keith Tester (1992) attributes the changing attitudes to the influence of new knowledge about the classification of animals. First available only to the nineteenth-century elite, knowledge about the differences and similarities between humans and other animals shaped kinder sensibilities. Adrian Franklin (1999) brings the analysis into the late twentieth century. He argues that, up to the 1970s, human–animal relationships followed an anthropocentric, modern agenda. Animals were vehicles for human progress (or demonstrations thereof), whether through experimentation, consumption, or entertainment. After the 1970s, the social, economic, and cultural changes that arguably constitute postmodernity "resulted in a shift from anthropocentric instrumentality to zoocentric empathy" (175). Granted, this shift should not be understood as a society wide attitudinal change. Attitudes toward animals still vary widely and are fraught with ambiguity (Arluke and Sanders 1996). For example, while some species live comfortably in human households, the majority are still exploited and tortured for food, hide, entertainment, sport, and research. Nevertheless, Franklin calls attention to how conditions of postmodern life have produced a new, more compassionate attitude toward animals, and he marshals evidence from several sites of human–animal interaction, including pet-keeping, hunting and fishing, and the food industry, to name a few.

This paper builds upon Franklin's analysis of pet-keeping. Although I cannot do justice to the argument here, Franklin maintains that ontological insecurity—the sense that one can no longer count on stability and permanence in key areas of one's life—manifests itself not only in rising rates of pet-keeping, but in new kinds of relationships with companion animals. That is, pets provide the stable, emotional relationships that other people cannot reliably offer. However, this is not to say that companion animals are surrogates for human relationships. Rather, evidence suggests that many people "have learned to appreciate their animal pets as *animals*," rather than as decorations or entertainment (86; emphasis added). Put another way, postmodern social conditions have made "pets" into "companion animals" and "owners" into "guardians." Dogs and cats are considered beings whose needs and characteristics are indeed "other," but in a sense worth honoring, not in a modern sense of inferiority. I have observed at least seven examples of this new sensibility:

- New knowledge about animals' nutrition, behavior, emotions, and cognition
- A trend toward nonviolent, compassionate methods of training
- Increased awareness of the problem of pet overpopulation, resulting in affordable spay and neuter programs
- Increased visibility of homeless animals to encourage adopting from shelters instead of purchasing from "puppy mills"
- Technological advances such as the implanted microchip, which reunites stray animals with their guardians
- Veterinarians who practice holistic and alternative medicine
- New things for animals (especially dogs) and guardians to do together, such as agility and flyball

This paper examines another example of this new sensibility: the everyday activity of play. I argue that, through play with companion animals, human caregivers challenge and even dissolve the human–animal divide. My analysis is informed by Foucault's (1977) depiction of power.[3] Foucault portrays modern power as working through a circulatory system. Tiny points of resistance in the system create capillaries that divert power along the way. In the social context, these points of resistance take the form of "micropractices," which are habits and activities that individuals engage in during the routine of everyday life.

Micropractices are not revolutionary; they seldom occur at the centers of power, but more often entail negotiations at the margins. Still, they can gradually undermine hegemonic ideologies—or at least aspects of them—and a growing body of research documents their political efficacy in the arenas of gender, race, and ethnic inequality (e.g., Fisher and Davis 1993). Micropractices can offer powerful indicators of cultural knowledge, social relations, and power.

This paper extends that analysis to the anthrozoological domain. Through the framework of micropractices, the common activity of play between adults and companion animals constitutes an individualized act of political resistance to society's disregard for nonhuman life.

What Is Play?

Researchers who study the behavior of human and nonhuman animals agree on the importance of play. They disagree on its definition and its impact on those who engage in it. The range of activities that can constitute play makes it hard to define as a distinct behavioral phenomenon (Bekoff and Byers 1981). For example, dedicated athletes work very hard at sports, sometimes without much enjoyment. Conversely, my idea of "play" often involves sitting at a desk for hours, "working" on an intellectual problem. I find the work fun, whereas I do not enjoy "playing" sports. This muddle has led some scholars to abandon the task of defining play, opting instead for basic principles of behavior that can easily account for and describe play without need for special theories and concepts. To be sure, play involves physical and cognitive activities that, at other times or in other instances, have other meanings. However, most of us can distinguish between, say, fighting and play-fighting, or between a friendly chat and the discussion at a committee meeting. Something makes the two contexts different. But what is that "something?"

Since a definition of play would help, and since a definition that pins play to behavior offers none, an alternative is to look at what play accomplishes. The literature on play often uses definitions in which play activities accomplish one of two functions (Burghardt 1998): they either sharpen skills in preparation for the future or provide an outlet for evolutionary vestiges of those used in the past. In the case of the former, for example, young animals' play behaviors might later be involved in hunting. Likewise, children's play prepares them for adult behaviors. Moreover, as George Herbert Mead (1934) claimed, play not only primes skills for the future, it also makes possible the development of the self.[4] In the case of the latter, recapitulation theory maintained that the kicking, hitting, and throwing games of boys were outlets for vestiges of behaviors once used in hunting and war. Among girls, playing with dolls supposedly expressed vestiges of behaviors necessary for caring for younger siblings.

Play, however, does not necessarily have to serve a purpose, either at the time or later in life. As Bekoff and Allen (1998) point out, functional definitions are problematic because of the lag between when play is performed and when it is manifested in adult activities. This "ontogenetic gap" makes for uncertain correlations between play behaviors and later life consequences. In this light, Bekoff and Byers (1981, 300–301) offer a non-functional definition. They describe play as "all motor activity performed postnatally that appears to be purposeless, in which motor patterns from other contexts may often be used in modified forms and altered temporal sequencing. If the activity is directed toward another living being it is called social play." Along similar lines, Hinde (1966) defines play as "activities which seem to the observer to make no immediate contribution to survival." Keeping in mind that these definitions could include compulsive behaviors such as grooming or pacing, and, in humans, religious practices or artistic endeavors, the non-functional definition is a reminder that play is a state of its own.

It is this quality—the play-state—that makes it recognizable to researchers as well as to players. Nonhuman animals have ways, such as the dog's play bow, of indicating that they are—or wish to be—playing (Bekoff 1977; 1995). One of the advantages of studying humans is that they can articulate their intentions and experiences. They can say, "This is play"; "I am playing now." The advantage of language makes it possible to study play phenomenologically. As "the study of the subjective experiences of human beings—how things seem or feel to them" (DeGrazia 1996, 78), phenomenology directs attention not so much at what is done during play (i.e., behaviors), but at the unique experience that play entails. In Goffman's (1974) terms, play constitutes a "frame" of experience. "Frame" refers to "a situational definition constructed in accord with organizing principles that govern both the events themselves and the participants" (10–11). Play constitutes a "protective frame" (Apter 1991) or a psychologically "enchanted zone" between players and the serious world. This allows for the same behaviors to constitute play in one instance, but not in another.

For example, it accounts for how the "work" at my desk can feel like "play" under some circumstances, but not others.

Methods

"Like many other beautiful things, play is ephemeral, and often difficult to study." (Bekoff and Byers 1998, xiii)

Data for this paper come from two sources. One is ethnographic fieldwork at an urban dog park.[5] This is a five-acre, fenced-in plot of land open to the public exclusively for offleash dog play. At peak times, especially after 4:30 p.m., as many as 20 dogs and their guardians use the space. Over the course of four months, I regularly visited the park with my companion dogs. I observed guardians and dogs at play and supplemented the observational data with field conversations. I talked at length with five guardians about play routines, objects, amount of time spent playing, frequency of visits to the park, and their interpretations of their dogs' play behavior. The second source of data is semi-structured interviews with 26 people who had adopted companion dogs and cats from a local shelter within the preceding three months. Whereas the dog park data revealed play behavior in public, the interview data explored play at home, which largely involved cats. The interview topics varied somewhat from those of the field conversations, but still probed into animals' play routines and the amount of time guardians spent playing with their new companions or watching them at play.

In a phenomenological approach to play, "the basic idea is to take, more or less at face value, the apparently sincere testimony of apparently normal human beings about how things seem to them" (DeGrazia 1996, 79). In short, I asked people how they played with their animal companions, what they enjoyed about it, and how it made them feel. I took their claims seriously as data about their experience. In analyzing the data, I used grounded theory methods (see Glaser and Strauss 1967; Glaser 1978; Charmaz 1983; Strauss and Corbin 1997), inductively developing theoretical concepts through coding the field and interview notes.

Results

Researchers have distinguished several different forms or types of play.[6] In this study, I focus on social object play, which refers to two partners playing with a toy (or an object that serves as one). When guardians played with their animals, they most often engaged in social object play, as in when they threw a ball for a dog or dangled a string for a cat. The play practices identified in this research represent three forms of resistance to hegemonic ideology: Resisting the notion of animal "otherness," Resisting trends to dominate other species, and Resisting the "iron cage" of life in an advanced technological society.

Resisting the Notion Of Animal "Otherness"

As a species, humans have adapted to the exploitation of other animals by using a variety of psychological distancing devices (see Maccoby 1982; Plous 1993). One of the most effective of these is detachment, or dissociation. This refers to the avoidance of emotional and physical contact with animals. Detachment makes it easier (for some) to eat meat wrapped in a supermarket package than from a cow one had known and raised.

One of the ideological mechanisms that sustains detachment is the notion that animals are "other" than human. The primary basis for this otherness has been the illusion that animals lack reasoning abilities. As Serpell (1986, 189) explains, "Aristotle's concept of a natural hierarchy, and Descartes's view of animals as machines were both myths that aided the process of detachment by creating an absolute rather than a relative distinction between humans and nonhumans." Animal consciousness, intelligence, and experience were not only cast as fundamentally different from our own, they were seen as so different as to be unknowable, and therefore dismissed as not worth knowing. Thus, humans could remain detached from animals.

In contrast, I observed guardians who recognized and gave voice to the subjectivity of their animal playmates. One of the ways they did so was through what Arluke and Sanders (1996) call "speaking for" the animals. In the dog park, guardians often said what they thought (or wished) their dogs could say if he or she could speak. Sometimes this took the form of very simple proclamations, such as "I'm ready to run!" or "I'm tired. Let's go home." Other times, it attributed more complex subjective states to animals. For example, when one dog repeatedly chased a ball but would not retrieve it, the woman "speaking for" portrayed the dog as seeing the whole fetching activity as ridiculous. As the guardian put it, "[The dog] says, 'Why do I have to bring [the ball] back, when you keep throwing it away!' " A guardian who speaks for an animal in such a way "demonstrates the intimacy of his or her relationship—the animal other is known so well that the owner can effectively discern what is 'on his or her mind' " (Arluke and Sanders 1996, 67).[7]

Another way that guardians gave voice to animals' subjectivity was by honoring the language that animals use. Although animals cannot speak, they do use recognizable gestures and vocalizations. Guardians can understand what their animals "say" by reading the symbolic evidence. Arluke and Sanders (78) explain that "through understanding the bodies and behaviors of companion animals, we actively construct a view of their minds." Here, dogs offer wonderful examples. With familiarity, we can easily read their play bows, their pant-smiles, and their expressive ears and tails. Even cats, with their reputation for inscrutability, give their guardians ample symbolic material, as these examples show:

- When she has that look on her face, she's ready to play
- She has a way of walking that says playtime is over. She's bored or just ready to do something else
- When we're playing, he'll sometimes stop to lick or scratch himself. I've seen him with mice and bugs, and when he means business he doesn't stop to scratch

By recognizing animals' subjectivity, these guardians challenge society's disregard for nonhuman life—or at least some forms of it. Some scholars would find the idea of "recognizing animals' subjectivity" absurd. Tester (1992), for example, claims that relationships with nonhuman animals are impossible since they cannot convey their perception of the relationship in ways that are meaningful to humans. However, the findings from this fieldwork suggest that people are far more willing to learn animals' means of communicating than Tester gives them credit for. Instead of believing that creatures who do not communicate on human terms have nothing important to say, they honor the means that animals use to communicate. One consequence of recognizing interspecies interconnections in this way is that it casts animals as deserving of moral concern. Another is that it raises strong possibilities of animal selfhood. If one of the capacities essential for a self is what Mead (1934) called "taking the role of the other," play offers evidence that companion animals indeed do this. For example, humans and nonhuman animals alike initiate play through gestures—the dog play bows, the cat bats at a hand or an object, the person offers a ball or toy—that signal that what follows will be play and subsequent behaviors will follow play's rules. The capacity to do this indicates that animals can define situations and expect intersubjectively shared definitions. With dogs, this goes even further, since dog–human play often includes elements of pretense. This comes not only from the human side, as when a person throwing a ball "fakes" a throw, but from the dog side, as well. For instance, one of my canine companions, Skipper, and I play a game I call "Pinecone Soccer." I kick a pinecone; he snatches it, runs, and drops it for me to kick again. He likes to feign snatching the pinecone so that I will quickly kick it in another direction. Behavior such as this suggests that animals not only share situational definitions, but also manipulate them based on their expectations of the other's behavior. The implications of this are vast, for, as Sanders (1999) writes, "if we remain open to the practice evidence afforded by our experience, [we] can reasonably come to see dogs [and cats] as intelligent and full-fledged partners in social interaction" (147).

Resisting Trends to Dominate Other Species

Domination implies that the needs of the dominator supersede those of the dominated. Play is a micropractice that resists—or at least renegotiates—this arrangement. Regularly making time for play with a companion animal tempers the certainty of human superiority. Many guardians placed their animals' need for play on an equal basis with their own needs. This was especially the case for dogs. A guardian at the dog park offered this illustrative example: This is her time. She needs time to be a dog, with other dogs, without a leash around her neck. We're here together, but this is for her. Sure, I've got lots of things I could be doing, but she needs this hour or so.

To be sure, I do not want to overstate this argument. While those who take time from their day to see to the needs of their companions have adopted a less anthropocentric standpoint, it is likely that human needs still typically take precedence. Nevertheless, the point I wish to make is the consciousness-raising that data such as these evince.

Another example of how play represents opposition to the domination of other species comes from a guardian who regularly plays with groups of dogs. Here, she recounts how she feels at one with the dogs:

> Sometimes, when there are lots of other dogs here, it's like we're all playing together. I'm in the game. I'll throw the ball, and a bunch of dogs run after it, but I don't know which dog will get it, and I don't think they know either. Then sometimes there'll be a little dodge and chase go on, and another dog will steal the ball. Then they'll all come running back to me at some point, because I have a part in this, too. I have to keep watching the action along with them.

The interconnection that she feels is an alternative to human superiority, which would have her running the game. In contrast, her perspective has all the players actively involved. To be sure, she can put the ball in her pocket and walk away, but any of the dogs could stop playing at any time, too. The point is that the two species are moving together, in what Sheldrake (1999) has called a "morphic field." This is a type of connection between animals that coordinates their activity. Sheldrake proposes that morphic fields are channels for telepathic communication among animals.

Sheldrake's work focuses primarily on how morphic fields between humans and non-humans allow for occurrences such as that which prompted the title of his book: *Dogs That Know When Their Owners Are Coming Home*. Other examples of morphic field phenomena include the migration of flocks of birds, and the movement of schools of fish, packs of wolves, and human groups.[8] The setting aside of land for urban dog parks itself represents an animal-inclusive standpoint. As Wolch (1998, 123) explains, "cities are perceived as so human-dominated that they become naturalized as just another part of the ecosystem, that is, the human habitat." Without taking the point too far, I argue that dog parks represent something of a borderland: certainly part of the human habitat, but dedicated to animals. Granted, dog parks are developed with the needs of humans in mind. But the consideration of the needs of animals—albeit via the humans who care for them—is striking. Dog park land could be developed in profitable ways, or ways that benefit humans directly. Devoting space to the needs of animals offers enormous potential for challenging that status quo.

Play practices in the home also show resistance to human domination of the household environment. Animal companions require their guardians to modify their "deeply rooted inclination for maintaining a neat and hygienic living space" (Sanders 1999, ix). Including animals in one's family means living with fur on every surface, muddy paw prints, clawed furniture, and various bodily fluids and solids, including what one guardian called "snoot goo" on car windows.[9] Living an animal-inclusive life requires compromising the hegemonic view of the home as a showplace, a view that receives ample legitimization from Martha Stewart and Home and Garden Television. For example, the guardian of a multi-cat household describes how her sense of sharing her home with cats (rather than "having" cats) keeps her from imposing human standards:

> Paper grocery bags are what my cats love. I always leave some around, open on the floor. When I go away, and I have someone come in to look after them, I imagine that person thinking, "What a slob. She leaves trash all over the place!" I don't care, though. The cats have to have things to do. After all, they live here, too.

Resisting the "Iron Cage"

As already discussed, the ability to reason has long justified the unequal treatment of nonhuman animals. Yet, human reason is as much a curse as it is a blessing. Our ability to think of ways to do things ever faster and more efficiently becomes, in Weber's (1954) apt phrase, an "iron cage." While the "iron cage" conjures up the sense of being trapped, Gergen (1991) offers a term that describes the feeling of never being caught up, never having time to catch one's breath. He calls this "the vertigo of the valued," attributing the sensation to an increasingly technological world.

Numerous scholarly studies propose ways to develop more humane economic practices (e.g., Ritzer 1993), and hundreds, if not thousands, of popular books offer advice on how to live more satisfying lives. Companion animal guardians have a clear advantage here. Playing with dogs and cats provides an escape—albeit temporary—from the "rat race." Many, many guardians saw play as something mutually beneficial that their animal companions added to their lives.

For example, a woman who lives with two dogs had this to say:

> Tomorrow is my day off, and I'm just going to play with my dogs all day. I'm going to take them to the park, and we'll play in the snow, and we'll have the whole day together. It'll be great for all of us. That's what I'm looking forward to. That's what got me through this day.

A similar sentiment comes from my reflections about play with one of my canine companions:

> But for Skipper, I would have stayed inside today. Skipper keeps me outdoors. He gets me out in the fresh air and keeps me moving. He makes me take breaks. He never seems to notice what we people would call "bad" weather, and more than a few times when I have dreaded taking him out, doing so has brought me to moments of extraordinary natural beauty. But for Skipper, I would not have seen the hawk that roosts in the trees around the park.

According to my interview data, much of the appeal of companionship with dogs is that they offer people excuses to play. Likewise, a Swedish study of dog guardians revealed that 80% of the respondents agreed with the statement, "The dog gives me an outlet for playfulness" (Adell-Bath et al. 1979). Although dogs require far more play than cats, a detailed study of 298 cat guardians nevertheless found that 23% of the men and 45% of the women claimed to spend between 30 and 120 minutes playing with their cats each day (Berghler 1989). Here, a guardian I interviewed describes how her cat lets her out of the "iron cage":

> I have a crystal paperweight on my desk, and if I hold it in the light just right, it throws rainbows on the floor. [The cat] chases them, and sometimes he "catches" the rainbow, and then seems to wonder why it's on top of his paw when he just caught it. When I'm working, it's a nice way for me to remember what's important. We start playing that way,

and there's no goal, no competition, either one of us can stop whenever we feel like it. Cats are totally in the moment, you know, and what
could be more that way than chasing a rainbow? It's a wonderful lesson
for me not to take work too seriously.

In a world that makes spiraling demands on adults and, increasingly, on children,
it is not surprising that animal companionship has increased. Play with dogs and cats
is one of the few outlets that people have for non-competitive fun. In this light, animal companionship is "adaptive" in the evolutionary sense of the word, since it contributes to individual health and survival by ameliorating the stresses and strains of
everyday life" (Serpell 1986, 148).

Conclusion

Considerable research examines play among children and young animals. Research
on play among adults is less plentiful, perhaps because adults favor formalized
games. Little extant literature explores play between adults and companion animals
(but see Sanders 1999 for an exception). People who play with companion animals
can see "play, laughter, and friendship burst across the species barrier" (Masson and
McCarthy 1995, 132).

It would be more accurate to talk about bursting across the species barrier *in
some places*. For this paper offers evidence of the need for a more nuanced idea of
the human–animal divide itself. While play with companion animals challenges the
separation between humans and animals, the separation remains untouched in other
contexts. People who play enthusiastically with their dogs and cats might still sit
down to a steak dinner, wear leather, and benefit from the suffering of animals in
laboratories. The accusation that someone behaved "like an animal" still implies
inferiority to humans and their moral codes. To return to the issue set out at the
beginning of this paper, the distinction between humans and animals may be the oldest social construction. It has proven itself incredibly malleable, responding to
social, economic, cultural, and other factors that continually change the distance
between humans and (some) animals. Moreover, the purpose of the divide changes,
since sometimes (but not always) it serves to define what is human by distinguishing what is not. The findings presented here suggest that, in other instances, people
recognize that animals' ways of being in the world are different, but they honor those
ways by accepting them and even attempting to understand them. To do so is to see
animals differently, which in turn requires humans to see themselves differently.
Therefore, play has the power to transform how people understand their lives, and,
perhaps, their world.

Following Foucault, this analysis suggests that, since the power of human supremacy resides in everyday practices, then that is precisely where challenges to that ideology must occur. Thus, when guardian-playmates honor animals' subjectivity, their activities, or micropractices, entail what Foucault calls a "politics of everyday life" that resists the devaluation of animals. Building on Franklin's idea that postmodern social conditions engendered a new sensibility toward animals, this must then be "played out" (pun intended) in everyday interaction.

To be sure, this study does not presume to describe a trend among companion animal guardians, nor does it suggest a norm. The sample is biased in favor of those who enjoy and seek out animal companionship, as opposed to those who "have pets." People who use dog parks are probably more likely to be sympathetic to dogs' needs for play, and people who adopt animals from a humane shelter typically do so from different standpoints than those who purchase from breeders or pet shops. Moreover, the region of the country in which this study took place has the highest proportion of companion animal guardianship in the US (64.3%). While the play practices examined in this study are neither universally descriptive nor generalizable, they nevertheless indicate what is possible. By highlighting both the malleability of the human–animal divide and the ways that play with companion animals reshapes it, this paper broadens the political arena and redefines what counts as political activity. Such is the power of play.

Questions for Discussion

1. How have our attitudes toward other animals changed over the past century, and what factors have led to those changes?
2. How does human–companion animal play challenge how we have traditionally thought about other animals compared to ourselves?
3. How does play with other animals transform the way we see our own lives?

12 There's Not Enough Room to Swing a Dead Cat and There's No Use Flogging a Dead Horse

Tracey Smith-Harris

Our language is filled with references to other animals. This article, by Tracey Smith-Harris, examines the use common animal idioms, metaphors, and euphemisms in the English language that depict or reinforce the exploitation and abuse of animals. These taken-for-granted words and phrases have become so much a part of our culture that we are unaware of the violence that they condone. Smith-Harris examines language the justifies the maltreatment of companion animals, particularly cats, and of animals in more socially approved arenas, such as science, hunting, and farming. She argues that our language not only shapes our perceptions of other animals, but maintains human dominance over them.

Human use of symbols and language help us to share and teach our cultural values and norms and allow us to socially construct the world around us, including our representations and constructions of other animals. While not the only means of symbolic interaction, language remains a powerful and effective means of teaching cultural values and norms, and this is true for the values assigned to other animals and the norms associated with human use of other animals. Robert Prus tells us "realities are created and transmitted, in the course of human interaction, through the development of shared sets of symbols" (1996, 53). In communication between humans, language remains an important feature of this sharing and transmission. This article examines the use of common animal sayings—idioms, metaphors, and euphemisms—that either describe or advocate animal cruelty and abuse. The theoretical underpinning of this research is symbolic interaction with a particular focus on meanings and sym-

ReVision, vol. 27, no. 2, pp. 12–15, 2004. Reprinted with permission of the Helen Dwight Reid Educational Foundation. Published by Heldref Publications, 1319 Eighteenth St., NW, Washington, DC 20036-1802. Copyright © 2007.

bols. Many researchers from a variety of viewpoints have expressed real concern for the speciesism inherent in our language used to describe animals so called animal industries. Carol Adams, Joan Dunayer, David Nibert, and Arran Stibbe, among others, caution us to carefully choose the language we utilize to discuss animals and animal industries. As Nibert tells us, "language is yet another powerful force that both reflects and conditions human perceptions and attitudes toward devalued humans and other animals" (Nibert 2002, 219).

Animal Idioms, Metaphors, and Euphemisms

Although the historical meaning is often hidden or forgotten, negative animal idioms, metaphors, and euphemisms are pervasive and indicate that there is a societal permissiveness to implied cruelty toward nonhuman animals. Both the power dynamic demonstrated in particular animal sayings and the importance of language itself—in expressing perceptions and socially constructing "normal" animal use—are examined in this article. While such language usage is not responsible for violence or abusive actions *per se*, it is an important tool in the social construction of a permissive societal attitude toward such treatment of animals; allowing humans to accept the normalness of having control over other animals, including cruelty and the ability to inflict violence. Interestingly, in such negative animal phrases violence is often explicit in the description but the meaning has been radically altered and the saying normalized, so that we no longer hear the implications of human violence against nonhuman animals, unless it is brought to our attention.

Why are we unaware of the violence in our everyday language? What are the implications for using such phrases and failing to acknowledge the dominance inherent in them? Why is it that in a post-industrial society we still discuss "flogging a dead horse" or the many ways to "skin a cat"? These phrases no longer mean what they once did—no longer a literal translation as they are stand-ins that underscore a very different lesson or meaning—but they still endorse a power differential between human and other animals and imply that violence against animals is acceptable, even natural. The violence explicit in the language to describe human relationships with other animals, including animal food industries, science, and hunting, represents the power of dominant human groups and their hegemonic control over perceptions of other animals and the use of animals in particular "socially approved" ways. In a previous study, Arran Stibbe examined how language influences the ways in which animals are socially constructed and therefore treated in human society, with a particular focus on the discourse of animal products industries (2001, 149). Stibbe found that language at all levels—from the personal to the collective use of descriptive terms for animals constructed as food—help to maintain the oppression of animals used in large-scale animal production. It is interesting to note that with the use of animal idioms, metaphors, and euphemisms, the phrases describe violence against animals but the words are interpreted to mean something completely unrelated, in a sense ignoring the message about animal use/abuse. But one cannot help but wonder is the message really lost? This article will examine negative animal idioms, euphemisms, and metaphors that can be broken into the two related sections: those that advocate violence against companion animals, with a particular focus on cats (for example, "There's not enough room to swing a cat") and those that advocate the continued use of animals in socially approved ways, with a focus on animals in science, farming, and hunting (for example, "guinea pig," "running around like a chicken with its head cut off," or "stool pigeon"). I will begin with a discussion of some of the common language that advocates or describes violence against animals kept as companions.

Phrases That Advocate or Describe Violence against Companion Animals

Companion animals have a special place in many North Americans' homes and hearts. We form close and often prolonged social relationships with them. Arluke and Sanders discuss the sociozoologic scale to help form an understanding of people's perceptions of animals and why particular types of animals are socially constructed in particular ways. They place "pets" at the top of the animal hierarchy as "good animals," as we might expect, since animals that humans form lose relationships with and live in close proximity to will undoubtedly be assigned a higher status than either animals who are constructed as utilitarian (for example, animals constructed as food) or those with a negative social construction (for example, animals that attack and kill humans and have thus forgotten their place in the species hierarchy) (1996, 171). Given the feelings of love that so many people express about their companion animals, what are we to make of the phrases that describe violent treatment toward animals we consider to be companions? First, when it comes to negative animal idioms and metaphors, it is important to note that the majority of such sayings regarding companion animals are related to cats. In fact, in an exploration of negative animal idioms, cats far outweigh all other animal species as the subject of disgust or the brunt of brutality. This may be surprising to some but given the shaky historical treatment of cats in human societies, perhaps it is not as difficult to understand. Although there have been cultures and time periods in which the cat was revered, for most of human history cats have been mistrusted and mistreated. The fact that we have sayings that discuss which way a cat will jump when shot at (for example, "see which way the cat jumps"), taking cats and kittens and placing them in a container and suspending them from a tree, to beat them to death with a stick or club (for example, "hang me in a bottle like a cat") tells us a great deal about the historical treatment of cats. They also come from a time and place in which cats were viewed as a dangerous part of paganism or in a much more utilitarian capacity as workers (mousers), not pampered companions.

Although the above idioms are less known, there are many others that are common today and tell of an equally brutal history of human treatment of cats. More common cat idioms are: "there's more than one way to skin a cat," "let the cat out of the bag," and "not enough room to swing a cat." Second, it is important to note that there is still considerable ambivalence in human relationships with all companion animals. In some human families, companion animals are treated well, but in many others animals suffer abuse and neglect on a regular basis. In addition, while some humans may really believe that their companion animals are family, in many families they exist in a strange object-being status, as such animals are often referred to as "it" and are routinely surrendered to animal shelters, left behind to fend for themselves when human families move, or taken to veterinarians to be unnecessarily killed. Such treatment is often tied to perceived or real behavioral problems or convenience. Third, negative animal idioms and metaphors not only reflect the social construction of other animals, but relate also to the use of animal metaphors to devalue marginalized human groups as well. Dunayer tells us that, "although nonhuman animals cannot discern the contempt in the words that disparage them, this contempt legitimates their oppression. Like sexist language, speciesist language fosters exploitation and abuse" (1995, 17). While language is used to negatively construct nonhuman animals and justify violent treatment of them, animal imagery is also used to negatively construct marginalized human groups. Negative animal imagery is often used to disparage human females,1 especially female sexuality and as racial and ethnic slurs. This, I believe, points to the power of language to maintain and reinforce social inequality, whether devaluing marginalized human groups or other animals.

Language That Condones or Even Endorses the Continued Use of Animals in Violent Yet Socially Approved Ways—Animals in Science, Hunting, and Farming

It is not uncommon to lose sight of the animal when it comes to animal-use industries. Science, hunting, and farming all advocate the use of animals for human benefit and tend to gloss over the inherent violence in these industries and activities. Many have written about the absence of individualized animals from documents related to science, farming, and hunting (Phillips 1994; Arluke and Sanders 1996; Adams 1991) and instead they are constructed as inanimate objects, tools, or human creations. Researchers have long since been aware of the power of language to shape perceptions and to allow humans to acquiesce to the unjust treatment of others, whether the "other" is another animal or a marginalized human. In animal industries, the individual animal is replaced by phrases such as "grain processing machines" and "culling stock." Carol Adams, for instance, uses the concept of the absent referent to examine the way that animals are ignored or lost in the social construction and consumption of meat. Adams states that, "without animals there would be no meat eating, yet they are absent from the act of eating meat because they have been transformed into food" (Adams 1991, 40). Animals become "it" or "meat" and are therefore relegated to the position of a thing, an inanimate object. As Adams states, "when we eat animals we change the way we talk about them" (Adams 1991, 41–42) and Dunayer adds that "clichés like beat a dead horse, bleed like a stuck pig, and run around like a chicken with its head cut off trivialize violence toward nonhuman animals" (Dunayer 2001, 167).

Metaphorically, the cruel treatment of other animals is marginalized in language usage. In the language discussed in this section, I will examine the image of animals being used to represent cruelty and unjust treatment toward humans, even though cruelty toward other animals in farming, hunting, and science is still widespread and is institutionalized. Adams states that "[w]hen we talk about victimization of humans we use animal metaphors derived from animal sacrifice and animal experimentation: someone is a scapegoat or a guinea pig. Violence undergirds some of our most commonly used metaphors that cannibalize the experience of animals: beating a dead horse, a bird in the hand, I have a bone to pick with you" (Adams 1991, 64–65). Dunayer tells us that our use of animal idioms as "metaphors obscure the reality from which they arose. Hunters tied the first 'stool pigeons' to a stool as a way of luring other pigeons to their death. People who 'lived high on the hog' ate the most expensive parts of pigs' bodies. During eighteenth-century riverside picnics, a 'fine kettle of fish' consisted of salmons boiled alive" (Dunayer 2001, 166–167). Therefore, we need to bring the inequality of other animals to the forefront in our language usage and become aware of the real implications of our use of animal idioms and other types of words and phrases that inadvertently advocate or condone the use of violence against animals as socially approved. Part of this social approval comes from our use of language. Dunayer states that "if our treatment and view of nonhuman beings became caring, respectful, and just, nonhuman-animal metaphors quickly would lose all power to harm" (2001, 167). Since the chance of that happening in the immediate future seems slim, another route to consider is becoming mindful of our language choices and their relationship to oppression and marginalization. In discussing language usage and its relationship to the oppression of women, Dale Spender says that it is not enough to simply change language usage. Changes to language can be viewed as part one of a two-part process. To facilitate longstanding changes to systems of oppression, social organizations must first be changed if the changes to language are to be sustained (Spender 1989, 31). And so, for concrete changes to occur in human perceptions and treatment toward other animals, both language and societal institutions must be altered to include a real ethic of caring and respect for other animals.

Conclusion

In much the same way that humans have become sensitized to the power of language in the marginalization and eventual emancipation of human groups, we need to become aware of the power of words in shaping human perceptions and treatment of other animals. We should increase awareness of the power of language in maintaining human dominance over other animals and the possibility of using language to shift and reshape human attitudes and perceptions toward other animals. Although language on its own does not have the power to change animal industries or even individual treatment of companion animals, it is an important step toward challenging and hopefully changing perceptions that could eventually help shape the treatment of other animals. It becomes harder to accept cruel and violent acts toward other animals, when we alter our language and refer to animals and animal industries as they really are and what they really represent. For instance, the use of euphemisms helps conceal human treatment and use of other animals, as euthanizing companion animals because of overcrowding at a shelter sounds rather peaceful. Killing cats and dogs by lethal injection because no one wanted them sounds quite different. Eating pâté sounds refined, whereas eating the swollen liver of a force-fed goose sounds quite different. Becoming aware of negative animal idioms, metaphors, and euphemisms and how they may provide justifications for the oppression of other animals represents a simple step toward an eventual solution to human oppression of other humans and animals. By being more careful with our language choices and consciously avoiding oppressive language, whether directed toward oppressed human groups or other animals, we make an important step toward not only making oppression visible, but also our decision not to partake in the symbolic justification of the oppression of less powerful groups by those that are more privileged and powerful. As Kenneth Shapiro states, "speciesism, like racism and sexism, is partially formed in and maintained by linguistic use," and, further, "we resolve to use language that enhances the social and moral status of animals from objects or things to individuals with needs and interests of their own" (1998, 1).

Questions for Discussion

1. What role does language play in the oppression of other animals?
2. Are there parallels between language that exploits other animals and racist or sexist language?
3. Can you think of other examples of animal references in our language that reveal their subordinate status?

Part V: Attitudes toward Other Animals

For many children, companion animals become honorary family members and it is difficult to imagine how such early and significant bonds could fail to engender at least some sense of kinship or affinity with other nonhuman species.

Elizabeth Paul and James Serpell

13 Gender, Sex-role Orientation, and Attitudes toward Animals

Harold A. Herzog, Jr., Nancy S. Betchart, and Robert B. Pittman

In examining our attitudes toward other animals, one of the most consistent research findings is that women have more favorable attitudes than men. This study, by psychologist Harold Herzog and his colleagues, looks at sex role orientation as one possible factor in explaining these gender differences. Is there something about a feminine orientation that leads to greater sensitivity toward other animals? Does a more masculine orientation result in less concern? This study attempts to answer these questions and suggests possible explanations for the observed differences between males and females.

Sex-role Identity and Attitudes toward Animals

One of the more intriguing aspects of changing societal views concerning our ethical responsibilities toward other species is the existence of large sex differences in attitudes toward the treatment of animals. Attitude surveys have consistently found that, compared to men, women are less tolerant of abuses of animals and have less utilitarian views concerning other species. For example, Gallup and Beckstead (1988) reported that female undergraduates showed more concern for pain and suffering of laboratory animals than male students, and Tennov (1986) found that more females than males claimed that they would refuse to shock an animal as part of a hypothetical experiment. Using the most extensive data set available on the attitudes of Americans toward animals, Kellert and Berry (1987) found sex differences on almost all dimensions of attitudes and knowledge about animals and concluded that sex differences were so large as to suggest that men and women have different emotional and cognitive orientations toward animals. They reported that women's attitudes

Originally published in 1991 in *Anthrozoös*, vol. 4, no. 3, pp. 184–191. Reprinted with permission, International Society for Anthrozoology (ISAZ).

toward animals were characterized by humanistic and moralistic orientations, where-as men's were more utilitarian and "dominionistic."

Gender differences in knowledge of and attitudes toward animals appear to develop during or before adolescence, depending on the dimension investigated. Sex differences in knowledge of animals, fears of animals, and species preference have been reported to emerge by the elementary school years (Bowd 1984; Kidd and Kidd 1990; Ollila, Bullen, and Collis 1989). Melson and Fogel (1989) recently reported that boys, but not girls, develop more detailed knowledge of animal young and ani-mal caregiving between preschool and the second grade. Gender differences in moral concern for animals, however, may not be evidenced until later in adolescence (Kellert and Berry 1987).

Males and females also behave differently toward animals. Kindergarten boys and girls exhibit different behaviors toward some species (Nielsen and Delude 1989), male and female horse owners treat their animals differently (Brown 1984), and female children assume more responsibility for pets than do their male counterparts (Kidd and Kidd 1990). Not surprisingly, gender differences are also reflected in the relative involvement of men and women in the animal rights movement. While pre-cise numbers are lacking, there is a substantial female bias in membership of both animal welfare and animal rights organizations (Sperling 1988). A recent survey of vegetarians, most of whom reported that the ethics of consuming animal flesh were a consideration in their dietary preferences, produced a sample composed of 71% women and 29% men (Amato and Partridge 1989).

The existence of sex differences in both attitudes and behavior toward animals seems to be a widespread phenomenon. However, little is known about how various aspects of gender and sex role produce the observed differences between males and females. In this study, we used the Bem Sex Role Inventory (BSRI) (Bem 1974, 1977, 1981) to examine the relationship among gender, sex role, and attitudes toward other species. The BSRI is one of the most commonly used personality inventories in the current psychological literature, and, while not without criticism (e.g., Lenney 1979; Spence and Helmreich 1979; 1980; see also Cook 1985), it has the advantage of being the subject of a considerable body of research, including a number of valid-ity studies (e.g., Taylor 1984; Ramanaiah and Martin 1984; Wilson and Cook 1985).

The BSRI conceptualizes sex roles along a two-dimensional matrix rather than the traditional male–female dimension. One dimension of the BSRI is an affec-tive–expressive dimension with men stereotypically lying on the non-expressive side of the continuum and females falling on the expressive side. The second dimension reflects instrumentality, with men having higher scores. Therefore, an individual

could score high on both instrumental (masculine) and expressive (feminine) characteristics. Individuals who score high on both dimensions are referred to as *androgynous* and are presumed to have sex role orientations that allow for more flexibility
with regard to sex-stereotyped behaviors (Bem 1975). Individuals who score low on
both dimensions are referred to as *undifferentiated*.

As mentioned, sex role orientation has been found to be related to how individuals respond to animals; for example, feminine and androgynous males were reported to be more likely to play with a kitten than males with traditional sex role orientation (Bem 1975). But the relation between sex role orientation and attitudes toward
the use of other species has largely been neglected. We hypothesized that both the
instrumental (masculine) and the expressive (feminine) dimensions of the BSRI
would be related to attitudes toward the use of animals. Specifically, we predicted
that both gender and sex role orientation would be related to (a) general attitudes
toward the use of animals and animal suffering, (b) the tendency to report a willingness to become actively involved in helping animals in distress, and (c) the degree of
comfort touching animals of different species. In addition, we hypothesized that there
would be a positive relationship between concern for the treatment of animals and the
degree of comfort subjects felt with them.

To test these hypotheses, we developed two scales to be used in conjunction
with the BSRI. The first was designed to measure general attitudes toward concern
for and use of other species and contained two subscales. One was designed to
assess the tendency to take action to further the welfare of mistreated animals, and
the other concerned the ethics of their treatment. The second scale measured how
comfortable the subjects felt around other species as reflected by their self-reported
comfort touching them.

Methods

Subjects

The subjects were 144 male and 222 female undergraduate students recruited from
introductory psychology and biology classes at three colleges in North Carolina: a
midsized regional state university and two small, private liberal arts colleges. A few
students did not complete all of the survey items, and thus group sizes vary slightly
for some of the analyses. The subjects ranged in age from 17 to 48, with a mean age
of 21 (SD=4.9 years). The majority of the subjects (335) were white, with 12 blacks
and 18 "others" (Hispanics and Native and Asian Americans). Forty-two percent
characterized the area in which they were raised as rural, 37% as suburban, and 15%
as urban. About 90% (332) were from the southern United States.

Instruments

In addition to questions designed to elicit demographic information such as age, race, state in which subjects were raised, and political orientation, the following instruments were used to collect data.

Bem Sex Role Inventory. The BSRI is a list of 20 characteristics typically attributed to women (e.g., love children, sensitive to needs of others, gentle), 20 characteristics usually attributed to men (e.g., competitive, defend my own beliefs, have leadership abilities), and 20 neutral characteristics (e.g., conscientious, moody, truthful). Subjects rate the degree to which each trait describes their personalities on a seven-point scale (1=never or almost never true, 7=always or almost always true). Two methods have been used to analyze BSRI data. In the original version of the BSRI, each subject was assigned a sex role orientation category (masculine, feminine, or androgynous) based on median splits. However, Bem (1977) later advocated the use of multiple regression techniques for the analysis of BSRI data, and we applied this approach in the present study.

Note that it is somewhat misleading to refer to males describing themselves as gentle and sensitive as "feminine" and women describing themselves as leaders as "masculine." However, according to convention, we will use these terms in the following contexts: The term *masculine* refers to a constellation of traits associated with instrumentality, achievement, dominance, and competitiveness. *Feminine*, on the other hand, refers to traits associated with expressiveness, sensitivity, and nurturance. The terms do not refer to sexual preference or transgender behavior patterns (i.e., effeminate males or masculine females).

Animal Attitude Scale. The Animal Attitude Scale designed for this study consisted of 29 Likert scale statements assessing attitudes toward the use of animals. Each of the items was scored on a five-point scale (strongly agree, agree, undecided, disagree, strongly disagree). The scale had acceptable psychometric properties, with a Cronbach's alpha of .88, indicating high internal consistency (Poresky 1989). Nine of the items were written to assess the tendency to become actively involved in animal welfare (e.g., "I would be unlikely to stop my car to help an injured dog" or "If I had the opportunity, I would sign a petition in support of stricter animal welfare laws"). These are referred to as the Take Action Subscale. The remaining 20 items measured attitudes toward the treatment and use of animals, including their use as food, clothing (furs), recreational resources (hunting, zoos), and research. Typical items included: "There is something morally wrong about hunting wild animals just for sport," "I do not think there is anything wrong with using animals in medical research," and "Too much fuss is made over the welfare of animals these days when there are many human problems that need to be solved." These 20 items are collectively referred to as the Ethics Subscale. High scores on these attitude measures reflected greater concern for the welfare of other species.

Comfort Scale. A second instrument was developed to assess the extent to which people felt comfortable with animals by having them indicate how they would feel about touching them. It consisted of a list of 15 species (butterfly, hamster, canary, earthworm, nonpoisonous spider, kitten, toad, duck, horse, harmless snake, mouse, turtle, large dog, chicken, bat) that subjects rated along with a five-point scale on which 1 indicated "would be very comfortable touching" and 5 indicated "would be very uncomfortable touching." Each individual's total Comfort score was determined by summing the circled number for each of the 15 species. In the analysis, the item values were reversed so that a high score indicated a higher degree of comfort touching the animal. Thus, the minimum score of 15 would be given to a person who said she or he would feel uncomfortable touching all of the species, whereas the maximum score of 75 would be characteristic of a person who said she or he would feel very comfortable touching any of the species.

Factor analysis of the scale indicated that there were two distinct factors, one corresponding to animals that are generally perceived positively (butterfly, hamster, canary, kitten, duck, horse, dog) and the other consisting of animals typically viewed more negatively (worm, spider, toad, snake, mouse, bat). Two animals failed to load clearly on either factor—chicken and turtle. We subsequently divided the Comfort Scale into two subscales. The first consisted only of the positive animals, and the second consisted of the negative animals. Responses to chickens and turtles were included on the overall Comfort Scale but not on the positive and negative animal subscales.

Data Analysis

Data were analyzed using standard parametric procedures (t-tests, Pearson correlation coefficients, multiple regression) with two-tailed statistical tests. Since one of our primary interests was male/female differences, it was necessary to consider whether the interaction between gender and sex role orientation was an important contributor to predicting the measures of attitudes toward animals. The multiple regression indicated that this interaction was not significant; therefore, it was not included in the analysis.

Results

There were highly significant gender differences for all of the attitude measures except closeness to positively perceived animals (Table 1). As hypothesized, males showed less concern for animal welfare issues than did females both in terms of the self-reported tendency to take action to help members of other species and in sensitivity to their use by humans.

Table 1   Mean (and Standard Deviations) of Males and Females on Scales Related to Sex Role Orientation and Attitudes toward Animals

| | Males | | Females | | |
Scale	Mean	SD	Mean	SD	T-test
BSRI Feminine	4.6	0.5	5.2	0.5	9.27**
BSRI Masculine	5.2	0.6	4.8	0.7	5.16**
Take Action	30.5	5.2	33.2	5.1	4.77**
Ethics	63.7	11.6	68.3	10.6	3.86**
Total Attitude[a]	94.3	15.5	101.3	14.5	4.35**
Negative animals	20.5	6.8	16.0	7.0	5.98**
Positive animals	31.5	5.7	31.9	4.5	0.68
Total Comfort[b]	60.5	12.6	56.1	11.1	3.54**

[a] Refers to combined Take Action and Ethics subcsales.
[b] Refers to all of the species included in the Comfort Scale.
** $p<.01$

Table 2 shows how various species were evaluated by males and females on the Comfort Scale. Generally, women were as likely as men to report that they were comfortable touching "nice" animals such as kittens and butterflies but were less comfortable than men with animals having more negative reputations (e.g., spiders, snakes, toads). The only closeness scores that were significantly higher for female than male subjects were for horses and dogs.

The correlations between the attitude measures and the closeness to animal measures are shown in Table 3. Note that correlations between the total Animal Attitude Scale and the two subscales (Ethics and Take Action) are high by definition. This is also true for the high correlations between the two subscales measuring how various species are perceived (positively and negatively perceived animals) and the total Comfort Scale. The data in this table indicate that there was a strong relationship between the self-reported tendency to take action and ethical sensitivities concerning the use of animals ($R=.68$). There was a moderate positive correlation between the comfort scores for the positively and negatively perceived animals ($R=.40$). However, the other correlations were either not significant or statistically significant but low. In contrast to our expectations, the correlation between the total Animal Attitude Scale and the Comfort Scale was not significant ($R=.08$), indicating that perceived comfort around animals is not necessarily related to attitudes about how we should treat them.

Table 2 Mean Comfort Scale Scores for Male and Female Subjects

Species	Males (N=143)		Females (N=221)	
	Mean	SD	Mean	SD
Kitten	4.81	0.68	4.86	0.63
Horse**	4.55	0.98	4.79	0.66
Dog*	4.31	1.21	4.58	0.87
Duck	4.50	0.99	4.50	0.85
Buterfly	4.46	1.01	4.36	1.04
Hamster	4.46	1.01	4.37	1.04
Canary	4.41	1.01	4.41	0.92
Turtle	4.48	0.97	4.34	1.01
Chicken	4.04	1.21	3.81	1.24
Worm***	4.13	1.18	3.07	1.50
Toad***	3.92	1.26	3.31	1.43
Mouse***	3.68	1.44	3.10	1.59
Snake***	3.32	1.63	2.62	1.64
Spider***	3.04	1.51	2.09	1.39
Bat***	2.38	1.49	1.84	1.23

Note: The species were rated from 5 ("I would feel very comfortable touching the animal")
to 1 ("I would feel very uncomfortable touching the animal").
* $p<.05$
** $p<.01$
*** $p<.001$

Table 3 Correlations between Attitude and Closeness to Animals Scales

Scale	Take Action	Ethics	Total Attitude	Negative animal	Positive animal
Ethics	.68**				
Total Attitude	.85**a	.97**a			
Negative animal	.13*	-.04	.02		
Positive animal	.20**	.07	.12*	.40**	
Total Comfort	.20	.02	.08	.88**a	.77**a

Note: See text for explanation of the scales.
a Indicates correlations between scale and subscale.
* $p<.05$
** $p<.01$

The overall relationship among gender, sex role orientation (BSRI Feminine and
Masculine scale scores), and attitudes toward animals was investigated using a two-
step analytical strategy. In the first step, a canonical correlation was used to determine
the degree of relationship between gender-related variables and attitude variables.

The overall correlation between the gender-related variables (gender, BSRI Masculine score, BSRI Feminine score) and the attitude scores was 0.47. Examination of the standardized canonical weights indicated that the variables that contributed most to understanding the relationship were gender, the Feminine Scale scores, the Take Action Scale score, and the Negative Animals score. This analysis was followed by a series of multiple regression analyses in which gender and the BSRI Masculine and Feminine scores were used as predictor variables with the following dependent variables: the Take Action Subscale score, the Ethics Subscale score, the total Animal Attitude score, and the scores for the negatively and positively perceived animals as well as those for the total Comfort Scale.

Table 4   Correlations Among Gender, Sex Role Orientation, and Attitude Scales

Scale	BSRI Feminine	BSRI Masculine	Gender[a]
Take Action	.25**	-.02	-.24**
Ethics	.19**	-.16**	-.19**
Total Attitude	.23**	-.13*	-.22**
Negative animal	-.22**	.12*	.31**
Positive animal	-.03	-.01	-.04
Total Comfort	-.15**	.09	.19**

[a] Gender was coded 0 for female, 1 for male.

* $p<.05$

** $p<.01$

Table 5   Multiple Regressions and Standardized Regression Weights Describing How Gender and BSRI Feminine and Masculine Scales Contribute to the Prediction of the Dependent Variables

Scale	Multiple regression	Standard regression weights		
		BSRI Feminine	BSRI Masculine	Gender
Take Action	.295	.18**	.02	-.17**
Ethics	.259	.14*	-.13*	-.10
Total Attitude	.277	.17**	-.09	-.13*
Negative animal	.323	-.12*	.07	.22**
Positive animal	.059	-.06	.00	-.05
Total Comfort	.206	-.10	.05	.12*

* $p<.05$

** $p<.01$

Results from these analyses and the accompanying correlations are presented in Tables 4 and 5. Together, gender and BSRI Feminine and Masculine scores predicted relatively small but statistically significant portions of variation on the following measures: the Take Action Subscale (9% of the variance), the Ethics Subscale (7% of the variance), the total Animal Attitude Scale (8% of the variance), and closeness to negatively perceived animals (10% of the variance). The intercorrelations in Table 4 and the regression results in Table 5 indicate that gender and the BSRI Feminine Scale were the best predictors for most of the attitude scores. Greater concern for animal welfare was associated with being female and having higher BSRI Feminine Scale scores. The importance of the BSRI Feminine Scale in the prediction of attitudes held with the effect of gender partial led out for both males and females. Only for the Ethics Subscale was the BSRI Masculine Scale a significant predictor variable. It is interesting to note that, in all cases, the BSRI Masculine and Feminine scales were related to the dependent variables in opposite directions. Comfort with positively perceived animals was not significantly predicted by either gender or sex role orientation.

Discussion

In this study, we found significant sex differences in attitudes toward animals and their use. Regression analysis indicated that gender and feminine sex role orientation predict a fairly small but statistically significant portion of individual differences in several such attitudes. Male and female subjects differed on all of the attitude measures except perceived comfort touching positive animals. Feminine sex role orientation as measured by the BSRI was positively correlated with concern for the well-being of other species and inversely correlated with comfort touching them (particularly negatively perceived species). With the exception of the Ethics Subscale, the degree of masculine sex role orientation did not predict attitudes toward other species. However, in all cases, feminine and masculine sex role orientation measures were related to animal attitude scales in opposite directions.

Scores on the BSRI Feminine Scale correspond to nurturance/warmth and expressive components of personality whereas the BSRI Masculine Scale appears to represent the dominance/poise and instrumental aspects (Baldwin et al. 1986). Our results suggest that the nurturance-expressive dimension of personality is more highly related to concern for animal welfare than is the dominance-instrumental dimension. The relation is also in the opposite direction; higher femininity is related to increased concern about other species, whereas increased masculinity is related, though to a lesser degree, with lower sensitivity to the ethical treatment of other creatures. These findings are particularly interesting in light of the explosive growth in the membership of animal rights groups in recent years. Women are disproportionately represented in these organizations (e.g., Sperling 1988; Kaplan and Herzog unpublished data). In a series of interviews with rank-and-file animal rights activists, Herzog (1990) found that the themes of nurturance and concern were especially evident in the thinking of the female interviewees.

There is no shortage of possible explanations as to why women generally show greater sensitivity to the treatment of animals. Sociocultural theorists would no doubt argue that women are socialized from birth for nurturant and caring roles while men are trained to be less emotional and more utilitarian and this manifests itself in their respective feelings about the use of animals. For example, Hills (1989) recently reported that females were more "person oriented" and favored cute, cuddly animals, whereas males tended to be more "thing oriented" and preferred less attractive species.

Those with a penchant for biological explanations (see Burghardt and Herzog 1989) would argue that the roots of sex differences might ultimately reside in differing evolutionary pressures. (Females may be attracted to some animals by a misfiring of maternal urges, and the attraction of men to blood sports is perhaps a result of selection favoring males with hunting skills.) Cognitive developmental psychologists, on the other hand, might interpret gender difference in terms of differing moral orientations (care versus justice) (e.g., Gilligan and Attanucci 1988; Kellert and Berry 1987; Lyons 1983; but see Walker 1984; 1986).

Like all studies, this study has certain limitations and also suggests areas in which additional research is warranted. Our sample consisted largely of southern, white college students, and, while we anticipate that the results will be generally applicable, more research needs to be done with other populations. In addition, there is controversy over the adequacy of measures such as the BSRI that attempt to reduce complex concepts like masculinity or femininity to unidimensional scales (Myers and Gonda 1982). Finally, roughly 90% of the individual variation in the various attitude measures was not accounted for by gender or sex role orientation. This finding suggests that researchers seeking to explicate factors predicting sensitivity, cruelty, and kindness toward other creatures will have enough work to remain busy for the foreseeable future.

Questions for Discussion

1. Summarize some of the gender differences in attitudes toward the treatment of other animals that researchers have uncovered.
2. What was the relationship between masculinity, femininity, and attitudes toward animals that was found in this study?
3. What are the possible explanations for why women tend to have more favorable or sensitive attitudes toward the treatment of animals than men?

14 Childhood Pet Keeping and Humane Attitudes in Young Adulthood

Elizabeth S. Paul and James A. Serpell

Are children who grow up with pets more likely to have more humane attitudes as adults? This age-old question was investigated in this study of young adults in England by Elizabeth Paul and James Serpell. As the authors suggest, it seems plausible that caring for pets during childhood may be associated with pet ownership and thus positive attitudes toward pets as an adult. But does growing up with companion animals also lead one to have more positive attitudes toward other kinds of animals as an adult? And further, could it be related to having more concern and empathy in adulthood for other humans? If these relationships do exist, then they may have important implications for the well-being of both humans and other animals.

Introduction

Data presented in this paper come from a questionnaire survey of university students in which subjects were asked to report retrospectively on their childhood histories of pet ownership, as well as their current attitudes to animals. The information collected from students in this survey was designed to investigate the possibility that childhood involvement with pets is associated with the development of more humane attitudes in later life. That is, more positive adult attitudes toward—and empathy with—pet animals, other animals and human beings.

This idea has a long historical pedigree (Serpell and Paul 1994). Locke (1699), one of the founders of modern educational theory, advocated the keeping of pets by children in order to encourage the development of tender feelings toward animals and people alike. Toward the end of the last century, the notion that childhood pet keeping was causally related to humane attitudes came to particular prominence when it was adopted as a central tenet of the humane education movement (Finch 1989). Since then, school-based humane education programs have been practiced on the

Originally published in 1993 in *Animal Welfare*, vol. 2, pp. 321–337. Reprinted with permission from the Universities Federation for Animal Welfare.

basis of this idea, despite equivocal findings from the few studies that have attempted to measure their efficacy (e.g., Vockell and Hodal 1980, Ascione 1992).
Nowadays, many parents also express the firm belief that caring for pets in childhood
encourages respect for all kinds of animals, and instills a more caring nature in general (Macdonald 1981, Salomon 1981, Paul 1992).

The idea that caring for pets in childhood will help to inculcate a greater respect
and empathy for *pet animals* is a reasonably plausible one. Childhood pet keeping is
positively correlated with adult pet ownership levels (Serpell 1981) and therefore,
presumably, with positive attitudes toward pets during adulthood (see also Poresky *et
al.* 1988). The further idea of a relationship existing between childhood pet ownership and adult attitudes to *other kinds of animals*, however, has received very little
research attention, although Bowd (1984b) found that during childhood, pet ownership was associated with more positive attitudes to a number of non-pet animals, such
as lions, pigs, chickens and snakes. The idea that learning to care for pet animals during childhood may lead to a greater concern for, or emotional empathy[1] with, *humans*
in adulthood is perhaps particularly ambitious. It has nevertheless received at least
some support from research looking at the relationship between pet ownership and
empathy during childhood itself. Poresky and Hendrix (1988), for example, found
that three- to six-year-old, pet owning children achieved higher empathy scores than
their non-pet owning counterparts. Bryant (1986) found that ten-year-old children
who used pets for social support when stressed had higher empathy scores than those
who did not. Bailey (1988), on the other hand, found no differences between pet owning and non-pet owning pre-schoolers, using a role-taking task as a test of empathy.
She did, however, find that exposing the same children to a puppy within the pre-
school curriculum significantly increased scores on the same empathy test.

Methods

Subjects and Procedure

The childhood pet ownership questionnaire (see below), with accompanying letter
and prepaid return envelope, was circulated to approximately 1,200 students in three
University of Cambridge colleges, one of which was solely attended by postgradu-
ates. Four hundred and twenty questionnaires were completed and returned, representing a 35% response rate. Although this is a reasonable response rate for a relatively long and unsolicited questionnaire, the sample does suffer the disadvantage of
being a self-selected population. Nevertheless, a complete range of pet owning and
non-pet owning subjects responded (54% reported pets of their own during childhood
and 88% reported family pets), which suggests that the self-selection process did not

result in any major biases due to subjects' pet keeping experiences. Thirty-five questionnaires completed by non-Western nationals were excluded from the present analysis (i.e. 8.3% of completed questionnaires), in order to avoid problems associated with cultural differences in attitudes toward and ownership of pet animals. This left a sample of 230 men and 155 women, of British (91%), other European (4%), and other Western (5%) nationalities. The sexes and nationalities of respondents were representative of the college populations surveyed. The mean age of the subjects was 22.2 years (this is relatively high due to survey of students from the postgraduate college and mature students).

Questionnaire

In the first part of the questionnaire, subjects were asked to give information concerning all the pets that they and their families had owned during their childhoods (0–16 years). Seven categories of pet were distinguished: (a) horses, ponies, or donkeys; (b) dogs; (c) cats; (d) small mammals; (e) birds; (f) fish, reptiles, amphibians, insects, spiders etc; (g) other pets. Subjects were also asked to list any of these pets that they considered to have been important to them in some way during childhood. Data from these questions were used to create the independent variables listed below.

In the second part of the questionnaire, subjects were required to answer a number of questions and complete attitude scales aimed at finding out about their current attitudes toward pets, other animals and human beings. These were used as dependent variables in the analysis and are also described in the section below.

Data and Analyses

Independent Variables

It has been noted (e.g., Poresky *et al.* 1987, Melson 1989, 1990) that many empirical studies of pet ownership have been blighted by over-simplified classification of subjects as, for example, either pet owners or non-pet owners. The retrospective approach used in this study offered an opportunity to assess the whole of a subject's childhood pet experiences in a more detailed way. Data from the first part of the questionnaire were used to create three separate, although not mutually exclusive, measures of subjects' overall levels of childhood pet involvement. These were used as *independent* variables for the purposes of the present analyses:

Pets owned

The number of pets owned *specifically by the subject*, i.e., not by other members of the family or by the family as a whole, during childhood. (n.b. For the purposes of this and the following category, multiple fish, reptiles, amphibians, insects, spiders etc. were counted as equivalent to one pet per sub-category of animal).

Family pets owned

The *total* number of pets owned in the subject's family during childhood (this included pets owned by the subject, by siblings, by parents and by the family as a whole).

Important pets

The number of pets reported as having been important to the subject in some way during childhood (these pets could have belonged to any member of the family). Data for this variable were obtained by asking subjects to list any pets owned by themselves or their family that had been important to them in some way during childhood.

Dependent variables

The second part of the questionnaire consisted of questions and attitude scales designed to assess subjects' attitudes toward pets, other animals and other human beings. These were used as *dependent* variables for the present analyses:

Animal-related involvements

These were a series of questions concerning: what pets were currently owned and what pets subjects would like to own in the future; whether or not subjects would encourage their own future children to keep pets; whether subjects took part in any animal-related hobbies or activities (fishing, hunting, horse-riding, and bird-watching); whether subjects were members of animal welfare or environmental organizations or charities; whether subjects practiced any sorts of ethical food avoidances such as vegetarianism.

Attitude scales

Pet Attitude Scale (Templer *et al.* 1981). This aimed to measure a person's "favorableness of attitudes toward pets" in general. Higher scores represented more favorable attitudes toward pets.

Scale of Attitudes toward the Treatment of Animals. A modified, updated and Anglicized scale from Bowd (1984a). This modified version fulfilled statistical conventions of validity and reliability in the student population surveyed. Three sub-scales were included; these concerned attitudes toward the treatment of (a) farm, (b) wild and (c) laboratory animals. Higher scores on all these scales represented greater concern about the welfare and treatment of animals.

Empathy Scale (Mehrabian and Epstein 1972). This was designed to measure *emotional* empathy as defined as "a vicarious emotional response to the perceived emotional experiences of others." Higher scores represented greater empathy with other human beings.[2] For the purposes of the present analyses, scores from the two pet animal empathy questions of the scale were excluded.

Charity donations test

Subjects were asked to indicate how they would distribute £100 among eight different hypothetical charities. Two of these charities were concerned with animal welfare, two with conservation of the natural environment and four with human health and welfare.

Analyses and Presentation of Results

Non-normality of the pet ownership and involvement data (both before and after transformations) and the ordinal nature of the data available from the attitude scales, meant that the assumptions needed to perform parametric statistics were not fully met (see Snedecor and Cochran 1976). All statistical analyses were therefore conducted using non-parametric, two-tailed tests (Chi-squares, Kendall correlations, Kruskal-Wallis one-way analyses of variance and Mann-Whitney U tests).

Results

Animal-related Involvements

The number of pets that subjects listed as wanting to own in the future (as students, most of them were unable to keep pets currently) was significantly positively correlated with the number of pets owned during childhood (Kendall's $T=0.1973$, $P<0.001$); the number of pets owned by subjects' families as a whole during childhood $(T=0.2545, P<0.001)$, and the number of important childhood pets they reported having had $(T=0.3834, P<0.001)$. Subjects who said they would encourage their own future children to keep pets were found to have had significantly more pets of their own during childhood (Mann-Whitney $U=7033$, $P<0.0005$[3]; more family pets $(U=5197.0, P<0.0001)$, and more important pets $(U=4290.0, P<0.0001)$ than those who did not.

Subjects who reported regularly going fishing were not significantly different in their childhood pet involvements from those who did not regularly fish. Hunters and bird-watchers, however, both owned more pets (specifically of their own) during childhood than their non-hunting and non-bird-watching counterparts $(U=914.5,$ $P<0.05$; and $U=2545.5, P<0.05$ respectively).

Current horse-riders, when compared with non-riders, showed greater childhood involvement with pets on all three measures considered *(Pets owned, U=3106.0, P<0.0001; Family pets owned, U=3237.0, P<0.0001; Important pets, U=4089.0, P<0.0005).*

Members of organizations or charities concerned with animal welfare reported having had more pets of their own *(U=8618.0, P<0.005)*; more family pets *(U=7293.0, P<0.0001;* and more important pets *(U=8004.0, P<0.005)* during their childhood than non-members. Similarly, members of organizations or charities concerned with conservation and the environment reported more family pets *(U=13626.0, P<0.05;* and more important pets than non-members *(U=13486.5, P<0.05).* However, when the sample was split by sex, this latter relationship held for male subjects only *(Family pets owned, U=4543.5, P<0.05; Important pets, U=4467.5, P<0.05).*

Subjects who currently avoided eating at least one type of animal-based food product for ethical or moral reasons (e.g., vegans; vegetarians; those who do not eat veal, battery eggs, and so forth, reported having had more pets of their own during childhood *(U=13848.0, P<0.05)*, although this association was found to apply only to female subjects *(U=2310.5, P<0.05)* when the sample was split by sex. This may be explained in part by the fact the female subjects were considerably more likely than males to report some kind of food avoidance practice[4] (Females 42.5%, Males 26.3%, X^2=10.14, P<0.005). However, both male and female food avoiders reported having had more important pets *(U=12030.5, P<0.0005* during childhood than non-food avoiding subjects.

Attitude scales

Table 1 gives a full summary of the results of correlations between the pet involvement measures and the three attitude scales administered.

Current attitudes toward pets, as measured by the Pet Attitude Scale (Templer *et al.* 1981) were significantly positively correlated with pet ownership, family pet ownership and number of important pets reported as having been kept during childhood.

Total scores on the Scale of Attitudes toward the Treatment of Animals (modified from Bowd 1984a) were significantly and positively correlated with levels of childhood pet ownership, family pet ownership, and the number of important childhood pets. Scores on the sub-scales concerning the treatment of farm and wild animals showed significant positive correlations with all three pet involvement measures, while attitudes toward the treatment of laboratory animals were significantly correlated with the number of family pets owned and the number of important pets owned, but showed no relationship with the number of pets owned by subjects themselves during childhood.

Empathy Scale (Mehrabian and Epstein 1972) scores were significantly positively correlated with childhood pet ownership levels, family pet ownership levels and the number of important pets kept during childhood. However, when the sample was broken down by sex, these correlations were found only among male subjects *(Pets owned, T=0.1088, P<0.05; Family pets owned, T=0.1096, P<0.05; Important pets, T=0.1455, P<0.005;* see Discussion).

Table 1   Kendall Correlations between Attitude Scale Scores and the Number of *Pets Owned* During Childhood; Number of *Family Pets Owned*, and Number of *Important Pets* Kept During Childhood.

	Kendall correlation (T)		
Attitude scale	*Pets owned*	*Family pets owned*	*Important pets*
1) *Pet Attitude Scale*	0.1723****	0.2279****	0.4190****
2) *Scale of Attitudes toward the*			
Treatment of Animals	0.0846*	0.1083***	0.2604****
a) Farm animals	0.0813*	0.0888*	0.2320****
b) Wild animals	0.0967*	0.0685*	0.2184****
c) Laboratory animals	0.0518	0.1117***	0.2024****
3) *Empathy Scale*	0.1134***	0.0896*	0.1421****

* *p<.05*
*** *p<0.005*
**** *p<0.0001*

Charity donations test

The amount of money hypothetically donated to animal welfare charities in the charity test was significantly positively correlated with the number of family pets *(T=0.1057, P<0.0l)* and the number of important childhood pets *(T=0.2149, P<0.001)* reported. Money donated to environmental charities did not correlate significantly with any of the childhood pet experience measures, but the amount of money donated to human welfare charities was significantly negatively correlated with the number of important childhood pets reported, particularly among male subjects *(T=0.0972, P<0.05; Men, T=0.1324, P<0.05; Women, T=0.0410,* nonsignificant).

Discussion

Results obtained in this survey tend to support the view that keeping pet animals in childhood helps to develop more positive and caring attitudes toward pets in adulthood. Students' attitudes toward pets were found to be positively correlated with all three of the childhood pet involvement measures considered (*Pets owned*, *Family pets owned*, and *Important pets*). Likewise, the positive relationship found between childhood pet ownership and the number and types of pets that subjects reported wanting to own in the future, seems to confirm previous findings that early experience of pet ownership tends to set a pattern for adult life (Serpell 1981, Poresky *et al.* 1988, Kidd and Kidd 1989). The additional finding of a link between subjects' childhood pet keeping experiences and their intentions concerning whether or not to encourage their own future children to keep pets is consistent with the inter-generational continuity of attitudes to pet dogs found by Gage and Magnuson-Martinson (1988).

The relationship between childhood pet involvement and adult attitudes does not stop at attitudes toward pets. A positive association was also found between involvement with pet animals in childhood and self-reported concern about the treatment and welfare of laboratory, farm, and wild animals. This relationship was further confirmed by the positive association found between childhood pet involvement and ethical food avoidance practices such as vegetarianism, and the finding that childhood pet involvement was also positively associated with membership of animal welfare and environmental organizations. The charity donations test also demonstrated a positive correlation between the amount of money hypothetically donated to animal welfare charities and childhood involvement with pets.

The finding that empathy with humans was correlated with childhood pet involvement is also in keeping with the predictions outlined in the introduction to this paper. However, the association was weak and was only detected amongst male subjects when the sample was split by sex. Although this latter result can be explained in large part by a ceiling effect (the majority of female subjects obtained high scores on the empathy scale), the fact remains that the association between childhood pet keeping and adult empathy with humans is able to account for only a very small proportion of the overall variance in empathy scores. Whether the connection between childhood pet keeping and adult empathy for human beings is quantitatively or qualitatively different from that found with adult concern for animals is an important question that has yet to be resolved.

In summary, the results presented here demonstrate that more humane adult attitudes, toward both animals and people, are indeed associated with higher levels of reported childhood pet ownership. Moreover, those subjects who reported having had important childhood pets were particularly likely to express more humane attitudes in adulthood. The data also suggest that childhood pet involvement may be related to heightened environmental concerns in adulthood. As yet, however, these findings shed little light on the causal relationships underlying these statistical associations.

The self-selected nature of the survey population means that certain groups, such as those with little experience of childhood pet keeping, might have been under-represented in the sample. However, the generally broad range found in the number of childhood pets owned by subjects suggests that no major biases were operating in this respect. Perhaps a more important problem concerns the above average socioeconomic status and educational level of the students surveyed. Data obtained from students at a prestigious university cannot be assumed to be applicable to the wider population. Replication of this study amongst a representative sample is needed before firm conclusions can be drawn concerning its more general relevance. Nevertheless, previous studies have shown that socioeconomic status exhibits neither a strong nor consistent association with overall pet ownership levels (e.g., Godwin 1975, Franti *et al.* 1980, Wise and Kushman 1984, Marx *et al.* 1988). There is, therefore, no *a priori* reason for expecting the sampled population to differ significantly from the norm in terms of any relationship between childhood pet keeping and adult attitudes.

The fact that the data used here relied on retrospective reporting of childhood experiences and feelings also means that the present findings need to be interpreted with some caution. Subjects may have been inaccurate or selective in their recollections of childhood pets, although this seems unlikely to have been a major or widespread problem, since no respondents indicated having any difficulties remembering what pets were owned, and by whom, during childhood. Memories concerning what childhood pets were important, however, concern the recall of *feelings* and may therefore be especially vulnerable to bias. For example, the sort of person who is willing to admit that they had pets that were important to them during childhood may also be more likely to respond sensitively and empathetically to questions on the attitude scales. This argument is unlikely to apply, however, to responses to more factual questions concerning membership of animal welfare or environmental organizations, vegetarianism, and so on. In addition, subsequent analysis showed that the majority of pets nominated as important were either cats or dogs (Paul 1992) suggesting that something about the actual *quality* of the relationship that can be developed with certain types of pet may play a considerable part in determining whether or not a childhood companion animal is remembered as having been important.

With these various provisos in mind, we can suggest a range of possible explanations for the present findings. First, it is conceivable that the results were affected by subjects' preconceptions regarding the benefits of pet ownership. For example, a number of the students who took part in the survey reported believing that childhood pet ownership encourages "respect for animals" and a "caring" nature in general (Paul 1992). Subjects who personally held such beliefs may therefore have responded to the questionnaire in an "appropriate" manner. Subjects may also have responded in such a way as to give the investigator what they perceived to be the "right" answers. Potential biases of this kind, however, are unlikely to have affected answers to more factual questions concerning, say, membership of organizations or vegetarianism.

Second, it is possible that the present findings are largely a product of parental attitudes. Research on other topics suggests that certain attitudes, such as political and religious orientation, are transmitted from parents to their children (e.g., Oskamp 1977). Likewise, the sorts of parents who encourage their children to have pets and to perceive them as important may also be the kinds of parents who would be keen on inculcating kindness and sympathy toward both animal and human others. This explanation, however, begs the question as to why this particular constellation of attitudes and behavior existed in the parents to begin with. Unfortunately, it was not possible to measure parental attitudes to animals or other people directly in the present study. However, the relationship between parents' and children's attitudes to animals and animal-related issues represents a potentially fruitful area for future research.

Third, it may be that some people are essentially predisposed to be more animal-orientated than others, and that this personality trait is relatively stable throughout an individual's development. Young adults who identify strongly with animals now may also have been more animal-orientated as children, and hence more likely to report more important childhood pets. They may also have been more effective in childhood at influencing the purchase of more interesting and important pets such as dogs and cats. This idea would not, however, explain why such people tend also to score higher on a human empathy scale, unless of course a direct link between animal orientation and overall empathetic tendencies could be postulated. Nevertheless, since both children and adults vary considerably in their overall liking for animals, work investigating the possible endogenous sources of such variation is likely to prove valuable in the future.

Finally, it is possible that the humane educationalists are substantially correct, and that childhood relationships with pets do indeed have a direct formative influence on the development of humane attitudes. The mechanism by which such an effect might be operating still remains to be elucidated, although one could postulate a process of generalization from particular feelings toward individual pets to a more global concern for animals as a group. Even then, however, it is not at all clear how such a process could include empathy with humans, unless one proposes some sort of general identification or sympathy with vulnerable individuals, regardless of species (e.g., ten Bensel 1984). Further research, focusing on the ways in which people structure their beliefs about the welfare of both animals and people, should offer some valuable insights into the processes underlying the development of humane and animal welfare–orientated attitudes.

Conclusions

It is evident that public opinion is the all-important driving force for improvements in animal welfare at both an individual and societal level. Although humane education has been directed for many years toward improving people's (and particularly children's) concerns about the welfare of animals, recent research has revealed that such work is considerably less successful than had originally been hoped (Ascione 1992). The main problem seems to be a simple lack of understanding of the processes by which humane attitudes develop. As Bowd (1989) pointed out, "*if we are to change the way people behave toward animals, we must first learn about the origins of that behaviour in childhood*". Although the present study can give no definitive answers in this respect, it has provided further evidence of a possible link between childhood experience of animals and the development of subsequent adult attitudes toward both animals and fellow humans. It has also opened up a number of potentially fruitful avenues of future research.

For many children, companion animals become honorary family members and it is difficult to imagine how such early and significant bonds could fail to engender at least some sense of kinship or affinity with other nonhuman species. The precise causal mechanisms underlying the process of generalization from individual pets to animals as a group are as yet unclear, and further research is needed to improve our understanding of the relevant developmental processes involved. The information gained from such studies is likely to assist programs of humane education to become better focused and more effective in the future.

Animal Welfare Implications

Future improvements in the welfare of animals depend crucially on the attitudes and beliefs of society—this includes the animal users as well as the general public. Yet almost nothing is known about the reasons why some people feel great concern about the welfare of animals while others appear largely indifferent to such issues. Knowledge of the experiences that underlie existing variation in humane attitudes will greatly assist the development of more effective humane education programs in the future.

Questions for Discussion

1. Did you have companion animals growing up? If so, do you think it affected the way you currently think about pets? About animals in general? About other people?

2. What are some possible explanations for the relationship found in this study between childhood pet keeping and positive attitudes toward pets, other animals, and humans in adulthood?

3. Do you think that humane education could help bring about more concern and empathy for both animals and people? Why or why not?

15 Animal Rights and Human Social Issues

David Nibert

*What is the relationship between attitudes toward animals and attitudes toward peo-
ple? Are so-called animal rights supporters anti-people? Or does compassion and
tolerance toward one group generalize to compassion and tolerance toward other
groups? In this selection, David Nibert attempts to answer these questions, asking if
support for animal rights is linked to support for social justice issues related to sex,
race, sexual orientation, and violence. In general, opponents of animal rights were
much more likely to oppose the rights of minority groups and to accept violence.
What are the implications of these relationships?*

Opponents of animal rights frequently have trivialized the concerns expressed by animal activists, suggesting that their time should be spent on more important human
issues. However, concern for humans and concern for animals may not be as distinct
as some contend. It has long been suggested that the ethical treatment of other animals may benefit humans as well. For example, Immanuel Kant, although not a
strong supporter of animal welfare, recognized the relationship between people's callous treatment of animals and their treatment of each other (Midgley 1984). Early
feminist writers, including Mary Wollstonecraft Shelley, Margaret Fuller, Susan B.
Anthony, Elizabeth Cady Stanton, and others, highlighted the similarities and relationship between men's domination of nonhuman animals and men's domination of
women (Donovan 1990). Contemporary feminist scholarship continues to illuminate
this relationship (Adams 1992; Birke 1991; Clifton 1990).

Albert Schweitzer noted, "Anyone who has accustomed himself to regard the life
of any living creature as worthless is in danger of arriving also at the idea of worthless human lives." Margaret Mead stated, "One of the most dangerous things that can
happen to a child is to kill or torture an animal and get away with it" (Lockwood and
Hodge 1986). In the early part of this century, the American Humane Society under-

Originally published in 1994 in *Society and Animals*, vol. 2, no. 2, pp. 115–124. Reprinted
with permission from Brill Academic Publishers.

took a nationwide education program to promote kindness to animals, based on the assumption that people who treat nonhuman animals well also will treat human beings well (Moulton, Kaufmann, and Filip 1991).

Recent anecdotal information has provided some support for these assumptions. Studies of domestic violence have revealed cases where attacks against the family pet preceded wife abuse (Gelles and Strauss 1988), and threats against pets have been used by child sexual abusers as a method of silencing children they assault (Faller 1990; Finkelhor, Williams, and Burns 1988). Additionally, an examination of the backgrounds of recent serial killers has revealed that several had histories of abusing animals (Lockwood and Hodge 1986).

The few quantitative studies conducted to date have also shown a relationship between humans' treatment of animals and their treatment of each other. A study of 23 cruelty reports compiled by the Royal Society for the Prevention of Cruelty to Animals in one community in England found that 83% of the reported households had also been identified by human service agencies as having a child at risk for abuse or neglect (Hutton 1983). Another study examined 57 families with companion animals being treated for child abuse by New Jersey's Division of Youth and Family Services. In 88% of these cases, at least one family member had abused and in two-thirds of the cases an abusive parent had killed or injured an animal (DeViney, Dickert and Lockwood 1983). An examination of the history of animal cruelty among three groups of men labeled as aggressive criminals, nonaggressive criminals, and noncriminals found that 25% of the group labeled aggressive criminals reported five or more early acts of animal cruelty, compared to 6% of those labeled nonaggressive criminals and none of the noncriminals (Felthous and Kellert 1985). Additionally, a 1989 examination of Congressional voting revealed that members of Congress who supported animal welfare legislation were also likely to support legislation protecting the rights and needs of individual citizens and workers (Kimball 1989). . . .

If there is a relationship between human behavior toward humans and nonhuman animals, it would be reasonable to expect that human dispositions toward animals are related to positions on certain social issues, particularly violence and the acceptance of rights for minority groups. This question was explored using data from an opinion survey conducted in a Midwestern community.

Method

Five hundred and one residents of Clark County, Ohio, aged eighteen and older, responded to a telephone survey conducted April 16–18, 1993. Clark County has a population of 147,548. A systematic sample of telephone numbers was selected from the area telephone directory; the last number was changed by the "plus one" method to increase randomness and the probability of obtaining new or unlisted numbers (Landon and Banks 1977; Frey 1983). A respondent from within the household was selected by alternately asking for the youngest woman, youngest man, oldest woman, or oldest man who resided in the household.

The survey was designed to explore respondents' opinions on several social issues. One of the questions was, "Some people say that animals have rights that people should respect. Would you agree or disagree?" Respondents were also asked eleven questions adapted from the General Social Survey (Wood 1990). One of these questions pertained to gun control, one to acceptance of violence, four to issues of particular concern to women (domestic violence, rape, abortion, and employment of women), three to rights for people who are homosexual, and two to race relations. These questions, along with the names of the variables, are listed below:

- Would you favor or oppose a law that would require a person to obtain a police permit before he or she could buy a gun? (permit)
- Are there any situations you can imagine in which you would approve of a man punching an adult male stranger? (punch)
- Would you say that domestic violence in our area is a very serious problem, a somewhat serious problem, or not a serious problem? (domestic)
- Are there any situations you can imagine where rape would be the fault of the victim? (rape)
- Do you approve of a married woman working and earning money if she has a husband capable of supporting her? (work)
- Please tell me whether or not you think it should be possible for a pregnant woman to obtain a legal abortion if the woman wants to for any reason? (abortion)
- Consider someone who is a homosexual. Suppose this person wanted to make a speech in your community. Should this person be allowed to speak, or not? (speech)
- Should a person who is a homosexual be allowed to teach in a college or university? (teach)
- Do you believe gay people should be allowed in the military? (military)
- White people have a right to keep blacks out of their neighborhoods and blacks should respect that right (agree or disagree). (neighbor)
- Do you think there should be laws against marriages between blacks and whites? (marriage)

Table 1   Cross-tabulations of Support for Animal Rights with Various Demographic Variables

Animals have rights (N=457)

variables	agree	disagree	$\chi2$	df	sig.	φ	N
age							
18–29 yrs.	93 (95%)	5 (5%)	20.08	2	.000	.206	455
30–49 yrs.	161 (82%)	35 (18%)					
50 yrs. +	117 (73%)	44 (27%)					
income							
<$20,000	93 (85%)	17 (15%)	1.51	2	.470	.061	402
$30–49,000	165 (82%)	37 (18%)					
>$50,000	70 (78%)	20 (22%)					
school							
not H.S. grad	57 (84%)	11 (16%)	1.87	2	.393	.064	456
1 year college	210 (83%)	43 (17%)					
college grad	105 (78%)	30 (22%)					
sex							
male	176 (76%)	56 (24%)	9.65	1	.002	.151	457
female	197 (88%)	28 (12%)					
race							
with color	25 (81%)	6 (19%)	.00	1	1.00	.008	454
without color	346 (82%)	77 (18%)					
residence							
city	172 (86%)	28 (14%)	3.97	1	.046	.099	453
not in city	198 (78%)	55 (22%)					
religion							
Protestant	188 (77%)	56 (23%)	8.07	2	.018	.133	451
Catholic	56 (84%)	11 (16%)					
other	124 (89%)	16 (11%)					

The data obtained was at the nominal level; cross-tabulations were conducted to examine the nature of the relationship between support for animal rights and each of the eleven variables. Respondents who answered "undecided" to a specific question, or refused to respond, were withheld from cross-tabulations of that variable.

Results

Of the 501 respondents, 49.1% were male and 50.9% were female. One-fifth (20.8%) were less than 30 years of age, 41.6% were between 30 and 49 years old, and 36.8%

were over 50. 15.2% had not graduated from high school, 55.3% were high-school graduates and 29.6% were college graduates. The sample was predominantly white (92%) and married (66.7%).

In response to the animal rights question, 74.5% of respondents agreed, 16.8% disagreed, 7.4% were undecided, and 1.4% refused. For purposes of convenience, the respondents who agreed that animals have rights will be referred to as "animal rights supporters."

Examination of demographic variables, shown in Table 1, reveals that age, sex, place of residence, and religion were significantly related to support for animal rights. Younger people were more likely to support animal rights than older people, women more than men, and city residents more than those living in more rural areas of the county. Catholics were more likely to agree than Protestants, whereas respondents who selected the "other" category for their religious affiliation supported animal rights more than both Protestants and Catholics. Income, education, and race appear to be unrelated to support for animal rights.

Cross-tabulations of respondents' support for animal rights and other survey questions are shown in Table 2. The findings reveal a statistically significant relationship for seven of the eleven variables. The strongest relationship was the one between support for animal rights and support for a law requiring permits for purchasing guns ($\chi2=21.74$, p=.000). Respondents supporting animal rights were also less likely to report that they could imagine a situation where they would approve of a man punching an adult male stranger ($\chi2=4.96$, p=.023).

Mixed results were found for the items pertaining to issues of particular concern to women. Animal rights supporters were significantly less likely to imagine a situation where rape would be the fault of the victim ($\chi2=4.90$, p=.027), and they were significantly more likely to support the ability of a woman to obtain an abortion ($\chi2=8.31$, p=.004). Although animal rights supporters were more likely than nonsupporters to consider domestic violence a serious issue, this difference did not achieve a level of statistical significance ($\chi2=4.98$, p=.083). Respondents' answers to the question about a woman working when her husband could support her revealed no significance difference between those who supported animal rights and those who did not ($\chi2=1.38$, p=.240), although on this question animal rights supporters were slightly less likely to support a woman working in such a situation.

Two of the three questions pertaining to the rights of people who are homosexual were also answered differently by those who supported animal rights and those who did not. Animal rights supporters were significantly more likely to support the rights of a person who is homosexual to make a speech ($\chi2=3.92$, p=.048) and to

Table 2   Cross-tabulations of Support for Animal Rights with Various Social Issues

Animals have rights (N=457)

variables	agree	disagree	$\chi2$	df	sig.	φ	N
permit							
yes	286 (87%)	41 (13%)	21.74	1	.000	.230	437
no	74 (67%)	36 (33%)					
abortion							
yes	224 (65%)	122 (35%)	8.31	1	.004	.147	420
no	34 (46%)	40 (54%)					
neighbor							
yes	26 (63%)	15 (37%)	8.13	1	.004	.147	436
no	328 (83%)	67 (17%)					
punch							
yes	182 (78%)	52 (22%)	4.96	1	.023	.114	428
no	168 (87%)	26 (13%)					
rape							
yes	88 (74%)	31 (26%)	4.90	1	.027	.114	429
no	260 (84%)	50 (16%)					
military							
yes	190 (86%)	32 (14%)	4.15	1	.042	.109	397
no	135 (77%)	40 (23%)					
speech							
yes	299 (87%)	46 (13%)	3.92	1	.048	.106	418
no	56 (77%)	17 (23%)					
domestic							
very	170 (85%)	30 (15%)	4.98	2	.083	.106	438
somewhat	164 (80%)	41 (20%)					
not	23 (70%)	10 (30%)					
teach							
yes	271 (79%)	70 (21%)	1.59	1	.208	.070	412
no	51 (72%)	20 (28%)					
work							
yes	279 (78%)	77 (22%)	1.38	1	.240	.064	436
no	68 (85%)	12 (15%)					
marriage							
yes	44 (12%)	312 (88%)	.00	1	1.00	.000	437
no	10 (12%)	71 (88%)					

serve in the military ($\chi2$=4.15, p=.042). While animal rights supporters were somewhat more likely to support the right of a person who is homosexual to teach at a college or university, the difference was not statistically significant ($\chi2$=1.59, p=.208).

On the two questions that pertained to race relations, the two groups were identical in their response to the question about laws prohibiting marriage between blacks and whites; however, animal rights supporters were significantly less likely to agree with the statement that blacks should not push themselves into neighborhoods where they are not wanted ($\chi2=8.13$, p=.004).

Discussion

These findings suggest that support for animal rights is related to other social issues, notably issues regarding gun control, acceptance of violence, and acceptance of diversity and rights for women, persons who are homosexual, and persons of color. People who believed animals have rights answered differently than people who did not share that belief on seven out of the eleven questions, generally reporting less tolerance for violence and more acceptance of human diversity and choice. It should be noted that the variables where no significant differences were found, particularly variables "teach" and "marriage," were not very discriminating.

Although the measures of association on almost all of the seven items indicated the strength of the relationships was modest, and the causal direction of the relationships are unclear, these preliminary findings provide support for the assumption that the way people regard animals is related to the way they regard people.

Because only a single item was used to measure support for animal rights, and that item was not very discriminating (nearly three-fourths of the respondents agreed that animals had rights), this study does not identify the social opinions of strong animal rights supporters. Rather, it highlights the social opinions of a group opposed to animal rights.

Those in this anti-animal rights group, constituting nearly 17% of the sample, were more likely than other respondents to favor easy public access to guns, to oppose abortion rights, to exhibit racial prejudice, to be more approving of interpersonal violence, to blame the victims of rape, and to exhibit prejudice against homosexuals, and less likely to give people with different sexual orientations a right to free speech. Demographically, this group tended to be older, Protestant, and male and to live outside the urban area.

In their book, *The Animal Rights Crusade*, Jasper and Nelkin (1992) suggest that the moral sentiments of animal rights activists are largely independent of traditional political cleavages. While this study does not address that assertion, it does support the research by Kimball (1989), which found opposition to animal rights is closely aligned with political conservatism.

Overall, this research question has very important implications. To the extent that attitudes and behavior are related—a complex question—the possibility of a relationship between disrespect for nonhuman animals and disrespect for humans is an important one for clinicians, educators, and policy makers. Future research should seek to develop questions about the level of respondent support for animal rights and should examine such views relative to important human relations issues, especially the acceptance of and tendency toward violence.

Questions for Discussion

1. Do you think animal rights supporters care about animals more than they care about people?

2. What are the social characteristics of people who are most likely to oppose animal rights?

3. Why might opponents of animal rights be less likely to support human rights?

Part VI: Criminology and Deviance

The dangerous environments children endure can lead them to seek out animals for affection or to train animals to be weapons. . . . Parents know that cruelty to animals may be serious; children seem to know as well.

Frank R. Ascione

16 Children Who Are Cruel to Animals

A Review of Research and Implications for Developmental Psychology

Frank R. Ascione

In this 1993 article, psychologist Frank Ascione presents the first comprehensive review of the research on children's cruelty to animals. Ascione provides a definition of cruelty that has been employed by numerous scholars in their studies of childhood animal abuse. His review includes an examination of several key issues, including the association of animal cruelty with (a) subsequent violence against humans, (b) psychiatric diagnoses, (c) family violence, and (d) empathy. Ascione concludes with suggestions for future research.

Introduction

Cruelty, which can be defined as an emotional response of indifference or taking pleasure in the suffering and pain of others or as actions that unnecessarily inflict such suffering and pain, has long been considered a sign of psychological disturbance. Children's cruelty toward other people is a diagnostic sign included in psychiatric nosology related to antisocial and conduct disorders. Yet, only recently has cruelty to animals been added to the list of diagnostic criteria for Conduct Disorder (American Psychiatric Association, DSM-III-R 1987) in children and adolescents.

As a result, in part, of increased attention to animal cruelty, we are becoming aware that very basic information and data are lacking about the prevalence (existing cases) and incidence (new cases) of such behavior. Questions about the age of onset of cruelty toward animals, potential gender differences among perpetrators, relations to child and family interaction patterns, stability from childhood to adolescence to adulthood, and the design and evaluation of prevention and intervention programs are among the many issues that require research attention.

Originally published in 1993 in *Anthrozoös*, vol. 6. no. 4, pp. 226–247. Reprinted with permission, International Society for Anthrozoology (ISAZ).

This article begins with an examination of definitional issues followed by a brief review of examples of the renewed focus on childhood cruelty to animals and research on its link to antisocial behavior in adolescence and adulthood. Next, the relevance of childhood cruelty to animals for the diagnosis of conduct disorder in children and adolescents will be highlighted since this disorder is one of the best examples of the continuity of psychological disturbance from childhood to adulthood. The focus will then be directed to ecological factors in families and communities that can shed light on processes that may be operative in cases of childhood animal cruelty. This focus will lead to consideration of various forms of family violence, including the physical abuse and/or neglect of children and spouse abuse, sexual abuse of children, both within the family and in alternative care settings, and the relation of these conditions to distortions in the development of empathy. The article concludes with a discussion of prevention and intervention issues and directions for future research.

Definition of Cruelty to Animals

The dance of bloodless categories that broad theories present to us cannot show us the particular textures of the horrors.—P. P. Hallie

The task of defining cruelty to animals (for the sake of simplicity, "animals" will be used to refer to nonhuman animals) is, in many respects more daunting than defining cruelty to children. There are also common features of cruelty to animals and to children that may facilitate resolution of definitional issues. Categories of child maltreatment often include the following forms of abuse: physical, sexual, emotional/psychological, and neglect. It is not difficult to produce a litany of examples in which animals have experienced each of these forms of abuse. Each of these forms, however, requires further elaboration since the commissions and omissions they denote vary in form and severity. For example, physical abuse may range from teasing to torture, with gradations in this range being more subjective than objective in nature (from the perspectives of the victim, the victimizer, and potential observers).

The Compact Edition of the Oxford English Dictionary (1971, 614) includes the following characteristics of persons who display cruelty: "disposed to inflict suffering . . . indifferent to or taking pleasure in another's pain or distress . . . destitute of kindness or compassion . . . merciless, pitiless, hardhearted. . . . " This definition and a similar version in the *Random House Dictionary of the English Language* (1987, 438), suggest both behavioral and affective dimensions of cruelty.

Definitions that focus specifically on cruelty to animals have also been offered. Felthous and Kellert (1987) defined "substantial cruelty to animals" as a "pattern of deliberately, repeatedly, and unnecessarily hurting vertebrate animals in a manner likely to cause serious injury" (1715). This definition includes limitations on the species considered and introduces a quantitative dimension (frequency of cruelty). Brown (1988) defined cruelty as "unnecessary suffering knowingly inflicted on a sentient being (animal or human). . . . The suffering may be a sensation of pain induced by physical means, or it may be distress resulting from acts of enforced confinement, for instance, or of maternal deprivation. Cruelty to animals has both positive and negative forms, the first referring to an act committed against an animal, the second to omission or failure to act, as in neglecting to provide adequate food, water, or shelter. . ." (3). Both Felthous and Kellert and Brown introduce "deliberately" and "knowingly" as characteristics of cruelty, presumably to exclude accidental acts. This is not the case, however, in a definition provided by Vermeulen and Odendaal (1992): "the intentional, malicious and irresponsible, as well as the unintentional and ignorant infliction of physiological or psychological pain, suffering, deprivation, death or destruction of a companion animal, by both single or repeated incidents."

Although developing a widely accepted definition of cruelty to animals is probably as difficult as defining human interpersonal aggression, the following working definition is offered for the purpose of this review:

> Cruelty to animals is defined as socially unacceptable behavior that intentionally causes unnecessary pain, suffering, or distress to and/or death of an animal.

Excluded by this definition are socially approved practices related to the treatment or use of animals in veterinary practices and livestock production (including humane slaughter) or other animal husbandry practices. The definition also excludes activities involved in more controversial uses of animals, for example, in hunting and in laboratory research [see Arluke (1992) for descriptions of both compassionate and cruel treatment of laboratory primates].

Some elaboration of terms chosen for the definition may be helpful. "Behavior" is meant to include acts of commission (e.g., striking a dog's head with an iron bar) and acts of omission (e.g., depriving a house-bound cat of food). "Socially unacceptable" behavior may, in some cases, be general across cultures (e.g., setting a live bird on fire); however, there should be sensitivity to cultural variations in judgments of acceptability (as there is variation, for example, in the species of mammals judged acceptable for human consumption). "Intentional" denotes acts of commission or omission that are performed willfully and on purpose as distinct from acts performed accidentally or unknowingly (this admittedly complex distinction will be addressed below when the concept of culpability is examined).

"Pain, suffering, or distress" refer, most often, to the effects of noxious physical acts performed on an animal's body either directly or with some instrument or other agent (e.g., weapon, caustic solution, poison). Pain, suffering, and distress are judged from knowledge of species-characteristic response patterns. Physical pain, suffering, and distress may be distinguished from emotional or psychological pain, suffering, and distress, the latter being more subjective and difficult to define and verify. However, attention should also be paid to cruelty that may be psychological in nature (e.g., maintaining an animal separated from but in physical proximity to its natural predator).

Passive behavior and affective signs of pleasure when witnessing cruelty to animals are not directly addressed in the definition. However, a child who delights in the pain a peer may be producing by torturing an animal should be an object of concern. Also, bestiality may be considered cruel even in cases when physical harm to an animal does not occur (this is similar to the case of adult sexual activity with children where consent is presumed to be impossible).

Research Context

Links between Childhood Cruelty to Animals and Later Antisocial, Aggressive Behavior

The relation between violence toward animals and violence toward humans, especially children, has been the subject of philosophical and theoretical attention for centuries (Baenninger 1991; Mead 1964; Menninger 1951; Robin and ten Bensel 1985). Fictional accounts that have incorporated this presumed relation range from William Golding's 1954 *Lord of the Flies*, in which violence toward animals becomes a prelude to the stranded, young boys' interpersonal cruelty and aggression, to Andrew Vachss' 1991 novel *Sacrifice*, in which a sexually abused child, forced to observe animal mutilations, later turns his rage toward an infant victim. The scientific study of this relation, however, is relatively recent.

A variety of efforts have been made to illustrate the association between repetitive acts of severe cruelty in childhood and severe antisocial behavior in adulthood. These include press reports outlining the reported childhood cruelty to animals in the histories of a number of serial or multiple murderers (e.g., [Flynn 1988] "Torturing pets could be prelude to human murder," *San Francisco Examiner*, October 27, 1988), electronic media coverage of childhood animal cruelty (National Public Radio report, June 23, 1990), more extensive treatments in animal-welfare society periodicals (e.g., Lockwood and Hodge 1986), and published research reports. The latter are represented by case studies and a few prospective and retrospective studies below.

There are numerous case studies of cruelty to animals by children and adolescents, cruelty that fits Fromm's (1973) category of "malignant" aggression (distinguished from defensive, instrumental, or "benign" aggression). Early examples include Krafft-Ebing's (1906) descriptions of sadistic behavior toward animals associated with various forms of bestiality and Ferenczi's (1916) analysis of "A Little Chanticleer":

> The case was that of a five-year-old boy, Árpâd by name. . . . Whenever fowl were offered for sale . . . Árpâd . . . gave no peace until his mother bought some. He wanted to witness their slaughter. . . . Árpâd's curious sayings and actions . . . mostly display an unusual pleasure in phantasies about the cruel torturing of poultry. . . . His cruelty was often displayed in regard to human beings also. . . .

More recent case studies include Bettelheim's (1955) analysis of the case of Mary (157), who, at approximately five years of age, attempted to kill animals and set them on fire and who assaulted other children and Redl and Wineman's (1951) predictions of cruelty to animals (in contrast, Levinson 1969) in the antisocial children attending their Pioneer House therapeutic setting. In actual observations of some of the boys interacting with a dog, Redl and Wineman note, "The fascinating thing . . . is that each child duplicates in his relationship to him some of the essential symptomatic patterns that occur in the relationships to humans. . . ." (113). These case studies provide rich descriptions of childhood cruelty to animals but do not directly examine the developmental continuity or discontinuity of such behavior.

The case histories of 18 children referred for clinical evaluation, in part, for cruelty to companion (pets) and noncompanion animals were detailed by Tapia (1971). These children, aged 5 to 15 years, were reported to have engaged in varying degrees of cruelty toward family pets, livestock, farm animals, and wild animals. In a follow-up study of these children and adolescents (2 to 9 years later), Rigdon and Tapia (1977) reported that, of the 13 original clients who could be relocated, 62% were reported still to display abusive behavior toward animals (a more conservative 38% were reported to be engaging in clearly cruel animal treatment). Unfortunately, verification of cruelty incidents was not included in either report, nor was there any attempt to scale the severity of cruelty displayed by these children, problems common to research in this area. In addition, comparisons with clinic-referred children who were not reported to be cruel and with non-clinic children were not made. These early case studies were important in providing prospective information on childhood animal cruelty and rich clinical detail about familial factors possibly related to such behavior.

Critical retrospective research has been conducted by Alan Felthous, Stephen Kellert, and their associates. Childhood histories of animal cruelty (reported percentages are in parentheses) were examined in men who were psychiatric patients (25%) (Felthous 1980), aggressive men (25% "substantial cruelty") in prison and a comparison group of non-incarcerated men (0%) (Kellert and Felthous 1985), and assaultive (36%) and non-assaultive (0%) women offenders (Felthous and Yudowitz 1977). These studies generally support the relation between contemporary patterns of chronic interpersonal aggression and childhood histories of animal cruelty. Although this and related research have been acknowledged to contain some inconsistencies and to share some methodological shortcomings (Felthous and Kellert 1987), a case for the prognostic value of childhood animal cruelty has been made.

Retrospective research with more "select" samples of adults yield even higher rates of reported cruelty to animals. In a study of 28 convicted and incarcerated sexual homicide perpetrators (all men), Ressler, Burgess, and Douglas (1988) found that prevalence of cruelty to animals was 36% in childhood and 46% in adolescence. Tingle, Barnard, Robbins, Newman, and Hutchinson (1986) found that, in their sample of 64 men, 48% of convicted rapists and 30% of convicted child molesters admitted to cruelty to animals in their childhood or adolescence. In some cases, killing animals may follow killing humans. Hickey (1991) observed, "one offender admitted killing several puppies in order to relive the experience of killing his first child victim" (11).

With the assistance of the Utah Division of Youth Corrections, data were gathered, in the spring of 1992, on youth undergoing evaluations (Observation and Assessment) and youth currently incarcerated (Secure Facilities). Nearly all of these 96 participants were boys and their ages ranged from 14 to 18 years (65% were either 16 or 17). Twenty-one percent of the youths being evaluated and 15% of the incarcerated youth reported torturing or hurting animals on purpose within the past 12 months. Two other studies provide examples of research with clinical samples of youth in which cruelty to animals was assessed (primarily from review of case histories—a problematic methodology since failure to find mention of cruelty to animals is an ambiguous outcome). Lewis, Shanok, Grant, and Ritvo (1983) studied 51 eight-to-twelve-year-olds on an inpatient ward; 21 had been judged homicidally aggressive, 30 were not. The prevalence of reported cruelty to animals for these two groups was 14% and 3%, respectively. Wochner and Klosinski (1988) selected 50 children and adolescents, from inpatient and outpatient settings, half of whom had records of cruelty to animals and half who did not. The prevalence of sadistic behavior toward people was 32% and 12% for these two groups, respectively.

Lest the reader think that cruelty to animals is confined to prison samples and patients in psychiatric care, it should be noted that the breadth of the problem includes adult tolerance of child cruelty toward and abuse of animals at livestock auctions (Grandin 1988) and anecdotal evidence that children exposed to chronic wartime violence display violent and cruel behavior toward animals (Randal and Boustany 1990).

A final, yet significant, example of renewed attention to this area is a series of professional-conference sessions, sponsored by societies devoted to humane animal treatment, on the childhood animal cruelty/later violence link. Such sessions have been included in the meetings of the Animal Protection and Child Protection Divisions of the American Humane Association (September 1990), the Delta Society (October 1990), and in a workshop sponsored by the Latham Foundation. In November 1991, a conference, jointly sponsored by the Child Protection and Animal Protection Divisions of the American Humane Association, focused specifically on violence to children and animals (Moulton, Kaufmann, and Filip 1992). Presentations have also been made at the Sixth International Conference on Human–Animal Interactions (Ascione 1992, July) and a conference sponsored by the Geraldine R. Dodge Foundation (Ascione 1992, September).

The Relation between Childhood Animal Cruelty and the Psychiatric Diagnostic Category Conduct Disorder (*DSM-III-R*)

> *Cruelty to animals and other children is a characteristic, though not common, feature of the affectionless delinquent, and occasional outbursts of senseless cruelty are well known in some forms of mental illness.*—J. Bowlby

Included in a description of conduct disorder in the most recent revision of the *Diagnostic and Statistical Manual of Mental Disorders* (American Psychiatric Association 1987) is the following:

> The essential feature of this disorder is a persistent pattern of conduct in which the basic rights of others and major age-appropriate societal norms or rules are violated. . . . Physical aggression is common. Children or adolescents with this disorder usually initiate aggression, may be physically cruel to other people or to animals, and frequently deliberately destroy other people's property (this may include fireset-

ting). They may engage in stealing with confrontation of the victim, as in mugging, purse snatching, extortion, or armed robbery. At later ages, the physical violence may take the form of rape, assault, or, in rare cases, homicide. . . The child may have no concern for the feelings, wishes, and wellbeing of others, as shown by callous behavior, and may lack appropriate feelings of guilt or remorse. (53)

It is important to note that the 1987 edition of *DSM-III-R* is the first to list specifically physical cruelty to animals among the symptoms indicative of conduct disorder. Had the current diagnostic criteria been in effect when the prospective and retrospective animal cruelty studies cited earlier were conducted, the conduct disorder diagnosis might have been applied to many of the subjects in those studies.

Because cruelty to animals is only one of several symptoms of conduct disorder (Spitzer, Davies, and Barkley 1990), the prevalence of such cruelty is difficult to estimate. Research using checklists of behavior problems in children suggests that cruelty to animals is reported more frequently by parents of children being seen at mental health clinics than by parents of a nonclinic sample (Achenbach and Edelbrock 1981; Achenbach, Howell, Quay, and Conners 1991). A recent Canadian study reports an approximate 2% prevalence rate in a census-based sample of 12–16-year-olds (less than 2% in 4–11-year-olds), using mothers' reports; however, when the children in this sample self-reported cruelty to animals, the rate was closer to 10% (Offord, Boyle, and Racine 1991). This discrepancy may be due to differences between respondents in interpretation of "cruelty to animals" and/or to the often covert nature of the cruelty. Nevertheless, a recent meta-analysis of studies of oppositional defiant and conduct disorders reveals that cruelty to animals loads very strongly on the destructive pole of a destructive–nondestructive dimension derived from a multidimensional scaling and that hurting animals is one of the earliest reported symptoms of conduct disorder (median age of onset reported by parents=6.5 years of age) (Frick, Lahey, Loeber, Tannenbaum, Van Horn, Christ, Hart, and Hanson 1993).

Not all children diagnosed with conduct disorder will display the symptom of animal cruelty. However, certain issues addressed by research on conduct disorder and, more specifically, interpersonal aggression in children and adolescents may have relevance for our understanding of animal cruelty.

Kazdin (1990) has summarized definitional, theoretical, conceptual, and research issues pertaining to the prevention and treatment of conduct disorder. He notes that 1989 Institute of Medicine data suggest that 2–6% of American children display symptoms that fit the conduct disorder diagnosis. Data provided by Rosenstein (1990, personal communication) at the Statistical Research Branch of the National Institute of Mental Health suggest that, in 1986, nearly 100,000 children under the age of 18, diagnosed with this disorder, were admitted to inpatient and outpatient mental health facilities. If even a small percentage (assume 5%) of these children and adolescents displayed animal cruelty, the problem would involve thousands of children in the United States.

Kazdin emphasizes that conduct disorder is (1) often stable over time, (2) related to the prediction of adult disorders, and (3) often present across generations within families. Although these features are not always or consistently characteristic of this disorder, other researchers have also called attention to their significance (e.g., Loeber 1988; Widom 1989). Recent research on conduct disorder has focused on risk and protective factors in childhood that may increase and reduce, respectively, the likelihood and severity of conduct disordered behaviors (Garmezy 1988; Robins 1988; and Rutter 1988). Two theory-based approaches describe risk factors related to the development and escalation of aggression in children: coercive family interaction patterns and children's attributional biases.

The first approach is illustrated in the work of Gerald Patterson and colleagues (Patterson, DeBaryshe, and Ramsey 1989), which provides a research-based model of the escalation of aggression in families. Ineffective parenting styles, relying heavily on punitive or aversive control, present children with models of coercion such that family members become enmeshed in a cycle where parent and child use aversive techniques to terminate each others' behavior. This pattern is often coupled with an absence of parental behavior directed at fostering prosocial behavior. The implication for childhood animal cruelty is that children reared in such families may learn to generalize aversive control techniques to their companion animals, if present.

The second approach is exemplified in the work of Price and Dodge (1989) on peer rejection and social maladjustment in boys. These authors suggest that rejected boys who display atypical levels of aggression often show deficits in intention-cue detection. That is, in situations where peers' intentions may be ambiguous, these socially rejected boys display an attributional bias and impute hostile intentions to peer behavior that may be neutral (e.g., being accidentally bumped in a lunch line). This bias may lead such boys to respond to such situations with aggression, with subsequent retaliation by peers. Repetitions of such interactions may reinforce the rejected child's negative self-perceptions and belief in a hostile peer environment and reinforce the rejecting peers' aggressive stereotype of the child. Again, potential parallels to children who display cruelty toward animals are not difficult to conceive. If peers' intention cues are at times ambiguous to rejected children, intention cues provided by animals, both companion and noncompanion, may be even more difficult to discern. A vivid example of this possibility was included in the National Public Radio report referred to above. A young boy who brutalized, sexually assaulted, and eventually killed a stray dog reported how, when he heard the dog barking at him, he interpreted the dog's behavior as personally directed aggression, something the boy was not going to allow. There was no sensitivity to the possibility that the animal's behavior reflected being startled or frightened. Clearly, such attributional bias toward animals needs to be examined empirically.

Before leaving this topic, one additional parallel between conduct disorder research and research on childhood animal cruelty needs to be highlighted. Child and adolescent firesetting is also included in *DSM-III-R* diagnostic criteria for conduct disorder. (The firesetting–enuresis–cruelty to animals "triad," has received inconsistent support [see, for example, Hellman and Blackman 1966; Wax and Haddox 1974a; Wax and Haddox 1974b; in contrast, see Justice, Justice, and Kraft 1974] and its discussion, which is beyond the scope of this review.) Kolko and Kazdin (1989), in elaborating a risk model for children displaying such behavior, developed the *Children's Firesetting Interview* to ascertain qualitative information about children's firesetting as distinct from simplistic presence–absence ratings. They note that firesetting is a relatively low frequency behavior and is often covert, characteristics it shares with childhood animal cruelty. Wooden and Berkey (1984) found that young (4–8 years old) firesetters were more likely to be cruel to animals than older (9–17 years old) firesetters.

The development of an assessment instrument, patterned after Kolko and Kazdin's, for animal cruelty would assist our definition and understanding of qualitative variations in childhood animal cruelty. Current assessment instruments (Achenbach 1988; Achenbach and Edelbrock 1981; Kazdin and Esveldt-Dawson 1986) are lacking in this regard. The intensity, duration, and breadth of certain antisocial behaviors may be more important than their frequency (Kazdin 1990). Information about these dimensions for childhood animal cruelty would allow us to move beyond anecdotal evidence (e.g., Magid and McKelvey 1987).

Relations to Family Violence and Violence in Alternative Child Care Settings

"We have talked with two young women each of whom told us that when her father was angry with her he killed her favorite pet." (68) "Cindy remembers seeing her father hit her mother on many occasions. Bill (the father) rarely spanked Cindy. When he did, it was rather mild. But his other punishments were extraordinarily cruel. Cindy's clearest childhood memory was of her father shooting her pet cat." (119) These anecdotes from Gelles and Straus' (1988) book *Intimate Violence* are two of many references to the abuse, torture, and killing of companion animals that one encounters in the literatures on family violence and alternative child care sexual abuse.

A number of review articles have appeared recently on family violence (e.g., Emery 1989), characteristics of abusing and/or neglecting parents (e.g., LaRose and Wolfe 1987), and the psychological effects of abuse on children (Cicchetti 1990). In addition, there have been reports dealing with sexual abuse of children in day care (e.g., Faller 1990; Finkelhor, Williams, and Burns 1988) that include reference to the torture and killing of animals by adults as a coercive technique. In this section, I will not attempt to summarize the extensive research in these areas but rather will highlight how aspects of this research have relevance for our understanding of childhood animal cruelty. Special note will be made of potential distortions of children's empathic development that may result from their observation and direct experience of family violence.

Illustrating the relation between the violent and abusive environments in which some children are reared and the children's own violent reactions, Besharov (1990) reminds us of the case of Wayne Dresbach who, when 15 years of age, killed both of his parents (Mewshaw 1980). Wayne had been subjected to years of verbal and physical abuse at the hands of his father and had witnessed his father's beatings of his mother. Mewshaw describes an incident involving cruelty to animals by Wayne's father that no doubt included Wayne's psychological abuse:

> But one weekend morning his father scooped the kittens into a paper sack, picked up the .22, and headed out the back door. Worried, Wayne went with him.
>
> "What are you doing?" he asked as they crossed the yard, passed the stables, and set off toward a creek at the property line.
>
> "Going to get rid of these fucking things," Dresbach said.
>
> "I thought we were going to give them away."
>
> "I'm tired of waiting. Tired of them whining all night and stinking up the house."
>
> At the creek Dresbach rolled the top of the bag tight, then tossed it into the shallow water. While the kittens screeched, and pawed to get out, and Wayne sobbed for him not to do it, his father took aim and emptied the rifle. At that range he couldn't miss. The slugs tore the sack to pieces, and blood poured out in trickles, then in a great rush as the bottom gave way.
>
> Wayne wanted to bury the kittens, but Pat told him not to bother. Dogs and buzzards would take care of them.

It is also increasingly more common to find cruelty to animals (especially pets) listed in behavioral checklists used in domestic violence assessment. For example, Klingbeil and Boyd (1984, referred to in Jaffe, Wolfe, and Wilson [1990]) note that "Children in violent homes are characterized by . . . frequently participating in pecking order battering (maim or kill animals, batter siblings)" (30).

In addition to experiencing the abuse of their pet animals, battered women may be forced to perform acts of bestiality by their husbands or boyfriends (Dutton 1992, Walker 1979). We do not know how often children witness these abuses. In a study of partner abuse in lesbian relationships, Renzetti (1992) reports, "At least 35 of the respondents lived with children either their own or their partners'. In almost 30% of these cases, the children also were abused by the partner. Pet abuse was frequent as well; 38% of the respondents who had pets reported that their partners had abused the animals" (21). These phenomena are not limited to the admittedly violent nature of American society. In a major cross-cultural analysis, Levinson (1989) observed, "Women are more likely to be permanently injured, scarred, or even killed by their husbands in societies in which animals are treated cruelly." (45).

Hughes (1988) studied 3–12-year-olds accompanying their mothers to a shelter for abused women; 60% of the children were reported, by mothers, to have been physically abused. She notes that these child witness victims were least well adjusted (as measured by the Eyberg Child Behavior Inventory) when compared with either child witnesses who were not themselves abused or a control group of children. Jouriles, Murphy, and O'Leary (1989) reported that marital aggression (as distinct from marital discord) was associated with conduct-disordered behavior in 5–12-year-old boys whose parents were in marital therapy. One may speculate that witnessing marital aggression may be a form of observational learning through which children may learn violent problem-"solving" behaviors. If companion animals are present in such situations and are also targets of parental aggression, children may imitate parents' behavior. Evidence for this relation in non-distressed families has been provided by Zahn-Waxler, Hollenbeck, and Radke-Yarrow (1984).

Cicchetti (1990) has outlined a number of negative psychological correlates of child maltreatment including deficits in children's emotion language, problematic attachment relationships, and deficits in children's ability to decode facial expressions of emotions in others (see also, Camoras, Ribordy, Hill, Martino, Sachs, Spaccarelli, and Stefani 1990). A more commonly reported correlate of child maltreatment is victims' disordered and aggressive peer relations (e.g., prospective research by Dodge, Bates, and Pettit 1990). Mueller and Silverman (1989) note that maltreated preschoolers may respond to peer distress either by ignoring or in some cases aggressing toward the child displaying the distress (e.g., Klimes-Dougan and Kistner 1990). Although the processes involved in such atypical reactions are not clear, maltreated children may be hypersensitive to displays of distress (because of their own experiences associating distress with maltreatment) and may resort to aggression in an effort to terminate such displays. No information (beyond case study reports, e.g., Furman 1986) is available on how maltreated children might respond to animals in distress.

Although most cases of child abuse involve perpetrators who are parents or parent figures, in some cases, children suffer abuse from siblings. Wiehe (1990), in a study of 150 adult respondents to a questionnaire on sibling abuse, described how emotional abuse by siblings either took the form of or accompanied the torture or killing of the victim's pet (neither an uncommon nor only a recent phenomenon—see Burk 1897). The immediate effects of such trauma included the inability to care for another pet and, in some cases, the victim's emotional abuse of younger siblings. Although exposure to distressing childhood experiences may be related to higher levels of empathy in adulthood (Barnett and McCoy 1989), negative effects may be more likely when the distressing experiences take the form of physical, emotional, or sexual abuse. The factors leading to these differential outcomes are, as yet, unclear.

Only one published study exists (to my knowledge) that has directly addressed the relation between child abuse and neglect and companion animal abuse and neglect. Deviney, Dickert, and Lockwood (1983) studied 53 families who met New Jersey legal criteria for child abuse or neglect and who also had companion animals in their homes. Although only one observer was present, precluding reliability assessment, observations during home interviews revealed that pets were abused or neglected in 60% of these families. As potential support for observational learning of abusive tactics, one finds that 26% of the children in these families abused or were cruel to their pets. When the sample was categorized into physically abused (40%), sexually abused (10%), and neglected (58%), an alarming finding was that in 88% of families displaying child physical abuse (in contrast to 34% in sexually abusing or neglecting families), pet abuse was also present. An unpublished study by Walker (1980) examined records of families' contacts with child protection and animal protection agencies. Appearance in the records of both agencies was found for 9% of the families studied.

Some case studies of sexual abuse of children include reports of forcing children to interact sexually with animals or warning a child to maintain silence about abuse by threatening to harm or destroy the child's pet animals (Faller 1990; Finkelhor, Williams, and Burns 1988; Kelley 1989; Hunter 1990). Although Faller (1990) notes that the killing of animals at a day care facility occurred in only 4% of the cases she directly studied, Finkelhor, Williams, and Burns (1988) reported such coercion in 14% of their cases. Faller also describes a study (in Waterman, Kelly, Oliveri, and McCord 1993) in which 80% of the child victims in the Manhattan Beach molestation case reported exposure to the killing of animals as a part of teachers' threats to maintain secrecy. The long-term effects of these experiences on the child victims are, of course, not yet known. Sexual or violent "play" with animals is mentioned as a potential sign that a child has been sexually or physically abused—one report of such inappropriate play involved a three-and-one-half-year-old child (Hewitt 1990). Adult homicide perpetrators who report being sexually abused as children report higher rates of childhood animal cruelty (58%) than perpetrators not reporting sexual abuse (15%) (Ressler, Burgess, Hartman, Douglas, and McCormack 1986; Ressler, Burgess, and Douglas 1988).

The relation between physical and sexual abuse of children and children's dysfunctional interactions with animals has received attention in the clinical literature. Sterba (1935) related the case of a severe dog phobia in a seven-and-one-half-year-old girl who had been given daily enemas for over a month. Weil (1989) has reviewed a hundred case studies involving children exposed to erogenous and erotic contact with adults and to beatings and violent yelling. Examples of destructive behavior toward objects, other children, and animals were common among the symptoms many of these children presented. Cruelty to animals and sexual behavior with animals are listed in an assessment for adult and juvenile sex offenders (Hindman, n.d.). Hindman (1992) also includes in her *Juvenile Culpability Assessment* (to be used in judging responsibility in youth who act out sexually) an index of "social capacity for empathy" that includes whether a young person "indicates understanding of needed concern or sensitivity for animals."

Although much of the information we have on the relation between sexual abuse of children and children's cruelty toward animals is derived from retrospective research, some existing data sets (e.g., Friedrich, Urquiza, and Beilke 1986) allow for contemporary analysis of this relation. William Friedrich (April, 1992, personal communication) provided data from a large-scale study of substantiated cases of sexual abuse in children 2–12 years of age. Most of these children had been victimized within twelve months of data collection that included administration of the Child Behavior Checklist (Achenbach 1988). Parental reports of cruelty to animals were 35% for abused boys and 27% for abused girls; the percentages were 5% for non-abused boys and 3% for non-abused girls, a highly significant difference based on clinical status.

Anecdotal reports of animal cruelty also surface in the literature on alternate child care where allegations of molestation are present. The reports are present in cases where there may be a single perpetrator and victim but are even more prominent in "multidimensional child sex ring" reports (or in cases reported to involve so-called ritual abuse) (Boat 1991; Lanning 1989a, 1989b; Uherek 1991). Determining the degree of validity of such reports remains controversial (Lanning 1991, Putnam 1991), yet it is difficult to ignore common threads describing animal cruelty. Reports include mutilation and killing of animals, threatening to destroy or actually destroying animals to frighten children into secrecy, and forcing children to engage in sexual activity with animals (Jonker and Jonker-Bakker 1991). A recent study of 37 adult clients diagnosed with dissociative disorders noted that all of the clients reported witnessing animal mutilation or killing as part of their own childhood abuse experiences (Young, Sachs, Braun, Watkins 1991). In reviewing the relation between severe abuse and the development of dissociative problems in children, Peterson (1990) notes that cruelty to animals is one of a number of conduct disorder problems listed among other symptoms of dissociation. In constructing his Child Dissociation Problem Checklist, Peterson (1991) has included the item "hurt animals" along with a variety of antisocial behaviors. On balance, it should also be noted that abuse victims may find interactions with a family pet a source of comfort (Zimrin 1986) and that learning to touch pets appropriately may be a useful adjunct to therapy (Lew 1988). It is not clear what factors would allow us to predict whether animals would be the target of affectional or disordered behavior in cases of abuse.

Cruelty and Empathy

Finally, the potential relation between empathy and childhood animal cruelty will be examined. In earlier work (Ascione 1992, Weber and Ascione 1992), I have reviewed research, with non-distressed children and adults, showing a positive relation between children's empathy (ability to understand and relate to the emotional experiences of others) toward animals and other aspects of their psychological development. In Ascione (1992), I reported that, at certain elementary grades, a year-long humane education program not only enhanced children's attitudes toward animals (Ascione 1988a, 1988b) but this change generalized to a measure of human-directed empathy. Similar research with distressed children (e.g., abused, conduct-disordered) has not yet been accomplished. Feshbach (1989), however, reviewed a small number of studies of empathy in abusing parents and abused children (without, unfortunately, consideration of animal-directed empathy). She notes that "the relationship between empathy and prosocial behavior and empathy and aggression suggests that the abusive parent should be low in empathy and that the abused child should also manifest a lack of empathy" (355).

Studies show that even in non-abusing families, toddlers exposed to frequent maternal child-directed anger are less empathic when witnessing others' distress (Crockenberg 1985). Reporting on unpublished data, Feshbach (1989, 369) notes that "Abusive parents appear more indifferent to emotional pain in others than do the control or psychiatric patients." Low maternal empathy has also been found to be more strongly related to physical child abuse than a measure of maternal stress (Letourneau 1981). Parental deficits in empathy warrant attention since there is consensus that empathy development in children is strongly related to parental socialization practices (Zahn-Waxler, Hollenbeck, and Radke-Yarrow 1984) and evidence that higher levels of empathy in children are associated with greater prosocial behavior (Strayer and Roberts 1989). There is a critical need for research relating both human- and animal-directed empathy in children to child abuse and childhood animal cruelty.

Freud (1905), noting that clinicians should attend to "children who are distinguished for evincing especial cruelty to animals and playmates" also observed that "The absence of the barrier of sympathy carries with it the danger that a connection found in childhood between cruelty and the erogenous impulses will not be broken later in life" (594).

Research Needs

Companion animals are an integral part of the lives of children in the United States. Pet ownership has been found to be significantly more common in families with school-aged children and adolescents than in families without children (Albert and Bulcroft 1988). In samples from California and Connecticut, children reported pet ownership ranging from 52%, for kindergartners, to 75%, for fifth graders (Ascione, Latham, and Worthen 1985). Seventy-seven percent of a northern Utah sample of first, second, fourth, and fifth graders (Ascione 1992) reported having at least one pet at home. Higher rates of pet ownership in a sample of older children have been reported by Bryant (1990). The numbers confirm the importance of attending to the human–companion animal bond (Kidd and Kidd 1987, Levinson 1972, National Institute of Health 1988). Given the demonstrated or potential implication of childhood animal cruelty in a variety of psychological disturbances in children, adolescents, and adults, it is regrettable that we have so little information about the prevalence and incidence of seriously dysfunctional human–animal relations.

Given the infancy of research development in this area, many basic issues have yet to be addressed. For example, although "cruelty" and "maltreatment" may be used to describe behavior toward animals, operational definitions of these terms have yet to be developed or accepted (Arkow, Walker, Ascione, and Boatfield 1990). Clearly, these terms may refer to a spectrum of behavior that will vary in severity, intensity, and generality of contexts where it is displayed. There may even be differences in judgments of cruelty severity based on the species of animal(s) involved. Adult and child-adolescent differences in definitions may also make comparisons of parent reports and self-reports by children problematic.

An operational definition should include qualitative dimensions of cruelty to animals (e.g., forms of physical cruelty [sexual and nonsexual], whether it was performed overtly or covertly, whether it was performed alone or with the help of other individuals) with a measure of severity (perhaps based on degree of pain/distress as well as physical injury inflicted). Once a definition has been developed, other characteristics that should be addressed would include estimates of the onset or first occurrence of cruelty, listing of the types of animals (e.g., farm, companion, wild/stray) toward which the behavior was directed, describing opportunities to have contact with animals (including whether the individual currently has or has had companion animals), and some measure of positive behaviors toward animals (attending to patterns of behavior that include cruelty and kindness may be important).

> Lennie sat in the hay and looked at a little dead puppy that lay in front of him. . . . And Lennie said softly to the puppy, "Why do you got to get killed? You ain't so little as mice. I didn't bounce you hard."
> —John Steinbeck, Of Mice and Men, 85

Combinations of kindness and putative cruelty raise the issue of judging responsibility or culpability for acts of cruelty. (Lennie Small's desire to caress is overwhelmed by his inability to control the intensity of his touches, with tragic consequences.) One approach that could serve as a model has been used to judge culpability in cases of juvenile sex offending (Hindman 1992). The method considers a youth's cognitive and social skill levels as well as the youth's own history of abuse to assess level of responsibility. This general approach would be helpful in distinguishing cruelty derived from developmental immaturity from cruelty that may be malicious.

Process-oriented research that is sensitive to developmental issues is also needed. Childhood animal cruelty has been discussed in the context of observational learning, [children may learn both the roles of victim and victimizer (see Wertsch 1991, 234–236)], displacement of aggression (Bandura and Walters 1959, 91), as an outcome of psychological trauma (Green 1985, Terr 1990) [one report notes higher rates of parent-reported animal cruelty for children who lived near the Three Mile

Island accident (Davidson and Baum 1990)], and in relation to distortions in empathic development in children (Crockenberg 1985, Feshbach 1989). Basic developmental research in a number of these areas could inform studies on the ontogeny of animal maltreatment in children. Such research could also help identify factors that place children at risk for or protect them from developing cruelty toward animals.

Prevention and intervention issues will no doubt be related to our understanding of the processes of different forms of animal cruelty. Primary prevention may focus on educational programs (Ascione 1992) that provide children with clear guidelines for acceptable behavior with animals (Zahn-Waxler, Hollenbeck, and Radke-Yarrow 1984). Parents and other significant adults may also need to be informed that certain forms and/or patterns of cruelty should be of concern and not summarily dismissed as typical childhood exploration. Intervention for children who already display cruelty toward animals will need to consider ecological factors that may be related to such behavior, including family violence (Dodge, Bates, and Pettit 1990; Emery 1989; Jouriles, Murphy, and O'Leary 1989; Widom 1989; 1991), dysfunctional peer relations (Cicchetti 1990; Dodge, Bates, and Pettit 1990; Klimes-Dougan and Kistner 1990; Mueller and Silverman 1989), and the specific modeling of animal cruelty, live and in various forms of media.

Final Comments

In Ramon's classroom . . . at least four of the children face significant problems or are evidencing developmental harm: four-year-old Jamilla, who killed her brother's pet bird, plucking out its feathers one by one and stomping on it because it "made too much noise. . . ."
                            —Garbarino, Dubrow, Kostelny, and Pardo, 163

We are in the final years of a century of great promise and yet we are still struggling to understand and prevent violence (Reiss and Roth 1993). Violent environments, such as the one that envelops Jamilla, can foster cruelty or caring. The dangerous environments children endure can lead them to seek out animals for affection or to train animals to be weapons (Kotlowitz 1991, 6, 43, 78). A better understanding of how cruelty to animals is related to the more general domain of interpersonal violence may facilitate prevention and intervention efforts. Parents know that cruelty to animals may be serious (Weisz and Weiss 1991); children seem to know as well (Triplett 1903).

Questions for Discussion

1. Critique Ascione's definition of animal cruelty. What kinds of behaviors are not included in this definition?
2. Do you think that children who abuse animals are more likely to be violent later against other people? Why or why not?
3. If cruelty to animals is related to the inhibition of empathy and the potential for harmful treatment of others, could kindness toward other animals be related to enhanced empathy and the positive treatment of others? Justify your answer.

17 Childhood Cruelty to Animals and Subsequent Violence against Humans

Linda Merz-Perez, Kathleen M. Heide, and Ira J. Silverman

In recent years, animal advocates and some scholars have championed a relationship that has come to be known as "the link." In its most common form, known as the "graduation hypothesis" or the "progression thesis," those who are cruel to animals, especially in childhood, are predicted to move on to harm humans. This study tested this hypothesis by comparing the incidence of past acts of animal cruelty among violent and nonviolent inmates. As expected, violent inmates were significantly more likely than nonviolent ones to have abused animals in the past. The authors suggest that the findings provide support for "the link."

A substantial amount of literature with respect to cruelty to animals and its relationship to human violence appeared during the period between the 1960s and 1990s. Some of the literature focused specifically on the factor of cruelty to animals with respect to its relationship to violence perpetrated against humans (see e.g., Arkow 1998; Ascione 1993; 1998; DeViney, Dickert, and Lockwood 1983; Felthous and Kellert 1987; Lockwood and Church 1998; Lockwood and Hodge 1997; Ressler, Burgess, Hartman, Douglas, and McCormack 1998; Spiegel 1988; Tapia 1971). Other studies included cruelty to animals as one of several factors investigated (Bender 1959; Climent, Hyg, and Erwin 1972; Douglas, Burgess, Burgess, and Ressler 1997; Douglas and Olshaker 1995; Easson and Steinhilber 1961; Heide 1992; Heller, Ehrlich, Saundra, and Lester 1984; Hellman and Blackman 1966; Holmes and De Burger 1988; Holmes and Holmes 1996; Justice, Justice, and Kraft 1974; MacDonald 1964; Mead 1964; Wax and Haddox 1974a; 1974b; 1974c). Some studies have concluded that cruelty to animals is a significant factor, whereas others have found it to be insignificant. The latter studies have frequently cited such factors as familial vio-

Linda Merz-Perez, Kathleen M. Heide, and Ira J. Silverman, *International Journal of Offender and Comparative Criminology* (*vol.* 45), pp. 556–573, Copyright © 2001 by Sage Publications. Reprinted with permission of Sage Publications, Inc.

lence, school difficulties, and peer problems as more salient predictors of violent behavior. The literature itself, however, has often concluded that further research is needed to facilitate more meaningful understanding of this complex phenomenon.

This study was designed to investigate whether the phenomenon of cruelty to animals might serve as an early warning sign of predictable future violence against humans. It is frequently overlooked in discussions of the relationship between animal cruelty and subsequent violent behavior that cruelty to animals encompasses varying dimensions. A problem in the definition results from regional differences in its perception and identification due to cultural factors and varying definitions under law. According to most laws in the United States, failure to provide adequate food, water, and shelter or the use of physical force to leave a mark or otherwise cause injury constitutes cruelty to animals. The penalties under these laws, however, vary greatly from state to state.

Kellert and Felthous (1985) established precise definitions of animal cruelty. As a result of their study, the authors described the following nine motives for cruelty to animals: (a) to control an animal, (b) to retaliate against an animal, (c) to satisfy a prejudice against a species or breed, (d) to express aggression through an animal, (e) to enhance one's own aggressiveness, (f) to shock people for amusement, (g) to retaliate against another person, (h) displacement of hostility from a person to an animal, and (i) nonspecific sadism.

Kellert and Felthous (1985) emphasized the importance of identifying motives for animal abuse and establishing any applicable patterns of abuse. The authors reported that an understanding of the motive for any given act of animal cruelty is imperative. For example, two boys may each kill a mouse. One boy lives on a farm and finds the mouse in question in a feed bin. The other boy lives in a city and the mouse that he kills is his sister's pet. Within the context of motive, there is a broad qualitative difference between the two acts of violence just cited. In fact, the difference is broad enough to suggest that only one act of cruelty may have been committed. In this context, the farm boy might be appropriately viewed as having eliminated a pest that had the potential of contaminating feed. The city boy, however, killed a pet, an animal that was cherished and loved by his sister, and was thus, in the words of Mead (Lockwood and Hodge 1997, 80), a *good* animal. Some of the literature had emphasized the significance of cruelty to pet animals with respect to the relationship of cruelty to animals and later violence against humans (Kellert and Felthous 1985; Mead 1964).

It is also conceivable, however, considering the importance of precise definition as advocated by Kellert and Felthous (1985), that the farm boy may also have committed a cruel act. Did the farm boy kill the mouse swiftly and expediently, or did he torture the mouse and make it suffer? If the latter scenario were the case, Kellert and Felthous would consider that the boy's act was indeed an act of cruelty.

The importance of motive and precise definition cannot be overstated. Kellert and Felthous (1985) compared criminals and noncriminals with respect to cruelty to animals. In addition, the authors further distinguished the criminal group with respect to aggressive and nonaggressive criminals. They concluded that aggressive criminals committed cruelty to animals with greater frequency when compared to nonaggressive criminals and noncriminals.

The present study postulated that seven of the nine motives for cruelty would be particularly important with respect to the correlation between animal cruelty and human cruelty. These seven motives are: Motive 1: to control an animal; Motive 2: to express aggression through an animal; Motive 5: to enhance one's own aggressiveness; Motive 6: to shock people for amusement; Motive 7: to retaliate against another person; Motive 8: displacement of hostility from a person to an animal; and Motive 9: nonspecific sadism.

It was hypothesized from the available literature that a statistically significant greater proportion of violent offenders will have committed past acts of cruelty to animals when compared to the proportion of nonviolent offenders who will have committed past acts of cruelty to animals.

Method

Fifty violent and 50 nonviolent inmates who were incarcerated in a maximum-security facility located in Sumter County, Florida, were randomly selected by institutional staff members on the basis of their current commitment offenses for possible participation in this study. Careful attention focused on the verification of the participants' nonviolent as differentiated from violent offense status. Nonviolent participants found to have a violent offense in their criminal histories were eliminated from the study. A total of 45 nonviolent participants and 45 violent participants participated in the study. Qualitative summaries of both the participants' instant and most serious committed offenses indicated a broad range of offenses. With respect to the nonviolent participants' instant offenses overall, the offenses included unoccupied burglary (33%), property crimes (24%), drug-related offenses (36%), and other offenses such as escape and possession of a firearm by a felon (7%).

The most serious offenses committed by the violent offenders all reflected violent crimes. Close to two-thirds of these offenses included murder (33%) or attempted murder (2%) and sex offenses (30%). Other offenses included assault and/or battery or resisting a law enforcement officer with violence (21%), burglary of an occupied dwelling and armed burglary (9%), and robbery with a dangerous weapon or firearm (5%). The most serious offenses committed by 75% of the nonviolent offenders consisted of burglary of unoccupied structures (40%) or drug offenses (35%). The remaining offenses included property crimes (23%) or possession of a firearm (2%).

As depicted in Table 1, the median age with respect to both groups was similar, 31.8 years for nonviolent participants and 32.3 years for violent participants. No statistically significant differences were found between the two groups in terms of race ($\chi2=3.629$; $df=1$; $p=.058$), education ($\chi2=3.242$; $df=1$; $p=.072$), marital status ($\chi2=2.248$; $df=1$; $p=.134$), or the participants' known number of children ($\chi2=.382$; $df=1$; $p=.536$). All participants were male.

Table 1   Quantitative Summary of Respondents' Demographic and Personal Data

Variable	Percentage Nonviolent[a]	N	Percentage Violent[a]	N	$\chi2$ Results
Median age in years	31.8		32.3		
Race					
White	36	45	56	45	3.629[b]; $df=1$ $p=.058$ (ns)
Non-White	64		44		
Education					
High school grad./GED	36	45	55	44	3.242; $df=1$ $p=.072$ (ns)
Non-high school grad.	64		45		
Marital status					
Married	20	45	9	45	2.248; $df=1$ $p=.134$ (ns)
Not married	80		91		
Number of known children					
None	66	41	72	43	.382; $df=1$ $p=.536$ (ns)
One or more	34		28		

[a] Values, other than age, are in percentages.
[b] Not significant but demonstrates a tendency toward significance.

Data Collection and Coding

Two data collection instruments were used in the study. The Survivors' Coping

Strategies (SCS) Survey, developed by Kathleen M. Heide and Eldra P. Solomon (1991), was used to gather demographic and social history background data about the participants. The second instrument, the Children and Animals Assessment Instrument (CAAI), developed by Frank R. Ascione (Ascione, Thompson, and Black 1997), was used to gather data with respect to the participants' experience with animals, including cruelty to animals either committed or observed by the study participants. The CAAI instrument divided animals into the following four categories: wild, farm, pet, and stray. Ascione variables collected information on the frequency and severity of cruelty committed by the participant. Other Ascione variables, covert, isolate, and empathy, coded whether the offender tried to conceal the cruelty, whether he committed the cruelty alone, and whether he felt any sensitivity toward the animal, respectively. Additional data coded in this study included the seriousness of act committed variable, which qualitatively assessed the specific types of acts of cruelty to animals committed, and the participant's response to cruelty committed (remorse, not cruel or no effect, emotional/psych release/thrill, sex satisfaction, power/control, sadism, or other).

Both data collection instruments were used in the context of face-to-face interviews. Information about the participants and their offenses was also made available for review by the Department of Corrections. These documents included the police reports; charging, conviction, and sentencing materials; presentence investigations; and correctional assessment forms. These agency record data typically served as official accounts of the offense and the offender's history and on occasion, provided additional insight into the offender and his past. In some cases, psychological evaluations had previously been conducted, and summary reports were available in the participants' files. Standardized psychological tests, however, were not typically included in the participants' files. Any diagnostic terms that appeared in the participants' files typically reflected the clinicians' selection of diagnoses in use at the time of their assessment of these offenders.

...The interview process began in July 1995 and concluded in April 1996. . . . Variables were designed to collect both comprehensive quantitative and qualitative data with respect to the participants' histories. To establish validity, interrater reliability was measured by having 20% of the coded interviews ($N=20$) coded by a second rater. A comparison of the two sets of coded interviews revealed an interrater reliability of 99%. . . .

Data Analysis Plan

The primary goal of the study was to determine what relationship, if any, existed between past acts of cruelty to animals among violent and nonviolent offenders. The first set of analyses tested the relationship between cruelty committed to animals and later acts of violence committed against humans. The second set of analyses tested the relationship of cruelty committed against each of the four animal types and later violence committed against humans. Much of the literature supporting a relationship between cruelty to animals and later violence committed against humans has emphasized the significance of cruelty committed against pet animals.

Many of the variables were expressly designed to facilitate both quantitative and qualitative analyses. This design proved useful because quantitative analyses with respect to specific animal category variables (i.e., wild, farm, pet, and stray animals) were often insufficient to yield statistical significance given the overall sample size of 90. In such cases, qualitative data, often suggesting possible trends worthy of further investigation, were discussed.

Results

As depicted in Table 2, there was a statistically significant difference in the proportion of violent participants who committed past acts of cruelty to animals compared to the proportion of nonviolent participants who committed past acts of cruelty to animals ($\chi2=12.100$; $df=1$; $p=.00$). The proportion of violent participants who committed past acts of cruelty to animals was significantly greater (56%) than the proportion of nonviolent participants (20%).

Furthermore, a comparison of the Ascione summary scores comparing cruelty to animals committed by nonviolent and violent participants with respect to severity, frequency, covert, isolate, and empathy also yielded statistically significant results. The summary scores variable was designed to provide a qualitative comparison of summary scores with respect to nonviolent and violent participants who had committed acts of cruelty against animals. (This variable was recoded to quantify the overall test of the hypothesis as discussed earlier.) The summary scores revealed that a statistically significant greater proportion of violent participants had scored higher with respect to cruelty to animals committed (summary score 414) when compared to the proportion of nonviolent participants (summary score 101) ($\chi2=25.142$; $df=1$, $p=.033$).

Cruelty by Animal Type

Quantitative analyses with respect to the four types of animals were compared with respect to the two groups of offenders and are also reported in Table 2.

Pet Animals

Consistent with theoretical predictions, statistical significance was demonstrated with respect to the category of pet animals when nonviolent and violent participants were compared (χ2=6.132; df=1; p=.013). The proportion of violent offenders who committed past acts of cruelty to pet animals was significantly greater (26%) than the proportion of nonviolent offenders who committed past acts of cruelty to pet animals (7%) when violent (N=42) and nonviolent participants (N=45) were compared.

With respect to three of the violent offenders, the data reported by the participant were insufficient to establish that cruelty had been committed. Furthermore, in the case of violent offenders, contradictory information had been sometimes reported. However, cruelty committed was only coded as such in this study if the participant had positively articulated a committed act of animal cruelty. For example, one violent offender reported that his sister had purposely broken the neck of a kitten when he and his sister were children. The participant reported that the incident had taken place in the backyard of their home. At first the participant reported that his sister had been alone at the time of the incident because the participant was not at home. The participant later reported that he and his sister had been together when the incident occurred. The contradictions with respect to the participant's story suggested complicity. However, the participant reported that he had not participated in the cruel act committed. Therefore, the incident reported by the participant was coded as no cruelty committed by participant.

The strength of the revealed relationship with respect to cruelty to pet animals when nonviolent and violent offenders were compared would have been stronger if dog fighting had not been found to be a confounding variable. As depicted in Table 3, among nonviolent offenders, dog fighting (forced fighting) was the most serious form

Table 2   Summary of Quantitative Analysis of Cruelty Committed by
(Table extends across facing pages.)

	Nonviolent		
Category	*Percentage Cruelty Committed*	*Percentage No Cruelty Committed*	*N*
All categories	20	80	45
Wild Animals	13	87	45
Farm Animals	2	98	45
Pet Animals	7	93	45
Stray Animals	0	100	45

[a] Levels .05 through .07 are not statistically significant but indicate a tendency toward significance.

[b] Analyses nonapplicable: Cells<5; Fisher's Exact Test, one tail, used to determine statistical significance.

*p indicates significance.

of animal cruelty reported against pet animals. Furthermore, in the case of nonviolent offenders, dog fighting was the only form of cruelty to pet animals reported. In addition, two of the three nonviolent offenders who reported this act also reported that they shared their lives with pet dogs at the same time that they owned dogs for the expressed purpose of dog fighting. The participants spoke of their pet dogs with fondness. One of the participants described how his German Shepherd, named Brownie, slept in his bed with him and lived to the age of 10, an age indicating that the dog received appropriate care during its lifetime.

Another factor indicating the confounding nature of dog fighting is the fact that all three of the nonviolent offenders who reported this act of cruelty were African American. All three participants described dog fighting as a popular neighborhood activity that despite its illegality was attended by both adults and children. In most instances, gambling was the main attraction. In addition, the participants claimed that the dogs involved were aggressive and wanted to fight. One offender reported that he considered it "cruel" to stop a fight because the methods that had to be used could injure a dog, "like poking a stick in the dog's ear to make him back down."

The information reported by the nonviolent offenders suggests that dog fighting within the context of race (African American) and environment (urban) may be a confounding variable due to cultural factors. Interestingly, among the violent offenders, the only act of dog fighting committed was reported by a White participant who did not elaborate as to the particulars of motive or cultural context.

Although cruelty committed to pet animals was limited to dog fighting among the nonviolent offenders, acts of cruelty committed by violent offenders included a

Participant by Animal Category

	Violent			
Percentage Cruelty Committed	*Percentage No Cruelty Committed*	*N*	*χ2 Results*	*Fisher's Exact Test*
56	44	45	12.100; df=1; p=00*	p=.00*
29	71	45	3.269; df=1; p=07[a]	p=.06[a]
14	86	45	4.000; df=1; p=05[b]	p=.05[a]
26	74	45	6.133; df=1; p=01*	p=.01*
11	89	45	5.294; df=1; p=02[b]	p=.03*

Table 3 Qualitative Summary of Most Serious Acts of Cruelty to Animals
(Table extends across facing pages.)

	Wild		Farm	
Specific Act of Cruelty	Nonviolent Offender	Violent Offender	Nonviolent Offender	Violent Offender
Articulated fear	1	0	0	0
Killed for food	0	1	0	0
Killed for sport	0	2	0	0
Tease/torment/deprive	0	0	0	1
Throw object(s) at	0	0	0	1
Sex with animals	0	0	0	1
Forced fighting	0	0	0	0
Beatings/kicking/stomping	0	1	0	2
Tying animals together	0	0	0	0
Shooting	5	7	1	1
Stabbing	0	1	0	0
Pouring chemical irritants on	0	0	0	0
Burning	0	0	0	0
Dismembering	0	1	0	0
Missing data	0	0	0	0
Total number	**6**	**13**	**1**	**6**

Table 4 Qualitative Summary of Participant Responses to Cruelty to Animals
(Table extends across facing pages.)

	Wild		Farm	
Specific Response to Cruelty	Nonviolent Offender	Violent Offender	Nonviolent Offender	Violent Offender
Remorse	2	1	1	0
Not cruel or no effect	3	5	0	4
Emotional/psych release/thrill	1	5	0	1
Power or control	0	0	0	0
Sadism	0	1	0	0
Missing data	0	0	0	1
Total number	**6**	**12**	**1**	**6**

Committed by Participants (In Real Numbers)

Pet		Stray	
Nonviolent Offender	Violent Offender	Nonviolent Offender	Violent Offender
0	0	0	0
0	0	0	0
0	0	0	0
0	1	0	0
0	0	0	0
0	2	0	0
3	1	0	0
0	1	0	1
0	0	0	1
0	1	0	0
0	0	0	0
0	2	0	0
0	0	0	1
0	0	0	1
0	2	0	1
3	**10**	**0**	**5**

Committed by Participant (In Real Numbers)

Pet		Stray	
Nonviolent Offender	Violent Offender	Nonviolent Offender	Violent Offender
0	1	0	0
1	7	0	1
2	1	0	2
0	1	0	1
0	1	0	1
0	0	0	0
3	**11**	**0**	**5**

broad range of acts such as stomping a kitten to death, setting a dog on fire, and having sex with an animal. One violent offender reported having done something "very bad" to a puppy but "could not say" what it was. A similar reporting was made by another violent offender who related that he had once "done something" to a pet animal, but that he "could not talk about it."

As depicted in Table 4, comparative differences with respect to participant response to cruelty committed were not revealed as a result of the confounding factor of dog fighting. All three nonviolent offenders who reported participating in dog fighting did not view dog fighting as cruel but viewed dog fighting within the context of a socially accepted activity within their cultural context. Therefore, the responses provided by the nonviolent offenders with respect to the cruelty committed were also influenced by the confounding factor of dog fighting.

Wild Animals

The fact that significance was not demonstrated when nonviolent and violent offenders were compared with respect to wild animals ($\chi2=3.269$; $df=1$; $p=.070$) was likely due to the fact that both violent and nonviolent offenders described acts of cruelty to wild animals in various contexts. As depicted in Table 2, although statistical significance was not established, the proportion of violent offenders who had committed cruelty to wild animals was greater (29%) when compared to nonviolent offenders (13%) when violent offenders ($N=45$) and nonviolent offenders ($N=45$) were compared.

As depicted in Table 3, twelve of the nineteen acts of cruelty committed against wild animals by the participants involved the shooting of an animal. Some of the participants reported these acts within the context of acts that conformed to acceptable levels of behavior within certain cultural parameters, such as the shooting of wild birds as a prelude to legitimate hunting or in the playing of "war games." Four of the six nonviolent offenders who reported cruelty committed to a wild animal described their committed acts within this context. These four participants described their acts of cruelty to wild animals within the following contexts. One participant reported that at the age of nine, he shot a bird while "playing army" and felt remorse. A second participant reported that while an adolescent, he had hunted rabbits, birds, and wild ducks with his brother. The participant described these acts as something he "grew out of." A third participant reported that when he was 13 or 14 years old, he had hunted rabbits for "target practice." The participant described these acts as "ridiculous if you don't need food." A fourth participant reported that he learned how to hunt with a BB gun as a young child and that he later hunted rabbits, quails, and raccoons "mostly for food," using rifles and shotguns. The participant further reported that he had since lost all interest in hunting and that he "could no longer buy meat because there's not many animals left."

Many of the participants reported that they had committed such acts with peers. The only accounts, however, of cruelty committed to a wild animal when the participant was alone were reported by violent offenders. For example, one violent offender reported that he would go off on his own "to shoot squirrels for the fun of it." Another violent offender reported that when he was in the sixth grade he would "go into the woods alone to shoot birds and other animals just to kill them." In contrast, one nonviolent offender reported that when he was nine years old he shot a bird with a BB gun while "playing war games with friends." He also reported that he "felt so bad" he broke his gun.

Among the two remaining nonviolent offenders who reported cruelty committed against wild animals, one of the participants reported that when he was between eight and 10 years old, he had shot raccoons with a BB gun "just as something to do" because he was a "spoiled brat" and cared little for the feelings of others. The participant further reported that as an adult he remained "self-centered" and blamed the latter on his "permissive upbringing." The second participant reported that as an adolescent he "beat up a big snake out of fear" although the snake had attempted to escape. The participant reported that he had "held up the dead snake for neighborhood kids to see," presumably to demonstrate that he was brave and had overcome his fear. The participant reported no other acts of cruelty to animals.

Of the 13 violent respondents who reported cruelty to a wild animal, only two of them reported that they committed acts as a prelude to legitimate hunting. Most often, the participants reported that they committed acts as either "just something to do" or as acts committed "just to kill." For example, one violent offender reported that he and his friends had killed "whatever" wild animals they could find with "rocks, BB guns, slingshots, and rocket launchers." This individual also reported that often the animals were not killed but "merely wounded and left to die." The participant further reported that to the present day he "had no regrets." Violent respondents also reported such acts of cruelty as stabbing and dismembering. One participant reported that as a child, he had enjoyed dismembering live fish he had caught while fishing.

Distinct qualitative differences between the participants' responses were apparent when nonviolent and violent participant responses were compared. As depicted in Table 4, whereas a response of remorse was reported by two of the six nonviolent offenders who had reported committed acts of cruelty to wild animals, a response of remorse was reported by only one of the eleven violent offenders who had reported cruelty committed to wild animals. Four of the nonviolent offenders described these childhood acts of cruelty as "foolish" or "childish" acts or as behavior that they "grew out of." Whereas most of the nonviolent offenders suggested that these acts had been inappropriate, most of the violent offenders either did not pass judgment as to their acts or reported that the cruelty they committed was "fun." Ten of the thirteen violent offenders reported a response of not cruel or no effect or emotional/psych release/thrill. Furthermore, the only sadistic act committed against a wild animal was reported by a violent offender.

Farm Animals

As depicted in Table 2, the reported numbers of cruelty to farm animals were insufficient to establish statistical significance when violent and nonviolent offenders were compared using chi-square, so Fisher's Exact Test, one tail, was used ($p=.05$). Only one of the nonviolent offenders (2%) had reported cruelty committed to a farm animal compared to six (14%) of the violent offenders. Furthermore, the context in which the reported acts of cruelty occurred provided significant qualitative comparisons when nonviolent and violent offenders were compared. Comparisons with respect to the participants' responses to cruelty committed also revealed compelling qualitative differences.

As depicted in Table 3, the only act of cruelty to a farm animal reported by a nonviolent offender involved the act of shooting an animal. The respondent described the shooting of a pig when he was eight years old. The respondent's grandfather had given him his first "real gun," a rifle, as a birthday gift. Prior to this occasion, the participant had only used a BB gun, and he reported that he wanted to "test what the gun could do." To this end, the participant shot and killed a neighbor's pig. The individual reported that he had not given any thought to the pig with respect to it being a sentient creature. Rather, he had viewed the animal merely as an object to test his new rifle. His grandfather, however, viewed the act differently. He broke the participant's gun and ordered the participant to assist with chores on the neighbor's farm for a period of one year. The participant reported that as a result of the way this incident was handled, he felt remorse for killing the animal and not simply regret that he had been caught. This particular act of reported cruelty is highly significant in light of Mead's (1964) warning that a lack of punishment with respect to an act of cruelty committed to an animal by a child is worse than punishment that is too harsh.

As depicted in Table 3, the most serious acts reported by the six violent offenders who reported cruelty committed to a farm animal were varied. (To reiterate, the variables with respect to the seriousness of act committed were designed to indicate the most serious act of cruelty committed by a given offender. Therefore, a given offender may have reported more than one act of cruelty committed within any of the four animal categories.) One of the six violent offenders who had reported cruelty committed to farm animals reported that he had teased animals. Another of the participants reported that he had thrown rocks at a cow "to hurt it." One of the participants reported having had sex with a farm animal. Two participants reported acts that involved the beating of an animal. Among the latter two participants, one of the participants reported that when he was eight years old he had beaten a baby chick to death with a Coke bottle; the other reported that he had shot an animal to death.

As depicted in Table 4, none of the violent offenders reported a response of remorse. For example, despite the brutality of the act involving the baby chick (which according to the participant was rendered unidentifiable), the participant reported only that he was "not an animal person" and that he "liked to throw stuff." The latter participant's response was coded as not cruel or no effect. Three of the remaining violent participants who had reported cruelty to farm animals also reported a response of not cruel or no effect. One of the six participants did not provide a response, and the latter was coded as missing data, and one participant reported a thrill response.

Stray Animals

As depicted in Table 2, no acts of cruelty to stray animals were reported by nonviolent offenders. Cruelty was reported by five (11%) of the violent offenders. Fisher's Exact Test, one tail, a better test to use, indicated that these differences were statistically significant.

As depicted in Table 3, the acts of cruelty reported by the five violent offenders included beating an animal, tying animals together (to watch them panic and fight to separate themselves), setting an animal on fire or otherwise burning an animal, and dismembering an animal. One of the violent offenders reported that he had committed many acts of violence toward animals but did not wish to be specific. The latter reported cruelty was coded as missing data.

Although none of the nonviolent offenders reported cruelty committed to a stray animal, one nonviolent offender reported an act of self-defense involving a stray animal. The participant described being attacked by a stray dog while riding his bicycle and hitting the dog with a stick to make him "back off." Despite the circumstances of the incident, the participant reported that hitting the dog made him "feel sad." Among those violent offenders who reported cruelty committed to a stray animal, none reported a response of remorse. Rather, as depicted in Table 4, the responses reported by the violent offenders included not cruel or no effect, thrill, power or control, and sadism. The one violent offender who reported a response of power or control

described how when he was an adolescent, he would "frequently" go into the woods with his hunting dogs "to stalk and overpower" his prey. The participant reported that he spear-hunted both wild animals and stray dogs "for the joy of the kill." The fact that the participant articulated that "control" was the primary motivation for the acts of cruelty committed distinguishes the power or control response from the thrill response in this case. A police report of the participant's crimes described how the participant "killed his victims in the woods and then dragged the bodies deeper into the woods." The participant's psychological evaluation noted that the participant reported, "Many of my dreams are about the woods." The evaluation concluded that the participant had "a sociopathic personality." In addition to first-degree murder, the participant's crimes included kidnapping and rape.

Discussion

The purpose of this study was to examine the relationship of cruelty to animals and later violence against humans. Cruelty to animals has long served as a red flag in law enforcement circles with respect to extremely violent offenders. For example, the expansive literature with respect to serial killers has often cited cruelty to animals as a precursor to the violence later targeted against human victims (Lockwood and Church 1998). Furthermore, some of the recent literature with respect to domestic violence has cited cruelty to animals as part of an insidious cycle of violence that victimizes families. In this view, cruelty to pet animals has been viewed as a barometer of familial abuse. In addition, pet animals, which often are loved and treated like children in our culture, have been viewed as victims in their own right. Therefore, many advocates of children and animals have come to view cruelty to animals as a serious matter due to the analogous human victimization it often represents (Lockwood and Hodge 1997).

The overall results of the study support previous research efforts indicating a relationship between cruelty to animals committed during childhood and later violence perpetuated against humans. The findings indicate that offenders who committed violent crimes as adults were significantly more likely than adult nonviolent offenders as children to have committed acts of cruelty against animals in general and pet and stray animals in particular. Furthermore, even when reported numbers with respect to some of the animal cruelty variables used in this study were insufficient to generate quantitative analyses (as in the case of the farm and stray animal variables), the qualitative findings derived from these variables suggested consistent and pronounced differences when the two groups of participants were compared. Clearly, the qualitative results of this study both stimulate and provide direction for further inquiry.

These findings raise a very critical question, one that increasingly demands an answer as more studies show a correlation between animal cruelty and subsequent violence toward people: Is aggression against animals committed as children predictive of subsequent adult aggression against human beings? Our results underscore the need for a longitudinal study of children through their adult years to see to what extent violence toward specific types of animals as children is causally connected to adult violence against humans.

This study found that cruelty to animals is a complex phenomenon. Furthermore, it reinforced that any meaningful inquiry into its dynamics requires the application of rigorous methodological standards and conceptual precision. The results of this study provide both implications and ramifications with respect to the phenomenon of cruelty to animals and its relationship to human violence. The motivations for cruelty to animals are as diverse and complicated as those that provide the impetus for interpersonal violence. However, this study demonstrated that cruelty committed against animals often reveals insightful analogies with respect to violence that is committed against humans by humans.

It is interesting to note that past acts of cruelty to animals resembling either the participants' instant or most serious offense, as suggested by the case just referenced, were reported only by violent offenders. One violent offender, a repeat sex offender, had been convicted while an adolescent of a crime against nature for sodomizing a reformatory pig. Another participant, convicted of sexual battery on a person 65 years or older, described how he would throw stones and bricks at stray animals "to beat and hurt them like my parents hurt me." According to the police report, the victim's face had been severely beaten.

The results of this study indicate that cruelty to animals committed by children can provide insights into violent behavior that may or may not translate into later violence directed against humans. Therefore, cruelty to animals must be investigated in terms of its complex dynamics if useful and meaningful insight is to be extrapolated. In this view, the type of cruelty committed, the type of animal targeted, the motivation for the cruelty, and the perpetrator's response to the cruelty committed are critical factors that must be considered.

To dismiss cruelty to animals as incidental acts committed by "troubled kids" is to dismiss an opportunity to identify behavior that might indeed be a precursor of violence against humans to follow. Findings reported in this article strongly suggest that each act of cruelty to animals, which is but one expression of violence, should be investigated with rigorous attention to the specifics involved.

Each and every act should be investigated as a specific act committed by a specific individual against a specific animal. It would appear that through this approach, acts of cruelty to animals that are relevant to the relationship of cruelty to animals and later violence against humans could be distinguished from those that are not.

Clearly, the phenomenon of violence is as complicated as the physiology and psychology of human beings, the sources from which it derives. At this point in time, it is not known to what extent violence is the product of nature or nurture or both interactively. Its manifestations, however, often appear as unique as the individuals who commit it. Likewise, the reasons that many individuals avoid violence are highly individualized. Both must be examined systematically to detect patterns, intervene early, and prevent violence.

Questions for Discussion

1. What do scholars, criminologists, and animal advocates mean by "the link?"
2. How strong is the evidence from this study in support of the connection between animal abuse and interhuman violence? What are the implications for social policy if there is such a connection?
3. What categories of animals were particularly likely to have been harmed in the past by violent inmates? What is the significance of these findings?

18 Woman's Best Friend

Pet Abuse and the Role of Companion Animals in the Lives of Battered Women

Clifton P. Flynn

As the previous articles indicate, researchers are finding that animal abuse is relat-ed to other forms of family violence, especially violence against women and children. In this essay, I surveyed clients in a battered women's shelter about their relation-ships with their companion animals and whether their pets had been abused by their batterers. As the title suggests, most women considered their companion animals as important sources of emotional support, and many delayed leaving their abusive partner out of concern for the well being of their pets. What are the implications of battered women's close relationships with their companion animals, both for policy and for how we think about other animals?

Only recently have scholars begun to focus on the relationship between animal mal-treatment and interpersonal aggression, particularly violence within families (DeViney, Dickert, and Lockwood 1983; Lockwood and Ascione 1998). Several writ-ers have argued that animal cruelty may accompany, and thus be a marker of, vio-lence against women and children in families (Arkow 1996; Ascione 1993; Boat 1995). Further, researchers have found that aggressive criminals and troubled youth have high rates of perpetrating animal cruelty during their childhoods, and that the perpetrators often were victims of child abuse themselves (Felthous and Kellert 1986; Kellert and Felthous 1985; Rigdon and Tapia 1977; Tapia 1971).

With few exceptions, researchers have largely ignored the relationship between animal abuse and wife or partner abuse, addressing it only secondarily and anecdo-tally. Several authors refer to instances of animal abuse, including bestiality, by bat-terers attempting to intimidate, terrorize, or control their female partners (e.g.,

Clifton P. Flynn, *Violence against Women* (vol. 6, no. 2) pp. 150–175, Copyright © 2000 by Sage Publications. Reprinted with permission of Sage Publications, Inc.

Browne 1987; Dutton 1992; Renzetti 1992; Walker 1979). For example, Browne (1987) noted that battered women who had killed their husbands frequently reported the killing of pets and the destruction of animals by their batterers. A study of lesbians who had been victimized by their partners found that 38% of the women reported that their partners had abused their pets (Renzetti 1992).

A recent national survey of 48 shelters for battered women suggests that many of those who work with this population may have ignored pet abuse as well. Ascione, Weber, and Wood (1997a) surveyed the largest shelter in each state that had both residential and children's programs. They found that for the vast majority of shelters, staff had heard clients talk about incidents of pet abuse (85.4%) and had observed the coexistence of domestic violence and pet abuse (83.3%). Nearly two-thirds (63%) reported that staff had heard children talking about incidents of pet abuse. Yet, despite this awareness, only 13 of the 48 shelters (27%) asked any questions in their intake interview, and only six had arrangements with animal welfare organizations or veterinarians to provide temporary shelter or care to companion animals.

The current study seeks to build on the limited research in this area by examining pet abuse, along with the roles of pets, in the lives of battered women. Specifically, this study focused on four questions: What is the nature and extent of pet abuse suffered by battered women? How important are pets as sources of emotional support to victims of abuse? Do women continue to worry about their pets after seeking shelter? And does concern for the welfare of their pets cause some women to delay seeking shelter?

Review of the Literature

The first study specifically designed to explore the extent and impact of pet abuse among battered women was conducted by Ascione (1998). He surveyed 38 women who sought shelter at a safe house for battered women about their partners' and children's cruelty to companion animals. Seventy-four percent of the sample either currently owned pets or had owned them in the past year, and two-thirds owned more than one pet. Of those women, 71% reported that their partner had threatened to hurt or kill and/or had actually hurt or killed at least one of their pets.

More than half of the women (57%) reported that their pets had been physically harmed or killed by a partner. Approximately one-third of the women with children (7 of 22) said that their child had hurt or killed one or more pets. In five of the seven cases, the partner had also threatened or perpetrated harm against their pets. Nearly one-fifth (18%) of the women with pets reported that they had delayed seeking shelter due to concerns for the safety of their pets.

In a second study, Ascione, Weber, and Wood (1997b) compared animal maltreatment in samples of battered women from five shelters in Utah and nonbattered women from the community. The women were preselected on the basis of current or past pet ownership. Battered women were approximately three times more likely than women in the community sample to report that their partners had threatened to hurt their pets (52% vs. 16.7%). Even more dramatically, 54% of women at the shelter said that their partners had actually hurt or killed a pet, compared with only 3.5% in the community sample. Among battered women with children, nearly seven out of ten (69.2%) reported pets being hurt or killed by their partners. Not only were women in the shelters more than fifteen times more likely to experience pet abuse from their intimate partners (twenty times more likely if they had children), but the majority had to endure multiple incidents of pet maltreatment.

The vast majority of shelter women reported feeling "numb" or "terrible" after their pets were threatened or harmed, and they were significantly more likely to report these feelings than women in the community sample. The negative emotional and psychological impact of experiencing animal cruelty is likely to have been great, particularly because more than 80% of the shelter women indicated that they were "very close" to the pet that was victimized.

Because of their concern for the welfare of their companion animals, nearly one-fourth of the shelter women delayed coming to the shelter. This delay obviously increased their exposure, along with their children's and pets', to the possibility of further violence.

Ascione and colleagues (1997b) also looked at children's experiences with pet abuse. Target children of the shelter women were nearly twenty times more likely to have witnessed pet abuse than children of women in the community sample (61.5% vs. 3.3%). Further, although there was not much difference between shelter and community-sample women in the rate of children perpetrating animal abuse, the children of shelter women were more likely to engage in more severe pet maltreatment. "The results of this study illustrate the landscape of terror in which many women, children, and their pets reside and should prompt renewed attention to the confluence of family violence and animal maltreatment" (Ascione *et al.* 1997b, 2).

Sample and Data Collection

From March through August 1998, 111 women sought help at a South Carolina shelter for battered women. In all but four cases, the abuser was a current or former intimate male partner. The other perpetrators were a mother's boyfriend, a mother-in-law, a boss who was providing living quarters, and an unknown assailant. For the purposes of this study, these women were removed from the data set in order to focus solely on partner abuse, leaving a total of 107 women who served as subjects.

Nearly six out of ten respondents (59.8%) were White, whereas more than a third (36.5%) were Black. Three women were Hispanic (2.8%) and two were Asian (1.9%). Their ages ranged from 17 to 61 years, with a mean age of 32.4 years. Almost 70% of the women (68.2%) were unemployed. More than one-fourth of the women (28.0%) had been previous clients at the shelter, with six women coming twice during the six months the study was being conducted, and one other woman who came three times.

As part of the routine intake procedures, clients are required by shelter staff to complete a questionnaire detailing important demographic information about themselves and their abusers, as well as other data regarding the history and nature of the abusive relationship. A series of questions about the presence of factors such as child abuse, drugs, alcohol, and weapons are included. In addition to the standard questionnaire, the shelter staff agreed to ask subjects to complete a short nine-question survey concerning the women's experiences with pets. Because the agency believed data on pets and pet abuse was important to their service provision, this survey was incorporated into the routine intake process.

The specific questions were:

- Have you ever had any pets in this relationship?
- Do you currently have any pets?

If the subjects said yes to either of the first two questions, then they responded to the following questions:

> In dealing with the abuse, how important has your pet been as a source of emotional support: very important, somewhat important, not at all important?
>
> Has your partner ever threatened to harm your pet, actually harmed your pet, or killed your pet?
>
> Has your child ever threatened to harm your pet, actually harmed your pet, or killed your pet?
>
> Where is your pet now? (Possible responses included with a family member, with a friend/neighbor, with my partner/ex-partner, no longer alive, took to the animal shelter, gave pet away, and other.)
>
> Do you worry about your pet's safety?
>
> Did concern about your pet's safety keep you from seeking shelter sooner?

If [you responded] Yes to question 8, approximately how long did you delay seeking shelter due to your concern for your pet's safety? (Possible responses were less than one week, 1–2 weeks, 3–4 weeks, 5–8 weeks, and more than 8 weeks.)

Results

Characteristics of Pet Owners

Four out of ten women (40.2%) reported either currently owning pets or owning them at some time during the abusive relationship. Race, marital status, and employment status were three factors that were found to be related to pet ownership (see Table 1). More than half of the White respondents (54.7%) but only 15.8% of the Black respondents were or had been pet owners. Two of the three Hispanic women and neither of the two Asian women had pets.

Table 1   Comparison of Pet Owners and Nonowners among Battered Women by Race, Marital Status, Employment Status, and Presence of Children (%)

	Pet Owners (n=43)	Nonowners (n=64)
Race		
White	81.4	45.3
Nonwhite	18.6	54.7
Marital status		
Married	76.7	42.2
Not married	23.3	57.8
Woman's employment status		
Employed	44.2	23.4
Unemployed	55.8	76.6
Partner's employment status		
Employed	78.6	54.8
Unemployed	21.4	45.2
Presence of children		
Children	34.9	40.6
No children	65.1	59.4

More than 80% of pet owners were White, compared with only 45.3% of nonowners. Pet owners were more likely than nonowners to be married. Three fourths of the women with pets were married, whereas less than half (42.2%) of nonowners were married. The presence of children was largely unrelated to pet ownership. Nearly two-thirds of pet owners (65.1%) and six out of ten nonowners

(59.4%) had children. The average number of children among those women with children was 2.37 for pet owners and 2.03 nonowners.

Although unemployment was high for both groups, women with pets were nearly twice as likely to be employed than those without pets. Only 23.4% of nonowners were employed, compared with 44.2% of pet owners. Partner unemployment was also higher for nonowners. More than three fourths of the abusive partners of pet owners (78.6%) were employed, whereas slightly more than half of the partners of women with no pets (54.8%) were employed.

In short, pet owners were more likely to be White, married, employed, and to have a partner/batterer who is employed. Given that the care of pets can be costly, and given the relationship between race, marital status, and economic status, these findings are not surprising.

Extent and Nature of Pet Abuse

Of the 43 women with pets, 20 (46.5%) reported that their male abuser had threatened to harm and/or had actually harmed their pets. Nine women said their abusers had only threatened harm against pets, whereas eleven had actually inflicted harm. Eight of the eleven perpetrators of pet abuse had also threatened to hurt the pets. No pets had been killed by an abusive partner.

There were only two instances of pet abuse by children. One woman whose partner had threatened her pet reported that her child had also threatened to harm a pet. In the other case, a child had harmed a pet but the abusive partner had not. An interesting finding emerged regarding pet abuse and children. Women whose companion animals had been abused were less likely to have children than women whose pets had not suffered abuse, yet only somewhat less likely than those who did not have pets. Slightly less than half of women reporting pet maltreatment had children (45.0%), compared with 82.6% percent of owners of nonabused pets, and 59.4% of women who did not have pets. Yet, women whose pets had experienced cruelty were more likely to report that their children had suffered abuse than women in either of the other groups. One-third (three out of nine) of the women with abused pets said that their children had also been abused. The comparable figures for women with nonabused pets and women with no pets were 15.8% (three out of nineteen) and 10.5% (four out of thirty-eight), respectively.

Pet Issues and Concerns

Table 2 summarizes the findings related to the issues and concerns battered women had regarding their pets. Approximately three fourths of pet owners (73.2%) found their pets to be either very important (46.3%) or at least somewhat important (26.8%) as sources of emotional support in dealing with their own abusive situations. Only 26.8% said their pets were not at all important in this role.

Table 2 Issues and Concerns of Battered Women With Pets by Pet Abuse Status (%)

	Pet Abuse (n=20)	No Pet Abuse (n=22)	Total (n=42)
Pet as source of emotional support			
Very important	55.0	38.1	46.3
Somewhat important	35.0	19.0	26.8
Not at all important	10.0	42.9	26.8
Where is pet now?			
With partner/ex-partner	55.0	50.0	52.4
With family member, friend, neighbor	25.0	27.3	26.2
No longer have (gave away, died, took to animal shelter, abandoned)	20.0	22.7	21.4
Worry about pet's safety now?			
Yes	65.0	15.0	40.0
No	35.0	85.0	60.0
Delayed seeking shelter[a]			
Yes	40.0	0.0	20.0
No	60.0	100.0	80.0

[a] Of those women delaying shelter, one delayed 1–2 weeks, one delayed 3–4 weeks, one delayed 5–8 weeks, and five women delayed for more than 8 weeks.

The degree to which women viewed their companion animals as sources of emotional support varied based on whether the pets had been abused. Interestingly, women whose pets were abused indicated stronger emotional attachment to their pets than women who did not report pet abuse. Of the 20 battered women with abused pets, 11 said that the pets were very important sources of emotional support, seven said they were somewhat important, and only two said that their pets were not at all important. However, abused women whose pets were not maltreated were about as likely to say their pets were not important in terms of providing emotional support ($n=9$) as they were to say they were very important ($n=8$). The remaining four said that the pets were somewhat important in this regard.

Ratings of the emotional support of pets were also related to whether the woman had children. Among women with children, 37.0% said their pets were very important emotionally, whereas one-third said they were not at all important. For women with no children, nearly two-thirds (64.3%) reported that their pets were very important sources of emotional support, whereas only 18.2% felt they were not important.

Slightly more than half of the pets (52.4%) were still with the abusive partner or ex-partner. About one-fifth ($n=8$) of the women reported their pets were with other family members, and three said that the pets were with friends or neighbors. Others experienced more permanent loss. Five women had given their pets away, two reported that their pets had died, one pet had been taken to the animal shelter, and one pet had been abandoned. Women were about as likely to leave their pets with partners who had perpetrated pet abuse than with those who had not. Among women whose pets had not been abused, 50.0% of the pets were still with the women's partners. However, 55% of abusive partners who had also abused pets still had the pet in their possession.

Given that many pets are still with abusive partners, some of whom had previously inflicted harm on the pets, and that pets had served as significant sources of emotional support for battered women, it is not surprising that many women continued to worry about their companion animals after arriving at the shelter. Forty percent of the women with pets were worried about their pets' safety. Understandably, this was especially true if the pets had also been abused. Women whose pets were maltreated were more than four times more likely to be worried about their pets than those whose pets had not (65% vs. 15%). Eight women reported that they delayed seeking shelter due to their concern for their pets' safety, and each of them also had pets that had been abused. Five of the eight women delayed seeking shelter for more than two months.

Discussion

In the current study, 40% of clients at a shelter for battered women reported having pets presently or at some point in their abusive relationship, and 46.5% of those with pets said that their pets had also been threatened or harmed by the batterer. These rates are somewhat lower than those found by Ascione (1998). This may be due to sociodemographic differences between shelter clients in South Carolina compared to Utah. It seems likely that few, if any, of the women in the Utah study were African American, whereas more than one-third of the South Carolina sample was Black. The relationship between race, marital status, and socioeconomic status may explain the decreased likelihood of pet ownership among this sample.

Almost one-fifth (18.7%) of all clients and almost half of those with pets had experienced threats of, or actual, pet abuse. Women reporting pet abuse were much less likely to have children than women whose pets were not abused, and somewhat less likely than abused women without pets. However, women whose pets were harmed or threatened were more likely than either of the other groups to report that their children had been abused as well. Because of the small number of women whose pets and children had been abused, this finding must be interpreted cautiously. Nonetheless, it is consistent with the notion that different forms of violence often coexist in families. The presence of pet abuse may signify child abuse, just as the presence of domestic violence may also be a marker of animal maltreatment (Arkow 1996; DeViney *et al.* 1983).

There was little evidence of child pet abuse. One child had threatened a pet and one child had actually hurt a pet. However, it seems highly unlikely that at least some children did not either witness the abuse of pets or observe the effects of such abuse. It may be possible that some incidents of pet abuse were directed at the child (such as the father punishing the child's misbehavior by hitting a pet) and not the woman. Experiencing pet abuse, particularly by a loved one, is likely to be very traumatizing for children.

Many of the women with pets reported that their companion animals had been important to them emotionally as they coped with their violent relationship. This was particularly true for those women whose pets had been abused. Perhaps male batterers are more likely to target the pets if their partners are strongly attached to them. It may also be that women may form close bonds with companion animals who have been similarly victimized. Whatever the dynamics, it is clear that many batterers create a climate of terror that encompasses both human and nonhuman victims.

In American society, most pet owners view their companion animals as members of the family (Albert and Bulcroft 1988). Further, pet owners tend to report high levels of attachment to pets and often attribute human characteristics to them. Albert and Bulcroft (1988) found pets to be important sources of affection and support during critical life transitions such as divorce, remarriage, and widowhood. They argued that as individuals experience stress from losing or adding statuses and roles, affection from pets may be all the more valuable. This same reasoning could be applied to victims of domestic violence. If pets are granted human status, if they serve as emotional substitutes for family members, then they may be particularly important companions for battered women. This may be especially true, given the isolation that is known to frequently accompany abuse (e.g., Straus, Gelles, and Steinmetz 1980). In the current study, pet owners who did not have children were particularly likely to view their pets as important sources of emotional support. As one respondent wrote, "I can't have children so I have had a dog since she was 6 weeks old. She is really my life. My life revolves around [dog's name]."

If it is true that pets may take on special significance for victims of domestic violence, then being separated from or losing one's pet may create additional trauma. Unfortunately, slightly more than half of the women in this sample (52.4%) reported that their pets were still with the abusive partners, and therefore still at risk. If the woman is close to her pet, and if the pet lives with the batterer, then the animal could be used to control the victim. By threatening to harm the companion animal, abusers may be able to intimidate victims into dropping charges and/or returning home. According to one staff member, the woman who had come to the shelter three times during the study returned to her abuser because of concern for her pet.

Male partners may be resentful toward pets if they perceive that the pets are more important to their partners than they are. Nearly half of the pets that had not been abused continued to reside with the abuser, but that does not mean that they were free from harm. Once his partner has gone to a shelter, an angry batterer may decide to target a companion animal that had previously escaped harm. It also seems probable that pets that remain with abusive partners may be neglected. Because women are more likely to have been the pets' caretakers, their male partners may be less inclined to assume these responsibilities. Given these realities, it is clear why more than 40% of all women with pets, and two-thirds of women whose pets had been abused reported worrying about their pets' safety.

Coming to the shelter meant at least a temporary separation from their pets, whereas other women suffered a more permanent loss. Some women were able to place their pets with family members, friends, or neighbors. However, even knowing that their pets may be safe, neither pet nor woman is able to have the emotional support of the other. For whatever reasons, some women gave their pets away, took them to the animal shelter, or abandoned them. Two women reported that their pets had died. Thus, in addition to the trauma of enduring and trying to escape an abusive relationship, these women suffered yet another loss. Beyond that, regardless of the status of their pets, guilt may be a common emotion for women who feel that they have somehow let their animal companions down.

Eight of the women with abused pets delayed seeking shelter out of concern for their pet. Five women delayed coming to the shelter for more than two months. Women, and in some cases children, may literally have risked their lives in an effort to protect their pets. This sacrifice signifies how invaluable companion animals can be in the lives of battered women, and how crucial it is for professionals to recognize that fact.

Conceptual and Theoretical Animal/Human Connections

Veevers (1985) categorizes the roles that companion animals play in families in terms of three major functions:

> The projective function concerns the extent to which the selection of a pet is interpreted as making a statement about the owner. The sociability function concerns the extent to which having a pet acts as a social lubricant, and affects the quantity and quality of interaction with other humans. Finally, the surrogate function concerns the extent to which pet–human interaction may serve as a supplement to human–human interaction or even, in some extreme cases, as an alternative to it. (12–13)

It is this third function, that of surrogate, that is most relevant to the role of pets in the lives of battered women.

Veevers points out that the surrogate function may exist in positive and negative forms. Individuals may substitute pets for human interaction in their lives, with pets serving as surrogate friends and confidants, mates, children, or parents. The findings from this study suggest that this role may be especially relevant for victims of domestic violence. Male batterers often isolate their female victims, denying them opportunity for human social contact. Companion animals may substitute for human companions both as a critical source of emotional support and as a reliable and trusted friend.

Pets may also serve as surrogate enemies, as the evidence of pet abuse among battered women shows. Pets may be targeted for abuse by batterers in order to inflict emotional abuse or to control their female partners, a process referred to as "triangling" (DeViney et al 1983).

A feminist analysis by Adams (1994, 1995) illustrates the connection between the victimization of women, children, and animals, and the violence that is manifested in a patriarchal culture. The empirical evidence:

> . . . details a shocking hostility to the bodies of disenfranchised others— women, children, nondominant men, and animals. . . . Clearly women's oppression is interwoven with that of animals, so that women and animals are both trapped by the control exercised over their own and each other's bodies. (Adams 1994, 70)

Finally, Solot (1997) warns us not to forget the animals in our efforts to fight abuse against humans. She argues that "the published research on animal abuse—

unlike the published research on any other form of violence—is motivated almost without exception by the connection to human violence" (262). It is essential to remember that animal abuse is a serious social problem deserving of scholarly and public attention.

> Even as we validate the connections among all forms of violence, we must take care not to invalidate each separate form. The woman who beats her children, the teen who rapes his girlfriend, and the adolescent who sets a cat on fire all need attention because they have committed horrific acts of violence against other living beings—not because some-day they might do something worse. (Solot 1997, 262)

Implications for Domestic Violence and Other Professionals

Both the presence of pets and the abuse of pets in the lives of battered women are phenomena that shelter staff must incorporate into their intake interviews and servic-es. Although shelter staff are generally aware of the connection between domestic violence and animal abuse, few ask about pet abuse at intake, or offer psychological or practical services related to pets (Ascione *et al.* 1997a).

Counseling should include support for the complex feelings of loss, guilt, and worry that battered women with pets may feel. Counseling programs for children should determine whether children have witnessed or inflicted animal abuse, and pro-vide the needed services to help alleviate their trauma. Shelter services could be expanded to address the practical needs of pet owners as well. Most shelters fail to provide any kind of emergency or temporary shelter or veterinary services for clients (Ascione *et al.* 1997a). This is particularly problematic, given that pets of shelter clients are likely to have received lower levels of both regular and emergency veteri-nary care than typical pets (Ascione *et al.* 1997b), and that many pets are still with the abusive partner and thus still at risk. Collaborative arrangements could be estab-lished with local animal shelters or foster-care volunteers to house pets temporarily, and with local veterinarians to provide medical services, perhaps at a reduced rate (Arkow 1996).

Awareness of animal abuse could also have important legal implications. Evidence of animal cruelty could be used to enhance the chances of securing an order of protection, temporary custody of the home and children, or even the arrest of the batterer. This strategy could be quite effective if, as Boat (1995) argues, society often has less tolerance for animal abuse than it does for violence toward humans. Further, stiffer penalties for animal maltreatment have been implemented in some jurisdictions, in part because of claims that animal cruelty is an indicator of an individual's potential to engage in interpersonal violence (Ascione 1998).

Finally, it is important that cross-training and cross-referrals occur between animal protection personnel and social service agency professionals. The link between violence toward human and nonhuman animals makes it imperative for those whose work focuses on one population to be aware that there may be other victims who are in serious need of assistance. Victims of interpersonal violence include both human and nonhuman animals. Efforts to prevent and end such violence must not only recognize the interconnections, but grant legitimacy to all victims, human and animal.

Questions for Discussion

1. What might batterers gain by threatening or actually harming a woman's companion animal?
2. What factors are related to whether a pet is harmed and whether a woman delays leaving an abusive relationship?
3. Why might a companion animal be particularly important to a battered woman?

19 Hoarding of Animals

An Under-recognized Public Health Problem in a Difficult-to-study Population

Gary J. Patronek

Unlike most forms of animal cruelty, hoarding, or "pathological collecting" of animals, is committed primarily by females. As the title suggests, hoarding is a phenomenon that has received little attention from researchers or policy makers, in part because of the difficulty of studying these individuals. This study, by veterinarian Gary Patronek, helps to correct this oversight, providing an estimate of the prevalence of hoarding and identifying several significant socio-demographic characteristics of hoarders.

The hoarding, or pathological collecting, of animals is a phenomenon that is poorly described in the scientific literature. MEDLINE searches using the terms "hoarder," "collector" (the term used by animal control agencies and humane societies), and "animal" revealed only one paper, published in 1981 (Worth and Beck 1981). Perhaps as a result of this lack of scientific attention, there has been no formal recognition of the syndrome and no systematic reporting of cases. Nevertheless, anecdotal reports from animal control agencies and humane societies suggest that animal hoarding occurs sporadically in almost every community in the United States. It is important to note that the phenomenon transcends the ownership of multiple pets and is not defined by the number of animals in a household. Collecting a large number of animals becomes a concern when the number overwhelms the ability of the hoarder to provide acceptable care. It is not uncommon for hoarders to have from dozens to hundreds of animals, often both living and dead, confined in apartments, trailers, cars, and houses (Worth and Beck 1981; Handy 1994; Lockwood and Cassidy 1988; Lockwood 1994; Magitti 1990; Mullen 1991). Sanitary conditions often deteriorate

Originally published in 1999 in *Public Health Reports*, vol. 114, pp. 81–87. Reprinted with permission from the Association of Schools of Public Health.

to the extent that dwellings must be condemned by public health authorities as unfit for human habitation. Unfortunately, because of ill health, contagious diseases, and the large numbers involved, euthanasia is often the only option for many of the animals rescued from such situations (Handy 1994; Lockwood and Cassidy 1988; Lockwood, 1994; Magitti 1990; Mullen 1991). By the time these situations have deteriorated to the point they cannot be ignored, expenses for veterinary services and housing of animals, litigation, and clean-up or demolition of premises can run into the tens of thousands of dollars.

Animal hoarding cases tend to fall within multiple jurisdictions or into the jurisdictional cracks between state and local government agencies and departments (for example, mental health, public health, aging, child welfare, zoning, building safety, animal control, sanitation, fish and wildlife), so it is the rule rather than the exception that they are procedurally cumbersome, time consuming, and costly to resolve. Although common sense suggests that the accumulation of large numbers of animals in human living spaces can have important public health implications, including placing neighborhoods at risk due to unsanitary living conditions, facilitating the spread of zoonotic diseases, and endangering the health of vulnerable household members, particularly children or dependent elderly, the potential for these consequences in animal hoarding cases is not widely appreciated by government agencies. As a result, systematic procedures for resolving these cases are lacking, as are effective preventive strategies.

Little information exists to guide communities. The author undertook the present study to obtain a rough estimate of the prevalence of animal hoarding, to characterize the pattern of interactions among agencies within the public health and social service systems in responding to these cases, and to stimulate greater awareness of this under-recognized problem.

Methods

One barrier to better characterizing the problem of hoarding of animals is that there is no identifiable sampling frame from which to obtain a random sample of cases. There is no standard definition of a hoarding case, no single type of public or private agency responsible for investigating these cases, and no standard investigative or reporting format. For this study, I used the following definition of a hoarder: someone who accumulates a large number of animals; fails to provide minimal standards of nutrition, sanitation, and veterinary care; and fails to act on the deteriorating condition of the animals (including disease, starvation, and even death) or the environment (severe overcrowding, extremely unsanitary conditions) or the negative effect of the collection on their own health and well-being and on that of other household members.

To obtain a sufficient number and geographically varied sample of cases, I identified large, well-established humane societies and animal control agencies likely to have animal cruelty investigative divisions through consultation with the Humane Society of the United States (HSUS), a national advocacy organization that often assists, but does not operate, local animal shelters and humane societies. Five regional offices of the HSUS provided a short list of approximately 25 organizations believed to have high quality investigative divisions, good case records, and a sufficient investigative caseload. I attempted to contact each of these organizations by telephone during April 1997 to introduce the study and screen them for their willingness and ability to participate. I ascertained whether each agency had an investigative division between 1992 and 1996 that had investigated animal hoarder cases and whether it was possible to retrieve and abstract case records. Reasons for non-participation included: failure to respond to my phone calls; lack of hoarder cases; lack of an investigative division; inability to retrieve case records; investigative staff employed between 1992 and 1996 no longer with the agency; or staff too busy to complete case reports.

Thirteen of the agencies met the criteria for participation and initially expressed interest in participating in the study. I asked each to retrospectively identify as many animal hoarder cases as possible from 1992 to 1996 and to complete a pretested standardized case report form. Ten agencies sent in a total of 54 completed case report forms. By state, the number of cases reported were: California 10, Colorado 4, Indiana 11, Michigan 11, Missouri 4, Pennsylvania 6, Texas 5, Vermont 3. The officer who investigated the case completed the case report form for 50 of the 54 cases. No personal identifiers were used in the case report forms. The case report form consisted predominantly of multiple choice questions that addressed the nature of the complaint and how the case came to the attention of the investigating agency; the number, type and condition of the animals present; the location of the animals and condition of the premises; whether the collector acknowledged the lack of sanitation; the extent (none, moderate, extensive) of hoarding of a variety of inanimate objects; the genders and ages of household members; the nature and timing of interaction with government agencies; and the final resolution of the case. Respondents were asked to rank, in order of decreasing frequency, the methods by which the hoarders acquired animals. In addition, there were several open-ended questions allowing respondents to elaborate on details or provide explanations for unique features of the case. In order to derive a rough estimate of prevalence, I also asked each agency to estimate the approximate human population served and, as a measure of caseload, the total number of animals taken in each year.

Results

Agencies' estimates of the number of hoarding cases investigated each year ranged from zero to 16. The mean number of new hoarding cases per year per 100,000 human population served was 0.80 (median 0.25). Based on a U.S. population of 265 million, this extrapolates to approximately 700 to 2000 cases per year in the United States. The mean number of new hoarding cases per year per 1000 animals handled was 0.27 (median 0.20). Based on the estimated national animal shelter population of six million (Patronek and Rowan 1995), this extrapolates to approximately 1200 to 1600 cases per year in the United States, within the range estimated based on the human population. Thirty-two (59.3%) cases involved repeated investigations of the same individual, and the median number of visits per case was 7.5. Cases came to the attention of authorities primarily through complaints from neighbors (Table 1). The most commonly reported reason for complaints was unsanitary conditions (Table 2).

Table 1 Method by Which Cases of Pathological Hoarding of Animals Were Brought to the Attention of Investigative Agencies (N=54 Cases)

Source of complaint	Number	Percent
Neighbor	31	57.4
Social service agency	12	22.2
Police	8	14.8
Service person visiting the household	5	9.3
Anonymous complaint	5	9.3
Friend	4	7.4
Landlord	4	7.4
Another humane agency	4	7.4
Relative	3	5.6
Household member	1	1.9
Veterinarian	1	1.9

NOTE: Percentages do not total 100 because complaints could come from more than one source.

Demographics of Hoarders and Households

The majority (76%) of the 54 hoarders were female. Ages were often approximate and were not recorded in three cases; 46.3% were described as 60 years of age or older; 37.0% were described as between 40 and 59 years of age; and 11.1% as younger than 40 years of age. Almost three-quarters (39, or 72.2%) were reported to be single, divorced, or widowed. Just over half (30, or 55.6%) were described as living in single-person households, and eight (14.8%) were reported as married or living with a significant other; marital status was unknown for seven (13%). There was a mean of 1.6 (median 1.0) people per household. Only three households included children, ranging in age from two to fifteen years. In the open-ended comments of officers completing the case report forms, two hoarders were described as having dependent elderly household members. Employment information was often unknown or missing, but when it was provided, hoarders were typically described as being on disability, retired, or unemployed. Most (38, or 71.7%) of the residences were single-family homes, seven (13.2%) were house trailers, five were apartments or condominiums, and three were other types of housing. As described by the officer completing the case report forms, 28 households (51.9%) were in urban areas, 15 (27.8%) in rural areas, and 11 (20.4%) in suburban areas.

Animals

Cats were involved in 65% of cases, dogs in 60%, farm animals in 11%, and birds in 11%. Officers reported a median of 39 animals per case, but there were four cases of more than 100 animals in a household. Nineteen (35.2%) cases involved a single species, 17 (31.5%) involved two species, 12 (22.2%) involved three species, and six (11. 1 %) involved four or more species. According to those completing the case reporting forms, animals were acquired primarily through unplanned breeding in the household or intentionally seeking or acquiring animals from outside the household (for example, advertising for animals in newspapers or picking up strays) (Table 3). Intentional breeding was relatively uncommon in these cases. In 43 cases (80%), animals were reportedly found dead or in poor condition (very malnourished, poor haircoat, with obvious disease or injury), and in 58% of these cases, the hoarder would not acknowledge to the investigating officer that a problem existed, according to the officers completing the case reports. Twenty-three (42.6%) hoarders reportedly knew all of their animals by name, whereas 18 (33.3%) knew few, if any, by name. It was routine for officers to inquire about the hoarder's motivation for acquiring so many animals. Open-ended questions on the case report form indicated that justifications for having the animals typically revolved around the hoarder's love for animals, the animals as surrogate children, feelings that no one else would care for the animals, and fear that they would be euthanized if taken to an animal shelter.

Table 2   Reasons for Complaints about Pathological Hoarding of Animals Being Brought to the Attention of Investigative Agencies (N=54 cases)

Problem stated in complaint	Number	Percent
Unsanitary conditions	41	75.9
Excessive number of animals	33	61.1
Animals needing medical attention	32	59.3
Odor	27	50.0
Malnourished animals	22	40.7
Accumulation of junk	15	27.8
Odd human behavior	9	16.7
Loose animals	8	14.8
Damage to buildings	7	13.0
Noise	4	7.4

NOTE: Percentages do not total 100 because more than one problem could be reported in a given case.

Table 3   Frequency Ranking of Methods by Which Animal Hoarders Acquired Animals (N=54 cases)

Method of accumulation of animals	RANKED FIRST		RANKED SECOND	
	Number	Percent	Number	Percent
Deliberate breeding	7	13.0	5	9.3
Unplanned breeding	21	38.9	13	24.1
Brought by public, unsolicited	5	9.3	7	13.0
Purchased	4	7.4	6	11.1
Sought from public or strays taken in	14	25.9	7	13.0

Household Characteristics

According to case reports, the living areas of the residences were inspected in 49 cases (90.7%). In 38 cases (77.6% of those inspected), the premises were described as heavily cluttered and unsanitary, and in 34 (69.4%) investigators reported finding accumulations of animal feces and urine in the human living areas (Table 4). Lack of a working bathroom was confirmed in 16 (32.7%) of the 49 cases, lack of working cooking facilities in 10 (20.4%), no electricity in three (6.1 %), no working refrigerator in 10 (20.4%), and no working heat in seven (14.3%). The hoarder's bed was reported by the investigator as having been soiled with human or animal urine or feces or both in 13 (26.5%) of the cases in which the premises were inspected.

Dead animals were found in 32 (59.3%) of residences. Respondents assigned unsanitary ratings (ratings 3–5) to 38 cases (70.4%) (Table 4). The clutter reportedly inhibited normal movement about the home in 32 (84.2%) of the 38 cases, inhibited access to the furniture in 27 (73.0%), to the kitchen in 25 (71.4%), and to the bathroom in 22 (62.9%), and interfered with basic human hygiene in 33 (89.2%). The hoarder acknowledged the lack of sanitation to the investigating officer in 10 (26.3%) of the 38 cases. Extensive accumulation of newspapers was noted in 14 (25.9%), of trash in 31 (38.9%), of pet food in nine (16.7%), and of human food items in five (9.3%). Other items noted as being hoarded included holiday decorations, paperback books, dolls and toys, pornography, plastic milk jugs, medicines, and clothing.

Table 4   Sanitary Rating of Animal Hoarders' Residences (N=54 cases)

Rating	Condition of human residence	Number	Percent
1	Reasonably clean and tidy	3	5.6
2	Moderately cluttered and some trash or garbage, but no urine or feces present in living and food preparation area	8	14.8
3	Heavily cluttered with trash and garbage, with unsanitary living and food preparation areas. Noticeable odor. Any urine or feces confined to animal cages	4	7.4
4	Heavily cluttered with trash and garbage, with unsanitary living and food preparation areas. Strong odor and fresh feces or urine in human living areas	12	22.2
5	Heavily cluttered with trash and garbage. Filthy environment with profuse urine or feces in living areas	22	40.7
	Unknown	5	9.3

Case Outcomes

Respondents' open-ended comments indicated that cases were often protracted and difficult to resolve and that even after removal of the animals, resumption of hoarding was common. In some cases, the hoarders simply disappeared and resurfaced months or years later in a neighboring jurisdiction, either with the same or new animals. One woman was reported as purchasing a new home every few years after each residence became uninhabitable.

In the open-ended comments, respondents noted that in 14 cases (26%), the hoarder was ultimately placed under guardianship, institutional care, or some form of supervised living, and in six (11%) the hoarder's premises were condemned as unfit for human habitation.

Results of prosecution included nine (17%) hoarders being prohibited from owning animals for a period, court-ordered ongoing monitoring for 10 hoarders (18%), and psychiatric evaluation of 13 of the hoarders (24%), while three individuals received short jail terms (10 days, 90 days, and six months). One hoarder was prohibited from owning more than three pets at a time for the remainder of his/her life.

According to the respondents, government agencies (public health, department of aging, child welfare, mental health, fire, and sanitation) were involved or consulted at some stage in 36 (66.7%) cases, and in 23 of these, some action or intervention was eventually taken. Several respondents expressed frustration at the perceived inability or unwillingness of mental health, social service, and public health authorities, including departments of aging, to intervene. The rationale frequently offered by these agencies was that hoarding is a lifestyle choice and not a public health or mental health issue.

However, in one case, according to the case report form, a woman initially evaluated and determined to be mentally competent subsequently died as a result of a wound on her foot that became infected in the contaminated environment of her home.

Discussion

These results are in agreement with other reports that animal hoarders tend to be female, older, and solitary, to concentrate on one or two species of animal, and to fail to acknowledge the extent of the lack of sanitation and animal suffering (Worth and Beck, 1981; Handy 1994; Lockwood and Cassidy 1988; Lockwood 1994; Magitti 1990; Mullen 1991). In the present study, there were a few cases in which minor children or dependent elderly relatives or housemates were present, which is of particular concern given the extent of the unsanitary conditions and lack of basic necessities (such as heat, a working bathroom, or a functional kitchen) in many of the residences. Unlike the hoarding of inanimate objects, which may be linked with a variety of psychiatric conditions animal hoarding has not yet been linked with any specific disorder (Greenburg 1987; Rasmussen and Eisen 1992; Frost, Hartl, Christian, and Williams 1995; Damecour and Charron 1998). This may be an additional factor that precludes or delays intervention through conventional mental health or social service avenues, leaving cases in the hands of animal control officials or humane societies. In fairness, the response of mental health agencies may be limited by laws requiring evidence of danger to the hoarder or other people before an intervention that infringes on civil liberties can be made. Studies to document the extent and nature of psychopathology in hoarders could provide justification for more rapid action.

In many communities, if a hoarder resists recommendations to improve conditions, the only recourse may be for humane societies or animal control departments to prosecute under animal cruelty laws. Besides being inefficient and expensive, this moves what may be a mental or public health issue into the criminal justice arena, which can impede timely recognition of important health issues and delivery of needed services. It does not help that, because of the bizarre nature of these situations, the eccentricity of some hoarders, and the sheer numbers of animals involved, the cases are often sensationalized in the media. Prosecution offers at best an incomplete solution in the majority of these cases, and it is no surprise that anecdotal reports from humane societies and animal control agencies indicate resumption of the behavior is common in those cases in which animals are removed as a result of prosecution. While it is premature to attach any diagnostic labels to animal hoarders, reports that at least a quarter of the hoarders were subsequently institutionalized or placed in guardianship or in a supervised living situation suggest that the behavior should at least be considered a warning sign for early stages of dementia or for as yet unspecified psychiatric conditions.

Because of the lack of an identifiable sampling frame from which to select humane societies and to identify those with investigative divisions, the great variability in the training and experience of investigators, the lack of consistent record keeping or inability to retrieve records, and difficulty in getting agreement from overburdened animal shelters to participate, a case series format using a convenience sample was the only feasible approach to begin to study this issue. In addition to the inability to obtain a random sample, other methodological limitations associated with studying this hard to reach population preclude making generalizations from this case series. Animal shelters are often not geared to data collection, and it was not possible to gather data for they vary considerably in the thoroughness with which they seek out, respond to, and monitor hoarder cases. Therefore, the prevalence estimate of 0.25 to 0.80 reported cases per 100,000 people is rough. It is, however, similar to the 0.40 per 100,000 estimated in 1981 in New York City using case records from 1973 to 1979 (see Worth and Beck 1981). Because of the secretive nature of hoarders, their tendency to repeat the behavior, and the lack of an investigating agency in some communities, the true prevalence is undoubtedly much higher.

These limitations have been a barrier to the study and recognition of the problem of animal hoarding and the development of coordinated, consistent, and effective responses by municipal agencies. Some communities have passed laws that attempt to place the burden for paying for animal care and rehabilitation on the owner when animals are placed under protective custody, but this approach fails to address many other problems related to human health and well-being and is moot when the hoarder is destitute. Others have attempted to prevent these situations by regulating the maximum number of pets owned in a community. A broad coalition representing the pet industry, breeders, and some animal welfare groups typically vigorously resists such actions on the grounds that they unfairly penalize responsible pet owners.

The present report will hopefully stimulate discussion of hoarding behavior; better record keeping and prospective surveillance by humane societies, animal control agencies, and health departments; and additional studies to characterize the psychological underpinnings of animal hoarding. More timely assessment and coordinated intervention would result in less trauma for the hoarder, would be less expensive for municipalities, could prevent substantial animal suffering, and could provide needed services for the humans and animals involved.

Questions for Discussion

1. Hoarding is one of the few forms of animal cruelty that is committed primarily by women? Why do you think that is so?
2. How serious a problem do you think animal hoarding is? Why is the estimated prevalence of 700–2000 cases likely an underestimate?
3. What do you think of the rationale for not intervening used by mental health, social service, and public health agencies, that "hoarding is a lifestyle choice and not a public health or mental health issue?"

Part VII: Inequality— Interconnected Oppressions

The animals of the world exist for their own reasons. They were not made for humans any more than black people were made for whites or women for men.

Alice Walker
(from the foreword to *The Dreaded Comparison* by Marjorie Spiegel)

20 An Historical Understanding

Marjorie Spiegel

In the first chapter to her classic book, The Dreaded Comparison: Human and Animal Slavery, *Marjorie Spiegel lays out the argument that both African Americans and animals have been treated in similar ways as a result of systems of domination in which religion, science, and other social institutions reinforce oppression of less powerful groups with ideologies that define members of those groups as inferior. Spiegel's book was the first to tackle the controversial undertaking of comparing a system of human oppression with our treatment of animals. She demonstrates that, historically and currently, social systems reproduce inequality for subordinate groups, whether they are defined by race or species.*

Pain is pain, whether it be inflicted on man or on beast; and the creature who suffers it, whether man or beast, being sensible to the misery of it, whilst it lasts, suffers evil. . . . The white man . . . can have no right, by virtue of his color, to enslave and tyrannize over a black man. . . . For the same reason, a man can have no natural right to abuse and torment a beast.—Dr. Humphrey Primatt, 1776

[The tyranny of human over nonhuman animals] has caused and today is still causing an amount of pain and suffering that can only be compared with that which resulted from the centuries of tyranny by white humans over black humans. The struggle against this tyranny is a struggle as important as any of the moral and social issues that have been fought over in recent years.—Peter Singer, 1974

Comparing speciesism with racism? At first glance, many people might feel that it is

---

insulting to compare the suffering of nonhuman animals to that of humans. In fact, in our society, comparison to an animal has come to be a slur.

Why is it an insult for anyone to be compared to an animal? In many cultures, such a comparison was an honor. In Native American cultures, for example, individuals adopted the names of admired animals, and had spirit guides—in animal form—who served both as teachers and escorts into the realms of the spirit world. Names such as Sitting Bull, Running Deer, and Hawkeye are familiar to us, expressive of the admiration Native Americans had for the animals with whom they shared both the earth and the afterlife. Native Americans, Ancient Egyptians, some African tribes, and many other ancient and aboriginal cultures the world over have worshiped various animals as gods or messengers to god. So how is it that we find ourselves in a time when comparison to a nonhuman animal has ceased to be an honor and is instead hurled as an insult?

By the time the New World was "discovered" and colonization began, Europeans had "subdued" most of the land which they had for centuries inhabited (Edlin 1947, 1958). Europe's wildernesses were long-gone, replaced with a very "managed" countryside comprised of "English gardens," rolling hills where mighty forests had long ago stood, and relatively few stands of woods, often maintained as hunting grounds.

Understandably, it came as quite a shock to the British colonists' psyches when they encountered the unbridled and deeply forested North American wilderness. The white Puritan colonists measured "progress" and "civilization" in terms of (among other things) how far a people could distance themselves from Nature. "Countless diaries, addresses and memorials of the frontier period," writes historian Roderick Nash, attest to this in their representations of "the wilderness as an 'enemy' which had to be 'conquered,' 'subdued,' and 'vanquished' by a 'pioneer army'" (Nash 1967, 27). To the average colonist, explains Nash,

> Wilderness . . . acquired significance as a dark and sinister symbol. [The pioneers] shared the long Western tradition of imagining wild country as a moral vacuum, a cursed and chaotic wasteland. As a consequence, frontiersmen acutely sensed that they battled wild country not only for personal survival but in the name of nation, race and God. Civilizing the New World meant enlightening darkness, ordering chaos, and changing evil into good. (Nash 1967, 24)

Holding these beliefs, white Christians were convinced that it was virtually a moral obligation to conquer any people who were still living in harmony with the devil-ridden, moral wasteland of nature—as "savages," in their opinion. Paying no regard to the level of cultural sophistication or even to the general happiness of the people living within their native societies, the conquerors merely saw "heathens" while proceeding to destroy entire cultures, along with the ancient ecosystems which had long supported them.

In 1688, the idea of the "noble savage" was introduced by English playwright and novelist Aphra Behn in *Oroonoko*. The noble savage hated his fellow slaves because they were

> by Nature Slaves, poor wretched Rogues, fit to be used as Christian Tools; Dogs, treacherous and cowardly, fit for such Masters; and they wanted only but to be whipped into the knowledge of the Christian Gods, to be the vilest of all creeping things. (Behn 1973, 66)

The slave who had thus capitulated to his master personified the beliefs about nature and the denizens of the natural world held by the Christian conquerors, who maintained that they were serving God by whipping nature, animals, and black people into submission. And how convenient that they could obtain a slave work force while performing their sanctimonious acts. After all, there could exist no moral obligation toward any of those in league with the forces of chaos, darkness, or the devil.

In the above passage by Aphra Behn we also see sign of the trend toward using comparison to an animal as an insult: "dogs, treacherous and cowardly. . . ." Centuries later, an excerpt from an essay by James Baldwin exemplifies the integral part which this comparison has come to play in blacks' consciousness as they continue to struggle for equality:

> The American triumph—in which the American tragedy has always been implicit—was to make Black people despise themselves. When I was little I despised myself; I did not know any better. And this meant, albeit unconsciously, or against my will, or in great pain, that I also despised my father. And my mother. And my brothers. And my sisters. Black people were killing each other every night out on Lenox Avenue, when I was growing up: and no one explained to them, or to me, that it was intended that they should; that they were penned where they were, like animals, in order that they should consider themselves no better than animals. Everything supported this sense of reality, nothing denied it; and so one was ready, when it came time to go to work, to be treated as a slave. (Baldwin 1971, 20–21)

All of this has a negative effect on the lives of human and nonhuman animals alike. As long as humans feel they are forced to defend their own rights and worth by placing someone beneath them, oppression will not end. This approach, at the very best, results only in an individual or group of people climbing up the ladder by pushing others down. There is evidence of this approach in the world today: racially motivated gang-wars among impoverished youth; in the United States, white working-class racist violence directed at working-class blacks, who suffer from the residual effects of slavery in the form of prejudice and job discrimination; in Britain, black youths attack Indian-owned businesses. It is unfortunately common that those who feel trapped within circumstances they feel powerless to change often quarrel among themselves, feeling even more powerless to impact those who actually make the laws, profit from the system, and exert great influence over economic opportunities.

But winding its way through the history of inequality within our culture has been another approach, which today grows ever stronger; its main tenet is that we cannot maintain that oppression is fine for some simply because they are not like us. Only through a rejection of violence and oppression *themselves* will we ever find a long-term "freedom and justice *for all*." It is not an "either-or" situation; the idea that one group will have its rights protected or respected only after another "more important" group is totally comfortable is finally being widely recognized as a delay tactic used by those resisting change. Women were told to keep waiting for years for their right to vote because other issues were "more important." Black people in the United States were told that their slavery was an "economic necessity" to be continued for the good of the country. Until the reforms of the early 1990s, blacks in South Africa were still being told that apartheid was necessary. Necessary for whom? Surely not the people who were living under this form of slavery.

With the exception of those who still cling—either overtly or subtly—to racist thought, most members of our society have reached the conclusion that it was and is wrong to treat blacks "like animals." But with regard to the animals themselves, most still feel that it is acceptable to treat them, to some degree or another, in exactly this same manner; to treat them, as we say, "like animals." That is, we have decided that treatment which is wholly unacceptable when received by a human being is in fact the *proper* manner in which to treat a nonhuman animal.

A line was arbitrarily drawn between white people and black people, a division which has since been rejected. But what of the line which has been drawn between human and nonhuman animals? We often behave as if there were a wide and bridge-less chasm, with humans on one side and all the rest of the animals on the other. Even our terminology reflects this attitude: we speak of "humans" in one breath, and in the next, lump all other animals into one grab-bag of a category entitled "nonhuman animals." On what basis was this line drawn? Surely the line, if it need be drawn at all, could have been placed with equal or greater accuracy in any one of a number of places. We are, for instance, much closer genetically and behaviorally to other primates than nonhuman primates are to toads. So perhaps the line could be drawn *after* other primates. Or, the line could just as reasonably be drawn so as to separate all mammals from other creatures, for mammals share common attributes which other animals lack.

But one problem with this approach is that it presupposes some sort of "worst-to-best" ascension list, ranging from the "simplest" beings straight up to human beings—at the top, of course. This attempt to rank species reflects a chronic misinterpretation and misapplication of Darwin's evolutionary theory, falsely concluding that humans are evolution's "finished product." On the contrary, Darwin's *Origin of Species* implied that humans were evolutionary first cousins to modern-day apes and orangutans, all distinctly and simultaneously evolving from a common ancestor, just as, for example, distinct species of cats branched off from an ancient feline form. Darwin went further, writing in his notebook that "animals may partake from our common origin in one ancestor . . . we may all be netted together."

Darwin was even more specific in his views about the commonalities between other animals and the human species. "The senses and intuitions," wrote Darwin in 1871, "the various emotions and faculties, such as love, memory, attention, curiosity, imitation, reason, etc. of which man boasts, may be found in an incipient, or sometimes even well-developed condition in," as they were often called in Darwin's day, "the lower animals" (Darwin 1871, 105). He concluded that "there is no fundamental difference between man and the higher mammals in their mental faculties" (Darwin 1871, 35).

Nevertheless, from the misconstrued concept that humans are evolutionarily better than animals it easily followed (to those who were predisposed to this position) that whites could be evolutionarily superior to blacks. In fact, based on the popularized (mis)interpretation of evolutionary theory came the trend of "Social Darwinism." Darwin had spoken of natural selection in relation to adaptation, but the Social Darwinists—usually the powerful or wealthy—adopted natural selection as the key to "progress." Darwin himself took great exception to this application of his theory, by which ruthless behavior toward different races, classes, or species could be rationalized and justified as being only a demonstration of evolution in action, a manifestation of "nature red in tooth and claw."

Before the concept of evolution was widely known and accepted, religious doctrine—which placed ("civilized," white, Christian) humans above all other beings—

served as a justification for the subjugation of both blacks (whom pro-slavery writers and orators often claimed were of a different species!) and nonhuman animals; this subjugation was said to be ordained by God. Later, under the banner of Social Darwinism, both the unmitigated violence toward the "lower" animals and the enslavement of black "savages" in Africa were looked at as expressions of an evolutionary birthright.

Common only a quarter-century ago were charts depicting the evolution of primates from distant ancestors, up through various hominids, to a black person, and finally to a fully upright Aryan male. Without much of an uproar over their scientifically cloaked, subtly racist message (nor their poor science with regard to human evolution, human biology, and our relation to other modern primates), these charts were quietly retired. But they might give us some reason to pause as we consider a similar ranking system which places *all humans* up on the evolutionary pedestal, to the exclusion of other animals.

As we have seen, Darwin himself believed that evolutionary history is no basis for deciding "who is better than whom." Evolution occurs as the result of genetic mutations and there is no moral basis for declaring that the mutated form is better than the unmutated ancestral form. But even comparison of a modern species to its own evolutionary predecessors makes better sense than what is usually attempted: comparison of humans to other animals from completely different biological families, in an effort to determine "which is best." Actually, in evolutionary time, humans are relatively new additions to the landscape; our current stage of development finds us without a harmonious or stable position within an ecosystem. Nor have we yet "worked out" all the quirks in our physiology or behavior, leaving our species with significant problems which simply don't exist for the members of most other highly complex species.

But is any of this relevant in determining if humans or any other animals are "worthy" of moral consideration? What are the qualities which a being need possess before treating them "like an animal" would be unacceptable? The more we learn about the earth's environment, its ecosystems, and the creatures who live here, the more we see the absurdity in the concept of ranking species against one another. All life on earth is inextricably bound together in a web of mutual interdependence. Within that web, each species of animal has a niche for which it is more or less adapted, and attributes which others lack. It is only an anthropocentric worldview which makes qualities possessed by humans to be those by which all other species are measured.

If the earth was suddenly colonized by a species more powerful and bellicose than human beings, they could just as easily use attributes special to themselves when devising their ranking system. Let us suppose that by chance the aliens closely resembled a member of the cat family. They might decide to use the ability to see in near-darkness as the determining factor for who was worthy of freedom and who would be exterminated or enslaved. Measured against the standards of the alien cats, virtually all humans would be miserably lacking and, if those cats were anything like us when it came to ethics, humans would spend their lives in bondage. Their use of night-vision as a criterion would only be as *self-biased* as the criteria which we have decided to use. But it is we rather than the alien cousins of cats who are presently calling the shots, and as such we have made those characteristics which are claimed to be *exclusively human attributes* the requirements for moral consideration.

Many philosophers have clearly comprehended our bias. In the sixteenth century, Michel Eyquem de Montaigne wrote extensively on the subject. "I see some animals," Montaigne reflected, "that live so entire and perfect as life, some without sight, others without hearing: who knows whether to us also one, two, or three, or many other senses, may not be wanting" (Montaigne 1580–8a, 353). Some two centuries later, Lichtenberg made it clear that he thought it foolish to unfavorably judge another creature by human standards. Equally foolish was it to believe that human attributes were any more or less remarkable than those special to another species. "The most accomplished monkey," observed Lichtenberg, "cannot draw a monkey, this too only man can do; just as it is also only man who regards his ability to do this as a distinct merit" (Lichtenberg 1764–99, 6). It is only human arrogance that is able to find beauty and perfection exclusively in those things human. "Just as foolish," continued Lichtenberg, "as it must look to a crab when it sees a man walk forward" (Lichtenberg 1764–99, 4).

Despite periodic voices of reason, action and tradition still demanded proof of our "superiority," in the form of vital differences, that would provide justification for man's dominion over the animals. What are those elusive solely human qualities? Included among a veritable laundry list of attributes compiled in this exhaustive search for exclusivity are the ability to feel pain, to feel emotions, to reason, the possession of a soul, the ability to make free choices, and to speak a language—all claimed at one time or another to be features unique to human beings.[1]

In direct conflict with Darwin's views on the subject were those espoused, two centuries earlier, by René Descartes, a stalwart proponent of human superiority over nonhuman animals. Descartes believed animals lacked souls (whereas humans possessed them), intelligence, and even the ability to feel—pleasure, pain, or *anything*. If you struck one, the animal would cry out only in the same manner as a clock would chime, as a result of the workings of similar internal mechanisms. Bolstered by such Cartesian philosophy, physiological experiments on animals became an even more macabre endeavor, since any cries, any displays of suffering or efforts to escape, were viewed as the sounds and movements of veritable wind-up toys.

While very few people today would publicly declare themselves in agreement with such extreme views, in our treatment of most nonhuman animals, we still behave like true Cartesians. And while most people, I believe, informally and in theory agree with Darwin's views which recognize that animals are thinking, feeling beings, we still search for the moral loophole—the quality or qualities possessed by humans and lacked by nonhuman animals—that will enable us to find a defensible reason to justify continuing to treat animals "like animals." Yet all false claims of behavioral uniqueness and exclusivity are easily dismissed with common sense and unprejudiced observation. On the subject of *reason*, one modern essayist argued:

> Although animals are unable to do algebra, they are able to make rational decisions regarding their own interests. Dogs, for example, would never be so irrational as to intentionally inhale smoke; they must be forced to do this by contemporary "researchers." I think it is safe to say that animals, in their own way, are at least as reasonable — that is, rational in pursuit of their own interests—as human beings (Phillips 1986).

Attempts at moral disqualification on the basis of reason have not been used to exclude only nonhuman animals from the sphere of consideration. For centuries, black people were called "irrational," and this was used both as a reason to continue their "protective custody" (in the form of slavery), and to justify their virtually limitless abuse. Just as this claim has been popularly abandoned with regard to blacks, so too is it finally being widely disproved and retired with regard to animals.

Anyone who has spent time around animals knows that they both communicate with each other and try, with varying degrees of success, to communicate with our species. Montaigne suggested that both *they and we* fail equally at attempts to bridge the inter-species communication gap, and are equally frustrated. "This defect that hinders communication between them and us, why is it not just as much ours as theirs?" he asked. "We have some mediocre understanding of their meaning; so do they of ours, in about the same degree. They flatter us, threaten us, implore us, and we them" (Montaigne 1580–8b).

Not a hundred years later, Descartes, in his determined way, drew an altogether different conclusion. "All human beings," he began, "no matter how dull or stupid, even madmen, can arrange various words together and fashion them into a discourse. . . . Contrariwise," he continued,

> no animal however perfect or well-bred can do anything of the sort. This is not simply because they lack the right organs, because magpies and parrots can learn to utter words as well as we can . . . and people born deaf and mute—who are at least as handicapped as the beasts are—have the custom of inventing their own signs, with which they communicate.

"It seems incredible," concluded Descartes, "that the very best and brightest of monkeys or parrots could not learn to speak as well as the stupidest child . . . unless their souls were of an entirely different nature from our own" (Descartes 1953).

With the continued exception of some species of birds, animals still lack, of course, the vocal chords needed for verbal communication on our terms. Yet some of us are communicating with animals in ways which would make even Descartes take notice. Chimpanzees, orangutans, and gorillas have all been taught to communicate with humans through American Sign Language. Washoe, the first chimp to learn ASL, taught her adopted baby to sign. Perhaps best known is a gorilla named Koko, who since 1972 has been communicating with scientist Francine Patterson. Koko has a vocabulary in ASL of over 1000 words and understands spoken English, using ASL to respond. She can also read some printed words, including her own name, and creates new compound words to express thoughts and feelings her taught vocabulary did not provide for.

It's not only primates who are capable of such "human" communication. Jeffrey Moussaieff Masson cites the case of a parrot who unquestionably disproves the accepted belief that these birds can only repeat, devoid of context, remembered phrases. Left by his trainer at a veterinarian's office, the parrot pleaded, "Come here. I love you. I'm sorry. I want to go back" (Masson and McCarthy 1995, 229).[2]

Yet even if some vast, undeniable distinction between humans and animals could finally be found, would that mean that we could then justify using, mistreating, even torturing, animals? Could we then say, as did eighteenth-century writer Thomas Love Peacock, that "nothing could be more obvious, than that all animals were created solely and exclusively for the use of man"?[3] From any perspective other than one predisposed to slave-holding, we could not; that special, mythical quality or attribute that was the sole domain of humans would still be irrelevant. For what does someone's ability to speak French, drive a car, see in the dark, do algebraic equations, or use a tool, have to do with whether or not it is acceptable or just to enslave, torture, or in some other way inflict cruelty upon them? The only *relevant* requirement which should be necessary to keep us from unnecessarily inflicting pain and suffering on someone is that individual's ability to feel pain and to suffer. Similarly, the only qualification individuals should need to make it wrong for us to dominate their lives is that they *possess life*, that they are alive. All of these other questions of abilities and attributes can fill philosophy books, but are, for these issues, irrelevant.

This is not intended to oversimplify matters and to imply that the oppressions experienced by any human group and animals have taken *identical* forms. A complex web of social, political, and economic factors sustained slavery and made possible the life of a slave as it was known. This book in no way attempts to make the case that these factors are the same for animals; there are distinct social, political, and economic factors which create and support the subjugation of animals, as well as differences between the possible manners in which enslaved humans and animals could respond to their respective enslavements. But, as divergent as the cruelties and the supporting systems of oppression may be, there are commonalities between them. They share the same basic essence, they are built around the same basic relationship—that between oppressor and oppressed.

So, while the experiences of black slaves in the antebellum United States were unique to that system, there are many disturbing similarities between their treatment at the hands of white people during that period, and the treatment of animals at the hands of a large sector of the American population. Indeed, just as humans are oppressed the world over, animals receive poor treatment in nearly every human culture on earth.

Further, any oppression helps to support other forms of domination. This is why it is vital to link oppressions in our minds, to look for the common, shared aspects, and work against them as one, rather than prioritizing victims' suffering—(what we have already identified as the "either-or" pitfall). For when we prioritize we are in effect becoming one with the "master." We are deciding that one individual or group is more important than another, deciding that one individual's pain is less important than that of the next. A common result of prioritization is infighting among the oppressed or defenders of the oppressed, doing tragically little to upset the very foundations of cruelty.

Comparing the suffering of animals to that of blacks, women, or any other historically oppressed group is offensive only to the speciesist: one who adheres to such a severely prejudicial view of the other beings with whom we share this earth as to see them as not even worthy of our consideration, much less their own freedom. Those who are offended by the comparison of one's own suffering, or other forms of human suffering, to that experienced by a fellow sufferer have unquestioningly accepted the biased worldview presented by the masters. To deny the commonalities between the injustices inflicted upon animals and those which we as humans have suffered is to side with the oppressors, and to adopt the master mentality. It is to continue actively struggling to prove to our masters, past or present, that we are *similar to those who have abused us*, rather than to our fellow victims, those whom our masters have also victimized.

Let us remember that to those with a master mentality, there is often very little difference between one victim and the next. When blacks or another group of humans and animals are viewed as being "oppressible," the cruelties perpetrated upon them take similar forms. In later chapters we will explore whether these similarities are due to mere chance or to something which operates deep in the minds of the masters. In the meantime, let us note that the domination of animals, which was being honed to a clumsy science centuries before black slavery in America began, was in many cases used as a prototype for the subjugation of blacks. So observed Keith Thomas in his important study *Man and the Natural World*:

> Once perceived as beasts, people were liable to be treated accordingly. The ethic of human domination removed animals from the sphere of human concern. But it also legitimized the ill-treatment of humans who were in a supposedly animal condition. In the colonies, slavery, with its markets, its brandings and its constant labor, was one way of dealing with men thought to be beastly. The Portuguese, reported one English traveler, marked slaves "as we do sheep, with a hot iron," and at the slave market at Constantinople, Moryson saw the buyers taking their slaves indoors to inspect them naked, handling them "as we handle beasts, to know their fatness and strength" (Thomas 1983).[4]

The suffering animals currently endure at the hands of human beings in laboratories, on "factory farms," as pets, and in the wild, sadly parallels that endured by black people in the antebellum United States and during the lingering postbellum period. The parallels of experience are numerous. Both humans and animals share the ability to suffer from restricted freedom of movement, from the loss of social freedom, and to experience pain at the loss of a loved one. Both groups suffer or suffered from their common capacity to be terrified by being hunted, tormented, or injured. Both have been "objectified," treated as property rather than as feeling, self-directed individuals. And both blacks, under the system of slavery, and animals were driven to a state of total psychic and physical defeat, as a result of all or some of the variables mentioned above. (With animals, of course, this continues today in its most extreme form.)

From all of this we see that the liberation of animals, while a pressing and worthy goal in its own right, is not of importance only to nonhuman animals. While people are no longer branded, inspected at auction, or displayed in zoos, subtler forms of oppression are still in operation which have their counterparts in animals' slavery. Advances toward releasing animals from our domination and control of their lives will also serve to lessen the oppression of human groups who are viewed prejudicially, and who suffer under the weight of someone else's power. By eliminating the oppression of animals from the fabric of our culture, we begin to undermine some of the psychological structures inherent in a society which seems to create and foster masters. With a philosophy of universal respect for others' lives, treating anyone—human or nonhuman—in a cruel manner begins to be unthinkable.

The views . . . of such eminent thinkers, writers, and activists as Frederick Douglass, Harriet Beecher Stowe, Richard Wright, Paul Lawrence Dunbar, and many others, show us that they were acutely aware of the similarities between human and animal slavery. Let us follow their example and begin to reject oppression in all its forms.

> [Slaves] have been treated by the law upon the same footing as in England, for example, the . . . animals are still. The day may come when the rest of animal creation may acquire those rights which could never have been withholden from them but by the hand of tyranny. [Some] have already discovered that the blackness of skin is no reason why a human being should be abandoned without redress to the caprice of a tormentor. It may come one day to be recognized, that the number of legs, the villosity of the skin, or the termination of the os sacrum, are reasons equally insufficient for abandoning a sensitive being to the same fate. . . . The question is not, Can they reason? nor, Can they talk? but, Can they suffer?—Jeremy Bentham, *The Principles of Morals and Legislation*, 1789

Questions for Discussion

1. According to Spiegel, how are racism and speciesism similar?
2. What role did religion play in shaping our attitudes toward blacks and nonhuman animals?
3. Why might progress in the treatment of other animals be related to better treatment of human "others"?

21 The Sexual Politics of Meat

Carol J. Adams

In this chapter from her groundbreaking book of the same title, Carol Adams skillfully makes the connection between meat and power. Adams reveals that meat eating has always been associated with privilege, particularly male privilege. The Sexual Politics of Meat *identifies and analyzes the link between the oppression of women and the oppression of other animals. The association of femininity with vegetables and weaknesses is juxtaposed to the association of masculinity with meat and power. Meat, says Adams, is a symbol of patriarchy.*

Myth from the Bushman:

In the early times men and women lived apart, the former hunting animals exclusively, the latter pursuing a gathering existence. Five of the men, who were out hunting, being careless creatures, let their fire go out. The women, who were careful and orderly, always kept their fire going. The men, having killed a springbok, became desperate for means to cook it, so one of their number set out to get fire, crossed the river and met one of the women gathering seeds. When he asked her for some fire, she invited him to the feminine camp. While he was there she said, "You are very hungry. Just wait until I pound up these seeds and I will boil them and give you some." She made him some porridge. After he had eaten it, he said, "Well, it's nice food so I shall just stay with you." The men who were left waited and wondered. They still had the springbok and they still had no fire. The second man set out, only to be tempted by female cooking, and to take up residence in the camp of the women. The same thing happened to the third man. The two men left were very frightened. They suspected something terrible had happened to their comrades. They cast the divining bones but the omens were favorable. The fourth man set out timidly, only to end by joining his comrades. The last man became very frightened indeed and besides by now the springbok had rotted. He took his bow and arrows and ran away (Hays 1964).

Originally published in 1990 in *The Sexual Politics of Meat*, pp. 25–38. Reprinted with permission from Continuum International.

I left the British Library and my research on some women of the 1890s whose feminist, working-class newspaper advocated meatless diets, and went through the cafeteria line in a restaurant nearby. Vegetarian food in hand, I descended to the basement. A painting of Henry VIII eating a steak and kidney pie greeted my gaze. On either side of the consuming Henry were portraits of his six wives and other women. However, they were not eating steak and kidney pie, nor anything else made of meat. Catherine of Aragon held an apple in her hands. The Countess of Mar had a turnip, Anne Boleyn—red grapes, Anne of Cleaves—a pear, Jane Seymour—blue grapes, Catherine Howard—a carrot, Catherine Parr—a cabbage.

People with power have always eaten meat. The aristocracy of Europe consumed large courses filled with every kind of meat while the laborer consumed the complex carbohydrates. Dietary habits proclaim class distinctions, but they proclaim patriarchal distinctions as well. Women, second-class citizens, are more likely to eat what are considered to be second-class foods in a patriarchal culture: vegetables, fruits, and grains rather than meat. The sexism in meat eating recapitulates the class distinctions with an added twist: a mythology permeates all classes that meat is a masculine food and meat eating a male activity.

Male Identification and Meat Eating

Meat-eating societies gain male identification by their choice of food, and meat textbooks heartily endorse this association. *The Meat We Eat* proclaims meat to be "A Virile and Protective Food," thus "a liberal meat supply has always been associated with a happy and virile people" (Ziegler 1966). *Meat Technology* informs us that "the virile Australian race is a typical example of heavy meat-eaters" (Gerrard 1945). Leading gourmands refer "to the virile ordeal of spooning the brains directly out of a barbecued calf's head" (Root and de Rochemont 1976). *Virile: of or having the characteristics of an adult male*, from *vir* meaning *man*. Meat eating measures individual and societal virility.

Meat is a constant for men, intermittent for women, a pattern painfully observed in famine situations today. Women are starving at a rate disproportionate to men. Lisa Leghorn and Mary Roodkowsky surveyed this phenomenon in their book *Who Really Starves? Women and World Hunger*. Women, they conclude, engage in deliberate self-deprivation, offering men the "best" foods at the expense of their own nutritional needs. For instance, they tell us that "Ethiopian women and girls of all classes are obliged to prepare two meals, one for the males and a second, often containing no meat or other substantial protein for the females (Leghorn and Roodkowsky 1977).

In fact, men's protein needs are less than those of pregnant and nursing women and the disproportionate distribution of the main protein source occurs when women's need for protein is the greatest. Curiously, we are now being told that one should eat meat (or fish, vegetables, chocolate, and salt) at least six weeks before becoming pregnant if one wants a boy. But if a girl is desired, no meat please, rather milk, cheese, puts, beans, and cereals (Shearer 1982).

Fairy tales initiate us at an early age into the dynamics of eating and sex roles. The king in his counting-house ate four-and-twenty blackbirds in a pie (originally four-and-twenty naughty boys) while the Queen ate bread and honey. Cannibalism in fairy tales is generally a male activity, as Jack, after climbing his beanstalk, quickly learned. Folktales of all nations depict giants as male and "fond of eating human flesh" (Baring-Gould and Baring-Gould 1962, 103). Witches—warped or monstrous women in the eyes of a patriarchal world—become the token female cannibals.

A Biblical example of the male prerogative for meat rankled Elizabeth Cady Stanton, a leading nineteenth-century feminist, as can be seen by her terse comment on Leviticus 6 in *The Woman's Bible*: "The meat so delicately cooked by the priests, with wood and coals in the altar, in clean linen, no woman was permitted to taste, only the males among the children of Aaron" (Stanton 1898, 91).

Most food taboos address meat consumption and they place more restrictions on women than on men. The common foods forbidden to women are chicken, duck, and pork. Forbidding meat to women in non-technological cultures increases its prestige. Even if the women raise the pigs, as they do in the Solomon Islands, they are rarely allowed to eat the pork. When they do receive some, it is at the dispensation of their husbands. In Indonesia "flesh food is viewed as the property of the men. At feasts, the principal times when meat is available, it is distributed to households according to the men in them. . . . The system of distribution thus reinforces the prestige of the men in society" (Simoons, 1961).

Worldwide this patriarchal custom is found. In Asia, some cultures forbid women from consuming fish, seafood, chicken, duck, and eggs. In equatorial Africa, the prohibition of chicken to women is common. For example, the Mbum Kpau women do not eat chicken, goat, partridge, or other game birds. The Kufa of Ethiopia punished women who ate chicken by making them slaves, while the Walamo "put to death anyone who violated the restriction of eating fowl."

Correspondingly, vegetables and other non-meat foods are viewed as women's food. This makes them undesirable to men. The Nuer men think that eating eggs is effeminate. In other groups men require sauces to disguise the fact that they are eating women's foods. "Men expect to have meat sauces to go with their porridge and will sometimes refuse to eat sauces made of greens or other vegetables, which are said to be women's food" (O'Laughlin 1974).

Meat: For the Man Only

There is no department in the store where good selling can do so much good or where poor selling can do so much harm as in the meat department. This is because most women do not consider themselves competent judges of meat quality and often buy where they have confidence in the meat salesman.—Hinman and Harris (1939)

In technological societies, cookbooks reflect the presumption that men eat meat. A random survey of cookbooks reveals that the barbecue sections of most cookbooks are addressed to men and feature meat. The foods recommended for a "Mother's Day Tea" do not include meat, but readers are advised that on Father's Day, dinner should include London Broil because "a steak dinner has unfailing popularity with fathers." In a chapter on "Feminine Hospitality" we are directed to serve vegetable salads and soups (Sunset Books 1969). The New *McCall's* Cookbook suggests that a man's favorite dinner is London Broil. A "Ladies' Luncheon" would consist of cheese dishes and vegetables, but no meat. A section of one cookbook entitled "For Men Only" reinforces the omnipresence of meat in men's lives. What is for men only? London Broil, cubed steak, and beef dinner.[1]

Twentieth-century cookbooks only serve to confirm the historical pattern found in the nineteenth century, when British working-class families could not afford sufficient meat to feed the entire family. "For the men only" appears continually in many of the menus of these families when referring to meat. In adhering to the mythologies of a culture (men need meat; meat gives bull-like strength) the male "breadwinner" actually received the meat. Social historians report that the "lion's share" of meat went to the husband.

What then was for women during the nineteenth century? On Sunday they might have a modest but good dinner. On the other days their food was bread with butter or drippings, weak tea, pudding, and vegetables. "The wife, in very poor families, is probably the worst-fed of the household," observed Dr. Edward Smith in the first national food survey of British dietary habits in 1863, which revealed that the major difference in the diet of men and women in the same family was the amount of meat consumed (Smith 1864). Later investigators were told that the women and children in one rural county of England, "eat the potatoes and look at the meat (Oren 1973).

Where poverty forced a conscious distribution of meat, men received it. Many women emphasized that they had saved the meat for their husbands. They were articulating the prevailing connections between meat eating and the male role: "I keep it for him; he has to have it." Sample menus for South London laborers "showed extra meat, extra fish, extra cakes, or a different quality of meat for the man." Women ate meat once a week with their children, while the husband consumed meat and bacon, "almost daily."

Early in the present century, the Fabian Women's group in London launched a four-year study in which they recorded the daily budget of thirty families in a working-class community. These budgets were collected and explained in a compassionate book, *Round About a Pound a Week*. Here is perceived clearly the sexual politics of meat: "In the household which spends 10s or even less on food, only one kind of diet is possible, and that is the man's diet. The children have what is left over. There must be a Sunday joint, or, if that be not possible, at least a Sunday dish of meat, in order to satisfy the father's desire for the kind of food he relishes, and most naturally therefore intends to have." More succinctly, we are told: "Meat is bought for the men" and the leftover meat from the Sunday dinner, "is eaten cold by him the next day" (Reeves 1913). Poverty also determines who carves the meat. As Cicely Hamilton discovered during this same period, women carve when they know there is not enough meat to go around (Hamilton 1909).

In situations of abundance, sex role assumptions about meat are not so blatantly expressed. For this reason, the diets of English upper-class women and men are much more similar than the diets of upper-class women and working-class women. Moreover, with the abundance of meat available in the United States as opposed to the restricted amount available in England, there has been enough for all, except when meat supplies were controlled. For instance, while enslaved black men received half a pound of meat per day, enslaved black women often found that they received little more than a quarter pound a day at times (Savitt 1978, 91). Additionally, during the wars of the twentieth century, the pattern of meat consumption recalled that of English nineteenth-century working-class families with one variation: the "worker" of the country's household, the soldier, got the meat; civilians were urged to learn how to cook without meat.

The Racial Politics of Meat

The hearty meat eating that characterizes the diet of Americans and of the Western world is not only a symbol of male power, it is an index of racism. I do not mean racism in the sense that we are treating one class of animals, those that are not human beings, differently than we treat another, those that are, as Isaac Bashevis

Singer uses the term in *Enemies: A Love Story:* "As often as Herman had witnessed the slaughter of animals and fish, he always had the same thought: in their behavior toward creatures, all men were Nazis. The smugness with which man could do with other species as he pleased exemplified the most extreme racist theories, the principle that might is right" (Singer 1972, 257). I mean racism as the requirement that power arrangements and customs that favor white people prevail, and that the acculturation of people of color to this standard includes the imposition of white habits of meat eating.

Two parallel beliefs can be traced in the white Western world's enactment of racism when the issue is meat eating. The first is that if the meat supply is limited, white people should get it; but if meat is plentiful all should eat it. This is a variation on the standard theme of the sexual politics of meat. The hierarchy of meat protein reinforces a hierarchy of race, class, and sex.

Nineteenth-century advocates of white superiority endorsed meat as superior food. "Brain-workers" required lean meat as their main meal, but the "savage" and "lower" classes of society could live exclusively on coarser foods, according to George Beard, a nineteenth-century medical doctor who specialized in the diseases of middle-class people. He recommended that when white, civilized, middle-class men became susceptible to nervous exhaustion, they should eat more meat. To him, and for many others, cereals and fruits were lower than meat on the scale of evolution, and thus appropriate foods for the other races and white women, who appeared to be lower on the scale of evolution as well. Racism and sexism together upheld meat as white man's food.

Influenced by Darwin's theory of evolution, Beard proposed a corollary for foods; animal protein did to vegetable food what our evolution from the lower animals did for humans. Consequently:

> In proportion as man grows sensitive through civilization or through disease, he should diminish the quantity of cereals and fruits, which are far below him on the scale of evolution, and increase the quantity of animal food, which is nearly related to him in the scale of evolution, and therefore more easily assimilated (Beard 1898, 272–278).

In his racist analysis, Beard reconciled the apparent contradiction of this tenet: "Why is it that savages and semi-savages are able to live on forms of food which, according to the theory of evolution, must be far below them in the scale of development?" In other words, how is that people can survive very well without a great deal of animal protein? Because "savages" are little removed from the common animal stock from which they are derived. They are much nearer to the forms of life from which they feed than are the highly civilized brain-workers, and can therefore subsist on forms of life which would be most poisonous to us. Secondly, savages who feed on poor food are poor savages, and intellectually far inferior to the beef-eaters of any race.

This explanation—which divided the world into intellectually superior meat eaters and inferior plant eaters—accounted for the conquering of other cultures by the English:

The rice-eating Hindoo and Chinese and the potato-eating Irish peasant are kept in subjection by the well-fed English. Of the various causes that contributed to the defeat of Napoleon at Waterloo, one of the chief was that for the first time he was brought face to face with the nation of beef-eaters, who stood still until they were killed.

Into the twentieth century the notion was that meat eating contributed to the Western world's preeminence. Publicists for a meat company in the 1940s wrote: "We know meat-eating races have been and are leaders in the progress made by mankind in its upward struggle through the ages" (Hinman and Harris 1939, 1). They are referring to the "upward struggle" of the white race. One revealing aspect of this "upward struggle" is the charge of cannibalism that appeared during the years of colonization.

The word "cannibalism" entered our vocabulary after the "discovery" of the "New World." Derived from the Spaniards' mispronunciation of the name of the people of the Caribbean, it linked these people of color with the act. As Europeans explored the continents of North and South America and Africa, the indigenous peoples of those lands became accused of cannibalism—the ultimate savage act. Once labeled as cannibals, their defeat and enslavement at the hands of civilized, Christian whites became justifiable. W. Arens argues that the charge of cannibalism was part and parcel of the European expansion into other continents (Arens 1979).

Of the charges of cannibalism against the indigenous peoples, Arens found little independent verification. One well-known source of dubious testimony on cannibalism was then plagiarized by others claiming to be eyewitnesses. The eyewitnesses fail to describe just how they were able to escape the fate of consumption they report witnessing. Nor do they explain how the language barrier was overcome enabling them to report verbatim conversations with "savages." In addition, their reports fail to maintain internal consistency.

One cause of cannibalism was thought to be lack of animal protein. Yet most Europeans themselves during the centuries of European expansion were not subsisting on animal protein every day. The majority of cultures in the world satisfied their protein needs through vegetables and grains. By charging indigenous peoples with cannibalism (and thus demonstrating their utterly savage ways, for they supposedly did to humans what Europeans only did to animals) one justification for colonization was provided.

Racism is perpetuated each time meat is thought to be the best protein source. The emphasis on the nutritional strengths of animal protein distorts the dietary history of most cultures in which complete protein dishes were made of vegetables and grains. Information about these dishes is overwhelmed by an ongoing cultural and political commitment to meat eating.

Meat Is King

During wartime, government rationing policies reserve the right to meat for the epitome of the masculine man: the soldier. With meat rationing in effect for civilians during World War II, the per capita consumption of meat in the army and navy was about two-and-a-half times that of the average civilian. Russell Baker observed that World War II began a "beef madness . . . when richly fatted beef was force-fed into every putative American warrior" (Baker 1973). In contrast to the recipe books for civilians that praised complex carbohydrates, cookbooks for soldiers contained variation upon variation of meat dishes. One survey conducted of four military training camps reported that the soldier consumed daily 131 grams of protein, 201 grams of fat, and 484 grams of carbohydrates (Altschul 1965). Hidden costs of warring masculinity are to be found in the provision of male-defined foods to the warriors.

Women are the food preparers; meat has to be cooked to be palatable for people. Thus, in a patriarchal culture, just as our culture accedes to the "needs" of its soldiers, women accede to the dietary demands of their husbands, especially when it comes to meat. The feminist surveyors of women's budgets in the early twentieth century observed:

> It is quite likely that someone who had strength, wisdom, and vitality, who did not live that life in those tiny, crowded rooms, in that lack of light and air, who was not bowed down with worry, but was herself economically independent of the man who earned the money, could lay out his few shillings with a better eye to a scientific food value. It is quite as likely, however, that the man who earned the money would entirely refuse the scientific food, and demand his old tasty kippers and meat (Reeves 1913, 131).

A discussion of nutrition during wartime contained this aside: it was one thing, they acknowledged, to demonstrate that there were many viable alternatives to meat, "but it is another to convince a man who enjoys his beefsteak" (Hunscher and Huyck 1944). The male prerogative to eat meat is an external, observable activity implicitly reflecting a recurring fact: meat is a symbol of male dominance.

It has traditionally been felt that the working man needs meat for strength. A superstition analogous to homeopathic principles operates in this belief: in eating the muscle of strong animals, we will become strong. According to the mythology of patriarchal culture, meat promotes strength; the attributes of masculinity are achieved through eating these masculine foods. Visions of meat-eating football players, wrestlers, and boxers lumber in our brains in this equation. Though vegetarian weight lifters and athletes in other fields have demonstrated the equation to be fallacious, the myth remains: men are strong, men need to be strong, thus men need meat. The literal evocation of male power is found in the concept of meat.

Irving Fisher took the notion of "strength" from the definition of meat eating as long ago as 1906. Fisher suggested that strength be measured by its lasting power rather than by its association with quick results, and compared meat-eating athletes with vegetarian athletes and sedentary vegetarians. Endurance was measured by having the participants perform in three areas: holding their arms horizontally for as long as possible, doing deep knee bends, and performing leg raises while lying down. He concluded that the vegetarians, whether athletes or not, had greater endurance than meat eaters. "Even the *maximum* record of the flesh-eaters was barely more than half the *average* for the flesh-abstainers" (Fisher 1907).

Meat is king: this noun describing meat is a noun denoting male power. Vegetables, a generic term meat eaters use for all foods that are not meat, have become as associated with women as meat is with men, recalling on a subconscious level the days of Woman the Gatherer. Since women have been made subsidiary in a male-dominated, meat-eating world, so has our food. The foods associated with second-class citizens are considered to be second-class protein. Just as it is thought a woman cannot make it on her own, so we think that vegetables cannot make a meal on their own, despite the fact that meat is only secondhand vegetables and vegetables provide, on the average, more than twice the vitamins and minerals of meat. Meat is upheld as a powerful, irreplaceable item of food. The message is clear: the vassal vegetable should content itself with its assigned place and not attempt to dethrone king meat. After all, how can one enthrone women's foods when women cannot be kings?

The Male Language of Meat Eating

Men who decide to eschew meat eating are deemed effeminate; failure of men to eat meat announces that they are not masculine. Nutritionist Jean Mayer suggested that "the more men sit at their desks all day, the more they want to be reassured about their maleness in eating those large slabs of bleeding meat which are the last symbol of machismo."[2] The late Marty Feldman observed, "It has to do with the function of the male within our society. Football players drink beer because it's a man's drink, and eat steak because it's a man's meal. The emphasis is on 'man-sized portions,' 'hero' sandwiches; the whole terminology of meat-eating reflects this masculine bias."[3] Meat-and-potatoes men are our stereotypical strong and hearty, rough and ready, able males. Hearty beef stews are named "Manhandlers." Chicago Bears' head football coach, Mike Ditka, operates a restaurant that features "he-man food" such as steaks and chops.

One's maleness is reassured by the food one eats. During the 1973 meat boycott, men were reported to observe the boycott when dining out with their wives or eating at home, but when they dined without their wives, they ate London Broil and other meats (*New York Times* 1973). When in 1955 Carolyn Steedman's mother "made a salad of grated vegetables for Christmas dinner," her husband walked out (Steedman 1985, 114).[4]

Gender Inequality/Species Inequality

> *The men . . . were better hunters than the women, but only because the women had found they could live quite well on foods other than meat.*
> (Walker 1989)

What is it about meat that makes it a symbol and celebration of male dominance? In many ways, gender inequality is built into the species inequality that meat eating proclaims, because for most cultures obtaining meat was performed by men. Meat was a valuable economic commodity; those who controlled this commodity achieved power. If men were the hunters, then the control of this economic resource was in their hands. Women's status is inversely related to the importance of meat in non-technological societies:

> The equation is simple: the more important meat is in their life, the greater relative dominance will the men command. . . . When meat becomes an important element within a more closely organized economic system so that there exist rules for its distribution, then men already begin to swing the levers of power. . . . Women's social stand-

ing is roughly equal to men's only when society itself is not formalized
around roles for distributing meat (Leakey and Lewin, 1978)

Peggy Sanday surveyed information on over a hundred non-technological cultures and found a correlation between plant-based economies and women's power
and animal-based economies and male power. "In societies dependent on animals,
women are rarely depicted as the ultimate source of creative power." In addition,
"When large animals are hunted, fathers are more distant, that is, they are not in frequent or regular proximity to infants" (Sanday 1981, 65, 66)

Characteristics of economies dependent mainly on the processing of animals for
food include:

- sexual segregation in work activities, with women doing more work
  than men, but work that is less valued
- women responsible for child care
- the worship of male gods
- patrilineality

On the other hand, plant-based economies are more likely to be egalitarian. This
is because women are and have been the gatherers of vegetable foods, and these are
invaluable resources for a culture that is plant-based. In these cultures, men as well
as women were dependent on women's activities. From this, women achieved autonomy and a degree of self-sufficiency. Yet, where women gather vegetable food and
the diet is vegetarian, women do not discriminate as a consequence of distributing the
staple. By providing a large proportion of the protein food of a society, women gain
an essential economic and social role without abusing it.

Sanday summarizes one myth that links male power to control of meat:

> The Mundurucu believe that there was a time when women ruled and
> the sex roles were reversed, with the exception that women could not
> hunt. During that time women were the sexual aggressors and men
> were sexually submissive and did women's work. Women controlled
> the "sacred trumpets" (the symbols of power) and the men's houses.
> The trumpets contained the spirits of the ancestors who demanded ritu-
> al offerings of meat. Since women did not hunt and could not make
> these offerings, men were able to take the trumpets from them, thereby
> establishing male dominance (Sanday 1981, 39).

We might observe that the male role of hunter and distributor of meat has been
transposed to the male role of eater of meat and conclude that this accounts for meat's

role as symbol of male dominance. But there is much more to meat's role as symbol than this.

"Vegetable": Symbol of Feminine Passivity?

Both the words "men" and "meat" have undergone lexicographical narrowing. Originally generic terms, they are now closely associated with their specific referents. Meat no longer means all foods; the word *man*, we realize, no longer includes *women*. Meat represents the *essence or principal part of something*, according to the American Heritage Dictionary. Thus we have the "meat of the matter," "a meaty question." To "beef up" something is to improve it. Vegetable, on the other hand, represents the least desirable characteristics: *suggesting or like a vegetable, as in passivity or dullness of existence, monotonous, inactive*. Meat is *something one enjoys or excels in*, vegetable becomes representative of someone who does not enjoy anything: a *person who leads a monotonous, passive, or merely physical existence*.

A complete reversal has occurred in the definition of the word vegetable. Whereas its original sense was *to be lively, active*, it is now viewed as dull, monotonous, passive. To vegetate is to lead a passive existence; just as to be feminine is to lead a passive existence. Once vegetables are viewed as women's food, then by association they become viewed as "feminine," passive.

Men's need to disassociate themselves from women's food (as in the myth in which the last Bushman flees in the direction opposite from women and their vegetable food) has been institutionalized in sexist attitudes toward vegetables and the use of the word *vegetable* to express criticism or disdain. Colloquially it is a synonym for a person severely brain-damaged or in a coma. In addition, vegetables are thought to have a tranquilizing, dulling, numbing effect on people who consume them, and so we cannot possibly get strength from them. According to this perverse incarnation of Brillat-Savarin's theory that you are what you eat, to eat a vegetable is to become a vegetable, and by extension, to become woman-like.

Examples from the 1988 Presidential Campaign in which each candidate was belittled through equation with being a vegetable illustrates this patriarchal disdain for vegetables. Michael Dukakis was called "the Vegetable Plate Candidate" (Grady 1988). Northern Sun Merchandising offered T-shirts that asked: "George Bush: Vegetable or Noxious Weed?" One could opt for a shirt that featured a bottle of ketchup and a picture of Ronald Reagan with this slogan: "Nutrition Quiz: Which one is the vegetable?"[5] (The 1984 Presidential Campaign concern over "Where's the Beef?" is considered in the following chapter.)

The word *vegetable* acts as a synonym for women's passivity because women are supposedly like plants. Hegel makes this clear: "The difference between men and women is like that between animals and plants. Men correspond to animals, while women correspond to plants because their development is more placid."[6] From this viewpoint, both women and plants are seen as less developed and less evolved than men and animals. Consequently, women may eat plants, since each is placid; but active men need animal meat.

Meat Is a Symbol of Patriarchy

In her essay "Deciphering a Meal," the noted anthropologist Mary Douglas suggests that the order in which we serve foods, and the foods we insist on being present at a meal, reflect a taxonomy of classification that mirrors and reinforces our larger culture. A meal is an amalgam of food dishes, each a constituent part of the whole, each with an assigned value. In addition, each dish is introduced in precise order. A meal does not begin with a dessert, nor end with soup. All is seen as leading up to and then coming down from the entree that is meat. The pattern is evidence of stability. As Douglas explains, "The ordered system which is a meal represents all the ordered systems associated with it. Hence the strong arousal power of a threat to weaken or confuse that category" (Douglas 1975). To remove meat is to threaten the structure of the larger patriarchal culture.

Marabel Morgan, one expert on how women should accede to every male desire, reported in her *Total Woman Cookbook* that one must be careful about introducing foods that are seen as a threat: "I discovered that Charlie seemed threatened by certain foods. He was suspicious of my casseroles, thinking I had sneaked in some wheat germ or 'good-far-you' vegetables that he wouldn't like" (Morgan 1980).

Mary McCarthy's *Birds of America* provides a fictional illustration of the intimidating aspect to a man of a woman's refusal of meat. Miss Scott, a vegetarian, is invited to a NATO general's house for Thanksgiving. Her refusal of turkey angers the general. Not able to take this rejection seriously, as male dominance requires a continual recollection of itself on everyone's plate, the general loads her plate up with turkey and then ladles gravy over the potatoes as well as the meat, "thus contaminating her vegetable foods." McCarthy's description of his actions with the food mirrors the warlike customs associated with military battles. "He had seized the gravy boat like a weapon in hand-to-hand combat. No wonder they had made him a brigadier general—at least that mystery was solved." The general continues to behave in a bellicose fashion and after dinner proposes a toast in honor of an eighteen-year-old who has enlisted to fight in Vietnam. During the ensuing argument about war the general defends the bombing of Vietnam with the rhetorical question: "What's so sacred about a civilian?" This upsets the hero, necessitating that the general's wife apologize for her husband's behavior: "Between you and me," she confides to him, "it kind of got under his skin to see that girl refusing to touch her food. I saw that right away" (McCarthy 1965).

Male belligerence in this area is not limited to fictional military men. Men who batter women have often used the absence of meat as a pretext for violence against women. Women's failure to serve meat is not the cause of the violence against them. Yet, as a pretext for this violence, meat is hardly a trivial item. "Real" men eat meat. Failing to honor the importance of this symbol catalyzes male rage. As one woman battered by her husband reported, "It would start off with him being angry over trivial little things, a trivial little thing like cheese instead of meat on a sandwich" (Dobash and Dobash 1979, 100). Another woman stated, "A month ago he threw scalding water over me, leaving a scar on my right arm, all because I gave him a pie with potatoes and vegetables for his dinner, instead of fresh meat" (Pizzey 1974, 35).

Men who become vegetarians challenge an essential part of the masculine role. They are opting for women's food. How dare they? Refusing meat means a man is effeminate, a "sissy," a "fruit." Indeed, in 1836, the response to the vegetarian regimen of that day, known as Grahamism, charged that "Emasculation is the first fruit of Grahamism" (Whorton 1977, 122).

Men who choose not to eat meat repudiate one of their masculine privileges. The *New York Times* explored this idea in an editorial on the masculine nature of meat eating. Instead of "the John Wayne type," epitome of the masculine meat eater, the new male hero is "Vulnerable" like Alan Alda, Mikhail Baryshnikov, and Phil Donahue. They might eat fish and chicken, but not red meat. Alda and Donahue, among other men, have not only repudiated the macho role, but also macho food. According to the *Times*, "Believe me. The end of macho marks the end of the meat-and-potatoes man" (*New York Times* 1981). We won't miss either.

Questions for Discussion

1. What does the title of this chapter mean to you?
2. How is meat and eating meat associated with masculinity and male privilege?
3. Why are meat-based economies more likely to have greater levels of inequality?

22 Humans and Other Animals
Sociology's Moral and Intellectual Challenge
David Nibert

*In this insightful selection, David Nibert makes a powerful argument for the intercon-
nected oppressions of devalued humans and other animals. Modifying Noel's theory
of ethnic stratification, Nibert shows how it can be applied to the exploitation of nonhuman animals. Specifically, economic self-interest by corporations in a capitalist
economy combines with the power of the state and an ideology of speciesism, to
reproduce the systematic oppression of other animals. Nibert goes on to show how
the treatment of animals is entangled with the treatment of humans, with the primary
beneficiaries being society's powerful (male) elites. Ultimately, Nibert argues, sociology needs to expand its definition and focus to include other animals.*

Introduction

Anthropology is profoundly anthropocentric, as Barbara Noske has observed:

> [A]nimals tend to be portrayed as passive objects that are dealt with and
> thought and felt about. Far from being considered agents or subjects in
> their own right, the animals themselves are virtually overlooked by
> anthropologists. They and their relations with humans tend to be con-
> sidered unworthy of anthropological interest. Most anthropologists
> would think it perfectly natural to pay little or no attention to the way
> things look, smell, feel, taste or sound to the animals involved.
> Consequently, questions pertaining to animal welfare in the West or in
> the Third World rarely figure in anthropological thought (1993, 185).

The same can be said of sociology, particularly in the United States. While many
sociologists bring the power of sociological analysis to a range of social issues and
to different forms of oppression, challenging tradition, convention and existing polit-

Originally published in 2003 in the *International Journal of Sociology and Social Policy*, vol.
23, no. 3, pp. 5–25. Reprinted with permission from Emerald Publishing.

ical-economic arrangements, as a rule most sociologists in the U.S. accept human treatment of other animals[1] as normal and natural. The reluctance of most sociologists to recognize the elite-driven arrangements that oppress other animals and to bring them into scholarly and public focus highlights the question asked by Alfred McClung Lee: "Sociology for Whom?" (Lee 1978). Sociological acquiescence in the socially constructed perception and treatment of other animals only perpetuates the grotesque consequences for countless numbers of both humans and other animals and does little to challenge an unjust and unsustainable global political economy—one that is decidedly *dysfunctional*. This paper will suggest a theoretical device to further the development of a more inclusive sociology—one that advances the study of *society*, not just *human* society—and will use this device to make a case for including other animals as subjects in the realm of sociological inquiry.

Linkages of Racism, Sexism, and Speciesism

Most social scientists, and many liberation activists around the world, promote the idea that the oppression of various groups is deeply grounded in the institutional arrangements and belief systems of human societies. This is to say that oppressive treatment of groups of humans is not natural or inevitable; rather, it is part of the cultural practices that are deeply established in social arrangements. Daniel Rossides summarizes the findings and perspectives of such scholars and activists when he writes that discrimination against devalued groups is "socially induced and maintained" (1997, 19).

Many sociologists now accept the idea that the oppression of various devalued groups in human societies is not independent and unrelated; rather, the arrangements that lead to various forms of oppression are intricately woven together in such a way that the exploitation of one group frequently augments and compounds the mistreatment of others. Margaret Andersen and Patricia Hill Collins are at the forefront of a rapidly growing number of sociologists who regard race, class, and gender as "interlocking" and "interactive systems" that should be analyzed in the context of "social institutions and belief systems" (1992, xii). Social activist and writer Suzanne Pharr puts it this way:

> It is virtually impossible to view one oppression . . . in isolation because they are all connected. . . . They are linked by a common origin—economic power and control—and by common methods of limiting, controlling and destroying lives. There is no hierarchy of oppressions. Each is terrible and destructive. To eliminate one oppression successfully, a

movement has to include work to eliminate them all or else success will always be limited and incomplete (Pharr 1988, 53).

Over the past three decades a number of scholars and activists have denounced "speciesism" and compared it explicitly to racism and sexism (Singer 1990; Regan 1982, Spiegel 1996). The application of sociological ideas furthers an examination of the legitimacy of such comparisons. First, though, a challenge to the customary definition of two important terms is necessary. The appropriateness of the term *minority group* must be reconsidered; a more accurate and inclusive term is recommended in its place. Then, the term *speciesism* will be interpreted from a sociological vantage point.

The term minority group was coined early in the twentieth century to refer to groups that differed from the one that controlled society. Initially used to refer to *ethnic* minorities, sociologists now commonly use the term to refer to any group in human society whose members differ from the controlling group (Sagarin 1971). Unfortunately, for many years most sociologists portrayed controlling group members as normative or typical members of society, while minority group members have been viewed as "alien" or "special" (Nibert 1996). What is more, traditional academic definitions of minority group have largely soft-pedaled the causes, consequences, and realities of the frequently oppressive social arrangements imposed on minority groups, often making them appear to be both natural and inevitable. As a result, the term minority group has been used extensively because it does not imply a critique of basic social arrangements.

Not surprisingly, due in part to the widespread use of the euphemistic term minority group, most who benefit from the privilege that stems from the exploitation of such groups seldom are motivated or encouraged to become aware of and reflect on their material and psychological stake in oppressive social arrangements. Consequently, the ostensibly objective term minority groups should be replaced with one that is more accurate and straightforward—"oppressed groups."

The following definition of "oppressed group" is derived in large part from an analysis of oppression developed by Iris Young (1990). *An oppressed group shares physical, cultural, or economic characteristics and is subjected, for the economic, political, and social gain of a privileged group, to a social system that institutionalizes its exploitation, marginalization, powerlessness, deprivation, or vulnerability to violence.* This term is more forthright than "minority group," its euphemistic counterpart, and is inclusive of humans of color, humans living in poverty, women, humans who are older, humans with disabilities, and humans with different sexual orientations, and also can include *other animals*. The term "oppressed group" not only is more appropriate and honest but also avoids the human-centered concept of minority groups and helps examine the prevailing view that human use and mistreatment of other animals lies in the realm of the "natural affairs."

The second theoretical adjustment needed for examination of the comparison of racism, sexism, and speciesism is a clear conceptualization of the term *speciesism*. The view that speciesism is prejudice or discrimination, a view promoted by many advocates and defenders of other animals, impedes an examination of the social structural causes of oppression of other animals. Sociologists tend to use the suffix "ism" in a more specific way than what is generally meant by those talking about speciesism. Most sociologists consider racism, as well as sexism, classism, and other "isms," to be ideologies. That is, they are neither prejudice nor mistreatment. Rather, an ideology is *a set of socially shared beliefs that legitimates an existing or desired social order*. Treatment of the term speciesism as ideology will thus assist in furthering an understanding of the causes of human mistreatment of other animals and in comparing their treatment with that of other devalued groups.

The application of the sociological perspective in general, then, and selected minority group theory in particular, to the oppression of other animals holds a great deal of promise for expanding the understanding of the causes of speciesism and its relationship to, and entanglement with, the oppression of devalued groups of humans. In exploring the parallels and entanglements of racism, sexism, and speciesism it is helpful to turn to Donald Noel's 1968 theoretical framework to explain the origin of ethnic stratification (Noel 1968). Noel maintained that ethnic stratification was the product of three interactive forces: (1) competition for resources, or some form of exploitation of one group by another, (2) unequal power and (3) ethnocentrism—"the view of things in which one's own group is the center of everything, and all others are scaled and rated with reference to it" (Sumner 1906, 13). While his theory made room for social-psychological considerations, they were placed in the context of structural forces. The value of Noel's theory is not just its close linking of material motivation with issues of power and belief systems but also its distillation of complex and interdependent social forces into a compact and readily understood model.

Noel's model will be revised somewhat in this analysis of the comparison of the oppression of humans and other animals into a three-pronged theoretical device that accentuates the economic context of most episodes of competition and exploitation. Moreover, the consideration of unequal power will be focused largely on the use of the various powers that are vested in those who control the state. Finally, the concept of ethnocentrism will be regarded here as a process primarily fueled by a larger system of ideological control.

This modified version of Noel's theory of ethnic stratification, which the author has referred to previously as the *Theory of Oppression* (Nibert 2002), has substantial application to an analysis of the oppression of other animals. The motivating factor—the pursuit of economic self-interest—is easily applied to humans' displacement, exploitation, and extermination of other animals as human society expands. First, humans compete with other animals for economic resources, including the use of land. Second, exploitation of other animals serves numerous economic ends for human animals, providing sources of food, power, clothing, furniture, entertainment, and research tools.

This theory also points to the importance of power. One important aspect of power is the ability of one group to exert its will over another, regardless of resistance. Abuses of power are seen throughout history as various human groups have devised weapons and techniques to dominate other animals and to displace, control, capture, exploit, or exterminate them. The most concentrated form of power for most of the past 10,000 years has been the *state*.

Finally, ideological conditioning is the third essential requirement for oppressive social arrangements. Oppression requires rationalization and legitimation; it must appear as the right thing to do, both to the oppressing group and in the eyes of others. A set of ideas that devalues an entire group—an ideology such as racism, sexism, or speciesism—thus is socially constructed. That ideology explains and supports the development and perpetuation of social institutions that foster the elimination or exploitation of the oppressed group. Moreover, the ideology justifying that action is promulgated throughout the social system in order to garner public acceptance and reduce dissent. Over time, these socially constructed ideas will come to be accepted as real and true, and the "lower" or "special" position of the oppressed group will be viewed as the natural order of things, promoting ethnocentrism and anthropocentrism.

Generally speaking, then, humans tend to disperse, eliminate or exploit a group they perceive to be unlike themselves (an outgroup or the "other"), particularly when it is in their economic interests to do so. Next, the oppressing group must have the power to subordinate members of the at-risk group. While physical force is the key to this subordination, such force is usually vested in part in political control. Those who exercise political control wield the power of the state, with the ability to make and oversee the implementation of law. Finally, ideological manipulation fuels prejudiced attitudes and discriminatory acts, which help protect and maintain oppressive economic and social arrangements by making them appear natural and, thus, acceptable. This model is based on the supposition that oppressive treatment of entire groups, including other animals, is a systemic phenomenon and cannot be explained by biological reductionism. Significantly, while this model depicts systemic oppression as occurring in a linear fashion, in reality the various aspects of the system are largely interdependent and operate more or less simultaneously. The reciprocal influences are not entirely symmetrical, due to the primary influence of material and economic considerations.

Historical Roots of Oppression

The economic factors that primarily cause the oppression of humans and other animals can be traced to the latter stages of hunting and gathering society. Systematic stalking and killing of other animals contributed to other inequalities, such as the devaluation of women. Hunting shaped relations between female and male humans largely because the bodies of other animals became a prized asset and killing them enhanced male prestige and privilege. Men achieved elevated prestige through the acquisition and distribution of resources derived from the bodies of other animals, even though women generally provided more reliable, if more mundane, forms of nourishment and resources through foraging. What is more, the decrease that hunting caused in men's participation in foraging and in caring for children and others needing assistance no doubt required women to devote more of their time to these tasks—resulting in less time for rest and leisure. Concomitantly, the increased labor and caretaking exacted from women freed males to increase the time they could devote to hunting. The developing mistreatment and exploitation of women and of other animals each was based upon and compounded by the other—a constant historical pattern.

The advent of early agricultural society brought with it opportunities for individual privilege and power—primarily for elite males—by increasing the possibilities for systematic oppression. Countless humans were assigned to hegemonically created social positions of "slave" and "serf" that devalued them, collectively and personally. So it was with other animals, who were relegated to such social positions as "livestock" and "game" and whose exploitation greatly facilitated the development of highly stratified and oppressive agricultural societies. Untold numbers of "others" were yoked to pestles, plows, wagons, and chariots for their entire lives, while countless other individuals were used as currency or devoured as victuals—primarily by the privileged. Humans and other animals were forced to fight each other to the death to amuse elites and to distract the masses from their daily experiences and from consideration of the sources of their deprivation. Similar entertainment and diversionary uses of devalued others occurred during the Middle Ages, when manorial lords and high-placed Church officials continued mass exploitation. Under such conditions, devalued others were also scapegoated for system ills, as in the case of women and cats who were scapegoated for individual or collective misfortunes and executed as witches and witches' accomplices.

Capitalism largely continued the 10,000-year-old tradition of exploiting humans and other animals to create wealth and privilege for the few, exploitation that continued to bind the fate of devalued humans and other animals. For instance, the enclosure movements in Europe forced exploited humans out of the countryside, where the land they used was taken to raise captive sheep. The hair of sheep was taken and sent to developing urban areas where those displaced from the land, transformed into an urban proletariat, suffered in textile mills. The Irish, subjugated by the British military, were forced off their land; much of it then was used to raise cows, whose bodies were sent back to feed the elite in England. In the Western hemisphere, humans such as John Jacob Astor killed innumerable other animals—whose skin and hair were worn largely by elites to advertise their elevated social status—while exploiting indigenous humans. Meanwhile, countless other animals were massacred or "cleared" from the land so that humans of color could be forced to produce profitable cash crops there. Cattle barons accrued great wealth raising cows for slaughter while the "meat producers" exploited workers who had the task of killing and dismembering other animals; contaminated and tainted "meat" was sold to the public and the U.S. military at inflated prices.

The twentieth century brought corporate dominance of the economy, and millions of farmers were forced from the countryside as the capitalist imperative for growth and expansion fueled large-scale factory farming. Food, especially "meat," is very abundant in affluent nations today, an availability supplemented by nonstop, widespread, and manipulative advertisements.

Few are aware of the terrible costs associated with the food abundance in advanced capitalist nations, and of the inherent unsustainability of the affluents' culinary opulence, particularly their consumption of "meat." Numerous agencies and organizations, including the Office of the U.S. Surgeon General, the National Academy of Sciences, the National Cancer Society, and the American Heart Association, have linked high levels of "meat" consumption to such conditions as diabetes, high blood pressure, arteriosclerosis, stroke, and certain forms of cancer (U.S. Department of Health and Human Services 1988). The increasing consumption of "meat" and "dairy" products is also linked to the growing problem of obesity in the United States. A 1999 study conducted by the Centers for Disease Control found that the number of citizens considered obese—defined as being more than 30 percent over ideal body weight—was one in five, up from one in eight in 1991 (Crossette 2000).

The U.S. hamburger culture has also taken a toll on the nation's youth. According to the Centers for Disease Control, the number of overweight children increased more than 50 percent during the last two decades of the twentieth century, and the number of extremely obese children nearly doubled during the same period (Schmidt 1999). Diets based largely on the consumption of "meat" and "dairy" products have serious effects for the young. Children's health care providers are taking notice, particularly of the health problems associated with rising rates of obesity in children.

Due to corporate machinations in an economic system characterized by greed and an incessant drive to maximize profits, the Worldwatch Institute's 2000 report estimated that 1.2 billion humans, *the largest number it ever reported*, are "underfed and undernourished," while another 1.2 billion are "eating too much or too much of the wrong food." The United States has become the most overfed, undernourished, and overweight society in the world.

It is believed that, when humans consume the flesh or secretions of other animals, they are consuming antibiotic residues that compromise their own bodies' immune systems and increase the risk that antibiotic-resistant strains of bacteria will develop. Moreover, there is a risk that new bacteria in other animals that are unresponsive to existing antibiotics could be passed on to humans. Due to factory farming practices, and the powerful presence of corporate agribusiness inside the U.S. Department of Agriculture, increasing production and consumption of tainted "meat" also is related to several food-borne illnesses, including the potentially lethal E. coli bacteria.

In a nation that is supposed to be the epitome of capitalist progress, nearly half of Americans suffer at least one chronic disease, and that number is expected to grow by 30 million within the next 20 years (Associated Press 2000). Preventive care and less refined, plant-based diets are inconsistent with the production of food under modern capitalism and with the profitable "treatment" of the diseases linked to its consumption. Meanwhile, the vast majority of the oppressed individuals defined as "food" are faceless, nameless, and largely invisible.

Humans, Other Animals and the Environment

When natural scientists report on the costs of concentrated agricultural production and predict the further effects of agribusiness practices, they usually voice their warnings using such terms as "further reductions in biodiversity," "further destruction of ecosystems," and "Third World population migrations." Such abstract and arcane expressions do not make real or visible to the public the pain, suffering, and death of countless humans and other animals that both underlie and result from what Vandana Shiva calls the "rotten food culture" (Shiva 1997). Powerful transnational corporations use ubiquitous advertisements to exhort everyone to consume "hamburgers" and "fried chicken," whereas Third World elites create poverty in their nations by taking over the land to send feed and other animals raised to be food to countries like the United States.

Feeding a privileged portion of the human population, especially under contemporary agribusiness with its emphasis on "meat" production, necessitates high levels of deforestation and desertification (the destruction of soil, rendering it infertile and desert-like), adds to air pollution (caused in no small part by the vast amounts of methane gas generated by huge populations of other animals, particularly hundreds of millions of cows), exhausts fresh water supplies, and compounds already critical levels of water pollution. Few life-sustaining resources will remain for future generations of humans and other animals as long as agricultural production under capitalism exists to make profits rather than to feed the world.

A report by a panel of scientists whose work appeared in a 2001 article in the journal *Science* projects an increase in the human population from six billion in 2000 to nine billion by 2050 (Tilman 2001). This increase will double the world's food demands by mid-century, partly because people in wealthy countries will want diets rich in "meat", which takes more resources to produce. The report suggests that, if contemporary forms of agriculture persist, by 2050 the global agricultural land base will have to increase by at least 109 hectares of land, resulting in the worldwide loss of forests and natural ecosystems in a total area larger than the United States. The displacement, destruction, and death brought on by appropriation of so much of the remaining homeland of devalued humans and other animals would be cataclysmic. The panel writes:

> Because of regional availabilities of suitable land, this expansion of
> agricultural land is expected to occur predominantly in Latin America
> and sub-Saharan Africa. This could lead to the loss of about a third of
> remaining tropical and temperate forests, savannas, and grasslands and
> of the services, including carbon storage, provided by these ecosystems
> (Tilman 2001, 283).

Pharmaceuticals and Entangled Oppressions

Economic motivation for oppression of humans and other animals can also be brought into focus by a brief look at the pharmaceutical industry. In the 1990s, the medical and biomedical-pharmaceutical industries led the successful resistance to creation of a national system of health care in the United States, leaving tens of millions in the U.S. uninsured or underinsured. At the same time, the industry staunchly defended using millions of other animals every year in horrific experiments, ostensibly for the public good. While drug companies aggressively market and promote expensive products that purport to have some therapeutic value for populations who are affluent or have health insurance, they all but ignore the tens of millions of United States citizens who are uninsured or under-insured, as well as the masses of humans around the world with few resources and little power. For example, because of the enormous demand for medicine in Africa (due in no small part to colonialist and imperialist-caused disruption and poverty), prices for drugs are higher than in the United States and Europe. According to a United Nations report, even painkillers are scarce in many Third World countries, and "many are left to die in agony from cancer and other diseases" (Crossette 2000a).

Further, while drug companies will defend research on other animals as necessary to fight diseases such as AIDS (advocates of other animals, progressive physicians, and gay-rights groups like ACT UP San Francisco dispute the efficacy of AIDS research using other animals), the companies are little interested in getting their anti-AIDS products to the millions around the world, particularly in sub-Saharan Africa, who are infected but are cash poor. Not only has the Western drug industry kept its own AIDS-related products out of reach of those in the Third World, who cannot afford them, but it also has aggressively defended patent rights to forestall Third World countries from developing generic forms of these drugs. Largely out of sight are millions of other animals whose existence and suffering is eclipsed by Madison Avenue advertising, their agony entangled with the exploitation of consumers as each form of mistreatment fuels the other.

The entangled oppression of groups of devalued humans and other animals is the material fodder for existing and emerging global disparities, exploitation, and violence. What is more, structurally imposed austerity programs in debt-ridden countries have led millions of individual humans to continue, if not increase, the exploitation of other animals. They supplement their incomes by trapping, exhibiting, breeding, slaughtering, stuffing, smuggling, and poaching other animals. Desperate humans sell gorillas and chimpanzees, kill elephants bearing ivory, and use any other being whose exploitation and death can help them survive, or gain an edge, in the "new economic order."

Such practices are inevitable in a selfish and profit-driven global economic system that has fostered agricultural concentration, megamergers, corporate flight, sweatshops, child labor, and other problems of the new century.

The examples of the interdependent nature of oppression of humans and other animals just mentioned scarcely begin to cover the actual economic entanglement. Still, they should make clear that the treatment of devalued humans and other animals is deeply imbedded in economic arrangements and that the forms of oppression are causally connected, profoundly intertwined, and reinforcing.

The State As a Primary Tool of Oppression

These economic arrangements—which are largely created by elites and which certainly facilitate their interests—have been sanctioned and protected by the various powers of the state. Military force and chauvinistic political systems have created and solidified oppression for thousands of years. From legal sanctioning of slavery to the creation of "humane" slaughter policy, the power of the state usually has been controlled by the beneficiaries of oppression. The fairly recent rise of capitalist-based globalization seeks to further reduce impediments to profit-taking as the governments of the most powerful nations package and promote trade agreements that weaken or eliminate protections for workers, consumers, other animals, and the environment.

They purport to "aid" less powerful and affluent nations through such international financial institutions as the International Monetary Fund and the World Bank, which in many instances require desperation inducing austerity plans and support the development of such land-intensive and oppressive enterprises as "cattle" ranching and "animal feed" production. In the event that indigenous peoples and displaced populations in the oppressed nations of the world resist expropriation of the land they call home and rely on for their survival, military forces of dictatorial leaders violently repress such dissent—frequently with assistance from the United States (Blum 1995).

Less obvious forms of structural violence in the economic arena result from U.S. government policies that protect agribusiness and other corporate interests through agricultural subsidies. Agribusiness in the United States receives public funds to produce "major commodities like sugar, corn, and wheat below cost" (Oxfam 2002, 3). The prices of these crops are so low that small farmers in Third World countries cannot compete or make a living and these nations become unable to be self-sufficient food providers—facilitating hunger and famine and the many diseases that follow malnutrition. Many oppressed nations have become dependent upon exports of cash crops to pay increasing debts to banking institutions in powerful capitalist nations and to purchase food.

At another level, minimalist government regulations in the United States that purport to oversee the welfare of other animals subjected to the practices of agribusiness, pharmaceutical, entertainment and other industries are underfunded, underenforced, and serve primarily as ideological subterfuge to quiet public concern.

The Social Construction of Speciesism

Oppression usually is naturalized—that is, it is made to appear as a normal and innate part of worldly existence. The metaphysical and theological ideologies that for thousands of years explained the "natural" place of the enslaved, women, children, other animals, and other devalued and oppressed groups today largely have been replaced with "scientific" ideologies that justify and naturalize the contemporary socioeconomic order. The benefits and success of capitalism, the desirability of wealth and the "inferior" qualities of women, humans of color, those with disabilities, those of advanced age, and other animals are deeply woven into contemporary reality. Powerful messages coming from such diverse sources as church, school, family, state, peers, and the mass media create widespread and deep acceptance—and internalization—of this socially constructed reality.

Over the past hundred years many oppressed groups have been disparaged for their alleged "low mental caliber" and consequently scaled low in a hierarchy of worth. The measurement of an individual's or group's value was based on the purported level of intelligence, measured or attributed in ethnocentric, anthropocentric ways. In addition, ecofeminists have observed that ideas about the hierarchy of worth are deeply entwined with patriarchy, a system of social organization in which masculinity is valued over femininity (both being social constructions). Ecofeminist Janis Birkeland put it this way:

> In the dominant Patriarchal cultures, reality is divided according to gender, and a higher value is placed on those attributes associated with masculinity, a construction that is called "hierarchical dualism." In these cultures, women have historically been seen as closer to the earth or nature. . . . Also, women and nature have been juxtaposed against mind and spirit, which have been associated in Western cosmology with the "masculine" and elevated to a higher plane of being. . . . [I]t is clear that a complex morality based on dominance and exploitation has developed in conjunction with the devaluing of nature and "feminine" values (1993, 18–19).

General acceptance of the existence and naturalness of such a hierarchy continues to legitimate oppression of other animals, women, humans of color, humans with disabilities, and other devalued groups. The denigration of some groups, generated to a large degree by cupidity, is increased by high levels of socially cultivated egocentrism and is woven into both the culture and individual psyches in a way that shapes personal identities. Those who perceive themselves to be superior to others sometimes display their socially induced prejudice by acts of discrimination, frequently by creating physical, social, and emotional distance between themselves and the devalued. At times, discriminatory acts are perpetrated only for the amusement value of denigrating and harming the "lowly other" and to display the perpetrator's power. The prevailing beliefs and values required to legitimize widespread institutionalized oppression, such as that practiced by agribusiness and the pharmaceutical and chemical industries, shape the reality and cultivate the general personality types of human members of society. In an often predatory system, where the prevailing ideology glorifies wealth and power, more humans will be inclined to accept or tolerate, if not practice, violence against those "others" who are perceived as poor, weak, or powerless. The widespread acceptance of the general concept of the hierarchy of worth of living beings both rationalizes oppressive acts and arrangements and thoroughly entangles the various beliefs that arise from a hierarchical worldview. Only the rejection of the entire notion of such hierarchy can remove the ideological support for oppression of any group and begin to make all groups secure.

The important point to take from this analysis, particularly for those interested in challenging and reducing oppression, are that the principal causal factor underlying the oppression of humans and other animals is material in nature and that oppression primarily serves the interests of elites—particularly male elites. Oppression is supported by the state, and an ideological support system is manufactured to legitimate the tyrannical treatment of others.

The Future of Sociology

The social construction of speciesism is deeply entangled with the oppression of devalued humans, and such oppression has only intensified with the rapid advance of modern global capitalism. However, the unethical and chauvinistic treatment of other animals, the entanglement of oppressions and the unsustainability of the current prevailing arrangements based on this oppression all have been largely overlooked by the sociological community. Reflecting on the nature of capitalist society, R. H. Tawney observed, "The appeal of [capitalist] society must be powerful, for it has laid the whole modern world under its spell" (Tawney 1948, 29–30). Sociologists, particularly in the United States, certainly are not entirely immune from this spell. Members of the discipline, who like most other humans in society partake in the privileges derived from entangled oppressions—such as eating and drinking substances derived from the bodies of "others," wearing their skin and hair, and enjoying the entertainment value their exploitation provides—can do so only by accepting the self-interested realities crafted by powerful agribusiness, pharmaceutical, and other industries that rely on public acquiescence in oppressive social arrangements. Privilege is not easy to give up. Silence, denial, and substantial intellectual acrobatics are necessary for oppression of all forms to continue.

Once sociologists are capable of recognizing and reducing their own privilege, privilege fueled by exploitation legitimated by hegemonically constructed and deeply entrenched realities and buttressed by quasi- and pseudo-scientific ideas, the challenge then becomes one of crafting a more inclusive sociology. For example, instead of emphasizing the purported "lowliness" of other animals, as is frequently done in introductory textbooks, the discipline must present other animals in the spirit of embracing diversity and developing respect for difference. This paper has called for the inclusion of other animals in the study of oppressed groups and has provided a glimpse of how the exploitation of humans and other animals is inextricably tangled.

This twenty-first century variation of "the new sociology" (Horowitz 1964) should begin by treating other animals as subjects who have personalities, wills, desires, and social relations and who are capable of experiencing both pleasure and suffering. Their lives should be studied both in relation to human animals and—to the extent that they can be—in the absence of human imposition. While the lives of other animals can be studied in the context of their own communities and societies, it is also necessary to include them in the broader use of the term *society*. The tremendous power that humans, particularly the elite, exert over the other inhabitants of the earth and the social positions assigned to groups of other animals—"livestock," "game," "zoo animal," "lab animal" and so forth—require their substantive inclusion in the concept of society that has hitherto referred only to human society.

A major paradigm shift is necessary to set the discipline on a new course. To further the creation of a sustainable and just world, and for the advancement of science, the question posed by Alfred McClung Lee, "sociology for whom?" should be answered: *sociology for all humans and other animals*.

Questions for Discussion

1. Why does Nibert prefer the term *oppressed group* over *minority group*?
2. How did Nibert modify and apply Noel's theory of ethnic stratification to explain the oppression of nonhuman animals?
3. Analyze the interconnections between the exploitation of other animals and the exploitation of humans?

Part VIII: Living and Working with Other Animals

Researchers believe that all animals are capable of feeling pain, but what they actually see when they look at lab animals is a scientific objective, not the animal's subjective experience. The result is that it rarely occurs to them to consider whether an animal is in pain, is suffering, or whether it is feeling anything at all. . . .

Mary T. Phillips

23 The Health Benefits
of Human–Animal Interactions

Andrew N. Rowan and Alan M. Beck

Andrew Rowan and Alan Beck summarize the powerful evidence for the benefits to human health resulting from relationships with animals. Yet they also bemoan the limited response to these findings, particularly from the research community, in terms of the small number of studies and the lack of research funding. Much could be learned, they argue, that could benefit both individuals, as well as the larger society from intensified investigation into this area. And, Rowan and Beck remind us, let's not forget to study the health benefits that other animals derive from their relationships to us.

Over two years ago, one of us (ANR) drew attention to several research reports that highlighted the benefits of interactions with animals for individual humans (Rowan 1991), the most striking of which was the finding that pet owners had a reduced risk of cardiovascular disease when compared with nonowners (Anderson *et al*. 1992). Pet owners had lower systolic blood pressures, plasma cholesterol, and triglyceride values. While pet owners engaged in more exercise, they also ate more meat and "take-out" foods than nonowners and the socioeconomic profiles of the two groups were very similar. It appears that pet ownership reduces the risk factors associated with cardiovascular disease, possibly even for reasons that go beyond simply influencing risk behaviors. For example, it has been hypothesized that pet ownership improves survival because it influences psychosocial risk factors that lessen the risk of coronary heart disease (Patronek and Glickman 1993).

Whatever the mechanism of the influence of pets on the incidence of and survival after cardiovascular disease, the report by Anderson *et al*. (1992) has not caused a sudden flurry of interest in funding studies on the links between human–animal interactions and cardiovascular health. Similarly, the other major observation on the link

Originally published in 1994 in *Anthrozoös*, vol. 7, no. 2, pp. 85–89. Reprinted with permission, International Society for Anthrozoology (ISAZ).

between pet ownership and cardiovascular health, the report a decade earlier that pet owners experienced increased one-year survival after discharge from a coronary care unit (Friedmann *et al*. 1980), did not lead to an increased availability of research funds. As far as we are aware, both reports have had only a very limited impact on subsequent epidemiological projects on cardiovascular health because very few have added a question or two on pet ownership and attachment to animals to their studies. There is one independent ancillary study to the Coronary Arrhythmia Suppression Trial (CAST), a National Institutes of Health (NIH) clinical trial, which is finding that pet ownership, lower anxiety, and social support are all associated with an increased likelihood of one-year survival after a myocardial infarction (E. Friedmann—personal communication 1994). The CAST protocol and early findings have been published (CAST 1989).

At the final presentation of the 1987 NIH Technology Assessment Workshop, Beck and Glickman (1987) proposed that "All future studies of human health should consider the presence or absence of a pet in the home and, perhaps, the nature of this relationship with the pet, as a significant variable. No future study of human health should be considered comprehensive if the animals with which they share their lives are not included."

The need to conduct detailed and serious research of human–animal interactions on reasonably large study populations is as pressing as ever. The strong indications of benefits to individuals provided by Friedmann *et al*. (1980) and Anderson *et al*. (1992) would have generated enormous research interest if the intervention (pet ownership) could have been patented and sold as a drug. Perhaps we should suggest that a few simple "improvements" in the basic pet (that would be patentable since animals can now be patented!) might lead to an animal that could be prescribed by doctors to ameliorate cardiovascular disease. There are other possible benefits of pet ownership that are even less amenable to commercial exploitation by the medical profession. For example, Wilson (1991) reported that the presence of companion animals alleviates anxiety and has a relaxing effect on college students of all ages and races. However, Wilson (1991) also reported that reading quietly was less stressful than interacting with a pet, which was not consistent with previous data from other studies. While measuring the anxiolytic effect of a pet on a human companion is not a simple task, nonetheless there appears to be a real effect.

We should not focus exclusively on individual benefits. A case can also be made that companion animals could have a positive impact on societal health. A group in Miami has described at Delta Society meetings how their use of animals in the classrooms of inner city communities has dramatically reduced pupil truancy rates and increased scores on standardized tests. In the same vein, Aaron Katcher reports that his work with disturbed children at the Deveraux School in Pennsylvania indicates that animals can have profound positive effects on children who have become trapped in a cycle of antisocial and violent behavior (Katcher, A.H.—personal communication 1994).

We are all now familiar with the links between animal abuse and abusive behavior toward other humans (see review by Ascione 1993) but there are tantalizing hints of the opposite effect. For example, a friend tells me (ANR) how she was abused by her father as a child and how her animals have helped to rid her of the nightmares of her youth and have helped her to learn "tenderness." However, there are no studies of this effect of animals on people despite the widespread but largely untested belief that we should teach children to be "kind" to animals. For example, children exposed to humane education programs displayed enhanced empathy for humans compared with children not exposed to such programs. (Ascione 1992). Animals may also have less dramatic effects than increasing survival rates or reducing anxiety. Serpell (1991) reported that dog owners experienced fewer minor health problems and increased the number and durations of their recreational walks. The effects persisted over the 10-month study period and there was no clear explanation for the results.

Much of the early literature documents nothing more than fortuitous interactions with animals that happen to be present in a therapeutic setting. The animals were brought in to provide a diversion or the joys traditionally associated with pet care. These expectations may not have been incorrect; often the best medicines are appropriate concentrations of what is generally beneficial (Beck and Katcher 1984). One role, perhaps the major role of animal contact, is that it enhances one's sense of well-being.

Just under one thousand Medicare patients were evaluated prospectively, and those with dogs reported fewer physician visits than nonowners (Siegel 1990). Most of the people noted that the pets provided them with companionship and a sense of security and the opportunity for fun/play and relaxation. Animals allow people to experience bonding. Pets are nonjudgmental in their love and pets facilitate a child's learning about responsibility. Siegel (1993) suggested that pets have a stress-reducing effect. However, another study reported that pet ownership did not reduce stress in working women (Watson and Weinstein 1993). The different results obtained with this younger study population may have been due to the fact that the women had relatively little time to spend with their pets and so they did not realize the therapeutic benefits.

There is every reason to believe that animals may decrease a sense of loneliness. Kidd and Kidd (1994) interviewed 106 homeless people and report that pets were very important for companionship, friendship, and love. Providing food and veterinary care for the animals was, however, a problem for this population.

There is also a need for more study on some of the difficulties that can occur in human–animal contact. We need a better appreciation of the diseases and injuries that are or might be associated with animal interactions as well as more data on the problems of human psychological dependence on companion animals—for example, excessive grief responses on the death of a companion animal and the accumulation of large numbers of "companion" animals to the point where they constitute a threat to animal and human welfare.

The symbolic role of animals in society may be as important as some of the more physiological roles of companion animals. For example, many police forces carry teddy bears in their cruisers as part of their trauma kits. Advertising is full of animal images, as are our everyday lives and speech, and yet very little attention has been given to trying to understand how these symbols are important to us as individuals and to society as a whole. In the real world, even rabbits and turtles can encourage approaches by other people and stimulate conversations between children and unfamiliar adults (confederates) in a community park setting. This is an example of animals as "social lubricants" (Hunt *et al.* 1992).

In the past ten to fifteen years, much more attention has been given to the scholarly investigation of human–animal interactions but significant support still eludes the field. Although Elizabeth Marshall Thomas's (1993) *The Hidden Life of Dogs* sells hundreds of thousands of copies and publishers hurry to become part of the latest publishing fad (dogs), large-scale scholarship on human–animal interactions still languishes, mainly because of a lack of funds. Today, serious epidemiological studies cost hundreds of thousands of dollars but most grants to study human–animal interactions are for $10,000 or less. Admittedly, such an amount would be sufficient to support the addition of a few questions on human–animal interactions to larger epidemiological surveys, but only if those controlling the large study are amenable. Unfortunately, they are usually not interested. A few large grants would, however, change the negative or neutral attitudes of many academics since there is nothing quite like the lure of significant research funding to concentrate the mind and convert even the most cynical of skeptics.

The lack of funding is not a problem exclusive to human–animal interactions. People who pray and participate more actively in their religions have better health at all ages. People associated with conservative religious affiliations have poorer health than those with more liberal affiliations (Ferraro and Albrecht-Jensen 1991). While society generally believes that being religious is valuable to health, there have been few studies. There is more evidence that animal contact is beneficial than being religious, yet we still have trouble accepting animals as more than the "therapeutic clown" of society (Beck and Katcher 1983).

Lastly, future studies should include the health benefits for the animals involved of human–animal interaction. Such an expansion of the study scope would not only be humane but might provide a better model for understanding the impact of animals on humans. There is some support for the idea that human–animal interactions benefit the animals as well as the people (Lynch and McCarthy 1969; Lynch et al. 1974; Sato et al. 1993). If social companionship is an evolutionary development, then it is only logical that both sides of the social interaction will benefit.

In sum, there is solid evidence that animal contact has significant health benefits and that it positively influences transient physiological states, morale, and feelings of self worth. The impact may be mediated directly, or by influencing psychosocial or risk behaviors. Long term effects of animal companionship and interaction include an influence on the attitudes and behaviors of young children. Presumably, this influence has value for the future. Research is needed to identify the scope of the influence of animal contact, and how to better focus the effect for people at risk.

Questions for Discussion

1. Summarize the major research findings regarding the benefits of human–animal interaction to human health.
2. What mechanisms might help to explain some of these findings?
3. Propose an area of research that you think might have potential for producing important findings regarding the health benefits from our relationships with other animals.

24 Personality Characteristics of Dog and Cat Persons

Rose M. Perrine and Hannah L. Osbourne

Do you consider yourself a dog person? A cat person? A common belief is that peo-ple with dogs are different from those with cats. Is this the case? And do dog or cat persons differ from individuals without companion animals? These are the questions explored in this study by Rose Perrine and Hannah Osbourne. They expected dog and cat persons to differ on several dimensions of personality, including sex role (mascu-line versus feminine), athleticism, independence, and dominance. They also expected people to perceive dog and cat persons the way they perceived themselves. Were they right? The results may surprise you.

Introduction

Although the fact of owning a pet would seem to reveal aspects of one's personality, research findings are mixed. Some research suggests that there are no differences between pet owners and nonowners on personality variables such as self-acceptance, self-esteem, social self-esteem, extraversion or neuroticism (Martinez and Kidd 1980; Friedmann *et al.* 1984; Johnson and Rule 1991). Additionally, Johnson and Rule (1991) found no differences in self-esteem, social self-esteem, or extraversion among owners with different levels of attachment to their pets. However, other research suggests that pet owners have higher self-esteem than do nonowners (e.g., Messent 1983; Savishinsky 1983), and that years of pet ownership is negatively relat-ed to neuroticism and alienation (Paden-Levy 1985).

Most of us have heard of people who do not fit in socially with others, but love, and are loved by, animals. How common is such a person? Cameron and Mattson (1972) found that pet owners claimed not to like people as much as nonowners, nor did they feel as liked by others. Their findings suggest that pet owners may not be as

Originally published in 1998 in *Anthrozoös*, vol. 11, no. 1, pp. 33–40. Reprinted with permis-sion, International Society for Anthrozoology (ISAZ).

socially adept as nonowners. However, other research suggests the opposite. For example, compared with nonowners, pet owners scored higher on measures of social sensitivity and interpersonal trust (Hyde *et al*. 1983), spent significantly more time each day in socializing with others (Joubert 1987), and were less independent and less likely to avoid lasting obligations (Guttman 1981). Furthermore, Poresky and Hendrix (1990) found that children with strong bonds with a pet had higher social competency and empathy scores.

Mere ownership of dogs versus cats does not appear to be related to personality. For example, dog and cat owners did not differ on self-esteem, social self-esteem, extraversion (Johnson and Rule 1991), or self-acceptance (Martinez and Kidd 1980). However, research suggests that preference for dogs or cats may be related to personality. Kidd and Kidd (1980) found that male cat lovers were higher on autonomy than were male dog lovers or female cat and dog lovers; male dog lovers were higher, and female cat lovers were lower, on dominance than the other groups; male and female cat lovers were lower on nurturance than male and female dog lovers, and male dog lovers were higher on aggression than the other groups. Edelson and Lester (1983) found that among males (but not among females), extraversion was related to a higher preference for dogs than for cats.

Why should dog and cat lovers differ in personality? One possibility is that childhood pet ownership affects adult personality. Kidd and Kidd (1980) found that people tend to label themselves as loving the type of pet with which they grew up, and for many people the preference for one type of pet is exclusive: 40% of dog lovers indicated that they disliked cats, and 34% of cat lovers said that they disliked dogs. Kidd and Kidd suggest that an environment which produces a dominant and aggressive adult male may be created by parents who prefer dogs over cats; or it may be that dog-ownership by a child elicits responses from others that reinforce personality traits like dominance and aggression. Podberscek and Serpell (1997) found a relationship between personality traits of owners and prevalence of aggression in their English cocker spaniels. Owners of high aggression dogs were significantly more likely to be tense, emotionally less stable, shy, and undisciplined than the owners of low aggression dogs. Furthermore, Miller and Lago (1990) found a positive correlation between friendliness of pet dogs and the friendliness of their owners. Thus, the personality of a dog lover may be influenced by an environment in which a dog is present, others' reactions to the dog owner, and the interaction between the dog's and owner's personalities. These same possibilities exist for cat lovers. Cats have less social needs than do dogs (Lorenz 1954) and the child-rearing environment of adult cat-lovers may have been created by parents who valued autonomy. The child may have been reinforced for independence, and/or the cat's behavior may have elicited and reinforced autonomy.

Category-based expectancies are stereotypes that we have of others based on groups to which they belong (Jones and McGillis 1976). Many people perceive others as either dog people or cat people (Fox 1981), and because they mentally categorize people into these groups they are likely to have stereotypes about the characteristics of these group members. Some research suggests that stereotypes about dog and cat lovers are based on the perceptions people have of dogs and cats. Cats are perceived as more independent, aloof, and less affectionate than dogs (Zasloff and Kidd 1994), and people were rated as more likable when they were accompanied by a dog than when accompanied by a cat (Geries-Johnson and Kennedy 1995). Hirschman (1994) found that people often described a companion animal's personality as matching or representing the personality of the animal's human owner. Whether these similarities in personality are real or simply perceived on the basis of stereotypes was one focus of the present research.

There are gender differences in preferences for dogs versus cats. Females are more likely to own cats than dogs, and rank cats higher in preference to own than dogs (Edelson and Lester 1983). Some of the characteristics of dog lovers, such as being physically active (Rogers *et al.* 1993) and high in dominance and aggression (Kidd and Kidd 1980) are traditional masculine sex-role characteristics (Bem 1974). Bem (1975) found that males with masculine sex-role orientations were less likely to play with a kitten than were males with feminine or androgynous sex role orientations. Furthermore, Budge *et al.* (1996) found that women were perceived as more confident, professional, and active (traditional masculine characteristics) in the presence of a dog rather than a cat. In contrast, men were seen as more warm, loving, and gentle (traditional feminine characteristics) in the presence of a cat rather than a dog. Stereotypically, females are paired with cats and males are paired with dogs (Lockwood 1985); therefore, cats may be perceived as more feminine and dogs as more masculine. In the company of a dog a woman may be perceived as more masculine simply because the dog is perceived as masculine. Likewise, in the company of a cat a man may be perceived as more feminine simply because the cat is perceived as feminine. Taken together these research findings suggest that dogs, and dog lovers, may be perceived as masculine, while cats, and cat lovers, may be perceived as feminine. In addition, dog lovers may perceive themselves as masculine and cat lovers may perceive themselves as feminine.

In the present study, participants who were self-labeled as dog person, cat person, both or neither, rated their own personality, and the personality of a fictitious character who was described as either a dog person or cat person. We expected dog persons to rate themselves higher on masculinity, athleticism, and dominance than cat persons. The characteristic of dominance was of particular interest because previous research, 18 years ago, found that only male dog lovers rated themselves high on dominance (Kidd and Kidd 1980). We expected that sex roles would have changed to the extent that now both male and female dog lovers would rate themselves high in dominance. Athleticism was of interest because both previous research (Rogers et. al. 1993) and anecdotal evidence suggest that people who are physically active may prefer dogs because the dog and owner can engage in physical activity together.

We also expected cat persons to rate themselves higher on femininity and independence than dog persons. The characteristic of independence was of interest because one defining characteristic of cats is their independence (Lorenz 1954) and we expected cat lovers to perceive themselves in similar terms. Previous research found that only male cat lovers rated themselves high on autonomy (Kidd and Kidd 1980), but, again, because of changing sex roles we expected high scores on independence for all cat persons, regardless of gender.

We expected subjects to perceive dog and cat persons in the same way that dog and cat persons perceive themselves. Specifically, we expected dog persons to be perceived as more masculine, athletic, and dominant than cat persons, and cat persons to be perceived as more feminine and independent than dog persons. These expectations are based on previous research suggesting that people view dogs and cats in masculine and feminine terms (Lockwood 1985; Budge *et al.* 1996).

Methods

Participants

Participants were 126 undergraduate students, 48 males and 78 females, at Eastern Kentucky University (EKU). Ages ranged from 18 to 52, with a median age of 21. Participants were recruited from introductory psychology and psychology research methods courses, and most received course credit for participating.

Materials and Procedure

Participants came to a laboratory in groups of three to five, and completed the following questionnaires, which were presented in counterbalanced order. All responses were anonymous.

Dog/Cat Attitudes

We developed a questionnaire assessing participants' experience with, and current attitudes toward, dogs and cats. Separate questions asked participants (a) whether they had at least one dog (cat) as a pet while they were growing up, (b) whether their past experience with dogs (cats) were positive or negative (6-point scale), (c) whether they currently owned a dog (cat), and (d) to classify themselves as either a dog person, cat person, neither or both. The choices for categories were: I really like dogs and consider myself a "dog person;" I really like dogs but do not consider myself a "dog person;" I feel neutral about dogs; I don't like dogs; I hate dogs; and other. The same choices were given for cats. Participants were classified as a dog person or cat person only if they chose the first category.

Liking Scale

Participants rated how much they liked other people, how much people liked them, how much they liked pets, and how much they liked their pet, using the same four questions that Cameron and Mattson (1972) developed for their study. Responses were rated on a six-point scale from one (not at all) to six (very much).

Descriptions of Other

Each participant read one of four descriptions, which were developed for the study. Either a male or female was portrayed as either a dog or cat lover: *Jim (Jane) is a 25-year old college student who attends EKU. Jim considers himself to be a dog (cat) lover. He thinks of his German Shepherd (cat) as part of his family. Jim (Jane) spends many hours each week with his dog (cat).*

Because perceptions of a dog's characteristics are probably related to breed, we held this variable constant by specifying German Shepherd, which is considered a prototypical dog (Gleitman 1986). We did not specify a breed of cat because perceptions of cats' characteristics were not expected to differ much as a function of breed. In addition, no research has explored prototypicality of cat breeds.

Sex Role and Personality

We used an abbreviated version of the Bem Sex-Role Inventory (BSRI) (Bem 1974) which consisted of 24 adjectives rated on a six-point scale from one (almost never) to six (very often or always). Twelve of the items were masculine adjectives and twelve were feminine adjectives. Separate masculine and feminine scores were obtained by summing the responses to the appropriate twelve items. Three items—independent, athletic, and dominant—also were analyzed separately. The masculinity and femininity scales of the BSRI have an internal consistency reliability of approximately 0.80 and a four-week retest reliability of approximately 0.90 (Bem

1974). In the present study, participants completed the BSRI twice, once rating them-selves and once rating their perception of the character in the description.

Results

Participants classified themselves as either dog persons, cat persons, neither or both. Results were: 40% dog persons, 19% cat persons, 27% neither dog nor cat persons, and 14% both dog and cat persons. A chi square test of association showed a signifi-cant gender difference in self-labeling. More females (65%) than males (23%) classi-fied themselves as cat persons ($\chi2(1)$=6.77, n=126, p=0.009). Classification as a dog person did not differ significantly as a function of gender (males=60%; females=50%). Forty-six percent of the participants reported currently owning a cat and 52% current-ly owning a dog; there was no gender difference in current pet ownership.

Most people (80%) reported either positive or neutral feelings toward dogs and cats, however some people reported that they either 18% reported that they disliked cats (males=23%; females=18%); this was not a significant gender difference. Dog persons were no more likely than non–dog persons to say that they disliked cats. The only participants who reported that they disliked dogs were two females who disliked both dogs and cats.

Liking people versus liking pets. Results showed no significant differences between pet owners (n=90) and nonowners (n=36) on how much they liked people, or how much people liked them. However, dog/cat persons reported liking other peo-ple more (M=2.4; SD=0.2) than did non–dog/cat persons (M=1.7; SD=0.2), (F(3, 125)=4.00, p=0.009). Also, dog/cat persons were more likely to report that people liked them more (M=2.3; SD=0.2) than did non–dog/cat persons (M=1.9; SD=0.2).

As might be expected, pet owners indicated that they liked pets more (M=2.3; SD=0.8) than did the non–pet owners (M=1.6; SD=0.8) (t(44)=2.61, p=0.01). There were no significant differences between dog persons and cat persons on any of the liking variables.

Past Experience

Participants were asked if, while they were growing up, their families had at least one dog/cat for a pet; 95% had at least one dog and 42% had at least one cat. Participants also rated the quality of their past experience with dogs/cats, from one to six, with higher numbers indicating more positive past experiences. There was a significant difference in past experience with dogs (M=5.3) versus cats (M=4.4) (t(130)=5.10, p<0.0001). There were no significant gender differences in family ownership of, or past experience with, dogs/cats.

Past experience with dogs and cats was related to current pet ownership and self-label. Compared with people who did not currently own cats ($n=68$), people who currently owned cats ($n=58$) reported having more positive past experiences with cats ($t(124)=5.11, p<0.001$). Mean past experience was 5.2 ($SD=1.6$) for people who currently owned cats, and 3.7 ($SD=1.8$) for people who did not currently own cats. Past experience with cats also differed as a function of self-label ($F(3,122)=26.23$, $p<0.001$). People who labeled themselves cat persons or both dog and cat persons reported more positive past experiences with cats than did people who labeled themselves dog persons only, or neither dog nor cat persons (See Table 1).

Table 1   Mean Past Experience with Dogs and Cats As a Function of Self

		SELF LABEL				
		Dog Person	Cat Person	Both	Neither	F
	N	50	24	18	34	
Cats	M	3.7a	6.0b	5.8b	3.6a	26.23***
	SD	.2	.3	.3	.2	
Dogs	M	5.7a	4.9b	5.5a	4.7b	9.81***
	SD	.1	.2	.2	.2	

*** $p<.001$ Means with different letters (a, b) are significantly different from each other.

Compared with people who did not currently own dogs ($n=60$), people who currently owned dogs ($n=66$) reported having more positive past experiences with dogs ($t(124)=2.88, p=0.005$). Mean past experience was 5.5 ($SD=0.8$) for people who currently owned dogs, and 4.9 ($SD=1.2$) for people who did not currently own dogs. Past experience with dogs also differed as a function of self-label ($F(3, 122)=9.81$, $p<0.001$). People who labeled themselves dog persons or both dog and cat persons reported more positive past experiences with dogs than did people who labeled themselves cat persons only, or neither dog nor cat persons (See Table 1).

Personality and Self-Label

Data were analyzed using the General Linear Model; personality variables were entered as separate dependent variables (masculine, feminine, independent, athletic, or dominant). The independent variables were self-label (dog person, cat person, both, or neither) and gender. The main effect of gender was not of interest but the interaction between gender and self-label was. For example, would male cat lovers rate themselves differently than male dog lovers? If the omnibus F was significant means were compared using Fisher's LSD test. Means and standard deviations for the personality variables can be seen in Table 2.

Masculinity and femininity scores had a possible range of 12–72, with higher scores indicating higher masculinity and femininity. The range in these data were: masculinity 31–68, and femininity 30–67. There was a significant main effect of self-label for masculinity ($F(3,118)=2.83, p=0.04$). As expected, dog persons rated themselves as more masculine than did cat persons, with participants in the neither and both categories falling in-between. Contrary to the hypothesis for femininity, neither the main effect of self-label nor the interaction between self-label and gender were significant.

Scores for the variables of independent, athletic, and dominant ranged from one to six. Higher scores indicated higher self-ratings of independence, athleticism, and dominance. There was a significant main effect of self-label for independence ($F(3,118)=2.68, p=0.05$). Opposite to the hypothesis, dog persons rated themselves as more independent than did cat persons, with participants in the neither and both categories falling in-between. On athleticism we expected dog persons to rate themselves higher than cat persons. Instead people who labeled themselves dog persons, or dog and cat persons, were higher in athleticism than were participants who were neither dog nor cat persons ($F(3, 118)=3.06, p=0.03$). Cat persons did not differ significantly from any other group on athleticism. For the variable of dominant, we expected dog persons to be higher than cat persons, but neither the main effect of self-label nor the interaction between self-label and gender were significant.

Personality and Dislike of Cats

In order to explore the relationship between dislike of cats and personality, the personality variables were entered as separate dependent variables. The independent variables were dislike of cats (yes or no) and gender. The interaction between dislike of cats and gender was also tested.

Compared with people who liked cats, people who disliked cats rated themselves lower in femininity ($F(1,118)=3.82, p=0.05$). Mean femininity for people who liked cats was 52.7 ($SD=0.7$) and for people who disliked cats, 49.9 ($SD=1.2$). However, this main effect was driven by the significant interaction between dislike of cats and gender ($F(1,118)=5.63, p=0.02$). Males who disliked cats rated themselves lower in femininity ($M=46.0; SD=1.9$) than any other group: Males who liked cats ($M=52.2; SD=1.1$), females who like cats ($M=53.3; SD=0.8$), and females who disliked cats ($M=53.9; SD=1.7$).

Table 2 Mean Personality Scores As a Function of Self

		SELF LABEL				
		Dog Person	Cat Person	Both	Neither	F
Masculine	M	54.3a	47.9b	51.2ab	51.3ab	2.83*
	SD	1.1	1.9	1.9	1.4	
Feminine	M	52.6	54.4	52.4	50.6	n.s.
	SD	6.8	6.6	7.0	5.1	
Independent	M	5.4a	4.6b	5.2ab	5.2ab	2.68*
	SD	.1	.2	.2	.2	
Athletic	M	4.1a	3.4ab	4.1a	3.1b	3.06*
	SD	.2	.3	.4	.3	
Dominant	M	3.6	3.5	3.5	3.6	n.s.
	SD	.2	.3	.3	.2	

Note: Possible range: Masculine and Feminine=12–72; Independent, Athletic and Dominant=1–6. *p<.05 Means with different letters (a, b) are significantly different from each other. "ab" signifies that the mean is not significantly different from either means a or b.

Perceptions of Dog versus Cat Persons

Participants read a description of a male or female dog or cat person and rated this person's personality. The personality variables (masculine, feminine, independent, athletic, and dominant) were entered as separate dependent variables. The independent variables were: character gender, character label (dog person or cat person), participant gender, and participant self-label. There were no significant differences in perceptions of dog versus cat persons as a function of the participants' gender or self-label. No interactions were significant. For the significant main effects, Fisher's LSD was used for the post hoc analysis of means. Participants' perceptions of the character's masculinity differed as a function of character gender ($F(1,120)=4.91, p=0.03$), and character label ($F(3,120)=4.26, p=0.04$). Males were perceived as more masculine ($M=47.0$; $SD=1.1$) than females ($M=43.6$; $SD=1.1$) and dog persons were perceived as more masculine ($M=46.9$; $SD=1.1$) than cat persons ($M=43.7$; $SD=1.0$).

Participants' perceptions of the character's femininity did not differ as a function of character gender, but there was a trend for character label to have an effect ($F(1,120)=3.33, p=0.07$). Dog persons were perceived as less feminine ($M=56.3$; $SD=0.9$)) than were cat persons ($M=58.5$; $SD=0.8$). This main effect was driven by a trend for an interaction between character gender and label ($F(1,120)=2.77, p=0.09$). Male dog persons were perceived as less feminine ($M=54.3$; $SD=0.8$) than were male cat persons, female dog persons and female cat persons (M=58.5, 58.2 and 58.1; SD=0.8, 0.9, 0.8, respectively).

Perceptions of the character's athleticism differed as a function of character gender ($F(1,120)$=6.84, p=0.01) and character label ($F(1,120)$=35.31, p<0.001). Males were perceived as more athletic (M=3.7; SD=0.2)) than females (M=3.1; SD=0.2), and dog persons were perceived as more athletic (M=4.1; SD=0.2) than cat persons (M=2.7; SD=0.2). Perceptions of the character's dominance differed as a function of character gender ($F(1,120)$=6.72, p=0.02) and character label ($F(1,120)$=5.29, p=0.03). Males were perceived as more dominant (M=3.3; SD=0.2) than females (M=2.7; SD=0.2) and dog persons were perceived as more dominant (M=3.3; SD=0.2) than cat persons (M=2.8; SD=0.2). These main effects were driven by a trend for an interaction ($F(1,120)$=3.28, p=0.07). Male dog persons were perceived as more dominant (M=3.8) than were male cat persons, female dog persons and female cat persons (M=2.8, 2.8 and 2.7, respectively). Contrary to our expectation, perception of the character's independence did not differ as a function of label.

Discussion

The purpose of the present study was to explore personality as a function of pet ownership and self-labeling (dog person or cat person). Other people's perceptions of dog and cat persons were also explored. Results showed no differences in personality between people who owned dogs/cats and people who did not. However, several differences were found as a function of label. Dog persons rated themselves higher on masculinity than did cat persons, independent of gender. Similarly, dog persons were perceived as more masculine than cat persons. Dog and cat persons did not rate themselves differently on femininity, but the perceptions of others did not match the self reports: Male dog persons were perceived as lower on femininity than any other group. On independence, dog persons rated themselves higher than did cat persons. However, other people did not perceive dog and cat persons differently on independence. On the other hand, dog and cat persons did not rate themselves differently on dominance, but others perceived male dog persons to be more dominant than male cat persons, and female dog and cat persons. On athleticism, dog and cat persons did not rate themselves differently, but dog persons were perceived as more athletic than cat persons.

In this sample of college students approximately half currently owned dogs and/or cats. The present findings suggest that the decision to own dogs/cats is not related to personality. This finding supports previous research by Martinez and Kidd (1980) and Johnson and Rule (1991). On the other hand, personality does appear to be related to labeling oneself a dog person or cat person. Furthermore, other people appear to attribute different personality characteristics to dog persons than to cat persons. Interestingly, the self reported personality characteristics and the perceptions of others do not always agree. The most notable differences are others' perceptions of male cat persons, who were perceived as more feminine and less dominant than male dog persons. In fact, the ratings for males were nearly identical to the ratings for dog persons on four out of the five variables: masculinity, femininity, athleticism, and dominance. Male cat persons were perceived to be more similar to females than to other males. Given these perceptions it may not be surprising that more women than men labeled themselves cat persons, even though there were no gender differences in past experiences with, or current ownership of, cats. The stereotype of a male cat person as a "wimp" may be enough to discourage self-application of the label.

One limitation of this study is that participants were rating a dog person who supposedly owned a German Shepherd. Some of the perceived personality differences between dog and cat persons may be a function of perceptions of German Shepherd lovers rather than perceptions of dog lovers, in general. Indeed, it is unlikely that lovers of all breeds of dogs would be perceived in the same terms. We intend to explore these differences in future research. Other questions arise from these findings: Do self-labeled dog and cat persons rate other dog and cat persons differently than do non dog cat people? Do self-labeled dog and cat persons attribute to other dog and cat persons the same personality characteristics they perceive in themselves? The present study suggests that the answer to both of these questions may be yes, but the cell sizes are too small to draw any conclusions. We currently are collecting data to address these questions.

In previous research people tended to label themselves as a lover of the type of pet with which they grew up (Kidd and Kidd 1980). Our results modify this previous finding. In the present study almost all (95%) of the participants grew up with dogs and 42% grew up with cats. There was no relationship between past and present ownership of dogs or cats, but there was a relationship between the quality of one's past experience with these animals and current ownership. Compared with participants who currently did not own cats, participants who currently owned cats reported more positive past experiences with cats. Likewise, compared with participants who currently did not own dogs, participants who currently owned dogs reported more positive past experience with dogs. Kidd and Kidd (1980) also reported that many dog lovers indicated that they disliked cats, and many cat lovers said that they dislike dogs. In contrast, we found that self-labeled dog persons did not indicate that they disliked cats, nor did self-labeled cat persons say that they disliked dogs.

Cameron and Mattson (1972) found that pet owners claimed not to like people as much as nonowners, nor did they feel as liked by others. Their findings suggest that pet owners may not be as socially adept as nonowners. The present data do not support Cameron and Mattson's findings. We found no differences between pet owners and nonowners on how much they liked others or how much they perceived others to like them. In fact we found that people who labeled themselves dog persons or cat persons liked people more than did people who labeled themselves neither dog nor cat persons. In addition, dog and cat persons perceived that others liked them more than did people who were neither dog nor cat persons. The present findings suggest that positive feelings about dogs/cats may engender positive feelings about people, or vice-versa. Indeed, positive feelings about animals and people may have common developmental origins, as suggested by previous research showing a relationship between empathy for children and empathy for pets (Poresky 1990).

Questions for Discussion

1. What did previous studies find with regard to whether there were differences in dog persons compared to cat persons and why?
2. What did the researchers expect to find? What was the basis for their hypotheses?
3. How different do you think dog persons really are from cat persons? What about people with pets compared to those without pets?

25 Human Grief Resulting from the Death of a Pet

Gerald H. Gosse and Michael J. Barnes

The death of a companion animal can be a very traumatic event in many households. Yet how much do we know about how and why people grieve the loss of a pet? This study by Gerald Gosse and Michael Barnes identifies variables that help to predict the level of grief expressed by individuals whose pets have died. Grief, which was measured in three ways—feelings of despair, social isolation, and somatization (bodily symptoms like headaches that occur due to stress)—was predicted by three major variables: level of attachment to the deceased pet, level of support from others, and stressful life events during the previous year. But there were other hypothesized variables that were surprisingly unrelated to level of grief. As you read this study, think about how society responds to those who openly show their overwhelming sadness at the death of their pet.

Introduction

Pet keeping is a widespread phenomenon in our culture (Serpell 1983). Pets are often perceived by their owners as family household members; and, they are kept for companionship as well as enjoyment in the nurturing opportunities that they provide (Katcher and Beck 1987). As a result of these types of relationships between people and their pets, there is the likelihood that when a pet dies the owner may experience feelings that would ordinarily be associated with loss through the death of a significant other (Katcher and Beck 1983; Keddie 1977; Rynearson 1978).

The literature has suggested that there are specific characteristics of pet owners and their personal situations which would affect the grief reaction, as it results from the death of a household pet (Bloom 1986; Harris 1983; Quackenbush 1984; Quackenbush and Glickman 1983; Stewart 1983). Furthermore, it has been suggested that the impact of this type of loss can be fundamentally similar to the death of a

Originally published in 1993 in *Anthrozoös*, vol. 7, no. 2, pp. 103–112. Reprinted with permission, International Society for Anthrozoology (ISAZ).

human family member for the pet owner (Quackenbush 1985; Stewart 1983). To date, however, there has been relatively little scientific research in this area. Hence, the present study employed several validated instruments in attempting to provide knowledge about this important part of human emotion/behavior, in the hope that specific antecedents/correlates of the grief response could be identified.

Method

Subjects

A convenience sample of two hundred and seven adult (i.e., 21 years of age or older) pet owners, from Long Island, New York, provided personal information, which was analyzed for this study. Each volunteer had lost a pet cat or dog within the one year prior to participation. Seventy-one of the owners were obtained from two private veterinary practices; and the other 136 owners were obtained from announcements in a variety of other sources, such as newsletters of animal welfare organizations and the "personals" section of a major Long Island newspaper.

The majority of participants (79%) were women. The average age of subject was 41 years, with two-thirds between 28 and 54 years. The average number of other family members living in the household at the time of pet death was 2.1 and the average number of dependent children was less than one (0.6). The sample represented a fairly well educated portion of the population (approximately 70% indicated a college level or advanced degree), and the level of primary caretaker responsibilities and degree of attachment to the deceased pet were both high (on scales of one to five, respective means were 4.5 and 4.6). Sixty-three percent of the owners lost a pet dog, 37% lost a pet cat, 61% were multiple pet owners, and the overall average of other cats/dogs in the home at the time of pet death was 2.4.

Procedure

During the initial phase, veterinarians from twelve small animal clinics were contacted by mail and asked for help in obtaining potential subjects for the intended study. From these contacts, veterinarians from two practices responded and ultimately agreed to participate. These veterinarians were then provided with a detailed description of the methodology and procedures to be followed.

In the next phase, letters that briefly described the study were sent by the veterinarians to client/owners who had lost a pet dog or cat through death over a previous one-year time period. Owners who were interested in participating returned a pre-addressed/stamped postcard to their respective veterinarians. After this, the author sent study materials and communicated directly with the responding owners.

The owner/participants who were obtained from other sources also received materials and communication directly from the author. Eventually, 71 of the 300 owners contacted from the two veterinary clinics and 136 of 139 owners from the other sources completed materials and were qualified as subjects. All materials were distributed and collected between July 1987 and November 1987.

Instruments

Grief Experience Inventory

The Grief Experience Inventory (GEI) was developed by Sanders, Mauger, and Strong (1985). Although the GEI was normed on populations of people who had experienced the death of a close human family member, it had also been used successfully in a previous study that examined the grief experience of people who had lost a companion animal through death (Lenior 1986). Three clinical bereavement scales were used to measure predictor variables: (1) Despair (DES); (2) Social Isolation (SI); and (3) Somatization (SOM). The DES scale measured thoughts and feelings that would be associated with a pessimistic outlook on life (e.g., apathy); the SI scale measured indications of social withdrawal (e.g., a need to be alone); and the SOM scale measured the presence of somatic symptoms that tend to occur under stress (e.g., headaches).

Three validity scales from the GEI were also used in order to eliminate data from subjects that would not be valid for research purposes. These scales eliminated profiles of people who would have a hesitancy to admit to common, but socially undesirable, weaknesses and feelings (i.e., Denial Scale), an unusual response set (i.e., Atypical Response Scale) and a tendency to try to make a good impression (i.e., Social Desirability Scale).

Censhare Pet Attachment Survey-Intimacy Scale.

The Censhare Pet Attachment Survey (PAS) was developed by researchers from the Center for the Study of Human Animal Relationships and Environments at the University of Minnesota (Holcomb, Williams and Richards 1985). In its entirety the PAS has two scales; (1) a Relationship Maintenance scale with 16 items; and (2) an Intimacy scale with 11 items. Because validation studies by the authors revealed dog owners as obtaining significantly higher scores than cat owners on the Relationship Maintenance scale, and this study included data from both dog and cat owners, only the Intimacy scale was used for data collection. The present study was retrospective; that is, pet death occurred within one year prior to participation. Therefore, it was also necessary to re-write each item on the Intimacy scale from its original present tense to the past tense. For example, "When you feel bad, you seek the comfort of your pet." became "When you felt bad, you sought the comfort of your pet." The owner's total score on the PAS Intimacy scale was assumed to represent his/her level of attachment to the deceased pet.

Schedule of Recent Experience.

The Schedule of Recent Experience (SRE) was developed by Amundson, Hart, and Holmes (1986) to collect data about people's life experiences within 42 types of stress-producing events. Each event carries an assigned weight according to the estimated impact and personal adaptation it would require. For example, death of a spouse has a value of 100; a divorce 73; and a change in residence 20. Each subject's score was calculated by multiplying the number of times each event occurred over the one-year period prior to participation in this study by its weighted value. Then, the item products were summed to derive a total Life Change Units score or the level of other stressful events.

Questionnaire for Pet Owners.

The Questionnaire for Pet Owners (QPO) was developed by the author of this study. The QPO contained 27 short-answer type items. Twenty-one of these items were designed to gather demographic data and information about personal attitudes. The other six items were designed to measure the owner's perception of the degree of understanding received from others about the loss of the pet (social support). Each of these six items was assessed on a Likert type scale and a total score was derived. (It should be noted that inter-item correlations for these six items indicated a level of consistency that allowed for their combined use in hypothesis testing.)

Design and Statistical Analyses

The main predictor variables that were used for hypothesis testing in this study were: (1) Strength of owner-pet bond in attitudes and feelings about intimacy; (2) Number of family members; (3) Living alone; (4) Living without children; (5) Single-pet ownership; (6) Sudden/unexpected cause of death; (7) Understanding received from others; and (8) Other stressful events. The criterion variables used were Despair (DES), Social Isolation (SI) and Somatization (SOM). Experimental questions involving length of ownership, age of owner, length of time since the pet's death, type of final arrangement (e.g., private cremation), gender of owner, and special support (e.g., counseling) were also examined to determine their relationship with the criterion variables. Finally, a supplemental analysis was conducted on the three criterion variable scores between owners who had been living alone or with one other adult, and those who had been living with more than one other adult and/or with one or more children. Pearson correlation coefficients, two-tailed t-tests, and multiple regression analyses were utilized where appropriate.

Results and Discussion

Main Predictors of Grief

As originally predicted in the study, a significant relationship was found between the main set of predictor variables taken together and the owner's grief response. This relationship was found on all three of the grief response measures; however, only the owner's level of attachment to the deceased pet, the level of perceived support from others and the level of other stressful events during the year prior to participation in the study were significant in accounting for up to 28% of outcome variance. Since these three predictor variables occurred in different combinations of relative strength on the three outcome measures, and the greatest amount of variance accounted for in the grief response by any single predictor variable was only 16% (i.e., pet attachment rating by level of somatization), it was apparent that for making the best prediction of the grief response over pet-loss these variables would be the most important ones to consider.

Household Makeup and Family Size

A prediction was made that pet owners living without children would have a more intense grief response than owners living with a child or with children. This prediction was partially supported, in that a significant difference was found in the expected direction in Social Isolation only. Because the analyses did not indicate a similar pattern for Despair and Somatization, it appeared that owners who did not have children in the household may have been predisposed toward social isolation and/or their pets may have played a role as a social stimulus. These results would be in agreement with other research which found that owners without children living in the home were more likely than others to believe that their pets helped them to make friends within the social environment (Albert and Bulcroft 1987).

A hypothesis that predicted that owners living alone would have a higher grief response than other owners was not supported on any of the response measures. However, when the sample was reorganized so that those living alone and those living with only one other adult were combined and then compared to owners living with more than one other adult and/or with a child or children, the grief response for the former group was higher in Social Isolation. This result was similar to the findings of Quackenbush and Glickman (1983). In their investigation, they found that those who received a social work service after the death of a pet were more likely to either live by themselves or with a spouse; and non-bereaved owners were more likely to live as a couple with at least one child or in an extended family unit.

A hypothesis that stated that there would be an inverse relationship between the total number of family members living in the household at the time of pet death and the owner's grief response also failed to receive any support on the grief measures. Based upon this result, in combination with the other findings about household make-up, it was apparent that family structure would be more essential than family size in predicting grief outcome.

Number of Pets in Household

A prediction was made that owners of single pets would have a more intense grief response than owners of multiple pets. This prediction was not supported on any of the grief response measures. Based upon these results, it appeared that the loss of a pet was as important to owners who had lost their only dog or cat as it was to owners who had another or others in the household. In fact, based upon the mean scores of the outcome variables, the intensity of the grief response for the multiple pet owners was higher on all three measures (i.e., Despair, Social Isolation, and Somatization).

Gender of Owner

One research question suggested that there would be a significant difference in the grief response between female owners and male owners. Interestingly, the data for the sub-sample of female owners revealed a more intense grief response on one of the three outcome measures only. Specifically, the female group was significantly higher than the male group on Despair. In that there was no significant difference on the Social Isolation and Somatization scales, there appeared to have been a qualitative difference in how the female pet owners experienced the death of a pet as compared to their male counterparts. Speculation was that certain cultural/gender stereotypes may have resulted in females being more willing than males to subscribe to thoughts and feelings of despair. In comparison, this type of bias may not have existed for items on the Social Isolation and Somatization scales. Another way to look at this male–female difference in response pattern would be to assume that the male grief response was underrepresented (or "masked") in a reluctance to express feelings of despair.

Table 1 Multiple Regression Analysis for Significant Predictors of Despair,
(Table extends across facing pages.)

	Variable		*Coefficient*	
Despair	SRE		.0019	
	PAS		.3624	
	Support		−.4023	
		R=.53		R^2=.28
Social Isolation	PAS		.3375	
	Support		−.4340	
	SRE		.0057	
		R=.42		R^2=.17
Somatization	PAS		.5486	
	SRE		.0082	
	Support		−.2915	

Note: SRE=total score for Survey of Recent Events, PAS=total score for Pet Attachment Scale, Support=total score for six support items on questionnaire for Pet Owners.

Age of Owner

An investigation of the possibility that there was a linear relationship between the age of owner and the grief response was completed. However, no such relationship was found on any of the grief scales. A possible explanation for this may be that other types of owner demographics that would have a strong association with grief outcome may have varied considerably within the chronological age groups of the present sample. Along these lines, Albert and Bulcroft (1987) have found that in comparison to chronological age, particular stages in the family life cycle, such as the "prospective parent" stage and the "empty nest" stage, have been helpful in understanding the psychological role and function of the family pet. These authors have suggested that in contemporary society one woman of 40 years might be married for two decades and have grown children, while another woman of the same age might be married for only a short period of time and be pregnant with her first child. Thus, differences in the social structure of these types of family units would lead to corresponding differences in attitudes and interactions with family pets (Bulcroft and Albert 1986).

Length of Ownership

An investigation of how length of ownership might directly influence the pet owner's grief response was conducted. This relationship, however, was not found on any of

Social Isolation and Somatization (*N*=207)

BETA		F		P
.3536		31.0082		.000***
.2555		16.322		.000***
−.2076		11.095		.000***
	F=9.458		P=.000***	
.1990		8.668		.004**
−.1873		7.908		.006**
.1840		3.375		.007**
	F=5.206		P=.000***	
.3379		28.052		.000***
.2275		18.810		.000***
.1315		4.371		.036*

* *p*<.05; ** *p*<.01; *** *p*<.001

the grief outcome measures. One possible explanation for this was offered by one of the veterinarians who participated in the study. He said that on the basis of his professional experience, many pet-owning clients have appeared to form a strong bond with a dog or cat immediately after purchasing or adopting it. Hence, whenever an owner of this type has had a pet die early in the relationship, the grief response has resembled what might have generally been expected to occur after a more lengthy period of time.

Time Since Pet's Death

An investigation was conducted into the possibility that there might be a significant relationship between the length of time since the pet died and the grief response. This relationship was found on each of the grief measures. Surprisingly, however, as there was an increase in the length of time up to one year, there was a corresponding increase in the level of grief. A possible explanation for this was that some pet owners may have experienced relatively high levels of grief which remained stable over time. Hence, the absence of a diminishing grief response in this type of owner may have been a factor in volunteering for participation in the study itself. Based upon the results of this research question and personal conversations with some of the participants in the study, it appeared that the grief process would vary considerably from individual to individual overtime.

Table 2 Means, Standard Deviations and *t* Values on the Three Clinical Scales between Pet Owners Living without Children (W/OC) and Pet Owners Living with Children (WC)

| | Mean | | Standard Deviation | | |
| | W/OC | WC | W/OC | WC | |
Scale	N=131	N=76	N=131	N=76	t
Despair	45.23	44.83	8.08	8.08	.34
Social Isolation	48.18	44.92	10.38	7.88	2.36*
Somatization	45.37	42.99	9.59	8.41	1.80

*p<.05

Table 3 Means, Standard Deviations and *t* Values on the Three Clinical Scales between Pet Owners Living Alone or with One Other Adult (GR1) and Pet Owners Living with More Than One Other Adult and/or with Children (GR2)

| | Mean | | Standard Deviation | | |
| | GR1 | GR2 | GR1 | GR2 | |
Scale	N=80	N=127	N=80	N=127	t
Despair	45.34	44.92	9.03	7.42	.36
Social Isolation	49.28	45.54	9.89	9.23	2.74*
Somatization	45.40	43.93	9.43	9.09	1.11

*p<.01

Table 4 Means, Standard Deviation and *t* Values on the Three Clinical Scales between Male Owners (MO) and Female Owners (FO)

| | Mean | | Standard Deviation | | |
| MO | FO | MO | FO | MO | |
Scale	N=44	N=163	N=44	N=163	t
Despair	42.16	45.87	6.69	8.19	2.74*
Social Isolation	46.50	47.12	8.59	9.93	.37
Somatization	42.18	45.12	8.67	9.30	1.88

*p<.01

Special Support

An investigation of the possibility that there might be a difference in the grief response between owners who had received special support, such as from a counselor, and those who did not resulted in an absence of significance on each of the grief scales. In view of this outcome, the following explanations were offered: (1) owners who had received special support may have derived some benefit from this; consequently, their grief response may have been brought into line with the response levels of owners who did not receive special support; (2) there may not have been a difference in levels of grief between the two groups in the first place; (3) special support may have been relatively unimportant in comparison to an owner's perception of support from others in general; and (4) the single item on the questionnaire which asked whether special support had been received may have been ambiguous; and, therefore, confounded the attempt to construct two dichotomous groups.

Type of Final Arrangements

An investigation of the possibility that there might be a significant difference between private cremation or burial and other types of disposal was conducted. This difference was not found on any of the clinical scales. Thus, the type of disposal for the deceased pet was not a significant predictor for an owner's level of grief response in the present study.

Table 5   Correlations between Length of Time Since the Pet's Death and the Grief Response on the Three Clinical Scales (N=207)

Scale	r	r	ρ
Despair	.15	.0225	.028*
Social Isolation	.24	.0576	.001**
Somatization	.16	.0256	.017*

*$p<.05$
**$p<.01$

Summary and Conclusions

The overall findings of this study suggested that the pet owner's level of attachment to a deceased pet, the perceived degree of understanding received from others about the loss, and the level of other stressful events would combine to have a significant predictive value in grief outcome. In other words, high attachment, low social support, and an accumulation of other stressful events would be associated with high levels of grief. Other findings suggested the following: (1) bereaved pet owners who live by themselves, as adult couples and/or without a child or children in the household, may be predisposed toward social isolation; (2) bereaved female owners may experience a qualitatively stronger response in feelings of despair than male owners; (3) the loss of a pet would be as important to a multiple pet owner as it would be to a single pet owner; and (4) the grief process may vary considerably from owner to owner over time. Additionally, age of owner, length of ownership, the presence of special support, and type of final arrangement were not found to be predictive of grief outcome. Given the instruments and sample size used, the results of this study appear to be meaningful in predicting the grief response of pet owners. Hence, it is expected that the present findings would be valuable in helping veterinary staff and mental health professionals to improve their understanding of this special type of human experience.

Questions for Discussion

1. What variables were important for predicting grief resulting from the loss of a pet? What variables were not related? Did any of these findings surprise you?
2. Some people grieve the loss of their pet in much the same way that others express their grief at the death of a human loved one. Yet often, friends and family don't offer the same level of support and comfort. Why do think this is? And what are the consequences for those who have suffered the loss?
3. If you were a veterinarian or bereavement counselor, how would the findings from this study help you deal with clients whose pets had died?

26 Loving Them to Death

Blame-displacing Strategies of Animal Shelter Workers and Surrenderers

Stephanie S. Frommer and Arnold Arluke

Every year, millions of cats and dogs are surrendered to shelters, where most of them will be killed. Do people who surrender their pets feel guilty, knowing the animals' likely fate? Do the shelter workers who do the killing feel guilty about their job, especially if they think of themselves as "animal lovers"? This selection, by Stephanie Frommer and Arnold Arluke, examines the strategies that both groups use to manage their guilt, finding similar patterns of placing all of the blame on others, while accepting none for themselves. Interestingly, Frommer and Arluke argue that these blame-management strategies make it possible for the cycle of surrendering and killing to be perpetuated.

Millions of healthy animals are euthanized each year in American shelters. Estimates of yearly euthanasia rates vary from 2.4 million dogs (Patronek and Rowan 1995) to 11.1 to 18.6 million cats and dogs (Nassar, Talboy, and Moulton 1992). Even a 5% euthanasia rate, a conservative estimate, shows that an unacceptably large number of animals are being euthanized (Rowan 1992).

One might suppose that many of the animals turned in to shelters are strays. Alternatively, one might suppose they represent the remnants of puppy and kitten litters, those for whom a home could not be found. But the truth is that many euthanized animals are companion animals surrendered by their caregivers (Patronek and Glickman 1994).

Research suggests that surrenderers who relinquish companion animals may experience feelings of conflict, doubt, regret, and shame—key components of guilt (Henry 1973). DiGiacomo, Arluke, and Patronek (1998) report that the vast majority

Originally published in 1999 in *Society and Animals*, vol. 7, no. 1, pp. 1–16. Reprinted with permission from Brill Academic Publishers.

of surrenderers find relinquishment a difficult and complex decision. McNicholas and Collis (1995) point out that many pet owners have strong feelings of doubt about the necessity or inevitability of euthanasia when discussing its elective possibility for their ill or elderly pets—even when they are convinced that it's the kindest thing to do.

Arkow and Dow (1984) claim that those who acquire dogs for companionship rather than for utilitarian purposes, such as guarding a home, regret surrendering their pets and acknowledge that they would choose to keep them if the problems leading to relinquishment could be resolved. Dorr Research Corporation (1994) and Patronek (1995) even contend that many pet owners are unwilling to admit to relinquishment, suggesting that they were ashamed of their actions.

Research also shows that surrenderers are not the only ones who experience guilt about euthanizing animals brought to shelters. Euthanasia appears to arouse various emotions among shelter workers that would indicate guilty feelings. A number of studies, for example, have found that euthanizing animals causes stress for many shelter workers (Cochran 1989; White and Shawhan 1996) because they feel a conflict between caring for and killing animals (Arluke 1991; Arluke 1994). More specifically, this research documents that euthanizing healthy animals violates an ideal conception held by many workers regarding the proper treatment of animals. A nagging inner reproach has led some shelter workers to deny or conceal the practice of euthanasia to outsiders. According to Henry (1973), these feelings are indicators of guilt.

This study began with the finding that the prospect of euthanasia creates guilty feelings for both surrenderers and shelter workers. Rather than further documenting the guilt of these actors, this article focuses on understanding how they cope with it. Strategies used to diffuse this guilt are important in understanding how the relinquishment–euthanasia cycle is perpetuated. Companion animals, given up by people who have a sense of attachment or duty to them, continually arrive at shelters. There, many of the companion animals will be euthanized by people who also care about their welfare. Surrenderers and shelter workers will continue this cycle as long as they can cope with their emotions about the deaths they cause. To the extent that both parties experience guilt in this situation, understanding how they manage this emotion is essential to unpacking the relinquishment–euthanasia cycle and allowing concerned individuals to discuss and debate it.

Research Site and Methods

In order to understand how surrenderers and shelter workers cope with the guilt of euthanasia, an ethnographic study was conducted of a full-service shelter serving a major, northeastern city and its surrounding areas. This shelter received nearly 7,000 animals in 1995, the majority of whom were cats and dogs. Of the animals received, 2,195 were adopted, and, following a holding period, 2,422 were euthanized. The rest, if not dead on arrival, were either returned to their owners, sent to the city's animal control facility, or euthanized immediately at an owner's request. In 1995, the shelter achieved an adoption rate of 52.7% for cats and dogs.

Open-ended interviews were conducted with surrenderers and shelter workers. Informal and semi-structured, the interviews allowed interviewees to direct the conversations and recount stories of their experiences. Interviews varied in length from five to 45 minutes, depending on the interviewees' comfort and willingness to talk. All interviews were tape-recorded with permission, and conversations were later transcribed verbatim along with detailed observations.

Eight, paid shelter workers were interviewed, including the shelter manager, animal care supervisor, and the animal caregivers. Staff members were overwhelmingly female (one male) and young (average age in the early twenties). All were high school graduates, and half had college degrees. Volunteers were excluded from this study because they were not directly involved either in selecting animals for euthanasia or for carrying out the euthanasia. Ten surrenderers were also interviewed. Six men and four women, ranging in age from young adulthood to middle age, represented a mix of racial and socioeconomic groups. Half of the interviewees surrendered dogs. The remainder surrendered cats.

In addition to interviews, observations, and informal interactions with shelter staff and surrenderers, shelter staff provided information about the daily operations of the shelter and allowed researchers to access parts of the shelter closed to the general public. During a seven-month period, researchers visited the shelter at least once a week, occasionally alternating the days on which the visits occurred, in order to observe typical busier days. Visits usually lasted three to four hours. All in all, the fieldwork involved more than 70 hours of interviewing, observing, and note taking. Research showed that surrenderers and shelter workers experienced guilt over the euthanasia of surrendered animals and managed their guilt by displacing blame. Although both groups relied on the same general coping strategies, some specific techniques for accomplishing displacement were unique to each group.

Displacing Blame

Sociologists have long documented a variety of techniques such as vocabularies of motive and accounts that people use to protect themselves psychologically when they consider their own acts immoral, strange, or untoward (Mills 1940; Scott and Lyman

1968; Sykes and Matza 1957). To avoid real or anticipated negative attributions of others as well as self recriminations, people seek to present themselves in a favorable light by constructing explanations—excuses, justifications, apologies, and absolutions (Arluke and Hafferty 1996; Hewitt and Stokes 1975; Tavuchis 1991).

Guilt feelings, in particular, may spur people to construct these accounts as they try to minimize the perceived blame of others and/or self-blame. Forced to manage ensuing guilt, they rely on after-the-fact, damage-control tactics or blame-management strategies. Studies of legislators (McGraw 1991), suicide survivors (Henslin 1970), and convicted rapists (Scully and Marolla 1984) have demonstrated the use of blame management as a way to forestall emotional and social injury. In these studies, however, blame management is usually examined as only one of a variety of accounting techniques people use. Nevertheless, in some situations, blame management may be a master accounting scheme that overshadows or excludes other types of accounts in terms of their complexity or effectiveness.

Unfortunately, researchers have not examined guilt-instilling situations, such as the surrender of animals to shelters, where blame-management strategies might be used as a master-accounting scheme. By examining such guilt-instilling situations, a more complete description of the types of blame-management strategies used might come to light. The interaction of those who mutually instill guilt in each other may elicit blame management. Blame-management strategies, then, may be more complex than prior studies suggest.

Surrenderers' Approaches

Although all surrenderers presented reasons for relinquishing their pets, their reasons entailed *blaming someone else*, *passing the buck*, or *blaming the victim*.

Blaming Others

To relinquish a pet for any reason was considered the same as to surrender the animal, knowing a high likelihood of euthanasia existed. By refusing to admit alternatives to shelter relinquishment, surrenderers could avoid self-blame. Thus, if animals were to be killed, the fault would lie with those who made the surrenderers give up their pets, not with the surrenderers who had neglected to explore safer options.

Some respondents claimed that they had to relinquish their animals because their landlords did not allow pets. One interviewee told a shelter worker that her landlady would not let her keep [her] pet: "It's either my dog or my house." Other interviewees blamed companions. One surrenderer, for instance, credited his wife with the decision to surrender their dog to the shelter:

> She called me at work and says, "You know, you should do it." . . .
> [S]he's the one . . . holding the decision. . . . So, when she called she
> said, "Well, you should go and do it," and I said, "If it's what you want
> to do, fine, I'll do it, but . . ."

Also, when displacing blame, surrenderers often pointed to an undefined other or
others who were responsible for a large pet overpopulation that necessitated the
euthanasia of surplus companion animals. According to one surrenderer, "Nobody
wants dogs," so his hand was forced. Bringing his dog to the shelter, where she was
subsequently euthanized, was his only option. Another surrenderer discussed her
family's role as the neighborhood foster family for strays. She and her children regularly took care of homeless animals until new homes for them could be found. She
explained her daughter's frustration over not being able to find a home for the stray
she had just surrendered:

> [My daughter] gets mad that people get animals and they can't take care
> of them and that's what she gets mad about. But that's one of the rea-
> sons I've told her [that] we can't keep on taking animals, because we
> can't keep on worrying about this. It's not fair to us. So, you know. And
> I think we're better off doing it now, 'cause if I keep it any longer it's
> gonna be harder for her.

A woman faulted an adoption agency for not answering her request to find a home
for her cat: "Rather than have her put to sleep, I thought they could find a home for
her, which I had been trying to do for two months myself. But if the adoption agency
had answered me, she never would have got here."

Passing the Buck

Using another strategy for displacing blame over possible euthanasia, surrenderers
emphasized their animals' attractiveness to make sure the shelter workers were at
fault if adoptions did not materialize. By building a strong case for their animals'
adoptability, surrenderers could shift blame for euthanasia to the shelter staff who,
presumably, failed to adopt out these special animals. To build their case, surrenderers described their animals in appealing terms. When filling out shelter identification
cards, they pointed out aspects of their animals' physical characteristics that set them
apart from the other animals in the shelter. One man, for example, distinguished his
cats by telling a shelter employee, "They're kind of unusual because they're big."
Surrenderers also considered youth a marketable quality that would ensure the adop-

tion of animals. One woman noted, "He's a puppy, so someone should . . . if no one claims him, someone should adopt him, you know. I hear they kill old cats and dogs, but he's a puppy, he should be OK."

Other surrenderers would try to endear their animals to the staff by describing their pets' attractive personalities. Comments such as, "She's very playful," "A great dog," or "She's a very caring, loving dog . . . a real caring dog," were commonly overheard. One small dog was described as better than a cat: "She doesn't do anything in the house." Her caregiver used the dog's low activity level and unobtrusiveness as a bargaining point. Another woman even threw in the fact that her cats were "free of parasites" and had pleasant personalities. According to her, "They [are] friendly, no fleas, you know—everything. Somebody'll probably adopt them. Nice cats."

Using another device for passing the buck, surrenderers chose shelters that they believed held the greatest likelihood of placement. In their minds, surrenderers could then feel they had done their best to avoid euthanasia by placing their animals' fates into the hands of the shelters most likely to obtain adoptions. A number of surrenderers said that they had chosen the shelter under study because they thought it was highly visible in the general community, had more visitors than other shelters, and, thus, would provide their animals with a better chance of being adopted. One man claimed, "I chose the [shelter] because the [affiliated] hospital is so well known—so the shelter would have more resources for placement." Another surrenderer, asked why she had chosen this particular shelter, replied, "I knew this was more of a safer place to bring her than to bring her to one of those other places that there's more of a chance of her being put to sleep. I think they try harder."

. . . Making their animals special on the basis of physical or personality characteristics in a shelter with the most resources seemed to further alleviate the surrenderers' guilt. By assuring themselves that their pets would be adopted, surrenderers could avoid dealing with the guilt of knowing that their relinquishments might, in reality, have caused their pets' deaths.

Blaming the Victim

Many surrenderers, considered euthanization a better solution for their pets than allowing them to live in poor situations. In the surrenderers' eyes, death was preferable to sacrificing the quality of life that the animal deserved and, indeed, had come to expect. Although animals were not held culpable for these expectations in a strict sense, their needs were nonetheless at the root of this justification. Although humans were also faulted in these justifications, the animals were implicated, as though their presumed needs forced the surrenderers to risk euthanasia.

For example, some surrenderers felt that euthanasia would be necessary if animals could not be placed in acceptable homes. Presumably, the animals would be neither sufficiently content nor well cared for in such homes. One surrenderer explained that because her kids weren't helping to take care of her pet dog, the possibility of euthanasia was preferable to their neglect. Another man surrendered his dog because she did not receive enough attention in his home. He admitted that he did not want the dog euthanized. When asked if he felt that bringing the dog to the shelter was best for the dog, he responded, "I feel that it is, 'cause she was home alone. I work early and come home late and she's home alone all the time. So I don't think that it's a good idea."

One woman justified the possible euthanasia of the puppy she had found as a price for keeping him off the street and safe. Another man said that he wouldn't want to take the chance of just letting [an animal] go . . . because life as a stray would be worse than death. A woman who had started feeding a stray cat, whom she subsequently relinquished to the shelter, did not want to turn him "back loose in the street." For this woman, dying in the shelter was better for the cat than returning him to his former life.

In several cases, surrenderers considered euthanasia preferable to placing animals in situations where they might put people or other animals in danger. Here, blaming the animal victim is more apparent. . . . One surrenderer explained about the stray she was relinquishing: "She can't get along with our cats . . . she can't get along with our dog. So . . . I don't want them to get in a big fight and one of the kids get bitten or anything—trying to break it up—and then she has to be put to sleep." Another decided midway through the surrender process to have his dog euthanized immediately rather than placed for adoption. He noted, "I'd rather just put her to sleep, you know, 'cause she's mean. I feel they'll do the humane thing. If I gave her to someone and, you know—God forbid she ever bit someone." In this man's eyes, the possibility of the dog's being put into a potentially dangerous situation where others could be hurt and the dog neglected or punished outweighed the chance that the dog could find a good home. . . .

Shelter Workers' Approaches

Like surrenderers, shelter employees displaced blame to lessen or manage the guilt they experienced over killing animals. Surrenderers often blamed others, and shelter employees often blamed the surrenderers. Shelter workers were observed trying to instill guilt into the surrenderers and often took the moral high ground. Yet, like the surrenderers, they too blamed the victim.

Blaming Surrenderers

Most shelter workers' comments about euthanasia were made in the context of their feelings about, and views of, surrenderers. The two were inextricably linked in their minds. Shelter employees considered surrenderers responsible for the deaths of unadopted animals because they were directly responsible for the behavior problems that made the animals inappropriate for adoption or because they had failed to carry out their lifetime responsibility to these animals. As one shelter employee remarked,

> If somebody comes in to surrender an animal, I feel like they did some-thing wrong. [This worker feels like saying to surrenderers,] "You failed. You're bringing this thing that you, you know, adopted as a life-long companion, back to us, and we might have to kill it."

Another worker narrated an example of a typical, aggravating surrender:

> I guess the biggest, all-time aggravating situation that I can think of is somebody who comes in with a cat that is declawed—they just had it declawed, say, a year ago, and now it's peeing all over the carpet. That is one situation, you know, or it's peeing all over the sofa or the furni-ture or the rugs and it's not using its litter box, or it's getting snitty. It doesn't have the same personality, they say, since before it was declawed. But then, I guess I do get aggravated with those surrenderers because once they realize that now the cat is mutilated and it's behav-ing badly, probably because it's mutilated, they don't . . . they just give up on the cat and they bring it to a shelter where we inevitably have to kill it, and . . . they're not interested in doing anymore.

In the example above, the shelter worker blamed the surrenderers' actions for the behavior of declawed cats. The declawed cats would have to be euthanized because these relinquishers had caused the intolerable behavior, but then had refused to deal with it and keep them. . . .

Sometimes the shelter workers were very straightforward in placing blame on surrenderers. One shelter employee stated, "Every time I see someone come in, I think, 'God, you know, we might have to put that animal to sleep. You're so irrespon-sible!'" Another worker said, "I just want them to realize that they were responsible for it." Not only did workers blame the individuals who brought their animals in for having to euthanize them, they also wanted surrenderers to accept the blame. If sur-renderers were held responsible for what happened to their animals, shelter workers would not have to feel that the killings were actually their fault.

Another way in which shelter workers blamed the victims was by viewing the global problem of pet overpopulation and recognizing that most animals in shelters are euthanized simply because there are too many of them and not enough good homes. If this were not the case, shelters might be more like adoption agencies than death row and each relinquishment would seem less like a death sentence for the animal. In this scenario, workers blamed not only the abundance of animals but also the general public for creating the surplus pet population that necessitates euthanasia. Comments such as "I'm mad at whoever it is that's created this problem" and "We're never gonna beat this problem until everybody takes a small amount of responsibility" indicate the shelter workers' frustrations with the public's lack of concern over the killings that shelters are forced to do. . . .

Instilling Guilt

When surrenderers failed to display the proper guilt or grief over their relinquishments, shelter workers often sought to make them feel guilty. As one shelter worker said, "I try really hard not to let a person walk out the door without knowing that 'Gee, this could have been corrected.' " By reminding surrenderers that relinquishment was only one of several options, workers placed the responsibility, blame, and guilt on surrenderers. One shelter worker commented, "I don't want to make people feel bad," but it was clear that making surrenderers feel guilty was precisely what she was trying to do. She continued,

> Sometimes, I feel like it comes across that way. But I'm not trying to make [them] feel guilty. I'm just trying to let [them] know that as a result of [their] actions, this animal may die. Um, generally when someone says to me, "I don't want you to kill my animal," I say, "Then don't sign that piece of paper [and give] it to me, cause there's a big chance that it's gonna happen." And then they look at me and say, "But what am I supposed to do?" "Well, A-B-C-D-E-F-G. I can give you 20 different things that you could do. If you're not willing to do them, then you're gonna have to accept [it], if your choice is to give me the animal, then you're gonna have to accept that this might happen."

This worker came back to this point later, explaining how she would come across to a surrenderer to whom she had given problem-solving options.

> Now you make another choice. Are you definitely going to leave this animal with me or are you going to try to work it out? If you're not

going to try to work it out—if you're definitely gonna leave it with me—understand that this might happen.

Another shelter worker's approach to making surrenderers feel guilty was somewhat more passive because she did not assuage surrenderers' guilty feelings. As she said, "If they come in and act like this is a bag of trash that they want to hand me . . . I tend to be much shorter with them and, um, much less consoling, you know?" One worker noted that she was not intentionally rough on surrenderers, but recognized that she could come across that way. As she explained, "I don't ever try to be mean but, God, I would walk out of there feeling like, maybe I could have tried something else. Maybe I—I should have tried something else."

Taking the Moral High Ground

By blaming surrenderers, shelter workers set themselves apart from and above those who surrendered animals to them. In a sense, they took the moral high ground, claiming that they would never make the kinds of mistakes or decisions that people who surrender animals to them make regularly (Weaver 1986). By insisting that they would never break their lifelong commitment to their own animals, they separated themselves from the group of people who were actually responsible for the need to kill animals placed in shelters.

In fact, workers were quite aware of using this strategy. One shelter worker admitted that she did this at the beginning of her career but implied that she had softened over time as she encountered more surrenderers.

> When I started working here, I think I was pretty much the typical self-righteous, I-know-everything-about-animals [type] and [felt that] none of my animals would ever end up in a shelter, and [that] these people [surrendering animals] must be ignorant and uncaring both at the same time.

Another worker expressed frustrated over a situation that she could not fathom touching her own life:

> And, you know what I mean? Moving—moving as a reason. Well, jeeze, you know what I mean? I've moved three times with two cats and two dogs. How is it that I can manage to find an apartment that allows animals, but [they] can't?

This shelter worker would consider moving to a new home only if she could take her pets. Another shelter employee made the same assessment of her commitment to her pets, swearing,

> I would never move anywhere without my animals. I would protect them, you know. I would do anything I could for them. I have five animals at home that I have to take care of on a daily basis and—and damn it all—they'll never be in a shelter. I don't care if I'm sleeping in—in [the street] tomorrow—my dogs will be sleeping next to me.

Claiming the moral high ground also enabled shelter workers to judge the actions of surrenderers and conclude that they had neither tried hard enough to solve their problems nor properly cared for their animals. One shelter worker spoke for her colleagues when she said, "It aggravates us when we think they haven't put the effort into taking care of their animals to make it work, when it's obvious that they can." Another employee developed an answer:

> People have really simple problems or, you know, that are more annoyances than problems, with their animals, and they just don't examine their situation and solve it before they come to us. And then they come to us as if the world has collapsed and they're frustrated beyond belief, when all it is, is [that] they need to come home and walk the dog first before they sit down and watch the news, or so it's having a piddle accident, you know, and it's really basic things that are easily solved and they're not willing to do it.

By viewing the surrenderers problems as minor and solvable and depicting them as stubborn and uncaring, shelter workers emphasized the wrongdoing of surrenderers who relinquished pets. Magnifying this wrongdoing made workers seem all the more kind and helpful, particularly considering the people they helped. This served not only to reverse the workers' guilt but also to commend them for the job.

Blaming the Victim

Shelter workers, like surrenderers, coped with euthanasia by viewing it as necessary for the animals' sakes, a better alternative to a bad quality of life or painful death. Every time I kill an animal," a worker remarked, "I think to myself, 'What a shame, what a shame. This is so unfair.' But, thank God it wasn't getting smushed by a car, or getting shot in the head, or whatever could have happened." Another worker, almost as graphic in describing the possible horrors an animal could meet outside the shelter, said, "It's better, you know. I have to realize that it's better than what a lot of people would do: leave it or, you know, drown it or something. You know," she continued, "people drown cats." By assuming that the animals would meet a worse fate as a stray or with uncaring people, shelter workers enabled themselves to view euthanasia as merciful. By viewing killing as an act of mercy, shelter workers absolved themselves of their guilt.

A related strategy considered animals' deaths both ongoing and inevitable. Shelter workers resolved their guilt by seeing that the animals were slowly dying in the shelter—euthanasia served merely as an earlier endpoint to eventual death. One shelter worker accomplished this, even putting a positive spin on her participation, by viewing the deaths of the animals in her shelter as a process that she just helps along.

> And I'm not actually killing the animal. I'm just giving it an injection. I'm just helping the process speed up. It—I really feel that most of these animals are dying as we speak. Um, sitting in those cages, the kennel stress that goes on, the frustration . . . the fear, loneliness, and boredom. I mean, I—I can't call it living. Um, so by euthanasia, I think that we're only helping the process along. It's already started, long before we decided to.

This outlook made euthanasia a morally neutral action, if not an act of kindness, in the minds of the shelter staff. By stripping euthanasia of its negative connotation, shelter workers reduced their own feelings of guilt about killing.

Discussion

Surrenderers and shelter workers were bound by a common concern for animals taken to shelters. Both groups were very much concerned about the euthanasia of valued animals, experienced guilt over it, and used the same general strategy to mitigate their guilt—namely, both groups refused to accept blame for euthanasia. That these groups resorted to blame-reducing strategies is not surprising. They appeared to patch together an intricate web of these strategies and made their defenses in tandem, each group unaware of the depth or complexity of the other's perspectives.

Both groups relied on several blame-management strategies. Both surrenderers and shelter workers resorted to blaming the victim (Ryan 1976) by pointing to problems with animals that justified their euthanasia.

Unlike conventional victim blaming, however, which fault individuals rather than the social systems creating the problems, both surrenderers and shelter workers had a sophisticated view of the problem. In their views, society at large is at fault for the need to euthanize some animals because society created the pet-overpopulation problem. Both surrenderers and shelter workers also blamed specific others. Surrenderers would blame the person or persons who made it necessary for them to relinquish their pets, such as their landlord or spouse, while shelter workers blamed individual surrenderers for failing to live up to a lifelong commitment to their companion animals. Finally, shelter workers tried to minimize blame by conveying positive character information about themselves (Weaver 1986).

Second, previous studies of guilt-mitigating techniques have demonstrated that, in order to reduce responsibility for particular acts, individuals commonly diffuse blame in a guilt hierarchy by attributing the major responsibility of their act to others, yet feeling some degree of blame (Henslin 1970). In this study, surrenderers and shelter workers appeared to accept no blame and externalized all responsibility for euthanasia. In short, they placed virtually all the blame on others. . . .

These findings contribute to our understanding of both sides of the shelter blame-game. By resorting to a host of blame-management strategies, both groups avoided personal responsibility for the problem and failed to construct a common ground for promoting communication between them. Yet it is this very communication that could stop the cycle of surrender and euthanasia. Shelter managers and administrators can use these strategies to improve the effectiveness of staff members' interactions with the public, curbing certain guilt-producing strategies that alienate the public. To make surrenderers feel actively guilty or otherwise offended only serves the workers' short-term purpose of relieving their own guilt and stress. . . . To make shelter workers more aware of surrenderers' feelings of guilt may improve the morale of shelter staff, helping them to recognize that many surrenderers are not callous and uncaring toward animals. Also, shelter workers may feel less alone in their concerns for the animals. By being sensitive to surrenderers' guilt and loss, shelter workers may feel more willing to converse with them and provide the supportive, educational experience that could improve the surrenderers' opinion of the humane community and help them to make better decisions regarding future pet ownership.

The humane community, as a whole, may benefit from understanding the guilt that surrenderers experience as they relinquish their companion animals. Such understanding helps those who look for ways to implement both public awareness and educational programs that promote responsible pet ownership. Knowing why people surrender pets may be helpful in determining ways to prevent the problem situations that underlie relinquishment. Understanding how people manage their feelings once they have decided to surrender an animal, however, may be just as important. After all, in many cases, the why can be solved? Pet owners can learn how to train cats not to destroy furniture, individuals can look for apartments that allow pets, and professional dog walkers can take a puppy out during the middle of the day until he or she is housebroken—simple solutions to common pet problems. Yet these problems are reasons why caregivers surrender companion animals to shelters.

Information about surrenderers' coping strategies can be invaluable in the design of future educational efforts to make pet owners think more seriously before they relinquish their pets. Making the public aware that youth does not guarantee an animal's adoption may result in an owner's considering the reality of a pet's future before deciding to surrender that companion animal. It may also inspire people to think more carefully about the long-term commitment needed to care properly for pets. These are important and useful tools in promoting the humane community's ultimate mission of improving companion animal welfare through responsible pet ownership and public awareness.

Questions for Discussion

1. What are the three blame-management strategies used by surrenderers?
2. In what ways are the strategies used by the surrenderers and shelter workers similar?
3. How difficult to do you think it would be to work in an animal shelter and regularly kill perfectly healthy animals? Could you do it?

27 Savages, Drunks, and Lab Animals

The Researcher's Perception of Pain

Mary T. Phillips

Thousands of researchers undertake studies involving millions of animals every year. But how do the researchers think about these animals? What is the researcher's perception of whether and to what degree their experimental animals experience pain? In this ethnographic study of two New York laboratories, Mary Phillips discovered that animal researchers defined pain very narrowly, and carefully distinguished laboratory animals from other animals, such as their own pets. Since laboratory animals are seen as research tools, as objects, scientists rarely considered whether they ever suffered or felt pain.

As Martin Pernick tells it, "The Case of McGonigle's Foot" is a horror story (Pernick 1985, 3–8). On a summer day in 1862 a Philadelphia laborer named McGonigle took a fall and fractured his ankle. He was rushed to a hospital, where doctors immediately amputated the man's foot *without anesthesia.* This occurred 16 years after a public demonstration of ether anesthesia at the Massachusetts General Hospital had shown an astonished world that surgery could be painless. The Pennsylvania Hospital, where McGonigle was taken, had been among the last of the major medical institutions in the United States to introduce anesthetic drugs, but even there ether had been in use for a good 10 years. Chloroform and nitrous oxide had been in general use for almost as long as ether, and all were inexpensive and readily available in 1862. So why no anesthesia for poor McGonigle? (Who, incidentally, died of shock two days later.)

The case was not an isolated incident. For several decades after its discovery, anesthesia was withheld in a large proportion of surgical operations. According to records unearthed by Pernick and discussed in his fascinating study of nineteenth-

---

Originally published in 1993 in *Society and Animals*, vol. 1, no. 1, pp. 61–81. Reprinted with permission from Brill Academic Publishers.

century attitudes toward pain, about 32 percent of all major limb amputations performed at the Pennsylvania Hospital from 1853 to 1862 were done without anesthesia. Pernick gives a comparable figure for amputations done at New York Hospital during the five years following the introduction of ether there (Pernick 1985, 4).

The reasons for this drew upon a complex ideology of pain that attributed sensitivity to pain selectively, according to social status (sex, race or ethnic origin, age, education, social class) and personal habits (especially alcohol and drug use) as well as the nature of the surgical operation. People considered most sensitive to pain (and therefore the most likely to receive anesthesia) were women, the educated and wealthy classes, whites (except for recent immigrants), children and the elderly, and people with no history of alcohol or drug abuse. Their social opposites—males, the uneducated, the poor, "savages" (meaning blacks and Indians), Irish and German immigrants, young adults, and alcoholics were considered least likely to need anesthesia because of their relative insensitivity to pain. McGonigle fit perfectly the model for insensitivity: the man was an uneducated Irish immigrant who had been drinking when he fell (Pernick 1985, 4, 148–167).

Down at the bottom of the hierarchy of sensitivity, along with the lower classes, was the place of animals. Silas Weir Mitchell, nineteenth-century physician and pioneer in neurology, wrote: "[I]n our process of being civilized we have won, I suspect, intensified capacity to suffer. The savage does not feel pain as we do; nor, as we examine the descending scale of life, do animals seem to have the acuteness of pain-sense at which we have arrived" (quoted in Dimock 1996).

This hierarchical view of life, so much a part of the nineteenth-century ethos of colonialism, casts differences of skin color and class and culture (and species, the extreme case) as unbridgeable chasms. Such a perspective did not foster much empathy for the suffering of others, as this episode from the history of anesthesia illustrates. "The descending scale of life," however, is a metaphor from a bygone age. Already in the Victorian era (a time of great humanitarian and antivivisectionist movements), the scope of empathy was growing. Social historians have remarked upon the dawning, at about this time, of a distinctly modern sensitivity to the feelings of a widening circle of others. By the turn of the century, social station was no longer considered a relevant consideration in the decision to administer anesthetic drugs. Today we would no more condone operating on a Native American without anesthesia (or an Irish immigrant, drunk or not) than we would condone calling him or her a savage.

If we were to document the use of anesthesia in veterinary surgery over the past century, we would probably find a pattern similar to that of the less fortunate classes of humans. Animal surgeons in the nineteenth century were slow to adopt surgical anesthesia, in spite of a strong campaign by the British antivivisection movement to counter the belief that animals were insensitive to pain (Pernick 1985, 178). Antivivisectionist pressure prompted the British Association for the Advancement of Science to publish guidelines in 1871 that contained a requirement for the use of anesthetics in experimentation, but a study by Stewart Richards (1986; 1987) suggests that even the authors of these guidelines often did not follow them. John Scott Burdon Sanderson, who was one of the authors of the 1871 guidelines, omitted any mention of anesthesia in describing many experiments in his *Handbook for the Physiological Laboratory* (1873). Richards's detailed analysis of the *Handbook* reveals that about 15% of the potentially painful experiments did not specify the use of any anesthetic.

Nevertheless, the use of anesthesia for all major surgery, both animal and human, is now routine. This says something about how attitudes have changed, but it is hardly the end of the story. In a three-year study of animal research laboratories in New York, I found that the administration of pain-relieving drugs to animals used in scientific experiments differs considerably from the standards for human patients—and, I suspect, for pets in veterinary hospitals. In the remainder of this paper, I will present some empirical findings from the study, and I will suggest a framework for understanding scientists' beliefs and practices regarding pain in laboratory animals. As will be seen, researchers tend to view lab animals as somehow different from other animals, belonging to an altogether distinct category of being. Now, as in centuries past, such rigid categorization schemes can have far-reaching consequences. Among these consequences are beliefs about the other's pain, and measures taken—or not taken—for its relief.

Methods and Procedures

This report is based on an ethnographic study of laboratories located in two research institutions in the New York City area. At one of the institutions (hereafter referred to as the Institute), participants were selected using a random sampling technique, weighted to assure adequate representation of behaviorists and of those using species other than mice and rats. At the other, smaller, institution (hereafter referred to as the University), every eligible researcher was selected. A total of 27 scientists in 23 laboratories participated in the study, for an overall participation rate of 77% of those selected.

From January 1985 through November 1987, I spent hundreds of hours observing experiments on rats, mice, hamsters, toads, birds, rabbits, cats, monkeys, and fish. I took notes during these observations, from which I later typed a detailed account of each session. After several weeks or months (or, in one case, years) in a given laboratory, I interviewed the lab's study participant, using a structured, open-ended interview guide. Interviews, which lasted about two hours, were tape-recorded, and later transcribed. In addition, each study participant filled out a questionnaire, which provided background information on such variables as gender, age, marital status, pet ownership, and educational background. All data reported below are from observation notes, interview transcripts, or background questionnaires.

Anesthesia in Animal Research

Until the passage of the Laboratory Animal Welfare Act (PL 89-544) in 1966, experimenters in this country had free rein to do whatever they wanted to animals in their laboratories. Even after 1966, researchers were not required to use anesthesia or any other pain-relieving drugs, since the Act was primarily intended to ensure that animals purchased by scientific laboratories were not stolen pets. The legislation also established some minimum standards for the humane care of animals awaiting experimentation. However, it covered only facilities that used dogs and cats, and it expressly exempted from regulation the treatment of animals "during actual research or experimentation." (For a more detailed discussion of the Animal Welfare Act and relevant guidelines, see Phillips and Sechzer 1989, 17–34.)

The Act has been amended three times: in 1970, 1976, and 1985. The 1970 amendments changed its name to the Animal Welfare Act (dropping "Laboratory"), extended coverage to zoos and circuses and to many more species, and inserted a provision requiring "the appropriate use of anesthetic or tranquilizing drugs, when such use would be proper in the opinion of the attending veterinarian of such research facilities." This was backed by a requirement (still in effect) that each research facility covered by the Act submit an annual report to the government showing how many animals of each species were used in experiments during the previous year, how many of these animals received pain-relieving drugs, and how many animals were used in painful experiments without receiving any pain relief. The report must include an explanation for any instances of the latter. These annual reports are public record, available by request under the Freedom of Information Act. I will return to this subject presently for a close look at the reports filed by the particular institutions examined in this study.

The 1976 amendments were concerned with issues irrelevant to this discussion (interstate transportation of animals and animal fighting ventures), but in 1985 the pain-relief provisions were strengthened somewhat. An explicit prohibition was placed on the use of paralytic drugs without anesthesia (once a popular procedure in vision research), and more authority was vested in the facility's veterinarian to make decisions about pain relief. In addition, the 1985 amendments required that an Institutional Animal Committee be established at each facility to review experiments that might involve pain, and to ensure that research meets all the standards of the Act, including these other new provisions: that the principal investigator consider alternatives to painful procedures; that animal pain and distress be minimized; and "that the withholding of tranquilizers, anesthesia, analgesia, or euthanasia when scientifically necessary shall continue for only the necessary period of time."

These regulations merely codified recommendations already established in the animal research guidelines of numerous professional scientific societies, as well as the guidelines of the National Institutes of Health (NIH). Compliance with the NIH guidelines, first published in 1963, is mandatory for researchers receiving NIH funds—and that means the majority of them (USDHHS 1985). Moreover, the NIH guidelines cover *all* warm-blooded animals used in research, thus filling a gap left by the Animal Welfare Act's exclusion (until recently) of mice, rats, and birds from its coverage.

The cumulative effect of these regulations and guidelines is constraining, despite the loophole that allows scientists to withhold anesthesia when "scientifically necessary." I observed no instances in which surgery was performed on unanesthetized animals, and without exception researchers told me they would consider it unacceptable to do so. Legal, political, and technical/scientific reasons for using anesthesia are overwhelming, quite aside from the ethical qualms that many researchers expressed. They feared the consequences of breaking the law and bringing down the wrath of animal advocates. They pointed out that it is more convenient to operate on anesthetized animals than on struggling ones. In addition, scientists have come to appreciate the many ways in which pain and stress can alter physiological functions and thereby affect the validity of research results. The clincher, perhaps, is that most reputable scientific journals will not publish results of painful research done on unanesthetized animals. One researcher told me frankly that he had wanted to curarize some monkeys without anesthesia for vision experiments, but he was deterred by the knowledge that he could never get the work published.

However, none of these rules or regulations can prevent a researcher from becoming inattentive or careless in monitoring an animal's level of anesthesia during surgery. While one laboratory I visited had an elaborate array of equipment to monitor the physiological state of the cats and monkeys undergoing surgery there, many scientists who worked with rats and mice relied on nothing more than the animal's general appearance. Unlike human operating rooms, animal laboratories have no full-time anesthesiologist standing by whose sole responsibility is to administer and monitor the anesthesia. Sometimes, during very long experiments, anesthetized animals are even left alone for hours at a time.

One morning when I arrived at a neuroscience laboratory to observe the finale of an experiment on a cat that had begun the day before, I found the investigators sitting around glumly. They had worked until about 1:00 the early morning before, they told me, leaving the cat anesthetized with a combination of drugs (urethane and surithal) administered continuously through a vein. When a graduate student arrived the next morning at about 6:00 am, the cat was dead. There is no reason to suppose that the cat ever gained consciousness, but if it had, its open wounds would have caused intense suffering. Leaving anesthetized animals unattended through the night was standard practice in this laboratory, and is apparently so in many neuroscience labs, where experiments often last for 36 hours or longer. The intention is never to cause pain (nor, certainly, to kill the animal prematurely), but it is implausible to believe it never happens.

In another laboratory, I was present when a rat regained consciousness during brain surgery. The rat was one of 20 given brain transplants on one day by a team consisting of the senior investigator (study participant), a postdoctoral fellow, the facility's veterinarian, and an undergraduate student. The procedure was for the veterinarian to inject each rat with anesthetic (chloropent, a commercially available drug containing pentobarbital and chlorohydrate) about 10 minutes prior to surgery. Then an incision was made in the top of the rat's head, the skin drawn back, and a drill used to make a small hole in the skull. Into this opening the researcher injected a tiny amount of material that had been extracted from the brain of a rat fetus a few hours earlier. The incision was then closed with surgical staples and the rat was placed on a warming pad to recover. The whole procedure took about 20 minutes.

My notes for the afternoon show that at 2:35 p.m., the postdoctoral fellow began drilling into the skull of a rat, which immediately began to squirm and struggle. The rat's hind legs began scrambling in a coordinated running movement, eventually running right off the small cardboard box being used as a makeshift operating platform. While its hindquarters were hanging over the edge of the platform, the rat's head was still held firmly in place by ear bars, part of the stereotaxic device that keeps the animal's head correctly aligned for precise placement of the drill. The researcher kept on working on the skull, paying no attention to the rat's frantic struggles. After several minutes of this, the rat managed to kick over the box-platform, making it impossible for the researcher to continue. At that point, he asked the veterinarian for more anesthesia, which the latter immediately injected. The researcher righted the box, repositioned the rat on it, and at once resumed drilling. The rat again struggled until half of its body had slipped off the box. The researcher continued drilling for about 30 seconds, then once more repositioned the rat. By this time it was 2:45, ten minutes after the rat's first movements; the booster dose of anesthesia had taken effect, and the animal became quiet, and remained so for the duration of the surgery. During all this lime, the senior investigator, seated a few feet away performing an identical operation on another rat, did not look up from his work. The others paid no attention, either. They all acted as though nothing unusual or untoward was going on.

I asked the senior investigator about this incident when I interviewed him some three months later. I described what I had seen, and asked if he thought the rat had been in pain. He replied that "in that kind of situation, it's probably more uncomfort than anything else." But then he asked, rhetorically, "Is it worthwhile giving a general anesthetic to prevent the animal from feeling those two minutes of pain that would be involved in surgery and risk killing the animal?" He continued, explaining at some length the statistical probability of accidents due to anesthetic overdose. Out of every 20 animals, he said, one or two are likely to be more resistant to the anesthesia than the others. But "99% of the animals that die before you want to terminate them, it's because of anesthetic." "I think that in order to eliminate all pain," he concluded, "the chances are that you would be killing a lot more animals."

This scientist did not seem very convinced, himself, that the rat felt "more uncomfort than anything else." But the question was not really important for him. Much more important was the possibility of losing data by inadvertently killing animals with too much anesthesia. The risk is not that animals might die—they were all to be killed a week or two later—but that they might die "before you want to terminate them." In this passage, the scientist has subtly clothed his interest in the success of his experiment in the nobler garb of concern for the animal's life.

Analgesia in Animal Research

In spite of these kinds of lapses, there is a wide consensus among researchers that anesthetics should be used in pretty much the same situations as for humans, and in practice this is usually followed. At any rate, researchers have virtually no latitude in deciding when to administer anesthetics. Analgesics—painkillers, such as aspirin— are an entirely different matter. The use of analgesics in animal research, in practice, if not in theory, is left almost entirely to the discretion of the investigator. For this reason, the administration of analgesics can provide us with a far more sensitive indicator of the view of animal pain and suffering held by scientific researchers than can the use of anesthetics.

On the face of it, the federal regulations require the use of analgesics no less than anesthetics. The Animal Welfare Act mandates that "animal pain and distress [be] minimized, including adequate veterinary care with the appropriate use of anesthetic, analgesic, tranquilizing drugs, or euthanasia" (1966, PL 89-544 Sec. 13 [3] [A]) and that "in any practice which could cause pain to animals (i) that a doctor of veterinary medicine [be] consulted in the planning of such procedures; (ii) for the use of tranquilizers, analgesics, and anesthetics" (1966, PL 89-544 Sec. 13 [3] [C] [i, ii]). The National Institutes of Health *Guide* is more specific. It states: "Postsurgical care should include observing the animal to ensure uneventful recovery from anesthesia and surgery; administering supportive fluids, analgesics, and other drugs as required . . ." (USDHHS 1985, 38).

Analgesics are routinely given to human patients following surgery, and in fact a number of commentators have made much of modern Westerners' dependence on painkillers (e.g., Illich 1976; see also Pernick 1985, 233–234). In the animal laboratories, however, analgesics were rarely used. No one (with the possible exception of some animal welfare advocates) considers this a violation of the regulations, but rather a (more or less) legitimate interpretation of the "appropriate use" and "as required" clauses. Whereas the regulations were invariably interpreted to require anesthesia for surgery, they were not construed to require analgesic drugs under any specific conditions. Analgesics were considered—when they were considered at all— to be a matter for individual judgment.

In the 23 laboratories I visited, I never saw an analgesic administered, although two researchers reported regular analgesic use: monkeys were said to be given Tylenol (acetaminophen) after brain surgery in one laboratory; and rats that had had brain surgery in another laboratory were reportedly given Talwin (pentazocine, a potent nonnarcotic analgesic), at the veterinarian's suggestion. I was not present immediately after surgeries in either laboratory, but I have no reason to doubt these reports.

In a third laboratory, the senior investigator told me that he gives post-operative rats an aspirin in their water "all the time." (He later modified this claim to "sometimes," and, when pressed, "not normally.") However, this laboratory chief had his graduate students do all the surgeries, and the student I had observed not only did not administer aspirin, but she told me that she never did so because aspirin is not appropriate for rats. It was her belief that "there just are no analgesics appropriate for rats." In a fourth laboratory, monkeys received no analgesics after head surgery at the time of my visits, but both scientists interviewed here stated their intention to begin the use of opiates for this purpose soon.

It should be noted that in five laboratories there was really no opportunity to administer analgesics, either because the animals were killed while still under surgical anesthesia or because nothing that would nominally be considered painful was done to them. This discussion, which assumes that the question of whether or not to administer an analgesic is an applicable one, should be understood to refer only to the remaining 18 laboratories. In most of the latter, major survival surgery provided a situation in which one could reasonably wonder if an analgesic might be appropriate (see Table 1).

Table 1   Use of Analgesics by Study Participants

Category	No. of Labs
A. Inapplicable (Animals killed before regaining consciousness from surgical anesthesia; or no painful procedures)	5
B. Analgesic use after surgery reported on a regular basis	2
C. Analgesic use after surgery (for monkeys only) to be instituted soon	1
D. Analgesic use reported but contradicted by observations	1
E. No analgesic use reported or observed, nor any plans to consider it	14

The large majority of researchers interviewed for the present study who did not administer analgesics (Table 1, Category E) appeared surprised when I asked about them. Some answered as though they thought I meant anesthetics; others said the idea had never occurred to them; many assured me that their animals did not seem to need painkillers; a few, like the graduate student performing rat surgery, thought none was available; and a sizable proportion added that, in any event, they would not want to introduce the unpredictable effects of a new variable into their research results.

The following interview excerpts are drawn from many that illustrate these themes:

MTP:	Do the rats suffer much coming out of anesthesia, after the surgery?
RESEARCHER:	Well, I can imagine they have a headache.
MTP:	Do they ever get analgesics?
RESEARCHER:	Um [pause] No, I don't think so. Of course, they are certainly anesthetized for surgery. Um [trails off]
MTP:	Is that something you've ever given any thought to?
RESEARCHER:	I've never given it any thought. I'm not sure I would, anyway. I give myself as few drugs as possible, even when I'm in pain. . . . That's tricky, to dwell on that issue. One could turn down all sorts of alleyways of thought.

* * *

MTP: Is there any pain recovering from that surgery [rats recovering from ovariectomies]?

RESEARCHER: I would imagine that after any surgery there must be some pain. They don't seem to show any discomfort. They eat as well. They drink as well. They walk around as well as before. But I can't ask them.

MTP: Do you ever use, or have you ever considered using, analgesics?

RESEARCHER: No, we don't use that.

MTP: Is there any particular reason?

RESEARCHER: I think simply because it would add another variable to the experiment. And because you don't see the animal in any apparent discomfort.

                              * * *

MTP: Do you ever give analgesics to rodents or monkeys, or cats when you work with them?

RESEARCHER: Anesthetics.

MTP: No, analgesics. Painkillers. [pause] Things like aspirin, Tylenol.

RESEARCHER: Uh [pause] No. I never have. . . . You would first have to ask the question, is the aspirin going to affect any phenomena you're looking at. In order to investigate that, and what dose, and how long . . . you'd have to do an experiment. . . . You'd have to add an extra control group. . . . It would just be adding another variable.

MTP: Has this ever been a subject of discussion with anybody?

RESEARCHER: Never. [chuckles] Never mentioned whether animals should take aspirin or not. . . . If you give an animal an aspirin to overcome its discomfort, then what about sleeping on a wire mesh floor? I mean, shouldn't you have some shavings for the animal to sleep on? Wouldn't they be more comfortable if you did that? . . . The goal of your research then becomes providing a pleasant surrounding for your animals.

Most researchers had never sought a veterinarian's advice on this subject, and the last quoted above even seemed amused by the idea. Yet they had had very little training in this area, and often admitted ignorance about available drugs. The only scientist who did consult a veterinarian—an endocrinologist who was worried about the poor appearance of her rats after surgery—was advised to administer a painkiller, a practice that she told me had since become routine in her laboratory (this was the laboratory in which I was told Talwin was given). In only two other laboratories were discussions about the issue reported to have taken place, and in both cases the decision was subsequently made to give analgesics. Elsewhere, the question was not treated as worthy of serious discussion.

Inaccurate beliefs were sometimes given as reasons for not considering analgesics. For instance, a scientist told me that he could not give cats morphine-related analgesics, because "cats don't tolerate morphine drugs." Another told me that "Demerol drives [cats] crazy; they go bananas if you give them Demerol." In fact, a standard veterinary manual recommends Demerol (the trade name for meperidine, a morphine-like narcotic) and other opioids, such as buprenorphine, for cats (Flecknell 1987). In another laboratory, a neuroscientist assured me that the nembutal anesthesia he used in monkey surgery had an analgesic effect that lasted for "half a day" after the animals regained consciousness. On the contrary, the veterinary manual states that one of nembutal's undesirable characteristics is its *poor* analgesic activity (Flecknell 1987, 35). Recovery from nembutal anesthesia (as from other barbiturates) is prolonged, causing the animal to remain groggy for hours afterwards; that effect may have led the researcher to think, mistakenly, that nembutal is also an analgesic.

I do not mean to imply that all of the animals were in pain after the surgical operations I observed or that they *should* have been given painkillers. I am not claiming a privileged position from which to judge such matters. In fact, I was amazed, just as some scientists said they were, by how active and normal many of the animals appeared as they emerged from anesthesia. (On the other hand, there were also some that looked miserable.) However, at the time of my fieldwork, there was growing discussion of this issue in the animal science and veterinary literature. Elsewhere I have documented a sharp rise in publications on this topic beginning in the mid-1970s (Phillips and Sechzer 1989, 58–60). Experts in the field of animal pain were pointing out that pain may be present in spite of an animal's "normal" appearance (Dawkins 1980), and many were urging the use of analgesics, especially after surgery. Manuals and papers with advice on appropriate drugs and dosages for various species were readily available (e.g., Heidrich and Kent 1985; Kitchell *et al.* 1983; Soma 1985; Wright *et al.* 1985). The new climate of opinion was summed up in one pain specialist's comment that "one of the psychological curiosities of therapeutic decision making is the withholding of analgesic drugs, because the clinician is not absolutely certain that the animal is experiencing pain. Yet the same individual will administer antibiotics without documenting the presence of bacterial infection. Pain and suffering constitute the only situation in which I believe that, if in doubt, one should go ahead and treat" (Davis 1983, 175).

This attitude toward analgesics can be found in at least two sets of interdisciplinary animal research guidelines drawn up by organizations with a broad representation (including veterinarians and pain specialists). One adopted at an international conference on animal research held under the auspices of the World Health Organization and UNESCO, stated that "Postoperative pain should be prevented or relieved by analgesics" (CIOMS 1983, VIII). The other is the New York Academy of Sciences' Interdisciplinary Principles and Guidelines for the Use of Animals in Research, Testing, and Education, which states that "Post-surgical analgesia must be provided appropriate for the type of surgical intervention" (NYAS 1988, 5).

It is against this background that one must consider the almost total lack of interest in animal analgesia that I found among researchers. The subject was being treated very seriously by specialists in veterinary medicine and pain, while researchers in the laboratories included in this study were ignoring it. The point being made here is not so much that analgesics were withheld, but that so few researchers even considered the subject worth thinking about.

USDA Data on Pain in Animal Experimentation

Statistics compiled by the United States Department of Agriculture show that nationwide, scientists report that the majority of research animals are not exposed to painful or distressing procedures: the percentage of animals in this category has ranged from about 58% to 62% in recent years. Of the others, most received "appropriate pain relief." The percentage of animals reported to have actually experienced pain or distress, without any pain relief, ranges from about 6% to 8% each year (see Table 2). These figures are provided by the animal facilities themselves, in the annual reports mentioned earlier that are required under the provisions of the Animal Welfare Act.

Comparable data for the University and the Institute alone are given in Table 3. The years 1985–1987 represent the period during which my fieldwork was carried out (most of it in 1985). University scientists reported *no* animals subjected to "pain or distress without administration of appropriate anesthetic, analgesic, or tranquilizer drugs" (Category D) during all three years. Researchers are required to attach explanations for all Category D cases; the explanations attached to the Institute's reports for these years reveal that none of the experiments in Category D was performed in any laboratory included in this study. We can only conclude that *not one* investigator included in the present study reported *any* instances of unrelieved pain for *any* of the experiments performed during this three-year period. These experiments included not only many instances of major survival surgery (with no post-operative analgesics), but also mice injected with cobra venom, LD-50 tests in which rats died from large doses of a toxic substance, and cancers in mice and rats. No anesthetics or analgesics were administered in these non-surgical situations.

Table 2   Use of Pain-Relieving Drugs in Animal Research: U.S. Data (1982–1986)[a]

(A) Total no. of federally protected animals[b] used by reporting facilities

(B) Percent of federally protected animals not exposed to painful or distressing procedures

(C) Percent that received appropriate pain relief

(D) Percent that did not receive pain relief because it would have interfered with test results

Date	A	B	C	D
1982	1,576,556	62%	30%	8%
1983	1,680,242	61%	31%	8%
1984	2,074,133	62%	32%	6%
1985	2,153,787	57.6%	35.6%	6.8%
1986	1,778,403	59.4%	34.2%	6.3%

[a] Data are for the period October 1–September 30. This table was compiled from annual reports published by the United States Department of Agriculture (USDA-APHIS 1982–1986, Animal Welfare Enforcement). The USDA compiles its report from the annual reports filed by individual research facilities (see USDA-APHIS 1982–1987, Annual Reports of Research Facilities.

[b] Until recently, "federally protected animals" included only dogs, cats, nonhuman primates, guinea pigs, hamsters, and rabbits. Birds, rats, mice, horses and other farm animals were explicitly excluded from regulation and facilities were not required to include them (or any cold-blooded animals) in their annual reports. A January 1992 court decision may mean that henceforth birds, rats and mice will also have to be included in annual reports.

Category D experiments go unchallenged by the USDA as long as a "brief explanation" for withholding pain-relieving drugs is attached. It is possible that for some investigators this is simply too much trouble, but judging from the attachments to the Institute reports, an explanation acceptable to the USDA requires precious little thought or effort. The following samples are typical, and constitute about a third of all the explanations attached to the Institute reports for 1985–1987:

Table 3   Use of Pain-relieving Drugs in Animal Research: University and Institute Data (1985–1987)[a]

(A) Total no. of animals

(B) Percent of animals used in research, experiments, or tests involving no pain or distress

(C) Percent of animals used in research, experiments, or tests where appropriate anesthetic, analgesic, or tranquilizer drugs were administered to avoid pain or distress

(D) Percent of animals used in research, experiments, or tests involving pain or distress without administration of appropriate anesthetic, analgesic, or tranquilizer drugs

Date	A	B	C	D
UNIVERSITY[b]				
1985	3,413	8%	92%	0
1986	2,648	88.9%	11.1%	0
1987	3,942	28%	72%	0
INSTITUTE[c]				
1985	30,654	73.2%	21.5%	5.3%
1986	1,983	46.4%	51.5%	2.1%
1987	3,284	19.5%	77.3%	3.3%

[a] The figures in this table are adapted from the Annual Report of Research Facilities filed by each institution with the United States Department of Agriculture and obtained by the author under the Freedom of Information Act. The reporting period is from October 1 through September 30. (USDA-APHIS 1982–1987)

[b] Rats and mice are included in University data for all years.

[c] Rats and mice are included in Institute data for 1985 only. The inclusion of data for rats and mice was voluntary.

Dogs are used to study treatment of heart worms

Rats are used in studies of aortic occlusion and Trypansoma [sic] infection (Annual Report 1985)

Seventeen rabbits were utilized in 2 studies of Toxic Shock Syndrome prevention (Annual Report 1986)

Fourty[sic]-four rabbits were required for use in a study of Toxic Shock syndrome prevention (Annual Report 1987)

In 1987, an atypical explanation also was submitted: *Sixty-three hamsters were decapitated without prior anesthesia as anesthesia would alter neuroendocrine data* (Annual Report 1987)

The last is atypical because it alone mentions why no anesthesia could be administered; the others simply state the general type of research that was done. The hamster explanation is also noteworthy for another reason: I saw scores of rats and mice decapitated without anesthesia at both the University and the Institute, as well as unanesthetized mice killed by cervical dislocation or a blow to the head. And yet none of these researchers made any entries in Category D on their annual reports.

Since the USDA data reflect only the scientists' own evaluations of animal pain and distress in their research, these figures cannot be used to "prove" that there is very little painful experimentation. All they show is that researchers *report* very little painful experimentation. When the biomedical research establishment uses USDA figures uncritically to refute complaints about animal pain, as the American Medical Association did in a recent white paper, one cannot but wonder if the authors are really as unsophisticated as all that. The AMA paper smugly states, "The fact that most experiments do not expose animals to pain was confirmed by a report issued by the Department of Agriculture. . ." (AMA 1989, 17). This gives the impression that the USDA conducts independent evaluations using standardized criteria, which is far from the case.

One can easily understand why scientists might not want to fan the flames of the animal research controversy by reporting many Category D animals. Animal rights activists can easily obtain copies of these reports under the Freedom of Information Act just as I did, and target individual research facilities for harassment. These fears probably underlie some decisions to report animals in Category B (no pain or distress) rather than Category D; and to put all animals that received anesthetics in Category C (pain relieved by drugs), regardless of whether analgesics had been withheld. However, the researchers I studied appeared convinced and they clearly hoped that, by opening their laboratories to me, I would also become convinced that nothing painful or distressing was going on.

Over and over researchers assured me that in their laboratories, animals were never hurt. "I love animals. . . . I would not feel that I'm doing the right thing if I would do anything to animals that is not being done to human beings," said one. "I do believe in not causing pain to them," said another. "We certainly aren't inflicting pain on the animals," said a third. Another insisted, "I limit the kinds of experiments that I think about [doing] to those that are not going to cause pain and suffering to the animal."

Scientists could tell me these things with apparent conviction because they defined pain and suffering very narrowly. "Pain" meant the acute pain of surgery on conscious animals, and almost nothing else. Most felt that their humane obligations were fulfilled when they relieved that pain with anesthesia. Although the USDA reporting forms refer to "pain or distress" and ask for information regarding "anesthetic, analgesic, or tranquilizer drugs," no annual report for any of half a dozen research facilities that I examined ever included a category D explanation of why analgesics were not administered. As we have seen, one certainly cannot assume that this is because analgesics always *were* administered.

Conclusions

The scientists I studied were full participants in "the modern sensibility." There were no latter-day Cartesians among them who claimed that animals do not feel pain. The majority of them had pets at home, with whom they seemed capable of empathizing enormously. But their pets were individuals whom they knew by name, and whom they would *never* use in an experiment. Laboratory animals were (usually) nameless, deindividualized creatures, whose sole purpose in life was to serve in a scientific experiment. Researchers continually made distinctions between lab animals and pets, on the one hand, and between lab and wild animals on the other.

Although researchers always acknowledged the ability of animals to feel pain, this knowledge remained an abstraction for most. Scientists rarely saw any pain or suffering in their labs. Their view of lab animals as statistical aggregates overshadowed any perception of an individual animal's feelings at any given moment. And when I went beyond the issue of physical pain to ask about psychological or emotional suffering, many researchers were at a loss to answer. Typical was the comment of one neuroscientist who, when asked about possible boredom of monkeys kept in bare metal cages, answered with a palpable lack of interest: "We can speculate about these things, but I think it's pointless." Another responded more impatiently: "Oh, how would anybody know that? I mean, anybody? How could anybody know that? There's a danger of being anthropomorphic about anything. I just, I wouldn't even venture a guess."

The savage and the drunk of yesteryear find their counterpart in the twentieth-century laboratory, but not because of any simple belief that the lab animal is insensitive to pain. Laboratory animals are categorized and perceived as distinctive creatures whose purpose and meaning is constituted by their role as bearers of scientific data. Researchers believe that all animals are *capable* of feeling pain, but what they actually *see* when they look at lab animals is a scientific objective, not the animal's subjective experience. The result is that it rarely occurs to them to consider whether an animal is in pain, is suffering or whether it is feeling anything at all, outside the boundaries of the research protocol.

Questions for Discussion

1. What is the importance of a name? And thus, why is the absence of naming significant for animals in the laboratory?
2. What factors operate to constrain the naming of animals used in research?
3. What general conclusions can be reached about the social construction of other animals (e.g., pets, "wild animals," "farm animals," and so forth)?

Part IX: Animal Rights— Philosophy and Social Movement

We should not kill, eat, torture, and exploit animals because they do not want to be so treated, and we know that. If we listen, we can hear them.

Josephine Donovan

28 All Animals Are Equal

Peter Singer

With the publication his groundbreaking book Animal Liberation *in 1975, philosopher Peter Singer is often credited with starting the modern animal rights movement. This selection is taken from the first chapter of that important book, in which Singer spells out the philosophical argument for the ethical treatment of animals. Interestingly, Singer never speaks of animal rights, but rather of their interests. Any being who suffers has an interest in not suffering, and to place the interests of humans over animals, simply on the basis of species, would be akin to favoring the interests of men over women or whites over blacks. Singer thus argues that we must apply a principle of equal consideration, whereby the suffering of all beings is treated equally, regardless of species. And as we consider how to respond to the suffering of other beings, we should be guided by the utilitarian philosophy which espouses" the greatest good for the greatest number."*

"Animal Liberation" may sound more like a parody of other liberation movements than a serious objective. The idea of "The Rights of Animals" actually was once used to parody the case for women's rights. When Mary Wollstonecraft, a forerunner of today's feminists, published her *Vindication of the Rights of Woman* in 1792, her views were widely regarded as absurd, and before long an anonymous publication appeared entitled *A Vindication of the Rights of Brutes*. The author of this satirical work (now known to have been Thomas Taylor, a distinguished Cambridge philosopher) tried to refute Mary Wollstonecraft's arguments by showing that they could be carried one stage further. If the argument for equality was sound when applied to women, why should it not be applied to dogs, cats, and horses? The reasoning seemed to hold for these "brutes" too; yet to hold that brutes had rights was manifestly absurd. Therefore the reasoning by which this conclusion had been reached must be unsound, and if unsound when applied to brutes, it must also be unsound when applied to women, since the very same arguments had been used in each case.

In order to explain the basis of the case for the equality of animals, it will be helpful to start with an examination of the case for the equality of women. Let us assume that we wish to defend the case for women's rights against the attack by Thomas Taylor. How should we reply?

One way in which we might reply is by saying that the case for equality between men and women cannot validly be extended to nonhuman animals. Women have a right to vote, for instance, because they are just as capable of making rational decisions about the future as men are; dogs, on the other hand, are incapable of understanding the significance of voting, so they cannot have the right to vote. There are many other obvious ways in which men and women resemble each other closely, while humans and animals differ greatly. So, it might be said, men and women are similar beings and should have similar rights, while humans and nonhumans are different and should not have equal rights.

The reasoning behind this reply to Taylor's analogy is correct up to a point, but it does not go far enough. There are obviously important differences between humans and other animals, and these differences must give rise to some differences in the rights that each have. Recognizing this evident fact, however, is no barrier to the case for extending the basic principle of equality to nonhuman animals. The differences that exist between men and women are equally undeniable, and the supporters of Women's Liberation are aware that these differences may give rise to different rights. Many feminists hold that women have the right to an abortion on request. It does not follow that since these same feminists are campaigning for equality between men and women they must support the right of men to have abortions too. Since a man cannot have an abortion, it is meaningless to talk of his right to have one. Since dogs can't vote, it is meaningless to talk of their right to vote. There is no reason why either Women's Liberation or Animal Liberation should get involved in such nonsense. The extension of the basic principle of equality from one group to another does not imply that we must treat both groups in exactly the same way, or grant exactly the same rights to both groups. Whether we should do so will depend on the nature of the members of the two groups. The basic principle of equality does not require equal or identical treatment; it requires equal consideration. Equal consideration for different beings may lead to different treatment and different rights.

So there is a different way of replying to Taylor's attempt to parody the case for women's rights, a way that does not deny the obvious differences between human beings and nonhumans but goes more deeply into the question of equality and concludes by finding nothing absurd in the idea that the basic principle of equality applies to so-called brutes. At this point such a conclusion may appear odd; but if we examine more deeply the basis on which our opposition to discrimination on grounds of race or sex ultimately rests, we will see that we would be on shaky ground if we were to demand equality for blacks, women, and other groups of oppressed humans while denying equal consideration to nonhumans. To make this clear we need to see, first, exactly why racism and sexism are wrong. When we say that all human beings, whatever their race, creed, or sex, are equal, what is it that we are asserting? Those who wish to defend hierarchical, inegalitarian societies have often pointed out that by whatever test we choose it simply is not true that all humans are equal. Like it or not we must face the fact that humans come in different shapes and sizes; they come with different moral capacities, different intellectual abilities, different amounts of benevolent feeling and sensitivity to the needs of others, different abilities to communicate effectively, and different capacities to experience pleasure and pain. In short, if the demand for equality were based on the actual equality of all human beings, we would have to stop demanding equality.

Still, one might cling to the view that the demand for equality among human beings is based on the actual equality of the different races and sexes. Although, it may be said, humans differ as individuals, there are no differences between the races and sexes as such. From the mere fact that a person is black or a woman we cannot infer anything about that person's intellectual or moral capacities. This, it may be said, is why racism and sexism are wrong. The white racist claims that whites are superior to blacks, but this is false; although there are differences among individuals, some blacks are superior to some whites in all of the capacities and abilities that could conceivably be relevant. The opponent of sexism would say the same: a person's sex is no guide to his or her abilities, and this is why it is unjustifiable to discriminate on the basis of sex.

The existence of individual variations that cut across the lines of race or sex, however, provides us with no defense at all against a more sophisticated opponent of equality, one who proposes that, say, the interests of all those with IQ scores below 100 be given less consideration than the interests of those with ratings over 100. Perhaps those scoring below the mark would, in this society, be made the slaves of those scoring higher. Would a hierarchical society of this sort really be so much better than one based on race or sex? I think not. But if we tie the moral principle of equality to the factual equality of the different races or sexes, taken as a whole, our opposition to racism and sexism does not provide us with any basis for objecting to this kind of inegalitarianism.

There is a second important reason why we ought not to base our opposition to racism and sexism on any kind of factual equality, even the limited kind that asserts that variations in capacities and abilities are spread evenly among the different races and between the sexes: we can have no absolute guarantee that these capacities and abilities really are distributed evenly, without regard to race or sex, among human beings. So far as actual abilities are concerned there do seem to be certain measurable differences both among races and between sexes. These differences do not, of course, appear in every case, but only when averages are taken. More important still, we do not yet know how many of these differences are really due to the different genetic endowments of the different races and sexes, and how many are due to poor schools, poor housing, and other factors that are the result of past and continuing discrimination. Perhaps all of the important differences will eventually prove to be environmental rather than genetic. Anyone opposed to racism and sexism will certainly hope that this will be so, for it will make the task of ending discrimination a lot easier; nevertheless, it would be dangerous to rest the case against racism and sexism on the belief that all significant differences are environmental in origin. The opponent of, say, racism who takes this line will be unable to avoid conceding that if differences in ability did after all prove to have some genetic connection with race, racism would in some way be defensible.

Fortunately there is no need to pin the case for equality to one particular outcome of a scientific investigation. The appropriate response to those who claim to have found evidence of genetically based differences in ability among the races or between the sexes is not to stick to the belief that the genetic explanation must be wrong, whatever evidence to the contrary may turn up; instead we should make it quite clear that the claim to equality does not depend on intelligence, moral capacity, physical strength, or similar matters of fact. Equality is a moral idea, not an assertion of fact. There is no logically compelling reason for assuming that a factual difference in ability between two people justifies any difference in the amount of consideration we give to their needs and interests. *The principle of the equality of human beings is not a description of an alleged actual equality among humans: it is a prescription of how we should treat human beings.*

Jeremy Bentham (1789), the founder of the reforming utilitarian school of moral philosophy, incorporated the essential basis of moral equality into his system of ethics by means of the formula: "Each to count for one and none for more than one." In other words, the interests of every being affected by an action are to be taken into account and given the same weight as the like interests of any other being. A later utilitarian, Henry Sidgwick (1907/1963, 382), put the point in this way: "The good of anyone individual is of no more importance, from the point of view (if I may say so) of the Universe, than the good of any other." More recently the leading figures in contemporary moral philosophy have shown a great deal of agreement in specifying as a fundamental presupposition of their moral theories some similar requirement that works to give everyone's interests equal consideration—although these writers generally cannot agree on how this requirement is best formulated (see Hare 1963, 1972; Rawls 1972).

It is an implication of this principle of equality that our concern for others and our readiness to consider their interests ought not to depend on what they are like or on what abilities they may possess. Precisely what our concern or consideration requires us to do may vary according to the characteristics of those affected by what we do: concern for the well-being of children growing up in America would require that we teach them to read; concern for the well-being of pigs may require no more than that we leave them with other pigs in a place where there is adequate food and room to run freely. But the basic element—the taking into account of the interests of the being, whatever those interests may be—must, according to the principle of equality, be extended to all beings, black or white, masculine or feminine, human or nonhuman.

Thomas Jefferson, who was responsible for writing the principle of the equality of men into the American Declaration of Independence, saw this point. It led him to oppose slavery even though he was unable to free himself fully from his slaveholding background. He wrote in a letter to the author of a book that emphasized the notable intellectual achievements of Negroes in order to refute the then common view that they had limited intellectual capacities:

> Be assured that no person living wishes more sincerely than I do, to see a complete refutation of the doubts I myself have entertained and expressed on the grade of understanding allotted to them by nature, and to find that they are on a par with ourselves. . . but whatever be their degree of talent it is no measure of their rights. Because Sir Isaac Newton was superior to others in understanding, he was not therefore lord of the property or persons of others.[1]

Similarly, when in the 1850s the call for women's rights was raised in the United States, a remarkable black feminist named Sojourner Truth made the same point in more robust terms at a feminist convention:

> They talk about this thing in the head; what do they call it? ["Intellect," whispered someone nearby.] That's it. What's that got to do with women's rights or Negroes' rights? If my cup won't hold but a pint and

yours holds a quart, wouldn't you be mean not to let me have my little half-measure full?[2]

It is on this basis that the case against racism and the case against sexism must both ultimately rest; and it is in accordance with this principle that the attitude that we may call "speciesism," by analogy with racism, must also be condemned. Speciesism—the word is not an attractive one, but I can think of no better term—is a prejudice or attitude of bias in favor of the interests of members of one's own species and against those of members of other species. It should be obvious that the fundamental objections to racism and sexism made by Thomas Jefferson and Sojourner Truth apply equally to speciesism. If possessing a higher degree of intelligence does not entitle one human to use another for his or her own ends, how can it entitle humans to exploit nonhumans for the same purpose?[3]

Many philosophers and other writers have proposed the principle of equal consideration of interests, in some form or other, as a basic moral principle; but not many of them have recognized that this principle applies to members of other species as well as to our own. Jeremy Bentham was one of the few who did realize this. In a forward-looking passage written at a time when black slaves had been freed by the French but in the British dominions were still being treated in the way we now treat animals, Bentham wrote:

> The day may come when the rest of the animal creation may acquire those rights which never could have been withholden from them but by the hand of tyranny. The French have already discovered that the blackness of the skin is no reason why a human being should be abandoned without redress to the caprice of a tormentor. It may one day come to be recognized that the number of the legs, the villosity of the skin, or the termination of the os sacrum are reasons equally insufficient for abandoning a sensitive being to the same fate. What else is it that should trace the insuperable line? Is it the faculty of reason, or perhaps the faculty of discourse? But a full-grown horse or dog is beyond comparison a more rational, as well as a more conversable animal, than an infant of a day or a week or even a month, old. But suppose they were otherwise, what would it avail? The question is not, Can they *reason*? nor Can they *talk*? but, Can they *suffer*?

In this passage Bentham points to the capacity for suffering as the vital characteristic that gives a being the right to equal consideration. The capacity for suffering—or more strictly, for suffering and/ or enjoyment or happiness—is not just another characteristic like the capacity for language or higher mathematics. Bentham is not saying that those who try to mark "the insuperable line" that determines whether the interests of a being should be considered happen to have chosen the wrong characteristic. By saying that we must consider the interests of all beings with the capacity for suffering or enjoyment Bentham does not arbitrarily exclude from consideration any interests at all—as those who draw the line with reference to the possession of reason or language do. The capacity for suffering and enjoyment is a pre-requisite for having interests at all, a condition that must be satisfied before we can speak of interests in a meaningful way. It would be nonsense to say that it was not in the interests of a stone to be kicked along the road by a schoolboy. A stone does not have interests because it cannot suffer. Nothing that we can do to it could possibly make any difference to its welfare. The capacity for suffering and enjoyment is, however, not only necessary, but also sufficient for us to say that a being has interests—at an absolute minimum, an interest in not suffering. A mouse, for example, does have an interest in not being kicked along the road, because it will suffer if it is.

Although Bentham speaks of "rights" in the passage I have quoted, the argument is really about *equality* rather than about rights. Indeed, in a different passage, Bentham famously described "natural rights" as "nonsense" and "natural and imprescriptable rights" as "nonsense upon stilts." He talked of moral rights as a shorthand way of referring to protections that people and animals morally ought to have; but the real weight of the moral argument does not rest on the assertion of the existence of the right, for this in turn has to be justified on the basis of the possibilities for suffering and happiness. In this way we can argue for equality for animals without getting embroiled in philosophical controversies about the ultimate nature of rights.

In misguided attempts to refute the arguments of this book, some philosophers have gone to much trouble developing arguments to show that animals do not have rights (Fox 1978a; Levin 1977; Perry and Jones 1982). They have claimed that to have rights a being must be autonomous, or must be a member of a community, or must have the ability to respect the rights of others, or must possess a sense of justice. These claims are irrelevant to the case for Animal Liberation. The language of rights is a convenient political shorthand. It is even more valuable in the era of thirty-second TV news clips than it was in Bentham's day; but in the argument for a radical change in our attitude to animals, it is in no way necessary.

If a being suffers there can be no moral justification for refusing to take that suffering into consideration. No matter what the nature of the being, the principle of equality requires that its suffering be counted equally with the like suffering—insofar as rough comparisons can be made—of any other being. If a being is not capable of suffering, or of experiencing enjoyment or happiness, there is nothing to be taken into account. So the limit of sentience (using the term as a convenient if not strictly accurate shorthand for the capacity to suffer and/or experience enjoyment) is the only defensible boundary of concern for the interests of others. To mark this boundary by some other characteristic like intelligence or rationality would be to mark it in an arbitrary manner. Why not choose some other characteristic, like skin color?

Racists violate the principle of equality by giving greater weight to the interests of members of their own race when there is a clash between their interests and the interests of those of another race. Sexists violate the principle of equality by favoring the interests of their own sex. Similarly, speciesists allow the interests of their own species to override the greater interests of members of other species. The pattern is identical in each case.

Most human beings are speciesists. . . . [O]rdinary human beings—not a few exceptionally cruel or heartless humans, but the overwhelming majority of humans—take an active part in, acquiesce in, and allow their taxes to pay for practices that require the sacrifice of the most important interests of members of other species in order to promote the most trivial interests of our own species.

There is, however, one general defense of the[se] practices . . . that needs to be disposed of before we discuss the practices themselves. It is a defense which, if true, would allow us to do anything at all to nonhumans for the slightest reason, or for no reason at all, without incurring any justifiable reproach. This defense claims that we are never guilty of neglecting the interests of other animals for one breathtakingly simple reason: they have no interests. Nonhuman animals have no interests, according to this view, because they are not capable of suffering. By this is not meant merely that they are not capable of suffering in all the ways that human beings are—for instance, that a calf is not capable of suffering from the knowledge that it will be killed in six months time. That modest claim is, no doubt, true; but it does not clear humans of the charge of speciesism, since it allows that animals may suffer in other ways—for instance, by being given electric shocks, or being kept in small, cramped cages. The defense I am about to discuss is the much more sweeping, although correspondingly less plausible, claim that animals are incapable of suffering in any way at all; that they are, in fact, unconscious automata, possessing neither thoughts nor feelings nor a mental life of any kind.

Although . . . the view that animals are automata was proposed by the seventeenth-century French philosopher René Descartes, to most people, then and now, it is obvious that if, for example, we stick a sharp knife into the stomach of an unanesthetized dog, the dog will feel pain. That this is so is assumed by the laws in most civilized countries that prohibit wanton cruelty to animals. Readers whose common sense tells them that animals do suffer may prefer to skip the remainder of this section. . . . Implausible as it is, though, for the sake of completeness this skeptical position must be discussed.

Do animals other than humans feel pain? How do we know? Well, how do we know if anyone, human or nonhuman, feels pain? We know that we ourselves can feel pain. We know this from the direct experience of pain that we have when, for instance, somebody presses a lighted cigarette against the back of our hand. But how do we know that anyone else feels pain? We cannot directly experience anyone else's pain, whether that "anyone" is our best friend or a stray dog. Pain is a state of consciousness, a "mental event," and as such it can never be observed. Behavior like writhing, screaming, or drawing one's hand away from the lighted cigarette is not pain itself; nor are the recordings a neurologist might make of activity within the brain observations of pain itself. Pain is something that we feel, and we can only infer that others are feeling it from various external indications.

In theory, we *could* always be mistaken when we assume that other human beings feel pain. It is conceivable that one of our close friends is really a cleverly constructed robot, controlled by a brilliant scientist so as to give all the signs of feeling pain, but really no more sensitive than any other machine. We can never know, with absolute certainty, that this is not the case. But while this might present a puzzle for philosophers, none of us has the slightest real doubt that our close friends feel pain just as we do. This is an inference, but a perfectly reasonable one, based on observations of their behavior in situations in which we would feel pain, and on the fact that we have every reason to assume that our friends are beings like us, with nervous systems like ours that can be assumed to function as ours do and to produce similar feelings in similar circumstances.

If it is justifiable to assume that other human beings feel pain as we do, is there any reason why a similar inference should be unjustifiable in the case of other animals?

Nearly all the external signs that lead us to infer pain in other humans can be seen in other species, especially the species most closely related to us—the species of mammals and birds. The behavioral signs include writhing, facial contortions, moaning, yelping or other forms of calling, attempts to avoid the source of pain, appearance of fear at the prospect of its repetition, and so on. In addition, we know that these animals have nervous systems very like ours, which respond physiologically as ours do when the animal is in circumstances in which we would feel pain: an initial rise of blood pressure, dilated pupils, perspiration, an increased pulse rate, and, if the stimulus continues, a fall in blood pressure. Although human beings have a more developed cerebral cortex than other animals, this part of the brain is concerned with thinking functions rather than with basic impulses, emotions, and feelings. These impulses, emotions, and feelings are located in the diencephalon, which is well developed in many other species of animals, especially mammals and birds (Brain 1962).

We also know that the nervous systems of other animals were not artificially constructed—as a robot might be artificially constructed—to mimic the pain behavior of humans. The nervous systems of animals evolved as our own did, and in fact the evolutionary history of human beings and other animals, especially mammals, did not diverge until the central features of our nervous systems were already in existence. A capacity to feel pain obviously enhances a species' prospects of survival, since it causes members of the species to avoid sources of injury. It is surely unreasonable to suppose that nervous systems that are virtually identical physiologically, have a common origin and a common evolutionary function, and result in similar forms of behavior in similar circumstances should actually operate in an entirely different manner on the level of subjective feelings.

It has long been accepted as sound policy in science to search for the simplest possible explanation of whatever it is we are trying to explain. Occasionally it has been claimed that it is for this reason "unscientific" to explain the behavior of animals by theories that refer to the animal's conscious feelings, desires, and so on—the idea being that if the behavior in question can be explained without invoking consciousness or feelings, that will be the simpler theory. Yet we can now see that such explanations, when assessed with respect to the actual behavior of both human and nonhuman animals, are actually far more complex than rival explanations. For we know from our own experience that explanations of our own behavior that did not refer to consciousness and the feeling of pain would be incomplete; and it is simpler to assume that the similar behavior of animals with similar nervous systems is to be explained in the same way than to try to invent some other explanation for the behavior of nonhuman animals as well as an explanation for the divergence between humans and nonhumans in this respect.

The overwhelming majority of scientists who have addressed themselves to this question agree. Lord Brain, one of the most eminent neurologists of our time, has said:

> I personally can see no reason for conceding mind to my fellow men and denying it to animals. . . . I at least cannot doubt that the interests and activities of animals are correlated with awareness and feeling in

the same way as my own, and which may be, for aught I know, just as vivid (1962, 11).

The author of a book on pain (Serjeant 1969) writes:

> Every particle of factual evidence supports the contention that the higher mammalian vertebrates experience pain sensations at least as acute as our own. To say that they feel less because they are lower animals is an absurdity; it can easily be shown that many of their senses are far more acute than ours—visual acuity in certain birds, hearing in most wild animals, and touch in others; these animals depend more than we do today on the sharpest possible awareness of a hostile environment. Apart from the complexity of the cerebral cortex (which does not directly perceive pain) their nervous systems are almost identical to ours and their reactions to pain remarkably similar, though lacking (so far as we know) the philosophical and moral overtones. The emotional element is all too evident, mainly in the form of fear and anger (72).

In Britain, three separate expert government committees on matters relating to animals have accepted the conclusion that animals feel pain. After noting the obvious behavioral evidence for this view, the members of the Committee on Cruelty to Wild Animals, set up in 1951, said:

> . . . we believe that the physiological, and more particularly the anatomical, evidence fully justifies and reinforces the commonsense belief that animals feel pain.

And after discussing the evolutionary value of pain the committee's report concluded that pain is "of clear-cut biological usefulness" and this is "a third type of evidence that animals feel pain." The committee members then went on to consider forms of suffering other than mere physical pain and added that they were "satisfied that animals do suffer from acute fear and terror." Subsequent reports by British government committees on experiments on animals and on the welfare of animals under intensive farming methods agreed with this view, concluding that animals are capable of suffering both from straightforward physical injuries and from fear, anxiety, stress, and so on.[4] Finally, within the last decade, the publication of scientific studies with titles such as *Animal Thought* (Walker 1983), *Animal Thinking* (Griffin 1984), and *Animal Suffering: The Science of Animal Welfare* (Dawkins 1980) have made it plain that conscious awareness in nonhuman animals is now generally accepted as a serious subject for investigation.

That might well be thought enough to settle the matter; but one more objection needs to be considered. Human beings in pain, after all, have one behavioral sign that nonhuman animals do not have: a developed language. Other animals may communicate with each other, but not, it seems, in the complicated way we do. Some philosophers, including Descartes, have thought it important that while humans can tell each other about their experience of pain in great detail, other animals cannot. (Interestingly, this once neat dividing line between humans and other species has now been threatened by the discovery that chimpanzees can be taught a language) [for example, Eckholm 1985; Linden 1976; *Newsweek* 1988] But as Bentham pointed out long ago, the ability to use language is not relevant to the question of how a being ought to be treated—unless that ability can be linked to the capacity to suffer, so that the absence of a language casts doubt on the existence of this capacity.

This link may be attempted in two ways. First, there is a hazy line of philosophical thought, deriving perhaps from some doctrines associated with the influential philosopher Ludwig Wittgenstein, which maintains that we cannot meaningfully attribute states of consciousness to beings without language. This position seems to me very implausible. Language may be necessary for abstract thought, at some level anyway; but states like pain are more primitive, and have nothing to do with language.

The second and more easily understood way of linking language and the existence of pain is to say that the best evidence we can have that other creatures are in pain is that they tell us that they are. This is a distinct line of argument, for it is denying not that non-language-users conceivably *could* suffer, but only that we could ever have sufficient reason to *believe* that they are suffering. Still, this line of argument fails too. As Jane Goodall has pointed out in her study of chimpanzees, *In the Shadow of Man*, when it comes to the expression of feelings and emotions language is less important than nonlinguistic modes of communication such as a cheering pat on the back, an exuberant embrace, a clasp of the hands, and so on. The basic signals we use to convey pain, fear, anger, love, joy, surprise, sexual arousal, and many other emotional states are not specific to our own species.[5] The statement "I am in pain" may be one piece of evidence for the conclusion that the speaker is in pain, but it is not the only possible evidence, and since people sometimes tell lies, not even the best possible evidence.

Even if there were stronger grounds for refusing to attribute pain to those who do not have a language, the consequences of this refusal might lead us to reject the conclusion. Human infants and young children are unable to use language. Are we to deny that a year-old child can suffer? If not, language cannot be crucial. Of course, most parents understand the responses of their children better than they understand the responses of other animals; but this is just a fact about the relatively greater knowledge that we have of our own species and the greater contact we have with infants as compared to animals. Those who have studied the behavior of other animals and those who have animals as companions soon learn to understand their responses as well as we understand those of an infant, and sometimes better.

So to conclude: there are no good reasons, scientific or philosophical, for denying that animals feel pain. If we do not doubt that other humans feel pain we should not doubt that other animals do so too.

Animals can feel pain. As we saw earlier, there can be no moral justification for regarding the pain (or pleasure) that animals feel as less important than the same amount of pain (or pleasure) felt by humans. But what practical consequences follow from this conclusion? To prevent misunderstanding I shall spell out what I mean a little more fully.

If I give a horse a hard slap across its rump with my open hand, the horse may start, but it presumably feels little pain. Its skin is thick enough to protect it against a mere slap. If I slap a baby in the same way, however, the baby will cry and presumably feel pain, for its skin is more sensitive. So it is worse to slap a baby than a horse, if both slaps are administered with equal force. But there must be some kind of blow—I don't know exactly what it would be, but perhaps a blow with a heavy stick—that would cause the horse as much pain as we cause a baby by slapping it with our hand. That is what I mean by "the same amount of pain," and if we consider it wrong to inflict that much pain on a baby for no good reason then we must, unless we are speciesists, consider it equally wrong to inflict the same amount of pain on a horse for no good reason.

Other differences between humans and animals cause other complications. Normal adult human beings have mental capacities that will, in certain circumstances, lead them to suffer more than animals would in the same circumstances. If, for instance, we decided to perform extremely painful or lethal scientific experiments on normal adult humans, kidnapped at random from public parks for this purpose, adults who enjoy strolling in parks would become fearful that they would be kidnapped. The resultant terror would be a form of suffering additional to the pain of the experiment. The same experiments performed on nonhuman animals would cause less suffering since the animals would not have the anticipatory dread of being kidnapped and experimented upon. This does not mean, of course, that it would be right to perform the experiment on animals, but only that there is a reason, which is not speciesist, for preferring to use animals rather than normal adult human beings, if the experiment is to be done at all. It should be noted, however, that this same argument gives us a reason for preferring to use human infants—orphans perhaps—or severely retarded human beings for experiments, rather than adults, since infants and retarded humans would also have no idea of what was going to happen to them. So far as this argument is concerned nonhuman animals and infants and retarded humans are in the same category; and if we use this argument to justify experiments on nonhuman animals we have to ask ourselves whether we are also prepared to allow experiments on human infants and retarded adults; and if we make a distinction between animals and these humans, on what basis can we do it, other than a bare-faced—and morally indefensible—preference for members of our own species?

There are many matters in which the superior mental powers of normal adult humans make a difference: anticipation, more detailed memory, greater knowledge of what is happening, and so on. Yet these differences do not all point to greater suffering on the part of the normal human being. Sometimes animals may suffer more because of their more limited understanding. If, for instance, we are taking prisoners in wartime we can explain to them that although they must submit to capture, search, and confinement, they will not otherwise be harmed and will be set free at the conclusion of hostilities. If we capture wild animals, however, we cannot explain that we are not threatening their lives. A wild animal cannot distinguish an attempt to overpower and confine from an attempt to kill; the one causes as much terror as the other.

It may be objected that comparisons of the sufferings of different species are impossible to make and that for this reason when the interests of animals and humans clash the principle of equality gives no guidance. It is probably true that comparisons of suffering between members of different species cannot be made precisely, but precision is not essential. Even if we were to prevent the infliction of suffering on animals only when it is quite certain that the interests of humans will not be affected to anything like the extent that animals are affected, we would be forced to make radical changes in our treatment of animals that would involve our diet, the farming methods we use, experimental procedures in many fields of science, our approach to wildlife and to hunting, trapping and the wearing of furs, and areas of entertainment like circuses, rodeos, and zoos. As a result, a vast amount of suffering would be avoided.

So far I have said a lot about inflicting suffering on animals, but nothing about killing them. This omission has been deliberate. The application of the principle of equality to the infliction of suffering is, in theory at least, fairly straightforward. Pain and suffering are in themselves bad and should be prevented or minimized, irrespective of the race, sex, or species of the being that suffers. How bad a pain is depends on how intense it is and how long it lasts, but pains of the same intensity and duration are equally bad, whether felt by humans or animals.

The wrongness of killing a being is more complicated. I have kept, and shall continue to keep, the question of killing in the background because in the present state of human tyranny over other species the more simple, straightforward principle of equal consideration of pain or pleasure is a sufficient basis for identifying and protesting against all the major abuses of animals that human beings practice. Nevertheless, it is necessary to say some thing about killing.

Just as most human beings are speciesists in their readiness to cause pain to animals when they would not cause a similar pain to humans for the same reason, so most human beings are speciesists in their readiness to kill other animals when they would not kill human beings. We need to proceed more cautiously here, however, because people hold widely differing views about when it is legitimate to kill humans, as the continuing debates over abortion and euthanasia attest. Nor have moral philosophers been able to agree on exactly what it is that makes it wrong to kill human beings, and under what circumstances killing a human being may be justifiable.

Let us consider first the view that it is always wrong to take an innocent human life. We may call this the "sanctity of life" view. People who take this view oppose abortion and euthanasia. They do not usually, however, oppose the killing of nonhuman animals—so perhaps it would be more accurate to describe this view as the "sanctity of human life" view. The belief that human life, and only human life, is sacrosanct is a form of speciesism. To see this, consider the following example.

Assume that, as sometimes happens, an infant has been born with massive and irreparable brain damage. The damage is so severe that the infant can never be any more than a "human vegetable," unable to talk, recognize other people, act independently of others, or develop a sense of self-awareness. The parents of the infant, realizing that they cannot hope for any improvement in their child's condition and being in any case unwilling to spend, or ask the state to spend, the thousands of dollars that would be needed annually for proper care of the infant, ask the doctor to kill the infant painlessly.

Should the doctor do what the parents ask? Legally, the doctor should not, and in this respect the law reflects the sanctity of life view. The life of every human being is sacred. Yet people who would say this about the infant do not object to the killing of nonhuman animals. How can they justify their different judgments? Adult chimpanzees, dogs, pigs, and members of many other species far surpass the brain-damaged infant in their ability to relate to others, act independently, be self-aware, and any other capacity that could reasonably be said to give value to life. With the most intensive care possible, some severely retarded infants can never achieve the intelligence level of a dog. Nor can we appeal to the concern of the infant's parents, since they themselves, in this imaginary example (and in some actual cases) do not want the infant kept alive. The only thing that distinguishes the infant from the animal, in the eyes of those who claim it has a "right to life," is that it is, biologically, a member of the species Homo sapiens, whereas chimpanzees, dogs, and pigs are not. But to use this difference as the basis for granting a right to life to the infant and not to the other animals is, of course, pure speciesism.[6] It is exactly the kind of arbitrary difference that the most crude and overt kind of racist uses in attempting to justify racial discrimination.

This does not mean that to avoid speciesism we must hold that it is as wrong to kill a dog as it is to kill a human being in full possession of his or her faculties. The only position that is irredeemably speciesist is the one that tries to make the boundary of the right to life run exactly parallel to the boundary of our own species. Those who hold the sanctity of life view do this, because while distinguishing sharply between human beings and other animals they allow no distinctions to be made within our own species, objecting to the killing of the severely retarded and the hopelessly senile as strongly as they object to the killing of normal adults.

To avoid speciesism we must allow that beings who are similar in all relevant respects have a similar right to life—and mere membership in our own biological species cannot be a morally relevant criterion for this right. Within these limits we could still hold, for instance, that it is worse to kill a normal adult human, with a capacity for self-awareness and the ability to plan for the future and have meaningful relations with others, than it is to kill a mouse, which presumably does not share all of these characteristics; or we might appeal to the close family and other personal ties that humans have but mice do not have to the same degree; or we might think that it is the consequences for other humans, who will be put in fear for their own lives, that makes the crucial difference; or we might think it is some combination of these factors, or other factors altogether.

Whatever criteria we choose, however, we will have to admit that they do not follow precisely the boundary of our own species. We may legitimately hold that there are some features of certain beings that make their lives more valuable than those of other beings; but there will surely be some nonhuman animals whose lives, by any standards, are more valuable than the lives of some humans. A chimpanzee, dog, or pig, for instance, will have a higher degree of self-awareness and a greater capacity for meaningful relations with others than a severely retarded infant or someone in a state of advanced senility. So if we base the right to life on these characteristics we must grant these animals a right to life as good as, or better than, such retarded or senile humans.

This argument cuts both ways. It could be taken as showing that chimpanzees, dogs, and pigs, along with some other species, have a right to life and we commit a grave moral offense whenever we kill them, even when they are old and suffering and our intention is to put them out of their misery. Alternatively one could take the argument as showing that the severely retarded and hopelessly senile have no right to life and may be killed for quite trivial reasons, as we now kill animals.

Since the main concern . . . is with ethical questions having to do with animals and not with the morality of euthanasia I shall not attempt to settle this issue finally (Kuhse and Singer 1985; Singer 1979). I think it is reasonably clear, though, that while both of the positions just described avoid speciesism, neither is satisfactory. What we need is some middle position that would avoid speciesism but would not make the lives of the retarded and senile as cheap as the lives of pigs and dogs now are, or make the lives of pigs and dogs so sacrosanct that we think it wrong to put them out of hopeless misery. What we must do is bring nonhuman animals within our sphere of moral concern and cease to treat their lives as expendable for whatever trivial purposes we may have. At the same time, once we realize that the fact that a being is a member of our own species is not in itself enough to make it always wrong to kill that being, we may come to reconsider our policy of preserving human lives at all costs, even when there is no prospect of a meaningful life or of existence without terrible pain.

I conclude, then, that a rejection of speciesism does not imply that all lives are of equal worth. While self-awareness, the capacity to think ahead and have hopes and aspirations for the future, the capacity for meaningful relations with others and so on are not relevant to the question of inflicting pain—since pain is pain, whatever other capacities, beyond the capacity to feel pain, the being may have—these capacities are relevant to the question of taking life. It is not arbitrary to hold that the life of a self-aware being, capable of abstract thought, of planning for the future, of complex acts of communication, and so on, is more valuable than the life of a being without these capacities. To see the difference between the issues of inflicting pain and taking life, consider how we would choose within our own species. If we had to choose to save the life of a normal human being or an intellectually disabled human being, we would probably choose to save the life of a normal human being; but if we had to choose between preventing pain in the normal human being or the intellectually disabled one—imagine that both have received painful but superficial injuries, and we only have enough painkiller for one of them—it is not nearly so clear how we ought to choose. The same is true when we consider other species. The evil of pain is, in itself, unaffected by the other characteristics of the being who feels the pain; the value of life is affected by these other characteristics. To give just one reason for this difference, to take the life of a being who has been hoping, planning, and working for some future goal is to deprive that being of the fulfillment of all those efforts; to take the life of a being with a mental capacity below the level needed to grasp that one is a being with a future—much less make plans for the future—cannot involve this particular kind of loss (Singer 1987).

Normally this will mean that if we have to choose between the life of a human being and the life of another animal we should choose to save the life of the human; but there may be special cases in which the reverse holds true, because the human being in question does not have the capacities of a normal human being. So this view is not speciesist, although it may appear to be at first glance. The preference, in normal cases, for saving a human life over the life of an animal when a choice has to be made is a preference based on the characteristics that normal humans have, and not on the mere fact that they are members of our own species. This is why when we consider members of our own species who lack the characteristics of normal humans we can no longer say that their lives are always to be preferred to those of other animals. This issue comes up in a practical way in the following chapter. In general, though, the question of when it is wrong to kill (painlessly) an animal is one to which we need give no precise answer. As long as we remember that we should give the same respect to the lives of animals as we give to the lives of those humans at a similar mental level, we shall not go far wrong. . . . [7]

Questions for Discussion

1. What does Singer mean by "equal consideration of interests"?
2. According to Singer, should humans and other animals be treated in identical ways? Or to put it another way, should they have the same "rights"?
3. Respond to this statement by Singer: "If a being suffers, there can be no moral justification for refusing to take that suffering into consideration."

29 The Case for Animal Rights

Tom Regan

Tom Regan, the top American animal rights philosopher, criticizes the two main approaches that have been used in philosophy to consider the rights of other animals—contractarianism and utilitarianism, as advocated in the previous selection by Peter Singer. Regan skillfully identifies the problems inherent in both of these approaches, and finds them both wanting. Instead, Regan proposes what he calls the "rights view." Here he introduces his famous term, "subjects of a life." All beings, including animals, who is aware of their existence, who has desires and preferences, feelings, and memories—i.e., a conscious awareness of one's life, beings whose lives are important to them—are considered to be subjects of a life and to have equal inherent value, which entitles them to be treated with respect, as ends and not means, irrespective of species. Regan's philosophy demands not that we improve the welfare of animals involved in currently accepted practices—factory farming, animal experimentation, etc., but rather that we abolish them altogether.

I regard myself as an advocate of animal rights—as a part of the animal rights movement. That movement, as I conceive it, is committed to a number of goals, including:

- the total abolition of the use of animals in science
- the total dissolution of commercial animal agriculture
- the total elimination of commercial and sport hunting and trapping

There are, I know, people who profess to believe in animal rights but do not avow these goals. Factory farming, they say, is wrong—it violates animals' rights—but traditional animal agriculture is all right. Toxicity tests of cosmetics on animals violates their rights, but important medical research—cancer research, for example—does not. The clubbing of baby seals is abhorrent, but not the harvesting of adult

---

Originally published in 1985 in *In Defense of Animals*, Peter Singer, Ed., pp. 13–26. Reprinted with permission of Blackwell Publishers, Inc.

seals. I used to think I understood this reasoning. Not any more. You don't change unjust institutions by tidying them up.

What's wrong—fundamentally wrong—with the way animals are treated isn't the details that vary from case to case. It's the whole system. The forlornness of the veal calf is pathetic, heart wrenching; the pulsing pain of the chimp with electrodes planted deep in her brain is repulsive; the slow, torturous death of a raccoon caught in the leg-hold trap is agonizing. But what is wrong isn't the pain, isn't the suffering, isn't the deprivation. These compound what's wrong. Sometimes—often—they make it much worse. But they are not the fundamental wrong.

The fundamental wrong is the system that allows us to view animals as *our resources*, here for *us*—to be eaten, or surgically manipulated, or exploited for sport or money. Once we accept this view of animals—as our resources—the rest is as predictable as it is regrettable. Why worry about their loneliness, their pain, their death? Since animals exist for us, to benefit us in one way or another, what harms them really doesn't matter—or matters only if it starts to bother us, makes us feel a trifle uneasy when we eat our veal escalope, for example. So, yes, let us get veal calves out of solitary confinement, give them more space, a little straw, a few companions. But let us keep our veal escalope.

But a little straw, more space, and a few companions won't eliminate—won't even touch—the basic wrong that attaches to our viewing and treating these animals as our resources. A veal calf killed to be eaten after living in close confinement is viewed and treated in this way: but so, too, is another who is raised (as they say) "more humanely." To right the wrong of our treatment of farm animals requires more than making rearing methods "more humane"; it requires the total dissolution of commercial animal agriculture.

How we do this, whether we do it or, as in the case of animals in science, whether and how we abolish their use—these are to a large extent political questions. People must change their beliefs before they change their habits. Enough people, especially those elected to public office, must believe in change—must want it—before we will have laws that protect the rights of animals. This process of change is very complicated, very demanding, very exhausting, calling for the efforts of many hands in education, publicity, political organization and activity, down to the licking of envelopes and stamps. As a trained and practicing philosopher, the sort of contribution I can make is limited but, I like to think, important. The currency of philosophy is ideas—their meaning and rational foundation—not the nuts and bolts of the legislative process, say, or the mechanics of community organization. That's what I have been exploring over the past ten years or so in my essays and talks and, most recently, in my book *The Case for Animal Rights*. I believe the major conclusions I reach in the book are true because they are supported by the weight of the best arguments. I believe the idea of animal rights has reason, not just emotion, on its side.

In the space I have at my disposal here I can only sketch, in the barest outline, some of the main features of the book. It's main themes—and we should not be surprised by this—involve asking and answering deep, foundational moral questions about what morality is, how it should be understood, and what is the best moral theory, all considered. I hope I can convey something of the shape I think this theory takes. The attempt to do so will be (to use a word a friendly critic once used to describe my work) cerebral, perhaps too cerebral. But this is misleading. My feelings about how animals are sometimes treated run just as deep and just as strong as those of my more volatile compatriots. Philosophers do—to use the jargon of the day— have a right side to their brains. If it's the left side we contribute (or mainly should), that's because what talents we have reside there.

How to proceed? We begin by asking how the moral status of animals has been understood by thinkers who deny that animals have rights. Then we test the mettle of their ideas by seeing how well they stand up under the heat of fair criticism. If we start our thinking in this way, we soon find that some people believe that we have no direct duties to animals, that we owe nothing to them, that we can do nothing that wrongs them. Rather, we can do wrong acts that involve animals, and so we have duties regarding them, though none to them. Such views may be called indirect duty views. By way of illustration: suppose your neighbor kicks your dog. Then your neighbor has done something wrong. But not to your dog. The wrong that has been done is a wrong to you. After all, it is wrong to upset people, and your neighbor's kicking your dog upsets you. So you are the one who is wronged, not your dog. Or again: by kicking your dog your neighbor damages your property. And since it is wrong to damage another person's property, your neighbor has done something wrong—to you, of course—not to your dog. Your neighbor no more wrongs your dog than your car would be wronged if the windshield were smashed. Your neighbor's duties involving your dog are indirect duties to you. More generally, all of our duties regarding animals are indirect duties to one another—to humanity.

How could someone try to justify such a view? Someone might say that your dog doesn't feel anything and so isn't hurt by your neighbor's kick, doesn't care about the pain because none is felt, is as unaware of anything as is your windshield. Someone might say this, but no rational person will, since, among other considerations, such a view will commit anyone who holds it to the position that no human being feels pain either—that human beings also don't care about what happens to them. A second possibility is that though both humans and your dog are hurt when kicked, it is only human pain that matters. But, again, no rational person can believe this. Pain is pain wherever it occurs. If your neighbor's causing you pain is wrong because of the pain that is caused, we cannot rationally ignore or dismiss the moral relevance of the pain that your dog feels. Philosophers who hold indirect duty views—and many still do— have come to understand that they must avoid the two defects just noted: that is, both the view that animals don't feel anything as well as the idea that only human pain can be morally relevant. Among such thinkers the sort of view now favored is one or other form of what is called *contractarianism*.

Here, very crudely, is the root idea: morality consists of a set of rules that individuals voluntarily agree to abide by, as we do when we sign a contract (hence the name contractarianism). Those who understand and accept the terms of the contract are covered directly; they have rights created and recognized by, and protected in, the contract. And these contractors can also have protection spelled out for others who, thought they lack the ability to understand morality and so cannot sign the contract themselves, are loved or cherished by those who can. Thus young children, for example, are unable to sign contracts and lack rights. But they are protected by the contract nonetheless because of the sentimental interests of others, most notably their parents. So we have, then, duties involving these children, duties regarding them, but no duties to them. Our duties in this case are indirect duties to other human beings, usually their parents.

As for animals, since they cannot understand contracts, they obviously cannot sign; and since they cannot sign, they have no rights. Like children, however, some animals are the objects of the sentimental interest of others. You, for example, love your dog or cat. So those animals that enough people care about (companion animals, whales, baby seals, the American bald eagle), though they lack rights themselves, will be protected because of the sentimental interests of people. I have, then, according to contractarianism, no duty directly to your dog or any other animal, not even the duty not to cause them pain or suffering; my duty not to hurt them is a duty I have to those people who care about what happens to them. As for other animals, where no or little sentimental interest is present—in the case of farm animals, for example, or laboratory rats—what duties we have grow weaker and weaker, perhaps to the vanishing point. The pain and death they endure, though real, are not wrong if no one cares about them.

When it comes to the moral status of animals, contractarianism could be a hard view to refute if it were an adequate theoretical approach to the moral status of human beings. It is not adequate in this latter respect, however, which makes the question of its adequacy in the former case, regarding animals, utterly moot. For consider: morality, according to the (crude) contractarian position before us, consists of rules that people agree to abide by. What people? Well, enough to make a difference—enough, that is, *collectively* to have the power to enforce the rules that are drawn up in the contract. That is very well and good for the signatories but not so good for anyone who is not asked to sign. And there is nothing in contractarianism of the sort we are discussing that guarantees or requires that everyone will have a chance to participate equally in framing the rules of morality. The result is that this approach to ethics could sanction the most blatant forms of social, economic, moral, and political injustice, ranging from a repressive caste system to systematic racial or sexual discrimination. Might, according to this theory, does make right. Let those who are the victims of injustice suffer as they will. It matters not so long as no one else—no contractor, or too few of them—cares about it. Such a theory takes one's moral breath away . . . as if, for example, there would be nothing wrong with apartheid in South Africa if few white South Africans were upset by it. A theory with so little to recommend it at the level of the ethics of our treatment of our fellow humans cannot have anything more to recommend it when it comes to the ethics of how we treat our fellow animals.

The version of contractarianism just examined is, as I have noted, a crude variety, and in fairness to those of a contractarian persuasion it must be noted that much more refined, subtle, and ingenious varieties are possible. For example, John Rawls, in his *A Theory of Justice*, sets forth a version of contractarianism that forces contractors to ignore the accidental features of being a human being—for example, whether one is white or black, male or female, a genius or of modest intellect. Only by ignoring such features, Rawls believes, can we ensure that the principles of justice that contractors would agree upon are not based on bias or prejudice. Despite the improvement of such a view over the cruder forms of contractarianism, it remains deficient; it systematically denies that we have direct duties to those human beings who do not have a sense of justice—young children, for instance, and many mentally retarded humans. And yet it seems reasonably certain that, were we to torture a young child or retarded elder, we would be doing something that wronged him or her, not something that would be wrong if (and only if) other humans with a sense of justice were upset. And since this is true in the case of these humans, we cannot rationally deny the same in the case of animals.

Indirect duty views, then, including the best among them, fail to command our rational assent. Whatever ethical theory we should accept rationally, therefore, it must at least recognize that we have some duties directly to animals, just as we have some duties directly to each other. The next two theories I'll sketch attempt to meet this requirement.

The first I call the cruelty-kindness view. Simply stated, this says that we have a direct duty to be kind to animals and a direct duty not to be cruel to them. Despite the familiar, reassuring ring of these ideas, I do not believe that this view offers an adequate theory. To make this clearer, consider kindness. A kind person acts from a certain kind of motive—compassion or concern, for example. And that is a virtue. But there is no guarantee that a kind act is a right act. If I am a generous racist, for example, I will be inclined to act kindly toward members of my own race, favoring their interests above those of others. My kindness would be real and, so far as it goes, good. But I trust it is too obvious to require argument that my kind acts may not be above moral reproach—may, in fact, be positively wrong because rooted in injustice. So kindness, notwithstanding its status as a virtue to be encouraged, simply will not carry the weight of a theory of right action.

Cruelty fares no better. People or their acts are cruel if they display either a lack of sympathy or, worse, the presence of enjoyment in another's suffering. Cruelty in all its guises is a bad thing, a tragic human failing. But just as a person's being motivated by kindness does not guarantee that he or she does what is right, so the absence of cruelty does not ensure that he or she avoids doing what is wrong. Many people who perform abortions, for example, are not cruel, sadistic people. But that fact alone does not settle the terribly difficult question of the morality of abortion. The case is no different when we examine the ethics of our treatment of animals. So, yes, let us be for kindness and against cruelty. But let us not suppose that being for the one and against the other answers questions about moral right and wrong.

Some people think that the theory we are looking for is utilitarianism. A utilitarian accepts two moral principles. The first is that of equality: everyone's interests count, and similar interests must be counted as having similar weight or importance. White or black, American or Iranian, human or animal—everyone's pain or frustration matter, and matter just as much as the equivalent pain or frustration of anyone else. The second principle a utilitarian accepts is that of utility: do the act that will bring about the best balance between satisfaction and frustration for everyone affected by the outcome.

As a utilitarian, then, here is how I am to approach the task of deciding what I morally ought to do: I must ask who will be affected if I choose to do one thing rather than another, how much each individual will be affected, and where the best results are most likely to lie—which option, in other words, is most likely to bring about the best results, the best balance between satisfaction and frustration. That option, whatever it may be, is the one I ought to choose. That is where my moral duty lies.

The great appeal of utilitarianism rests with its uncompromising *egalitarian-*

ism: everyone's interests count and count as much as the like interests of everyone else. The kind of odious discrimination that some forms of contractarianism can justify—discrimination based on race or sex, for example—seems disallowed in principle by utilitarianism, as is speciesism, systematic discrimination based on species membership.

The equality we find in utilitarianism, however, is not the sort an advocate of animal or human rights should have in mind. Utilitarianism has no room for the equal moral rights of different individuals because it has no room for their equal inherent value or worth. What has value for the utilitarian is the satisfaction of an individual's interests, not the individual whose interests they are. A universe in which you satisfy your desire for water, food, and warmth is, other things being equal, better than a universe in which these desires are frustrated. And the same is true in the case of an animal with similar desires. But neither you nor the animal have any value in your own right. Only your feelings do.

Here is an analogy to make the philosophical point clearer: a cup contains different liquids, sometimes sweet, sometimes bitter, sometimes a mix of the two. What has value are the liquids: the sweeter the better, the bitterer the worse. The cup, the container, has no value. It is what goes into it, not what they go into, that has value. For the utilitarian you and I are like the cup; we have no value as individuals and thus no equal value. What has value is what goes into us, what we serve as receptacles for; our feelings of satisfaction have positive value, our feelings of frustration negative value.

Serious problems arise for utilitarianism when we remind ourselves that it enjoins us to bring about the best consequences. What does this mean? It doesn't mean the best consequences for me alone, or for my family or friends, or any other person taken individually. No, what we must do is, roughly, as follows: we must add up (somehow!) the separate satisfactions and frustrations of everyone likely to be affected by our choice, the satisfactions in one column, the frustrations in the other. We must total each column for each of the options before us. That is what it means to say the theory is aggregative. And then we must choose that option which is most likely to bring about the best balance of totaled satisfactions over totaled frustrations. Whatever act would lead to this outcome is the one we ought morally to perform—it is where our moral duty lies. And that act quite clearly might not be the same one that would bring about the best results for me personally, or for my family or friends, or for a lab animal. The best aggregated consequences for everyone concerned are not necessarily the best for each individual.

That utilitarianism is an aggregative theory—different individuals' satisfactions or frustrations are added, or summed, or totaled—is the key objection to this theory. My Aunt Bea is old, inactive, a cranky, sour person, though not physically ill. She prefers to go on living. She is also rather rich. I could make a fortune if I could get my hands on her money, money she intends to give me in any event, after she dies, but which she refuses to give me now. In order to avoid a huge tax bite, I plan to donate a handsome sum of my profits to the local children's hospital. Many, many children will benefit from my generosity, and much joy will be brought to their parents, relatives, and friends. If I don't get the money rather soon, all these ambitions will come to naught. The once-in-a-lifetime opportunity to make a real killing will be gone. Why, then, not kill my Aunt Bea? Of course, I *might* get caught. But I'm no fool and, besides, her doctor can be counted on to cooperate (he has an eye for the same investment and I happen to know a good deal about his shady past). The deed can be done . . . professionally, shall we say. There is *very* little chance of getting caught. And as for my conscience being guilt-ridden, I am a resourceful sort of fellow and will take more than sufficient comfort—as I lie on the beach at Acapulco—in contemplating the joy and health I have brought to so many others.

Suppose Aunt Bea is killed and the rest of the story comes out as told. Would I have done anything wrong? Anything immoral? One would have thought that I had. Not according to utilitarianism. Since what I have done has brought about the best balance between totaled satisfaction and frustration for all those affected by the outcome, my action is not wrong. Indeed, in killing Aunt Bea the physician and I did what duty required.

This same kind of argument can be repeated in all sorts of cases, illustrating, time after time, how the utilitarian's position leads to results that impartial people find morally callous. It *is* wrong to kill my Aunt Bea in the name of bringing about the best results for others. A good end does not justify an evil means. Any adequate moral theory will have to explain why this is so. Utilitarianism fails in this respect and so cannot be the theory we seek.

What to do? Where to begin anew? The place to begin, I think, is with the utilitarian's view of the value of the individual—or, rather, lack of value. In its place, suppose we consider that you and I, for example, do have value as individuals—what we'll call *inherent value*. To say we have such value is to say that we are something more than, something different from, mere receptacles. Moreover, to ensure that we do not pave the way for such injustices as slavery or sexual discrimination, we must believe that all who have inherent value have it equally, regardless of their sex, race, religion, birthplace, and so on. Similarly to be discarded as irrelevant are one's talents or skills, intelligence, and wealth, personality or pathology, whether one is loved and admired or despised and loathed. The genius and the retarded child, the prince and the pauper, the brain surgeon and the fruit vendor, Mother Teresa and the most unscrupulous used-car salesman—all have inherent value, all possess it equally, and all have an equal right to be treated with respect, to be treated in ways that do not reduce them to the status of things, as if they existed as resources for others. My value as an individual is independent of my usefulness to you. Yours is not dependent on your usefulness to me. For either of us to treat the other in ways that fail to show respect for the other's independent value is to act immorally, to violate the individual's rights.

Some of the rational virtues of this view—what I call the rights view—should be evident. Unlike (crude) contractarianism, for example, the rights view *in principle* denies the moral tolerability of any and all forms of racial, sexual, or social discrimination; and unlike utilitarianism, this view *in principle* denies that we can justify good results by using evil means that violate an individual's rights—denies, for example, that it could be moral to kill my Aunt Bea to harvest beneficial consequences for others. That would be to sanction the disrespectful treatment of the individual in the name of the social good, something the rights view will not—categorically will not—ever allow.

The rights view, I believe, is rationally the most satisfactory moral theory. It surpasses all other theories in the degree to which it illuminates and explains the foundations of our duties to one another—the domain of human morality. On this score it has the best reasons, the best arguments, on its side. Of course, if it were possible to show that only human beings are included within its scope, then a person like myself, who believes in animal rights, would be obliged to look elsewhere.

But attempts to limit its scope to humans only can be shown to be rationally defective. Animals, it is true, lack many of the abilities humans possess. They can't read, do higher mathematics, build a bookcase, or make *baba ghanoush*. Neither can many human beings, however, and yet we don't (and shouldn't) say that they (these humans) therefore have less inherent value, less of a right to be treated with respect, than do others. It is the *similarities* between those human beings who most clearly, most non-controversially have such value (the people reading this, for example), not our differences, that matter most. And the real crucial, the basic similarity is simply this: we are each of us the experiencing subject of a life, a conscious creature having an individual welfare that has importance to us whatever our usefulness to others. We want and prefer things, believe and feel things, recall and expect things. And all these dimensions of our life, including our pleasure and pain, our enjoyment and suffering, our satisfaction and frustration, our continued existence or our untimely death—all make a difference to the quality of our life as lived, as experienced, by us as individuals. As the same is true of those animals that concern us (the ones that are eaten and trapped, for example), they too must be viewed as the experiencing subjects of a life, with inherent value of their own.

Some there are who resist the idea that animals have inherent value. "Only humans have such value", they profess. How might this narrow view be defended? Shall we say that only humans have the requisite intelligence, or autonomy, or reason? But there are many, many humans who fail to meet these standards and yet are reasonably viewed as having value above and beyond their usefulness to others. Shall we claim that only humans belong to the right species, the species *Homo sapiens*? But this is blatant speciesism. Will it be said, then, that all—and only—humans have immortal souls? Then our opponents have their work cut out for them. I am myself not ill-disposed to the proposition that there are immortal souls. Personally, I profoundly hope I have one. But I would not want to rest my position on a controversial ethical issue on the even more controversial question about who or what has an immortal soul. That is to dig one's hole deeper, not to climb out. Rationally, it is better to resolve moral issues without making more controversial assumptions than are needed. The question of who has inherent value is such a question, one that is resolved more rationally without the introduction of the idea of immortal souls than by its use.

Well, perhaps some will say that animals have some inherent value, only less than we have. Once again, however, attempts to defend this view can be shown to lack rational justification. What could be the basis of our having more inherent value than animals? Their lack of reason, or autonomy, or intellect? Only if we are willing to make the same judgment in the case of humans who are similarly deficient. But it is not true that such humans—the retarded child, for example, or the mentally deranged—have less inherent value than you or I. Neither, then, can we rationally sustain the view that animals like them in being the experiencing subjects of a life have less inherent value. *All* who have inherent value have it *equally*, whether they be human animals or not.

Inherent value, then, belongs equally to those who are the experiencing subjects of a life. Whether it belongs to others—to rocks and rivers, trees and glaciers, for example—we do not know and may never know. But neither do we need to know, if we are to make the case for animal rights. We do not need to know, for example, how many people are eligible to vote in the next presidential election before we can know whether I am. Similarly, we do not need to know how many individuals have inherent value before we can know that some do. When it comes to the case for animal rights, then, what we need to know is whether the animals that, in our culture, are routinely eaten, hunted, and used in our laboratories, for example, are like us in being subjects of a life. And we do know this. We do know that many—literally, billions and billions—of these animals are the subjects of a life in the sense explained and so have inherent value if we do. And since, in order to arrive at the best theory of our duties to one another, we must recognize our equal inherent value as individuals, reason—not sentiment, not emotion—reason compels us to recognize the equal inherent value of these animals and, with this, their equal right to be treated with respect.

That, *very* roughly, is the shape and feel of the case for animal rights. Most of the details of the supporting argument are missing. They are to be found in the book to which I alluded earlier. Here, the details go begging, and I must, in closing, limit myself to four final points.

The first is how the theory that underlies the case for animal rights shows that the animal rights movement is a part of, not antagonistic to, the human rights movement. The theory that rationally grounds the rights of animals also grounds the rights of humans. Thus those involved in the animal rights movement are partners in the struggle to secure respect for human rights—the rights of women, for example, or minorities, or workers. The animal rights movement is cut from the same moral cloth as these.

Second, having set out the broad outlines of the rights view, I can now say why its implications for farming and science, among other fields, are both clear and uncompromising. In the case of the use of animals in science, the rights view is categorically abolitionist. Lab animals are not our tasters; we are not their kings. Because these animals are treated routinely, systematically as if their value were reducible to their usefulness to others, they are routinely, systematically treated with a lack of respect, and thus are their rights routinely, systematically violated. This is just as true when they are used in trivial, duplicative, unnecessary, or unwise research as it is when they are used in studies that hold out real promise of human benefits. We can't justify harming or killing a human being (my Aunt Bea, for example) just for these sorts of reason. Neither can we do so even in the case of so lowly a creature as a laboratory rat. It is not just refinement or reduction that is called for, not just larger, cleaner cages, not just more generous use of anesthetic or the elimination of multiple surgery, not just tidying up the system. It is complete replacement. The best we can do when it comes to using animals in science is—not to use them. That is where our duty lies, according to the rights view.

As for commercial animal agriculture, the rights view takes a similar abolitionist position. The fundamental moral wrong here is not that animals are kept in stressful close confinement or in isolation, or that their pain and suffering, their needs and preferences are ignored or discounted. All these *are* wrong, of course, but they are not the fundamental wrong. They are symptoms and effects of the deeper, systematic wrong that allows these animals to be viewed as lacking independent value, as resources for us—as, indeed, a renewable resource. Giving farm animals more space, more natural environments, more companions, does not right the fundamental wrong, any more than giving lab animals more anesthesia or bigger, cleaner cages would right the fundamental wrong in their case. Nothing less than the total dissolution of commercial animal agriculture will do this, just as, for similar reasons I won't develop at length here, morality requires nothing less than the total elimination of hunting and trapping for commercial and sporting ends. The rights view's implications, then, as I have said, are clear and uncompromising.

My last two points are about philosophy, my profession. It is, most obviously, no substitute for political action. The words I have written here and in other places by themselves don't change a thing. It is what we do with the thoughts that the words express—our acts, our deeds—that changes things. All that philosophy can do, and all I have attempted, is to offer a vision of what our deeds should aim at. And the why. But not the how.

Finally, I am reminded of my thoughtful critic, the one I mentioned earlier, who chastised me for being too cerebral. Well, cerebral I have been: indirect duty views, utilitarianism, contractarianism—hardly the stuff deep passions are made of. I am also reminded, however, of the image another friend set before me—the image of the ballerina as expressive of disciplined passion. Long hours of sweat and toil, of loneliness and practice, of doubt and fatigue: those are the discipline of her craft. But the passion is there too, the fierce drive to excel, to speak through her body, to do it right, to pierce our minds. That is the image of philosophy I would leave with you, not "too cerebral" but *disciplined passion*. Of the discipline enough has been seen. As for the passion: there are times, and these not infrequent, when tears come to my eyes when I see, or read, or hear of the wretched plight of animals in the hands of humans. Their pain, their suffering, their loneliness, their innocence, their death. Anger. Rage. Pity. Sorrow. Disgust. The whole creation groans under the weight of the evil we humans visit upon these mute, powerless creatures. It is our hearts, not just our heads, that call for an end to it all, that demand of us that we overcome, for them, the habits and forces behind their systematic oppression. All great movements, it is written, go through three stages: ridicule, discussion, and adoption. It is the realization of this third stage, adoption, that requires both our passion and our discipline, our hearts and our heads. The fate of animals is in our hands. God grant that we are equal to the task.

Questions for Discussion

1. What is meant by the "indirect duty view?"
2. Summarize the contractarian and utilitarian approaches. What problems does Regan find with each?
3. Explain Regan's rights view. What does he mean by "subjects-of-a life?" What is the significance of the term "inherent value?"

30 Animal Rights and Feminist Theory

Josephine Donovan

One of the first comprehensive feminist theories of animal rights is presented in this selection by Josephine Donovan. Although recognizing the important contributions that contemporary animal rights theorists Peter Singer and Tom Regan have made, Donovan argues that both still use the same Cartesian logic that has been used to justify much of the abusive treatment of other animals. Rather than a masculinist approach that values reason and logic over emotion and relationship, Donovan calls for a feminist ethic of care that recognizes the interdependence of all lives, and that emerges out of what she calls "a women's relational culture of caring and attentive love. . . ."

> *This article is dedicated to my great dog Rooney (1974–87), who died as it was being completed but whose life led me to appreciate the nobility and dignity of animals.*

Peter Singer prefaces his groundbreaking treatise *Animal Liberation* (1975) with an anecdote about a visit he and his wife made to the home of a woman who claimed to love animals, had heard he was writing a book on the subject, and so invited him to tea. Singer's attitude toward the woman is contemptuous: she had invited a friend who also loved animals and was "keen to meet us. When we arrived our hostess's friend was already there, and . . . certainly was keen to talk about animals. 'I do love animals; she began . . . and she was off. She paused while refreshments were served, took a ham sandwich, and then asked us what pets we had."[1] Singer's point is not only to condemn the woman's hypocrisy in claiming to love animals while she was eating meat but also to dissociate himself from a sentimentalist approach to animal welfare. Speaking for his wife as well, he explains: "We were not especially 'interested in' animals. Neither of us had ever been inordinately fond of dogs, cats, or horses. . . . We didn't 'love' animals. . . . The portrayal of those who protest against cruelty to

Originally published in 1990 in *Signs*, vol. 15, no. 2, pp. 350–375. Reprinted with permission from University of Chicago Press.

animals as sentimental, emotional 'animal lovers' [has meant] excluding the entire issue . . . from serious political and moral discussion." In other words, he fears that to associate the animal rights cause with "womanish" sentiment is to trivialize it.[2]

Singer's concerns about the image and strategies of animal rights activists are shared by another major contemporary theorist of animal rights, Tom Regan. In his preface to *The Case for Animal Rights* (1983) Regan stresses that "since all who work on behalf of the interests of animals are . . . familiar with the tired charge of being 'irrational'; 'sentimental'; 'emotional'; or worse, we can give the lie to these accusations only by making a concerted effort not to indulge our emotions or parade our sentiments. And that requires making a sustained commitment to rational inquiry" (xii). In a later article Regan (1985) defends himself against charges of being hyper-rational by maintaining that "reason—not sentiment, not emotion—reason compels us to recognize the equal inherent value of . . . animals and . . . their equal right to be treated with respect" (24). Regan's and Singer's rejection of emotion and their concern about being branded sentimentalist are not accidental; rather, they expose the inherent bias in contemporary animal rights theory toward rationalism, which, paradoxically, in the form of Cartesian objectivism, established a major theoretical justification for animal abuse.

Women animal rights theorists seem, indeed, to have developed more of a sense of emotional bonding with animals as the basis for their theory than is evident in the male literature. Mary Midgley (1985, 60), for example, another contemporary animal rights theorist, urges, "What makes our fellow beings entitled to basic consideration is surely not intellectual capacity but emotional fellowship." Animals, she notes, exhibit "social and emotional complexity of the kind which is expressed by the formation of deep, subtle and lasting relationships." Constantia Salamone, a leading feminist animal rights activist, roundly condemns the rationalist, masculinist bias of current animal rights theory.[3] In the nineteenth century, women activists in the anti-vivisection movement, such as Frances Power Cobbe, viewed as their enemy the "coldly rational materialism" of science, which they saw as threatening "to freeze human emotion and sensibility. . . . Antivivisection . . . shielded the heart, the human spirit, from degradation at the hands of heartless science."[4]

Yet Singer's anecdote points up that one cannot simply turn uncritically to women as a group or to a female value system as a source for a humane relationship ethic with animals. While women have undoubtedly been less guilty of active abuse and destruction of animals than men (Virginia Woolf observes in *Three Guineas*: "The vast majority of birds and beasts have been killed by you; not by us"),[5] they nevertheless have been complicit in that abuse, largely in their use of luxury items that entail animal pain and destruction (such as furs) and in their consumption of meat. Charlotte Perkins Gilman, an animal welfare crusader as well as a feminist, criticized such hypocrisy decades before Singer in her "A Study in Ethics" (1933). Condemning women's habit of wearing "as decoration the carcass of the animal," Gilman remarks the shocking inconsistency that "civilized Christian women, sensitive to cruelty, fond of pets, should willingly maintain the greatest possible cruelty to millions of harmless little animals. . . . Furs are obtained by trapping. Trapping means every agony known to an animal, imprisonment, starvation, freezing, frantic fear and pain. If one woman hung up or fastened down hundreds of kittens each by one paw in her backyard in winter weather, to struggle and dangle and freeze, to cry in anguish and terror that she might 'trim' something with their collected skins . . . she would be considered a monster."[6] Recognizing that such problems are involved in women's historical relationship with animals, I believe that cultural feminism, informed by an awareness of animal rights theory, can provide a more viable theoretical basis for an ethic of animal treatment than is currently available.

Contemporary animal rights theory includes two major theoretical approaches, one based on natural rights theory and the other on utilitarianism. The major theoretician for the natural rights position is Tom Regan, whose primary statement appears in *The Case for Animal Rights*. In this lengthy, impressive, but sometimes casuistical document Regan argues that animals—in particular, adult mammals—are moral entities who have certain inalienable rights, just as humans do, according to the natural rights doctrine enunciated in the eighteenth century (particularly by Locke).[7]

Regan builds his case primarily by refuting Kant, who had stipulated in his second formulation of the Categorical Imperative that "man and generally any rational being exists as an end in himself—not merely as a means," that rational beings possess "absolute worth," and that therefore they are entitled to treatment as ends (1927, 308–309). It is on the basis of their rationality that humans are identified by Kant and other Enlightenment thinkers as moral agents who are therefore entitled to such natural rights as to be treated as ends.

In the articulation of Locke and the framers of the U.S. Declaration of Independence and Constitution not all humans were in fact considered sufficiently rational as to be considered "persons" entitled to rights: only white, male property holders were deemed adequately endowed to be included in the category of personhood. Indeed, much of the nineteenth-century women's rights movement was devoted to urging that women be considered persons under the Constitution (Donovan 1985, 4–5). Here as elsewhere in Western political theory women and animals are cast together. Aristotle, for example, linked women and animals in the *Nicomachean*

Ethics by excluding them from participation in the moral life. As Keith Thomas (1983) points out, the centuries-long debate over whether women have souls paralleled similar discussions about the moral status of animals (see also Midgley 1983).

In building his case for animal rights, Regan extends the category of those having absolute worth or inherent value to include non-rational but still intelligent non-human creatures. He does this by elaborating the distinction between moral agents (those who are capable of making rational, moral judgments) and moral patients (those who cannot make such formulations but who are nevertheless entitled to be treated as ends). This is contrary to Kant, who maintains that "animals . . . are there merely as a means to an end. That end is man" (Regan 1983, 177).

Regan makes his case by countering Kant's theory that human moral patients (i.e., those who are severely retarded, infants, or others unable to reason) need not be treated as ends. This to Regan is unacceptable. Therefore, if one accepts both moral agents and moral patients as entitled to the basic respect implied in the notion of rights, Regan argues, it follows that nonhuman moral patients (animals) must be included in the category of those entitled to be treated as ends. To argue otherwise is speciesist; that is, it arbitrarily assumes that humans are worth more than other life-forms. Speciesism is a concept borrowed from feminist and minority group theory. It is analogous to sexism and racism in that it privileges one group (humans, males, whites, or Aryans) over another. [8] Regan (1983) therefore, maintains an absolutist deontological non-consequentialist position; treating animals as ends is, he insists, a moral duty. It is a matter of justice, not kindness.

Although Regan rejects Kant's determination of rationality as the basis for entry into the "kingdom of ends," he specifies that those who have "inherent value" must have a subjective consciousness (be "subject of a life") and/or have the kind of complex awareness found in adult mammals. This criterion leaves open the question of severely retarded humans, humans in irreversible comas, fetuses, even human infants. Regan's criterion in fact privileges those with complex awareness over those without. Therefore, though it rejects Kantian rationalism, Regan's theory depends on a notion of complex consciousness that is not far removed from rational thought, thus, in effect, reinvoking the rationality criterion. I do not quarrel with the idea that adult mammals have a highly developed intelligence that may be appropriated to human reason; rather I question the validity of the rationality criterion. Regan's difficulty here stems in part, it seems, from natural rights theory, which privileges rationalism and individualism, but it may also reflect his own determined exclusion of sentiment from "serious" intellectual inquiry.

From a cultural feminist point of view the position developed by utilitarian animal rights theorists is more tenable in this regard because it dispenses with the higher-intelligence criterion, insisting instead on the capacity to feel—or the capacity to suffer—as the criterion by which to determine those who are entitled to be treated as ends.

The utilitarian position in animal rights theory has been developed principally by Peter Singer. Indeed, it is his admirable and courageous book *Animal Liberation* that largely galvanized the current animal rights movement. Singer's central premise derives from a key passage in Jeremy Bentham's *Introduction to the Principles of Morals and Legislation* (1789/1939). During a high tide of the natural rights doctrine, the French Revolution, Bentham wrote:

> The day may come when the rest of the animal creation may acquire those rights which never could have been withholden from them but by the hand of tyranny. . . . It may one day come to be recognized that the number of the legs, the villosity of the skin, or the termination of the os sacrum, are reasons . . . insufficient for abandoning a sensitive being to the same fate. What else is it that should trace the insuperable line? Is it the faculty of reason, or perhaps the faculty of discourse? But a full-grown horse or dog is beyond comparison a more rational, as well as a more conversable animal than an infant of a day, or a week, or even a month, old. But suppose the case were otherwise, what would it avail? The question is not, Can they *reason*? nor Can they *talk*? but, Can they *suffer*? (847)

A similar passage occurs in Rousseau's *Discourse on the Origin of Inequality* (1755/1967). It seems in part to be a rejoinder to the Cartesian view of animals as machines, discussed below.

> We may put an end to the ancient disputes concerning the participation of other animals in the law of nature; for it is plain that, as they want both reason and free will, they cannot be acquainted with that law; however, as they partake in some measure of our nature in virtue of that sensibility with which they are endowed, we may well imagine they ought likewise to partake of the benefit of natural law, and that man owes them a certain kind of duty. In fact, it seems that, if I am obliged not to injure any being like myself, it is not so much because he is a reasonable being, as because he is a sensible being. (172)[9]

Thus, both Bentham and Rousseau advocate that natural rights, or entrance into Kant's kingdom of ends, be accorded to creatures who can feel. Their assumption is that the common condition that unites humans with animals is sensibility, the capacity to feel pain and experience pleasure.

The utilitarian position proceeds from this premise to establish that if a creature is sentient, it has interests that are as equally worthy of consideration as any other sentient creature's interests when humans make decisions about their well-being. In Singer's (1975, 8) words, "The capacity for suffering and enjoyment is a *prerequisite for having interests.* A stone, for example, does not have interests in the question of being kicked because it cannot suffer, whereas a mouse does have such interests because it can experience pain as a result. "If a being suffers," Singer maintains, "there can be no moral justification for refusing to take that suffering into consideration. . . . The principle of equality requires that its suffering be counted equally with the like suffering . . . of any other being" (8). In short, "pain and suffering are bad and should be prevented or minimized, irrespective of the race, sex, or species of the being that suffers" (18). This is the essence of the utilitarian animal rights position.

Utilitarian animal rights theory has the virtue of allowing some flexibility in decision making, as opposed to Regan's absolutist stance that no animal's suffering is justifiable under any circumstances. As a utilitarian, Singer insists, for example, that an awareness of consequences can and should influence the evaluation of an individual's fate in any given situation. This leads him to admit that "there could conceivably be circumstances in which an experiment on an animal stands to reduce suffering so much that it would be permissible to carry it out even if it involved harm to the animal . . . [even if] the animal were a human being."[10] Elsewhere he says that if the suffering of one animal would have the result of curing all forms of cancer, that suffering would be justifiable. Singer's basic position is that "similar interests must count equally, regardless of the species of the being involved. Thus, if some experimental procedure would hurt a human being and a pig to the same extent, and there were no other relevant consequences . . . it would be wrong to say that we should use the pig because the suffering of the pig counts less than the suffering of a human being" (Singer 1985, 48).

Therefore, although Singer also uses the term "animal rights," his modifications take it even farther from traditional natural rights doctrine than do Regan's reconceptions. It is not a matter of political rights of a rational citizen, such as the right to free speech or to vote, nor is it the right of an intelligent creature to be treated as an end (in Kantian terms). Rather it is the right of a sentient creature to have its interests in remaining unharmed considered equally when weighed against the interests of another sentient creature.[11]

Singer's insistence that animals have interests equal to humans makes his argument as morally compelling as Regan's contention that animals have rights. Nevertheless, there are some weaknesses in the utilitarian position. One is that a precise value standard for decision making or weighing of interests is not provided, which allows unacknowledged prejudices to intrude. Second, it requires a quantification of suffering, a "mathematization" of moral beings, that falls back into the scientific modality that legitimates animal sacrifice. Thus, while it recognizes sensibility or feeling as the basis for treatment as a moral entity, the utilitarian position remains locked in a rationalist, calculative mode of moral reasoning that distances the moral entities from the decision-making subject, reifying them in terms of quantified suffering. Just as the natural rights theory proposed by Regan inherently privileges rationality, Singer's utilitarianism relapses into a mode of manipulative mastery that is not unlike that used by scientific and medical experimenters to legitimate such animal abuses as vivisection. It is for this reason that we must turn to cultural feminism for alternative theory.

Cultural feminism has a long history. Even during feminism's "first wave" thinkers otherwise as diverse as Margaret Fuller, Emma Goldman, and Charlotte Perkins Gilman articulated a critique of the atomistic individualism and rationalism of the liberal tradition.[12] They did so by proposing a vision that emphasized collectivity, emotional bonding, and an organic (or holistic) concept of life. In *Woman in the Nineteenth Century* (1845/1971), for example, Fuller argued that the "liberation" of women and their integration into public life would effect a feminization of culture, which would mean a reign of "plant-like gentleness," a harmonic, peaceful rule, an end to violence of all kinds (including, she specifies, the slaughter of animals for food) and the institution of vegetarianism (substituting, she urges, "pulse [beans] for animal food") (113). Gilman put forth a similar vision in her utopian novel *Herland* (1911). Indeed, in addition to Fuller and Gilman there is a long list of first-wave feminists who advocated either vegetarianism or animal welfare reform, including Mary Wollstonecraft, Harriet Beecher Stowe, Lydia Maria Child, Elizabeth Blackwell, Elizabeth Stuart Phelps Ward, Susan B. Anthony, Victoria Woodhull, Elizabeth Cady Stanton, the Grimké sisters, Lucy Stone, Frances Willard, Frances Power Cobbe, Anna Kingford, Caroline Earle White, and Agnes Ryan.[13]

In the second wave of feminist theory there have been a few articles specifically linking feminism with animal rights: in the 1970s Carol Adams's articles on vegetarianism and more recently Constantia Salamone's piece in *Reweaving the Web of Life* (1982).[14] There have been a number of other works that link feminism more generally with ecology, such as those by Susan Griffin (1978), Carolyn Merchant (1980),

Rosemary Radford Ruether (1975, 1983), Marilyn French (1985), Paula Gunn Allen (1986), Chrystos (1981), and Ynestra King (1981).

From the cultural feminist viewpoint, the domination of nature, rooted in postmedieval, Western, male psychology, is the underlying cause of the mistreatment of animals as well as of the exploitation of women and the environment. In her path-breaking study, *The Death of Nature: Women, Ecology, and the Scientific Revolution*, Carolyn Merchant (1980, xviii) recognizes that "we must reexamine the formation of a world view and a science that, by reconceptualizing reality as a machine rather than a living organism, sanctioned the domination of both nature and women."

Critiques of the logical fallacies inherent in the scientific epistemology are not new. Wittgenstein demonstrated the tautological nature of the analytic judgment in his *Tractatus* in 1911, indeed, a point Hume made in the *Enquiry Concerning Human Understanding* in 1748; but it was the critique offered by Max Horkheimer and Theodor Adorno in their *Dialectic of Enlightenment* (1944) that first made the connection between what Husserl called the "mathematisation of the world,"[15] and the derogation of women and animals (Horkheimer and Adorno 1944/1972).

The scientific or experimental method converts reality into mathematical entities modeled on the physical universe, which, as seen in Newton's laws, is cast in the image of a mechanism that operates according to fixed repetitions. No distinction is made between life-forms such as human and animal bodies, which are seen as machines in the Cartesian view, and non-life forms such as rocks.

Horkheimer and Adorno argue that the imposition of the mathematical model upon reality reflects a psychology of domination. "In [scientific] thought, men distance themselves from nature in order thus imaginatively to present it to themselves—but only in order to determine how it is to be dominated" (39). Using the term "enlightenment" to refer to the scientific viewpoint, they note that "enlightenment is as totalitarian as any system" (24); it operates "as a dictator toward men. He knows them in so far as he can manipulate them" (9).

The pretensions of universality of scientific knowledge and the generalizing character of the machine metaphor mean that differences and particularities are erased, subdued, dominated. "In the impartiality of scientific language, that which is powerless has wholly lost any means of expression" (Horkheimer and Adorno 1944/1972, 23). As Max Scheler noted, "Those aspects which cannot be represented in the chosen symbolic language of mathematics . . . are assigned a fundamentally different status: they belong to the realm of the 'subjective' and 'unscientific.'"[16] Thus, all that is anomalous—that is, alive and not predictable—is erased or subdued in the Newtonian/Cartesian epistemological paradigm. The anomalous and the powerless include women and animals, both of whose subjectivities and realities are erased or converted into manipulable objects—"the material of subjugation" (Horkheimer and Adorno 1944/1972, 84) at the mercy of the rationalist manipulator, whose self-worth is established by the fact that he thus subdues his environment. "Everything—even the human individual, not to speak of the animal—is converted into the repeatable, replaceable process, into a mere example for the conceptual models of the system" (84).

Horkheimer and Adorno conclude that this scientific epistemology is an ideological form that is rooted in the material conditions of social domination—particularly that of men over women. In "their nauseating physiological laboratories" scientists "force [information] from defenseless [animals]. . . . The conclusion they draw from mutilated bodies [is that] . . . because he does injury to animals, he and he alone in all creation voluntarily functions. . . . Reason . . . belongs to man. The animal . . . knows only irrational terror" (245). But the scientist feels no compassion for or empathy with his victims because "for rational beings . . . to feel concern about an irrational creature is a futile occupation. Western civilization has left this to women . . . [through] the division of labor imposed on her by man" (248).

The association of the postmedieval split between reason and the emotions with the division of labor and in particular with the rise of industrial capitalism is a well-developed thesis, particularly among Marxist theorists. Eli Zaretsky, in *Capitalism, the Family and Personal Life* (1976), suggests that the reification of public life occasioned by alienated industrial labor meant personal relationships were relegated to the private sphere: "The split in society between 'personal feelings' and 'economic production' was integrated with the sexual division of labour. Women were identified with emotional life, men with the struggle for existence" (64).

Women's connection with economic life has been nearly universally "production for use" rather than "production for exchange"—that is, their labor has prepared material for immediate use by the household rather than for use as a commodity for exchange or for monetary payment. Such a practice, theorists have argued, tends to create a psychology that values the objects of production emotionally in a way that alienated production for exchange cannot. Since in the capitalist era it is largely women who engage in use-value production, it may be a basis for the relational, contextually oriented epistemology that contemporary theorists ascribe to Western women.[17] The relegation of women, emotions, and values to the private sphere, to, the margins, allowed, as Horkheimer, Adorno, and others have noted, masculine practices in the public political and scientific sphere to proceed amorally, "objectively," without the restraint of "subjective" relational considerations, which are in any event elided or repressed by the dominant disciplines.

Like Carolyn Merchant, Horkheimer and Adorno recognize that the witch-hunts of the early modern period were symptomatic of the new need to erase and subdue anomalous, disorderly (and thus feminine) nature. Horkheimer and Adorno consider that the eradication of witches registered "the triumph of male society over prehistoric matriarchal and mimetic stages of development" and "of self-preserving reason . . . [in] the mastery of nature" (249). Merchant (1980) suggests witches represent that aspect of nature that did not fit into the orderly pattern of the mathematical paradigm; they therefore were seen as dangerously rebellious: "Disorderly woman, like chaotic nature, needed to be controlled" (127).

Merchant notes that Bacon, one of the formulators of the experimental method, used the analogy of a witch inquisition to explain how the scientist manipulates nature in order to extract information from it. He wrote: "For you have but to follow it and as it were hound nature in her wanderings, and you will be able when you like to lead and drive her afterward to the same place again" (168). The image of nature as a female to be dominated could not be more explicit.

The mathematical paradigm imposed the image of the machine on all reality. It was Descartes who most fully developed the idea that non-mental life-forms function as machines, which some of his followers (La Mettrie, e.g., in *L'homme machine*) carried to its extreme. Tom Regan critiques the Cartesian view at length in *The Case for Animal Rights*; it is clear that the notion of animals as feelingless, unconscious robots (which Rousseau, among others—see above—rejected) legitimated (and continues to legitimate) atrocious scientific experimentation. One early anonymous critic of Descartes noted: "The [Cartesian] scientists administered beatings to dogs with perfect indifference and made fun of those who pitied the creatures as if they felt pain. They said the animals were clocks; that the cries they emitted when struck were only the sound of a little spring that had been touched, but that the whole body was without feeling. They nailed the poor animals up on boards by their four paws to vivisect them to see the circulation of the blood which was a great subject of controversy" (Regan 1983, 5).

In a recent article, "The Cartesian Masculinization of Thought," Susan Bordo (1986) describes Cartesian objectivism as an "aggressive intellectual 'flight from the feminine.' " "The 'great Cartesian anxiety' [seen especially in the Meditations is] over separation from the organic female universe of the Middle Ages and the Renaissance. Cartesian objectivism [is] a defensive response to that separation anxiety" (441). In the process "the formerly female earth becomes inert *res extensa*: dead, mechanically interacting nature. . . . 'She' becomes 'it'—and 'it' can be understood. Not through sympathy, of course, but by virtue of the very *object*-ivity of 'it' " (451).

Natural rights theory, likewise an expression of Enlightenment rationalism, similarly imposes a machine grid upon political and moral reality. Recent feminist theorists have criticized the neutral and objective pretenses of the liberal theoretical tradition for leaving out the anomalous context in which events occur, inscribing them instead in an abstract grid that distorts or ignores the historical environment. For example, Catherine A. MacKinnon (1985) has criticized the traditional liberal interpretation of U.S. constitutional law for its neutral approach to justice. She urges that we "change one dimension of liberalism as it is embodied in law: the definition of justice as neutrality between abstract categories," for this approach ignores the "substantive systems"—that is, the real conditions in which the abstractions operate. MacKinnon therefore rejects, to use her example, the idea that "strengthening the free speech of the Klan strengthens the free speech of Blacks" (4). This thesis is invalid, she maintains, because it equates "substantive powerlessness with substantive power" (15) through the use of a mechanistic conceptual model. Thus, MacKinnon, like the cultural feminists discussed below, rejects the "mathematizing" elisions of Enlightenment rationalism in favor of a view that "sees" the environmental context. Had the vivisectionists described above allowed this epistemological shift, they presumably would have "seen" the pain—the suffering and emotions—of the animals, which the machine abstraction through which they were viewing them ignored.

Unfortunately, contemporary animal rights theorists, in their reliance on theory that derives from the mechanistic premises of Enlightenment epistemology (natural rights in the case of Regan and utilitarian calculation in the case of Singer) and in their suppression/denial of emotional knowledge, continue to employ Cartesian, or objectivist, modes even while they condemn the scientific practices enabled by them.

Two of the earliest critics of Cartesian mechanism were women: Margaret Cavendish, the Duchess of Newcastle (1623–1673), and Anne Finch, Lady Conway (1631–1679). Finch emphatically rejected the Cartesian view; she felt that animals were not "composed of 'mere fabric' or 'dead matter,' but had spirits within them 'having knowledge, sense, and love, and divers other faculties and properties of a spirit' " (Finch 1690, cited in Merchant 1980, 260). Cavendish, an untutored genius, challenged Descartes directly. She met him while she and her husband were in exile in France in the 1640s, and she later exchanged letters with him about his *Treatise on Animals*. In one of his letters, dated November 23, 1646, he is prompted by her to defend his notion of animals as machines: "I cannot share the opinion of Montaigne and others who attribute understanding or thought to animals" (Descartes 1957, 44).

As Keith Thomas (1983, in *Man and the Natural World*) recognizes, Cavendish was one of the first to articulate the idea of animal rights. Her biographer, Douglas Grant (1957, 4-1), notes: "Her writings . . . constantly illustrate her sensibility to nature [and] its creatures: how she felt for 'poor Wat,' the hunted hare . . . the stag; her pity for their unnecessary sufferings making her speak out in a century when cruelty to animals was all too common." "As for man, who hunts all animals to death on the plea of sport, exercise and health," she asked, "is he not more cruel and wild than any bird of prey?" (124) [18]

The resistance of Finch and Cavendish to the impositions of early modern science were not isolated accidents, I propose. Indeed, if we accept Michel Foucault's contention that the ascendancy of the scientific disciplines and their attendant institutions was a historical process of colonization that intensified through the postmedieval period, reaching a height in the late nineteenth century, we must read Finch and Cavendish's critiques as an early feminist resistance to a process that inevitably meant the destruction of women's anomalous worlds. The suppression of women's social realities effected by the pseudoscientific medical theories (especially those of the sexologists) of the late nineteenth century was the final stage in what Foucault has labeled the "medicalisation de l'insolite"—the medicalization of the anomalous.[19] This process itself involved the social imposition of sexologist paradigms analogous to the scientific imposition of the mathematical machine paradigm on all living forms.

Perhaps this is why many women of the period seem to have felt a kinship to animals. Both were erased (at best) or manipulated (at worst) to behave in accordance with paradigms imposed by the rationalist lords—whether vivisectors or sexologists. Women in fact became the primary activists and energizers of the nineteenth-century antivivisection movement, which should be seen, I propose, as one manifestation of a counter-hegemonic resistance undertaken by women against the encroachments of the new disciplines. Just as sexologists anatomized women's world "of love and ritual," "entomologizing" it (to use Foucault's term) into various species and subspecies of deviance, so vivisectors turned animal bodies into machines for dissection.

In her study of the nineteenth-century English antivivisection movement, *The Old Brown Dog*, Coral Lansbury (1985) argues that women activists thus identified with the vivisected dog: "Every dog or cat strapped down for the vivisector's knife reminded them of their own condition" (82). It was an image of dominance. Indeed, pioneer woman doctor Elizabeth Blackwell saw ovariectomies and other gynecological surgery as an "extension of vivisection" (89). For the suffragists, "the image of the vivisected dog blurred and became one with the militant suffragette being force fed in Brixton Prison" (24).

The dominance over nature, women, and animals inherent in this scientific epistemology, which requires that the anomalous "other" be forced into ordered forms, may be rooted in the Western male maturation process that requires men to establish their autonomous identity against the maternal/feminine. Hanna Fenichel Pitkin's (1984) recent analysis of the psychological development of Machiavelli, a prototypical formulator of postmedieval secularism, is most instructive in this regard. She reveals that "Machiavelli's writings show a persistent preoccupation with manhood."[20] "If *virtu* [manliness] is Machiavelli's favorite quality, *effeminato* . . . is one of his most frequent and scathing epithets" (25). In *The Prince* (1966), Machiavelli asserts that a leader rules "either by fortune or by ability (virtu)" (13). Virtu implies manipulative rationality and a certain macho willingness to exert military control. Fortuna, on the other hand, represents the non-rational, that which is unpredictable, all that is other to the exertion of rational control and masculine domination. In another celebrated passage in *The Prince*, Machiavelli asserts: "Fortune is a woman and in order to be mastered she must be jogged and beaten" (86–87).

In an unfinished poem that treats the Circe legend, Machiavelli opposes the world of women, nature, and animals to the civilized world of public order, the world of men. Pitkin (1984) notes that Circe is seen as a witch who has the power to turn men into beasts; much is made by Machiavelli of the "contrast between her feminine, natural world, and the world of men which is political and the product of human artifice. . . . Juxtaposed to the masculine world of law and liberty [is] the forest world where men are turned into animals and held captive in permanent dependence" (124, 128). "Male culture," therefore, "symbolizes control over nature" (Ruether 1983, 76).

Pitkin concludes, "Civilization . . . history, culture, the whole *vivere civile* that constitute the world of adult human autonomy are . . . male enterprises won from and sustained against female power—the engulfing mother . . . women as the 'other' . . . . The struggle to sustain civilization . . . thus reflects the struggle of boys to become men" (230). In "Gender and Science" (1978) Evelyn Fox Keller similarly argues that the autonomy and objectivity of the male scientist reflect the basic dissociation from the feminine affective world required in the male maturation process.[21]

Beyond this ontogenetic theory is the phylogenetic thesis developed by Rosemary Radford Ruether (1975) that patriarchal civilization is built upon the historical emergence of a masculine ego consciousness that arose in opposition to nature, which was seen as feminine. Sexism, she notes, is rooted in this "'war against the mother,' the struggle of the transcendent ego to free itself from bondage to nature" (25). Developing the existentialist notion of the transcendent masculine *pour soi*, and the immanent feminine *en soi*, Ruether urges (thereby rejecting Simone de

Beauvoir's thesis in *The Second Sex*) that the continual cultural attempt to transcend the feminine is what has led to our present ecological and moral crisis.

The fundamental defect in the "male ideology of transcendent dualism" is that its only mode is conquest. "Its view of what is over against itself is not that of the conversation of two subjects, but the conquest of an alien object. The intractability of the other side of the dualism to its demands does not suggest that the 'other' has a 'nature' of her own that needs to be respected and with which one must enter into conversation. Rather, this intractability is seen as that of disobedient rebellion." Thus, "patriarchal religion ends . . . with a perception of the finite cosmos itself as evil in its intractability" to technological, scientific progress (195–196).

In her recent book *Beyond Power* (1985) Marilyn French argues that "patriarchy is an ideology founded on the assumption that man is distinct from the animal and superior to it. The basis for this superiority is man's contact with a higher power/knowledge called god, reason, or control. The reason for man's existence is to shed all animal residue and realize fully his 'divine' nature, the part that seems unlike any part owned by animals—mind, spirit, or control" (34). [22] French sees a sadomasochism inherent in this cultural impulse to mutilate or kill off the animal/feminine in the self. According to French, patriarchal society has reached a frightening impasse: "Our culture, which worships above all else the power to kill, has reached the point of wishing to annihilate all that is 'feminine' in our world" (523).

Recent cultural feminist theorists have identified alternative epistemological and ontological modes that must, I believe, replace the mode of sadomasochistic control/dominance characteristic of patriarchal scientific epistemology. Ruether, for example, urges the development of new ways of relating to nature and to nonhuman life-forms. "The project of human life," she says, "must cease to be seen as one of 'domination of nature.' . . . Rather, we have to find a new language of ecological responsiveness, a reciprocity between consciousness and the world systems in which we live and move and have our being" (83). In *Sexism and God-Talk* (1983), Ruether suggests that human consciousness be seen not as different from other life-forms but as continuous with the "bimorphic" spirit inherent in other living beings.

> Our intelligence is a special, intense form of . . . radial energy, but it is not without continuity with other forms; it is the self-conscious or "thinking dimension" of the radial energy of matter. We must respond to a "thou-ness" in all beings. This is not romanticism or an anthropomorphic animism that sees "dryads in trees," although there is truth in the animist view. . . . We respond not just as "I to it," but as "I to thou," to the spirit, the life energy that lies in every being in its own form of

existence. The "brotherhood of man" needs to be widened to embrace not only women but also the whole community of life. (87)

Ruether calls for "a new form of human intelligence," one based on a relational, affective mode popularly called "right-brain thinking," which moves beyond the linear, dichotomized, alienated consciousness characteristic of the "left-brain" mode seen in masculinist scientific epistemology. Linear, rationalist modes are, Ruether enjoins, "ecologically dysfunctional" (89–90). What is needed is a more "disordered" (my term—if order means hierarchical dominance) relational mode that does not rearrange the context to fit a master paradigm but sees, accepts, and respects the environment.

In *The Sacred Hoop: Recovering the Feminine in American Indian Traditions* (1986), Paula Gunn Allen finds in those traditions attitudes toward nature that are quite different from the alienation and dominance that characterize Western epistemology and theology. God and the spiritual dimension do not transcend life but rather are immanent in all life-forms. All creatures are seen as sacred and entitled to fundamental respect. Allen, herself a Laguna Pueblo-Sioux, recalls that "when I was small, my mother often told me that animals, insects, and plants are to be treated with the kind of respect one customarily accords to high-status adults." Nature, in her culture, is seen "not as blind and mechanical, but as aware and organic." There is "a seamless web" between "human and nonhuman life."

Rather than linear, hierarchical, mechanistic modes, Allen proposes a return to the achronological relational sensibility characteristic of her people. Recognizing that "there is some sort of connection between colonization and chronological time," Allen observes that "Indian time rests on a perception of individuals as part of an entire gestalt in which fittingness is not a matter of how gear teeth mesh with each other but rather how the person meshes with the revolving of the seasons, the land, and the mythic reality that shapes all life into significance (154). . . . Women's traditional occupations, their arts and crafts, and their literatures and philosophies are more often accretive than linear, more achronological than chronological, and more dependent on harmonious relationships of all elements within a field of perception than western culture in general (243). . . . Traditional peoples perceive their world in a unified-field fashion" (244).

In her recent study of contemporary women's art, *Women as Mythmakers* (1984), Estella Lauter has identified the contours of a new myth that involves women and nature. "Many of these artists accept the affinity between woman and nature as a starting point—in fact, creating hybrid images of woman/animal/earth until the old distinctions among the levels in the Great Chain of Being seem unimportant."[23]

Recognizing Susan Griffin's *Woman and Nature* (1978) as prototypical, Lauter (1984, 19) detects in contemporary women's literature and art "an image of relationships among orders of being that is extremely fluid without being disintegrative."

In these works, boundaries between the human world and the vegetable and animal realm are blurred. Hybrid forms appear: women transform into natural entities, such as plants, or merge with animal life. Lauter finds "surprising numbers of women" poets have a "high degree of identification with nature, without fear and without loss of consciousness" (177). Many of these artists have revalidated ancient mythic figures that emblematize aspects of women's relationship with nature: Demeter/Kore, Artemis/Diana, Daphne, Circe. The earth is seen not as "dead matter to be plundered, but wounded matter from which renewal flows. The two bodies, women's and earth's, are sympathetic" (174).

The women artists and the feminist theorists cited here point to a new mode of relationship; unlike the subject–object mode inherent in the scientific epistemology and the rationalist distancing practiced by the male animal rights theorists, it recognizes the varieties and differences among the species but does not quantify or rank them hierarchically in a Great Chain of Being. It respects the aliveness and spirit (the "thou") of other creatures and understands that they and we exist in the same unified field continuum. It appreciates that what we share—life—is more important than our differences. Such a relationship sometimes involves affection, sometimes awe, but always respect.

In "*Maternal Thinking*" Sara Ruddick urges that a maternal epistemology, derived from the historical practice of mothering—that is, caring for an other who demands preservation and growth—can be identified. She calls it a "holding" attitude, one that "is governed by the priority of keeping over acquiring, of conserving the fragile, of maintaining whatever is at hand and necessary to the child's life." Ruddick contrasts the "holding" attitude to "scientific thought, as well as . . . to the instrumentalism of technocratic capitalism." Maternal practice recognizes "excessive control as a liability," in sharp distinction to scientific modes of manipulation (Ruddick 1980; 1989).

The maternal ethic involves a kind of reverential respect for the process of life and a realization that much is beyond one's control. Citing Iris Murdoch and Simone Weil as her philosophical predecessors, Ruddick (1980) calls this an ethic of humility. It is an attitude that "accepts not only the facts of damage and death, but also the facts of the independent and uncontrollable, developing and increasingly separate existences of the lives it seeks to preserve" (351). Ruddick calls such an attitude "attentive love," the training to ask, "What are you going through?" (359) Were vivisectionists to ask such a question, we would not have vivisection.

In a recent article Evelyn Keller (1982) draws similar distinctions to Ruddick's in her observations of Nobel Prize winner Barbara McClintock's "feminine" scientific practice (which contrasts so markedly to the aggressive manipulation of nature proposed by Bacon, seen at its worst in lab animal experimentation). McClintock believes in "letting the material speak to you," allowing it to "tell you what to do next." She does not believe that scientists should "impose an answer" upon their material, as required in the mathematical paradigm of traditional scientific epistemology; rather, they should respond to it and retain an empathetic respect for it (Keller 1982, 599). It is interesting that numerous women scientists and naturalists who have worked with and observed animal life for years—such as Jane Goodall, Dian Fossey, Sally Carrighar, Francine Patterson, Janis Carter—exhibit this ethic implicitly: a caring, respecting attitude toward their "subjects."[24]

Finally, Carol Gilligan's *In a Different Voice* (1982, 19) suggests that a feminine ethic is one rooted in a "mode of thinking that is contextual and narrative rather than formal and abstract."[25] What she names a "morality of responsibility" is in direct contrast to the "morality of rights" seen in Regan's animal rights theory. In the former, a feminine mode, "morality and the preservation of life are contingent upon sustaining connection . . . [and] keeping the web of relationships intact." She contrasts this with the "rights" approach (which is seen in her study as more characteristically masculine) that relies upon "separation rather than connection," and on a "formal logic" of hierarchically ranged quantitative evaluations.[26]

Gilligan, Ruddick, Lauter, Allen, Ruether, and French all propose an ethic that requires a fundamental respect for nonhuman life-forms, an ethic that listens to and accepts the diversity of environmental voices and the validity of their realities. It is an ethic that resists wrenching and manipulating the context so as to subdue it to one's categories; it is nonimperialistic and life affirming.

It may be objected that this ethic is too vague to be practicable in decisions concerning animals. My purpose here, however, is not to lay out a specific practical ethic but, rather, to indicate ways in which our thinking about animal/human relationships may be reoriented. Some may persist: suppose one had to choose between a gnat and a human being. It is, in fact, precisely this kind of either/or thinking that is rejected in the epistemology identified by cultural feminism. In most cases, either/or dilemmas in real life can be turned into both/ands. In most cases, dead-end situations such as those posed in lifeboat hypotheticals can be prevented. More specifically, however, it is clear that the ethic sketched here would mean feminists must reject carnivorism; the killing of live animals for clothing; hunting; the trapping of wildlife for fur (largely for women's luxury consumption); rodeos; circuses; and factory farming;

and that they must support the drastic redesigning of zoos (if zoos are to exist at all) to allow animals full exercise space in natural habitats; that they should reject the use of lab animals for testing of beauty and cleaning products (such as the infamous "LD-50" and Draize tests) and military equipment, as well as psychological experimentation such as that carried out in the Harlow primate lab at the University of Wisconsin; that they should support efforts to replace medical experiments by computer models and tissue culture; that they should condemn and work to prevent further destruction of wetlands, forests, and other natural habitats. All of these changes must be part of a feminist reconstruction of the world.

Natural rights and utilitarianism present impressive and useful philosophical arguments for the ethical treatment of animals. Yet, it is also possible—indeed, necessary—to ground that ethic in an emotional and spiritual conversation with nonhuman life-forms. Out of a women's relational culture of caring and attentive love, therefore, emerges the basis for a feminist ethic for the treatment of animals. We should not kill, eat, torture, and exploit animals because they do not want to be so treated, and we know that. If we listen, we can hear them.

Questions for Discussion

1. According to Donovan, how do the two major animal rights theories—utilitarianism (Singer) and natural rights theory (Regan)—still employ the same objectivist Cartesian rationalist bias that they claim to criticize?
2. How does feminist theory differ from these two contemporary animal rights theories?
3. Why do you think many feminists, both past and present, have been concerned with the treatment of nonhuman animals?

31 Caring about Blood, Flesh, and Pain
Women's Standing in the
Animal Protection Movement
Lyle Munro

Unlike most social movements, women have played a prominent role in the animal rights movement. Most studies show that women have much more favorable attitudes about other animals than men, are more likely to oppose practices involving the use or abuse of animals. Yet within the animal rights movement, men and women show much agreement in their attitudes toward the treatment of other animals. In this selection, Lyle Munro examines the history of women's involvement in animal activism and reviews the gender differences in animal attitudes. His survey of members of an Australian umbrella animal protection organization revealed that, for the most part, there is striking overlap in the attitudes of men and women within the movement. What explains the few differences that do emerge? That is the focus of Munro's analysis.

The animal rights movement in many ways is the kindred spirit of the environmental movement. Indeed, one writer has suggested that the former is an offshoot of the latter (Eckersley 1992). In terms of membership and activism, women have played a pre-eminent role in both movements. Most notably, Rachel Carson, author of *Silent Spring* is often lauded as the individual who launched the environmental movement in the United States in the 1960s. It is therefore surprising to read, "a good bit of feminist theory is either insensitive to environmental and animal rights issues or downright hostile toward them" (Slicer 1994, 35). Partly for this reason, ecofeminism emerged in the 1970s as a new and separate field of research that would herald an era of new relationships between men and women and between people and nature (Instone 1997, 136). Writing about the environmental movement in Australia, Instone

Originally published in 2001 in *Society and Animals*, vol. 9, no. 1, pp. 43–61. Reprinted with permission from Brill Academic Publishers.

claims that the majority of members and volunteers of the movement are women. She notes that women's numerical importance does not protect them from doing the lower status paid work or from being locked into the majority of voluntary jobs in the movement. "The male public face of the movement," she writes, "contrasts sharply with the behind the scenes reality of women doing most of the jobs" (138). In this respect at least, the animal movement is different. From the nineteenth century on, women historically have enjoyed a high standing as protectors of nonhuman animals.

A Brief History of Animal Activism

Women have been conspicuous in the animal protection movement from the outset as pioneers in the early antivivisectionist and animal protectionist organizations that were active in Victorian and Edwardian England. The early antivivisectionist movement in Victorian England attracted many women because they drew connections between the abusive treatment of especially poor women as gynecological patients, women's portrayal in pornography, and male vivisectors' dissection of nonhuman animals (Lansbury 1985). Despite their strength of numbers however, they were denied leadership positions in the early Royal Society for the Prevention of Cruelty to Animals (RSPCA), its counterpart, the American Society for the Prevention of Cruelty to Animals, and local SPCAs.

The early history of animal protection movement in Australia took a different route. According to MacCulloch (1993), the animal protection and conservation movements were irrevocably intertwined and culturally became feminized, which— at least organizationally—ironically led to the movement's gradual decline. MacCulloch's carefully researched thesis traces the history of both movements in Sydney between 1850 and 1930. The Animal Protection Society of New South Wales was established in 1873, a half-century after the SPCA had been founded in England. The Women's Society for the Prevention of Cruelty to Animals was founded in 1886. MacCulloch argues that in the twentieth century women and a shift in ideology increasingly would dominate the animal protection movement.

From a moralizing, reformist body, the movement was transformed into a society of pet lovers with a consequent change in direction from a campaign against cruelty to the more genteel approach of promoting kindness to animals. "This loss of purpose both mirrored and was reinforced by the growing feminization of the cause. Increasingly, the cause of animal protection was given over to women, and subsequently, children" (MacCulloch 1993, 45–46). Although these changes diluted the strength of the early movement, MacCulloch's account acknowledges the social legacy of animal protection's female pioneers that by the early twentieth century "had effectively changed the moral make-up of society," and the emotions that cruelty evoked had "overflowed into the preservation movement and fused them together at a popular level" (46).

This brief historical excursus suggests the organizational vulnerability of the modern animal protection movement with its predominantly female membership. The female of 1996 is altogether different from her 1886 counterpart, although to explain the fundamental changes affecting women's status over the past century is beyond the scope of this paper. At the end of the twentieth century, however, Western democracies no longer see women as a liability to animal protectionist and environmental causes. In the case of the animal movement, female animal protectionists at century's end can no longer be so easily dismissed as "dotty" cat lovers, or worse, diagnosed as suffering from "zoophil-psychosis" as they were both in the nineteenth and early twentieth century (Buettinger 1993).

Even so, a movement predominantly female in membership is likely to attract criticism as being "emotional" (stereotypical feminine trait) as opposed to "rational" (the masculine opposite). Indeed, stereotypes associated with labels such as "crazed spinsters", "sob sisters", and "idle, muddle-headed women" who are dismissed as "too emotional" to understand the rational endeavors of science and agriculture continue to crop up in the rhetoric of vilification used by critics of the animal movement (Munro 1999b). Yet, these enterprises are quick to use emotional appeals in their counterattacks against animal liberationists (Munro 1999a).

Gender, Attitudes, and Women's Standing

Reviews of both feminist (Adams and Donovan 1995) and ecofeminist (Vance 1993) writings indicate that the large body of literature on the themes of women, nature, and animals supports the argument that, when it comes to nature, there is a vast gender gap on attitudes and values. Much of the literature contains an implicit assumption that women and men vary fundamentally in the way they treat other life forms. There is ample empirical evidence in every context where humans use or abuse animals. It is evident that men, more than women, work or otherwise engage in animal-oriented occupations and leisure activities—in factory farms, abattoirs, science and veterinary practice, hunting, shooting, trapping and fishing, rodeos, horse and dog racing, and a host of similar pursuits. However, most studies of gender differences toward the treatment of animals focus on animal research rather than on other substantive areas such as hunting and farming (Pifer 1996). Furthermore, many of those studies are based on comparisons between movement insiders and outsiders—animal rights supporters and animal researchers (Hills 1993; Paul 1995). In addition, the typical study of gender differences in our relations with other animals focuses on individual attitudes and behavior rather than on broader sociological issues. Virtually no studies look at the significance of the gender gap in relation to the preponderance of women within the animal movement.

It would seem plausible to argue that women are the primary actors within the animal protection movement since they make up close to 80% of the membership (Richards 1990/1992; Jasper and Nelkin 1992). Put differently, women have a pre-eminent standing and legitimacy in the movement that may eclipse that of their male colleagues. Yet, standing is not determined by sheer weight of numbers alone. Women always have constituted the army of grassroots activists in the animal move-ment—the handmaidens or "midwives" to the movement (Jasper and Nelkin 1992, 90). Ironically, however, male philosophers, notably Tom Regan and Peter Singer, have predominated as the leading advocates of animal rights.

Indeed, a case can be made for describing the animal movement as "gender direct" rather than "non–gender direct" or "indirect" (Beckwith 1996). By gender direct, Beckwith means a social movement characterized by the primacy of women's gendered experiences, women's issues, and women's leadership and decision making in feminist and women's movements (1038). Strictly speaking, animal rights issues are gender neutral, although, in practice, many women believe that—especially in the predominantly male areas of science, hunting, and factory farming—their oppression parallels that of animal exploitation by men. The president of Animal Liberation (Victoria) sees that organization with its 95% female membership as fulfilling the requirements of a gender direct movement:

> I think we need to look at the politics of animal rights to see how they do converge quite clearly with feminist politics. . . . And they are issues of oppression, they're issues of abuse and the link is very easy to make for women because women have known what it is to live in patri-archies, to know what it is to confront that masculine scientific detach-ment that allows abuse to continue for abstract greater goals. . . . I'd have to say that people who care about animals and are prepared to politicise that caring, care about blood, flesh, pain, care about a partic-ular animal's suffering in this particular situation now. So they are sit-uating their caring, they're not abstracting it. (R. Linden, personal com-munication, 1997)

Most studies of everyday attitudes toward animals confirm the general femi-nist–ecofeminist thesis Linden articulates that women, more than men, care about nonhuman animals—a claim dramatically underlined by the massive over-representation of women in her own organization. Yet, within the context of animal movement membership the gender gap takes on a different complexion. In comparing the attitudes of animal rights supporters, farmers, and the urban public, Hills (1993) notes that there were gender differences between all three groups, with animal rights supporters scoring highest on empathy and lowest on instrumentality. These results were a direct contrast to males in general and to farmers in particular. For our purpose, the most pertinent result was the similarity in responses between male and female animal rights supporters, which was not the case for farmers and the urban public where gender differences were marked.

McAdam (1992) points out that in the context of social movements, sociologists have perceived activism as gender neutral. My own study of the attitudes of animal welfare supporters toward animals generally confirmed the finding by Hills (1993) that little or no difference exists between the views of men and women committed to the animal welfare cause. Although this might seem self-evident, the finding has important theoretical implications for the analysis of gender relations in other social movement organizations. According to McAdam, gender is arguably the most important factor mediating the experience of social movement activism. Although the worldviews of males and females may seem of a different order, when their attitudes and values are compared within a specific social movement context, there may be a degree of convergence within these movements and organizations that challenges conventional wisdom. More particularly, the convergence challenges the view, *pace* Gilligan (1982), that there is a different female voice in various moral contexts, such as within the animal protection movement. This argument about convergence is based on the results of an Animal and Social Issues Survey (ASIS) conducted among members of the Australian and New Zealand Federation of Animal Societies (ANZFAS) in late 1995.

About ANZFAS and ASIS

Widely representative of the animal protection lobby in Australia, ANZFAS covers the whole spectrum of animal protectionists from RSPCA welfarists and Australian Koala Foundation conservationists to the more radical animal liberationists, antivivisectionists, and animal rights advocates who belong to one of several campaigning groups such as Animal Liberation. ANZFAS is the umbrella organization for some 35 societies in Australia numbering about 33,000 members. An additional 500 individuals join as private rather than affiliated, members.

In late 1995, the ASIS, an eight-page questionnaire, was sent to these 500 private members throughout Australia. The response rate was 87% (n=437), well above the usual rate of around 30% for mail-out surveys (Fowler 1988, 49). The survey was designed to elicit the following information about members: attitudes toward animals; involvement in animal issues; views about ways to improve the treatment of animals; lifestyle and social attitude as well as a personal profile of the ANZFAS membership, including how members defined themselves in the movement—animal activist, advocate, or animal welfare supporter.

Two demographic variables in ANZFAS stood out. In relation to age and sex, there were major discrepancies between ANZFAS members and the rest of the Australian population: There was a disproportionately large number of females in the sample (79%), and the age distribution of the sample did not conform to the national figures. For example, the median age for the population in 1994 was 33.4 years as compared to 51 years for the sample. Structural factors may also be important in explaining the preponderance of older people in the organization. Biographical availability may account for the high proportion of older women in ANZFAS, since people who are willing to support such organizations must have the time to do so. For example, in Oliver's (1983) study of voluntary activists in the neighborhood movement, discretionary time was seen as a critical resource. People who are employed full-time or have heavy marital and familial responsibilities are less likely than retired seniors to engage in social movement activism.

Thus, while discretionary time is important for a person's availability to a cause, age made little difference to the level of self-designated activism. That is, age was not important when people described themselves as activists, advocates, or supporters, at least when the cohorts were categorized broadly as young (under 39 years) and old (over 40 years). The unusually high number of middle-aged people in ANZFAS suggests that members might be unwilling to engage in the direct action campaigns favored by younger activists. That this was not the case is supported by the evidence of the massive protests and militant actions of "middle England" where many of the activists were older people protesting against the United Kingdom's mid-1990s live animal–export trade. In the Australian sample, however, age was a significant variable affecting respondents' dietary habits. Not surprisingly, as vegans and vegetarians, younger cohorts had stricter dietary regimens than the older persons who made up the bulk of carnivores in the sample. Therefore, except for diet—where meat avoidance was strongest among the young—age was not a factor in determining the respondents' beliefs, attitudes, or behaviors toward animals.

Gender effects were only slightly more noticeable than age. The most striking feature about ANZFAS—as an organization—is its predominantly female membership (79%), a characteristic of the animal protection movement worldwide. In a sample taken from the readership of *Animals' Agenda*, Richard's (1990) study of a similar group of American animal welfare and rights supporters also reported a 79% female membership.

Wells and Hepper (1997) and Kruse (1999) report on greater female affinities with animal issues. Their studies demonstrate that women, more than men, express concern about the use of animals in research, are more likely to be members of animal welfare groups, are more inclined to abstain from eating meat or other selected animal produce, hold anthropomorphic views regarding animals, and support animal rights. They also report that women are more likely than men to take action to promote animal welfare.

How can we explain why women, more so than men, are active in the animal protection movement? According to McAdam (1992), activists in social movements appear to be distinguishable from nonactivists. Does this mean that high levels of consensus activists can characterize attitudes within the same social movement? At least in the case of the animal movement, the activists do share a common worldview for which there is a strong ideological consensus (Munro 1997). In fact, McAdam points out that very little research exists about activists within the same movement, a fact most evident in the case of animal protection and one that this paper seeks to redress.

That women have good standing in the contemporary animal movement can be seen in the increasing number of women in animal protection organizations who are taking up leadership roles that were not available to them in the nineteenth century. Women led more than half of the 27 animal protection organizations I studied in Australia, Britain, and the United States (Munro, 2000), although only three of these were large, prominent organizations with relatively well-paid staff. These gendered work patterns are reflected in the staffing of anti-environmental/animal rights groups such as Put People First. A sample of the same number of these organizations (Deal 1993) indicated that women headed only seven of the 27 groups sampled and that men headed the remaining 20. This can be explained sociologically by the industries and interests represented by these anti-green organizations. Most are male-oriented enterprises associated with the extractive industries (coal, gas, oil, timber), off-road vehicle manufacturers, hunting and fishing lobbies, chemical and pharmaceutical companies, and the cattle industry. There can be little doubt that leadership positions in these social movements and, especially, countermovement organizations reflect the structure of gendered employment opportunities in the wider society. Yet, leadership issues aside, this is where differentials cease to be important.

The ASIS data show a strong consensus among women and men on most of the issues covered in the survey. The ASIS findings suggest that the issue of animal cruelty blurs the differences between male and female protectionists and acts as a catalyst for bringing the two together. The moral standing of women in the movement is also strengthened by the movement's strong ideological consensus, specifically in what it condemns as the worst forms of animal exploitation (Munro 1997). In the remainder of the paper, I outline the main findings in connection with the role of gender in animal protection.

Discussion

The sex of the survey respondents in ASIS made a significant difference to fewer than 20% of the issues surveyed. For more than 80% of the issues examined in the survey, there was a strong consensus between the male and female members of ANZFAS. Ideological consensus in the movement as a whole has been reported elsewhere (Munro 1997). The purpose of the following discussion is to identify and explain the areas where there is a significant difference between women and men on the issues covered in the survey. Gender differences may have been relevant in four broad areas. As indicated in Table 1 below, there were only 12 instances in which this was the case.

Given the importance of gender differences in the way men and women are said to perceive nature and other life forms, the gaps identified in this study are of particular interest. Why is it that both men and women reject some abuses of animals with equal vehemence but not others? Thus, while the respondents agree on how to improve the welfare of animals in general, there are significant gender differences when it comes to specific issues (see Table 2). Respondents were asked to rate these issues on a scale from one (extremely wrong) to seven (not at all wrong). There were seven such issues identified in the questions on which there was significant gender divergence.

On the remaining 17 uses to which animals are put, there were no significant differences between the sexes. So how can the gender effects for these seven practices be explained? The practices can be further divided into four categories as indicated below.

Hunting

Hunting wild animals with guns ranked tenth (very high level of concern with a mean of 1.32) in the list of 24 practices involving the human use of animals. That female respondents, rather than their male counterparts, see sport hunting as more morally objectionable is supported in the feminist and ecofeminist literature, specifically in papers by Comninou (1995), Kheel (1995), Adams and Donovan (1995), and Collard and Contruccis (1988). They explicitly define "man" as male to argue that hunting is man's oldest profession and that it is pursued for "pleasure, status, profit, power and masculine identity" (52), a thesis challenged by Stange (1997). Stange's refutation of feminist discourse on women's estrangement from hunting is, however, a voice in the wilderness when measured against the empirical data on hunting that suggest that most forms of hunting remain primarily a male activity.

Table 1   Gender Effects on Animal and Social Issues

	Survey Item	No. of Items	Significant Gender Effect
1–24	Attitude toward animals	24	7
25–38	Involvement in animal issues	14	1
39–57	Improving the treatment of animals	18	0
57–69	Lifestyle and social attitudes	13	4
		N=69	N=12

Table 2   Gender Differences on Specific Issues

Items	Significant Gender Difference on Seven Issues	Females' Lower Mean and Tolerance
1.	Hunting wild animals with guns	p=<.015
2.	Using horses for steeple/jump racing	p=<.005
3.	Exposing an animal to a disease as part of a medical experiment	p=<.05
4.	Using animals' organs in human transplants	p=<.0006
5.	Killing kangaroos for their meat or skin	p=<.03
6.	Using poisons for feral animal control	p=<.002
7.	Performing operations on animals without anesthetics (e.g. branding/de-horning)	p=<.032

Hunting wild animals with guns in Australia typically means men killing indigenous animals like kangaroos, wild pigs, and ducks. Unlike the United Kingdom where fox hunting includes a smattering of female hunters, almost all Australia's recreational and professional hunters are male. According to Stange, (1997), roughly 10% of all American hunters are female and "these numbers seem to be growing exponentially (although) the precise number of female hunters nationally is impossible to determine" (179).

Steeple/Jump Horse Racing

This particular practice, glamorized in Australia as the sport of kings, ranked seventeenth in terms of moral reprehensibility. Nonetheless, a mean score of 1.79 places it in the second division of perceived atrocities to animals; that is, it represents a high, rather than very high, level of concern for the respondents. Like hunting, but less so, horse racing in Australia is largely a male preoccupation. There are few female jockeys, bookmakers, or trainers, and a visit to any betting shop will confirm that gambling is predominantly, though not exclusively, a male phenomenon. Furthermore, females tend to have a special relationship with horses through their childhood experiences in pony clubs and the like. These reasons no doubt explain a significant difference in attitudes toward the sport among the survey respondents.

Animal Experimentation: Disease, Animal Organs, and Branding

Three uses of animals came under the heading of animal experimentation: (a) operations without anesthetics (ranked 8, mean 1.20); (b) exposing an animal to a disease as part of a medical experiment (ranked 11, mean 1.33); and (c) using animal organs in human transplants (ranked 13, mean 1.73). Female respondents recorded lower means than their male counterparts. Given the pioneering role of women in the early antivivisectionist movements discussed above, it is hardly surprising that more women than men should oppose animal experimentation. As we have seen, the term animal experimentation arouses the passions more of women than of men. That female respondents had a significantly lower mean and tolerance for animal research than their male counterparts was reinforced elsewhere in the survey with more women than men believing that scientists cause more harm than good.

Wild Animals: Kangaroos and Feral Animals

Males and females differed on an additional two questions that concerned the killing of kangaroos for their meat and skins and the poisoning of feral animals as a means of control. Both tied for fifteenth place in the list of 24 practices and were seen as being of great concern to the respondents (mean 1.76). Thorne (1998) suggests that killing kangaroos for commercial reasons, although perceived as less morally objectionable than recreational hunting, is predominantly men's business:

> Four-wheel drive vehicles penetrate the darkness using light to freeze groups or individuals. A gunshot claps, echoing fear. Adult bodies fall to the dusty ground, often dead on impact. Young-at-foot, hurtling into the blackness, die alone. Pouched young stunned, but not killed outright, expire with time. The shooter, most likely a part-timer, hangs each carcass—legs tied vertically, head swinging—on the truck. The shooter proceeds to the next target. (174)

Cruelty seems to be the issue that explains the gender difference here. There is no need to refer to the sex of the part-time shooter in this passage, which focuses on the death of an Australian icon in the outback. The passage speaks for itself.

Movement Involvement, Lifestyle, and Social Attitudes

Gender differences also were significant in a number of other areas covered in the survey.

Involvement in Animal Issues

Female respondents belonged to significantly more animal welfare/rights organizations than their male counterparts (p=<.001). Apart from the ecofeminist claim that women are more in tune with nature than men and Gilligan's (1982) argument that women, more than men, seek a sense of inter-connectedness with others (including other animals), there is the historical fact concerning women's traditional involvement and standing in the animal protectionist movement. For many contemporary women, animal protection organizations still offer an outlet for social and professional development. This is particularly likely in the ANZFAS membership with its very high number of retired and elderly women.

Similarly, of the 330 life members in the RSPCA, just over 80%—roughly the same proportions as in ANZFAS—are female. Although pro-active groups like hunting fraternities mainly attract male enthusiasts, reactive animal protection organizations like ANZFAS and the RSPCA appeal more to women. In the nineteenth century, animal protection societies provided a rare opportunity for women to work outside the home. At the end of the twentieth century in Australia, animal protection still manages to attract women, but typically only as voluntary workers or part-time employees. Although this does not augur well for the future of the movement, it does say a lot for the commitment of females to the cause. In 1994 and 1995, women contributed just over 60% of all donations to the RSPCA Victoria in excess of $500. In that period in Victoria alone, the RSPCA received more than $1 million in bequests and over $60 million in donations, most of which, it is safe to assume, came from female benefactors (RSPCA 1994, 1995).

Lifestyle

In the western world, a high rate of pet ownership is a strong characteristic of animal rights supporters (Richards 1990/1992; Jasper and Nelkin 1992). In the ANZFAS sample, the rate was 81% compared to the national figure of 60%. Females (84%) are more likely than males (69%) to keep a companion animal, and the difference here is significant at the .0001 level. Although by no means an earth-shattering revelation, this may confirm the ecofeminist claim concerning female empathy with animals. In addition, companion animals function as honorary members in the family where women traditionally do much of the caring and nurturing, which may explain the discrepancy. Also, more divorced, separated, and widowed females than males comprise the ANZFAS membership. These women may have a greater need for companion animals. Although more male than female respondents were single at the time of the survey, this is not the same as a since-ended relationship.

Social Attitudes

The survey asked respondents to rate eight statements from strongly disagree to strongly agree (see Table 3). There was a significant gender gap in only three statements where females scored a higher mean than their male counterparts.

**Table 3. Survey Respondent Statements on Social Attitudes
(Rated from Strongly Disagree to Strongly Agree)**

Being Involved in the Animal Movement is	*Gender Difference*
a way of life to me	(p=<.005)
very satisfying to me	0
a personal sacrifice	(p=<.05)
From My Point of View	
religion is very important in my life	0
meat eating is the worst form of animal abuse	0
on the whole, scientists do more harm than good	(p=<.001)
moral support is more important for the movement than financial support	0
wide media coverage is important for the movement's success	0

The first two issues—belonging to the movement is a way of life and a personal sacrifice—may be idiosyncrasies of the survey respondents, many of whom are older women. Although animal welfare work in Australia does not provide daily bread, it does provide daily meaning for many people, especially older women. This is borne out in interviews with members of animal welfare organizations (Munro, personal communications 1994, 1995, 1996). Therefore, it is not surprising that for many women this work involves a high degree of commitment and sacrifice. A commonly expressed sentiment in the open-ended section of the questionnaire was that being a member of so many animal welfare groups often was financially taxing, especially for females on a pension.

Finally, in the question concerning scientists, females had a significantly higher mean than males in agreeing with the proposition that scientists do more harm than good. Again, as in opposition to vivisection, there is a strong historical precedent for this negative view of the scientist's work. Modern animal protectionists, like their antivivisection predecessors in the late nineteenth century, perceive the abuse of animals as a central moral dilemma confronting society. Sperling (1988 39) puts the contemporary position succinctly when she writes how for many animal activists "the animal as victim has become a symbol of both humanity and nature besieged (in the) vivisection of the planet."

If gender differences in activities associated with hunting, wild animals, horse racing, and animal experimentation explain the divergence of attitudes of male and female animal supporters, converging attitudes logically would mean equal or minimal differences in male and female involvement in these activities. This seems to be the case in the majority of practices ranked by the respondents at either very high or high levels of concern. For most of these practices, either a roughly equal involvement of men and women or some other factor made the issue of gender involvement less important. Thus, in condemning the use of steel-jawed leghold traps—ranked as the most morally objectionable practice in the entire list—males and females are equally concerned by the sheer cruelty of the practice; that the relatively small number of trappers is predominantly male is of little importance.

Nor does gender involvement appear to be the most important factor in the relatively low condemnation of the commercial use of wildlife (ranked 14) or the raising of cattle on open ranges (ranked 20). In Australia at least, these practices are viewed as relatively benign, often carried out as small-scale, family enterprises in contrast to the industrialized mass production of animal products in factory farming. Even in raising animals in feedlots (ranked 12), the most important factor in shaping attitudes concerns the purpose of intensive farming—the production and consumption of meat. The ASIS questionnaire revealed much ambivalence about this. Both male and female respondents saw meat eating (ranked 18) as only slightly more objectionable than containing animals in zoos (ranked 19). Because the sampled men and women consume meat equally, though perhaps not in the same quantities, we can expect that attitudes toward industries involving pig production (ranked 2), battery hens (ranked 4), and the live sheep trade (ranked 5) will share the same fate as raising cattle in feedlots. The equal numbers of males and females involved in the consumptive side outweigh the gender imbalance in the productive side of these industries. Similarly, for using animals in cosmetic/beauty product experiments and for fur coats the consumptive outweighs or equals the productive so that both males and females are equally involved in these activities.

For the purpose breeding of animals for research (ranked 9) and the use of unclaimed dogs in experiments (ranked 7) the respondents' convergence of attitudes calls for different explanations. One only can speculate that males and females equally see the use of unclaimed dogs as morally reprehensible because they associate dogs with companion animals. For purpose-bred animals, it may be that the gender involvement is about equal because both female animal technicians and male scientists perform this practice.

In the practices for which there are convergences of attitudes from the respondents, the relevance of gender involvement is either minimal or outweighed by some other factor. A strong male involvement and an almost complete absence of females characterize the seven practices in which there is divergence of attitudes between the sexes.

Conclusion

I have tried to show in this paper that women have high standing in the animal protection movement because of their longstanding commitment to animals and deep involvement in animal issues. By focusing on activism within the animal movement, the paper reveals much more convergence (80%) than divergence (20%) of attitudes and actions by male and female animal protectors. This ideological consensus reflects the high standing of women as activists and advocates in the animal movement. It means that women's ideas are the prevailing ideas of the movement. Issues of divergence results indicate that stronger female opposition to hunting and allegedly cruel practices—steeple/jump horse racing, experiments on animals, and the commercial exploitation of wildlife—is contingent on early socialization, gendered work and leisure patterns, affinity with companion animals, ambivalence about science, and a history of opposition to animal abuse by generations of female activists and animal advocates. Outside the feminist and women's movements, it is rare to find a social movement in which the standing of women—their gendered experiences, their issues, and their roles—eclipses those of their male colleagues. Much more than in the environmental movement, animal protection remains a bastion of female activism and advocacy. Unlike previous generations of activists, today's female animal protectors are seen as an asset in the animal protection cause, and their standing in the movement is increasingly reflected in leadership positions and decision-making.

Questions for Discussion

1. Why have women been, or are more likely to be, involved in the animal rights movement, compared to other social movements?
2. There is a great deal of agreement among male and female activists in the animal rights movement. What are the areas of divergence, and what accounts for these differences?
3. Do you think that the role and influence of women in the movement will change in the future? And if so, how?

Contributors

Carol J. Adams is the author of the pioneering *The Sexual Politics of Meat: A Feminist-Vegetarian Critical Theory*. Carol has published close to 100 articles in journals, books, and magazines on the issues of vegetarianism and veganism, animal advocacy, domestic violence, and sexual abuse.

Arnold Arluke is Professor of Sociology and Anthropology at Northeastern University and Senior Scholar at Tufts University Center for Animals and Public Policy. His research examines conflicts and contradictions in human–animal relationships.

Frank R. Ascione is a professor in the Department of Psychology and adjunct professor in Family and Human Development at Utah State University. Dr Ascione has co-edited two books: *Cruelty to Animals and Interpersonal Violence: Readings in Research and Application* (1998), *Child Abuse, Domestic Violence, and Animal Abuse: Linking the Circles of Compassion for Prevention and Intervention* (1998). He is also the author of *Children and Animals: Exploring the Roots of Kindness and Cruelty* (2005, Purdue).

Michael J. Barnes is Associate Professor of Psychology at Hofstra University.

Alan M. Beck is the Dorothy N. McAllister Professor of Animal Ecology and director of the Center for the Human–Animal Bond in the School of Veterinary Medicine, Purdue University, West Lafayette, Indiana.

Nancy S. Betchart is Dean of the Frost School of Continuing and Professional Studies at Plymouth State University.

Clifton Bryant is Professor of Sociology at Virginia Polytechnic Institute and State University (Virginia Tech).

Josephine Donovan is Professor Emeritus of English at the University of Maine. She is co-editor (along with Carol Adams) of *Beyond Animal Rights: A Feminist Caring Ethic for the Treatment of Animals*. (1996, Continuum) and *Animals and Women: Feminist Theoretical Explorations* (1995, Duke).

Clifton P. Flynn is Professor of Sociology at the University of South Carolina Upstate. His research has focused on animal abuse and its relation to family violence. He is the editor of this volume.

Stephanie S. Frommer earned her master's degree at the Center for Animals and Public Policy at Tufts University.

Gerald H. Gosse is Adjunct Professor of Psychology at Nassau Community College.

Kathleen M. Heide is Professor of Criminology at the University of South Florida.

Harold Herzog is Professor of Psychology at Western Carolina University. He has published numerous articles on human–animal interactions, including studies of cockfighting, attitudes toward animals, animal research, animal rights activists, and the cultural impact of popular dog breeds.

Leslie Irvine is Associate Professor of Sociology at the University of Colorado. She is the author of *If You Tame Me*: *Understanding Our Connection with Animals* (2004, Temple).

Aaron H. Katcher, MD, is a psychiatrist and professor emeritus at the University of Pennsylvania, where he taught in the medical, dental, and veterinary schools. His research has focused on the cognitive and physiological consequences of human animal interaction.

Andrew Linzey is a member of the Faculty of Theology in the University of Oxford, and Director of the Oxford Centre for Animal Ethics. He also holds the first Professorship in Animal Ethics at the Graduate Theological Foundation, Indiana. Professor Linzey has written more than 200 articles and authored or edited twenty books on theology and ethics, including several seminal works on animals.

Linda Merz-Perez is the former Executive Director of the Humane Society of Shelby County, Alabama. She has served as court-appointed Animal Cruelty Investigative Officer, and has been involved in the field of animal welfare for the last 14 years.

Lyle Munro teaches Sociology at the School of Humanities, Communications, and Social Sciences at Monash University Gippsland in Australia.

David Nibert is Professor of Sociology at Wittenberg University. His research interests include the historical and contemporary entanglement of the oppression of humans and other animals. He is the author of *Animal Rights/Human Rights: Entanglements of Oppression and Liberation* (2003, Rowman & Littlefield).

Barbara Noske is a Research Fellow at the Research Institute for Humanities and Social Science at the University of Sydney in Australia. Her publications include *Beyond Boundaries: Humans and Animals* (1997, Black Rose) and *Humans and Other Animals* (1989, Pluto).

Hannah L. Osbourne has a master's degree in industrial and organizational psychology from the University of South Florida.

Gary J. Patronek is Director of Animal Welfare and Protection at the Animal Rescue League in Boston. From 1997 to 2003, he was the Director of Tufts Center for Animals and Public Policy.

Elizabeth S. Paul is Research Associate for the Division of Farm Animal Science in the Department of Clinical Veterinary Science at the University of Bristol, UK.

Rose M. Perrine is Professor of Psychology at Eastern Kentucky University.

Mary T. Phillips is the Deputy Director of the Research Department of the New York City Criminal Justice Agency, a private, non-profit corporation providing pre-trial release services in New York City's Criminal Courts

Robert B. Pitman is Professor of Education at Western Carolina University.

Tom Regan is Emeritus Professor of Philosophy at North Carolina State University. Author of hundreds of professional papers and over twenty books, he is widely recognized as the intellectual leader of the animal rights movement.

Harriet Ritvo is the Arthur J. Conner Professor of History at the Massachusetts Institute of Technology. She is the author of *The Animal Estate: The English and Other Creatures in the Victorian Age* (1987), published by Harvard University Press.

Andrew N. Rowan is Senior Vice President, Research, Education and International Issues, Humane Society of the United States. He also serves as Adjunct Professor, Tufts University School of Veterinary Medicine, a Senior Fellow, Tufts Center for Animals and Public Policy, and a Faculty Member, Center for Alternatives to Animal Testing.

Clinton R. Sanders is Professor of Sociology at the University of Connecticut. He has numerous publications on human–animal interactions, including two award-winning books: *Regarding Animals* (1996, with Arnold Arluke) and *Understanding Dogs* (1999), both published by Temple University Press.

James A. Serpell is Professor of Humane Ethics and Animal Welfare and Director, Center for the Interaction of Animals and Society at the School of Veterinary Medicine at the University of Pennsylvania. He is the author of *In The Company of Animals*, as well as numerous scholarly articles on companion animals.

Kenneth J. Shapiro is the Co-Executive Director of the Animals and Society Institute. He is also the Editor and founder of *Society and Animals*, one of the premier academic journals in Human–Animal Studies, as well as the co-editor of the *Journal of Applied Animal Welfare Science*.

Ira J. Silverman is Professor of Criminology at the University of South Florida.

Peter Singer is the Ira W. DeCamp Professor of Bioethics at the University Center of Human Values at Princeton. His 1975 classic book, *Animal Liberation*, is widely credited as being the catalyst of the modern animal rights movement.

Tracey Smith-Harris is Assistant Professor of Sociology at Cape Breton University in Nova Scotia, Canada.

Marjorie Spiegel is the co-founder and executive director of IDEA, The Institute for the Development of Earth Awareness, a 501(c)(3) nonprofit think-tank and educational organization whose mission synthesizes human, animal and environmental issues. [www.ideaevolution.org].

Michael Tobias is the author of more than 30 books and has directed, written, and/or produced well over one hundred films for broadcast throughout the world. In 1996, Tobias received the "Courage of Conscience Award" for his commitment to animals.

Notes

Editor's note: Notes that contained only references were removed and incorporated into the reference section. Citations for references that were in press at the time of original publication have been updated to reflect the complete citation information. All references have been edited for consistency of style and presentation.

Reading 2—Bryant

1. We refer to sensitizing in a manner similar to that of Blumer (1954) in his use of the phrase "sensitizing concepts."
2. There has been a recent and excellent sociological study of the rodeo (Reid 1978).
3. Perhaps one of the most singular instances of becoming newsworthy because of involvement with animals is the case of Peter Snyman. Mr. Snyman is a South African who has been attempting to break the world record for living in a snake pit. He has been living in a cage with 24 poisonous snakes including black mambas and Egyptian cobras and hopes to continue his ordeal for 40 days to break the old record of 36 days. The snakes sometimes slither into bed with Mr. Snyman for a little body warmth. (Associated Press 1979). Another odd, animal-related record was set by Curtis Roe of Bakersfield, California who reportedly ate 32 earthworms and set a record in doing so. As a prize he won a role in an upcoming movie to be titled "Brain Suckers." (Associated Press 1977d).
4. Many colleagues in sociological circles have told me of a paper which Hugh Bain read at a professional meeting some years ago. The paper addressed the topic of the dog as a social problem. Unfortunately, I have never been successful in locating a copy of this paper. If anyone has this paper, I would very much appreciate receiving a copy.
5. One such effort is the program of research studies conducted at VPI and SU over the past six years. This research has addressed the occupational structure, role, and careers of ecologically related vocations, most of which are, incidentally, also animal related. Among the occupations studied are those of veterinarian, game warden, forest and park ranger, fish biologist, marine resources agent, and poultry processing worker. For an interview of this research program see Bryant *et al*. (1976).
6. Skinner, of course, had managed to train pigeons to operate missile guidance systems in World War II.
7. Only recently have social thanatologists begun to explore the parameters of grief and mourning attendant to the death of companion animals. For one excellent, pioneering study see the paper by Witt.
8. The emotional dependence of humans on animals has been noted by both folk peoples and contemporary romantic novelists. As one American Indian expressed it: "What is man without beasts? If all the beasts were gone, men would die from great loneliness of spirit, for whatever happens to the beast also happens to man. All things are connected. Whatever befalls the earth befalls the sons of earth." Chief Sealth of the Duwamish Tribe, State of Washington, Letter to the President of the United States, 1855 (quoted in Rynearson).

   In a similar vein Romain Gary, the French novelist, has the protagonist Morel, in The Roots of Heaven say: " 'Dogs aren't enough any more,' he was saying with satisfaction. 'You see, up to now, dogs were enough for a good many people. They consoled themselves in their company. But the way things have been going, people have been seized by such a need for friendship and company that the dogs can't manage it. We've been asking too much of them. The job has broken them down—they've had it. Just think how long they've been doing their damnedest for us, wagging their tails and holding out their paws—they've had enough. . . .' 'They've had enough, I tell you. It's natural: they've seen too much. And the people feel lonely and deserted, and they need something bigger that can really take the strain. Dogs aren't enough any more; men need elephants. That's the way I see it.' "

9. It is interesting to note that recently dogs are being used in therapy programs for alcoholics. As one alcoholic patient put it, "A dog is always your friend" (United Press International, a).

10. The phrase, "Son of Sam murders," became a household word. We have traditionally tended to use animal labels in referring to some kinds of crime and criminals. Examples might include "cat burglar," "mad-dog killer," and "werewolf killings."

Reading 6—Sanders

1. Despite the significant power difference symbolized by the terms "owner" and "caretaker," I use these designations interchangeably throughout the article.

2. The focus of this discussion on people's relationships with dogs flows, in part, from my own lifelong experience with dogs, my respect for them as a species, and the ready access afforded by my currently living intimately with them. Further, dogs are the nonhuman animals with which humans have the longest history of intimate association (Budiansky 1992; Porter 1989) and for whom people have the most intense attraction (Endenburg 1991). The dog's highly social nature accounts, in part, for this lengthy and emotional relationship with people and also means that human interaction with dogs lends itself ideally to sociological analysis.

3. My informants were not, as one anonymous reviewer skeptically put it, "wacky and lonely people who are over-involved with their pets, dress them in silly outfits, etc." At the veterinary clinic in which I participated, clients with this sort of over-involved orientation were identified as such, were commonly referred to as "animal nuts," and were frequently the focus of gentle derision. None of the data on which this discussion is based are drawn from observations of or conversations with this readily identifiable category of client.

4. One reviewer of an earlier version of this article expressed some concern with the apparent implication that dogs are "like" severely disabled human beings. Some discussions (e.g., Regan 1983) emphasize that infants, the mentally retarded, and others with limited or nonexistent verbal and social capacities are regarded as human and afforded a consequently appropriate moral place, whereas animals are typically denied similar considerations (see Frey 1980). I do not intend to imply necessarily that because dog owners consistently define their animal companions as minded and humanlike that, therefore, dogs and their interests are morally equivalent to those of humans. This discussion is about the social construction of the companion animal's identity in the context of intimate relationships. While not irrelevant to the issue of animal rights, this description focuses on a sociological phenomenon. The rights of companion animals and the attendant responsibilities of humans are matters of philosophical and legal debate beyond the scope of this article.

5. Of the owners interviewed by Cain (1985), 72% said that their dog usually or always had "people status" (see also Veevers 1985).

6. For interesting discussions of play interactions between dogs and people, see Mitchell and Thompson (1990, 1991) and Mechling (1989).

7. The most common categories used by caretakers to situate their relationships with their dogs was to regard them as either family members or close friends. General studies of pet owners show that this is extremely common. Somewhere between 70% (Beck and Katcher 1983) and 99% (Voith 1983) of pet caretakers define their animals as members of the family and from 30% (Nieburg and Fischer 1982) to 83% (Bryant 1982) consider the pet a "special" or "close" friend.

Reading 10—Linzey

1. First presented as a paper to a conference on "Faiths and the Environment" arranged by the Center

for Inter-Faith Dialogue at Middlesex University, and subsequently published in the conference Papers under the same title by Middlesex University in 1996 and edited by Christopher Lamb.

2. The notion of ahimsa, originally an emphasis of the Jain and Buddhist traditions, was translated in modern times by Gandhi as "nonviolence"; it provides for those traditions and Hinduism an expression of their common respect for all life, see Zaehner (1966). For an account of Gandhi's spiritual quest and his commitment to vegetarianism, see Gandhi (1929).

3. I am grateful to Brian Klug for this reference.

Reading 11—Irvine

1. Thomas (1983) lists other qualities that distinguished humans from and made them superior to animals. In addition to reason, speech, physical beauty, religion, and private property have been used to justify human superiority. Until Jane Goodall observed the chimpanzee David Greybeard not only using but *making* a tool, tool use typically set humans apart from other animals.

2. For a thorough treatment of the flaws in this argument, known as the *indirect duty view*, see DeGrazia (1996).

3. Here, I am influenced by, but taking great liberties with, Foucault's analysis of power.

4. For Mead, the acquisition of a sense of self was a uniquely human capacity. However, since play among animals requires many of the same processes evident in human play (e.g., taking the role of the other), there is reason to believe that nonhuman animals, too, possess self-awareness. Further evidence comes from research revealing deception, treachery, humor, cooperation, and empathy beyond the human realm (see Goodall 1990; Allen and Bekoff 1997; Linden 1999; Bekoff 2000).

5. For other research on interaction in dog parks, see Robins, Sanders, and Cahill (1991); West (1999).

6. For discussions of various types of play among animals, see Bekoff and Byers (1998) and Fagen (1981). For play among children, see Power (2000). Among adults, see Apter (1991).

7. Mitchell and Edmonson (1999) found that humans talk to dogs mostly to control them, as in "Get the ball" or "Be a good dog." However, Mitchell and Edmonson's study did not include the type of talk that I observed, which referred to dogs' mental states (as in "Gonna go say hi to that dog?").

8. An engaging discussion of morphic fields that acknowledges the scientific prejudices about what animals allegedly can and cannot do took place between Rupert Sheldrake and Marc Bekoff in *The Bark: The Modern Dog Culture Magazine*, Winter 2000, Number 10, 48–50.

9. For a witty, endearing account of the incorporation of a dog into a human household, see J. R. Ackerley's *My Dog Tulip* (1965, New York: New York Review Books).

Reading 14—Paul and Serpell

1. As opposed to cognitive empathy, which is simply the recognition of another's state of emotion rather than any vicarious experience of that person's actual emotion.

2. It is interesting that Mehrabian and Epstein included statements concerning pet animals in their emotional empathy scale. This suggests that they assumed pet and human empathy to be aspects of the same underlying construct. The fact that these two pet-based statements achieved reliability and validity within their scale, suggests that pet and human empathy are likely to be related, at least to some degree.

3. Sample sizes vary between analyses according to the number of subjects who answered or completed each particular question or attitude scale.

4. The predominance of women in the vegetarian movement has been noted and discussed by a number of commentators (e.g., Adams 1990; Herzog *et al.* 1991).

Reading 20—Spiegel

1. In *The Descent of Man*, Charles Darwin lists, in addition to those mentioned in the text of this book, several attributes claimed to belong to humans alone. They include: "that man alone is capable of progressive improvement; that he alone makes use of . . . fire, domesticates other animals, [or] possesses property. . .; that no other animal is self-conscious, comprehends itself, has the power of abstraction, or possesses general ideas; that man alone has a sense of beauty, is liable to caprice, has the feeling of gratitude, mystery, etc.; believes in God, or is endowed with a conscience." Darwin ably refutes those he merits as the most important of these points. (*Descent of Man*, 49–69.)
2. This book explores the great depth and breadth of animals' experiences.
3. Cited in The Princeton Language Institute, *21st Century Dictionary of Quotations*, (New York: Dell Publishing, 1993), 27.
4. Thomas is citing Moryson from Day, *Day's Descent*, 213.

Reading 21—Adams

1. The quotation in the following paragraph is found in Simoons, 73.
2. Quoted in "Red Meat: American Man's Last Symbol of Machismo," *National Observer* 10 July 1976, 13.
3. Marty Feldman, quoted in Rynn Berry Jr., *The Vegetarians*. Brookline, Mass.: Autumn Press, 1979, 32.
4. She concludes, "and I wish he'd taken us with him."
5. From a catalog from Northern Sun Merchandising, 2916 E. Lake Street, Minneapolis, MN, 55406.
6. From Hegel's *Philosophy of Right*, para. 166, p. 263, quoted in Nancy Tuana, "The Misbegotten Man: Scientific, Religious, and Philosophical Images of Women," unpublished manuscript.

Reading 22—Nibert

1. One of the ways in which oppression masquerades as somehow right and natural, particularly in more affluent nations, is through the use of language. The very words we use exert considerable control over our consciousness and our views of the world. I have struggled with the English language in my attempt to use words and phrases that do not automatically reflect hierarchical rankings of living beings. For example, I largely refrain from using the terms "people," "nonhuman," and "animals," choosing instead to use the phrase "humans and other animals." This wording emphasizes human commonality with other inhabitants of the planet, rather than fostering a perception of separate-ness and "other-ness" that helps to rationalize disregard and mistreatment of other animals.

Reading 28—Singer

1. Letter to Henry Gregoire, February 25, 1809.
2. Reminiscences by Francis D. Gage, from Susan B. Anthony, *The History of Woman Suffrage*, vol. 1; the passage is to be found in the extract in Leslie Tanner, ed., *Voices From Women's Liberation* (New York: Signet, 1970).
3. I owe the term "speciesism" to Richard Ryder. It has become accepted in general use since the first edition of this book, and now appears in *The Oxford English Dictionary*, second edition (Oxford: Clarendon Press, 1989).
4. See the reports of the Committee on Cruelty to Wild Animals (Command Paper 8266, 1951), paragraphs 36–42; the Departmental Committee on Experiments on Animals (Command Paper 2641, 1965), paragraphs 179–182; and the Technical Committee to Enquire into the Welfare of Animals Kept under Intensive Livestock Husbandry Systems (Command Paper 2836, 1965), paragraphs 26–28 (London: Her Majesty's Stationery Office).

5. *In the Shadow of Man* (Boston: Houghton Mifflin, 1971), 225. Michael Peters makes a similar point in "Nature and Culture," in Stanley and Roslind Godlovitch and John Harris, eds., *Animals, Men and Morals* (New York: Taplinger, 1972). For examples of some of the inconsistencies in denials that creatures without language can feel pain, see Bernard Rollin, *The Unheeded Cry: Animal Consciousness, Animal Pain, and Science* (Oxford: Oxford University Press, 1989).

6. I am here putting aside religious views, for example the doctrine that all and only human beings have immortal souls, or are made in the image of God. Historically these have been very important, and no doubt are partly responsible for the idea that human life has a special sanctity. Logically, however, these religious views are unsatisfactory, since they do not offer a reasoned explanation of why it should be that all humans and no nonhumans have immortal souls. This belief too, therefore, comes under suspicion as a form of speciesism. In any case, defenders of the "sanctity of life" view are generally reluctant to base their position on purely religious doctrines, since these doctrines are no longer as widely accepted as they once were.

7. The preceding discussion, which has been changed only slightly since the first edition, has often been overlooked by critics of the Animal Liberation movement. It is a common tactic to seek to ridicule the Animal Liberation position by maintaining that, as an animal experimenter put it recently, "Some of these people believe that every insect, every mouse, has as much right to life as a human." (Dr. Irving Weissman, as quoted in Katherine Bishop, "From Shop to Lab to Farm, Animal Rights Battle is Felt," *The New York Times*, January 14, 1989.) It would be interesting to see Dr. Weissman name some prominent Animal Liberationists who hold this view. Certainly (assuming only that he was referring to the right to life of a human being with mental capacities very different from those of the insect and the mouse) the position described is not mine. I doubt that it is held by many—if any—in the Animal Liberation movement.

Reading 30—Donovan

1. Peter Singer, *Animal Liberation* (New York: Avon, 1975), ix–x. Throughout I use the shorthand term "animal rights theory" to refer to any theorizing about humane treatment of animals, regardless of its philosophical roots. I would like to acknowledge contribution of Gloria Stevenson, who introduced me to the concept of animal rights years ago, and my dog Jessie.

2. In the *Ethics* Spinoza remarked that opposition to animal slaughter was based on "superstition and womanish pity" rather than on reason (as cited in Mary Midgley, *Animals and Why They Matter* [Athens: University of Georgia Press, 1983], 10). This is the kind of charge that disconcerts Singer.

3. Constantia Salamone, xeroxed form letter, July 1986.

4. James Turner, *Reckoning with the Beast: Animals, Pain* and *Humanity in the Victorian Mind* (Baltimore: Johns Hopkins University Press, 1980), 101, 103. Roswell C. McCrea, *The Humane Movement: A Descriptive Survey* (1910; reprint. College Park, Md.: McGrath, 1969), 117, notes that sentimentalism versus rationalism as a basis for animal rights theory was an issue in the nineteenth-century animal rights campaign: "As a rule humane writings [and] work, are based on a 'faith' rather than any rationalistic scheme of fundamentals. The emotional basis is a common one, and the kind treatment of animals is assumed to be a thing desirable in itself." The exception was the Humanitarian League under Henry Salt, which tried to place "humane principles on a consistent and rational basis." It was based "not merely on a kindly sentiment, a product of the heart rather than of the head." However, Frances Power Cobbe and other women theorists of the time were not afraid to privilege the heart. For an introduction to their ideas see Coral Lansbury, *The Old Brown Dog: Women, Workers, and Vivisection in Edwardian England* (Madison: University of Wisconsin Press, 1985).

5. Virginia Woolf, *Three Guineas* (1938; reprint, New York: Harcourt, Brace, 1963), 6. Woolf's note to this passage indicates she had done some research on the issue.

6. Charlotte Perkins Gilman, "A Study in Ethics" (Schlesinger Library, Radcliffe College, Cambridge, Mass., 1933, typescript). Published by permission of the Schlesinger Library. It must be noted that

the women criticized by Singer and Gilman are guilty of sins of omission rather than commission; they are not actively conducting atrocities against animals. Their failure is due to ignorance and habit, traits that are presumably correctable through moral education. In this article I focus mainly on the rationalist ideology of modern science because it is the principal contemporary legitimization of animal sacrifice and because its objectifying epistemology, which turns animals into "its," has become the pervasive popular view of animals, thus legitimizing other forms of animal abuse such as factory farming.

7. Despite his accent on rigorously rational inquiry, Regan throughout uses the term *counterintuitive* as a kind of escape clause whenever deductive reason *per se* proves inadequate. An example of where Regan's argument becomes (to me at least) illogical is his lifeboat hypothetical where he maintains that with four normal adult humans and one dog, it is the dog who must be sacrificed. His reasoning here suggests an unacknowledged hierarchy with humans still at the top. See Regan, *The Case for Animal Rights*, 324–325. See also Peter Singer's critique in "Ten Years of Animal Rights Liberation," *New York Review of Books* (January 17, 1985), 46–52, esp. 49–50, and "The Dog in the Lifeboat," *New York Review of Books* (April 25, 1985), 57.

8. The term *speciesist* was coined, according to Regan, by Richard D. Ryder in *Victims of Science* (London: Davis-Poynter, 1975). See also Singer, *Animal Liberation* (in 1 above), 7, 9.

9. Jean-Jacques Rousseau, The Social Contract and Discourse on the Original Foundation of Inequality among Mankind, ed. Lester G. Crocker (New York Washington Square, 1967), 172. See also Midgley, *Animals and Why They Matter*.

10. Peter Singer and Tom Regan, "The Dog in the Lifeboat: An Exchange," *New York Review of Books* (April 25, 1985), 57. It should be noted that however much Regan and Singer disagree in theory, in practice their positions are similar: each opposes animal experimentation, exploitation of animals for food and clothing, factory farming, trapping, hunting, rodeos, and circuses.

11. Peter Singer, "Ethics and Animal Liberation;' in Singer, ed., 1–10. Historically, utilitarianism developed as part of the wave of sentimentalism that emerged in late eighteenth-century Europe, which paved the way intellectually for the animal protection movement of the nineteenth century. See Turner (n. 4 above), 31–33. Of course, women's increasing participation in cultural life in the eighteenth century undoubtedly contributed to the emergence of sentimentalism and to the growing empathy for animals seen in Bentham's and Rousseau's statements.

12. For a full discussion, see Donovan, *Feminist Theory*, 31–63. The other major theoretical tradition that one might wish to turn to for alternative ideas about human relationship with the natural world is Marxism; however, as Isaac D. Balbus perceptively points out in *Marxism and Domination: A Neo-Hegelian, Feminist, Psychoanalytic Theory of Sexual, Political and Technological Liberation* (Princeton, N.J.: Princeton University Press, 1982), Marxism is rooted in a philosophy of domination. Marx indeed saw human identity as formed through labor that manipulates an objectified physical world. Balbus turns instead to Hegel, who urged that "all substance is subject," that is, motivated by a specific teleology, but all subjects are not identical (285). "Neither instrumental reason nor mere intuition or feeling but rather a new form of instrumental, empathic reason will guide the interactions between humans and the world on which they depend" (286). Such a "postobjectifying consciousness" (285) will emerge, Balbus believes, when new child-rearing practices are developed that intervene in the present male maturation process, which requires the development of enmity for the mother. Thus, Balbus turns in the latter part of his book to neo-Freudian cultural feminist theory—specifically that developed by Dorothy Dinnerstein—to substantiate his position.

13. Mary Wollstonecraft, *A Vindication of the Rights of Woman* (1792; reprint, Baltimore: Penguin, 1975), 291–292, and *Original Stories from Real Life* (London: J. Johnson, 1788); Harriet Beecher Stowe, "Rights of Dumb Animals;' *Hearth and Home* 1, no. 2 January 2, 1869): 24; Elizabeth Blackwell, *Essays in Medical Sociology* (London: Longmans Green, 1909); Elizabeth Stuart Phelps Ward, "Loveliness: A Story," *Atlantic Monthly* 84 (August 1899): 216–229, " 'Tammyshanty; " *Woman's Home Companion* 35 (October 1908): 7–9, Trixy (Boston: Houghton Mifflin, 1904),

Though Life Do Us Part (Boston: Houghton Mifflin, 1908), and various articles on vivisection; Frances Power Cobbe, *The Modern Rack* (London: Swann, Sonnenshein, 1899), *The Moral Aspects of Vivisection* (London: Williams and Margater, 1875); Anna Bonus Kingford, *The Perfect Way in Diet*, 2d ed. (London: Kegan, Paul, Trench, 1885), *Addresses and Essays on Vegetarianism* (London: Watkins, 1912). Anthony, Woodhull, the Grimké sisters, Stone, and Willard are mentioned by various sources as being vegetarian, and Child as being concerned with animal protectionism. See Singer, *Animal Liberation*, 234. Elizabeth Griffith, in her biography *In Her Own Right* (New York: Oxford, 1984), notes that Elizabeth Cady Stanton followed the Grahamite (largely vegetarian) regimen in her youth, following the practices of the Grimkés (34–35). Ruth Bordin, in *Frances Willard: A Biography* (Chapel Hill: University of North Carolina Press, 1986), 122, says Frances Willard believed flesh-eating was "savagery" and that the "enlightened mortals of the twentieth century [would] surely be vegetarians." Indeed, there is an interesting connection between the nineteenth-century temperance and humane movements. In 1891 the WCTU in Philadelphia (probably under the aegis of Mary F. Lovell) developed a "Department of Mercy" dedicated to antivivisectionism. According to Turner, 94, it was virulently antiscience. In *Letters of Lydia Maria* Child (1883; reprint, New York: Negro Universities Press, 1969), Child says she is a member of the SPCA and supports the humane movement. She stresses the close kinship between animals and humans as her rationale (letter of 1872, 213–214). Caroline Earle White was a leading animal protectionist in nineteenth-century Philadelphia; she wrote numerous articles on the subject. Much of Agnes Ryan's material is unpublished in the Schlesinger Library in Cambridge. It includes an "animal rights" novel, *Who Can Fear Too Many Stars?* Charlotte Perkins Gilman wrote numerous articles on animal issues, including "The Beast Prison," *Forerunner* 31 (November 1912): 128–130, and "Birds, Bugs and Women," *Forerunner* 4 (May 1913) 131–132. A further useful reference on women in the U.S. nineteenth-century animal welfare movement is Sydney H. Coleman, *Humane Society Leaders in America* (Albany, N.Y.: Humane Association, 1024).

14. Carol Adams, "The Oedible Complex: Feminism and Vegetarianism;' in *The Lesbian Reader,* ed. Gina Covina and Laurel Galana (Oakland, Calif.: Amazon, 1975), 145–152, and "Vegetarianism: The Inedible Complex;' *Second Wave* 4, no. 4 (1976): 36–42: Constantia Salamone, "The Prevalence of the Natural Law: Women and Animal Rights," in *Reweaving the Web of Life: Feminism and Nonviolence*, ed. Pam McAllister (Philadelphia: New Society, 1982), 364–375. See also the articles by Janet Culbertson, Cynthia Branigan, and Shirley Fuerst in "Special Issue: Feminism and Ecology," *Heresies,* no. 13 (1981); Joan Beth Clair (Newman), "Interview with Connie Salamone": *Woman of Power*, no. 3 (Winter/Spring 1986), 18–21; Andrée Collard, "Freeing the Animals," *Trivia*, no. 10 (Spring 1987), 6–23; Karen Davis, "Farm Animals and the Feminine Connection," *Animals' Agenda* 8, no. 1 (January/February 1988): 38–39, which provides an important feminist critique of the macho vein in the ecology movement; and Andrée Collard with Joyce Contrucci, *Rape of the Wild: Man's Violence against Animals and the Earth* (Bloomington: Indiana University Press, 1989). There is also Carol J. Adams, *The Sexual Politics of Meat: A Feminist-Vegetarian Critical Theory* (New York: Continuum 1991). Alice Walker has also recently embraced the animal rights cause. See her "Am I Blue?" *Ms.* (July 1986), reprinted in *Through Other Eyes: Animal Stories by Women*, ed. Irene Zahava (Freedom, Calif.: *Crossing,* 1988), 1–6: and Ellen Bring, "Moving toward Coexistence: An Interview with Alice Walker," *Animals' Agenda* 8, no. 3 (April 1988): 6–9.

15. As cited in Colin Gordon's afterword to *Power/Knowledge: Selected Interviews and Other Writings, 1972–1977*, by Michel Foucault (New York: Pantheon, 1980), 238. Max Horkheimer and Theodor F. Adorno, *Dialectic of Enlightenment* (1944; reprint, New York: Herder and Herder, 1972).

16. As cited in William Leiss, *The Domination of Nature* (New York: Braziller, 1972), 111. Sandra Harding similarly observes that "it is the scientific subject's voice that speaks with general and abstract authority; the objects of inquiry 'speak' only in response to what scientists ask them, and they speak in the particular voice of their historically specific conditions and locations" (*The Science Question in Feminism* [Ithaca, N.Y.: Cornell University Press, 1986], 124).

17. Nancy C. M. Hartsock, *Money, Sex and Power: Toward A Feminist Historical Materialism* (New York: Longman, 1983), 152, 246. On use-value production, see Karl Marx, *Capital*, in *Karl Marx: Selected Writings*, ed. David McLellan (Oxford: Oxford University Press, 1977), 422–423. See Harding, 142–161, for a useful summary of what she calls "feminist standpoint epistemologies." They are rooted, she notes, in the assumption derived from Hegel's notion of the master/slave consciousness that "women's subjugated position provides the possibility of a more complete and less perverse understanding" (26). Women's historical experience of silence, of being in the "slave" position vis-a-vis the "master" may provide a basis for empathy with other silenced voices, such as those of animals.

18. The principal sources of Margaret Cavendish's writings on animal rights are her *Poems and Fancies* (1653; 2d ed., 1664), *Philosophical Letters* (166-1), and *The World's Olio* (1655). Her empathetic imagination extends to plant life, to which she also imputes a form of consciousness (see esp. "Dialogue *between* an Oake, *and a* Man *cutting him downe*," in *Poems and Fancies*).

19. Michel Foucault, *La Volonté de savoir*, vol. 1 of *Histoire de la sexualité* (Paris: Gallimard, 1976), 61 (my translation). For studies of female sexual deviance as defined by nineteenth-century sexologists, see George Chauncey, Jr., "From Sexual Inversion to Homosexuality: Medicine and the Changing Conceptualization of Female Deviance," *Salmagundi* 58/59 (Fall 1982/Winter 1983): 114–45; and Lillian Faderman, "The Morbidification of Love between Women by Nineteenth-Century Sexologists," *Journal of Homosexuality* 4, no. 1 (Fall 1978): 73–90.

20. Hanna Fenichel Pitkin, *Fortune Is a Woman: Gender and Politics in the Thought of Niccolo Machiavelli* (Berkeley and Los Angeles: University of California Press, 1984), 125. Pitkin's analysis relies on the work of "object-relations" neo-Freudian feminists such as Nancy Chodorow, Dorothy Dinnerstein, and Jane Flax.

21. Evelyn Fox Keller, "Gender and Science" (1978), in *Discovering Reality: Feminist Perspectives on Epistemology, Metaphysics, Methodology, and the Philosophy of Science*, ed. Sandra Harding and Merrill B. Hintikka (Dordrecht: Reidel, 1983), 187–205, esp. 197. Hunting is, of course, the quintessential rite of passage in the male maturation process. As Barbara A. White notes in *The Female Novel of Adolescence* (Westport, Conn.: Greenwood, 1985), 126–127, "many initiation stories [involve] a hunt [where] the protagonist destroys a 'feminine principle: "Numerous feminist theorists have connected hunting with male dominance. See Charlotte Perkins Gilman, *His Religion and Hers* (1923; reprint, Westport, Conn.: Hyperion, 1976), 37–38. A more recent scholarly study is Peggy Reeves Sanday, *Female Power and Male Dominance: On the Origins of Sexual Inequality* (Cambridge: Cambridge University Press, 1981), 66–69, 128–130.

22. French, 341. Coral Lansbury recognizes the inherent connection between vivisection and sadomasochistic pornography and, indeed, analyzes a number of late nineteenth-century works of pornography that include scenes of vivisection (n. 4 above), chap. 7.

23. Estella Lauter, *Women as Mythmakers: Poetry and Visual Art by Twentieth-Century Women* (Bloomington: Indiana University Press, 1984), 18. A separate study could be written on animals in women's fiction. In a number of works animals are used to avenge injuries done to women; e.g., Edith Wharton's "Kerfol" (1916), in *The Collected Short Stories of Edith Wharton*, ed. R. W. B. Lewis (New York: Scribner's, 1968), 282–300; or Sylvia Plath's "The Fifty-ninth Bear" (1959), in *Johnny Panic and the Bible of Dreams* (New York: Harper and Row, 1979), 105–114. In others the woman/animal identification is explicit. See Mary Webb, *Gone to Earth* (fox) (1917; reprint, New York: Dalton, 1974); Radclyffe Hall, *The Well of Loneliness* (fox) (New York: Covice, Freed, 1929); Ellen Glasgow, *The Sheltered Life* (ducks) (Garden City, N.Y.: Doubleday Doran, 1932); Zora Neale Hurston, *Their Eyes Were Watching God* (mule) (1937; reprint, Urbana: University of Illinois Press, 1978); Willa Cather, *A Lost Lady* (woodpecker) (New York: Knopf, 1923); Hariette Arnow, *Hunter's Horn* (fox) (New York: Macmillan, 1949). In many of Glasgow's novels the animal/woman connection is a central issue. See Josephine Donovan, *The Demeter-Persephone Myth in Wharton, Cather, and Glasgow* (University Park: Pennsylvania State University Press, 1989), esp. chap. 5. In many

works by women, animals are women's closest companions and often there is a kind of psychic communication between them (especially when the women are witches). See Annie Trumbull Slosson, "Anna Malann," in *Dumb Foxglove and Other Stories* (New York: Harper, 1898), 85–117; Mary E. Wilkins (Freeman), "Christmas Jenny," in *A New England Nun and Other Stories* (New York: Harper, 1891), 160–177; Sarah Orne Jewett, "A White Heron" in *The Country of the Pointed Firs*, ed. Willa Cather (1925; reprint, Garden City, N.Y.: Doubleday Anchor, 1956), 161–171; Virginia Woolf, "The Widow and the Parrot: A True Story," in *The Complete Shorter Fiction of Virginia Woolf*, ed. Susan Dick (San Diego: Harcourt Brace Jovanovich, 1985), 156–163; Rose Terry (Cooke), "Dely's Cow;" in *"How Celia Changed Her Mind" and Selected Stories*, ed. Elizabeth Ammons (New Brunswick, N.J.: Rutgers University Press, 1986), 182–195; Susan Glaspell, "A Jury of Her Peers;" in *American Voices: American Women*, ed. Lee R. Edwards and Arlyn Diamond (New York: Avon, 1973), 359–381. Sarah Grand's *The Beth Book* (1897; reprint, New York: Dial, 1980) and various works by Elizabeth Stuart Phelps Ward (n. 13 above) are explicitly antivivisectionist. See Lansbury for further works in this area. Flannery O'Connor exposed the male hubris involved in hunting; see "The Turkeys" in *Complete Stories* (New York: Farrar Straus and Giroux 1971), 42–53. Other significant works include Colette's *Creatures Great and Small* trans. Enid McLeod (London: Seeker and Warburg, 1951); Virginia Woolf's *Flush: A Biography* (London: Hogarth, 1923); and May Sarton's *The Fur Person* (1957: reprint, New York: New American Library, 1970). See also Zahava, ed. (n. 14 above). Ellen Moers in *Literary Women* (Garden City, N.Y.: Doubleday, 1977) notes "a rich untapped field remains to yield a fortune in scholarly dissertations, and that is the animals in the lives of literary women. George Sand had a horse . . . named Colette; Christina Rossetti had the wombat; Colette had all those cats; Virginia Woolf was positively dotty about all sorts of animals. But it is their dogs who will serve the purpose best—Elizabeth Barrett's spaniel named Flush; Emily Dickinson's 'dog as large as myself' " (260). The most promising recent theoretical approach to the issue of women's connection with animals is that proposed by Margaret Homans in *Bearing the Word: Language and Female Experience in Nineteenth-Century Women's Writing* (Chicago: University of Chicago Press, 1986). Using Lacanian theory, Homans urges that women and nature are linked as "the absent referrent" in patriarchal discourse. Her discussion of Heathcliff's sadistic treatment of birds in *Wuthering Heights* is especially suggestive. She observes that Cathy's aim is "to protect nature from figurative and literal killing at the hand of androcentric law" (78).

24. See Jane Goodall, *In the Shadow of Man* (Boston: Houghton Mifflin, 1971), *The Chimpanzees of Gombe: Patterns of Behavior* (Cambridge, Mass.: Harvard University Press, 1986); Dian Fossey, *Gorillas in the Mist* (Boston: Houghton Mifflin, 1983); and Sally Carrighar, *Home to the Wilderness* (Boston: Houghton Mifflin, 1973). See Eugene Linden, *Silent Partners* (New York: Times Books, 1986), on Patterson and Carter. Janis Carter spent eight years trying to reintroduce Lucy, a chimpanzee who had learned sign language, to the wild in West Africa. She tells her moving story in "Survival Training for Chimps," *Smithsonian* 19, no. 5 (June 1988): 36–49. Goodall recently issued a sharp condemnation of the treatment of chimpanzees in American laboratories. See her "A Plea for the Chimps," *New York Times Magazine* (May 17, 1987). Also of interest is Cynthia Moss, *Elephant Memories: Thirteen Years in the Life of an Elephant Family* (New York: Morrow, 1988); and Sue Hubbell's relationship with her bees, seen in *A Country Year: Living the Questions* (New York: Random House, 1986).

25. For a further discussion of the ethic proposed in cultural feminist theory, see Donovan, "The New Feminist Moral Vision," in *Donovan, Feminist Theory* (n. 12 above), 171–86.

26. Gilligan, 59, 19, 73. Another important work that develops a cultural feminist ethic is Nell Noddings, *Caring: A Feminine Approach to Ethics and Moral Education* (Berkeley and Los Angeles: University of California Press, 1984). Unfortunately, however, while Noddings believes the caring ethic she endorses is enhanced by a celebratory attitude toward the female domestic world, which includes, she notes, "feeding the cat," she nevertheless specifically rejects the main tenets of animal rights theory, including not eating meat. It is clear that her "caring" ethic extends only to humans; the arbitrariness

of her position can only be attributed to an unexamined speciesism. Nodding's book, while admirable in other ways, is weakened by this bias, thereby illustrating how feminist theory must be informed by animal rights theory if we are to avoid the hypocrisies and inconsistencies of the tea-ladies condemned by Singer (for Noddings evinces affection for her pets while endorsing carnivorism [154]).

References

Achenbach, T. M. (1988). *Child Behavior Checklist* (for ages 2–3, for ages 4–16). Burlington, Vt.: Center for Children, Youth, and Families.

Achenbach, T. M., and C. S. Edelbrock (1981). "Behavioral Problems and Competencies Reported by Parents of Normal and Disturbed Children Aged Four through Sixteen." *Monographs of the Society for Research in Child Development*, *46* (1, Serial No. 188).

Achenbach, T. M., C. T. Howell, H .C. Quay, and C. K. Conners (1991). "National Survey of Problems and Competencies among Four to Sixteen-Year-Olds." *Monographs of the Society for Research in Child Development* 56, Serial No. 225.

Adams, C. J. (1991, 1992). *The Sexual Politics of Meat: A Feminist-Vegetarian Critical Theory*. New York: Continuum.

———. (1994). "Bringing Peace Home: A Feminist Philosophical Perspective on the Abuse of Women, Children, and Pet Animals." *Hypatia*, *9*, 63–84.

———. (1995). "Woman-Battering and Harm to Animals." In C. J. Adams and J. Donovan (eds.), *Animals and Women: Feminist Theoretical Explorations*, 55–84. Durham, N.C.: Duke University Press.

Adams, C. J., and J. Donovan (1995). *Animals and Women: Feminist Theoretical Explorations*. Durham, N.C.: Duke University Press.

Adell-Bath, M., A. Krook, G. Sandqvist, and K. Skantze (1979). *Do We Need Dogs?* Gothenburg: University of Gothenburg Press.

Albert, A., and K. Bulcroft. (1987). "Pets and Urban Life." *Anthrozoös*, *1*, *1*, 9–23.

———. (1988). "Pets, Families, and the Life Course." *Journal of Marriage and the Family 50*, 543–552.

Allen, C., and M. Bekoff (1997). *Species of Mind: The Philosophy and Biology of Cognitive Ethology*. Cambridge, Mass.: MIT Press.

Allen, K., B. E. Shykoff, and J. L. Izzo, Jr. (2001). "Pet Ownership but not ACE Inhibitor Therapy Blunts Home Blood Pressure Responses to Mental Stress." *Hypertension*, *38*, 815–820.

Allen, K. M., J. Blascovich, J. Tomaka, and R. M. Kelsey (1991). "Presence of Human Friends and Pet Dogs as Moderators of Autonomic Responses to Stress in Women." *Journal of Personality and Social Psychology*, *61*, 582–589.

Allen, P. G. (1986). The Sacred Hoop: Recovering the Feminine in American Indian Traditions. Boston: Beacon.

Altschul, Aaron M. (1965). *Proteins: Their Chemistry and Politics*. New York: Basic Books.

Amato, P. R., and S. A. Partridge (1989). *The New Vegetarians: Promoting Health and Protecting Life*. New York: Plenum.

American Medical Association (AMA) (1989). "Use of Animals in Biomedical Research: The Challenge and Response." AMA White Paper. Available from the AMA, 535 N. Dearborn St., Chicago, IL 60610.

American Pet Products Manufacturers Association (APPMA) (2003). *American Pet Products Manufacturers Association National Pet Owners Survey*. Greenwich, Conn.: Author.

American Psychiatric Association (1987). *Diagnostic and Statistical Manual of Mental Disorders* (3rd ed. rev.). Washington, D.C.: Author.

American Psychological Association (1994). *The Diagnostic and Statistical Manual of Mental Disorders-IV (DSM-IV)*. Washington, D.C.: Author.

Amundson, M. E., C. A. Hart, and T. H. Holmes (1986). *Manual for the Schedule of Recent Experience*. Seattle: University of Washington Press.

Andersen, M. L., and P. Hill Collins (1992). *Race, Class, and Gender: An Anthology*. Belmont, Calif.: Wadsworth.

Anderson, W. P., C. M. Reid, and G. L. Jennings (1992). "Pet Ownership and Risk Factors for Cardiovascular Disease." *Medical Journal of Australia, 157*, 298–301.

Animal Welfare Act. (1966, 1970, 1985). 7 U.S.C., 2131–2157. PL 89-544, Aug. 24, 1966,80 Stat 350-353; as amended by PL 91-579, Dec. 24, 1970, 84 Stat 15601565; PL 94-279, Apr. 22, 1976, 90 Stat 417-423; and PL 99-198, title XVII, subtitle F, Dec. 17, 1985, 99 Stat 1645-1650. Reprinted in Phillips and Sechzer 1989, 179–197.

Anonymous. (1879). *Sportman's Journal and Fancier's Guide: Stud and Stable and Kennel and Curtilage 129*, Feb. 15.

———. (1891a). "Review of the Past Year." *Kennel Gazette 12*, 5–6.

———. (1891b). "Collies." *Kennel Gazette 7*, 7–8.

———. (1894). "Dogs up to Date: The Bulldog." *Dogs, 1*, 43.

———. (1897). Report of the Departmental Committee to Inquire into and Report upon the Working of the Laws Relating to Dogs. *Parliamentary Papers*, c.8320 and c.8378, *XXXIV*, 63–64.

Antal, E., and J. Harthan (eds.) (1971). *Animals in Art and Thought to the End of the Middle Ages*. London: Routledge and Kegan Paul.

Apter, M. (1991). "A Structural Phenomenology of Play." In M. Apter and J. Kerr (eds.), *Adult Play: A Reversal Theory Approach*, 13–29. Amsterdam: Swets and Zeitlinger.

Arens, W. (1979). *The Man-Eating Myth: Anthropology and Anthropophagy*. New York: Oxford University Press.

Arkow, P. (1996). "The Relationships between Animal Abuse and Other Forms of Family Violence." *Family Violence and Sexual Assault Bulletin, 12*, 29–34.

———. (1998). "The Correlations between Cruelty to Animals and Child Abuse and the Implications for Veterinary Medicine. In R. Lockwood and F. R. Ascione (eds.), *Cruelty to Animals and Interpersonal Violence*, 409–414. West Lafayette, Ind.: Purdue University Press.

Arkow, P. S., and S. Dow (1984). "The Ties that Do Not Bind: A Study of the Human–Animal Bonds that Fail." In R. K. Anderson, B. L. Hart, and L. A. Hart (eds.), *The Pet Connection: Its Influence on Our Health and Quality of Life*, 348–354. Minneapolis: University of Minnesota.

Arkow, P., J. R. Walker, F. R. Ascione, and M. P. Boatfield (1990, April). *The Links between Animal Abuse and Child Abuse*. Panel presentation at the Delta Society Ninth Annual Conference, Houston, Tex.

Arluke, A. (1988). "Sacrificial Symbolism in Animal Experimentation: Object or Pet?" *Anthrozoös, 2*, 98–117.

———. (1990). "Moral Evaluation in Medical Research." *Advances in Medical Sociology, 1*, 189–204.

———. (1991). "Coping with Euthanasia: A Case Study of Shelter Culture." *Journal of the American Veterinary Medical Association, 198*, 1176–1180.

———. (1992, July). *The Ethical Cultures of Animal Labs*. Paper presented at the Sixth International Conference on Human–Animal Interactions, Montreal, Quebec.

———. (1994). "Managing Emotions in an Animal Shelter." In A. Manning and J. Serpell (eds.), *Animals and Society: Changing Perspectives*, 145–165. London: Routledge.

Arluke, A., and F. Hafferty (1996). "From Apprehension to Fascination with Dog Lab: The Use of Absolutions by Medical Students." *Journal of Contemporary Ethnography, 25*, 201–225.

Arluke, A., and C. Sanders (1996). *Regarding Animals*. Philadelphia: Temple University Press.

Arluke, A., J. Levin, C. Luke, and F. Ascione (1999). "The Relationship of Animal Abuse to Violence and Other Forms of Antisocial Behavior." *Journal of Interpersonal Violence, 14*, 9, 963–975.

Ascione, F. R. (1988a). *Primary Attitude Scale*. "Assessment of Kindergarten through Second Graders' Attitudes toward the Treatment of Animals." Logan, Utah: Wasatch Institute for Research and Evaluation.

———. (1988b). *Intermediate Attitude Scale*. "Assessment of Third through Sixth Graders' Attitudes toward the Treatment of Animals." Logan, Utah: Wasatch Institute for Research Evaluation.

———. (1992). "Enhancing Children's Attitudes about the Humane Treatment of Animals: Generalization to Human-Directed Empathy." *Anthrozoös*, 5, 3, 176–191.

———. (1992, July). "Cruelty to Animals in Childhood and Adolescence: An Overview of Research." Presentation at the "Risks for Animals Workshop," R. Arkow, C. Moulton, F. Ascione, J. Filip, and M. Kaufmann, *Cruelty to Animals and Child Abuse: Connections and Creative Community Strategies*. Sixth International Conference on Human–Animal Interactions, Montreal, Quebec.

———. (1992, September). *Cruelty to Animals in Childhood and Adolescence*. Presentation at the American Humane Association Conference, "Protecting Children and Animals: Agenda for a Nonviolent Future," Herndon, Va.

———. (1993). "Children Who Are Cruel to Animals: A Review of Research and Implications for Developmental Psychopathology." *Anthrozoös*, 6, 226–247.

———. (1998). "Battered Women's Reports of Their Partners' and Their Children's Cruelty to Animals." *Journal of Emotional Abuse*, 1, 119–133.

Ascione, F. R., and P. Arkow, (eds.) (1999). *Child Abuse, Domestic Violence, and Animal Abuse: Linking the Circles of Compassion for Prevention and Intervention*. West Lafayette, Ind.: Purdue University Press.

Ascione, F. R., G. I. Latham, and B. R. Worthen (1985). Final report, Year 2: An Experimental Study. *Evaluation of the Humane Education Curriculum Guides*. Report to the National Association for the Advancement of Humane Education.

Ascione, F. R., T. M. Thompson, and T. Black (1997). "Childhood Cruelty to Animals: Assessing Cruelty Dimensions and Motivations." *Anthrozoös*, 10, 4, 170–179.

Ascione, F. R., C. V. Weber, and D. S. Wood (1997a). "The Abuse of Animals and Domestic Violence: A National Survey of Shelters for Women Who Are Battered." *Society and Animals*, 5, 205–218.

———. (1997b). *Animal Welfare and Domestic Violence* [12 pages]. [On-line final report submitted to the Geraldine R. Dodge Foundation]. Available: http://vachss.com/mission/guests/~hascione_2.html

Associated Press. (1975a). "Horse Diapers 'Unreasonable' Judge Rules." *Roanoke Times and World News* (December 30).

———. (1975b). "Tampa Man Arrested in Pet Killing Spree." *The Atlanta Journal* (January 5).

———. (1977a). "Dallas Judge Fines Monkey Owner." *Lubbock Avalanche-Journal* (June 25).

———. (1977b). "Dolphin Liberator Goes on Trial." *Roanoke Times and World News* (November 30).

———. (1977c). "Frog Biting Must Stop in Huddle." *Lubbock Avalanche-Journal* (October 14).

———. (1977d). "Man Eats 32 Worms, Wins Role in Movie." *Roanoke Times and World News* (December 15).

———. (1977e). "Snake Smuggling Probe Leads to Prestigious Zoos." *Roanoke Times and World News* (April 11).

———. (1977f). "Teacher Must Prove Cougar is Educational." *Roanoke Times and World News* (December "15).

———. (1977g). "Vagrant Skunk Lands Chicagoan in Dilemma." *Roanoke Times and World News* (December 15).

———. (1978a). "Pet Craze Endangering Birds: Some Near Extinction." *Roanoke Times and World News* (March 29).

———. (1978b). "They Made News—Fur, Feathers and All." *Roanoke Times and World News* (January 1).

———. (1979). "Snakes Getting Next to Record Seeker." *Roanoke Times and World News* (April 22), A-7.

———. (2000). "Chronic Ills Hit Nearly 1 of 2 in U.S.," *Dayton Daily News*, 1 December, 4A.

Baker, R. (1973). "Red Meat Decadence." *New York Times*, 3 April, 43.

Baenninger, R. (1991). "Violence toward Other Species." In R. Baenninger (ed.), *Targets of Violence and Aggression*, 5–43. New York: North-Holland.

Bailey C. M. (1988). "Exposure of Pre-School Children to Companion Animals: Impact on Role Taking Skills." *Dissertation Abstracts International* 48 *(8-A): 1976.*

Baldwin, A. C., L. C. Stevens, J. W. Critelli, and S. Russell (1986). "Androgyny and Sex Role Measurement: A Personal Construct Approach." *Journal of Personality and Social Psychology, 51,* 1081–1088.

Baldwin, J. (1971). "An Open Letter to My Sister, Angela Y. Davis." In *If They Come in the Morning: Voices of Resistance*. New American Library.

Bandura, A., and R. H. Walters. (1959). *Adolescent Aggression*. New York: Ronald Press.

Banziger, G., and S. Roush (1983). "Nursing Homes for the Birds: A Control-Relevant Intervention with Bird Feeders." *The Gerontologist, 23, 5,* 527–531.

Baring-Gould, William S., and Ceil Baring-Gould (1962). *The Annotated Mother Goose*. New York: Bramhall House.

Barnett, M. A., and S. J. McCoy (1989). "The Relation of the Distressful Childhood Experiences and Empathy in College Undergraduates." *Journal of Genetic Psychology, 15,* 417–426.

Batson, K., B. McCabe, M. M. Baun, and C. Wilson (1997). "The Effect of a Therapy Dog on Socialization and Physiological Indicators of Stress in Persons Diagnosed with Alzheimer's Disease." In C. C. Wilson and D. C. Turner (eds.), *Companion Animals in Human Health*, 203–215. London: Sage.

Baun, M. M., N. Bergstrom, N. F. Langston, and L. Thomas (1984). "Physiological Effects of Human Companion Animal Bonding." *Nursing Research, 33,* 126–129.

Beach, K., R. Fouts, and D. Fouts (1984). "Representational Art in Chimpanzees." *Friends of Washoe 3, 4,* 2–4.

Beard, M.D., George (1898/1972). Sexual Neurasthenia [Nervous Exhaustion] Its Hygiene, Causes, Symptoms and Treatment with a Chapter on Diet for the Nervous. New York: E. B. Treat and Co., New York: Arno Press.

Beattie, W. A., and M. de Lacy Lowe (1980). *Australia's North-West Challenge*. Melbourne: Kimberly Publishing.

Beck, A. M. (2000). "The Use of Animals to Benefit Humans, Animal-Assisted Therapy." In A. H. Fine (ed.), *The Handbook on Animal Assisted Therapy: Theoretical Foundations and Guidelines for Practice*, 21–40. San Diego, Calif.: Academic Press.

Beck, A. M., and L. T. Glickman (1987). "Future Research on Pet Facilitated Therapy: A Plea for Comprehension before Intervention." *Health Benefits of Pets*, NIH Technology Assessment Workshop September 10–11.

Beck, A. M., and A. H. Katcher (1983). *Between Pets and People: The Importance of Animal Companionship*. New York: G. P. Putnam's Sons.

———. (1984). "A New Look at Pet-Facilitated Therapy." *Journal of the American Veterinary Medical Association, 184,* 414–421.

———. (1996). *Between Pets and People: The Importance of Animal Companionship*. West Lafayette, Ind.: Purdue University Press.

Beck, A. M., and N. M. Meyers (1987). "The Pet Owner Experience. *New England and Regional Allergy Proceedings, 8, 3,* 29–31.

Beck, A. M., L. Seraydarian, and G. F. Hunter (1986). "The Use of Animals in the Rehabilitation of Psychiatric Inpatients." *Psychological Reports, 8,* 63–66.

Beck, A. M., G. F. Melson, P. L. da Costa, and T. Liu (2001). "The Educational Benefits of a Ten-Week Home-Based Wild Bird Feeding Program for Children." *Anthrozoös, 14, 1,* 19–28.

Beckwith, K. (1996, Summer). "Lancashire Women against Pit Closures: Women's Standing in a Man's Movement." *Signs,* 1034–1068.

Behn, Aphra (1688/1973). *Oroonoko; or, The Royal Slave*. London: Will. Canning. Reprint, New York: W. W. Norton.

Beirne, P. (1995). "The Use and Abuse of Animals in Criminology: A Brief History and Current Review." *Social Justice*, *22*, *1*, 5–31.

Bekoff, M. (1977). "Social Communication in Canids: Evidence for the Evolution of a Stereotyped Mammalian Display." *Science*, *197*, 1097–1099.

———. (1995). "Play Signals as Punctuation: The Structure of Social Play in Canids." *Behaviour*, *132*, 419–429.

———. (2000). *The Smile of a Dolphin: Remarkable Accounts of Animal Emotions*. New York: Random House/Discovery.

———. (2006). "Animal Passions and Beastly Virtue." *Zygon*, *41*, *1*, 71–104.

Bekoff, M., and C. Allen (1998) "Intentional Communication and Social Play." In M. Bekoff, and J. Byers (eds.), *Animal Play: Evolutionary, Comparative, and Ecological Perspectives*, 97–114. Cambridge and New York: Cambridge University Press.

Bekoff, M., and Byers, J. (1981) "A Critical Reanalysis of the Ontogeny of Mammalian Social and Locomotor Play: An Ethological Hornet's Nest." In K. Immelmann, G. W. Barlow, L. Petrinovich, and M. Main (eds.), *Behavioral Development: The Bielefeld Interdisciplinary Project*, 296–337. Cambridge and New York: Cambridge University Press.

———. (1998). *Animal Play: Evolutionary, Comparative, and Ecological Perspectives*. Cambridge, U.K. and New York: Cambridge University Press.

Bem, S. L. (1974). "The Measurement of Psychological Androgyny." *Journal of Consulting and Clinical Psychology*, *47*, 155–162.

———. (1975). "Sex Role Adaptability: One Consequence of Psychological Androgyny." *Journal of Personality and Social Psychology*, *31*, 634–643.

———. (1977). "On the Utility of Alternative Procedures for Assessing Psychological Androgyny." *Journal of Counseling and Clinical Psychology*, *45*, 196–205.

———. (1981). *Bem Sex Role Inventory professional manual*. Palo Alto, Calif.: Consulting Psychologists Press.

Bender, L. (1959). "Children and Adolescents Who Have Killed." *American Journal of Psychiatry*, *116*, 510–513.

Bennett, D. H. (1983). "Some Aspects of Aboriginal and Non-Aboriginal Notions of Responsibility to Nonhuman Animals." *Australian Aboriginal Studies*, *2*, 19–24.

———. (1991). "Animal Rights and Aboriginal Concepts." In D. B. Croft (ed.), *Australian People and Animals in Today's Dreamtime, The Role of Comparative Psychology in the Management of Natural Resources*, 53–69. New York: Praeger.

Bentham, J. (1789/1939). "Introduction to the Principles of Morals and Legislation." In E. A. Burtt (ed.), *The English Philosophers from Bacon to Mill*. New York: Modern.

Berger, P., and T. Luckmann (1967). *The Social Construction of Reality*. Garden City, N.Y.: Doubleday Anchor.

Berghler, R. (1989). *Man and Cat: The Benefit of Cat Ownership*. Oxford (UK) and Cambridge, Mass.: Blackwell Scientific.

Berry Jr., R. (1979). *The Vegetarians*. Brookline, Mass.: Autumn Press

Besharov, D. J. (1990). *Recognizing Child Abuse*. New York: The Free Press.

Beston, H. (1928). The Outermost House: A Year of Life on the Great Beach of Cape Cod. Harmondsworth. Middlesex: Penguin.

Bettelheim, B. (1955). *Truants from Life*. New York: The Free Press.

Bewick, T. (1975). *A Memoir of Thomas Bewick, Written by Himself*, ed. I. Bain, 1862. Oxford: Oxford University Press.

Birke, L. (1991). "Science, Feminism and Animal Natures: Extending the Boundaries." *Women's Studies International Forum*, *14*, *5*, 443–449.

Birkeland, J. (1993). "Ecofeminism: Linking Theory and Practice."In Greta Gaard (ed.), *Ecofeminism: Women, Animals, Nature*, 13–59. Philadelphia: Temple University Press.

Bloom, M. (1986). *When the Bond Is Broken: Companion Animal Death and Adult Human Grief.* Unpublished master's thesis, California State University, Dominguez Hills.

Blum, W. (1995). *Killing Hope: U.S. Military and CIA Intervention since World War II*. Monroe, Me.: Common Courage Press.

Blumer, Herbert (1954). "What Is Wrong with Social Theory?" *American Sociological Review, 19* (February), 3–10.

Boat, B. W. (1991). "Caregivers as Surrogate Therapists in Treatment of a Ritualistically Abused Child." In W. N. Friedrich (ed)., *Casebook of Sexual Abuse Treatment*, 1–26. New York: W. W. Norton.

———. (1995). "The Relationship between Violence to Children and Violence to Animals: An Ignored Link?" *Journal of Interpersonal Violence, 10,* 229–235.

Bogdan, R., and S. Taylor (1989). "Relationships with Severely Disabled People: The Social Construction of Humanness." *Social Problems, 36,* 135–148.

Bogdan, R., S. Taylor, B. deGrandpre, and S. Haynes (1974). "Let Them Eat Programs: Attendants' Perspectives and Programming on Wards in State Schools." *Journal of Health and Social Behavior, 15,* 142–151.

Bordo, S. (Spring 1986). "The Cartesian Masculinization of Thought," *Signs: Journal of Women in Culture and Society, 11, 3,* 439–456.

Bowd A. D. (1984a). "Development and Validation of a Scale of Attitudes toward the Treatment of Animals." *Educational and Psychological Measurement, 44,* 513–515.

———. (1984, 1984b). "Fears and Understanding of Animals in Middle Childhood." *Journal of Genetic Psychology, 145,* 143–144.

———. (1989). "The Educational Dilemma". In D. Paterson and M. Palmer M (eds.), *The Status of Animals: Ethics, Education and Welfare*, 52–57. CAB International: Wallingford.

Bowlby, J. (1953). *Child Care and the Growth of Love*. Baltimore: Pelican Books.

Brain, L. (1962). "Presidential Address." In C. A. Keele and R. Smith, (eds.), *The Assessment of Pain in Men and Animals*. London: Universities Federation for Animal Welfare.

Brickel, C. M. (1979). "The Therapeutic Roles of Cat Mascots with a Hospital Based Geriatric Population: A Staff Survey." *The Gerontologist, 19,* 368–372.

Brickel, C. M. (1984). "Depression in the Nursing Home: A Pilot Study Using Pet-facilitated Therapy." In R. K. Anderson, B. L. Hart, and L. A. Hart (eds.), *The Pet Connection: Its Influence on Our Health and Quality of Life*, 407–415. Minneapolis: University of Minnesota.

Brown, D. S. (1984). *Human Gender, Age, and Personality Effects on Relationships with Dogs and Horses*. Ph.D. diss., Duke University, Durham, N.C.

Brown, L. (1988). *Cruelty to Animals: The Moral Debt*. London: Macmillan.

Brown, S., and A. Katcher (1997). "The Contribution of Attachment to Pets and Attachment to Nature to Dissociation and Absorption." *Dissociation, 10, 2,* 125–129.

———. (2001). "Pet Attachment and Dissociation." *Society and Animals, 9,* 25–42.

Browne, A. (1987). *When Battered Women Kill*. New York: Free Press.

Bryant, B. K. (1982). "Sibling Relationships in Middle Childhood." In *Sibling Relationships: Their Nature and Significance across the Lifespan*. In M. E. Lamb and B. Sutton-Smith, (eds.), 87–122. Hillsdale, N.J.: Lawrence Erlbaum.

———. (1990). "The Richness of the Child–Pet Relationship: A Consideration of Both Benefits and Costs of Pets to Children." *Anthrozoös, 3,* 253–261.

Bryant B. K. (1986). "The Relevance of Family and Neighbourhood Animals to Social-Emotional Development in Middle Childhood." Paper presented at the Delta Society International Conference, *Living Together: People, Animals and the Environment*. August 1986, Boston, Massachusetts.

Bryant, C. D. (1971). "Feathers, Spurs and Blood: Cockfighting as a Deviant Leisure Activity." Paper read at the annual meeting of the Southern Sociological Society.

———. (1972). "Sawdust in Their Shoes: The Carnival as a Neglected Sub-culture and Work Setting." In Clifton D. Bryant (ed.), *The Social Dimensions of Work*. Englewood Cliffs: Prentice-Hall.

_____. (1991). "Deviant Leisure and Clandestine Lifestyle: Cockfighting as a Socially Disvalued Sport." *World Leisure and Recreation, 33*, 17–21.

Bryant, C. D., and J. P. King (1979). " 'Fowl Work and Offal Activities': A Pilot Study of Morale and Disaffection among Poultry Processing Employees." Paper read at the annual meeting of the Southern Association of Agricultural Scientists.

Bryant C. D., and C. E. Palmer (1976). "Zoological Crime: A Typological Overview of Animal-related Laws and Deviant Behavior." Paper read at the annual meeting of the Southwestern Social Science Association.

Bryant, C. D., and W. E. Snizek (1976). "Practice Modes and Professional Role Playing among Large and Small Animal Veterinarians." *Rural Sociology, 41* (Summer), 179–192.

Bryant, C. D., W. E. Snizek, and D. J. Shoemaker (1976). "Ecological Work and Careers: An Overview of a Research Program for the Sociological Study of Environmentally-related Occupational Specialties." *Man–Environment Systems, 6* (March), 107–119.

Budge, R. C., J. Spicer, B. R. Jones, and R. St. George (1996). "The Influence of Companion Animals on Owner Perception: Gender and Species Effects." *Anthrozoös, 9, 1*, 10–18.

Budiansky, S. (1992). *The Covenant of the Wild: Why Animals Chose Domestication*. New York: Morrow.

Buettinger, C. (1993, Winter). "Antivivisection and the Charge of Zoophil-Psychosis in the Early Twentieth Century." *The Historian, 15, 2*, 277–289.

Bulcroft, K., and A. Albert (1986, August). *Pet Ownership Over the Family Life Cycle*. Paper presented at the annual international conference of the Delta Society, Boston.

Burd, S. (1992). "Federal Judge Says Scope of Animal-Welfare Laws Must Not Exclude Protection of Rats, Mice, Birds." *The Chronicle of Higher Education*, Jan. 15: A27, A30.

Burghardt, G. (1985). "Animal Awareness: Current Perceptions and Historical Perspective." *American Psychologist, 40*, 905–919.

———. (1998). "The Evolutionary Origins of Play Revisited: Lessons from Turtles." In M. Bekoff and J. Byers (eds.), *Animal Play: Evolutionary, Comparative, and Ecological Perspectives,* 1–26. Cambridge and New York: Cambridge University Press.

Burghardt, G. M., and H. A. Herzog, Jr. (1989). "Animals, Evolution, and Ethics. In R. J. Hoage (ed.), *Perceptions of Animals in American Culture*, 129–151. Washington, D.C.: Smithsonian Institution Press.

Burk, F. L. (1897). "Teasing and Bullying." *Pedagogical Seminary, 4*, 336–371.

Burtt, E. A. (ed.) (1955). *The Teachings of the Compassionate Buddha*. New York: New American Library "The Bodhisattva's Vow of Universal Redemption."

Buytendjik, F. J. J. (1936). *The Mind of the Dog*. Boston: Houghton-Mifflin.

Cain, A. O. (1983). "A Study of Pets in the Family System." In A. H. Katcher and A. M. Beck (eds.), *New Perspectives on Our Lives with Companion Animals*, 351–359. Philadelphia: University of Pennsylvania Press.

———. (1985). "Pets as Family Members." In M. Sussman (ed.), *Pets and the Family*, 5–10. New York: Haworth.

Caius, J. (Undated). *Of English Dogges: The Diversities, the Names, the Nature, and the Properties*, trans. Abraham Fleming, p. 13. London: A. Bradley.

Cameras, L. A., S. Ribordy, J. Hill, S. Martino, V. Sachs, S. Spaccarelli, and R. Stefani (1990). "Maternal Facial Behavior and the Recognition and Production of Emotion Expression by Maltreated and Nonmaltreated Children." *Developmental Psychology, 26*, 304–312.

Cameron, P., and M. Mattson (1972). "Psychological Correlates of Pet Ownership." *Psychological Reports, 30*, 286.

Carson, Gerald (1972). *Men, Beast, and Gods: A History of Cruelty and Kindness to Animals*. New York: Scribner.

Cartmill, M. (1993). *A View to a Death in the Morning*, Cambridge: Harvard University Press.

CAST: The Coronary Arrhythmia Suppression Trial Investigators. (1989). Preliminary report: "Effect of Encainide and Flexainide on Mortality in a Randomized Trial of Arrhythmia Suppression after Myocardial Infarction." *New England Journal of Medicine*, *321*, 406–412.

Cave, G. (1982). "Animals, Heidegger, and the Right to Life." *Environmental Ethics 4*, *3*, 249–255.

Charmaz, K. (1983). "The Grounded Theory Method: An Explication and Interpretation." In R. Emerson (ed.), *Contemporary Field Research*, 109–126. Boston: Little, Brown and Co.

Chaucer, G. *The Canterbury Tales: General Prologue*, Fragment 1, Group A, lines 146–147.

Chhabra, T. (1993, September). "A Journey to the Toda Afterworld." *The India Magazine of Her People and Culture*, 7–16.

———. (1995, February). "A Journey to Nyoolzn: A Toda Migration." *The India Magazine of Her People and Culture*, 62–71.

Chrystos (1981). "No Rock Scorns Me as Whore." In C. Morgan and G. Anzaldua (eds.), In *This Bridge Called My Back: Writings by Radical Women of Color*, Watertown, Mass.: Persephone.

Cicchetti, D. (1990). "The Organization and Coherence of Socioemotional, Cognitive, and Representational Development: Illustrations through a Developmental Psychopathology Perspective on Down Syndrome and Child Maltreatment." In R. A. Thompson (ed.), *Socioemotional Development*, Nebraska Symposium on Motivation, 259–366. Lincoln: University of Nebraska Press.

Clark, Anne (1975). *Beasts and Bawdy*. New York: Taplinger.

Clark, M., and T. Nater (1977). "La Rage in Europe." *Newsweek* (September 12).

Clark, S. (1984). *The Nature of the Beast*. New York: Oxford University Press.

Clarke, P., and A. Linzey (eds.) (1990). *Political Theory and Animal Rights*. London: Pluto Press.

Clifton, M. (1990). "Killing the Female: The Psychology of the Hunt." *The Animals' Agenda*. September.

Climent, C. E., R. Hyg, and F. R. Erwin (1972). "Historical Data in the Evaluation of Violent Subjects." *Archives of General Psychiatry*, *27*, 621–624.

Cochran, C. D. (1989). *A Study of Job-Related Stress at Halifax Humane Society of Volusia County, Inc.* Unpublished manuscript, Stetson University, Department of Psychology.

Cohen, J. (1989). "About Steaks Liking to Be Eaten: The Conflicting Views of Symbolic Interactionists and Talcott Parsons Concerning the Nature of Relations between Persons and Nonhuman Objects." *Symbolic Interaction, 12*, 191–214.

Cohen, S. P. (1998). *The Role of Pets in Some Urban American Families*. Unpublished doctoral dissertation, Columbia University, New York. (UMI 9910568).

———. (2002). "Can Pets Function as Family Members?" *Western Journal of Nursing Research*, *24*, 6, 621–638.

Collard, A., and Contrucci, J. (1988). *Rape of the Wild: Man's Violence against Animals and the Earth*. London: The Women's Press.

Collins, R. (1989). "Toward a Neo-Meadian Theory of Mind." *Symbolic Interaction, 12*, 1–32.

Comninou, M. (1995). "Speech, Pornography and Hunting." In C. J. Adams and J. Donovan (eds.), *Animals and Women: Feminist Theoretical Explorations*, 126–148. Durham and London: Duke University Press.

The Compact Edition of the Oxford English Dictionary. (1971). New York: Oxford University Press.

Cook, E. P. (1985). *Psychological Androgyny*. New York: Pergamon.

Corson, S. A., E. O. Corson, and P. H. Gwynne (1975). "Pet-facilitated Psychotherapy." In R. S. Anderson (ed.), *Pet Animals and Society*, 19–36. London: Baillière Tindall.

Council for International Organizations of Medical Sciences (CIOMS) (1983). "Proposed International

Guiding Principles for Biomedical Research Involving Animals." Ms. prepared at XVIIth CIOMS Round Table Conference, Geneva, Dec. 8–9.

Crist, E., and M. Lynch (1990). *The Analyzability of Human–Animal Interaction: The Case of Dog Training*. Paper presented at the annual meeting of the International Sociological Association, Madrid, Spain.

Crockenberg, S. (1985). "Toddlers' Reactions to Maternal Anger." *Merrill-Palmer Quarterly*, *31*, 361–373.

Crossette, B. (2000). "In Numbers, the Heavy Now Match the Starved." *New York Times*, January 18, A10.

————. (2000a). "Pain Relief Underused for Poor, Study Says." *New York Times*, February 23, A5.

Daanje, A. (1972). "On Locomotory Movements in Birds and the Intention Movements Derived from Them." In *Function and Evolution of Behavior*, ed. P. Klopfer and J. Hailman. Reading, Mass.: Addison-Wesley.

Dalziel, H. (1879–80). *British Dogs: Their Varieties, History, Characteristics, Breeding, Management and Exhibition*. London: Bazaar office.

Damecour, C. L., and M. Charron (1998). "Hoarding: A Symptom not a Syndrome." *Journal of Clinical Psychiatry*, *59*, 267–273.

Darwin, C. (1871). *The Descent of Man*. London: J. Murray.

Davidson, L. M., and A. Baum. (1990). "Posttraumatic Stress in Children Following Natural and Human-made Trauma." In M. Lewis and S. M. Miller (eds.), *Handbook of Developmental Psychopathology*, 251–259. New York: Plenum Press.

Davies, C. J. (1905). *The Kennel Handbook*. London: John Lane.

Davis, J. H. (1985). "Children and Pets: A Therapeutic Connection." *Pediatric Nursing*, *11*, 377–379.

Davis, L. E. (1983). "Species Differences in Drug Disposition as Factors in Alleviation of Pain." In R. L. Kitchell *et al.* (eds.), *Animal Pain: Perception and Alleviation*, 161–178. Bethesda, MD: American Physiological Society.

Dawkins, M. S. (1980). *Animal Suffering: The Science of Animal Welfare*. New York: Methuen.

Deal, C. (1993). *The Greenpeace Guide to Anti-Environmental Organizations*. Berkeley, Calif.: Odonian Press.

DeGrazia, D. (1996). *Taking Animals Seriously: Mental Life and Moral Status*. Cambridge and New York: Cambridge University Press.

Dembeck, H. (1965). *Animals and Men*. New York: Natural History Press.

Dent, A. A. (1974). *The Horse through Fifty Centuries of Civilization*. New York: Holt, Rinehart and Winston.

Denzin, N. (1989). *Interpretive Interactionism*. Newbury Park, Calif.: Sage.

DeViney, E., J. Dickert, and R. Lockwood (1983). "The Care of Pets within Child Abusing Families." *International Journal for the Study of Animal Problems*, *4*, 321–329.

DiGiacomo, N., A. Arluke, and G. Patronek (1998). "Surrendering Pets to Shelters: The Relinquishers Perspective." *Anthrozoös*, *11*, 41–51.

Dimock, Wai Chee (1996). *Residues of Justice: Literature, Law, Philosophy*. Berkeley: University of California Press.

Djerassi, C., A. Israel, and W. Jochle (1973). "Planned Parenthood for Pets." *Bulletin of the Atomic Scientists*, *29* (January), 10–19.

Dobash, R. E., and R. Dobash (1979). *Violence against Wives: A Case against the Patriarchy*. New York: The Free Press.

Dodge, K. A., J. E. Bates, and G. S. Pettit (1990). "Mechanisms in the Cycle of Violence." *Science*, *250*, 1678–1683.

Donovan, J. (1985). *Feminist Theory: The Intellectual Traditions of American Feminism*. New York: Ungar.

————. (1990). "Animal Rights and Feminist Theory." *Signs: Journal of Women in Culture and Society. 15, 2*, 350–375.

Dorr Research Corporation. (1994). *A Marketing Research Study of People/Pet Relationships That Have Ended*. Boston: Massachusetts Society for the Prevention of Cruelty to Animals.

Doughty, R. W. (1975). *Feather Fashions and Bird Preservation: A Study in Nature Protection*. Berkeley: University of California Press.

Douglas, J., and M. Olshaker (1995). *Mindhunter: Inside the FBI's Elite Serial Crime Unit*. New York: Simon and Schuster.

Douglas, J., A. W. Burgess, A. G. Burgess, and R. K. Ressler (1997). *Crime Classification Manual*. San Francisco: Jossey-Bass.

Draper, R. J., G. J. Gerber, and E. M. Layng (1990). "Defining the Role of Pet Animals in Psychotherapy." *Psychiatric Journal of the University of Ottawa*, *15*, *3*, 169–172.

Dunayer, J. (1995). "Sexist Words, Speciesist Roots." In C. J. Adams and J. Donovan (eds.), *Animals and Women: Feminist Theoretical Explorations*. Durham: Duke University Press.

———. (2001). *Animal Equality: Language and Liberation*. Derwood, Md.: Ryce Publications.

Dutton, M. A. (1992). *Empowering and Healing the Battered Woman*. New York: Springer.

Dwivedi, O. P. (1990). "Satyagraha for Conservation: Awakening the Spirit of Hinduism. " In J. R. Engel and J. G. Engel (eds.). *Ethics of Environment and Development: Global Challenge, International Response*. London: Bellhaven Press. 210–212.

Easson, W. M., and R. M. Steinhilber (1961). "Murderous Aggression by Children and Adolescents." *Archives of General Psychiatry*, *4*, 1–9.

Eckersley, R. (1992). *Environmentalism and Political Theory: Toward an Ecocentric Approach*, London: UCL Press.

Eckholm, E. (1985). "Pygmy Chimp Readily Learns Language Skill," *New York Times*, 24 June.

Eddy, J., L. A. Hart, and R. P. Boltz (1988). "The Effects of Service Dogs on Social Acknowledgements of People in Wheelchairs." *Journal of Psychology*, *122*, 39–44.

Edelson, J., and D. Lester (1983). "Personality and Pet Ownership: A Preliminary Study." *Psychological Reports*, *53*, 990.

Edlin, H. L. (1947). Forestry and Woodland Life. London: Batsford.

———. (1958). *England's Forests*. London: Faber and Faber.

Edwards, N. E., and A. M. Beck (2002). "Animal-assisted Therapy and Nutrition in Alzheimer's Disease." *Western Journal of Nursing Research*, *24*, *6*, 697–712.

Elkin, A. P (1967). "Religion and Philosophy of the Australian Aborigines." In E. C. B. McLaurin (ed.), *Essays in Honour of Griffithes Wheeler Thatcher 1863–1950*, 19–45. Sydney: Sydney University Press.

Ellis, C. (1991). "Sociological Introspection and Emotional Experience." *Symbolic Interaction*, *14*, 23–50.

Emery, R. E. (1989). "Family Violence." *American Psychologist*, *44*, 321–328.

Empson, W. (1951). *The Structure of Complex Words*. Ch. 7–8. New York: New Directions.

Endenburg, N. (1991). "Animals as Companions." Amsterdam: Unpublished Thesis.

Engell, J. (1981). *The Creative Imagination: Enlightenment to Romanticism*. Cambridge, Mass.: Harvard University Press.

Evans-Pritchard, E. E. (1940). *The Nuer, A Description of the Modes of Livelihood and Political Institutions of a Nilotic People*. Oxford: Clarendon Press.

Evernden, N. (1993). *The Natural Alien*. Toronto: University of Toronto Press.

Fagen, R. (1981). *Animal Play Behavior*. Oxford and New York: Oxford University Press.

Faller, K. C. (1990). *Understanding Child Sexual Maltreatment*. Newbury Park, Calif.: Sage Publications.

Farman, E. (1898). "The Bulldog Club." *Kennel Gazette 19*, 471.

Felthous, A. R. (1980). "Aggression against Cats, Dogs and People." *Child Psychiatry and Human Development*, *10*, 169–177.

Felthous, A. R., and S. R. Kellert (1985). "Childhood Cruelty toward Animals among Criminals and Noncriminals." *Human Relations*, *38*, *12*, 1113–1129.

———. (1986). "Violence against Animals and People: Is Aggression against Living Creatures Generalized?" *Bulletin of the American Academy of Psychiatry Law*, *14*, 55–69.

———. (1987). "Childhood Cruelty to Animals and Later Aggression against People: A Review." *American Journal of Psychiatry*, *144*, 710–717.

Felthous, A. R., and B. Yudowitz (1977). "Approaching a Comparative Typology of Assaultive Female Offenders." *Psychiatry*, *40*, 270–276.

Ferenczi, S. (1916). *Sex in Psycho-Analysis*, 240–252. Boston: Richard G. Badger, the Gorham Press.

Ferraro, K. F., and C. M. Albrecht-Jensen (1991). "Does Religion Influence Adult Health?" *Journal of the Scientific Study of Religion*, *30*, 193–202.

Feshbach, N. D. (1989). "The Construct of Empathy and the Phenomenon of Physical Maltreatment of Children." In *Child Maltreatment*, ed. D. Cicchetti and V. Carlson, 349–373. New York: Cambridge University Press.

Fick, K. M. (1993). "The Influence of an Animal on Social Interactions of Nursing Home Residents in a Group Setting." *American Journal of Occupational Therapy*, *47*, *6*, 529–534.

Filiatre, J. C., J. L. Millot, and H. Montagner (1983). "New Findings on Communication Behaviour between the Young Child and His Pet Dog." In *The Human–Pet Relationship: International Symposium on the Occasion of the 80th Birthday of Nobel Prize Winner Prof. Dr. Konrad Lorenz*, 50–57. Vienna: IEMT.

Finch P. (1989). "Learning from the Past." In D. Paterson and M. Palmer (eds.), *The Status of Animals: Ethics, Education and Welfare*, 64–72. CAB International: Wallingford.

Finkelhor, D., L. M. Williams, and N. Burns (1988). *Nursery Crimes: Sexual Abuse in Day Care*. Newbury Park, Calif.: Sage Publications.

Fisher, Irving (1907). "The Influence of Flesh Eating on Endurance." *Yale Medical Journal, 13*, 5 (March), 207.

Fisher, S., and K. Davis (ed.) (1993). *Negotiating at the Margins: The Gendered Discourses of Power and Resistance*. New Brunswick N.J.: Rutgers University Press.

Fitter, R., and P. Scott (1978). *The Penitent Butchers: 75 Years of Wildlife Conservation*. London: Fauna Preservation Society.

Flecknell, P. A. (1987). "Laboratory Animal Anesthesia: An Introduction for Research Workers and Technicians." London: Academic Press/Harcourt Brace Jovanovich.

Fleming, G. (1872). *Rabies and Hydrophobia: Their History, Nature, Causes, Symptoms, and Prevention*. London: Chapman and Hall.

Flynn, J. (1988, October 27). "Torturing of Pets Could Be Prelude to Human Murder." *San Francisco Examiner.*

Foucault, M. (1977). *Discipline and Punish: The Birth of the Prison*. New York: Vintage.

Fowler, F. (1988). *Survey Research Methods*. Newbury Park: Sage Publications.

Fox, M. A. (1978a). "Animal Liberation: A Critique," *Ethics*, *88*, 134–138.

Fox, M. W. (1978b). *The Dog: Its Domestication and Behavior*. New York: Garland.

———. (1978c). "How Your Problems Affect Your Pet." *McCalls* (October), 96 and 216.

———. (1981). *How to Be Your Pet's Best Friend*. New York: Coward, McCann, and Geoghegan.

Francis, G., J. T. Turner, and S. B. Johnson (1985). "Domestic Animal Visitation as Therapy with Adult Home Residents." *International Journal of Nursing Studies*, *22*, 201–206.

Franklin, A. (1999). *Animals and Modern Cultures*. London and Thousand Oaks, Calif.: Sage.

Franti C. E., J. F. Kraus, N. O. Borhani, S. L. Johnson, and S. D. Tucker (1980). "Pet Ownership in Rural Northern California (El Dorado County)." *Journal of the American Veterinary Medical Association*, *176*, *2*, 143–149.

French, M. (1985). *Beyond Power: On Women, Men, and Morals*. New York: Summit.

French, R. D. (1975). *Antivivisection and Medical Sciences in Victorian Society*. Princeton, N. J.: Princeton University Press.

Freud, S. (1905). "Three Contributions to the Theory of Sex." In A. A. Brill (ed.), *The Basic Writings of Sigmund Freud* (1938). New York: Random House.

Frey, J. (1983). *Survey Research by Telephone (Vol. 150)*. Sage Library of Social Research. Beverly Hills, Calif.: Sage Publications.

Frey, R. G. (1980). *Interests and Rights: The Case against Animals*. Oxford: Clarendon.

Frick, P. J., B. B. Lahey, R. Loeber, L. Tannenbaum, Y. Van Horn, M. A. G. Christ, E. A. Hart, and K. Hanson (1993). "Oppositional Defiant Disorder and Conduct Disorder: A Meta-Analytic Review of Factors Analyses and Cross-validation in a Clinic Sample." *Clinical Psychology Review*, *13*, *4*, 319–340.

Friedmann, E. (2000). "The Animal–Human Bond: Health and Wellness." In A. H. Fine (ed.), *The Handbook on Animal Assisted Therapy: Theoretical Foundations and Guidelines for Practice*, 41–58. San Diego, Calif.: Academic Press.

Friedmann, E., and A. H. Katcher (1978). "Pet Ownership and Coronary Heart Patient Survival." *Circulation*, *58* (November), 168.

Friedmann, E., and S. A. Thomas (1995). "Pet Ownership, Social Support, and One-Year Survival after Acute Myocardial Infarction in the Cardiac Arrhythmia Suppression Trial (CAST)." *American Journal of Cardiology*, *76*, 1213–1217.

Friedmann, E., A. H. Katcher, and D. Meislich (1983). "When Pet Owners are Hospitalized, Significance of Companion Animals during Hospitalization." In A. H. Katcher and A. M. Beck (eds.), *New Perspectives on Our Lives with Companion Animals*, 346–350. Philadelphia: University of Pennsylvania Press.

Friedmann, E., B. Z. Locker, and R. Lockwood (1993). "Perceptions of Animals and Cardiovascular Responses during Verbalizations with an Animal Present." *Anthrozoös*, *6*, 115–134.

Friedmann, E., A. H. Katcher, J. J. Lynch, and S. A. Thomas (1980). "Animal Companions and One Year Survival of Patients after Discharge from a Coronary Care Unit." *Public Health Reports*, *95*, 307–312.

Friedmann, E., A. H. Katcher, M. Eaton, and B. Berger (1984). "Pet Ownership and Psychological Status." In R. K. Anderson, B. K. Hart, and L. A. Hart (eds.), *The Pet Connection: Its Influence on Our Health and Quality of Life*, 300–308. Center to Study Human–Animal Relationships and Environment, University of Minnesota: Globe Publishing Company.

Friedmann, E., A. H. Katcher, S. A. Thomas, J. J. Lynch, and P. R. Messent (1983). "Social Interaction and Blood Pressure: Influence of Animal Companions." *Journal of Nervous and Mental Disease*, *171*, 461–465.

Friedrich, W. N., A. J. Urquiza, and R. L. Beilke (1986). "Behavior Problems in Sexually Abused Young Children." *Journal of Pediatric Psychology*, *11*, 47–57.

Fromm, E. (1973). *The Anatomy of Human Destructiveness*. New York: Henry Holt.

Frost R. O., T. L. Hartl, R. Christian, and N. Williams (1995). "The Value of Possessions in Compulsive Hoarding: Patterns of Use and Attachment." *Behaviour Research and Therapy*, *33*, 897–902.

Frumkin, H. (2001). "Beyond Toxicity: Human Health and the Natural Environment." *American Journal of Preventive Medicine*, *20*, *3*, 234–240.

Fuller, Margaret (1845/1971). *Woman in the Nineteenth Century*. New York: Norton.

Furman, E. (1986). "Aggressively Abused Children." *Journal of Child Psychotherapy*, *12*, 47–59.

Gage M. G., and S. Magnuson-Martinson (1988). "Intergenerational Continuity of Attitudes and Values about Dogs." *Anthrozoös*, *1*, 233–239.

Gallistel, C. R. (ed). (1992). *Animal Cognition*. Cambridge, Mass.: MIT Press.

Gallup, G. G., Jr., and J. W. Beckstead (1988). "Attitudes toward Animal Research." *American Psychologist*, *43*, 474–476.

Gandhi, M. K. (1929). *An Autobiography*. Ahmedabad, India: Navajivan Publishing House.

Garbarino, J., N. Dubrow, K. Kostelny, and C. Pardo (1992). *Children in Danger: Coping with the Consequences of Community Violence*. San Francisco: Jossey-Bass.

Garmezy, N. (1988). "Stressors of Childhood." In N. Garmezy and M. Rutter (eds.), *Stress, Coping, and Development in Children*, 43–48. Baltimore: Johns Hopkins University Press.

Gary, Romain (translated by Jonathan Griffin from the French) (1958). *The Roots of Heaven*. New York: Simon and Schuster.

Gelles R. J., and M. A. Straus (1988). *Intimate Violence*. New York: Simon and Schuster.

Gendlin, E. (1962). *Experiencing and the Creation of Meaning*. Toronto: Free Press of Glencoe.

Gergen, K. (1991). *The Saturated Self: Dilemmas of Identity in Contemporary Life*. New York: Basic Books.

Geries-Johnson, B., and J. H. Kennedy (1995). "Influence of Animals on Perceived Likeability of People." *Perceptual and Motor Skills*, *80*, 432–434.

Gerrard, Frank (1945, 1977). *Meat Technology: A Practical Textbook for Student and Butcher*. London: Northwood Publications, Inc.

Gilligan, C. (1982). *In a Different Voice: Psychological Theory and Women's Development*. Cambridge, Mass.: Harvard University Press.

Gilligan, C., and J. Attanucci (1988). "Two Moral Orientations: Gender Differences and Similarities." *Merrill-Palmer Quarterly*, *34*, 223–237.

Giorgi, A. (1970). *Psychology as a Human Science: A Phenomenologically Based Approach*. New York: Harper and Row.

Glaser, B. (1978). *Theoretical Sensitivity*. Mill Valley, Calif.: Sociology Press.

Glaser, B., and A. Strauss (1967). *The Discovery of Grounded Theory*. Chicago: Aldine.

Gleitman, H. (1986). *Psychology* (3rd Ed.). W. W. Norton and Co. New York.

Godwin R. D. (1975). "Trends in the Ownership of Domestic Pets in Great Britain." In R. Anderson (ed.) *Pet Animals and Society*. London: Baillière Tindall.

Goffman, E. (1959). *The Presentation of Self in Everyday Life*. Garden City, N.Y.: Doubleday.

———. (1961). *Asylums*. Garden City, N.Y.: Doubleday.

———. (1974). *Frame Analysis: An Essay on the Organization of Experience*. Cambridge, Mass.: Harvard University Press.

Golding, W. (1959). *Lord of the Flies*. New York: Capricorn Books.

Goodall, J. (1986). *The Chimpanzees of Gombe: Patterns of Behavior*. Cambridge, Mass.: Harvard University Press.

———. (1990). *Through a Window: My Thirty Years with the Chimpanzees of Gombe*. Boston: Houghton Mifflin.

Goode, D. (1992). "Who Is Bobby? Ideology and Method in the Discovery of a Down Syndrome Person's Competence." In P. Ferguson, D. Ferguson, and S. Taylor (eds.), *Interpreting Disability: A Qualitative Reader*, 197–213. New York: Teachers College Press.

Gould, S. J. (1987). "Animals and Us." *New York Review of Books 34*, *11*, 20–25.

Grady, Sandy (1988). "The Duke as Boring as Spinach." *Buffalo News*, 26 March.

Graham, A. D. (1973). *The Eyelids of Morning*. Greenwich, Conn.: New York Graphic Society.

Grandin, T. (1988). "Behavior of Slaughter Plant and Auction Employees toward Animals." *Anthrozoös*, *1*, 205–213.

Grant, Douglas (1957). *Margaret the First*. Toronto: University of Toronto Press.

Green, A. H. (1985). "Children Traumatized by Physical Abuse." In S. Eth and R. S. Pynoos (eds.), *Post-Traumatic Stress Disorder in Children*, 135–154. Washington, D.C.: American Psychiatric Press.

Greenburg D. (1987). "Compulsive Hoarding." *American Journal of Psychotherapy*, *41*, 409–417.

Grene, M. (1965). *Approaches to a Philosophic Biology*. New York: Basic Books.

Griffin, D. (1981). *The Question of Animal Awareness: Evolutionary Continuity of Mental Experience*. Los Altos, Calif.: William Kaufmann.

———. (1984). *Animal Thinking*. Cambridge, Mass.: Harvard University Press.

Griffin, S. (1978). *Woman and Nature: The Roaring inside Her.* New York: Harper and Row.

Gubrium, J. (1986). "The Social Preservation of Mind: The Alzheimer's Disease Experience." *Symbolic Interaction, 9,* 37–51.

Guttman, G. (1981). "The Psychological Determinants of Keeping Pets." In B. Fogle (ed.) *Interrelations between People and Pets,* 89–98. Springfield, Ill.: Charles C. Thomas.

Guttman, G., M. Predovic, and M. Zemanek (1983). "The Influence of Pet Ownership on Non-Verbal Communication and Social Competence in Children." In *The Human–Pet Relationship: International Symposium on the Occasion of the 80th Birthday of Nobel Prize Winner Prof. Dr. Konrad Lorenz,* 58–63. Vienna: IEMT.

Hallie, P. P. (1982). *Cruelty.* Middletown, Conn.: Wesleyan University Press.

Hamilton, A. (1990). *History of the Ancient and Honorable Tuesday Club,* ed. R. Micklus. Chapel Hill: University of North Carolina Press.

Hamilton, C. (1909/1981). *Marriage as a Trade.* London: The Women's Press.

Handy, G. L. (1994). "Handling Animal Collectors: Part 1: Interventions that Work." *Shelter Sense,* May/Jun, 3–10.

Hare, R. M. (1963). *Freedom and Reason.* New York: Oxford University Press.

———. (1972). "Rules of War and Moral Reasoning," *Philosophy and Public Affairs, 1,* 2.

Harris, J. (1983). "A Study of Client Grief Responses to Death or Loss in a Companion Animal Veterinary Practice." In A. Katcher and A. Beck (eds.), *New Perspectives on Our Lives with Companion Animals,* 370–376. Philadelphia: University of Pennsylvania Press.

Harris, M. (1974). *Cows, Pigs, Wars and Witches: The Riddles of Culture.* New York: Vintage Books.

———. (1985). *Good to Eat, The Riddles of Food and Culture.* New York: Simon and Schuster.

Harris, M. D., J. M. Rinehart, and J. Gerstman (1993). "Animal-Assisted Therapy for the Homebound Elderly." *Holistic Nurse Practice, 8, 1,* 27–37.

Harwood, D. (1928). *Love for Animals and How It Developed in Great Britain.* New York: Columbia University Press.

Hastings, Hester (1936). *Man and Beast in French Thought of the Eighteenth Century.* Baltimore; The Johns Hopkins Studies in Romance Literature and Languages.

Hayano, D. (1979). "Auto-Ethnography: Paradigms, Problems, and Prospects. *Human Organization, 38,* 99–104.

Hays, H. R. (1964). *The Dangerous Sex: The Myth of Feminine Evil.* New York: Pocket Books.

Hearne, V. (1986). *Adam's Task: Calling Animals by Name.* New York: Knopf.

Heide, K. M. (1992). *Why Kids Kill Parents.* Columbus: Ohio State University Press.

Heide, K. M., and E. P. Solomon (1991). *The SCS Survey (Survivors' Coping Strategies).* (Available from Kathleen M. Heide, Ph.D., University of South Florida, Department of Criminology, Social Sciences Building Room 107, 4202 East Fowler Avenue, Tampa, FL 33620-8100)

Heidegger, M. (1962). *Being and Time.* New York: Harper and Row.

Heidrich, J. E., and G. Kent (1985). "Use of Analgesics after Surgery in Animals." *Journal of the American Veterinary Medical Association, 187, 5,* 513–514.

Heiman, Marcel (1956). "The Relationship between Man and Dog." *Psychoanalytical Quarterly, 25,* 568–585.

Heller, M. S., S. Ehrlich, M. Saundra, and D. Lester (1984). "Childhood Cruelty to Animals, Firesetting, and Enuresis as Correlates of Competence to Stand Trial." *Journal of General Psychology, 110,* 151–153.

Hellman, D. S., and N. Blackman (1966). "Enuresis, Firesetting and Cruelty to Animals: A Triad Predictive of Adult Crime." *American Journal of Psychiatry, 122,* 1431–1435.

Helmer, J. (1991). "The Horse in Backstretch Culture." *Qualitative Sociology, 14,* 175–195.

Hendy, H. M. (1984). "Effects of Pets on the Sociability and Health Activities of Nursing Home Residents." In R. K. Anderson, B. L. Hart, and L. A. Hart (eds.), *The Pet Connection: Its*

Influence on Our Health and Quality of Life, 430–437. Minneapolis: University of Minnesota Press.

Henry, J. (1973). *On Sham, Vulnerability, and Other Forms of Self-Destruction*. New York: Vintage.

Henslin, J. (1970). "Guilt and Guilt Neutralization: Response and Adjustment to Suicide." In J. Douglas (ed.), *Deviance and Respectability*, 192–228. New York: Basic Books.

Herzog, H. (1990). *"The Movement is My Life": The Psychology of Animal Rights Activism*. Paper presented at the meeting of the Animal Behavior Society, Binghamton, New York.

Herzog H. A., N. S. Betchart, and R. B. Pittman (1991). "Gender, Sex Role Orientation, and Attitudes toward Animals." *Anthrozoös*, *4*, 184–191.

Hewitt, J., and R. Stokes (1975). "Disclaimers." *American Sociological Review*, *40*, 1–11.

Hewitt, S. (1990). "The Treatment of Sexually Abused Preschool Boys." In M. Hunter (ed). *The Sexually Abused Male: Application of Treatment Strategies*, Vol. 2, 225–248. Lexington, Mass.: Lexington Books.

Hiatt, L. R. (ed.) (1978). *Australian Aboriginal Concepts*. Canberra: Australian Institute for Aboriginal Studies and New Jersey: Humanities Press.

Hibbert, C., (ed.) (1984). *Queen Victoria in Her Letters and Journals*. London: John Murray.

Hickey, E. W. (1991). *Serial Murderers and Their Victims*. Belmont, Calif.: Wadsworth.

Hickrod, L. J. H., and R. L. Schmitt (1982). "A Naturalistic Study of Interaction and Frame: The Pet as 'Family Member.' " *Urban Life*, *11*, 55–77.

Hiller, E. T. (1933). *Principles of Sociology*. New York: Harper.

Hills, A. M. (1989). "The Relationship between Thing–Person Orientation and the Perception of Animals." *Anthrozoös*, *3*, 100–110.

———. (1993). "The Motivational Bases of Attitudes toward Animals." *Society and Animals*, *1*, 111–128.

Hinde, R. (1966). *Animal Behavior*. New York: McGraw-Hill.

Hindman, J. L. (1992). *Juvenile Culpability Assessment* (2nd Revision). Ontario, Ore.: Alexandria Associates.

———. (n.d.). *Adult and Juvenile Data Collection Form*. Ontario, Ore.: Alexandria Associates.

Hingley, A. T., and L. Ruggeri (1998). "Alzheimer's." *FDA Consumer*, *32*, *3*, 26–31.

Hinman, Robert B., and Robert B. Harris (1939, 1942). *The Story of Meat*. Chicago: Swift and Co.

Hirschman, E. C. (1994). "Consumers and Their Animal Companions." *Journal of Consumer Research*, *20*, 616–632.

Hobsbawm, E., and T. Ranger (eds.) (1983). *The Invention of Tradition*. Cambridge: Cambridge University Press.

Holcomb, R., R. Williams, and P. Richards (1985). "The Elements of Attachment: Relationship Maintenance and Intimacy." *Journal of the Delta Society*, *2*, *1*, 28–34.

Holmes, R. M., and J. De Burger (1988). *Serial Murder*. Newbury Park, Calif.: Sage.

Holmes, R. M., and S. T. Holmes (1996). *Profiling Violent Crimes*. Thousand Oaks, Calif.: Sage.

Hooper, F. (1976). *The Military Horse: The Equestrian Warrior through the Ages*. New York: Barnes.

Horowitz, I. L. (1964). *The New Sociology: Essays in Social Science and Social Theory in Honor of C. Wright Mills*. New York: Oxford University Press.

Hughes, H. C., and C. M. Lang (1983). "Control of Pain in Dogs and Cats." In R. L. Kitchell *et al.* (eds.). *Animal Pain: Perception and Alleviation*, 207–216. Bethesda, Md.: American Physiological Society.

Hughes, H. M. (1988). "Psychological and Behavioral Correlates of Family Violence in Child Witnesses and Victims." *American Journal of Orthopsychiatry*, *58*, 77–90.

Hundley, J. (1991). "Pet Project: The Use of Pet Facilitated Therapy among the Chronically Mentally Ill." *Journal of Psychosocial Nursing*, *29*, *6*, 23–26.

Hunscher, H., and and M. Huyck (1944). "Nutrition." In Dameron, Kenneth (ed.), *Consumer Problems in Wartime*. New York and London: McGraw-Hill.

Hunt, S. J., L. A. Hart, and R. Gomulkiewicz (1992). "The Role of Small Animals in Social Interactions between Strangers." *Journal of Social Psychology*, *132*, *2*, 245–256.

Hunter, M. (1990). *Abused Boys: The Neglected Victims of Sexual Abuse*. New York: Fawcett Columbine.

Hutton, J. S. (1983). "Animal Abuse as a Diagnostic Approach in Social Work." In A. H. Katcher and M. Beck (eds.), *New Perspectives on Our Lives With Companion Animals*, 444–447. Philadelphia: University of Pennsylvania Press.

Hyde, K. R., L. Kurdek, and P. Larson (1983). "Relationship between Pet Ownership and Self-Esteem, Social Sensitivity, and Interpersonal Trust." *Psychological Reports*, *42*, 110.

Iggo, A. (1979). "Experimental Study of Pain in Animals Ethical Aspects." In J. J. Bonica, J. C. Liebeskind, and D. G. Albe-Fessard (eds.), *Advances in Pain Research and Therapy*, *3*, 773–778. New York: Raven Press.

Illich, I. (1976). *Medical Nemesis: The Expropriation of Health*. New York: Pantheon Books.

Ingold, T. (1974). "On Reindeer and Men." *Man*, *9*, *4*, 523–538.

———. (1994). "From Trust to Domination: An Alternative History of Human–Animal Relations." In J. Serpell and A. Manning (eds.), *Animals and Human Society*, 1–22. London and New York: Routledge.

Instone, L. (1997). "Denaturing Women: Women, Feminism and the Environment." In K. P. Hughes (ed.), *Contemporary Australian Feminism*. Melbourne: Longman.

"Interdisciplinary Principles and Guidelines for the Use of Animals in Research, Testing and Education." (pamphlet) New York: New York Academy of Sciences. Reprinted in Phillips and Sechzer 1989, 200–234.

Iremonger, F. A. (1948). *William Temple, Archbishop of Canterbury: His Life and Letters*. London and Oxford: Oxford University Press.

Jaffe, P. G., D. A. Wolfe, and S. K. Wilson (1990). *Children of Battered Women*. Newbury Park, Calif.: Sage Publications.

Jager, J. (1983). "Theorizing and Elaboration of Place." In A. Giorgi, A. Barton, and C. Maes (eds.), *Duquesne Studies in Phenomenology*, vol. 4. Pittsburgh: Duquesne University Press.

Jasper, J. M., and D. Nelkin (1992). *The Animal Rights Crusade: The Growth of a Moral Protest*. New York: The Free Press.

Jersild, A. T. (1954). "Emotional Development." In L. Carmichael (ed.), *Manual of Child Psychology*, 2nd ed., 833–917. New York: Wiley.

Jesse, E. (1835). *Gleanings in Natural History: Third and Last Series*, p. vi. London: John Murray.

Johnson, S. B., and W. R. Rule (1991). "Personality Characteristics and Self-Esteem in Pet Owners and Nonowners." *International Journal of Psychology*, *26*, *2*, 241–252.

Jones, G. S. (1984). *Outcast London: A Study in the Relationship between Classes in Victorian Society*. New York: Pantheon.

Jones, E. E., and D. McGillis (1976). "Correspondent Inferences and the Attribution Cube: A Comparative Reappraisal." In J. H. Harvey, W. J. Ickes, and R. F. Kidd (eds.), *New Directions in Attribution Research (Vol. 1)*, 389–420. Hillsdale, N.J.: Erlbaum.

Jonker, F., and P. Jonker-Bakker (1991). "Experiences with Ritualist Child Sexual Abuse: A Case Study from The Netherlands." *Child Abuse and Neglect*, *15*, 191–196.

Jordan, J. W. (1975). "An Ambivalent Relationship: Dog and Human in the Folk Culture of the Rural South." *Appalachian Journal*, *2* (Spring), 238–248.

Joubert, C. E. (1987). "Pet Ownership, Social Interest, and Sociability." *Psychological Reports*, *61*, 401–402.

Jouriles, E. N., C. M. Murphy, and K. D. O'Leary (1989). "Interspousal Aggression, Marital Discord, and Child Problems." *Journal of Consulting and Clinical Psychology*, *57*, 453–455.

Justice, B., R. Justice, and I. A. Kraft. (1974). "Early Warning Signs of Violence: Is a Triad Enough?" *American Journal of Psychiatry*, *131*, 457–459.

Kalechofsky, R. (1991a). *Autobiography of a Revolutionary: Essays on Animal and Human Rights.* Marblehead, Mass.: Micah Publications.

———. (1991b). *Judaism and Animal Rights.* Marblehead, Mass.: Micah Publications.

Kant, I. (1927). "Theory of Ethics," In T. M. Greene (ed.) *Kant's Selections.* New York: Scribner's.

Kapleau, P. (1982). To *Cherish All Life: A Buddhist Case for Becoming Vegetarian.* New York: Harper and Row.

Katcher, A. H. (1981). "Interactions between People and Their Pets: Form and Function." In B. Fogle (ed.), *Interrelations between People and Sets.* Springfield, Ill.: Charles C. Thomas Press.

———. (2000). "The Future of Education and Research on the Animal–Human Bond and Animal Assisted Therapy." In A. H. Fine (ed.), *The Handbook on Animal Assisted Therapy: Theoretical Foundations and Guidelines for Practice,* 461–473. San Diego, Calif.: Academic Press.

Katcher, A. H., and A. M. Beck (eds.). (1983). *New Perspectives on Our Lives with Companion Animals.* Philadelphia: University of Pennsylvania Press.

———. (1987, Winter). "Health and Caring for Living Things." *Anthrozoös, 1, 3* 175–183.

Katcher, A. H., and G. Wilkins (1993). "Dialogue with Animals: Its Nature and Culture." In S. R. Kellert and E. O. Wilson (eds.), *The Biophilia Hypothesis,* 173–197. Washington, D.C.: Island Press.

———. (2000). "The Centaur's Lessons: Therapeutic Education through Care of Animals and Nature Study." In A. H. Fine (ed.), *The Handbook on Animal Assisted Therapy: Theoretical Foundations and Guidelines for Practice,* 153–177. San Diego, Calif.: Academic Press.

Katcher, A. H., E. Friedmann, A. M. Beck, and J. J. Lynch (1983). "Looking, Talking and Blood Pressure: The Physiological Consequences of Interaction with the Living Environment." In A. H. Katcher and A. M. Beck (eds.), *New Perspectives on Our Lives with Companion Animals,* 351–359. Philadelphia: University of Pennsylvania Press.

Katcher, A. H., E. Friedmann, M. Goodman, and L. Goodman (1983). "Men, Women, and Dogs." *California Veterinarian, 2,* 14–16.

Katcher, A. H., H. Segal, and A. M. Beck (1984). "Comparison of Contemplation and Hypnosis for the Reduction of Anxiety and Discomfort during Dental Surgery." *American Journal of Clinical Hypnosis, 27,* 14–21.

Katz, D. (1937). *Animals and Men: Studies in Comparative Psychology.* London: Longmans, Green.

Kazdin, A. E. (1990, June). *Prevention of Conduct Disorder.* Paper prepared for the National Conference on Prevention Research, National Institute of Mental Health, Bethesda, Md.

Kazdin, A. E., and K. Esveldt-Dawson (1986). "The Interview for Antisocial Behavior: Psychometric Characteristics and Concurrent Validity with Child Psychiatric Inpatients. *Journal of Psychopathology and Behavioral Assessment, 8,* 289–303.

Keddie, K. M. (1977). "Pathological Mourning after the Death of a Domestic Pet." *British Journal of Psychiatry, 131,* 21–25.

Keller, Evelyn Fox (Spring 1982). "Feminism and Science." *Signs, 7, 3,* 599.

Kellert, S. R. (1983). "Affective, Cognitive and Evaluative Perceptions of Animals." In I. Altman and J. F. Wohlwill (eds.), *Behavior and the Natural Environment,* 241–267. New York: Plenum Publishing Co.

Kellert, S. R., and A. R. Felthous. (1985) "Childhood Cruelty toward Animals among Criminals and Noncriminals." *Human Relations, 38,* 1113–1129.

Kellert, S. R., and J. K. Berry (1987). "Attitudes, Knowledge, and Behaviors toward Wildlife as Affected by Gender." *Wildlife Society Bulletin, 15,* 363–371.

Kellert, S. R., and E. O. Wilson (eds.). (1993). *The Biophilia Hypothesis.* Washington, D.C.: Island Press.

Kelley, S. J. (1989). "Stress Responses of Children to Sexual Abuse and Ritualistic Abuse in Day Care Centers." *Journal of Interpersonal Violence, 4,* 502–513.

Kheel, M. (1995). "License to Kill: An Ecofeminist Critique of Hunters Discourse." In C. J. Adams and

J. Donovan (eds.), *Animals and Women: Feminist Theoretical Explorations*, 85–125. Durham and London: Duke University Press.

Kidd, A. H., and R. M. Kidd (1980). "Personality Characteristics and Preferences in Pet Ownership." *Psychological Reports*, *46*, 939–949.

———. (1987). "Seeking a Theory of the Human/Companion Animal Bond." *Anthrozoös*, *1*, 140–145.

———. (1989). "Factors in Adults' Attitudes toward Pets." *Psychological Reports*, 65 (3): 903–910.

———. (1990). "Factors in Children's Attitudes toward Pets." *Psychological Reports*, *66*, 775–786.

———. (1994). "Benefits and Liabilities of Pets for the Homeless." *Psychological Reports*, *74*, 715–722.

Kimball, P. (1989). "Liberal/Conservative Voting Records Compared to Interest in Animal Protection Bills." *PsyETA Bulletin*, *9*, *1*, 7–9.

King, Y. (1981). "Feminism and the Revolt of Nature," *Heresies*, *13*, 812–816.

Kipling, R. (1912/1950). *Just So Stories*. Boston: Doubleday.

Kitchell, R. L., H. H. Erickson, E. Carstens, and L. E. Davis (eds.) (1983). *Animal Pain: Perception and Alleviation*. Bethesda, Md.: American Physiological Society. New York Academy of Sciences (NYAS). Ad Hoc Committee on Animal Research.

Klimes-Dougan, B., and J. Kistner (1990). "Physically Abused Preschoolers' Responses to Peers' Distress." *Developmental Psychology*, *26*, 599–602.

Klineberg, O. (1954). *Social Psychology*. Rev. ed. New York: Holt.

Klingbeil, K. S., and V. D. Boyd (1984). "Emergency Room Intervention: Detection, Assessment, and Treatment." In A. R. Roberts (ed.), *Battered Women and Their Families*, 5–32. New York: Springer.

Kolko, D. J., and A. E. Kazdin (1989). "The Children's Firesetting Interview with Psychiatrically Referred and Nonreferred Children." *Journal of Abnormal Child Psychology*, *17*, 609–624.

Kongable, J. G., K. C. Buckwalter, and J. M. Stolley (1989). "The Effects of Pet Therapy on the Social Behavior of Institutionalized Alzheimer's Clients." *Archives of Psychiatric Nursing*, *3*, 191–198.

Kotlowitz, A. (1991). *There Are No Children Here*. New York: Doubleday.

Krafft-Ebing, R. V. (1906). *Psychopathia Sexualis* rev. ed., 1934. Brooklyn, N.Y.: Physicians and Surgeons Book Company.

Kreemer, J. (1956). *De Karbouw, Zijn Betekenis Voor de Volken van de Indonesische Archipel*. 'S-Gravenhage/Bandung: Van Hoeve.

Kruse, C. R. (1999). "Gender, Views of Nature, and Support for Animal Rights." *Society and Animals*, *7*, 179–198.

Kuhse, Helga and Peter Singer (1985). *Should the Baby Live?* Oxford: Oxford University Press.

Lago, D. J., B. Knight, and C. Connell (1983). "Relationship with Companion Animals among the Rural Elderly." In A. H. Katcher and A. M. Beck (eds.), *New Perspectives on Our Lives with Companion Animals*, 328–340. Philadelphia: University of Pennsylvania Press.

Lambton, L. (1985). *Beastly Buildings: The National Trust Book of Architecture for Animals*. London: Jonathan Cape.

Landon, E. L., and S. K. Banks (1977). "Relative Efficiency and Bias of Plus-One Sampling." *Journal of Marketing Research*, *14*, 294–299.

Lane, C. (1900). *All about Dogs: A Book for Doggy People*. London: John Lane.

Lanning, K. V. (1989a). *Satanic, Occult, Ritualistic Crime: A Law Enforcement Perspective*.

———. (1989b). *Child Sex Rings: A Behavioral Analysis*. Arlington, Va.: National Center for Missing and Exploited Children, December.

———. (1991). "Ritual Abuse: A Law Enforcement View or Perspective." *Child Abuse and Neglect*, *15*, 171–173.

Lansbury, C. (1985). "Gynaecology, Pornography, and the Antivivisection Movement." *Victorian Studies*, *28*, *3*, 413–437.

————. (1985). *The Old Brown Dog: Woman, Workers, and Vivisection in Edwardian England*. Madison: University of Wisconsin Press.

LaRose, L., and D. A. Wolfe (1987). "Psychological Characteristics of Parents Who Abuse or Neglect Their Children." In B. B. Lahey and A. E. Kazdin (eds.), *Advances in Clinical Child Psychology* (Vol. 10), 55–97. New York: Plenum Press.

Lawrence, E. (1993). "The Sacred Bee, the Filthy Pig, and the Bat out of Hell: Animal Symbolism as Cognitive Biophilia." In S. R. Kellert and E. O. Wilson (eds.), *The Biophilia Hypothesis*. Washington, D.C.: Island Press.

Leach, Maria (1961). *God Had a Dog: Folklore of the Dog*. New Brunswick: Rutgers University Press.

Leakey, R. E., and R. Lewin (1978). *People of the Lake: Mankind and Its Beginnings*. New York: Doubleday and Co.; New York: Avon Books, 210–211.

Leavitt, Emily S. (1968). *Animals and Their Legal Rights*. Washington, D.C.: Animal Welfare Institute.

Leghorn, Lisa, and Mary Roodkowsky (1977). *Who Really Starves? Women and World Hunger*. New York: Friendship Press.

Lee, A. M. (1978). *Sociology for Whom?* New York: Oxford University Press.

Lee, R. B. (1893–4). *A History and Description of the Modern Dogs of Great Britain and Ireland 3*, 243. London: Horace Cox.

Leeds, A. (1965). "Reindeer Herding and Chukchi Social Institutions." In A. Leeds and A. P. Vayda (eds.), *Man, Culture and Animals: The Role of Animals in Human Ecological Adjustments*, 87–125. Washington, D.C.: The American Association for the Advancement of Science.

Le Guin, U. (1987). *Buffalo Gals and Other Animal Presences*. Santa Barbara, Calif.: Capra.

Leigh, D. (1966). "The Psychology of the Pet Owner." *Journal of Small Animal Practice*, 7, 517–521.

Lenior, L. (1986). *Grief Experiences Following Companion Animal Death*. Unpublished master's thesis, University of Alaska, Anchorage.

Lenney, E. (1979). "Androgyny: Some Audacious Assertions toward Its Coming of Age." *Sex Roles*, 5, 703–719.

Letourneau, C. (1981). "Empathy and Stress: How They Affect Parental Aggression." *Social Work*, 26, 383–389.

Levin, M. (July /August 1977). "Animal Rights Evaluated." *Humanist*, 37, 14–15.

Levinson, B. M. (1964). "Pets: A Special Technique in Psychotherapy." *Mental Hygiene*, 48, 243–248.

————. (1969). *Pet-oriented Child Psychotherapy*. Springfield, Ill.: Charles C. Thomas Press.

————. (1972a). *Pets and Human Development*. Springfield, Ill.: Thomas.

————. (1972b). "The Dog as a 'Co-therapist.' " *Mental Hygiene*, 46 (January), 59–65.

Levinson, D. (1989). *Family Violence in Cross-Cultural Perspective*. Newbury Park, Calif.: Sage Publications.

Levi-Strauss, C. (1962). *Totemism* (translated by R. Needham). London: Menlin.

_____. (1965). *Le totémisme aujourd'hui*. Paris: Presses universitaires de France.

————. (1966). *The Savage Mind*. Chicago: University of Chicago Press.

Lew, M. (1988). *Victims No Longer*. New York: Harper and Row.

Lewis, D. O., S. S. Shanok, M. Grant, and E. Ritvo (1983). "Homicidally Aggressive Young Children: Neuropsychiatric and Experiential Correlates." *American Journal of Psychiatry*, 140, 148–53.

Lewis, M. M. (1936). *Infant Speech*. New York: Harcourt, Brace.

Lichtenberg, G. C. (1764–1799). *Aphorisms*. Cited in John Gross, *The Oxford Book of Aphorisms*, New York: Oxford University Press, 1987.

Linden, E. (1976). *Apes, Men and Language*. New York: Penguin.

_____. (1999). *The Parrot's Lament: and Other True Tales of Animal Intrigue, Intelligence, and Ingenuity*. New York: Dutton.

Lindesmith, A. R., and A. L. Strauss (1956). *Social Psychology*. Rev. ed. New York: Dryden.

Locke J. (1699). *Some Thoughts Concerning Education*. Reprinted 1964, Garforth F. W. (ed.). Heinemann: London.

Lockwood, R. (1985). "The Role of Animals in Our Perception of People." *Veterinary Clinics of North America: Small Animal Practice*, 15, 2, 377–385.

Lockwood R. (1994). "The Psychology of Animal Collectors." *Trends*, 9, 18–21.

Lockwood, R., and F. R. Ascione (eds.) (1998). *Cruelty to Animals and Interpersonal Ciolence: Readings in Research and Application*. West Lafayette, Ind.: Purdue University Press.

Lockwood R., and B. Cassidy (1988). "Killing with Kindness." *Humane Society News* Summer, 1–5.

Lockwood, R., and A. Church (1998). "Deadly Serious: An FBI Perspective on Animal Cruelty." In R. Lockwood and F. A. Ascione (eds.), *Cruelty to Animals and Interpersonal Violence*, 241–246. West Lafayette, Ind.: Purdue University Press.

Lockwood, R., and G. R. Hodge (1986, Summer). "The Tangled Web of Animal Abuse: The Links between Cruelty to Animals and Human Violence." *The Humane Society News*. Also in R. Lockwood and F. A. Ascione (eds.), *Cruelty to Animals and Interpersonal Violence*, 77–82. West Lafayette, Ind.: Purdue University Press.

Loeber, R. (1988). "Natural Histories of Conduct Problems, Delinquency, and Associated Substance Abuse." In B. B. Lahey and A. E. Kazdin (eds.), *Advances in Clinical Child Psychology* (Vol. 11), 73–124. New York: Plenum Press.

Lopez, Barry Holstun (1978). *Of Wolves and Men*. New York: Scribner.

Lorenz, L. (1954). *Man Meets Dog*. New York: Penguin.

Lubow, Robert E. (1977). *The War Animals*. New York: Doubleday.

Lynch, J. J. (1977). *The Broken Heart: The Medical Consequences of Loneliness*. New York: Basic Books.

———. (2000). *A Cry Unheard: New Insights into the Medical Consequences of Loneliness*. Baltimore: Bancroft.

Lynch, J. J., and J. F. McCarthy (1969). "Social Responding in Dogs: Heart Rate Changes to a Person." *Psychophysiology*, 5, 4, 389–393.

Lynch, J. J., G. F. Fregin, J. B. Mackie, and R. R. Monroe, Jr. (1974). "Heart Rate Changes in the Horse to Human Contact." *Psychophysiology*, 11, 4, 472–478.

Lynge, F. (1992). *Arctic Wars, Animal Rights, Endangered Peoples*. Hanover, N.H.: University Press of New England.

Lyons, J. (1987). *Ecology of the Body*. Durham, N.C.: Duke University Press.

Lyons, N. P. 1983. "Two Perspectives: On Self, Relationships, and Morality." *Harvard Educational Review*, 53, 125–145.

Lytton, J. N. (1911). *Toy Dogs and Their Ancestors, Including the History and Management of Toy Spaniels, Pekingese, Japanese and Pomeranians*. London: Duckworth.

Maccoby, H. (1982). *The Sacred Executioner*. London: Thames and Hudson.

MacCulloch, J. (1993). "Creatures of Culture: The Animal Protection and Preservation Movements in Sydney 1880–1930." University of Sydney: Unpublished thesis.

Macdonald A. (1981). "The Pet Dog in the Home: A Study of Interactions." In Fogel B. (ed.) *Interrelations between People and Pets*, 195–206. Charles C. Thomas: Illinois.

MacDonald, J. M. (1964). "The Threat to Kill." *American Journal of Psychiatry*, 8, 125–130.

MacKinnon, C. A. (Winter 1985). "Pornography, Civil Rights, and Speech," *Harvard Civil Rights Civil Liberties Law Review*, 20, 1, 4.

Maddock, K. (1982). *The Australian Aborigines, A Portrait of Their Society*. Ringwood: Penguin Australia.

Magid, K., and C.A. McKelvey (1987). *High Risk: Children Without a Conscience*. New York: Bantam Books.

Magitti P. (1990). "Dog and Cat 'Collectors'." *The Animals' Agenda*, Jan./Feb., 20–24.

Marshall, W. E. (1989). *A Phrenologist Amongst the Todas or, The Study of a Primitive Tribe in South India*. Gurgaon, Haryana: Vipin Jain for Vintage Books. (Original work published 1873).

Martinez, R. L., and A. H. Kidd (1980). "Two Personality Characteristics in Adult Pet Owners and Nonowners." *Psychological Reports*, *47*, 318.

Marx M. B., L. Stallones, T. F. Garity, and T. P. Johnson (1988). "Demographics of Pet Ownership among US Adults 21 to 64 Years of Age." *Anthrozoös*, *2*, 33–37.

Masri, Al-Hafiz B. A. (1987). *Islamic Concern for Animals*. Petersfield: The Athene Trust.

Masson, J., and S. McCarthy (1995). *When Elephants Weep*. New York: Delta.

McAdam, D. (1992, Summer). "Gender as a Mediator of the Activist Experience: The Case of Freedom." *American Journal of Sociology*, *97*, 1211–1240.

McGraw, K. (1991). "An Exploratory Test of the Effects of Political Accounts." *American Political Science Review*, *85*, 1133–1157.

McNicholas, J., and G. M. Collis (1995). "The End of a Relationship: Coping with Pet Loss." In I. Robinson (Ed.), *The Waltham book of Human–Animal Interaction: Benefits and Responsibilities of Pet Ownership*, 127–143. Oxford: Pergamon.

McSpadden, Joseph Walker (ed.) (1972). *Famous Dogs in Fiction*. Freeport, N.Y.: Books for Libraries Press.

Mead, G. H. (1934/1964). *George Herbert Mead on Social Psychology*. Anselm Strauss (ed.). Chicago: University of Chicago Press.

———. (1934). *Mind, Self, and Society*. Chicago: University of Chicago Press.

Mead, M. (1964). "Cultural Factors in the Cause and Prevention of Pathological Homicide." *Bulletin of the Menninger Clinic*, *28*, 11–22.

Mechling, Jay. (1989). " 'Banana Cannon' and Other Folk Traditions between Human and Nonhuman Animals." *Western Folklore*, *48*, 312–323.

Mehrabian A., and N. Epstein (1972). "A Measure of Emotional Empathy." *Journal of Personality*, *40*, 525–543.

Melson G. F. (1989). "Dimensions of the Child–Pet Relationship and How to Measure Them." Paper presented at *Monaco '89: Fifth International Conference on the Relationship between Humans and Animals*. November 1989.

———. (1990). "Studying Children's Attachment to Their Pets: A Conceptual and Methodological Review." *Anthrozoös*, *3*, 91–99.

———. (2001). *Why the Wild Things Are: Animals in the Lives of Children*. Cambridge, Mass.: Harvard University Press.

Melson, G. F., and A. Fogel (1989). "Children's Ideas about Animal Young and Their Care: A Reassessment of Gender Differences in the Development of Nurturance." *Anthrozoös*, 2, 265–273.

Melson, G. F., R. L. Schwarz, and A. M. Beck (1997). "Importance of Companion Animals in Children's Lives: Implications for Veterinary Practice." *Journal of the American Veterinary Medical Association*, *211*, *12*, 1512–1518.

Menninger, K. A. (1951). "Totemic Aspects of Contemporary Attitudes toward Animals." In G. B. Wilbur and W. Muernsterberger (eds.), *Psychoanalysis and Culture*, 42–74. New York: International Universities Press, Inc.

Merchant, C. (1980). *The Death of Nature: Women, Ecology. and the Scientific Revolution*. New York: Harper and Row.

Merleau-Ponty, M. (1962). *Phenomenology of Perception*. New York: Humanities Press.

———. (1963). *The Structure of Behavior*. Boston: Beacon Press.

Messent, P. R. (1983). "Social Facilitation of Contact with Other People by Pet Dogs." In A. H. Katcher and A. M. Beck (eds.), *New Perspectives on Our Lives with Companion Animals*, 37–46. Philadelphia: University of Pennsylvania Press.

Mewshaw, M. (1980). *Life for Death*. Garden City, N.Y.: Doubleday.

Midgley, M. (1984). *Animals and Why They Matter*. Athens, Ga.: University of Georgia Press.

———. (1985). "Persons and Non-Persons." In P. Singer (ed.), *In Defense of Animals*. New York: Basil Blackwell.

Miller, A. (1990). *For Your Own Good*. New York: Noonday Press.

Miller, M., and D. Lago (1990). "Observed Petowner In-Home Interactions: Species Differences and Association with the Pet Relationship Scale." *Anthrozoös*, *4*, *1*, 49–54.

———. (1990). "The Well Being of Older Women: The Importance of Pet and Human Relations." *Anthrozoös*, *3*, 245–252.

Mills, C. W. (1940). "Situated Actions and Vocabularies of Motives." *American Sociological Review*, *5*, 904–913.

Mitchell, R., and E. Edmonson (1999). "Functions of Repetitive Talk to Dogs during Play: Control, Conversation, or Planning?" *Society and Animals*, *7*, 55–81.

Mitchell, R., and N. Thompson (1990). "The Effects of Familiarity on Dog–Human Play." *Anthrozoös*, *4*, 24–43.

———. (1991). "Projects, Routines, and Enticements in Dog–Human Play." In P. P. G. Bateson and P. Klopfer (eds.), *Perspectives in Ethology: Human Understanding and Animal Awareness*, 189–216. New York: Plenum.

Mizell, T. A., and H. Robboy (1979). "Soring in the Tennessee Walking Horse Industry." Paper read at the annual meeting of the Southern Sociological Society.

Moberg, G. P. (ed.) (1985). *Animal Stress*. Bethesda, Md.: American Physiological Society.

Montagu, A. (ed.). (1978). *Learning Non-Aggression: The Experience of Non-Literate Societies*. New York: Oxford University.

Montaigne, M. E. de (1580–8a). "Apology for Raimond Sebond," *Essays*. Cited in John Gross, *The Oxford Book of Aphorisms*, New York: Oxford University Press, 1987.

———. (1580–8b). "Apology for Raimond Sebond." In D. M. Frame (trans.), *The Complete Essays of Montaigne*, Garden City: Anchor Books, 1960.

Morgan, M. (1980). *Marabel Morgan's Handbook for Kitchen Survival: The Total Woman Cookbook*. New Jersey: Fleming H. Revell Co.

Morton, J. (1991). "Black and White Totemism: Conservation, Animal Symbolism, and Human Identification in Australia." In *Australian People and Animals in Today's Dreamtime: The Role of Comparative Psychology in the Management of Natural Resources*, 21–51, ed. D. B. Croft. New York: Praeger.

Moulton, C. (1976). "Snake Handlers Appealing State Ban." *Lubbock Avalanche Journal* (January 18).

Moulton, C., M. Kaufmann, and J. Filip (1991). *Report on the Summit on Violence toward Children and Animals*. Englewood, Colo.: American Humane Association.

Mountford, C. M. P. (1981). *Aboriginal Conception Beliefs*. Melbourne: Hyland House.

Mueller, E., and N. Silverman. (1989). "Peer Relations in Maltreated Children." In D. Cicchetti and V. Carlson (eds.), *Child Maltreatment*, 529–578. New York: Cambridge University Press.

Mugford, R. A., and J. G. M'Comisky (1975). "Some Recent Work on the Psychotherapeutic Value of Cage Birds with Old People." In R. S. Anderson (ed.), *Pet Animals and Society*. London: Baillière Tindall.

Mullen S. (1991). "Animal Collectors Unlimited." *Advocate*, Summer, 18–21.

Munro, L. P. (1997). "Animal Rights/Welfare Down Under." *International Society for Anthrozoology*, *ISAZ Newsletter*, *14*, 15–19.

———. (1999a). "Contesting Moral Capital in Campaigns against Animal Liberation." *Society and Animals*, *1*, *7*, 35–53.

———. (1999b) "From Vilification to Accommodation: Making a Common Cause Movement," *Cambridge Quarterly of Healthcare Ethics*, *8*, 46–57.

———. (2000). *Compassionate Beasts: The Quest for Animal Rights*. New York: Praeger.

Myers, A. M., and G. Gonda (1982). "Utility of the Masculinity–Femininity Construct: Comparison of Traditional and Androgyny Approaches." *Journal of Personality and Social Psychology*, *43*, 514–523.

Myers, G. (1998). *Children and Animals: Social Development and Our Connection to Other Species*. Boulder, Colo.: Westview.

Nagel, T. (1974). "What Is It to Be a Bat?" *Philosophical Review*, *83*, 435–450.

Nash, J. (1989). "What's In a Face? The Social Character of the English Bulldog." *Qualitative Sociology*, *12*, 357–370.

Nash, R. (1967). *The Wilderness and the American Mind*. New Haven/London: Yale University Press.

Nassar, R., J. Talboy, and C. Moulton (1992). *Animal Shelter Reporting Study: 1990*. Englewood: American Humane Association.

National Advisory Mental Health Council (1990). *National Plan for Research on Child and Adolescent Mental Disorders*. A report requested by the U.S. Congress, DHHS Publication No. (ADM)90-1683. Rockville, MD: National Institute of Mental Health.

National Institutes of Health (NIH). (1988). *Health Benefits of Pets: Summary of Working Group*. Washington, D.C.: U.S. Department of Health and Human Services.

New York Times (1973). 15 April, 38.

New York Times (1977). "Three Concerns Accused of Illegal Traffic in Alligator Skins." (December 11).

New York Times (1981). Editorial, 17 August.

New York Times. (2000). "Obesity Rate Rising Fastest in the South." October 27, A21.

New York Times News Service (1974). "Bird Expert's Fine Causes Stir." *Roanoke Times and World News* (July 16).

Newsome, A. E. (1980). "The Eco-Mythology of the Red Kangaroo in Central Australia." *Mankind 12*, *4*, 327–333.

Newsweek (1988). "The Wisdom of Animals," *Newsweek*, 23 May.

Nibert, D. (1996). Minority Group as Sociological Euphemism. *Race, Gender and Class*, 3, 129–136.

———. (2002). *Animal Rights/Human Rights: Entanglements of Oppression and Liberation*. Lanham, MD: Rowman and Littlefield.

Nieburg, H., and A. Fischer (1982). *Pet Loss*. New York: Harper and Row.

Nielson, J. A., and L. A. Delude (1989). "Behavior of Young Children in the Presence of Different Kinds of Animals." *Anthrozoös*, *3*, 119–129.

Niemeijer, N. (1994). *Gif(t) voor de gast, een onderzoek naar mens-dier relaties in Tamil Nadu, Zuid India* (research report Cultural Anthropology). Utrecht: Rijksuniversiteit Utrecht.

NIH Technology Assessment Workshop. (Publication 1988-216-107). Bethesda, Md.: U.S. Government Printing Office.

Noel, D. (1968). "The Theory of Ethnic Stratification." *Social Problems*, *16*, 157–172.

Norris, P. A., K. J. Shinew, G. Chick, and A. M. Beck (1999). "Retirement, Life Satisfaction, and Leisure Services: The Pet Connection." *Journal of Park and Recreation Administration*, *17*, 2, 65–83.

Noske, B. (1989). *Humans and Other Animals*. London: Pluto Press.

———. (1990). "The Question of Anthropocentrism in Anthropology." *Focaal, (Netherlands) Journal for Anthropology* (theme issue in English: "Animal Kingdom and Human Empire"), *13*, 66–84.

———. (1993). "Het andere racisme." *Filosofie Magazine* (Netherlands) *2*, *3*, 30–32.

———. (1993). "The Animal Question in Anthropology." *Society and Animals: Social Scientific Studies of the Human Experience of Other Animals*, *1*, 185–187.

———. (1994). Animals and the Green Movement: A View from The Netherlands." *Capitalism, Nature, Socialism: A Journal of Socialist Ecology 5*, *20*, 85–94.

———. (1997). *Beyond Boundaries: Humans and Animals*. Montreal/New York: Black Rose Books.

Odendaal, J. S. J., and S. M. C. Lehmann (2000). "The Role of Phenylethylamine during Positive Human–Dog Interaction." *ACTA Veterinaria Brno*, *69*, 183–188.

Offord, D. R., M. H. Boyle, and Y. A. Racine (1991). "The Epidemiology of Antisocial Behavior in Childhood and Adolescence." In D. J. Pepler and K. H. Rubin (eds.), *The Development and Treatment of Childhood Aggression* (eds.). Hillsdale, N.J.: Lawrence Erlbaum Associates.

O'Laughlin, Bridget (1974). "Mediation of Contradiction: Why Mbum Women Do Not Eat Chicken."

In Michelle Zimbalist Rosaldo and Louise Lamphere (eds.). *Woman, Culture, and Society*. Stanford: Stanford University Press.

Oliver, P. (1983). "The Mobilization of Paid and Volunteer Activists in the Neighborhood Movement." *Research in Social Movements: Conflict and Change*, *5*, 133–170.

Ollila, L., C. Bullen, and B. Collis (1989). "Gender-related Preference for the Choice of Particular Animals as Writing Topics in Grade 1." *Journal of Research and Development in Education*, *22*, 37–41.

Orgent, E. G. (1973). "The Sored Horse and the Horse Protection Act of 1970." *Journal of the American Medical Association*, *163* (November), 1097–1099.

Ory, M. G., and E. L. Goldberg (1983). "Pet Possession and Life Satisfaction in Elderly Women." In A. H. Katcher and A. M. Beck (eds.), *New Perspectives on Our Lives with Companion Animals*, 303–317. Philadelphia: University of Pennsylvania Press.

Oskamp S. (1977). *Attitudes and Opinions*. Prentice Hall: New Jersey.

Oxfam America (2002). "Oxfam Dumps Sugar at WSSD." *Oxfam Exchange*, Washington D.C., 2, 3.

Paden-Levy, D. (1985). "Relationship of Extraversion, Neuroticism, Alienation, and Divorce Incidence with Pet Ownership." *Psychological Reports*, *57*, 868–870.

Palmer, C. E. (1975). "Camouflage-Collar Crime and Green-Coat Cops: A Study of Wildlife Law Enforcement." Paper read at the annual meeting of the Mid-South Sociological Association.

Passmore, J. (1975). "The Treatment of Animals." *Journal of the History of Ideas 36*, 195–218.

Patronek, G. J. (1995). *Development and Evaluation of an Ecological Model for Describing the Pet Dog Population in the United States and an Epidemiologic Study of Risk Factors for an Owner's Failure to Retain Their Dog as a Pet in the Home*. Unpublished doctoral dissertation, Purdue University, Indiana.

———. (1999). "Hoarding of Animals: An Under-Recognized Public Health Problem in a Difficult-to-study Population." *Public Health Reports*, *114*, 81–87.

Patronek, G. J., and A. N. Rowan (1995). "Determining Dog and Cat Numbers and Population Dynamics." *Anthrozoös*, *8*, 199–205.

Patronek, G. J., and L. T. Glickman (1993). "Pet Ownership Protects the Risks and Consequences of Coronary Heart Disease." *Medical Hypotheses*, *40*, 245–249.

Patronek, G. J., L. T. Glickman, and M. R. Moyer (1995). "Population Dynamics and the Risk of Euthanasia for Dogs in an Animal Shelter." *Anthrozoös*, *8*, 31–43.

Patterson, G. R., B. D. DeBaryshe, and E. Ramsey (1989). "A Developmental Perspective on Antisocial Behavior." *American Psychologist*, *44*, 329–335.

Paul E. S. (1992). *Pets in Childhood*. PhD thesis, University of Cambridge.

———. (1995). "Us and Them: Scientists' and Animal Rights Campaigners' Views of the Animal Experimentation Debate." *Society and Animals*, *3*, 1–21

Paulson, R. (1979). "The English Dog." In *Polite Art in the Age of Hogarth and Fielding*, 54–56. Notre Dame: University of Notre Dame Press.

Perelle, I. B., and D. A. Granville (1993). "Assessment of the Effectiveness of a Pet Facilitated Therapy Program in a Nursing Home Setting." *Society and Animals*, *1*, *1*, 91–100.

Pernick, M. S. (1985). *A Calculus of Suffering: Pain, Professionalism, and Anesthesia in Nineteenth Century America*. New York: Columbia University Press.

Perry, C., and G. E. Jones (1982). "On Animal Rights," *International Journal of Applied Philosophy*, *1*, 39–57.

Peterson, G. (1990). "Diagnosis of Child Multiple Personality Disorder." *Dissociation*, *3*, 3–9.

———. (1991). "Children Coping with Trauma: Diagnosis of 'Dissociation Identity Disorder.' " *Dissociation*, *4*, 152–164.

Pharr, S. (1988). *Homophobia: A Weapon of Sexism*. Little Rock: Chardon Press.

Phillips, M. T. (1991). "Constructing Laboratory Animals: An Ethnographic Study in the Study of Science." Unpublished thesis: New York University.

———. (1994). "Proper Names and the Social Construction of Biography: The Negative Case of Laboratory Animals." *Qualitative Sociology*, *17*, 119–142.

Phillips, M. T., and J. A. Sechzer (1989). *Animal Research and Ethical Conflict*. New York: Springer-Verlag.

Phillips, P. (1986). *Ten Common Arguments against Animal Rights Refuted*. First Edition, Seattle: People For Animals Press.

Pifer, L. (1996). "Exploring the Gender Gap in Young Adults' Attitudes about Animal Research." *Society and Animals*, *4*, 37–52.

Pizzey, E. (1974). *Scream Quietly or the Neighbours Will Hear*. Harmondsworth, England: Penguin Books, 35.

Plous, S. (1993). "Psychological Mechanisms in the Human Use of Animals." *Journal of Social Issues*, *49*, 11–52.

Podberscek, A. L., and J. A. Serpell (1997). "Aggressive Behaviour in English Cocker Spaniels and the Personality of Their Owners." *The Veterinary Record*, *141*, 73–76.

Polanyi, M. (1967). *The Tacit Dimension*. New York: Doubleday.

Polkinghorne, D. (1988). *Narrative Knowing and the Human Sciences*. Albany: State University of New York Press.

Pollner, M., and L. McDonaid-Wickler (1985). "The Social Construction of Unreality: A Case of a Family's Attribution of Competence to a Severely Retarded Child." *Family Process*, *24*, 241–254.

Poresky, R. H. (1989). "Analyzing Human–Animals Relationship Measures." *Anthrozoös*, *2*, 236–244.

———. (1990). "The Young Children's Empathy Measure: Reliability, Validity and Effects of Companion Animal Bonding." *Psychological Reports*, *66*, 931–936.

Poresky R. H., and C. Hendrix (1988). "Developmental Benefits of Pets for Young Children." Paper presented at the Delta Society Seventh annual conference *People, Animals and the Environment— Exploring Our Interdependence*.

———. (1990). "Differential Effects of Pet Presence and Petbonding on Young Children." *Psychological Reports*, *67*, 51–54.

Poresky R. H., C. Hendrix, J. E. Mosier, and M. L. Samuelson (1987). "The Companion Animal Bonding Scale: Internal Reliability and Construct Validity." *Psychological Reports*, *60*, 743–746.

———. (1988). "Young Children's Companion Animal Bonding and Adults' Pet Attitudes: A Retrospective Study." *Psychological Reports*, *62*, 419–425.

Porter, V. (1989). *Faithful Companions: The Alliance of Man and Dog*. London: Methuen.

Power, T. (2000). *Play and Exploration in Children and Animals*. Mahwah N.J.: Lawrence Erlbaum Associates.

Price, J. M., and K. A. Dodge (1989). "Peers' Contributions to Children's Social Maladjustment." In T. J. Berndt and G. W. Ladd (eds.), *Peer Relationships in Child Development*, 341–370. New York: Wiley.

Prus, R. (1996). *Symbolic Interaction and Ethnographic Research: Intersubjectivity and the Study of Human Lived Experiences*. Albany, N.Y.: State University of New York Press.

Putnam, F. W. (1991). "The Satanic Ritual Abuse Controversy." *Child Abuse and Neglect*, *15*, 175–179.

Pybus-Sellon, J. S. (1885). "Bulldogs." *Kennel Gazette 5*, 144.

Quackenbush, J. (1984). "Pet Bereavement in Older Owners. In R. K. Anderson, B. L. Hart, and L. A. Hart (eds.), *The Pet Connection: Its Influence on Our Health and Quality of Life*, 292–299. Minneapolis: University of Minnesota. (Center to Study Human–Animal Relationships and Environments).

———. (1985). "The Death of a Pet: How It Can Affect Owners." In J. Quackenbush and V. Voith (eds.), *The Veterinary Clinics of North America: Small Animal Practice: Symposium on the Human–Companion Animal Bond*, 15, 2, 395–401. Philadelphia: W. B. Saunders.

Quackenbush, J., and L. Glickman (1983). "Social Work Services for Bereaved Pet Owners: A Retrospective Case Study in a Veterinary Teaching Hospital." In A. H. Katcher and A. M. Beck (eds.), *New Perspectives on Our Lives with Companion Animals*, 377–389. Philadelphia: University of Pennsylvania Press.

Quantico, V. A: "National Center for the Analysis of Violent Crime," FBI Academy, October.

Ramanaiah, N. J., and H. J. Martin (1984). "Convergent and Divergent Validity of Selected Masculinity and Femininity Scales." *Sex Roles, 10*, 493–504.

Randal, J., and N. Boustany (1990). "Children of War in Lebanon." In C. Moorehead (ed.), *Betrayal: A Report on Violence toward Children in Today's World*, 59–82. New York: Doubleday.

Random House Dictionary of the English Language. (1987). New York: Random House.

Rappaport, R. A. (1967). *Pigs for the Ancestors.* New Haven: Yale University Press.

Rasing, W. C. E. (1988). *On Hunting for Survival and the Survival of Hunting: Ethics and Enemies of Inuit Hunters in the Canadian Pacific.* Paper given for conference "Man and the Animal World", Berg en Dal, The Netherlands.

Rasmussen S. A., and J. L. Eisen (1992). "The Epidemiology and Clinical Features of Obsessive Compulsive Disorder." *Psychiatr Clinic North Am, 15*, 743–758.

Rawls, J. (1972). *A Theory of Justice.* Cambridge: Harvard University Press, Belknap Press.

Redl, F., and D. Wineman (1951). *Children Who Hate.* New York: The Free Press.

Reeves, Maud Pember (1913/1979). *Round About a Pound a Week.* G. Bell and Sons; London: Virago Press.

Regan, T. (1982). *All That Dwell There: Animal Rights and Environmental Ethics.* Berkeley: University of California Press.

———. (1983). *The Case for Animal Rights.* Berkeley: California University Press.

———. (1985). "The Case for Animal Rights." In P. Singer (ed.), *In Defense of Animals.* New York: Basil Blackwell.

Regan, T., and P. Singer (eds.) (1976). *Animal Rights and Human Obligations.* Englewood Cliffs: Prentice-Hall.

Reid, K. S. (1978). "Rodeo Rituals: A Look at the Superstitions of the Rodeo." Paper read at the annual meeting of the Mid-South Sociological Association.

Reiss, Jr., A. J., and J. A. Roth (eds.) (1993). *Understanding and Preventing Violence.* Washington, D.C.: National Academy Press.

Renzetti, C. M. (1992). *Violent Betrayal: Partner Abuse in Lesbian Relationships.* Newbury Park, Calif.: Sage Publications.

Ressler, R. K., A. W. Burgess, and J. E. Douglas (1988). *Sexual Homicide: Patterns and Motives.* Lexington, Mass.: Lexington Books.

Ressler, R. K., A. W. Burgess, C. R. Hartman, J. E. Douglas, and A. McCormack (1986). "Murderers Who Rape and Mutilate." *Journal of Interpersonal Violence, 1*, 273–287. Also in R. Lockwood and F. R. Ascione (eds.), *Cruelty to Animals and Interpersonal Violence*, 179–193. West Lafayette, Ind.: Purdue University Press.

Richards, R. (1990). *Consensus Mobilization through Ideology, Networks and Grievances: A Study of the Contemporary Animal Rights Involvement.* Doctoral dissertation. Printed by University Microfilms International in 1992, Ann Arbor.

Richards, S. (1986). "Drawing the Life-blood of Physiology: Vivisection and the Physiologist's Dilemma, 1870–1900." *Annals of Science 43*, 27–56.

———. (1987). "Vicarious Suffering, Necessary Pain: Physiological Method in Late Nineteenth-Century Britain." In N. A. Rupke (ed.), *Vivisection in Historical Perspective*, 125–148. London: Croom Helm.

Ricoeur, P. (1970). *Freud and Philosophy.* New Haven: Yale University Press.

Riddick, C. C. (1985). "Health, Aquariums, and the Non-Institutionalized Elderly." In M. B. Susman (ed.), *Pets and the Family*, 163–173. New York: Haworth.

Rigdon, J. D., and F. Tapia (1977). "Children Who Are Cruel to Animals: A Follow-Up Study." *Journal of Operational Psychology, 8*, 27–36.

Ristau, C. (ed.) (1990). *Cognitive Ethology: The Minds of Other Animals*. Hillsdale, N.J.: Lawrence Erlbaum.

Ritchie, C. I. A. (1981). *The British Dog: Its History from Earliest Times*. London: Robert Hale.

Ritvo, H. (1986). "Pride and Pedigree: The Evolution of the Victorian Dog Fancy." *Victorian Studies 29*, 227–253.

———. (1987). *The Animal Estate: The English and Other Creatures in the Victorian Age*, ch. 3. Cambridge, Mass.: Harvard University Press.

———. (1988). "The Emergence of Modern Pet-keeping." In A. Rowan (ed.), *Animals and People Sharing the World*, 13–31. Hanover N.H.: University Press of New England.

Ritzer, G. (1993). *The McDonaldization of Society*. Thousand Oaks, Calif.: Pine Forge.

Rivers, W. (1986). *The Todas* (2 volumes). Jaipur, India: Rawat. (Original work published 1906).

Robb, S. S. (1983). "Companion Animals and Elderly People: A Challenge for Evaluators of Social Support." *The Gerontologist, 23*, 277–282.

Robertson, Robert Blackwood (1954). *Of Whales and Men*. New York: Knopf.

Robin, M., and R. ten Bensel (1985). "Pets and the Socialization of Children." In M. B. Sussman (ed.), *Pets and the family*, 63–78. New York: Haworth Press.

Robins, D., C. Sanders, and S. Cahill (1991). "Dogs and Their People: Pet-Facilitated Interaction in a Public Setting." *Journal of Contemporary Ethnography, 20*, 3–25.

Robins, L. N. (1988). "Some Methodological Problems and Research Directions in the Study of the Effects of Stress on Children." In N. Garmezy and M. Rutter (eds.), *Stress, Coping, and Development in Children*, 335–346. Baltimore: Johns Hopkins University Press.

Robinson, N. (ed.) (1991). *The Sayings of Muhammad*. London: Duckworth.

Rogers, J., L. A. Hart, and R. P. Boltz (1993). "The Role of Pet Dogs in Casual Conversations of Elderly Adults." *Journal of Social Psychology, 133, 3*, 265–277.

Root, Waverley, and Richard de Rochemont (1976). *Eating in America: A History*. New York: William Morrow, 279.

Rossides, D. W. (1997). *Social Stratification: The Interplay of Class, Race, and Gender* (Third Edition). Upper Saddle River, N.J.: Prentice Hall.

Rowan, A. N. (1991). Editorial: "Do Companion Animals Provide a Health Benefit?" *Anthrozoös, 4*, 212–213.

———. (1992). "Shelters and Pet Overpopulation: A Statistical Black Hole." *Anthrozoös, 5*, 140–143.

Rowan, A. N., and A. M. Beck (1994). "The Health Benefits of Human–Animal Interactions." *Anthrozoös, 7*, 85–89.

RSPCA. (1994/1995). *Twelfth Annual Report of the Royal Society for the Protection of Animals (Victoria) Incorporated*. Melbourne: Author.

Rud, A. G., Jr., and A. M. Beck (1999). "Send Us Your Favorite Pet Stories: Moral and Development Dimensions of Children's Entries in a Newspaper Contest." *Anthrozoös, 122*, 115–120.

———. (2000). "Kids and Critters in Class Together." *Phi Delta Kappan, 82, 4*, 313–315.

Ruddick, S. (1980). "Maternal Thinking," *Feminist Studies 6*, no. 2 (Summer 1980): 350–351.

———. (1989). *Maternal Thinking: Toward a Politics of Peace*. Boston: Beacon.

Ruether, R. R. (1975). *New Woman/New Earth: Sexist Ideologies and Human Liberation*. New York: Seabury.

———. (1983), *Sexism and God-Talk: Toward a Feminist Theology*. Boston: Beacon.

Rumbaugh, D., E. Savage-Rumbaugh, and M. Hegel (1987). "Summation in the Chimpanzee." *Journal of Experimental Psychology: Animal Behavior Processes, 13*, 107–115.

Runyan, W. (1984). *Life Histories and Psychobiography*. New York: Oxford University Press.

Rutter, M. (1989). "Pathways from Childhood to Adult Life." *Journal of Child Psychology and Psychiatry, 30*, 23–51.

Ryder, R. D. (1989). *Animal Revolution: Changing Attitudes toward Speciesism*. Oxford: Basil Blackwell.

Ryle, G. (1949). *The Concept of Mind*. New York: Barnes and Noble.

Rynearson, E. K. (1978). "Humans and Pets and Attachment." *British Journal of Psychiatry, 133* (December), 550–555.

Sagarin, E. (1971). *The Other Minorities.* Toronto: Ginn and Company.

Salomon A. (1981). "Animals and Children: The Role of the Pet." *Canada's Mental Health June: 9–13.*

Sanday, P. (1981). *Female Power and Male Dominance: On the Origins of Sexual Inequality.* Cambridge and New York: Cambridge University Press.

Sanders, C. R. (1990). "Excusing Tactics: Social Responses to the Public Misbehavior of Companion Animals." *Anthrozoös, 4,* 82–90.

_____. (1999). *Understanding Dogs: Living and Working with Canine Companions.* Philadelphia: Temple University Press.

Sanders, C. M., P. A. Mauger, and P. N. Strong (1985). *Manual for the Grief Experience Inventory.* Palo Alto, Calif.: Consulting Psychologists Press.

Sato, S., K. Tarumizu, and K. Hatae (1993). "The Influence of Social Factors on Allogrooming in Cows." *Applied Animal Behaviour Science, 38,* 235–244.

Savishinsky, J. S. (1983). "Pet Ideas; The Domestication of Animals, Human Behavior, and Human Emotion." In A. H. Katcher and A. M. Beck (eds.), *New Perspectives on Our Lives with Companion Animals,* 112–131. Philadelphia: University of Pennsylvania Press.

Savitt, T. L. (1978). *Medicine and Slavery: The Diseases and Health Care or Blacks in Antebellum Virginia.* Urbana and Chicago: University of Illinois Press.

Schantz, P. M. (1990). "Preventing Potential Health Hazards Incidental to the Use of Pets in Therapy." *Anthrozoös, 4,* 14–23.

Scheler, M. (1954/1973). *The Nature of Sympathy.* Hamden, Conn.: Archon.

Schmidt, C. W. (1999). "Too Big, Too Soon?" *Child.* August, 28.

Schutz, A. (1970). *On Phenomenology and Social Relations.* Chicago: University of Chicago Press.

Schwartz, R. H. (1988). *Judaism and Vegetarianism.* Marblehead, Mass.: Micah Publications.

———. (1992), "Tsa'ar Ba'alei Chayim: Judaism and Compassion for Animal.s" In Roberta Kalechofsky (ed.). *Judaism and Animal Rights: Classical and Contemporary Responses,* 59–70. Marblehead, Mass.: Micah Publications.

Scott, M., and S. Lyman (1968). "Accounts." *American Sociological Review, 33,* 46–62.

Scott, P. S., and J. Fuller (1965). *Genetics and the Social Behavior of the Dog.* Chicago: University of Chicago Press.

Scullard, H. H. (1974). *The Elephant in the Greek and Roman World.* London: Thames and Hudson.

Scully, D., and J. Marolla (1984). "Convicted Rapists' Vocabulary of Motives: Excuses and Justifications." *Social Problems, 31,* 530–544.

Seligman, M. (1975). *Helplessness: On Depression, Development, and Death.* San Francisco: Freeman.

Serjeant, R. (1969). *The Spectrum of Pain.* London: Hart Davis.

Serpell J. A. (1981). "Childhood Pets and Their Influence on Adults' Attitudes." *Psychological Reports, 49,* 651–654.

———. (1983, 1986). *In the Company of Animals A Study of Human–Animal Relationships.* Oxford: Basil Blackwell. Also Cambridge and New York: Cambridge University Press.

———. (1988). "Petkeeping in Non-Western Societies: Some Popular Misconceptions." In A. N. Rowan (ed.), *Animals and People Sharing the World,* 33–52. Hanover, N.H.: University Press of New England.

———. (1991). "Beneficial Effects of Pet Ownership on Some Aspects of Human Health and Behaviour." *Journal Royal Society Medicine, 84,* 717–720.

Serpell J. A., and E. S. Paul (1994). "Pets and the Development of Positive Attitudes to Animals." In A. Manning and J. A. Serpell (eds.), *Animals and Human Society: Changing Perspectives.* Routledge: London.

Shapiro, K. J. (1985). *Bodily Reflective Modes: A Phenomenological Method for Psychology.* Durham, N.C.: Duke University Press.

———. (1990). "Animal Rights Versus Humanism: The Charge of Speciesism." *Journal of Humanistic Psychology*, *30*, 9–37.

———. (1990). "Understanding Dogs through Kinesthetic Empathy, Social Construction, and History." *Anthrozoös*, *3*, 184–195.

———. (1998). "Animal Liberation through Language." *ISAZ Newsletter 14* (November 1997): 20–23. Quoted in *PSYETA Newsletter 19* (Spring 1998).

———. (2002). "The State of Human–Animal Studies: Solid, at the Margin!" *Society and Animals*, *10*, *4*, 331–337.

Shearer, L. (1982). "Intelligence Report: Does Diet Determine Sex?", *Parade* 27 June, 7.

Sheldrake, R. (1999). *Dogs that Know When Their Owners Are Coming Home*. New York: Crown.

Shell, M. (1986). "The Family Pet." *Representations 15*, 121–153.

Shepard, P. (1978). *Thinking Animals: Animals and the Development of Human Intelligence*. New York: Viking Press.

Shiva, V. (1997). *Vandana Shiva on McDonald's, Exploitation and the Global Economy*. http://www.mcspotlight.org/people/interviews.

Sidgwick, H. (1907/1963). *The Methods of Ethics*, seventh edition. London: Macmillan.

Siegel, A. (1962). "Reaching the Severely Withdrawn through Pet Therapy." *American Journal of Psychiatry*, *118* (May), 1045–1046.

Siegel, D., L. Kuller, N. B. Lazarus, D. Black, D. Feigal, G. Hughes *et al.* (1987). "Predictors of Cardiovascular Events and Mortality in the Systolic Hypertension in the Elderly Program Pilot Project." *American Journal of Epidemiology*, *126*, 385–399.

Siegel, J. M. (1990). "Stressful Life Events and Use of Physician Services among the Elderly: The Moderating Role of Pet Ownership." *Journal of Personality and Social Psychology*, *58*, *6*, 1081–1086.

———. (1993). "Companion Animals: In Sickness and in Health." *Journal of Social Issues*, *49*, *1*, 157–167.

Simon, L. J. (1984). "The Pet Trap: Negative Effects of Pet Ownership on Families and Individuals." In R. K. Anderson, B. Hart, and L. Hart (eds.), *The Pet Connection: Its Influence on Our Health and Quality of Life*, 226–240. Minneapolis: University of Minnesota Press.

Simoons, Frederick J. (1961, 1967). *Eat Not This Flesh: Food Avoidances in the Old World*. Madison: University of Wisconsin.

Simoons, F. J., and E. S. Simoons (1968). *A Ceremonial Ox of India: The Mithan in Nature, Culture, and History*. Madison, Milwaukee, London: The University of Wisconsin Press.

Sing, K. (1993). *The Life of the People of India*. New Delhi: ASI, Government of India.

Singer, I. B. (1972). *Enemies: A Love Story*. New York: Farrar, Straus and Giroux.

Singer, P. (1977, 1990). *Animal Liberation: A New Ethics for Our Treatment of Animals*. New York: Avon.

———. (1979). *Practical Ethics*. Cambridge: Cambridge University Press.

———. (1987). "Life's Uncertain Voyage," in P. Pettit, R. Sylvan and J. Norman, eds., *Metaphysics and Morality*, 154–172. Oxford: Blackwell.

Skinner, B. F. (1960). "Pigeons in a Pelican." *American Psychologist*, *15* (January), 28–37.

Slicer, D. (1994) "Wrongs of Passage: Three Challenges to the Maturing of Ecofeminism." In K. J. Warren (ed.), *Ecological Feminism*, London and New York: Routledge.

Sloan, A. (1971). *Dog and Man: The Story of a Friendship*. New York: Blom.

Smith, M.D., E. (1864). *Practical Dietary for Families, Schools and the Labouring Classes*. London: Walton and Maberly.

Snedecor G. W., and W. G. Cochran (1976). *Statistical Methods*. Iowa State University Press: Ames.

Snizek, W. E., and C. D. Bryant (1975). "Intraoccupational Veterinary Specialties: Career Trends and Contingencies among Students and Practitioners." *Journal of Veterinary Medical Education*, *2* (Fall), 36–43.

Snizek, W. E., C. D. Bryant, J. A. Blake, and C. E. Palmer (1975). *Work Roles and Occupational*

Ideologies of Virginia Game Wardens. Blacksburg: Virginia Polytechnic Institute and State University.

Sokolowski, R. (1985). *Moral Action: A Phenomenological Study.* Bloomington: Indiana University Press.

Solot, D. (1997). "Untangling the Animal Abuse Web. *Society and Animals, 5*, 257–265.

Soma, L. R. (1985). "Analgesic Management of the Experimental Animal." In *National Symposium of Imperatives in Research Animal Use: Scientific Needs and Animal Welfare.* Pub. No. 85-2445. Bethesda, Md.: National Institutes of Health.

Spence, J. T., and R. L. Helmreich (1979). "On Assessing 'Androgyny.' " *Sex Roles, 5*, 721–737.

———. (1980). "Masculine Instrumentality and Feminine Expressiveness: Their Relationships with Sex Role Attitudes and Behaviors." *Psychology of Women Quarterly, 5*, 147–163.

Spender, D. (1980). *Man Made Language.* London: Pandora Press.

Sperling, S. (1988). *Animal Liberators: Research and Morality.* Berkeley: University of California Press.

Spiegel, M. (1988, 1996). *The Dreaded Comparison: Human and Animal Slavery.* New York: Mirror Books.

Spittler, G. (1983). "Ekkurs: Zur Soziologie Des Kamel- und Ziegenhütens bei den Kel Ewey-Tuareg." *Tuareg, Leben in der Sahara.* Dr. Foerst Expeditionen Gmbh: Zürich.

Spitzer, R. L., M. Davies, and R. A. Barkley (1990). "The *DSM-III-R* Field Trial of Disruptive Behavior Disorders." *Journal of the American Academy of Child and Adolescent Psychiatry, 29*, 690–697.

Stallones, L., M. Marx, T. Garrity, and T. Johnson (1990). "Pet Ownership and Attachment in Relation to the Health of U.S. Adults, 21 to 64 Years of Age." *Anthrozoös, 4*, 100–112.

Stange, M. Z. (1997). *Women the Hunter.* Boston: Beacon Press.

Stanner, W. E. H. (1972). "The Dreaming." In W. A. Lessa and E. Z. Vogt (eds.), *Reader in Comparative Religion: An Anthropological Approach*, 269–277. New York: Harper and Row.

Stanton, E. C. (1898/1974). *The Woman's Bible: Part I.* New York: European Publishing Co.; Seattle: Coalition Task Force on Women and Religion.

Steedman, C. (1985). "Landscape for a Good Woman." In Heron, Liz (ed.), *Truth, Dare or Promise: Girls Growing Up in the Fifties.* London: Virago Press.

Steinbeck, J. (1938). *Of Mice and Men.* New York: Viking Press.

Stenning, D. J. (1963). "Africa: The Social Background." In A. E. Mourant and F. E. Zeuner (eds.), *Man and Cattle*, 111–118. Glasgow: Royal Anthropological Institute of Great Britain and Ireland.

Sterba, E. (1935). "Excerpt from the Analysis of a Dog Phobia." *Psychoanalytic Quarterly, 4*, 135–60.

Stewart, M. (1983). "Loss of a Pet—Loss of a Person: A Comparative Study of Bereavement." In A. Katcher and A. Beck (eds.), *New Perspectives on Our Lives with Companion Animals*, 390–404. Philadelphia: University of Pennsylvania Press.

Stibbe, A. (2001). "Language, Power, and the Social Construction of Animals." *Society and Animals, 9*, 145–161.

Stillman, W. J. (1899). "A Plea for Wild Animals." *Contemporary Review 75*, 674.

Stott, J. R. W. (1978, February). "Christians and Animals." *Christianity Today, 22, 10*, 33–39.

Straatman, I., E. K. S. Hanson, N. Endenburg, and J. A. Mol (1997). "The Influence of a Dog on Male Students during a Stressor." *Anthrozoös, 10*, 191–197.

Straus, M. A., R. J. Gelles, and S. K. Steinmetz (1980). *Behind Closed Doors.* New York: Doubleday/Anchor.

Strauss, A., and J. Corbin (1997). *Grounded Theory in Practice.* Thousand Oaks, Calif.: Sage.

Strayer, J., and W. Roberts (1989). "Children's Empathy and Roletaking: Child and Parental Factors, and Relations to Prosocial Behavior." *Journal of Applied Developmental Psychology, 10*, 227–239.

Sumner, W. (1906). *Folkways.* Boston: Ginn and Company.

Sunset Books and Sunset Magazines (1969). *Sunset Menu Cook Book*. Menlo Park, Calif.: Lane Magazine and Book Co.

Sykes, G., and D. Matza (1957). "Techniques of Neutralization: A Theory of Delinquency." *American Sociological Review*, *22*, 664–670.

Tapia, F. (1971). "Children Who Are Cruel to Animals." *Child Psychiatry and Human Development*, *2*, 70–77.

Taplin, W. (1803). *The Sportsman's Cabinet 1*, 27–28. London.

Tavuchis, N. (1991). *Mea Culpa: A Sociology of Apology and Reconciliation*. Stanford, Calif.: Stanford University Press.

Tawney, R. H. (1948 [1920]). *The Acquisitive Society*. New York: Harcourt Brace Jovanovich.

Taylor, D. (1984). "Concurrent Validity of the Bem Sex Role Inventory: A Person–Environment Approach." *Sex Roles*, *10*, 713–723.

Templer D. I., C. A. Salter, S. Dickey, R. Baldwin, and D. M. Veleber (1981). "The Construction of a Pet Attitude Scale." *The Psychological Record*, *31*, 343–348.

ten Bensel R. W. (1984). "Historic Perspectives of Human Values for Animals and Vulnerable People." In Anderson R. K., B. L. Hart, and L. A. Hart (eds.), *The Pet Connection: Its Influence on Our Health and Quality of Life*. 2–14. Center to Study Human–Animal Relationships and Environments: Minneapolis.

Tennov, D. (1986). "Pain-Infliction in Animal Research." In H. McGiffin and N. Brownley (eds.), *Animals in Education*, 35–40. Washington, D.C.: Institute for the Study of Animal Problems.

Terr, L. (1990). *Too Scared to Cry*. New York: Harper and Row.

Terrace, H. (1985). "In the Beginning Was the 'Name.' " *American Psychologist 40*, *9*, 1011–1028.

———. (1987). "Thoughts without Words." In C. Blakemore and S. Greenfield (eds.), *Mindwaves: Thoughts on Intelligence, Identity and Consciousness*, 123–137. New York: Blackwell.

Tester, K. (1992). *Animals and Society: The Humanity of Animal Rights*. London: Routledge.

Thomas, E. M. (1989). *The Harmless People*. New York: Vintage Books.

———. (1993). *The Hidden Life of Dogs*. Boston: Houghton Mifflin Co.

Thomas, K. (1983). *Man and the Natural World: A History of the Modern Sensibility*. New York: Pantheon. Also titled: *Man and the Natural World: Changing Attitudes in England 1500–1800*. London: Allen Lane.

Thorne, L. (1998). "Kangaroos: The Non-Issue." *Society and Animals*, *6*, 167–182.

Thornhill, R.B. (1804). *The Shooting Directory*. London.

Tilman, D., J. Fargione, B. Wolff, C. D'Antonio, A. Dobson, R. Howarth, D. Schindler, W. H. Schlesinger, D. Simberloff, and D. Swackhamer (2001). "Forecasting Agriculturally Driven Global Environmental Change." *Science*, *292*, 281–284.

Time. (1978). "Cutting out Monkey Business: India's Ban on Exports Perils U.S. Medical Tests." (February 6), 50.

Tingle, D., G. W. Barnard, L. Robbins, G. Newman, and D. Hutchinson (1986). "Childhood and Adolescent Characteristics of Pedophiles and Rapists." *International Journal of Law and Psychiatry*, *9*, 103–116.

Tobias, M. (1985). *After Eden: History, Ecology and Conscience*. San Diego: Slawson.

———. (1987). "Ahimsa Non-violence" [Television]. KRMA/TV-Public Broadcasting System. Denver.

———. (1991). *Voice of the Planet*. New York: Bantam.

———. (1992). *Life-Force: The World of Jainism*. Fremont, Calif.: Asian Humanities.

———. (1993). *Environmental Meditation*. Freedom, Calif.: Crossing.

———. (1994a). *A Naked Man*. Fremont, Calif.: Jain.

———. (1994b). *Rage and Reason*. New Delhi: Rupa and Company.

———. (1994c). *World War III: Population and the Biosphere at the End of the Millennium*. Santa Fe: Bear and Company.

———. (1995a). *India 24 hours*. Bombay: CMM Studios and Mapin Publishing.

――――. (1995b). *A Vision of Nature: Traces of the Original World*. Kent, Ohio: Kent State University.

――――. (ed.). (1986). *Mountain People*. Norman: University of Oklahoma.

Tobias, M., J. Morrison, and B. Gray (eds.) (1995). *A Parliament of Souls: In Search of Global Spirituality*. San Francisco: KQED Books.

Townes, B. (1975). "Italian Boat First Victim of Shelf Act." *National Fisherman*, 55 (April).

Toynbee, J. M. (1973). *Animals in Roman Life and Art*. Ithaca: Cornell University Press.

Triplett, N. (1903). "A Study of the Faults of Children." *Pedagogical Seminary*, *10*, 200–238.

Tuan, Y-F. (1984). *Dominance and Affection: The Making of Pets*. New Haven: Yale University Press.

Turkle, S. (1984). *The Second Self*. New York: Simon and Schuster.

Turner, J. (1980). *Reckoning with the Beast: Animals, Pain and Humanity in the Victorian Mind*. Baltimore: Johns Hopkins University Press.

U.S. Department of Health and Human Services. (1988). *Surgeon General's Report on Nutrition and Health*. Pub. no. 88-50210. Washington, D.C.

Uherek, A. M. (1991). "Treatment of a Ritually Abused Preschooler." In W. N. Friedrich (ed.), *Casebook of Sexual Abuse Treatment*, 71–92. New York: W. W. Norton.

Ulrich, R. S. (1984, April 27). "View through a Window May Influence Recovery from Surgery." *Science*, *224*, 420–421.

――――. (1993). "Biophilia, Biophobia, and Natural Landscapes." In S. R. Kellert and E. O. Wilson (eds.), *The Biophilia Hypothesis.*, 73–137. Washington, D.C.: Island Press.

United Press International (1975). "Dogs Said to Help Cure Alcoholism." *New York Times* (May 4).

――――. (1978a). "Eagles Case: Three Fined in Death of Birds: Warning Issued." *Houston Post* (February 7).

――――. (1978b). "Unlawful Harvesting of Pink Coral Off Coast Is Laid to Jewelry Fad." *New York Times* (January 15).

United States Department of Health and Human Services (USDHHS). Public Health Service. National Institutes of Health. (1985). (Revised). *Guide for the Care and Use of Laboratory Animals*. NIH Pub. No. 85-23. Bethesda, MD: National Institutes of Health.

United States Department of Agriculture, Animal and Plant Health Inspection Service (USDA-APHIS). (1982–1986). *Animal Welfare Enforcement: Report of the Secretary of Agriculture to the President of the Senate and the Speaker of the House of Representatives*. Available from the National Technical Information Service, Springfield, VA 22161.

United States Department of Agriculture, Animal and Plant Health Inspection Service (USDA-APHIS). (1982–1987). Annual Reports of Research Facilities. Photocopies of reports filed by the University and the Institute as required of all research facilities by the Animal Welfare Act. Available under the Freedom of Information Act from the USDA-APHIS, Federal Building, Hyattsville, MD 20782.

Untitled. 199, 9, 124. Reprinted from *Journal of the American Medical Association*, *18* (Jan. 23, 1892), 108.

Vachss, A. (1991). *Sacrifice*. New York: Alfred A. Knopf.

Vail, D. (1966). *Dehumanization and the Institutional Career*. Springfield, Ill.: Charles C Thomas.

van der Post, L. (1966). *The Lost World of the Kalahari*. Harmondsworth: Penguin.

Vance, L. (1993, June). "Remapping the Terrain: Books on Ecofeminism." *Choice*, 1585–1593.

Vaughan, T., and G. Sjoberg (1970). "The Social Construction of Legal Doctrine: The Case of Adolf Eichmann." In J. Douglas (ed.), *Deviance and Respectability*, 160–191. New York: Basic Books.

Veevers, J. E. (1985). "The Social Meaning of Pets: Alternative Roles for Companion Animals." *Marriage and Family Review*, *8*, 11–30.

Verderber, S. (1991). "Elderly Persons' Appraisal of Animals in the Residential Environment." *Anthrozoös*, *4*, 164–173.

Verhave, T. (1966). "The Pigeon as a Quality Control Inspector." *American Psychologist*, *21* (February), 109–115.

Vermeulen, H., and J. S. J. Odendaal. (1992, July). *A Typology of Companion Animal Cruelty.* Paper presented at the Sixth International Conference on Human–Animal Interactions, Montreal, Quebec.

Veterinary Medical Association. (1988). *The Veterinary Services Market for Companion Animals.* Overland Park, Kan.: Charles, Charles Research Group.

Vockell E., and F. Hodal (1980). "Developing Humane Attitudes: What Does Research Tell Us? *Humane Education, 4,* 19–21.

Voith, V. L. (1983). "Animal Behavior Problems: An Overview." In A. H. Katcher and A. M. Beck (eds.), *New Perspectives on Our Lives with Companion Animals,* 181–186. Philadelphia: University of Pennsylvania Press.

———. (1985). "Attachment of People to Companion Animals." In J. Quackenbush and V. L. Voith (eds.), *Veterinary Clinics of North American, 15, 2,* 289–295.

Wagner, H. (ed.) 1970. *Alfred Schutz on Phenomenology and Social Relations: Selected Writings.* Chicago: University of Chicago Press.

Walker, A. (1986). *The Toda of South India.* Delhi: Hindustan.

Walker, A. (1989). *The Temple of My Familiar.* San Diego, New York: Harcourt Brace Jovanovich.

Walker, J. R. (1980). "A Study on the Relationship of Child Abuse and Pet Abuse." Unpublished Professional Project. University of Pennsylvania School of Social Work, Philadelphia.

Walker, L. E. (1979). *The Battered Woman.* New York: Harper and Row.

Walker, L. J. (1984). "Sex Differences in the Development of Moral Reasoning: A Critical Review." *Child Development, 55,* 677–691.

———. (1986). "Experiential and Cognitive Sources of Moral Development in Adulthood." *Human Development, 29,* 113–124.

Walker, S. (1983). *Animal Thoughts.* London: Routledge and Kegan Paul.

Walter-Toews, D. (1993). "Zoonotic Disease Concerns in Animal Assisted Therapy and Animal Visitation Programs. *Canadian Veterinary Journal, 34,* 549–551.

Wannenburgh, A. (1979). *The Bushmen.* Secaucus, N.J.: Chartwell Book.

Waterman, J., R. J. Kelly, M. K. Oliveri, and J. McCord (1993). *Behind the Playground Walls: Sexual Abuse in Preschools.* New York: Guilford Press.

Watson, N. L., and M. Weinstein (1993). "Pet Ownership in Relation to Depression, Anxiety, and Anger in Working Women." *Anthrozoös, 6, 2,* 135–138.

Watzlawick, P. (1977). *How Real Is "Real"?: Confusion, Disinformation, Communication.* New York: Vintage Books.

Wax, D. E., and V. G. Haddox (1974a). "Enuresis, Firesetting, and Animal Cruelty in Male Adolescent Delinquents: A Triad Predictive of Violent Behavior." *Journal of Psychiatry and Law, 2,* 245–271.

———. (1974b). "Enuresis, Firesetting, and Animal Cruelty: A Useful Danger Signal in Predicting Vulnerability of Adolescent Males to Assaultive Behavior." *Child Psychiatry and Human Development, 4,* 151–156.

———. (1974c). "Sexual Aberrance in Male Adolescents Manifesting a Behavioral Triad Considered Predictive of Extreme Violence: Some Clinical Observations." *Journal of Forensic Sciences, 19,* 102–108.

Weaver, R. (1986). "The Politics of Blame Avoidance." *Journal of Public Policy, 6,* 371–398.

Weber, C., and F. R. Ascione (1992, July). *Humane Attitudes and Human Empathy: Relations in Adulthood.* Paper presented at the Sixth International Conference on Human–Animal Interactions, Montreal, Canada.

Weber, M. (1954). *The Protestant Ethic and the Spirit of Capitalism.* New York: Free Press.

Weil, J. L. (1989). *Instinctual Stimulation of Children: From Common Practice to Child Abuse* (Vol. I: Clinical Findings). Madison, Conn.: International Universities Press.

Weisz, J. R., and B. Weiss (1991). "Studying the 'Referability' of Child Clinical Problems." *Journal of Consulting and Clinical Psychology, 59,* 266–273.

Wells, D. L., and P. G. Hepper (1997). "Pet Ownership and Adults' Views on the Use of Animals." *Society and Animals*, *5*, 45–63.

Wertsch, M. E. (1991). *Military Brats: Legacies of Childhood inside the Fortress*. New York: Harmony Books.

West, C. (1999). "Not Even a Day in the Life." In B. Glassner and R. Hertz (eds.), *Qualitative Sociology as Everyday Life*, 3–12. Thousand Oaks, Calif.: Sage.

White, D. J., and R. Shawhan (1996). "Emotional Responses of Animal Shelter Workers to Euthanasia." *Journal of the American Veterinary Medical Association*, *208*, 846–849.

Whorton, James C. (1977). "'Tempest in a Flesh-Pot': The Formulation of a Physiological Rationale for Vegetarianism." *Journal of the History of Medicine and Allied Sciences*, *32*, 2 (April), 122.

Widom, C. S. (1989). "Does Violence Beget Violence? A Critical Examination of the Literature." *Psychological Bulletin*, *106*, 3–28.

———. (1991). *Long-Term Consequences of Early Childhood Victimization*. Paper presented at the annual meeting of the American Association for the Advancement of Science, Washington, DC, February 16.

Wieder, D. L (1980). "Behavioristic Operationalism and the Life-World: Chimpanzees and Chimpanzee Researchers in Face-to-face Interaction." *Sociological Inquiry*, *50*, 75–103.

Wiehe, V. R. (1990). *Sibling Abuse*. Lexington, Mass.: Lexington Books.

Williams, M. D. (1974). *Community in a Black Pentecostal Church: An Anthropological Study*. Pittsburgh: University of Pittsburgh Press.

Wilson, C. C. (1987). "Physiological Responses of College Students to a Pet." *Journal of Nervous and Mental Disease*, *175*, 606–612.

Wilson, C. C. (1991). "The Pet as an Anxiolytic Intervention." *Journal of Nervous and Mental Disease*, *179*, 482–489.

Wilson, D., and P. Ayerst (1976). *White Gold: The Story of African Ivory*. London: Heinemann.

Wilson, E. O. (1984). *Biophilia*. Cambridge, Mass.: Harvard University Press.

———. (1993). "Biophilia and the Conservation Ethic." In S. R. Kellert and E. O. Wilson (eds.), *The Biophilia Hypothesis*, 31–41. Washington, D.C.: Island Press.

Wilson, F. R., and E. P. Cook (1985). "Concurrent Validity of Four Androgyny Instruments." *Sex Roles*, *11*, 813–837.

Wise J. K., and J. E. Kushman (1984). "Pet Ownership by Life Group." *Journal of the American Veterinary Medical Association*, *185*, 6, 687–690.

Wissler, Clark (1914). "The Influence of the Horse in the Development of Plains Culture." *American Anthropologist*, *16* (January–March), 1–25.

Witt, D. D. (1978). "Work and Interaction in a Pet Cemetery." Unpublished paper. Department of Sociology, Texas Tech University.

Wochner, M., and G. Klosinski (1988). "Kinder-und jugendpsychiatrisch auffällige Tierquäler." ("Children and Adolescents with Psychiatric Problems Who Mistreat Animals"). *Schweizer "Archiv für Neurologie und Psyfchiatrie"* *139*, 59–67.

Wolch, J. (1998). "Zoöpolis." In J. Wolch and J. Emel (eds.) *Animal Geographies: Place, Politics, and Identity in the Nature–Culture Borderlands*, 119–138, London and New York: Verso.

Wollstonecraft, Mary (1792/1975). *A Vindication of the Rights of Woman* (Baltimore: Penguin.

Wood, F. W. (1990). *An American Profile: Opinion and Behavior, 1972–1989*. New York: Gale Research.

Wooden, W. S., and M. L. Berkey (1984). *Children and Arson: America's Middle Class Nightmare*. New York: Plenum Press.

Worth, D., and A. M. Beck (1981). "Multiple Ownership of Animals in New York City." *Transactions and Studies of the College Physicians Philadelphia*, *3*, 280–300.

Wright, E. M., Jr., K. L. Marcella, and J. F. Woodson (1985). "Animal Pain: Evaluation and Control." *Lab Animal*, (May–June), 20–34.

Young, I. (1990). *Justice and the Politics of Difference*. Princeton: Princeton University Press.

Young, W. C., R. G. Sachs, B. G. Braun, and R. T. Watkins (1991). "Patients Reporting Ritual Abuse in Childhood: A Clinical Syndrome Report of 37 Cases." *Child Abuse and Neglect*, *15*, 181–189.

Zaehner, R. C. (1966). *Hinduism*. Oxford: Oxford University Press.

———. (ed. and trans.) (1969). *The Bhagavad Gita*. Oxford: Oxford University Press, ch. XII, 13, 89 and commentary, 329.

Zahn-Waxler, C., B. Hollenbeck, and M. R. Radke-Yarrow (1984). "The Origins of Empathy and Altruism." In M. W. Fox and L. D. Mickley (eds.), *Advances in Animal Welfare*, 21–41. Norwell, Mass.: Kluwer Academic.

Zaretsky, E. (1976). *Capitalism, the Family and Personal Life*. New York: Harper and Row.

Zasloff, R. L., and A. H. Kidd (1994). "Attachment to Feline Companions." *Psychological Reports*, *74*, 747–752.

Ziegler, P. T. (1966). *The Meat We Eat*. Danville, Ill.: The Interstate Printers and Publishers.

Zimrin, H. (1986). "A Profile of Survival." *Child Abuse and Neglect*, *10*, 339–349.

Zinsser, H. (1935). *Rats, Lice and History*. New York: Bantam Books.

Zuelke, R. (1965). *The Horse in Art*. Minneapolis: Lerner Publications.

Contributors Index

449

Contents Index